Economics Now

Second Edition

ISBN 978-1-55077-270-8

Information on how to obtain copies of this book is available at
www.thompsonbooks.com
Phone: 416.766.2763
Fax: 416.766.0398

We acknowledge the support of the Government of Canada.

Canada

Printed in Canada.
1 2 3 4 5 6 7   25 24 23 22 21 20 19

Economics Now

Second Edition

Angelo Bolotta | Charles Hawkes | Rick Mahoney | Brian Raposo

THOMPSON

Toronto

IV

Contents

Thinking like an Economist
List of Topics

Preface

Welcome to the second edition of **Economics Now**!

If you are new to economics, rest assured that this subject is both interesting and relevant to your life and future. If you find economics difficult to grasp, know that we have aimed to make this resource relatable. Even if you do not go on to study economics in college or university, this resource will give you a useful understanding of how the Canadian economy works and how it interacts within the global economy.

Once fundamental concepts, principles, and realities of economics are explained, the principal focus for this course is an analysis of economic issues. To broaden the investigation of these issues, activities and policies in the Canadian economy are sometimes compared to those in other countries. At the same time, we hope that this resource, and your class experience, will stimulate you to go on to further study—both to deepen your understanding of economic issues and to possibly prepare you for an economics-related career.

As you browse through the resource, you will notice that there are 22 chapters organized into six major units. Each unit begins with a brief overview of the content in the chapters to follow, and an inquiry question to focus and direct your thinking throughout the unit. Each unit ends with a performance task that asks you to apply the concepts and skills you have learned in the unit.

FEATURES

- **Unit-opening spreads** introduce the subject matter and its personal relevance through a short description, a strong visual, and an inquiry question to focus and frame the learning activities in the chapters that follow. The *Looking Ahead* spotlight invites students to begin thinking about the performance task that appears at the end of the unit.

- **Chapter-opening spreads** start you thinking about chapter contents. Subject matter is briefly introduced, and a colourful visual is used as a symbolic starting point for discussion. *Learning Goals* tell you what you can expect to learn in the chapter. All key terms used in the chapter are listed in order of appearance.

- **Thematic spreads** focus your thinking about a specific topic or theme with a blend of words, photos, diagrams, graphs, and data tables to build understanding.

- **Margin notes** are used to explain the key terms being used and to provide you with additional supports and reference points, including *Did You Know?* and *Check This Out!* features.

- **Self-Reflect** questions (which appear at the end of major sections in each chapter) prompt you to review your knowledge of the chapter's content.

- **Thinking like an Economist** is a skill-building feature that asks you to think about and apply the skills that economists use (such as graphing, calculating, and applying theories) to economic issues.

- **Consolidation Activities** at the end of each chapter are divided into four sections:

  › *Knowledge* questions allow you to strengthen and extend your understanding of the chapter's key terms, concepts, principles, and ideas.

  › *Thinking and Inquiry* questions ask you to think analytically and to investigate economic issues.

  › *Communication* questions allow you to be creative in clearly presenting economic ideas and issues from the chapter.

  › *Application* questions direct you to apply your knowledge and skills to problems and new situations.

- The **Glossary** at the end of this resource includes all of the key terms from each chapter with definitions.

Performance Tasks

All units end with a **Performance Task**. Each performance task puts you in a real-life role that requires you to draw on the content, theories, and skills from the chapters in that unit. The performance tasks closely resemble actual work tasks being completed by professionals in today's economy. Each task provides you with a realistic opportunity to demonstrate the full extent of your learning during the unit. A suggested method of evaluation is included with each performance task that you and your teacher can use and adapt for your work. Performance tasks include the following information:

- An outline of the task

- Suggested steps and recommendations to complete the task successfully

- Performance targets and/or other critical-thinking suggestions

- Suggestions on how you can adapt the task to incorporate personal interests and abilities

- Assessment criteria that will be used to evaluate the quality of your work

The **Course Culminating Performance Task** found at the end of this resource gives you an opportunity to creatively demonstrate the knowledge, ideas, and skills you have learned throughout the entire course.

We sincerely hope that this resource helps make your study of economics stimulating and enjoyable. Whether you end up pursuing a career in a field related to economics or not, may your interactions with this resource help you develop lifelong critical and economic thinking skills.

Acknowledgements

The publisher and the authors would like to thank the following individuals, who kindly reviewed all or parts of this resource prior to publication:

F. Byrne
SD36 Social Studies Educator

Jeff Clark
Durham District School Board

Sebastian Conti
Upper Grand District School Board

Melissa Hoadley
Harrison Trimble High School, Moncton, NB

Philip Lam
Economics 11/12 Teacher

Paul Massie
Delta School District

Kevin Moogk
Bluevale Collegiate Institute

Tim Rudan
Toronto District School Board

Andrew Lawrence Smith, OCT
Halton District School Board

Dedications

To Mara, Alissa, and Alanna for their understanding and support, and to my parents for impressing upon me from an early age the value of economic thinking. — **Angelo Bolotta**

To Pat. — **Charles Hawkes**

To my children Katie, Jacob, Danny, and Andrew for all the joy you have given me watching you grow; and to my wife Cathie for supporting and encouraging me in everything I choose to pursue. When it comes to family, I am truly blessed. — **Rick Mahoney**

To my wife and children: Luisa, Christian, Julian, and Alexandra. — **Brian Raposo**

Unit 1

Introduction to Economics

Welcome to the inescapable world of economics!

Most difficult and important decisions are economic decisions because they require the responsible allocation of limited resources. Economic thinking involves satisfying the most wants and needs possible, while consuming the fewest resources. Economic thinkers seek to be maximizers, achieving the most while consuming the least.

In this unit, we will investigate the nature of economics and economic reasoning and explore some key fallacies, theories, and laws of economics. We will also investigate the different types of resources and how they are used to satisfy as many human wants and needs as possible. We will compare how each ecnomic system addresses questions of production and distribution. The main economic goals of the Canadian economy are explained.

Since we will never have enough resources to address all human wants and needs, difficult decisions have to be made. Economists often prefer to make these decisions by carefully comparing the costs and benefits of each option to determine the wisest choice. Given the inevitable reality of scarcity, the need for carefully established priorities is examined to deal with conflicting goals, trade-offs, and sacrifices required.

How do you determine the most productive use of your time, and what can be done to improve your productivity?

Guess what? Tonight, you have an economic choice to make: deciding whether to study for a math test, work additional hours, or hang out with friends.

You may be thinking, "This isn't even remotely an economic decision!" Well, time is a precious commodity and a limited resource, and each minute that you do one thing, you sacrifice what you could have done instead. Each of your three options this evening will involve a sacrifice or trade-off. Each choice will also come with its own set of consequences. What would be the consequences of not studying for your test, not earning extra money, and not being with your friends?

When you manage scarce resources in a productive and responsible manner, you are making economic decisions. The world's resources are limited, so we need to use them efficiently. And because economic thinking involves careful analysis of available options to make a sound choice, it is a complicated business.

LOOKING AHEAD ──────▶

The performance task at the end of this unit will require you to investigate the inquiry question above. It provides an opportunity for you to:

- Assume the role of human resources manager asked to recommend a corporate strategy to improve worker productivity

- Apply economic knowledge and skills to conduct a thorough cost–benefit analysis of available options to support your recommendation to the owners

- Prepare and present an informative and persuasive argument

- Use a performance task rubric and feedback to prepare a high-quality report

1

What Is Economics?

INTRODUCTION

We constantly face economic decisions because our needs and wants are virtually unlimited, while our means to satisfy them (what economists call our *available resources*) are quite limited. For most of us, available resources consist of our skills, income, and savings, and since these are limited, we must economize, or use these resources wisely. We can define "wise use" as that which most furthers our personal or group goals while consuming the least amount of available resources. Since there is a relative scarcity of these resources, we will always live with the economic dilemma of our wants exceeding our ability to satisfy them. In its most basic form, economics is all about scarcity management.

Each of us has to make many difficult decisions every day. For this reason, and whether or not we realize it, economics is continually at work in our lives. If we use time, energy, money, or materials to do one thing instead of another, we are engaged in economic decision making. If we face questions about what we need, what we want, and what we can afford to do, we are engaged in economic decision making.

This chapter introduces you to the most basic concepts and principles of economics—the social science of scarcity and choice. It also presents several examples of disciplined economic reasoning and some common examples of faulty economic thinking. You will encounter a number of opportunities to apply the decision-making and graphing skills that you will need to complete this course successfully and to analyze current economic issues.

LEARNING GOALS

Once you have completed this chapter, you should be able to:

- Realize the importance of economics as a social science
- Understand the purpose and benefit of economic thinking
- Recognize that choices express priorities and have different types of consequences
- Begin thinking like an economist
- Use models to focus and direct economic decision making

KEY TERMS

effective (use of resources)

priority

consequence

efficient (use of resources)

economize

economics

social science

stakeholder

scientific method

economy

analytical (or positive) economics

normative (or policy) economics

utility

util

Why Study Economics?

Today, many students make the deliberate decision to study economics, and they do so for a number of reasons. First, it is difficult to read or watch the news without encountering a multitude of economic issues and interpretations. To make sense of all this information, you need a practical understanding of economic concepts and principles. You also need to understand the ways in which the Canadian and global economies work and the ways people, businesses, and governments function within them.

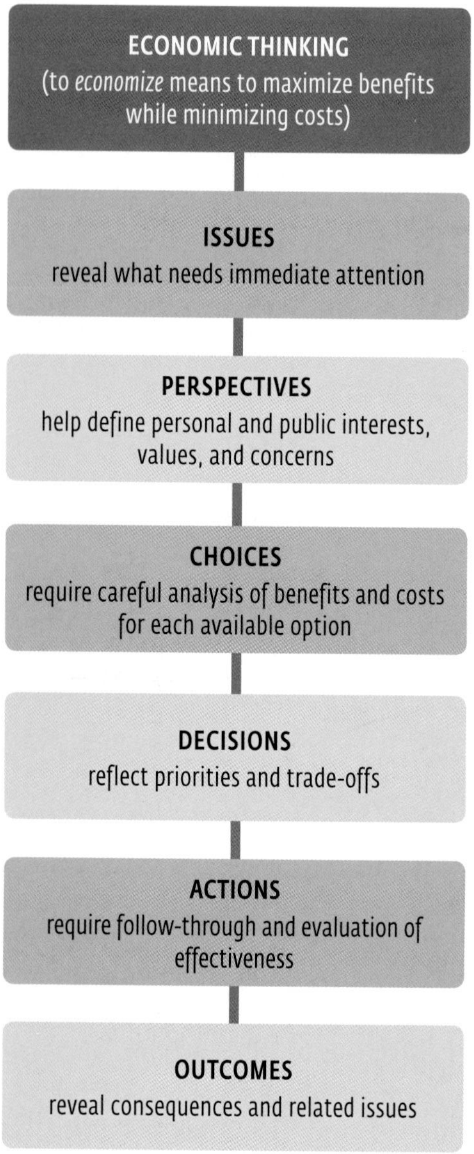

Second, since students have to make daily choices regarding the use of scarce resources (*Will I spend my entire paycheque or allowance this week, or will I put a part of it in my savings account? How badly do I need a new winter coat?*), they come to value the skills of economic reasoning. Throughout this resource, these skills will be profiled in feature spreads entitled *Thinking like an Economist*. In addition, there are many opportunities and activities for you to develop and apply decision-making and problem-solving strategies. These are lifelong skills that will always be useful and marketable.

Third, economic knowledge and skills can lead to more effective civic participation. If students are to vote wisely for the politicians who will make important collective decisions for them, they should be able to understand the interrelatedness of economic factors such as interest rates, foreign exchange rates, taxes, public debt, and laws protecting competition. Otherwise, how will they know whom to believe when issues arise?

Finally, since the study of economics develops problem-solving, analytical, and critical-thinking skills, successful students enjoy a wide variety of potential career paths in business, government, and education. Consult a job search site to identify jobs where economic thinking and knowledge might be useful assets.

FIGURE 1.1

Making difficult economic decisions
Economic choices involve the careful weighing of available options to determine what is most important and what must be sacrificed in order to achieve it.

ECONOMIC THINKING
(to *economize* means to maximize benefits while minimizing costs)

ISSUES
reveal what needs immediate attention

PERSPECTIVES
help define personal and public interests, values, and concerns

CHOICES
require careful analysis of benefits and costs for each available option

DECISIONS
reflect priorities and trade-offs

ACTIONS
require follow-through and evaluation of effectiveness

OUTCOMES
reveal consequences and related issues

MAKING DIFFICULT CHOICES

Given the many difficult choices you will have to make on a regular basis, economic thinking skills are worth developing, unless, of course, you prefer to be manipulated by others. The first rule of economics is that scarcity is inescapable. Therefore, it must be dealt with consciously and effectively. To be **effective** means to do the right things so that goals are achieved. Priority setting is required to determine the most appropriate use of available resources. Should I cook dinner or eat out tonight? Should we rent or buy a family home? Who will get to use the family car tonight? Will I study for my unit test or attend a friend's birthday party? All of these economic questions reflect personal and family **priorities**. Priorities involve favouring one thing in place of another when both are not possible. When we make our choices to eat in, save up to buy a larger home, and stay home to study, we reveal our priorities. Figure 1.1 illustrates the process of economic thinking—from issues to outcomes (the consequences of choices made).

When we make our choices, we must also accept the **consequences** that come along with them. Economic thinking requires careful analysis of all cause-and-consequence relationships. As Figure 1.2 illustrates, there are many different types of consequences. Too often we look only at immediate and direct consequences for our actions. The sad state of our natural environment today reveals the short-sightedness of this thinking. As global warming causes flooding and outbursts of extreme weather, Canadians continue to burn carbon-based fuels at one of the highest per capita rates in the world.

Positive consequences, like lower transportation costs, must be reconsidered in light of the negative consequences of climate change. Short-term consequences might include line ups at the gas pumps, while long-term consequences include the depletion of oil and gas reserves. Instant consequences are immediately felt, like when your car will not start because the gas tank is empty. Delayed consequences, like melting polar ice caps and rising sea levels are gradual.

Direct consequences can be traced directly back to the cause. For example, fire is the direct result of smoking while filling a car's gas tank. The fainting of a startled pedestrian walking by the gas station is an indirect consequence of smoking while refuelling your car. Intended consequences are deliberate and expected (reasonably foreseeable), while other consequences can be unexpected and accidental, like the fainting bystander. By their nature, some consequences, like noise pollution, have a very localized impact, while consequences like air pollution have a more universal or globalized impact. It is important to consider all types of consequences when making sound economic decisions. Sound economic decision making requires receiving maximum benefits from the resources being consumed. This requires the **efficient** use of resources.

effective (use of resources)
A particular use of resources that achieves a desired end, such as consumption.

priority
The favouring of one available option over another in making a decision or choice.

consequence
The result, effect, or outcome of an action taken or the refusal to take an action.

efficient (use of resources)
The use of a bare minimum of resources to achieve a desired end, such as consumption.

FIGURE 1.2
Economic consequences
Economic choices have many consequences. Economic thinking requires carefully determining the many related but different kinds of consequences for the choices being made.

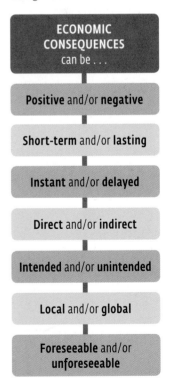

ECONOMIC CONSEQUENCES can be . . .

Positive and/or **negative**

Short-term and/or **lasting**

Instant and/or **delayed**

Direct and/or **indirect**

Intended and/or **unintended**

Local and/or **global**

Foreseeable and/or **unforeseeable**

economize
To use limited resources efficiently in production.

economics
The study of the way society makes decisions about the use of scarce resources.

social science
Sciences, such as economics, history, and sociology, that study some aspect of human behaviour.

stakeholder
A person with a vested or personal interest (or stake) in an economic decision.

scientific method
A method of study used to make discoveries in natural science and social sciences (such as economics) that has four steps: observation, data collection, explanation, and verification.

What Exactly Is Economics?

The dictionary dryly defines *economics* as a practical science dealing with the production, distribution, and use of goods, services, resources, and wealth. The word *economics* can be traced back to ancient Greece, where it was formed by joining the words *oikos*, meaning "house," and *nemo*, the verb for "to manage." In its root sense, then, *oikonomia* dealt with matters relating to the wise management of one's own household or estate.

Today, economics is often referred to as "the science of scarcity and choice." Since material wants always exceed available resources, scarcity must be managed. Each person, family, business, society, and government attempts to **economize** by making decisions that satisfy the largest number of material wants while using the smallest amount of resources possible. Therefore, **economics** is the study of the way we make decisions about the use of scarce resources.

ECONOMICS AS A SOCIAL SCIENCE

Because economics involves the study of people (either individually or in groups) making decisions about the choices available to them, it falls into the category of a **social science**. Other social sciences include history, geography, sociology, and psychology. Like economics, each of these sciences attempts to understand an important aspect of the human condition and of the world in which we live. This social aspect of the study gives economics both relevance and complexity.

When we broaden the study to consider the way economic decision making affects society as a whole, it becomes clear why economic decisions are key to the well-being of an entire country or group of countries. We can also see how complicated economics becomes when we try to balance the interests of one **stakeholder** group with those of another. For example, loggers seek to harvest forests; environmentalists seek to preserve them.

Unlike "natural" sciences such as physics and chemistry, social sciences are greatly complicated by human behaviour and value systems. An apple falling from a tree today behaves exactly as it did for Isaac Newton in 1665. The natural laws of physics remain unchanged, although human understanding of these laws has increased. On the other hand, human behaviour has changed significantly since 1665 and continues to change as society evolves. Refinements in economic theory, changes in social conditions, and evolving political systems (and priorities) produce considerable differences among economists on any given question: hence the cynical conclusion that the one thing economists know how to do best is disagree!

Having explained its social aspect, let's consider what it is about economics that makes it a science. A discipline, or field of study, is called a science based not on what it studies but on how it studies it—that is, based not on its subject matter but on its method. Economics, like all other natural and social sciences, uses a common investigative approach called the **scientific method**. The four basic components of the scientific method, as first outlined by English scientist

Francis Bacon (1561–1626), are observation, data collection, explanation, and verification. Even though scientists today use many different processes to make their discoveries, the four steps outlined by Bacon are almost always involved.

WHAT IS AN ECONOMY, AND HOW DOES IT WORK?

An **economy** can be described as a self-sustaining system in which many independent transactions by individuals, households, businesses, and institutions (often triggered by self-interest) create distinct flows of money and products.

An economy . . .

- Is a very complex or intricate system with many participants or stakeholders
- Is dynamic or subject to constant movements and exchanges
- Consists of interdependent people, groups, and institutions, each performing specialized roles
- Involves a series of independent transactions motivated by economic goals
- Involves numerous transactions that create two circular flows (goods and services move in one direction while money flows in the opposite direction to pay for what is received)

economy
A self-sustaining system in which many independent transactions in a society create distinct flows of money and products or services.

A big electronics store during one of the busiest shopping days of the year. How do retailers attract customers into their stores on Black Friday? What are these young consumers looking for?

Reconciling Materials, Facts, and Values in Economics

Some critics dismiss economics as being preoccupied with the study of material things and not showing enough concern for human values. Although economics is primarily concerned with such things as resources and products, at no time does it recognize them as ends in themselves. Remember that material things can be used for noble purposes, such as saving lives, eliminating poverty, and preserving peace. Not everyone takes satisfaction in piling up material possessions; people often use them to achieve ends determined by personal or societal value systems. Economics does not try to establish goals for the people who study it; rather, it gives them the tools they will need to achieve their own goals while wasting fewer resources.

It is important to realize that economic thinking distinguishes between the effective and the efficient use of resources. If we consume a certain amount of resources and, in the end, achieve the desired result, then our use of those resources can be called effective. However, if we use the bare minimum of resources necessary to achieve the desired end, then our use of these resources can also be considered efficient. Sound economic decisions must be both effective and efficient. Efficiency enables us to use the saved resources in achieving other goals—goals that we may not have been able to achieve unless we had economized previously. Although economics studies the material world, it does not place undue importance on material goods and maximizing consumption. Given the scarcity of most resources in our world, the economic imperative is to conserve and use things wisely.

Traditionally, the science of economics has attempted to explain human behaviour and assist in rational decision making by using both fact- and value-based considerations. Facts and values have long been considered as the two sides of economic currency. Let's explore the distinction between them to get an idea of the way they work together in economic decision making.

A homeless person on the streets of Vancouver. The fact that an increasing number of homeless persons can now be seen in Canadian cities is much more difficult to explain in normative terms because this extreme poverty exists in the midst of great affluence.

ANALYTICAL ECONOMICS

The branch of economics that deals with facts and direct observation of the world is called **analytical (or positive) economics**, and it is concerned with two types of statements: *descriptive* and *conditional*. Descriptive statements portray the world as it is or has been in the past. The following is a descriptive statement: "Automobile sales in Canada this quarter are 7 percent higher than the last quarter." This is a statement of fact that can be statistically verified.

Conditional statements are forecasts based on the careful analysis of economic behaviour. Often these statements take the form "If *x* occurs, then *y* will follow." This forecast can be either confirmed or refuted by referring to known facts and observing the accuracy of the prediction. For example, consider this conditional statement: "If the price of cigarettes decreases, the quantity purchased will increase." This forecast was confirmed in the early 1990s when the federal and provincial governments lowered taxes on cigarettes to combat organized smuggling operations that brought large quantities of American cigarettes into Canada. The tax cut lowered the price of Canadian cigarettes, and consumers did indeed purchase more. Cigarette taxes were never lowered again.

NORMATIVE ECONOMICS

The other branch of economics is called **normative (or policy) economics**, and it primarily concerns statements that contain value judgements. Normative statements express what economists think should be the case, based on their value judgements. These statements cannot be confirmed or refuted solely by reference to facts. Goals and policy statements of governments, businesses, and interest groups are often based on value judgements and, therefore, are normative statements. The following is an example of a normative statement: "Municipal governments should provide more housing for homeless people." Clearly, this is an expression of opinion reflecting a value judgement and policy preference. The word "should" often confirms that a statement is not factual and is therefore open to debate.

As we participate more actively in the global economy, it becomes necessary to use both facts and values in making wise economic decisions. One reason for this is that local decisions often have far-reaching consequences. Consider the following examples. When Canadians import inexpensive products from countries that violate human rights, we enable injustice. The financial crisis that rocked South Korea, Indonesia, Japan, and Russia in 1998 contributed to a weaker Canadian dollar, instability on Canadian stock markets, and increased prices for imported goods. During the "subprime mortgage crisis" in the United States (2007–2009), certain banks assumed extremely high-risk mortgages to increase profits. Eventually, some big banks needed government bailouts to avoid a disastrous collapse. This severe financial crisis helped launch the global economy into the deepest economic decline since the Great Depression (1929–1938).

analytical (or positive) economics
The branch of economics that deals with facts and direct observation of the world.

normative (or policy) economics
The branch of economics that deals with value judgements about economic subjects rather than facts and observations.

utility (*see next page*)
The usefulness, satisfaction, or benefit derived from each available option to help make a rational choice among them.

util (*see next page*)
A theoretical unit of satisfaction that a person gains from consuming an item.

Self-Reflect

1 Explain the four basic components involved in the scientific method as a thorough investigative approach.

2 Why are economic decisions often difficult?

Thinking like an Economist

Applying Economic Reasoning to a Decision-Making Model

When deciding among several possibilities, a well-thought-out decision-making model can make it easier to choose wisely. For example, Lani is in her final year of high school. She has to hand in a major research paper on Monday morning, but she also has an opportunity to work extended weekend hours at the ice cream parlour and a chance to go with friends to a concert featuring her favourite band. What should Lani do? Figures 1.3 and 1.4 illustrate the decision making in this example.

Economists use the concept of **utility** to help make a rational choice between available options. Utility refers to the usefulness, satisfaction, or benefit provided by each option. To determine this utility, appropriate decision-making criteria are determined by asking, "On what would a reasonable person base this decision?" Next, each criterion is weighted to establish its relative importance. In her matrix, Lani weighted both "marks" and "preparation for post-secondary studies" as highly important this weekend. **Utils** are units of satisfaction one gains from an item. They can be used to represent economic value and to help make a comparison. In Lani's matrix, a moderately satisfying item has two utils of satisfaction.

To determine the best use of her time, Lani multiplies the weighting of each criteria by the util score of each option. Attending the concert produces a total score of 6 (2 × 3); working extra hours produces a total score of 9 (3 × 3); and producing a better research paper produces a total score of 18 ([3 × 3] + [3 × 3]). When all criteria and the satisfaction provided are taken into account, the rational decision for this weekend is to work on the research paper. Not all decisions are rational. Sometimes decisions are emotional or spontaneous (impulsive).

APPLYING ECONOMIC THINKING

1   Do the steps of this decision-making model help to prevent mistakes and uninformed choices?

2   Does the use of utils or a weighted matrix help to recognize priorities?

3   Does this kind of disciplined economic thinking help focus thinking about the consequences for the choices being made? Does this mean that Lani should never go to another concert?

4   Use this model and matrix to help make a difficult decision you now face.

FIGURE 1.3 A decision-making matrix to determine the best use of time

A weighted decision-making matrix like this can help you establish your priorities.

Decision Criteria	Weighting*	Available Options					
		Attend the concert		Work extra hours		Write a better research paper	
		Util Score†	Weighted Utility	Util Score	Weighted Utility	Util Score	Weighted Utility
Marks	3	0	0	0	0	3	3 × 3 = 9
Preparation for post-secondary studies	3	0	0	0	0	3	3 × 3 = 9
Fun with friends	2	3	2 × 3 = 6	3	2 × 3 = 6	0	0
Extra income	1	0	0	3	1 × 3 = 3	0	0
Total Utils			**6**		**9**		**18**
Which option provides the most satisfaction or utility?							
* **Weighting:** 1 = low importance/priority; 2 = medium importance/priority; 3 = high importance/priority							
† **Util Scale:** 0 = no satisfaction; 1 = low satisfaction; 2 = moderate satisfaction; 3 = high satisfaction							

FIGURE 1.4 A decision-making model

What should Lani do this weekend? Although we apply this model to Lani's problem, it can also serve as a general model for deciding what to do with scarce resources. What scarce resource is Lani dealing with?

Model Steps	Details and Example(s)
1 **Define the problem**	At the heart of every decision, there is a choice to make—the selection of one alternative over others. State the problem in a clearly focused question. • What should Lani do over the weekend?
2 **Clarify goals and priorities**	Identify the most important issues involved in the problem. Establish goals and priorities in response to these issues. • Lani wants to go to university. • She needs to maintain good marks to be accepted at her university of choice. • She needs to save money to cover tuition and other expenses. • She enjoys spending time with her friends and listening to music.

3 **List the possible alternatives**	Identify all choices available to decision makers.
	• Lani's alternatives include the following:
	  ○ Attending the concert with her friends
	  ○ Working extra hours to make more money
	  ○ Producing a more thorough research paper

4 **Establish the criteria used to judge the alternatives**	Identify three or four standards that can be used to evaluate each alternative. • Lani's weekend can be spent in the pursuit of income, marks, fun, or preparation for post-secondary education. Each alternative includes positive and negative considerations. These considerations represent the criteria to be used in making a sound decision.
5 **Weight each criterion based on goals and priorities**	Use *goals* and *priorities* to determine the relative importance of each criterion and the ultimate *utility* (satisfaction or benefit) derived from each. Make value judgements. • Because of the importance of the research paper in determining her final grade and of effective research and writing skills in post-secondary education, Lani gives these two criteria more weight in making her decision. For this weekend, she gives fun with friends moderate weight and extra income a lower priority. Next weekend these weightings could change.
6 **Evaluate each alternative**	Use the weighted criteria to evaluate each alternative. Produce a decision-making matrix to weigh all options relative to established criteria. • In completing the matrix in Figure 1.3, Lani must consider the positive and negative aspects of each alternative and weight them according to her goals and priorities. She assigns important criteria triple weight in the decision, moderate criteria double weight, and lesser criteria single weight. By tabulating the results of this weighted analysis, Lani can determine her wisest alternative.
7 **Make a decision**	Select the best alternative based on the results of the weighted evaluation. • The decision matrix clearly identifies the third alternative as the best. It provides the most benefits (or positive aspects), while limiting the costs (or negative aspects). Lani will spend her weekend working on the research paper.
8 **Act on the decision**	Implement the selected alternative. • Lani invests extra time at the library and on her computer to acquire additional data, conduct a more thorough analysis of her findings, and produce a more polished written report.
9 **Assess effectiveness**	Assess the effectiveness of the action plan and revise it as needed. • Lani is pleased with the mark she receives on the major assignment because it improves her course grade. The concert she missed was described by friends as "the best of the year!"

Chapter 1
Consolidation Activities

KNOWLEDGE

1   Why is scarcity a constant, even in a resource-rich country like Canada?

2   Explain the difference between a natural science and a social science. Why is economics a social science?

3   Draw a flow chart or create a summary table to explain the difference between positive and normative economics.

4   Distinguish between being effective and being efficient in economic decision making. Explain why both are important.

THINKING & INQUIRY

5   Are all personal goals achievable at the same time? Use the decision-making matrix in Figure 1.3 to explain how complicated, conflicting, and less important goals can be addressed by setting economic priorities.

6   In the daily news, find three examples of analytical statements and three examples of normative statements. Explain your thinking.

7   "In decision-making situations, the key role of economists should not be to dictate values to others. Economists serve best by focusing attention on how to think rather than what to think." Do you agree or disagree with this statement? Use examples to justify your answer.

COMMUNICATION

8   Assume that you are writing an email to a friend about your economics class. In your own words, explain to your friend what economics is and why it is considered an important social science.

9   If you were the parent of a teenager, how would you explain to the teenager what it means to economize and why it is important?

10 Prepare a one-page, handwritten summary that your teacher would allow you to use during your first economics test. What information are you going to put in the limited space available?

APPLICATION

11 After graduation, do you plan to continue your education, get a job, or travel? What are the consequences of each choice? Remember to consider all types of consequences.

12 Give three examples of economic decisions you had to make this week. Explain why each was an economic decision. What priority was expressed by each decision?

13 Suppose you have $3 000 in your savings account. There are three things you would like to do, each of which will cost exactly $3 000:

a) Take a two-week, all-inclusive winter vacation on a Caribbean island.

b) Buy a 4K home-theatre system.

c) Buy a used motorcycle as affordable transportation to work and school.

d) Finance yourself to spend a summer working in Africa for a volunteer organization affiliated with Global Affairs Canada.

Whichever alternative you choose, you will have to do without the other three. Use a decision-making model to facilitate a sound economic decision.

2

Economic Fallacies, Theories, and Laws

INTRODUCTION

In the first chapter of this unit, we noted that the scientific method is used in economics to better understand the world of economics and its inherent realities. Like all scientists, economists use observation, data collection, analysis, explanation, and verification to prove hypotheses or to validate generalizations that attempt to explain economic realities. After they have been validated or proven, these generalizations become economic principles, laws, or theories.

We will begin by examining the three most common economic fallacies. A *fallacy* is an assumption that has been proven false but is still accepted by many people because it appears sensible. Next, we will investigate important theories and laws of economics to recognize their impact on decision making and production.

Economists use models and graphs for the following reasons:

- To simplify and explain complex patterns, relationships, and behaviours
- To outline and highlight the elements at work in an economic system or process
- To make supportable generalizations about economic behaviours
- To apply economic reasoning to issue analysis and decision making
- To identify general trends and tendencies to support forecasts and predictions

You will notice that mathematics is often used in the study of economics. Math is principally used to help us recognize and explain number patterns and statistical relationships. Since this is applied (rather than theoretical) mathematics, students who are not math majors have no cause for alarm. In fact, many students welcome the opportunity that economics provides to explore some practical applications of math.

LEARNING GOALS

Once you have completed this chapter, you should be able to:

- Realize the importance of economic fallacies, theories, and laws
- Understand the purpose and benefit of economic thinking
- Begin using graphs to support economic thinking and to explore patterns and relationships in the economic world
- Use simple models to understand and explain economic principles at work

KEY TERMS

fallacy

fallacy of composition

post hoc fallacy (or cause-and-effect fallacy)

fallacy of single causation

origin

inverse relationship

direct relationship

opportunity cost

production possibilities curve

trade-off

consumer goods

capital goods

relative cost

law of increasing relative cost

frontier

output

law of diminishing returns

input

law of increasing returns to scale

fallacy
A hypothesis that has been proven false but is still accepted by many people because it appears to be true.

fallacy of composition
A mistaken belief that what is good for an individual is automatically good for everyone, or what is good for everyone is good for the individual.

Identifying Economic Fallacies

The following fallacies reveal the kind of faulty thinking that economists must avoid. A **fallacy** is a hypothesis that has been proven false but is still accepted by many people because it appears, at first glance, to make sense. Like other scientists, economists must identify and test all assumptions incorporated into their thinking.

THE FALLACY OF COMPOSITION

In economics, what appears to be true from an individual perspective may, when examined in light of the economy as a whole, be proven false. For example, an individual farmer may decide to clear more land and plant more corn in an attempt to earn extra income. There is no question that this venture could be profitable for this particular farmer. However, suppose that every farmer in Canada attempts the same strategy simultaneously. The result would be an overproduction of corn that would drive its market price much lower. If the new price is so low that it does not allow the farmers to recover their operating expenses, many of them may go bankrupt. It would take several years for the Canadian corn market to recover from this type of collapse. We can see, then, that what is good for the individual is not automatically good for society as a whole. This mistaken belief that individual benefit automatically translates into societal benefit is called the **fallacy of composition**.

This fallacy also works the other way around—that is, what is good for society as a whole must be good for its individual members. Free trade can generally benefit Canadian society by resulting in lower prices for certain manufactured goods. This does not mean that everyone in Canada has benefited from free trade. In fact, some Canadians have lost their jobs because cheaper foreign goods are now available to compete with more expensive goods produced in Canada.

These Canadian workers produce luxury down-filled winter coats for export around the world. Many workers in the garment industry have lost their jobs to workers in China and Asia where wages are substantially lower. To claim that all Canadians benefit from freer global trade is an example of the fallacy of composition.

THE POST HOC FALLACY

The **post hoc fallacy** is derived from the Latin phrase *post hoc ergo propter hoc*, which means, "after this, therefore because of this." Sometimes people assume that, because it took place after event A, event B must have been caused by event A. We can use another agricultural example to illustrate this fallacy. A rooster wakes up every morning before dawn and instinctively crows. Moments later the sun rises. Would it not be ridiculous to assume that the rooster's crowing (and not the rotation of the earth) causes the sun to rise? Similarly, when a newly elected government takes credit for improving the economy, this, too, demonstrates post hoc thinking. Since the economy improved after the election, so the reasoning goes, the election result must have been responsible. Has the new government had time to implement new economic policies? Have the new policies had sufficient time to bring about economic improvement? Unfortunately, many people do not ask these critical questions, preferring instead the apparent logic of the post hoc argument.

This fallacy is also known as the **cause-and-effect fallacy** because of the false assumption that what comes before automatically causes what follows. Causation is very different from sequence. Some prior events are obviously not connected to later events in any meaningful way. As with our rooster crowing just before dawn, sometimes the relationship between two events is more a matter of coincidence than cause and effect.

THE FALLACY OF SINGLE CAUSATION

Closely related to the post hoc fallacy, the **fallacy of single causation** is based on the premise that a single factor or person caused a particular event to occur. For example, a historian might argue that the stock market crash of 1929 caused the Great Depression of the 1930s. This example of the single causation fallacy, like others, is an oversimplification. In reality, the stock market crash was a symptom of economic illness rather than a direct cause of the Great Depression. When the stock market did crash in October 1929, investors' confidence was devastated, which contributed to the Great Depression but was by no means its single cause. Reduced government and investment spending, as well as a marked decline in the rate of technological advancements, greatly contributed to the Depression. Had there been no meaningful connection between the crash of 1929 and the Depression of the 1930s, the argument would have been a good example of the post hoc fallacy. Since there was a meaningful connection, but other factors were also involved, this oversimplification best illustrates the fallacy of single causation.

post hoc fallacy (or cause-and-effect fallacy)
A mistaken belief that what occurs before some event is logically the cause of it.

fallacy of single causation
A mistaken belief, based on oversimplification, that a particular event has one cause rather than several causes.

Unemployed people march during the Great Depression, in Chicago, 1932. To claim that the Depression was caused by a single event is an example of the fallacy of single causation.

Thinking like an Economist

Using Graphs to Understand Relationships: Investigating Ice Cream Sales

Given their visual nature, graphs are an effective way to show the relationships that exist between two different variables. By plotting data along two axis lines, we can clearly see the relationship between the two sets of data. Let's look at a specific example to understand how economists use graphs. We will assume that the data table in Figure 2.1 reports changes in ice cream sales in your community as the selling price per cone fluctuates between $1 and $3.

While the table indicates a pattern, we can better understand the relationship between price and ice cream cone sales by graphing the data. Our graph requires an axis for both variables: price and quantity sold. The two axes are plotted to create a 90˚ angle. The point where the two axes intersect is called the **origin**. The vertical line is called the *y-axis*, and the

horizontal line is called the *x-axis*. Traditionally, in economics, price is plotted along the *y*-axis, with quantity along the *x*-axis. Each square along each axis must be assigned a constant value to maintain accuracy.

After examining the graph in Figure 2.1, answer the following questions:

- What is the value of each grid square along the *y*-axis?

- What is the value of each square along the *x*-axis?

- What would happen to your graph if you were to use one square to represent 1 000 cones along the *x*-axis?

FIGURE 2.1
Ice cream cone sales relative to price

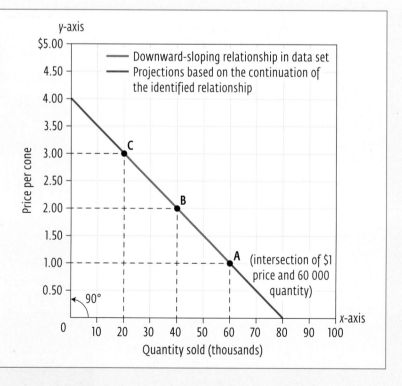

Data Table

Price per Cone	Number of Cones Sold	Point on Graph
$1	60 000	A
$2	40 000	B
$3	20 000	C

The data are plotted on the graph consistent with both axis scales. For example, the placement of point A on the graph represents a price of $1 and a quantity of 60 000 cones sold. No other placement on the grid would accurately represent both variables. A line is drawn to connect the three data points (A, B, and C). This line illustrates the relationship between the two variables. Since the line moves downward (from left to right), it is said to have a downward slope. This represents an **inverse relationship** between price and sales. As price increases, the quantity sold decreases. The two variables therefore change in opposite directions. Having shown the relationship between price and ice cream sales, the graph can now be used to determine additional information about this relationship:

- If the selling price is $1.50, how many cones will most probably be sold?

- If the price is increased to $2.50, how many cones will most probably be sold?

- If the price is increased to $3.50, how many cones will most probably be sold?

- Why can the price of an ice cream cone never be increased to $5 in this community?

The value of this graph as an economic tool is becoming clear. Now let's consider a case in which there is a **direct relationship** between variables; that is, a positive association between them. The table in Figure 2.2 presents data comparing ice cream cone sales to outdoor temperatures. When temperature increases, so do ice cream cone sales, reflecting a direct relationship.

FIGURE 2.2
Ice cream cone sales relative to temperature (data table)

Price per Cone	Number of Cones Sold	Point on Graph
12°C	20 000	X
24°C	50 000	Y
32°C	70 000	Z

APPLYING ECONOMIC THINKING

Draw a graph of the economic relationship between temperature and ice cream sales using the graph in Figure 2.1 as a model. Replace price with temperature on the y-axis of your graph, but use the same scale for the sales axis. Decide on an appropriate scale for the temperature axis. Use your new graph to answer the following questions.

1 If the temperature climbs to 38°C, how many ice cream cones will be sold in your community? Mark this as point A on your graph.

2 How many cones will be sold when the temperature drops to 8°C? Mark this as point B on your graph.

3 What temperature would generate sales of 35 000 cones? Mark this as point C on your graph.

4 At what temperature would ice cream sales stop completely in your community? Explain.

5 How does the slope of the curve help explain the kind of relationship that exists between temperature and ice cream sales and between price and sales? Explain.

origin
As used in graphs, the point at which the vertical and horizontal axes meet.

inverse relationship
A negative association between two variables where when one variable is increased the other decreases, and when one variable is decreased the other increase.

direct relationship
A positive association between two variables where when one variable is increased the other variable also increases, and when one variable is decreased the other also decreases.

opportunity cost
The value or benefit that must be given up to achieve something else. For example, by choosing to produce item A, a business gives up the benefit that it could have gained from producing item B using the same resources.

production possibilities curve
A graphical representation of the production choices facing an economy.

trade-off
The sacrifice of one resource or production choice for another.

consumer goods
Those goods or services that an economy produces to satisfy human needs.

capital goods
Goods, such as tools or machinery, used to produce consumer goods.

Opportunity Cost and Production Possibility Theories

In making any economic decision, we must consider not only what we expect to gain but also what we stand to lose. This is what economists call the **opportunity cost** of our actions. Any time we use resources to achieve one end, we have to do without something else we could have done with those resources instead. We can define *opportunity cost* as the sum of all that is lost from taking one course of action over another. This inescapable reality must be factored into all economic theories and choices.

   To make the concept of opportunity cost clearer, let's return to Lani's dilemma from Chapter 1 (page 12). Recall that she had the following options: working extra hours, attending a concert with her friends, or working on a major assignment. Whichever alternative Lani chooses, she will have to do without the other two. The opportunity cost of attending the concert is based on the satisfaction lost from the "next best" alternative use of her time and effort. In other words, the opportunity cost of going to the concert is either the satisfaction obtained from earning extra money at work or the higher grade earned by improving her research skills, but not both, since you can do only one or the other. Both staying home to study and going out with friends will include the opportunity cost of lost wages.

ECONOMIC LAWS AFFECTING PRODUCTION POSSIBILITIES

To improve your ability to think like an economist, let's look at some of the most important generalizations economists make. Economists use graphs of the **production possibilities curve** to illustrate the impact of scarcity. Since wants will always exceed available resources, people living in any economy must make production choices. The production possibilities curve provides a visual model of the production choices faced by people in a simple economy. Before examining a graph of this curve, we must understand the assumptions on which this model is based:

❶ *Only two products can be produced by this simple economy.*

In an economy capable of producing hundreds of thousands of different products, decision making is extremely complex. To reduce economic decision making to its most basic form, the model assumes that only two products can be produced by this economy. This assumption makes the classic economic **trade-off** very clear: the increased production of one good can be achieved only by sacrificing a sufficient quantity of the alternative product.

   In our model, we shall assume that the two goods that can be produced are bread and ploughs. Bread represents the production of **consumer goods**—those products and services that directly satisfy human wants. Ploughs, important agricultural tools, represent the production of **capital goods**—those goods used in the production of other goods. For example, ploughs are needed to prepare the soil for planting. The ploughs in operation today contribute to a successful wheat harvest tomorrow and, therefore, to the future production of bread.

❷ The economy has fixed technology and resources.

Since it is examining the economy over a short period of time, the model assumes that no technological innovations will be introduced to improve the rate of production. It also assumes that the amount of productive resources available does not change. Existing resources can be shifted, as desired, between the production of bread and ploughs, but no additional resources can be imported into the economy. For this reason, the only way to make more bread is to produce fewer ploughs, and vice versa.

❸ The economy is at full employment.

The model assumes that all productive resources, including labour, are fully employed and that they are being used effectively and efficiently to produce the maximum output possible.

What combination of ploughs and bread should our simple economy choose to produce? This question involves the concept of opportunity cost. Since the way we answer it will clearly reflect the values of our society, it is also a question that involves normative, or policy, economics.

The Law of Increasing Relative Cost

We can see by examining the production possibilities schedule in Figure 2.3 that the opportunity cost of increasing plough production is clearly reflected in the simultaneous decline in the production of bread. For example, in moving from alternative A to alternative B, the opportunity cost of producing one plough is the 1 000 loaves of bread that must be sacrificed. The production managers in the economy have effectively transformed the 1 000 loaves of bread into one new plough by shifting their resources from bread production to plough production. The economic cost of one plough relative to bread is not given in dollars but in the number of loaves, that is, 1 000 loaves. This is the plough's **relative cost** and is directly proportional to the opportunity cost of increased plough production.

relative cost
The cost of producing one item, A, expressed in terms of the numbers of another item, B, which must be given up to produce A (that is, A's opportunity cost).

FIGURE 2.3
A production possibilities schedule and the relative costs of producing ploughs and bread

Production Possibilities (alternatives)	Ploughs	Loaves of Bread	Opportunity Cost of Additional Plough Production (quantity of bread that must be given up)	Relative Cost to Society
A	0	15 000		
B	1	14 000	1 000	1 plough = 1 000 loaves*
C	2	12 000	2 000	1 plough = 2 000 loaves
D	3	9 000	3 000	1 plough = 3 000 loaves
E	4	5 000	4 000	1 plough = 4 000 loaves
F	5	0	5 000	1 plough = 5 000 loaves
* Since the production of one more plough will cost society 1 000 loaves of bread				

law of increasing relative cost

The increase in the relative cost of producing more of item A, measured by the numbers of another item, B, that could be produced with the same resources.

Figure 2.3, then, clearly reflects the existence of an important economic rule, known as the **law of increasing relative cost**. This law comes into play whenever a society, to get a greater amount of one product, sacrifices an ever-increasing amount of other products. It is reflected in the graph in Figure 2.4 by the bowed-out, or concave, line of the production possibilities curve. This curve is created by plotting the data from Figure 2.3. If the opportunity cost of each extra plough were constant at 1 000 loaves, the production possibilities curve would be a straight line.

The law of increasing relative cost causes this concave curvature of the production possibilities curve because, although plough production (the horizontal movement) changes by a constant amount each time, the quantity of bread production (the vertical movement) changes by an increasingly larger amount each time. (Look again at Figure 2.4.) In other words, the slope of the curve becomes steeper as a result of this ever-increasing vertical change.

To understand this economic phenomenon, we must take into account the nature of the goods being produced and the difference in the productive resources that each one requires. Our first product, bread, is an agricultural product made primarily from wheat. The principal resource required to grow wheat is fertile land. Labour is also involved but is not as important.

FIGURE 2.4

The production possibilities curve for ploughs and bread

This graph reveals how opportunity cost works.

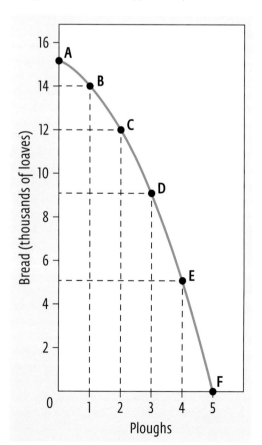

Our second product, the plough, is a farm tool. The principal resource required to manufacture ploughs is human labour. Land, which provides the natural resources required (such as wood and iron), is also necessary but not as important. Therefore, the production of bread and ploughs uses resources in different proportions. At point A, the economy produces no ploughs and 15 000 loaves of bread. It is easy to see that, from A to B, the opportunity cost of producing one plough is 1 000 loaves of bread. As we move from production alternative A to alternatives B and C, those resources more suited to producing ploughs and less suited to producing bread (such as carpenters and blacksmiths) will be shifted from making bread to making ploughs.

As society moves from alternative C to alternatives D, E, and F, however, resources more suited to producing bread are put to use producing additional ploughs. Bread production declines at a very rapid rate. The use of our limited resources has become less efficient and less effective. For instance, some farmland is being converted to woodlots, and some bakers are being retrained as blacksmiths. This inefficient use of resources is evident in the large amount of bread that must be sacrificed to produce the last two ploughs. From E to F, the opportunity cost of one more plough has grown drastically to 5 000 loaves of bread.

The Production Possibilities Curve as a Frontier

The production possibility schedule contains the maximum potential output that can be produced for each of the two products. The resulting curve, therefore, represents the outer limit, or **frontier**, of production possibility. This frontier is attainable only if all productive resources are fully employed. In reality, however, we know that resources are not always fully employed. For example, part of the labour force may be unemployed, some land may be left uncultivated, or some machines and factories may be idle. In addition, as a result of human error, some resources may be used ineffectively.

These realities will cause the economy to perform below the level of maximum potential output. In Figure 2.5, point L (inside and therefore below the frontier of maximum production) illustrates this situation. Most economies will achieve production levels below the frontier. Nevertheless, each society sets for itself economic goals that aim to reach the production possibility frontier in the short term and to force the frontier to grow outward in the long term.

frontier
The curve on a production possibilities graph representing the maximum numbers of two items that can be produced with a given amount of resources.

FIGURE 2.5
The production possibilities curve as a frontier
The curve is concave, or bowed out, because the opportunity cost of producing one extra plough (yellow arrows) increases constantly in terms of the quantity of bread that must be sacrificed each time (red arrows).

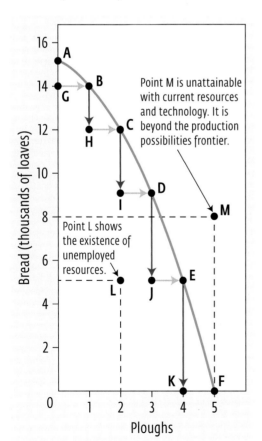

Point M on our graph (representing 8 000 loaves of bread and 5 ploughs) is clearly beyond the production possibility frontier and so is unattainable at this time. An economy's capacity to produce can be increased over the long term by such changes as population growth (which expands the labour force) and technological advances (such as the development of more efficient machinery). This kind of structural change will allow the economy to produce, simultaneously, more bread and ploughs in the long run, thereby shifting the production possibilities frontier outward as the productive capacity of the whole economy expands. In time, this expansion will make M an attainable point on the expanded production possibilities curve.

Self-Reflect

1 In your own words, explain the economic concept of opportunity cost.

2 Create a production possibilities schedule that reflects a constant trade-off between bread and ploughs (that is, 1 000 loaves of bread for each new plough) and then graph the production possibilities curve. How is your curve different from Figure 2.4? What is the cause of this difference?

output
The products produced by using resources or inputs such as land, labour, or capital.

law of diminishing returns
The eventual decline in the rate of extra outputs produced that occurs when one input used in production of the output is held constant and the others are increased.

input
A productive resource (such as land, labour, or capital) used to produce an output.

Working within Economic Laws

We have dealt with the law of increasing relative cost and looked at its effects on production possibilities. Just like our bread or ploughs example, if a society chooses to produce greater amounts of one product, it must sacrifice an ever-increasing amount of other products, because the increases lead to the efficient use of productive resources. This reality forces economic decision making to consider reasonable levels of production, at which the value of gains are comparable to what is sacrificed. For example, Canada could become self-sufficient in the production of orange juice, but the sacrifices required in lost production of other goods might never justify the venture as sound economic practice. It might be economically prudent to import our orange juice from producers in more tropical climates. Thus, the law of increasing relative cost helps to influence sound production decisions.

THE LAW OF DIMINISHING RETURNS

While the law of increasing relative cost deals with the relationship between two **outputs**, or products (in our case, bread and ploughs), the **law of diminishing returns** deals with the relationship between an **input** (a productive resource such as labour) and the resulting output. More specifically, the law of diminishing returns states that outputs will increase when a particular input is increased, but only to a point. After this point has been reached, increasing inputs will not have an appreciable effect on the production of outputs. Another agricultural example will give us a better idea of the way this law operates.

Suppose a farmer is working a farm that is 10 hectares (ha) without the use of machinery or hired help. There are only two productive resources, or inputs, involved in this enterprise: land and the farmer's labour. For the sake of our demonstration, assume that no additional land is available to the farmer. Further assume that the farmer is able to hire additional workers as needed. Therefore, the operation of this farm has one input that is variable (labour force) and one that is constant (land). Our farmer wants to increase the yield (or output) as a way of making the enterprise more profitable. For seven growing seasons in a row, the farmer experiments by hiring one additional person each year to help work the farm. Therefore, the workforce expands from one worker (the farmer alone) to seven (the farmer plus six hired hands) by year seven. Figure 2.6 outlines the results of this experiment.

In the second year, the additional worker contributes to a sizable increase in yield. After that, increases in the labour force result in less and less extra yield. Finally, a 10-ha farm can produce only so much yield, no matter how many workers are added. The law of diminishing returns is as follows:

For any productive enterprise, when at least one input is held constant [in our example, land] *while other inputs are increased* [in our example, labour force]*, there will be an eventual decline in the rate of extra output, or yield.*

FIGURE 2.6
Experiment A

A farmer's attempt to increase output, which illustrates the law of diminishing returns.

Year	Land (hectares)	Labour Force (workers)	Total Production (bushels of corn)	Increase in Yield (extra bushels)
1	10	1	1 000	
2	10	2	2 000	1 000
3	10	3	2 800	800
4	10	4	3 400	600
5	10	5	3 800	400
6	10	6	3 900	100
7	10	7	3 900	0

law of increasing returns to scale

The increase in the rate of extra outputs produced when all inputs used in production are increased and no inputs are held constant.

This decline may not be as immediate as in our example. Often, diminishing returns will appear only after several more increases in the variable resource have occurred. Because the amount of land remains constant, there will eventually be diminishing returns.

THE LAW OF INCREASING RETURNS TO SCALE

Examining another economic principle will help us to understand the law of diminishing returns even better. The **law of increasing returns to scale** tells us what happens when all productive resources are increased simultaneously. To see how this idea works, let's return to our cornfield and conduct a slightly different experiment. This time, as the farmer hires additional workers, additional parcels of land are being cultivated as well. Just as in our last example, we assume that all work is done manually. Figure 2.7 outlines the results of this second experiment.

FIGURE 2.7
Experiment B

A farmer's attempt to increase output, which illustrates the law of increasing returns to scale.

Year	Land (hectares)	Labour Force (workers)	Total Production (bushels of corn)	Increase in Yield (extra bushels)
1	10	1	1 000	
2	20	2	2 000	1 000
3	30	3	3 200	1 200
4	40	4	4 600	1 400
5	50	5	6 200	1 600
6	60	6	8 000	1 800
7	70	7	10 000	2 000

What economic law does this image of a corn harvest in Southwestern Ontario reflect?

In this experiment, the outcome is very different from that of the first experiment. Why? Have we refuted the law of diminishing returns? Not at all. In this second experiment, the farmer increases all productive resources each year and in the same quantity. Every time a new worker is added, another 10 ha of cultivated land are also added. As a result, the farmer increases the scale of operations. An operation that began as a single farmer working on a small parcel of land has grown into a large farm employing seven fulltime workers. The net result of this conversion to a larger-scale operation is a steady increase in yield.

When the farmer doubles the amount of all productive resources used in year two, total production also doubles. When the farmer doubles resource input again from year two to year four, output more than doubles (2 000 bushels of corn increased to 4 600 bushels of corn). By the end of the experiment, a sevenfold increase in inputs leads to a tenfold increase in total production. Clearly, the farmer's systematic increase in the amount of all productive resources results in greater returns. Through effective teamwork and specialization, economies of scale make the farmer's operations more efficient. In the real world, increased returns to scale (also referred to as *economies of scale*) help to explain why so many of the products we buy are produced by large companies. Even in agriculture, the large corporate enterprise is increasingly replacing the small family farm. In later chapters of this resource, we will explore various applications of the law of increasing returns to scale.

In the real world, productive resources are limited. As a result, it is not always possible for an enterprise to increase all resource inputs indefinitely. Ultimately, therefore, the availability of some productive resources will end, and the law of diminishing returns will once again prevail.

Self-Reflect

1 Explain each of the three economic laws in your own words.

2 Why is the law of diminishing returns considered inevitable? Explain.

3 What economic law does the image on the facing page confirm about farming in Canada? Explain.

Chapter 2
Consolidation Activities

KNOWLEDGE

1   Why are so many of the products that we buy manufactured by large-scale producers? Explain why most highly successful businesses today operate on a large scale.

2   Explain how the fallacy of composition helps to shed light on the tension that exists between individual self-interest and the common good.

3   Explain how increased relative costs relate directly to opportunity costs and diminishing returns.

THINKING & INQUIRY

4   Which economic law do you consider most significant? Justify your choice.

5   Working in small groups, discuss the following statements. Through group consensus, identify the type of reasoning error each statement contains: the fallacy of composition, the post hoc fallacy, or the fallacy of single causation. To keep you on your toes, one statement is fallacy-free.

   a) An economic crisis in Japan caused the 1998 decline of the Canadian dollar in international money markets.

   b) What is good for General Motors is good for the Canadian economy.

   c) Victoria, British Columbia, has one of the highest death rates in the country; therefore, it must be unhealthy to live there.

   d) Stephanie found the work experience she got through her school's co-operative education program to be of great personal benefit. Co-operative education should be a compulsory requirement for all secondary school students.

   e) A multi-car accident on the Trans-Canada Highway was caused by bad weather.

   f) If every Canadian worker received a 10 percent pay increase, the country as a whole would be better off.

   g) Curtis lost the student council election this morning because a black cat crossed his path while he was walking to school.

   h) The four components of the scientific method first outlined by Francis Bacon are observation, data collection and analysis, explanation, and verification. Although scientists today use many different processes to make their discoveries, they almost always make use of the four steps outlined by Bacon.

   i) Former prime minister Stephen Harper was responsible for the sluggish economic growth during the last years of his term in office.

   j) Ali's marks improved after she broke up with Evan. He was not a good influence.

COMMUNICATION

6   How would you explain to a friend, who does not study economics, why graphs are better than data tables to explain an economic relationship between price and the quantity of products sold?

7   Write a concise (one-page) summary note of the most important information from this chapter for a classmate who has been hospitalized.

APPLICATION

8 Identify three examples of economic fallacies that you have experienced personally, noticed in advertisements aimed at consumers, or seen in political messaging intended to persuade voters. Explain the faulty thinking embedded in each example.

9 Examine Figure 2.8 and answer the questions that follow.

FIGURE 2.8
Annual production possibilities for country X

Production Possibility	Bicycles	Cheese (kg)
A	0	170
B	1	160
C	2	140
D	3	110
E	4	60
F	5	0

a) Calculate the opportunity cost for each additional bicycle being produced.

b) Use the data in the table to graph a production possibilities curve.

c) Mark a point H on the graph that indicates widespread unemployment in country X.

d) Mark a point J that represents a production level that cannot be reached by country X's economy. Explain why this point is unattainable under present conditions. How might this production level be reached in the future?

e) Explain why this production possibility curve has a concave (bowed-out) curvature. What economic law is responsible for this curvature?

10 Figure 2.9 outlines some combinations of corn and beef that can be produced annually from a given parcel of farmland.

FIGURE 2.9
Annual production possibilities for an agricultural enterprise

Production Possibility	Corn (bushels)	Beef (kg)
A	16 000	0
B	8 000	900
C	6 000	1 200
D	4 000	1 400
E	2 000	1 450
F	0	1 500

a) Draw a production possibilities curve for this agricultural enterprise.

b) Can this farmland produce 6 000 bushels of corn and 1 500 kg of beef during the same year? Mark this production level as point H on your graph. Explain what must happen in order for this agricultural enterprise to reach this level of production.

c) What is the opportunity cost of expanding beef production from 900 kg to 1 200 kg annually?

d) What is the opportunity cost of expanding corn production from level B to level A annually?

e) If a decision is made to produce 5 000 bushels of corn, how much beef can be produced on this farm at the same time? Mark this production level as point K on your graph.

f) Given this set of production possibilities, should this enterprise specialize (in either corn or beef production) or produce ample quantities of both products? Justify your decision.

3

Productive Resources and Economic Systems

INTRODUCTION

Having examined the importance of productive resources in determining an economy's production possibilities frontier, we will now look more closely at the concept of productive resources to better understand the basic production choices that every economic system must make. Productive resources are the real wealth of a country and the key components that fuel growth and prosperity. We will also examine the way different types of economic systems answer the following three basic production questions: What to produce? How to produce? and For whom to produce? To consolidate economic thinking, we will distinguish between the related concepts of production, productivity, and value added. The concepts and skills developed in this chapter will help you successfully complete the performance task at the end of this unit.

LEARNING GOALS

Once you have completed this chapter, you should be able to:

- Recognize tangible and intangible productive resources as a country's real wealth
- Compare how different economic systems answer the three basic production questions and make choices about how productive resources are owned and used
- Compare different national economies with regard to their ability to produce and share wealth, respect individual economic freedom, and promote the common good
- Distinguish between production and productivity
- Explain the economic concept of value added

KEY TERMS

productive resources

factors of production

land

raw materials

labour

capital

real capital

money capital

productivity

entrepreneurship

tangible resources

intangible resources

environment for
  enterprise

economic system

traditional economy

barter

command economy

capital goods

market economy

private enterprise

mixed economy

mixed market economy

Crown land

value added

productive resources (or factors of production)
Resources (such as land, labour, and capital) that are used to produce goods and services.

land
A factor of production that includes all natural resources used to produce goods.

raw materials
All natural resources used in production.

labour
A factor of production comprising the physical and mental effort contributed by people to producing goods and services.

capital
A factor of production that refers to the machinery, factories, warehouses, and equipment used to produce goods and services.

real capital
A more precise term than *capital* for the machinery, factories, warehouses, and equipment used to produce goods and services. It is distinct from *money capital*.

money capital
The funds used to acquire real capital.

productivity
A firm's ability to maximize output from the resources available, usually measured as the firm's output per worker.

entrepreneurship
The contribution made by an owner, manager, or innovator who organizes land, labour, and capital to produce goods and services.

Making Resources Productive

By **productive resources**, economists mean anything that can be used to create or manufacture valuable goods or services. These resources are sometimes called **factors of production**. Originally, economists recognized only three types of productive resources: land, labour, and capital. Over time, the definitions of these three types of resources were broadened to include other related resources. As well, economists now recognize entrepreneurship and knowledge as productive resources. Entrepreneurship and knowledge allow for the more efficient use of land, labour, and capital.

Land includes not only the earth's surface but also natural resources found on or below the surface. Resources such as mineral deposits, groundwater, fossil fuels, and forests are extremely useful in providing the **raw materials** needed to produce the goods and services that people want.

Labour includes both the physical work and mental effort people contribute to the production process. In national surveys of business leaders, a majority of the chief executive officers interviewed consistently identify attracting and retaining high-calibre employees as major priorities. Economists recognize the importance of labour resources, whether they constitute a paid service (such as the work carried out on an automobile assembly line) or a volunteer service (such as the homemaking work done by a stay-at-home parent).

The third productive resource, **capital**, refers to the factories, warehouses, machinery, and equipment used in the production of goods and services. Since we also use the term *capital* to mean the money available in an enterprise to acquire these resources, we must be more precise in our terminology. For this reason, the factories, warehouses, machinery, and equipment are often referred to as **real capital**, while the funds to acquire them are referred to as **money capital**. Real capital is extremely important to a growing economy. An economy's investment in real capital today will allow it to expand its total production and improve its **productivity** (efficiency) in the future. The large amounts of tax dollars spent annually on public education in Canada represent a sizable investment in what is sometimes described as "human capital."

Entrepreneurship refers to the ability to develop and organize a business activity, assuming its risks, to achieve positive results. It is the contribution that an owner, a manager, or an innovator makes to the production process. The entrepreneur uses knowledge to organize and direct the other factors of production (land, labour, and capital), and seeks to develop new products, production processes, and marketing strategies. Although less tangible than physical labour, entrepreneurship and knowledge are today recognized as important factors of production.

Should labour that does not directly earn a wage be considered a valuable productive resource?

TANGIBLE AND INTANGIBLE RESOURCES

Productive resources can be classified as either tangible or intangible. **Tangible resources** have physical properties that can be seen and touched and are therefore easily quantified. Examples include a hundred tonnes of nickel, a thousand people in the labour force, or six punch presses on an industrial assembly line.

Intangible resources lack the physical properties that make them easy to quantify. Although economists cannot see or weigh something like entrepreneurship, they know it is important to the economy because of the positive effect that certain risk-taking and organizational activities have on production levels and on a company's ability to operate efficiently. Economists have concluded that, although it is difficult to quantify, entrepreneurship directly affects national productivity and is therefore an important intangible factor of production. Knowledge has become an important productive resource as well, given Canada's transformation from a manufacturing economy to an information economy. Information that is accurate and timely increases business productivity.

Economists also recognize a third, and even more intangible, factor as important in the production of goods and services—an economy's **environment for enterprise**. A country has an environment for enterprise when its social and cultural values and its political and economic institutions are conducive to doing business. For example, a stable government gives people and businesses the security they need to make sound planning and production decisions. It also bolsters both investor and consumer confidence, thereby creating a climate favourable to increased economic activity. As Figure 3.1 shows, most intangible resources involve productive human contributions—contributions that go beyond the physical, or tangible, form of labour.

In the final analysis, tangible and intangible resources work together to form the real source of a country's wealth and prosperity. The country's treasury can always print more money, but without goods and services to buy and sell, money means very little. An economy's capacity to produce goods and services in response to the wants and needs of its citizens—in other words, the sum total of its tangible and intangible productive resources—is a clear indicator of economic wealth and the cornerstone of long-term growth and prosperity.

tangible resources
Physical resources (such as land and labour) that are necessary for production and are visible.

intangible resources
Resources that are necessary for production, such as entrepreneurship, knowledge, and an environment for enterprise. Intangibles are not as visible as tangible resources, but they are no less important.

environment for enterprise
A society's social values and institutions, such as stable government, that are favourable to businesses attempting to produce and sell goods and services.

FIGURE 3.1

A summary listing of productive resources

TANGIBLE RESOURCES		INTANGIBLE RESOURCES	
LAND • Natural resources • Water • Raw materials • Fertile soils **LABOUR** • Skilled workforce **CAPITAL** • Facilities • Machinery } Real capital • Equipment • Money capital		**KNOWLEDGE** • Science • Experience • Technology (applied) • Education and training **ENTREPRENEURSHIP** • Organization • Risk taking • Management • Innovation • Direction **ENVIRONMENT FOR ENTERPRISE** • Political stability • Social values • Economic stability supporting enterprise • Work ethic	

Self-Reflect

1 Outline the difference between tangible and intangible productive resources, and explain why they are the real source of a country's wealth.

2 Explain the difference between real capital and money capital.

3 Why is political stability an important productive resource for an economy?

4 Although they are difficult to measure directly, how do economists know that entrepreneurship and technological know-how are valuable productive resources?

economic system
The laws, institutions, and common practices that help a country determine how to use its resources to satisfy as many of its people's needs and wants as possible.

Economic Systems and Production Questions

All societies have to determine how to make the best use of their limited resources. To address this issue, their economic system must answer the following three basic production questions:

❶ *What to produce?*

- What goods and services should our society produce, and in what quantities?
- What is worth producing, and what is not?
- What are we giving up to produce these goods and services?

❷ *How to produce?*

- By whom, with what resources, and in what way should goods be produced?
- Should goods be made in many small factories or in a few large operations?
- How much automation should be used? How much manual labour should be used?

❸ *For whom to produce?*

- How will total output be shared among the different members of society?
- Who will get which goods and services? Will goods be shared equally?
- On what basis should decisions concerning distribution be made?

Although every economy answers these questions, the way each economy answers them helps to identify the type of economic system that operates in a specific society. Economists define an **economic system** as the set of laws, institutions, and common practices that help a country determine how to use its scarce resources to satisfy as many of its people's needs and wants as possible. Over time, three distinctly different ways of approaching the basic questions of production have led to three types of economic systems: traditional economy, command economy, and market economy.

DID YOU KNOW?

The creation of Post-it® Notes by the 3M Corporation was an accident. In a failed attempt to create an inexpensive high-grade adhesive, 3M scientists developed a very low-grade adhesive. What first seemed like a useless material was transformed, through the ingenuity and inventiveness of 3M research lab technicians and marketing experts, into a marketable product that became one of the biggest success stories in company history.

FIGURE 3.2   The triangle of basic production questions

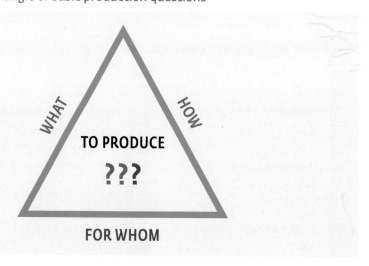

THE TRADITIONAL ECONOMY

In a pure **traditional economy**, practices of the past determine the answers to the three basic production questions. The goods and services produced today are the same as those produced in the past, and the manner of production remains unchanged. Traditional practices and skills are passed on from generation to generation, and the quantity of total output does not vary greatly from year to year. This type of economy is usually found in a relatively static subsistence society in which people engage in little long-term planning and focus primarily on surviving the challenges of each day.

In a traditional economy, each family's economic strategy is to be as self-sufficient as possible. Therefore, the question of what to produce is determined by the needs of the family, whose members produce goods for their own use. Surplus goods are usually traded to other families for essential items. This trading of goods (or services) without the use of a monetary system is known as **bartering**. In terms of how to produce these goods, parents teach their children the necessary skills so that they will be able to assume their parents' roles and responsibilities. As a result, people spend their lives as part of the same social class into which they were born.

Centuries ago, the traditional economy was the most common economic system throughout most of the world. People lived in small rural communities. They had modest needs, most of which could be met by using the natural resources provided by the local environment. They grew much of their own food, built their own homes, and made their own clothing and tools.

Over time, population growth as well as industrial, scientific, and technological advances transformed most traditional economies. For example, major advances in communications technology have introduced many indigenous populations living in remote areas (for example, Inuit in Canada's north and Aboriginal people in Australia's outback) to the practices and economic systems of other cultures. As a result, the pure traditional economy is more difficult to find. Those few that remain today are found in relatively isolated environments where indigenous populations carry on traditional practices largely unaffected by outside contact.

THE COMMAND ECONOMY

In a pure **command economy**, production decisions are made by a small group of political leaders with the power to enforce their decisions throughout the entire economy. In other words, the pure command economy is centrally planned. The central authority answers all production questions based on the best interests of the state. The state owns the productive resources; the central authority allocates them on behalf of the state. In this economic system, people are obligated to serve the state. State authorities draw up plans to meet individual needs such as food, housing, medicine, and education.

The central authority uses a system of reward and punishment to promote increased productivity. People who contribute to the betterment of the state are rewarded with extra goods and, sometimes, special privileges (such as more

traditional economy
An economic system in which production decisions are determined by the practices of the past.

barter
The trading of goods and services without the use of a monetary system; such transactions are common in traditional economies.

command economy
An economic system in which production decisions are made by government-appointed central planners.

DID YOU KNOW?

Today, traditional economies (with varying degrees of modification) are found within the following societies:

- The Bedouin of the Sahara
- The Bushmen of the Kalahari Desert
- The Mongols of the Gobi Desert
- The Lapps of the Scandinavian tundra
- The Masai of the African savannah
- The Waura and Yanomami of the Amazon rainforest
- The Mbuti of the African rainforest
- The Senoi and Negrito peoples of Malaysia.

capital goods
Goods, such as tools or machinery, used to produce consumer goods.

market economy
An economic system in which production decisions are made by the actions of buyers and sellers in the marketplace.

private enterprise
A term applied to the private ownership of productive resources, a characteristic of market economies.

comfortable living quarters). People who do not contribute are penalized for their lack of productivity. The central planning authority determines what products and quantities to produce, who will work where, what machinery will be available to assist production, and how much each worker will be paid. With many of their needs already covered by the state's central plan, workers usually spend their modest wages on consumer goods, such as food, clothing, and shelter. The state plan emphasizes the production of **capital goods** over consumer goods because capital goods increase the economy's ability to produce more in the future. Consequently, consumer goods are generally in short supply.

Very few pure command economies exist today. Modified examples are found in Cuba, China, North Korea, and Vietnam. Prior to 1991, when the former Soviet Union and the countries of Eastern Europe operated centrally planned economies under communist rule, one-third of the world's people lived under some version of a command economy.

THE MARKET ECONOMY

In a pure **market economy**, economic activity is co-ordinated by many individuals who make independent decisions in a free marketplace. Since people act for themselves, often out of self-interest, this system is also called *free enterprise*. Since resources are privately owned, the system is sometimes called **private enterprise**.

The actions of individual buyers and sellers in the marketplace determine the answers to the three basic production questions. What to produce is ultimately determined by consumer demand. Businesses will clear out their unwanted goods at discounted prices and no longer produce them. Instead, they will produce "in-demand" goods and services because these will fetch the highest prices and probably generate the highest profits.

The quest for profit also plays a key role in determining how to produce goods and services. Consumers prefer low prices. Producers can maximize their profits by using the least costly and most efficient methods of production. Inefficient producers will not be able to compete in the long run and be forced to improve their productivity or go out of business.

Distribution in a market economy is determined by the income people receive for their contributions (mostly labour) to the production process. Income levels, therefore, determine for whom to produce the economy's goods and services. People with high incomes can afford to buy more of the national output than those with low incomes.

An aerial view of Hong Kong, one of the closest examples of a market economiy that exist today.

The basic elements of a market economy are private property, freedom of enterprise, profit maximization, and competition. The government's role is only to provide law and order and to assist economic development. Very few pure market economies exist today. Perhaps the closest examples are the economies of Hong Kong and the United States. When Hong Kong was under British rule, it was recognized as the most liberal of market economies. In the United States, the federal government has expanded its role in the country's economic life, especially since the Great Depression.

MIXED ECONOMIES

By now, it should be obvious that very few "pure" economic systems exist today. There are two important reasons for this. First, no single type of economic system is perfect. To date, not one of the three types has managed to meet all of the needs and wants of its members. In other words, no system holds a monopoly on effectiveness and efficiency. Second, political leaders and economic decision makers have integrated the best elements of each type of economy to create their own **mixed economies**.

Canada: A Mixed Market Economy

The Canadian economy is a classic example of this cross-pollination of economic models because it contains many elements of a market economy along with some characteristics of command and traditional economies. For this reason, economists classify the Canadian economy as a **mixed market economy**. Our country's economy includes both private and state-owned enterprises. For example, in the television industry, the Canadian Broadcasting Corporation (CBC) is state-owned, while the Canadian Television Network (CTV) is privately owned. Although the non-profit, public service mandate of the CBC is different from that of the commercially motivated CTV, at times these two corporations are in direct competition with each other. A good example of this competition is the bidding war the two networks engage in for broadcast rights to the Olympic Games.

In the matter of land ownership, Canada has state-owned land (or **Crown land**), which is a feature of command economies. However, it also permits private ownership of land, which is a feature of market economies. The federal government has also established many reserve lands for Indigenous peoples, who tend to have more traditional economies.

Although there is a great amount of free enterprise in Canada's economy, there are also many government regulations that businesses must follow. In addition, over the years, the Canadian government has established a "social safety net" for the welfare of its most needy citizens. These social programs, which are not characteristics of a pure market economy, include guaranteed income supplements, government-funded medical care, employment insurance for workers, and social security for senior citizens. Partly because of this elaborate safety net, the United Nations Human Development Report has identified Canada as one of the best countries in the world in which to live.

mixed economy
An economic system, such as Canada's, that contains elements of market, command, and traditional systems.

mixed market economy
An economic system predominantly featuring characteristics of a free market system but also incorporating some qualities of command economies, such as government-owned enterprise.

Crown land
A Canadian term for government-owned land.

DID YOU KNOW?

The traditional practice of bartering is growing rapidly in Canada. For example, a cabinetmaker may agree with a bricklayer to exchange services. The bricklayer repairs the cabinetmaker's chimney, and the cabinetmaker provides the bricklayer with a set of cupboards. Since these services are being exchanged on a personal level, quality is guaranteed. Since no written contract is required and no money changes hands, this transaction might not be reported as income at the end of the year. Avoiding taxes is an additional benefit to both workers, but it reduces government revenues and the funds available for social programs.

China: An Emerging Industrial Giant

For decades, China maintained a command economy under a strong communist dictatorship. Since the 1980s, China's Communist Party has preferred to describe the Chinese model as a "socialist market economy." Elements of free and private enterprise have been introduced under the watchful eye of the Communist Party leadership, which is still firmly in charge of the economy. Under this mixed economic model, China has emerged as one of the world's fastest-growing major economies and the largest manufacturing economy and exporter of goods.

With a large population and workforce, wages have been kept low. Lower wages have allowed China to produce relatively inexpensive merchandise that competes favourably in world markets. Government assistance to key industries further improves competitiveness.

As it did as a command economy, the Chinese government continues to operate out of a series of ambitious five-year development plans. To meet the government's ambitious goals of developing industrial infrastructure and capacity, raising living standards for citizens, and redressing regional inequalities across the country, the economy is required to sustain a staggering 8 percent annual growth rate. To achieve this remarkable growth rate, often environmental protection, safety standards, and human rights are sacrificed. In the past, official economic statistics have been altered. At times, intellectual property and technology have been stolen from other economies. However, China's steady economic growth rate, even while other economies have been in sharp decline, is undeniable.

In Beijing, China, how has heay industrialization affected the environment?

Sweden: A Champion of Nordic Social Democracy

The Nordic economic model, practised with significant national variations in Denmark, Finland, Norway, Iceland, and Sweden, has gained global attention since 1950. The common trait of these mixed economic systems is an attempt to balance free enterprise with social responsibility. As a result, a "universalist" welfare state has emerged where citizens contribute effectively to economic growth and prosperity, and, in turn, they are well looked after. Economic security and opportunity are promoted within the framework of free enterprise, open markets, private ownership, and free trade.

In Sweden, a high percentage of the workforce is unionized. A three-party arrangement has evolved where representatives of labour, employers, and government work together to negotiate wages, working conditions, and market policies. The government mediates negotiations between the interests of labour and capital, not only to reduce conflicts but also to ensure that business practices support sustainable economic growth and shared prosperity. In this model, labour and capital are seen as economic partners rather than rivals. In addition, all citizens are entitled to health care, pensions, support for the unemployed, disability benefits, and child care.

The Swedish economy is focused on the efficient production of quality products for export around the world. Given its highly skilled labour force and rich natural resources, primary exports include automobiles, industrial machinery, chemicals and pharmaceuticals, paper products, iron and steel products, pulp and wood, and electronics. In addition, growth in information and communication technology has also been strong in Sweden. Both Skype® and Spotify® were founded in Sweden.

The Volvo Torslanda Works near Gothenburg, Sweden, has an impressive manufacturing capacity of 300 000 vehicles anually.

Self-Reflect

1 What are the three basic questions of production that all economic systems must answer?

2 Explain the importance of central planning in a command economy. Why is this not necessary in a market economy?

3 Explain why the Canadian economy can be accurately described as a mixed market economy.

4 How does the Swedish model differ from the Canadian model?

Thinking like an Economist

Differentiating between Production and Productivity

To understand what is meant by *productivity*, or "maximizing the output from the resources used," let's look at two competing manufacturers of quality shoes: Acme FootWare Company and ComfortMax Shoe Company. Figure 3.3 outlines weekly production figures for both firms.

As we can see in Figure 3.3, the total weekly production of shoes is identical for both firms; therefore, production levels are equal. Now let's consider the production efficiency of each firm. ComfortMax workers are more efficient because they are able to produce 2 600 pairs of shoes by employing a workforce of 36 shoemakers. On average, each worker produces 72 pairs of shoes per week. By comparison, each shoemaker at Acme produces an average of 52 pairs of shoes per week. If we were to calculate the productivity of capital goods (such as sewing machines), the position of the two competitors would be reversed. Acme is able to get more production out of each sewing machine.

FIGURE 3.3
Weekly production figures for competing shoe manufacturers

Weekly Production Data (based on five 8-hour work days)	Acme Footwear Co.	ComfortMax Shoe Co.
Number of shoemakers employed	50	36
Number of sewing machines used	14	20
Number of leather-stamping machines used	7	10
Number of pairs of shoes manufactured	2 600	2 600

APPLYING ECONOMIC THINKING

1 In your own words, explain the difference between *production* and *productivity*. Why would shoemakers at ComfortMax be more productive than shoemakers at Acme?

2 Calculate the average productivity of leather-stamping machines for both firms.

3 These two competitors use the same productive resources (shoemakers and machines), but in different proportions. Calculate the ratio of workers to sewing machines in each firm to identify the firm that uses a more *labour-intensive* production process.

4 Which firm uses the most *capital-intensive* production process? Explain your reasoning.

5 Suggest what ComfortMax might do to use its capital equipment more efficiently.

6 How might Acme increase its labour productivity? Suggest three changes that the firm might make to improve worker efficiency without exploiting workers.

COUNTING VALUE AT DIFFERENT PRODUCTION STAGES

Although productivity is very important to the bottom line of an enterprise, so is the market value of total production. Like productivity, this value also influences profitability at different stages. Figure 3.4 follows a wheat harvest through four production stages. Market value of product represents the dollar value that a product will fetch in the marketplace. **Value added** by contributor represents the increase in market value resulting from the additional processing or refinement of the product. Operating expenses represent all costs of processing incurred by a contributor. For example, the operating expenses of the farmer include land rental or property taxes, equipment rental or purchase, the cost of hired help, and the cost of technical expertise to improve soil quality, seed variety, and crop harvest.

Study the data to identify the relationships that exist between the market value of the product, value added by the contributor, and profit.

APPLYING ECONOMIC THINKING

1 Albert Einstein once said: "*Not everything that counts can be counted, and not everything that can be counted counts.*" Apply this principle to your experience. Provide two examples of things you value highly even though their economic benefit to you cannot be measured directly.

2 In Figure 3.4, how can the value of the economic contribution made at each production stage be measured?

3 Why is bread worth more to consumers on the supermarket shelf than on a baker's rack? What is the price of a loaf of bread on the store shelf?

4 Explain the relationship between value added and profit.

value added
The increase in market value of a product resulting from additional processing or refinement of that product.

FIGURE 3.4
Determining the economic value of different contributors to the production process

Stage	Contributor	Product	Market Value of Product	Value Added by Contributor	Operating Expenses	Profit
1	Farmer	Tonnes of wheat	$10 000	$10 000	$8 000	$2 000
2	Miller	Bags of flour	$14 000	$4 000	$2 000	$2 000
3	Baker	Loaves of bread	$20 000	$6 000	$3 000	$3 000
4	Retailer	Packaged bread on store shelf (20 000 loaves)	$28 000	$8 000	$3 500	$4 500

Chapter 3
Consolidation Activities

KNOWLEDGE

1   Compare how the different economic systems in Canada, China, and Sweden address the important questions related to national production and distribution. Investigate another national economy to expand your comparison.

2   Explain why a country's environment for enterprise is an important resource in the production of goods and services. Why is this resource considered intangible?

3   Complete a summary table titled "Canada's Mixed Economy" to explain why Canada is considered to be a mixed economy. Use these headings:

   • Market Characteristics
   • Command Characteristics
   • Traditional Characteristics

THINKING & INQUIRY

4   Research one group that appears in the *Did You Know?* feature about traditional economies of the world (page 37).

   a)   Make a list of important details in the economic system of your chosen group to explain how production decisions are made.

   b)   Explain what role the natural environment plays in the economic activities of this group.

   c)   List the advantages and disadvantages of the traditional economy used by this group. Maintain objectivity and avoid cultural judgements in your considerations. Make sure to spend as much time reflecting on the advantages as you do on the disadvantages.

   d)   As a class, discuss these advantages and disadvantages, and extend your list based on the discussion.

5   Research the problems Russia has encountered in the transition from a command economy to a market economy, and prepare a brief report.

6   Using information obtained through an Internet search, prepare a summary of two conflicting viewpoints (one positive and one negative) regarding the effectiveness of social democracy as practised in Sweden today. Assess the merits of the two viewpoints. If you wish, select a different Scandinavian country as your case study.

7   China has seen rapid economic growth in the twenty-first century. At what cost has this rapid transformation been achieved? Conduct Internet research to support your conclusions.

COMMUNICATION

8   Create a memory aid or mnemonic tool to help sort and explain tangible and intangible resources.

9   Create a comparison chart to show how the three different types of economic systems make basic production decisions. Be sure to outline strengths and limitations for each system.

10 Write or record an opinion piece outlining why command economies have declined since 1991, when one-third of the world's people lived under command systems. Be sure to use evidence to support your conclusions.

APPLICATION

11 Read the following interview comment from a company president after his lapel pin manufacturing company was named one of the "hottest new small businesses in America" by *BusinessWeek Magazine*, in 1996:

> *We have a factory in China where we have 250 people. We own them; it's our factory. We pay them $40 a month and they work 28 days a month. They work from 7 a.m. to 11 p.m., with two breaks for lunch and dinner. They eat all together, 16 people to a room, stacked on four bunks to a corner. Generally, they're young girls that come from the hills.*

While today's companies no longer boast about the direct exploitation of foreign workers, some do business with foreign companies that still exploit workers, including children, to keep costs down and profits up. This global problem will be investigated in Unit 6.

a) Would this business practice be considered acceptable in the United States, Canada, or Sweden? Explain.

b) Why has this company chosen to manufacture its lapel pins in China?

c) What does this practice reveal about how productive resources can sometimes be put to use?

12 Use the concept of the production possibilities frontier to explain why central planning in command economies traditionally favours the production of capital goods over consumer goods. Draw a graph to illustrate your answer.

13 China's rapid transformation into a manufacturing giant is sometimes referred to as an economic miracle and sometimes as an economic nightmare. Weigh both achievements and negative consequences to take a supportable position on this subject.

14 Often, productivity has negative connotations for labour. To increase productivity, workers may be forced to work longer hours or work for lower wages. Some factories in developing countries are more productive because they are "sweatshops"— their employees must work long hours for little pay. Suggest and explain three changes that a shoe company might make to improve worker efficiency without resorting to sweatshop tactics.

4
Political Economies and Policy Goals

INTRODUCTION

Economic systems rarely exist today outside a government framework, which means that political and economic decision making are closely connected. No study of an economic system is complete without an introduction to the political system that exists alongside it. Political systems can be broadly classified as either democracies or dictatorships. A **democracy** is a political system characterized by a freely elected government that represents, for a set term of office, the majority of citizens. It is open to many parties and political views. A **dictatorship** is a political system in which a single person or party exercises absolute authority over an entire country. There are no free elections to allow the people to change their leadership.

When you integrate these two types of political systems with market and command models of economic systems, four distinct political economies or "-isms" result. These -isms represent distinct politico-economic ideologies known as socialism, capitalism, communism, and fascism. As Figure 4.1 on the following page indicates, communism is a political economy featuring dictatorship within a command economy. By contrast, capitalism is a political economy featuring democracy within a free-market economy.

To better understand how the four -isms relate to one another, we must factor in the concept of **political orientation**. The political spectrum ranges from extreme-left thinking (represented by communism) to extreme-right thinking (represented by fascism). This is why these two ideologies are often considered mortal enemies. Socialism and capitalism, because they favour free elections, are considered to be moderate orientations. Extreme political orientations favour dictatorship, believing that people need to be controlled for their own good. Ask your teacher for a copy of the -isms survey to discover where your views fit among the -isms.

In this chapter, we will also investigate the main economic goals of the Canadian political economy and explore how governments make difficult decisions to set economic priorities and address economic challenges.

KEY TERMS

democracy

dictatorship

political orientation

capitalism

communism

socialism

nationalization

fascism

propaganda

public debt

economic growth

transfer payments

inflation

deflation

balance of payments accounts

consumer sovereignty

LEARNING GOALS

Once you have completed this chapter, you should be able to:

- Describe different political economies, their economic goals, and their approach to producing and sharing wealth, respecting individual economic freedom, and promoting the common good

- Provide examples of economic choices (both individual and collective) that Canadians must make as a result of scarce economic resources

- Recognize the advantages of cost-benefit analysis and how it is used to weigh economic options and make sound choices

- Understand how governments set economic priorities and respond to economic challenges

- Identify Canada's 10 principal economic goals and describe the links and trade-offs among them

- Conduct research using a variety of reliable sources (such as media, institutions, businesses, and interest groups) to address an inquiry question, and communicate economic information, research findings, analysis, and conclusions clearly, effectively, and accurately

democracy

A political system characterized by a freely elected government that represents the majority of its citizens.

dictatorship

A political system in which a single person exercises absolute authority over an entire country.

political orientation

The placement of specific ideas within a spectrum of political views ranging from extreme far-right thinking (fascism) to moderate views (capitalism and socialism) before extending to far-left thinking (communism).

capitalism

An economy characterized by private ownership of business and industry, the profit motive, and free markets.

Understanding Political Economies

CAPITALISM

When German philosopher Karl Marx called the free-enterprise system with democratic government **capitalism**, he meant to criticize its tendency to stress the accumulation of capital resources as a means to greater individual wealth and power. Capitalism requires a freely elected government to maintain public order and to keep competition free and fair. The private ownership of industry operating under free-market conditions is essential to capitalism. Producers are motivated to produce by the desire for profit. A business can maximize profits by making products that consumers are willing and able to buy. The opportunity for profit and the threat of loss, therefore, play the same role in capitalism that a dictator's edicts play in a command economy. Adam Smith (1723–1790), often called the father of capitalism, used the term *natural order* to describe this politico-economic system because he thought it was based on natural laws.

Capitalism occupies the moderate-right position on the political spectrum, although democratically elected governments can range from a moderate-right orientation (where free-enterprise is prioritized) to a moderate-left orientation (where social welfare is prioritized). Capitalist systems operate today in places such as Hong Kong, Singapore, the United States, and New Zealand. Since assuming control in 1997, the communist government of China has allowed Hong Kong's healthy free-market system to continue to operate. Countries such as Canada, Germany, France, Great Britain, and Italy have primarily capitalist systems blended with some socialist characteristics, such as welfare programs and government-owned enterprises. Economists often categorize these mixed systems as socially responsible "welfare capitalism."

FIGURE 4.1

An overview of politico-economic models making up the political spectrum (from extreme left to extreme right)

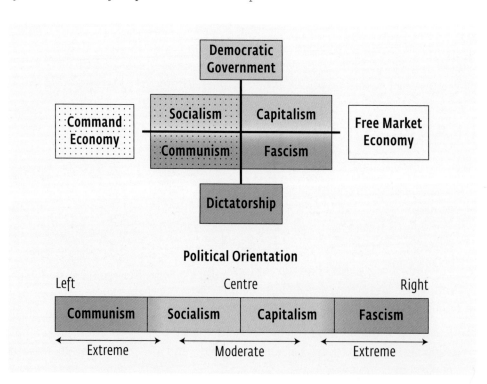

COMMUNISM

Communism is a politico-economic model based on the theory of Karl Marx. Communism grew out of the need for exploited working classes to rise up against their capitalist oppressors. It calls for government or community ownership of all means of production and wealth. Under communism, private property and free enterprise are abolished. Ideally, individuals produce according to their ability and consume according to their need. The communist ideology calls for an uncontested government with complete authority to plan for maximum economic growth. Opposition is often illegal. To safeguard the common good, opposing political parties and special interest groups (such as labour unions) have no part in the decision-making process. Since communists have historically used force to achieve their goals, they are seen as occupying the extreme-left wing of the political spectrum.

Under communist rule, the Soviet Union developed from a war-shattered Russian economy in the early stages of industrialization in 1917 into a military superpower 50 years later. This transformation was accomplished primarily through a series of five-year plans requiring citizens to make major personal sacrifices to help build the state. Government planning prioritized the manufacture of capital goods over consumer goods to expand the country's future capacity to produce.

By 1991, the Soviet economy had suffered a series of major economic setbacks. For decades, the quality of Russian goods was in sharp decline, and inefficient production processes failed to meet government targets. Citizens grew tired of the constant need to make personal sacrifices. As a result, the increasingly corrupt Communist Party lost its absolute power and the Soviet Union was dismantled. Today, the Russian economy continues the painfully inequitable transition to a market economy, while the government is controlled by a dictator and his closest associates. Communist systems are still in place in China, Cuba, North Korea, and Vietnam.

communism
A political system on the extreme left, founded on the theory of Karl Marx, that calls for government or community ownership of the means of production.

A commemorative military parade from 2018 in Moscow's Red Square, in Russia.

socialism

A political system of the moderate left that calls for public ownership of the principal means of production, to be achieved in a democratic and peaceful manner.

nationalization

Another term for state ownership of business enterprise.

DID YOU KNOW?

Did you know that French Prime Minister Georges Clemenceau (1917–1920) once stated: "If you are not a socialist at the age of 20 you have no heart; if you are still a socialist by the age of 40 you have no brain." What was his perspective on socialism as an ideology?

Pictured here at the height of the financial crisis in 2008 is a demonstration in London, England, by the Socialist Worker group of newspapers, with a distinct anti-capitalist message.

SOCIALISM

Socialism, too, is based on public ownership or control of the principal means of production. However, unlike communists, socialists favour democratic and peaceful methods to achieve their goals. Once they have been elected, socialists do not ban opposition parties. For this reason, they are often called *social democrats* and are considered to occupy the moderate-left position on the political spectrum.

Socialists aspire to the fair and equal distribution of available goods and services through a democratic decision-making process. They claim that free enterprise is inefficient, wasteful, and prone to conflicts between workers and capitalists resulting in exploitation. Under socialism, co-operation and worker solidarity theoretically replace the capitalistic ideals of self-interest and competition. Experiments with socialism in Britain and France in the 1970s and 1980s produced a measurable decline in national productivity. Some critics use such results to question whether human self-interest makes socialism ultimately unworkable.

The politico-economic systems in the Nordic (Scandinavian) countries of Norway, Sweden, Denmark, Finland, and Iceland have undergone a substantial transformation since 1950. They began under "free-enterprise socialism," the most moderate of socialist philosophies, and slowly evolved into a mixed capitalist system that attempts to balance free enterprise with social responsibility. In these countries, the focus is no longer on increasing state ownership (the **nationalization** of enterprise), but rather on private enterprise balanced by socialist government policies that address collective needs. As noted in Chapter 3, a key characteristic of the Nordic economic model is an arrangement whereby economic stakeholders work together to negotiate wages, working conditions, and market policies. National production levels and living standards in Norway and Sweden continue to grow under a free-enterprise system modified by a socialist perspective. Today, living standards in Nordic countries are among the highest in the world, while rates of government corruption are among the lowest.

FASCISM

Fascism, occupying the extreme-right position on the political spectrum, combines a free-market economy with a non-democratic, or authoritarian, form of government. Fascist governments use force as a means of political and social control. They believe that individuals need to be controlled for the collective good. As with the politics of the extreme left, fascist governments do not usually tolerate political opposition. Citizens are free to own property and businesses as long as they comply with all government dictates. There are clear restrictions on individual freedom. Military dictatorships that allow private ownership and enterprise can be categorized as fascist systems. Italy (1922–1945), Nazi Germany (1933–1945), Spain (1936–1975), Japan (1931–1945), Brazil (1937–1945), and Argentina (1946–1983) are historical examples of this ideology. The Second World War (1939–1945) was fought to repel the advancing forces of fascism in Europe and Asia.

Capitalists in a fascist state are very careful to fulfill the wishes and production demands of the government. In this manner, capitalists protect their privileged role in society. Fascist leaders expect industrialist and business leaders to promote economic growth and productivity. For this reason, fascist systems are sometimes referred to as "dictatorial capitalism." Often, these dictators are supported by sympathetic military leaders. **Propaganda** (grossly one-sided messaging intended to influence popular thinking) is heavily used to promote the greatness of the uncontested ruler and the fascist state. Capitalist systems that venture too deeply into uncontested rule, either by rigged elections where the ruling class always wins, or by suppressing the voices and rights of the opposition, can easily evolve into fascist states.

fascism
A political system on the extreme right, combining a free-market economy with a non-democratic form of government.

propaganda
Concerted messaging efforts used to influence thoughts and opinions by repeated emphasis, distortion, deception and misinformation.

General Francisco Franco (centre) stands with his senior officers before leading the 1936 coup d'état against the Republican Government in Spain and establishing a totalitarian military dictatorship.

Self-Reflect

1 What two factors are used to classify political economies? Explain how they help differentiate political economies.

2 Explain the difference between an extreme and a moderate political orientation.

3 What is the principal difference between socialism and communism?

4 Why is the Canadian system often referred to as "welfare capitalism"?

Setting Economic Goals: A Canadian Model

Every politico-economic system attempts to establish economic goals as targets to focus the use of productive resources. Some economic goals are *complementary*; that is, achieving one economic goal makes it easier to achieve another economic goal. For example, to reach employment rate targets, a government may lower interest rates on business loans to promote the creation of new jobs. In turn, the creation of new jobs will automatically help improve income levels in an economy and encourage consumer spending.

Unfortunately, some economic goals are *conflicting*; that is, achieving one economic goal makes it harder to achieve another economic goal. For example, government strategies to keep the economy's prices stable often have an adverse effect on employment rates and national production. Governments can promote price stability by raising interest rates to control the amount of money in circulation; as it becomes more expensive to borrow money for investment, businesses hire fewer workers and their production levels either remain constant or decline. Government policy-makers have to recognize this trade-off and decide whether the current priority is to achieve price stability or to put more people to work. They can't count on being able to have both. In this situation, increases in employment and production are the opportunity costs of stable prices.

The setting of economic goals, therefore, is a matter of normative, or policy, economics. In other words, governments must make value judgements when they set priorities for conflicting goals. On the whole, the economic goals that countries strive for are often similar. However, how each country prioritizes its conflicting goals will determine how it distributes its productive resources.

Since the 1960s, 10 economic goals have emerged as priorities in Canada (Figure 4.2). The following sections identify and explain each of them. The order of their appearance here does not indicate their order of priority. Each government has re-examined these economic goals and set its own priorities. In later chapters, we will examine these goals in greater detail.

❶ *Political Stability*

A stable government can help long-term planning and investment to flourish. Consistency in policy-making promotes both investor and consumer confidence and provides a climate conducive to economic growth. For example, each time a sovereignty referendum is conducted in the province of Quebec, consumer confidence (both foreign and domestic) is shaken, and the Canadian economy suffers. Similarly, in the United States, a political crisis in the White House usually upsets US stock markets. More often than not, political uncertainty has an adverse effect on a country's economy.

❷ *Reduced Public Debt*

With very few exceptions, since 1970, government spending in Canada has increased at a faster rate than the revenues being collected through taxes. Governments have had to borrow money to cover the difference. This has meant

FIGURE 4.2
Ten economic goals in Canada

① Political stability

② Reduced public debt

③ Economic growth

④ Increased productivity and efficiency

⑤ Equitable distribution of income

⑥ Price stability

⑦ Full employment

⑧ Viable balance of payments and stable currency

⑨ Economic freedom

⑩ Environmental stewardship

that Canada's **public debt** (and the interest payments to service it) has grown larger year after year. Just as individuals cannot continue to incur large personal debt without suffering for it economically, governments cannot continue to add to the public debt without adversely affecting the economy. Inevitably, interest rates climb higher, as do prices for consumer goods. As well, there is the moral issue involved in running up a debt that future generations of Canadians will have to pay. Concerned Canadians have begun to demand more balanced budgets from their elected governments.

public debt
The total debt held by federal and provincial governments accumulated from their past borrowings, on which interest must be paid.

economic growth
An increase in an economy's total production of goods and services.

③ Economic Growth

Economic growth is defined as an increase in the economy's total production of goods and services. Theoretically, it represents an outward shift in the economy's production possibilities frontier. This growth can result from the discovery of new natural resources, an increase in the skilled labour force, technological innovations, and more efficient production processes. As economic production expands, Canadians have more goods and services at their disposal, thereby increasing the average standard of living.

As a result of the periods of substantial growth that the Canadian economy has enjoyed since the Second World War, Canadian workers now have access to three times as many goods and services as they did in 1945. In addition, as the economy expands, the public debt (if held in check) becomes less significant and easier to manage. However, the sustainability of continued growth must be questioned in light of the limited quantity of productive resources ultimately available to the Canadian economy.

④ Increased Productivity and Efficiency

Maximizing productivity means that scarce productive resources are put to efficient use to get as much as possible out of them. Economic efficiency is often the result of healthy competition. As Canadian firms struggle to be competitive in both local and global markets, they must make their production processes more efficient. The companies with the most efficient practices will maximize profits, prevail in the marketplace, and set new standards for others. Increased productivity will allow these firms to get more out of existing resources. Workplace training programs, incentives, and bonuses (such as profit-sharing plans where workers receive a portion of the extra profits that their effort and efficiency have generated) are used by some progressive companies to improve the productivity of their workforce. Although increased productivity is generally good for the economy, it can also have negative consequences. For example, if worker productivity is increased, fewer workers will be needed to produce the same quantity of goods and services.

⑤ Equitable Distribution of Income

The equitable, or fair, distribution of income may be the most value-laden of all economic goals; it is certainly the most controversial. When it comes to dividing up total national output, there can be as many interpretations of what makes for a fair division of wealth as there are stakeholders. Is it fair that the annual income of a corporate executive in North America is many times higher than that of the

transfer payments
Direct payments from governments to other governments or to individuals; a mechanism for providing social security, income support, and alleviation of regional disparities.

inflation
A general rise in the price levels of an economy.

deflation
A general fall in the price levels of an economy.

average salaried worker in the same company? How much income should be taken away in taxes from someone who earns $10 million a year and redistributed among families whose gross annual income is less than $10 000?

In Canada, the issue of income equity is further complicated by regional differences. For example, average employment incomes for residents of Ontario are statistically higher than for people who live in the Atlantic provinces, a situation that has existed for years. Through **transfer payments** (using revenues from one province to make additional social program payments in another), the federal government attempts to redistribute national wealth.

Socialists advocate a more equal distribution of wealth. Others argue that income equalization will only reward inefficiency and remove the personal incentive to work harder and take risks. As the debate continues, more and more Canadians are forced to use food banks or live on the street. Canada is not alone in this regard; no country, not even the most affluent, has completely solved the problem of poverty. The Canadian model uses a social welfare system anchored on socialized health care, free public education, and social services for needy citizens to distribute national wealth more equitably. However, this social welfare system is sustained by a larger amount of government spending each year.

6 Price Stability

Stable prices generally indicate that an economy is healthy. Fluctuating prices complicate planning and discourage investment. Both **inflation**, a general rise in prices, and **deflation**, a general fall in prices, are symptoms of an unhealthy economy. Periods of price inflation erode the dollar's purchasing power and raise the cost of living for Canadians on fixed incomes. Deflation, though rare in Canada, is commonly associated with periods of great economic crisis, such as the Great Depression of the 1930s. It should come as no surprise, then, that government economic policy seeks to promote and maintain stable price levels.

7 Full Employment

In an attempt to reach their optimal production targets, governments try to promote the full employment of the labour force. Unemployed workers result in total output levels well below the national production possibilities curve. An unemployed labour force also represents a waste of human potential and can cause economic hardships for unemployed workers and their families. Sustained periods of high unemployment usually indicate that a country is in poor economic health. During the Great Depression, Canadian unemployment rates approached 20 percent, and during economic downturns in the 1980s and 1990s, rates were more than 10 percent.

"Full employment" is usually defined as between 6 and 7 percent of the labour force being out of work. However, full employment has become increasingly difficult to achieve in Canada: machines continue to replace people on production assembly lines, computers now perform tasks that were once performed by people, and many jobs have been outsourced to countries where labour costs are a fraction of Canadian costs. Since the late 1990s, unemployment rates in Canada have remained above 7 percent, despite sustained economic growth.

8 Viable Balance of Payments and Stable Currency

Canada is a major trading country. The annual dollar value of trade per person is higher in Canada than in any other country in the world. In a global economy, the international flow of goods and currency in transactions such as importing, exporting, borrowing, and lending has become increasingly more important. The **balance of payments accounts** summarize all currency transactions between Canadian and foreign economies. If Canadians import significantly more than we export, there will be a negative effect on employment rates in Canada as well as the foreign exchange value of the Canadian dollar. It is important, therefore, that imports and exports roughly balance one another. Similarly, money that flows in and out of the country needs to be balanced to foster a stable Canadian dollar in foreign money markets. As the value of the Canadian dollar declines in foreign money markets, Canadians will find that imported goods will become more expensive and their cost of living will rise.

9 Economic Freedom

Economic freedom refers to the freedom of choice available to workers, consumers, and investors in the economy. Canadian workers who want to improve their working conditions and income should be free to find and take another job. In a market economy, consumers should be free not only to purchase the goods and services of their choice but also, through their purchasing decisions, to determine what goods and services are produced. This is known as the principle of **consumer sovereignty**. In a market economy, people should be free to choose when and how to consume, save, or invest. Canadian public policy generally promotes economic freedom.

10 Environmental Stewardship

Economic activity must be carried out without significantly harming the natural environment. We have come to realize that the pollution of the air, water, and earth, the depletion of our natural resources, the destruction of the ozone layer that protects us from ultraviolet light, and the gradual warming of the planet are all additional costs of the decisions we make about economic development. If we wish to be more responsible stewards of our planet and protect it for future generations, we have to adjust the way we carry out our economic activities. Even if this means higher prices for consumers and lower profits for producers, we must find a way to reduce the negative effects we are having on the natural environment.

Potential problems can arise if Canada enacts environmental laws (such as a tax on carbon emissions) that make its products more expensive and its trading partners do not follow suit. This situation can make Canadian goods less competitive in world markets. It also raises a moral issue: If Canada trades with a country that has low environmental standards, does this mean that we are condoning the other country's harmful environmental policies? Clearly, on the normative side of economics, there is more to consider than just price!

balance of payments account

National account of international payments and receipts, divided into current account, and capital and financial account.

consumer sovereignty

A principle of market economies that the production choices of the economy are ultimately made by the buying decisions of consumers.

Self-Reflect

1 Explain why full employment and price stability can be conflicting goals for the Canadian economy.

2 Explain how both inflation and deflation are generally bad news for the Canadian economy.

3 Explain why the principle of consumer sovereignty is important in a market economy.

Thinking like an Economist

Using Cost-Benefit Analysis to Prioritize Difficult Choices

The cost-benefit analysis (also referred to as a *CBA*) is one example of disciplined economic thinking. This type of analysis is used to compare the benefits (advantages) and costs (trade-offs) of available options to determine the best course of action. When benefits are seen to outweigh costs, an option is seen to be economically viable. The option with the best benefit-to-cost ratio is said to represent the most economic choice. Cost-benefit analysis is often used early in a decision-making process to establish priorities and assess available options.

In a cost-benefit analysis, costs and benefits are converted to dollar values so that they can be compared and assessed. Let's say that a company wants to improve productivity by making workers more efficient (see Figure 4.3). One strategy for improving worker productivity is an efficiency training program. The training program fee multiplied by the number of participating workers would be the cost, while a 5 percent reduction in material waste and a 5 percent reduction in unit assembly time would be the benefits. Boosting worker morale is also recognized as helpful in improving productivity, so the costs and benefits of a suggestion box program and social events are also considered. From the available options, an economist may consider the costs of placing suggestion boxes around the plant and offering monthly cash prizes for the best ideas to improve efficiency to be the most economic choice. The option of social events for workers and their families might also be added to morale-building costs, but in this case the benefits are only slightly higher than the actual costs.

FIGURE 4.3
Sample cost-benefit analysis

Goal: To improve company productivity by making workers more efficient.			
Option	**Associated Costs** *(c)*	**Associated Benefits** *(b)*	**Net Benefits** *(b − c)*
1 Efficiency training	$500 training fee × 26 workers = $13 000	5% reduction in material waste = $13 000 5% reduction in unit assembly time = $12 000	$25 000 − $13 000 = $12 000
2 Suggestion box program	Purchase and installation of three boxes = $500 $500 monthly prizes = $6 000	Thinking and feedback about efficiency = $1 000 4% reduction in material waste = $10 400 4% reduction in unit assembly time = $9 600	$21 000 − $6 500 = $14 500
3 Social events	Christmas party (venue, entertainment, food, and gifts for 100 guests) = $5 000 Summer picnic (venue, activities, food, and prizes for 100 guests) = $4 000	1% reduction in material waste = $2 600 1% reduction in unit assembly time = $2 400 1% reduction in material waste = $2 600 1% reduction in unit assembly time = $2 400	$10 000 − $9 000 = $1 000

FIGURE 4.4
Steps in a cost-benefit analysis

Step	Focus Questions
❶ Define a need, issue, or goal.	• What needs our attention to achieve established targets?
❷ List available alternatives.	• What options are realistically available?
❸ Identify and consult stakeholders.	• Who will be affected by this decision? • What are their interests and views regarding this decision?
❹ Establish priorities for common and conflicting interests and goals.	• How can common interests be addressed? • How can conflicting views be reconciled or prioritized?
❺ Select measurement criteria.	• What considerations will help identify and value relevant costs and benefits?
❻ Measure all costs and benefits associated with each alternative.	• What are the benefits (positives) and costs (negatives) for each alternative or option?
❼ Convert all benefits and costs to a common currency (or tangible value).	• What dollar value can be determined for each benefit and cost?
❽ Compare alternatives to find the most favourable benefits-to-costs ratio.	• Which alternative maximizes benefits while minimizing costs?
❾ Implement the "most economic" option and assess outcomes.	• How is the decision working out? What adjustments are needed to address consequences or improve implementation?

When dollar values can be attributed to specific benefits and costs, a relative significance can be accurately determined. Often, especially when dealing with policy matters, a more normative value judgement is required when assessing costs and benefits. In these cases, individual costs and benefits are assessed as being highly, moderately, or minimally significant. When such value judgements are made in a cost-benefit analysis, they should be noted in the final decision.

Cost-benefit analysis can be used by a company to make economically viable business decisions and by government policy advisers to advocate for a particular prioritization of goals and strategies. Although cost-benefit analyses are sometimes customized to suit the programs, initiatives, or options being assessed, the general steps in Figure 4.4 are usually involved.

APPLYING ECONOMIC THINKING

1 How would you prioritize the three available options given a budget of $15 000? Explain your choice.

2 How would your decision change if your budget is expanded to $20 000?

3 Benefit calculations for options are based on the effect this strategy has had on other companies with similar workforces. To what degree can similar outcomes be guaranteed for this company?

4 How might government goals affect your productivity gains positively or negatively?

Setting Economic Priorities When Stakeholder Interests and Policy Goals Conflict

Finding common ground among people with different interests and viewpoints is challenging at the best of times. However, governments regularly consult with diverse stakeholders to determine shared public interests and set economic priorities. They also carefully assess what economic policies are most needed and what must be given up to achieve them. In both the political and economic worlds, every choice has consequences.

A GOVERNMENT PERSPECTIVE ON RESPONDING TO ECONOMIC CHALLENGES

Most governments equate economic growth with prosperity. Therefore, economic policies often include strategies intended to promote economic growth. For example, if a government wants to prioritize job creation to combat an unemployment rate approaching 9 percent of the workforce, it may decide to lower interest rates to encourage borrowing and investment spending. By increasing the circulation of money, both the demand for products and the labour required to produce them will increase. However, if production does not increase proportionately, the extra money in circulation can lead to higher prices. This price instability is just one trade-off that could result from a government job-creation policy.

Increased government spending on infrastructure projects (for example, highways, roads, bridges, schools, and public transit systems) will create jobs, but the trade-off will be increased public debt, unless taxes are also increased to pay for these new spending projects. Increasing taxes will take more money out of circulation and reduce both spending on consumer goods and investment spending by businesses. The consequences will generally be a negative effect on production and employment levels. As you can see, it is not easy to make economic policy decisions.

University students are seen protesting Canada's rapidly increasing federal government debt in 2016. At the time the accumulated federal debt was almost $620 billion, or $17 500 per person in Canada.

FIGURE 4.5
Unemployment rates for selected provinces, 1990, 2000, 2010, and 2017

Province	Unemployment Rate (%)			
	1990	2000	2010	2017
Alberta	6.9	5.0	8.1	7.8
British Columbia	8.4	7.2	7.6	5.1
New Brunswick	12.1	10.0	9.2	8.1
Newfoundland	17.0	16.6	14.7	14.8
Nova Scotia	10.7	9.1	9.6	8.4
Ontario	6.2	5.7	8.7	6.0
Quebec	10.4	8.5	8.0	6.1
Canada	**8.1**	**6.8**	**8.1**	**6.3**

To further complicate matters, some provinces or regions in the country will experience higher and more persistent unemployment rates than the rest of the country. Any economic priority with a trade-off of increased unemployment will have more severe consequences in provinces or regions where unemployment rates are already quite high.

Given the unemployment rates reflected in Figure 4.5, national economic policies to reduce public debt and to promote stable prices will have more serious consequences in provinces with relatively higher unemployment rates (such as Newfoundland, New Brunswick, and Nova Scotia). In addition, economic policies that prioritize job creation would have been more popular across Canada in 1990 and 2010, than in 2000 and 2017. Can you see why? It is important to note that policy priorities need to adapt to changing economic conditions. Provincial governments can help address regional issues and concerns. Intergovernmental co-operation is essential, since federal policy initiatives can be rendered less effective by the conflicting initiatives of provincial governments.

One of the traditional policy debates in Canada is centred on the economic trade-offs between debt reduction and the preservation of the national welfare safety net. Since welfare programs require increasing amounts of government spending, unless taxes are increased proportionately, these programs generally contribute to an increase in national debt. To illustrate the impact of this policy on future generations of Canadians, university students from British Columbia posed for a photo, struggling with a debt clock that travels across the country to draw attention to Canada's growing national debt and how much it will cost individual Canadians to repay it. This debt clock is funded by a special-interest group known as the Canadian Taxpayers Association, which is interested in reducing public debt.

Economic policy choices are so complex and value laden that Unit 5 has been reserved to investigate this topic much more closely.

Self-Reflect

1   What effect do regional differences have on the equitable distribution of income in Canada?

2   Explain how a government policy to reduce public debt will have more serious consequences in New Brunswick than in Ontario.

3   Identify the economic benefits and costs of a government policy to expand social welfare programs and create jobs for unemployed people in Canada.

Chapter 4
Consolidation Activities

KNOWLEDGE

1   Why has fascism historically been a bitter rival of communism? What makes them both extreme ideologies?

2   Explain why each of the following pairs represent either complementary or conflicting economic goals:

a)   Economic growth and reduced public debt

b)   Political stability and economic freedom

c)   Environmental stewardship and economic growth

d)   Reduced public debt and equitable distribution of income

THINKING & INQUIRY

3   Is the Nordic (Scandinavian) model primarily socialist or capitalist? Conduct Internet research to collect evidence to support your conclusion.

4   What economic problems led Sweden down the road of reform, ultimately creating one of the healthiest economies in the world? Conduct Internet research to investigate and explain this transformation.

5   Compare and assess the ability of capitalism, socialism, and communism to satisfy needs and achieve economic goals in a way that is consistent with human nature.

6   Using the Venn diagram in Figure 4.6 and a job search site, answer the following questions

a)   What kind of local job opportunities are there for people with a background in economics? At a job search site, find local job openings using three job titles that appear in Figure 4.6. Create a table with the following headings to summarize your findings:

• Company
• Job Title
• Salary
• Education Required
• Skills Required
• Background Required
• Nature of Work

b)   Why are companies willing to pay for expertise in economics? What makes a job related to economics both challenging and interesting?

c)   What kind of job opportunities related to economics most interests you? Why?

COMMUNICATION

7   As a study guide, create a comparison chart of political economies using the following headings: Government, Economy, Production Decisions, Strengths, Limitations, and Specific Examples.

8   Which political economy do you prefer? Explain and justify your choice.

9   How would you explain how cost-benefit analysis can be a useful decision-making or priority-setting tool to a schoolmate who is not taking this economics course?

APPLICATION

10 Collect several (6 to 10) articles from newspapers and magazines that reflect normative (or policy) decisions that the Canadian government has made. Using the 10 economic goals we considered in this chapter, identify the economic goals with which each article deals.

a)   Arrange the 10 economic goals in what you think is their order of importance, 1 being the most important and 10 being the least important. Justify your priorities by referring to the articles you have collected. Be sure to reassess these priorities once you have completed Unit 5.

b)   In the list of economic goals, identify those that conflict with each other. For each conflicting goal, identify the opportunity cost involved.

11 Explain the goal of environmental stewardship as it applies to three economic examples of responsible decision making based on research or personal experience.

12 Consider what would happen if the Canadian dollar plummeted to a new record low on world currency markets.

a)   Why does an unstable dollar create problems for the Canadian economy?

b)   What are the most likely causes of a declining dollar?

c)   What is the best way to achieve the economic goal of stable currency? Justify your decision.

d)   How important a priority is currency stability? Explain your answer.

FIGURE 4.6
Career opportunities related to economics exist in the business, government, and academic sectors of the economy

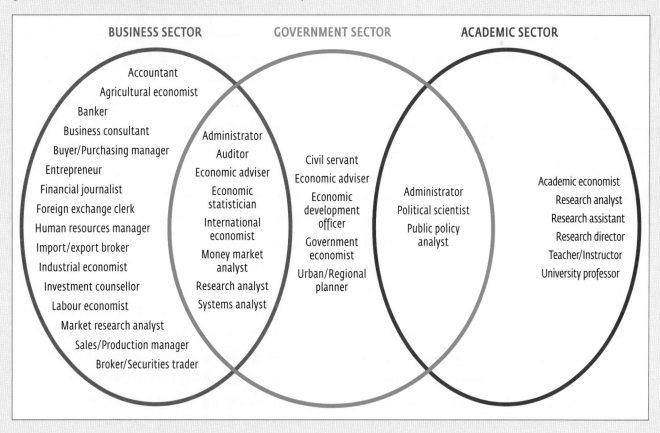

Unit 1   Performance Task

Developing a Strategy to Reach a Performance Target

Economists use their knowledge and skills to help clarify complex choices, explain human behaviour, evaluate available options, and support responsible decision making. At the start of this unit, you were asked "How do you determine the most productive use of your time, and what can be done to improve your productivity?" Now that you have completed the foundational learning activities in this first unit, your challenge is to put your knowledge and skills to effective use. The following task presents you with a realistic challenge, very much like the work carried out by many Canadians with a background in economics or related fields.

YOUR TASK

You are the manager of human resources for the Acme Sunshine Corporation, a young and growing Canadian company specializing in the design, manufacture, and installation of rooftop solar panels for homes and businesses. Acme is interested in expanding its business to other parts of Canada. To achieve this goal, the owners have set the following performance target to improve competitiveness.

PERFORMANCE TARGET

To position itself so that it can compete favourably in more markets, Acme Sunshine Corporation must generate efficiencies in all departments to achieve a 20 percent increase in corporate productivity within three years.

The four owners of the company are divided with regard to the best course of action for achieving this important target. The following four options have been identified:

1   Require all employees to work 10 hours longer per week, while freezing wages and salaries at current levels.

2   Reinvest a portion of corporate profits to fund ongoing employee training.

3   Pay employees in ownership shares in the company, instead of money, for all overtime work.

4   Start a profit-sharing plan to reward all employees for reaching productivity targets and for their direct contribution to higher profits for the company.

As manager of human resources, you are required to prepare a report to the owners that weighs the costs and benefits of each proposed option and makes a specific recommendation regarding the most appropriate course of action to make employees more productive and the company more competitive.

You have been promised a big bonus, depending on the outcome of your recommendation—not to mention that your job is on the line! Your report can be either a written report, documenting a thorough analysis and persuasive argument, or an oral report, visually supported by a presentation program such as PowerPoint or Prezi.

STEPS AND RECOMMENDATIONS

1 Review all the work you have done in this unit to refresh your understanding of related concepts and skills.

2 Use a decision-making model and include an analysis of both costs and benefits to make a sound decision.

3 In preparing your report, be sure to include the economic concepts, principles, and theories most appropriate to your analysis and most useful in supporting your recommendation.

4 Strive for high-quality economic thinking, thorough attention to detail, and a persuasive argument to support your recommendation.

5 Keep the language appropriate for a report to the owners of your company, your bosses.

ADAPTING THE TASK

Discuss format options for your report with your teacher. Select a format that capitalizes on your strengths. Interview local business leaders for practical input and suggestions. Share drafts with your teacher, classmates, and parents or guardians to obtain useful feedback.

ASSESSMENT CRITERIA

The following criteria will be used to assess your work:

- **Knowledge:** accurately using economic concepts, principles, and theories
- **Thinking and Inquiry:** using sound economic reasoning and thorough analysis; using a decision-making model effectively
- **Communication:** presenting economic information and analysis clearly and accurately, and in an appropriate format and style
- **Application:** presenting a persuasive argument to inform decision making

Use the rubric provided by your teacher as a coaching tool to help complete this task successfully.

Unit 2
History of Economic Thought

Over time, great thinkers have emerged to move economic thought forward. Aside from Xenophon's work in ancient Greece, economics as a scholarly discipline is about 250 years old. Economic thinking has evolved greatly and continues to evolve in response to changing times and priorities. Ultimately, all economic systems have strengths and weaknesses. To better understand contemporary economic systems, we need to trace the evolution of economic thought.

Economic thinkers seek to address the limitations, complications, and inequalities in the ways economies work. Often these ideas help to enrich the lives of many people. Sometimes, radical and thought-provoking ideas lead to the creation of an entirely new "school" of economic thinking. In this unit, we will investigate the evolution of economic thinking from Xenophon to the present day.

What is the connection between great economic thinkers, their ideas, and the times they lived in?

Do you prefer to work alone or with others? Do you put more emphasis on winning or playing the game? Do you prefer to follow others or do your own thing? You may be thinking, "What does any of this have to do with economics?" Unless you are planning to live on a deserted island, you are going to have to deal productively with others, and they are going to have deal effectively with you. How does your personality affect your thinking? How does your environment (family, circumstances, and friends) and your personal background and experience influence your thinking?

Economic systems have been created to address questions of production and distribution for all stakeholders. Throughout history, great thinkers have tried to address economic problems by alternating between competitive (free-enterprise) and collaborative (social-enterprise) approaches to the management of scarcity. Sometimes, the more difficult the times, the more radical or revolutionary the ideas coming forward. Often, in addressing one problem, another is created.

LOOKING AHEAD ⟶

The performance task at the end of this unit will require you to investigate the inquiry question above. It provides an opportunity for you to:

- Assume the role of a journalist trying to inform public opinion
- Apply economic knowledge and skills to outline the relationship between economic conditions and the important ideas that emerge and gain prominence
- Prepare and present an informative and persuasive argument
- Use a performance task rubric and feedback to prepare a high-quality news article

Early and Classical Economics

INTRODUCTION

The very first deep thinker of economic activities was Xenophon, the Greek citizen turned military general who was granted a family estate around 395 BCE. His past experiences led him to theorize about estate management, the division of labour between husband and wife, and the accumulation of personal wealth. His work, entitled *Oeconomicus* (published in 362 BCE), is recognized as one of the richest primary sources of the social, economic, and intellectual history of classical Greece. Among its numerous subjects, the *Oeconomicus* provides insight into the successful operation of an estate farm in ancient Greece. It reveals the value of marital partnership, appropriate treatment of workers (and slaves), the importance of agriculture to further civilization, and the shrewd use of productive resources, including enemies or competitors.

The **oikos**, the basic unit of classical Greek society, was a household or a large family estate, including land, crops, a house, family members, slaves, animals, and accumulated wealth. The economy of Greece was based on agriculture, and society consisted of two distinct, yet complementary, spheres. The public (or political) sphere was a world where men were dominant, and the private (or domestic) sphere was the realm of women.

Economic thinking started making significant advances during the second half of the eighteenth century with the progressive writings of Adam Smith, Thomas Robert Malthus, and David Ricardo. Karl Marx strongly reacted to the exploitation of workers during the second half of the nineteenth century. In this chapter, we will explore the ideas of these classical thinkers. For each featured economist, or "worldly philosopher," as the economic historian Robert L. Heilbroner calls them, our presentation will include the following: a brief biography, an account of the historical context in which the economist's ideas developed, and an explanation of some of the economist's major ideas and their political and economic impacts.

LEARNING GOALS

Once you have completed this chapter, you should be able to:

- Understand the major ideas and economic theories of Adam Smith, Thomas Robert Malthus, David Ricardo, and Karl Marx
- Understand how economic thinking has helped change the world
- Recognize cause and consequence relationships
- Begin thinking like an economist by testing hypotheses

KEY TERMS

oikos

physiocrat

laissez-faire

mercantilism

protectionist

tariff

Industrial Revolution

self-interest

invisible hand

division of labour

law of accumulation

law of population

geometrical progression

arithmetical progression

positive check

preventive check

Corn Laws

absolute advantage

comparative advantage

bourgeoisie

proletariat

labour value

surplus value

hypothesis

oikos
A Greek word meaning "household" or "estate," which historically was the first subject of economics analysis.

physiocrat
A believer in the eighteenth-century philosophy that argued that laws created by humans are artificial and unnecessary because they interfere with natural laws (such as an individual's pursuit of self-interest), which would ultimately benefit all of society.

laissez-faire
A French term meaning "leave to do" or "let alone," which became associated with the idea that an economy operates best if individuals are allowed to pursue their own self-interest without government interference.

Adam Smith (1723–1790)

Ideas that are significant enough to change the world usually emerge during turbulent times. Generally speaking, the more radical the idea, the more troubled the society it originates from, if only because it is during times of extreme crisis that people are most willing to listen to radically different ideas.

Adam Smith is known today as both the "father of modern economics" as well as the "founder of capitalism." He was the first thinker to outline in detail the characteristics and benefits of a complete economic system—in his case, the free-market economy. He did this in a two-volume work called *An Inquiry into the Nature and Causes of the Wealth of Nations*. Published in 1776, the same year that the American colonies declared their independence from Great Britain, this work is usually referred to as *The Wealth of Nations* and is recognized as the foundation of modern economic theory.

BIOGRAPHY

Adam Smith was born in 1723 to a middle-class family in a fishing village near Edinburgh, Scotland. He entered the University of Glasgow at 14 and, at 17, won a scholarship to Oxford University.

At the age of 27, Smith was offered a position as professor of logic at the University of Glasgow. Shortly afterwards, he earned the more prestigious position of professor of moral philosophy; in 1758, he became dean of the university. With his eccentric personality, the deep-thinking but absent-minded professor became Glasgow's most illustrious citizen.

In 1759, Smith's first book, *The Theory of Moral Sentiments*, made him famous throughout Great Britain. He accepted a lucrative offer in 1764 to become the private tutor of a young English aristocrat. This new position gave him the opportunity to live in France for two years. While visiting Switzerland, he met French philosopher Voltaire, and back in Paris he became acquainted with a new school of economic thought whose leaders were known as the **physiocrats**.

The physiocrats reasoned that if unchangeable natural laws governed the physical world, then natural laws also governed human behaviour and, therefore, the social, economic, and political worlds. They argued that if all human behaviour was controlled by natural laws, then all the artificial laws created by humans were unnecessary and ineffective. Since people have a natural tendency to serve their own best interests and to acquire wealth, the pursuit of self-interest would ultimately benefit all individuals if they were left alone to create more wealth. This doctrine of non-interference became known by the French term **laissez-faire**, which means literally "leave to do," or leave things alone so that matters can work themselves out naturally.

While travelling as a tutor, Smith began his most important project, *The Wealth of Nations*, which took him 12 years to complete and have published. Smith was greatly influenced by American politician and writer Benjamin Franklin, who provided much information about the economic situation in the American colonies. In 1778, Smith was appointed commissioner of customs for Edinburgh, where he lived for the rest of his life.

THE TIMES

Adam Smith was born into a world where **mercantilism** was the prevailing economic system. This system is based on the state's control of economic production and trade, with the goal of exporting as many goods as possible for sale abroad while, at the same time, importing as few foreign goods as possible. When this system is successful, it means that gold and silver from abroad (the money paid for the exported goods) are flowing into the country while very little money is flowing out of it. At the time, gold and silver reserves were thought to constitute the real wealth of any country.

To make mercantilism work, a country's government adopts a **protectionist** policy to safeguard its gold and silver reserves by limiting the entry of foreign goods. As a result, authorities impose stiff taxes, or **tariffs**, on imported goods to make them more expensive than the goods produced in the country. Problems arise, however, as more and more countries adopt this strategy. Trade between countries drops off, and prices of all but the most common domestic products go up. Mercantilism, a product of the Middle Ages, did not sit well with the established merchant class, the growing industrialist class, and the heavily burdened working class. All of these classes were feeling increasingly handcuffed by government regulations and taxes.

Laissez-faire philosophy provided a strong argument for replacing state control of the economy with a reliance on natural laws to regulate economic activity. This idea contributed to the political ferment in France that led, in turn, to the French Revolution. Smith learned from Benjamin Franklin that the growing mood of rebellion in the American colonies was a direct reaction to interference by the British government, through various taxes and regulations, in the economic life of the colonists. This interference led to the Declaration of Independence in 1776 and the American Revolution during the years 1775–1783.

Many of Smith's ideas developed in response to the rapid economic changes he observed in Great Britain. The Enclosure Movement broke up the large plots of land that towns had held in common since the Middle Ages and redistributed them in small plots to individual landholders. Owners began to run these farms for profit rather than subsistence. Inventions such as the spinning jenny, the power loom, and the steam engine made it possible for factory owners to increase both the scale of their operations and the level of their profits. In the new factories that sprang up, workers performed increasingly specialized tasks and used a variety of machines. This period of technological innovation and new means of production, which started during Adam Smith's lifetime, came to be known as the **Industrial Revolution**.

mercantilism

An economic system that emphasized state control of trade, with the goal of exporting as many goods as possible and importing as few foreign goods as possible.

protectionist

This is a term used to characterize an economic policy that restricts imports through tariffs, quotas, and regulations in an effort to boost domestic industry.

tariff

A tax on an import levied by a country; also called *custom duty*.

Industrial Revolution

The period of technological innovation and factory production, beginning in Britain in the late eighteenth century, that eventually changed an economy that was largely agricultural and rural to one that was industrial and urban.

IDEAS THAT ADVANCED ECONOMIC THOUGHT
Self-Interest

Adam Smith believed that human beings are motivated primarily by what he called **self-interest**, or the desire each of us has to better our condition in life. This means that the profit motive provides the major stimulus for economic growth and prosperity. When society requires greater production to satisfy its wants, it does not appeal to the generosity of producers, but rather to the desire of producers to increase their own profits.

The trick is to ensure that this desire for greater profits does not completely overwhelm a producer's sense of obligation to the rest of society. For this reason, in a free market, there is competition among many producers, none of whom can raise their prices too high without losing customers. In this way, self-interest and competition work together to advance the common good. Government regulation is not necessary to control the economy because the forces of market competition will serve, in Smith's famous phrase, as an **invisible hand**, or a natural control. To see how this works, let's consider a hypothetical situation.

Suppose an ambitious farmer decides to charge three times the going rate for a bushel of potatoes. Buyers will naturally do business with one of the many other farmers who sell their potatoes at lower market prices. The first farmer will have to reduce the price of his potatoes or face the economic consequence of lost sales. Even if all Ontario potato farmers conspire to sell their potatoes for exorbitant prices, entrepreneurs will bring potatoes into Ontario from other markets, such as Prince Edward Island, to realize a profit. At the same time, when local farmers realize that growing potatoes has become more profitable, they will replace some of their crops with potatoes. This increased supply of potatoes will naturally force the price of potatoes back down again. Smith believed that these natural "laws of the market" are at work in all openly competitive marketplaces.

Ongoing Progress and Prosperity

After reflecting on the substantial increases in wealth that had occurred in Britain during the previous 100 years, Smith outlined three reasons for the country's continued economic growth and increasing prosperity: the division of labour, the law of accumulation, and the law of population.

For Smith, the **division of labour**, or the specialization of workers in a complex and mechanized production process, led to increases in levels of production. These production increases provided greater profits for investors, more consumer goods for workers, and ultimately greater economic efficiency for society.

The **law of accumulation** worked naturally to fuel further rounds of growth and prosperity. The accumulated profits that industrialists invested in additional capital goods, such as factories and machinery, permitted increases in total production and efficiency for the economy as a whole. These increases in turn led eventually to greater profits for investor industrialists. The increased profits could then be reinvested in additional capital goods, providing the stimulus for further rounds of economic growth.

According to Smith, the **law of population** also contributed to the maintenance of this steady rate of growth and prosperity. The accumulation of capital naturally increases the demand for labour to operate the additional machinery that the industrialists purchase. To attract more workers, competing industrialists must offer higher wages. Wage increases lead to improved living conditions for workers, which in turn reduce mortality rates. As a result, there is an increase in the population and, therefore, in the labour force. Increases in the labour force mean that workers must compete with one another to find jobs, and this competition tends to keep wages from increasing. Thus, industrialists continue to make healthy profits.

law of population
Adam Smith's theory that the accumulation of capital by businesspeople requires more workers to operate the equipment, leading to higher wages, which in turn lead to better living conditions, lower mortality rates, and an increase in population.

A monument to Adam Smith on the Royal Mile in Edinburgh, Scotland.

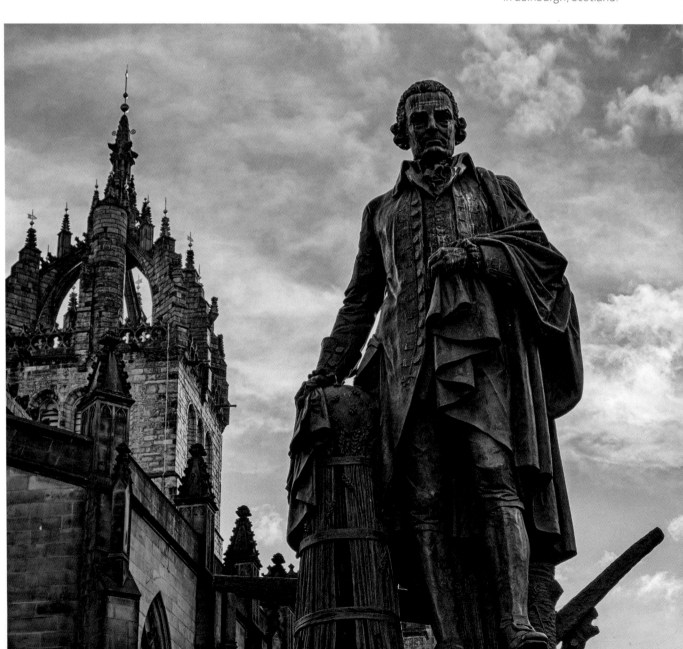

geometrical progression
A number sequence (such as 2, 4, 8, 16, 32, 64...) that has the same ratio (in this case, × 2) between each number in the sequence; it is associated with population growth in the pessimistic theories of Thomas Malthus.

Thomas Robert Malthus (1776–1834)

Recognized historically as the first professional economist, Thomas Robert Malthus was a mild-mannered cleric whose shyness was compounded by a severe speech impediment. He challenged Adam Smith's view of a world governed by natural laws that provided ever-increasing prosperity, and he predicted inevitable poverty and famine for the masses. Malthus first presented his pessimistic views in a book he published in 1798 called *An Essay on the Principle of Population, as It Affects the Future Improvement of Society*. He revised and expanded the text five times between 1803 and 1826. Although he softened his views slightly over the years, his pessimistic conclusions did not change. After reading Malthus, English writer Thomas Carlyle referred to economics as "the dismal science."

BIOGRAPHY

Malthus was born into an English upper-middle-class family in 1766. He was admitted to Jesus College at Cambridge University in 1784, where he studied a wide range of subjects and took prizes in Latin and Greek before earning a master of arts degree in 1791. In response to a religious vocation, Malthus took holy orders in the Anglican Church in 1797 and pursued the quiet life of an English country curate.

He was named professor of history and political economy at the East India Company's college at Haileybury, Hertfordshire, in 1805. This was the first time that the term *political economy* was used for an academic position, so Malthus can rightly be identified as the first professional economist.

THE TIMES

Malthus's thoughts and writings were greatly influenced by the existing economic conditions in Britain. The country was in the midst of the Industrial Revolution, a period when great numbers of workers left their farms and crowded into cities, where they hoped to find jobs in factories. They lived in congested and unsanitary quarters, struggling to survive on minimal wages. At the same time, a prolonged, expensive, and bloody war against Napoleon Bonaparte's France added to the misery of the British working class. Poor crop yields and a simultaneous population boom further aggravated the situation. It began to look as if Britain's once-rich farmlands could no longer feed the country's people.

IDEAS THAT ADVANCED ECONOMIC THOUGHT
Population and Food Production

Malthus based his ideas about population and food production on what he thought were two self-evident premises. The first is that food is necessary to sustain human life. The second premise is that human sexual instinct is constant. Starting with these two premises, Malthus built an argument that the population, if left unchecked, would double every 25 years (about one generation). This doubling effect meant that the population grew in what statisticians call a **geometrical progression**.

Food production, on the other hand, can only grow in an **arithmetical progression**. As more land is required for food production, less-fertile tracts of land will be employed out of necessity, and these less-fertile lands will yield fewer crops. At the same time, as more and more workers cultivate the lands more intensively, the productivity of the added workers also declines. Malthus used the economic principle of the law of diminishing returns (see Chapter 2) to explain why growth in food production would be limited to arithmetical increases from one generation to the next. That is, each generation's food production increases by an amount equal to the original quantity. Figure 5.1 illustrates what became known as the "Malthusian dilemma."

Malthus had a very pessimistic outlook. He thought that if wages went up, workers' improved standard of living would reduce infant mortality rates, which would lead to an increase in the population at a faster rate than the means of subsistence. Where Adam Smith saw a world of steadily increasing prosperity, Malthus believed that wages and the standard of living should hover around the subsistence level to keep the population from growing out of control.

Although Malthus admitted that two types of population control existed, he did not think they would prove strong enough to check the geometric progression of the world's population. **Positive checks**, which increase the death rate, include war, famine, disease, and epidemics. **Preventive checks**, which reduce the birth rate, include moral restraints such as late marriage and sexual abstinence.

In the end, Malthus failed to predict two developments that had major impacts on his theories of population. In the twentieth century, a series of technological breakthroughs in the field of agriculture, known collectively as the Green Revolution, increased food production rates beyond anything Malthus might have imagined. Also, continued urbanization has had a negative effect on the birth rate. Whereas additional children in farm families have always been seen as assets to help with the work, this has never been the case in urban families. Average family size in urban industrial countries continues to decline, to the point where several countries in the world today have reached zero population growth. Does this mean Malthus was wrong? Two hundred years after the publication of his ground-shaking text, the debate continues.

arithmetical progression
A number sequence (such as 1, 3, 5, 7, 9, 11, 13…) that has the same difference (in this case, by 1) between each number in the sequence; it is associated with food production in the pessimistic theories of Thomas Malthus.

positive check
Thomas Malthus's theory that war, famine, and disease would check population increases to some extent, but not enough to prevent the geometrical progression of the world's population to unsustainable levels.

preventive check
Thomas Malthus's theory that restraints such as late marriage and sexual abstinence would help reduce the birth rate to some extent, but not enough to prevent the geometrical progression of the world's population to unsustainable levels.

Generation	1	2	3	4	5	6	7	8	9	10
Year	1	25	50	75	100	125	150	175	200	225
Population	1	2	4	8	16	32	64	128	256	512
Food	1	2	3	4	5	6	7	8	9	10

Note: Each 25-year period refers to one generation. Each generation, the population doubles. Every 25 years, food production increases by an amount equal to the original quantity produced during the first year.

To keep this table simple, constant units of population and food production are used instead of actual figures. One unit of population might represent 1 million people, and 1 unit of food might represent enough wheat to sustain 1 unit of population from one harvest to the next.

FIGURE 5.1
The Malthusian dilemma
A balanced economic system (in which 1 unit of food is available for 1 unit of population) naturally transforms—if left unchecked—into an economically unbalanced situation. After 10 generations (or 225 years), 512 units of population must subsist on only 10 units of food. Unless population growth is controlled, famine awaits the entire human race!

David Ricardo (1772–1823)

Adam Smith's notion of humankind living in a harmonious world governed by natural laws was most effectively assailed by David Ricardo, the articulate son of a Dutch merchant banker who had immigrated to Britain and made a fortune on the London Stock Exchange.

BIOGRAPHY

David Ricardo was born into a prosperous family in London in 1772. At 14, he went to work in his father's investment business, but by the time he turned 22, he had established his own business with a capital base of £800. He retired 20 years later with over £1 million.

Recognizing that most investors tend to overreact and exaggerate the importance of events, Ricardo was able to use his knowledge of different kinds of securities to make great profits. For example, in the panic following Napoleon's return to power in France—and with the increased likelihood of war—the market for British government securities declined sharply. Ricardo, however, invested heavily in government securities prior to the Battle of Waterloo. When the Duke of Wellington defeated Napoleon's armies at Waterloo, Ricardo's profits were significant.

When Ricardo retired to the country at the age of 42, he devoted his attention to the new science of political economy. His most famous book, *On the Principles of Political Economy and Taxation*, exposed the bitter class conflicts at the heart of any society structured around free-enterprise capitalism. Published in 1817, it challenged the power of the aristocratic landlord class by questioning the contributions of this class to society. The book was hailed by the rising industrialist class and became an influential document of political reform.

Elected to the House of Commons in 1819, Ricardo argued on behalf of free trade and carefully outlined the complex laws of land rent that allowed the idle landlord class to exploit land, labour, and capital. In 1823, he died suddenly at the age of 51, before he could witness first-hand the full impact of his economic ideas.

THE TIMES

Ricardo lived during a period of great social conflict and political unrest in Britain. The British population grew rapidly, putting a strain on food supplies. The Napoleonic Wars and successive years of poor crops further drained food reserves.

Not surprisingly, where Adam Smith saw society as a family making great progress together, Ricardo saw clear divisions between conflicting groups. He identified the three main groups in British society as the working class, who lived on modest wages; the industrialist class, who made healthy profits by operating the factories they owned; and the aristocratic landlord class, who received substantial rent from the land titles they held. One group, Ricardo argued, could prosper only at the expense of the others.

Ricardo reasoned that, given their hold on the land, landlords were best positioned to compete effectively against the other classes. The working class would always struggle to live at or near subsistence levels. The rising industrialists had new-found riches but lacked sufficient representation in Parliament. Therefore, the powerful and entrenched landed aristocracy would always prevail.

To illustrate his case, Ricardo used the example of the landlord-dominated Parliament forcing through legislation known as the **Corn Laws**. These measures imposed stiff taxes on grains imported from other countries. Since there was a shortage of grain in England at the time, the taxes drove up the price of domestic grain to levels usually seen only in times of famine. By 1813, a bushel of wheat sold for twice the average worker's weekly wage. This forced the industrialists to pay higher wages (to ensure that their workers would survive), which, in turn, cut into their profits. High grain prices, however, guaranteed the payment of high rents to the landlords. When the industrialists finally succeeded in repealing the Corn Laws in the 1840s, they effectively broke the power of the landed aristocracy and slowly began replacing them as the dominant class in British society.

IDEAS THAT ADVANCED ECONOMIC THOUGHT
The Iron Law of Wages

Ricardo reasoned that, because of the working class's unchecked rate of reproduction, labour's natural wages would always remain at the subsistence level. Higher wages would increase the population by ensuring lower rates of infant mortality but would not raise living standards because the higher wages would have to be distributed among larger families.

Greedy industrialists seized on this economic principle to justify keeping their workers' wages at the lowest level possible, in some cases claiming that they were thereby performing a public service. Low wages became the figurative leg irons that shackled the working class to their slums. This was never Ricardo's intent. He always believed that wages should be determined by free-market conditions.

The Theory of the Comparative Advantage of Trade

It is a commonly accepted principle that when one community can produce grain more efficiently than another, while the other community can produce wool more efficiently, trade will provide an obvious or **absolute advantage** to both communities. Ricardo was the first person able to recognize and explain that even when one community can produce both wheat and wool efficiently, there remains a **comparative advantage** to be shared when both communities trade the products they can each produce most efficiently. (We'll explore both concepts in Unit 6.)

As a result of his belief in comparative advantage, Ricardo became a strong advocate of free trade at a time when Britain imposed high tariffs on many imports precisely to discourage trade with other countries. While these taxes often protected the earnings of the rich landlords, they hurt the workers and the industrialists. Once again, argued Ricardo, the interests of the landlords ran counter to the interests of the rest of the economy. From Ricardo's perspective, the landlord class grew very rich while others performed all the work and assumed all the risks. Ricardo quickly became the parliamentary champion of the previously unrepresented industrial capitalist.

Corn Laws
Early nineteenth-century taxes on grains imported into Britain that drove up the market price of domestic grain to benefit aristocratic landlords. These taxes became a focus of opposition for David Ricardo's wage and free trade theories.

absolute advantage
The capacity of one economy to produce a good or service with fewer resources than another.

comparative advantage
The capacity of one economy to produce a good or service with comparatively fewer resources than another (for example, having a lower opportunity cost).

bourgeoisie

The term used by Karl Marx for industrial capitalists who, he theorized, would be overthrown by the working class.

proletariat

The term used by Karl Marx to describe the working class who, he theorized, would rise up and overthrow the bourgeoisie, or industrial capitalists.

Karl Marx (1818–1883)

According to Karl Marx, all of human history is governed by economic laws and a series of struggles between people of different social classes. Marx believed that economics is central to people's lives. He held that people's need to eat, drink, and have shelter (the material means of existence) comes before other pursuits in life, such as politics, science, art, and religion.

In collaboration with his friend, wealthy capitalist Friedrich Engels, Marx founded an international workers' movement intended to overthrow the corrupt ruling class of industrial capitalists and aristocratic landlords. Marx called the ruling class the **bourgeoisie**. In 1848, Marx and Engels published the *Communist Manifesto*, in which they incited all exploited workers (whom they called the **proletariat**) to rise up against their oppressors: "Let the ruling classes tremble at a Communistic revolution. The proletariat have nothing to lose but their chains. They have a world to win. Workers of all countries unite!" And so was born the international revolutionary socialist movement of communism. Several rebellions followed in European countries, but none of them succeeded until the Russian Revolution in 1917.

For his radical views, Marx has come to be known as either "the prophet of the proletariat" or "the demonic philosopher." Either way, it is undeniable that he left an indelible mark on the science of economics and on the course of human history.

BIOGRAPHY

Karl Marx was born in the German Rhineland in 1818. An excellent scholar, he attended Bonn University, where he studied philosophy. Marx became the editor of a small, middle-class liberal newspaper. One of the first editorials to get Marx into trouble with the government denounced a new law that prevented peasants from exercising their traditional right to gather fallen timber in the forest for firewood. The authorities first censored and then closed down the newspaper. Marx became more and more outspoken as, one by one, the papers he edited were suppressed by the state.

As his views became more radical and even revolutionary, Marx had to flee Germany. He moved first to Paris and then to Brussels, but his troubles with the state followed him until he moved to London in 1849. Marx and his family lived in London in relative poverty for the rest of his life.

His most comprehensive work, *Capital* (*Das Kapital* in the original German text), was published in three volumes in 1867, 1885, and 1894. In this cold and complex critique of economics, Marx explained why capitalism would ultimately destroy itself. The book was completed by Engels after Marx died in 1883.

THE TIMES

Living in the second half of the nineteenth century, Marx witnessed first-hand the ill effects of the Industrial Revolution on the working class. By the time of Marx's death, England had been transformed from an agricultural and artisan-based economy to one in which the dominant mode of production was the steam-powered factory.

Workers lived in the slums of crowded cities and worked 18-hour days in unsafe and unclean factories. Since there were no laws against child labour, working-class children had to endure these same hardships. After working long hours, children rarely had the time to acquire the education that might lift them out of such deplorable circumstances.

To Marx, the capitalist system was immoral and the people who exploited it unspeakably evil. He saw a world in which all wealth was achieved on the backs of the workers. Yet, the working class received few of the benefits of their labour. Marx believed capitalism, as an economic system, was morally bankrupt and that its moral bankruptcy would one day bring about its own demise.

IDEAS THAT CHANGED ECONOMIC THOUGHT

The Economic Interpretation of History

Marx thought that the laws of economics determine the course of human history. He believed history was an ongoing series of class conflicts between exploiters and the exploited: free citizens against slaves, patricians against plebeians, lords against serfs, guild masters against journeymen, and industrial capitalists against workers. Whenever conditions become unbearable, the oppressed rise up in open rebellion against their oppressors. The capitalist system, based on exploitation and self-gratification, has sown the seeds of its own destruction. Capitalist exploitation will continually worsen the living standards of workers. Immersed in misery, workers will eventually unite to overthrow the corrupt ruling class.

The International Communist Revolution (Revolutionary Socialism)

According to Marx, this revolution would begin in the most industrialized countries of Western Europe (where capitalism was strongest and where workers were exploited most severely) and then would spread throughout the world. The violent overthrow of capitalism would lead to international socialism based on the common ownership of land and capital. Socialism, once fully evolved, would be transformed into its ideal state of communism: a worker-governed society based on the guiding principle "from each according to ability, and to each according to need."

A monument to Karl Marx at Teatralnaya Square, Moscow, Russia. The inscription reads: "Proletarians of all countries, solidarity!"

The Labour Theory of Value and the Impact of Marx

For Marx, the value of any item is the value of all labour used in its production (**labour value**). This includes the direct labour supplied by workers in the manufacturing process as well as the amount of indirect labour—that is, the labour embodied in the machinery and buildings used in the manufacturing process. In a capitalist system, workers receive only a portion of what their labour is worth. The difference, which Marx called **surplus value**, is stolen from the worker in the form of profit for the capitalist.

To better understand this concept, let's use a simple example. Assume that the production of a wool sweater requires $40 worth of labour, $5 worth of materials, and $5 worth of wear and tear on machinery (depreciation). If the industrial capitalist can sell the sweater for $80, then a surplus value of $30 is created in the form of profit for the capitalist. This surplus value arises from the market's determination that the real value of each sweater is $80. Since the value of the indirect labour is $10 ($5 + $5), the value of the direct labour must be $70. Since workers are only paid $40 for knitting the sweater, $30 represents the amount of worker *exploitation*.

Worker employment in a capitalist system is based on the premise that the worker will always produce more for the employer than the employer will have to pay in the form of wages. Workers are forced to sell their labour to capitalists for less than it is truly worth because there is always what Marx identified as a "reserve army of the unemployed." Capitalists always have the option of hiring desperate unemployed workers at lower wages, which ensures that wages will never rise above the subsistence level.

The impact of Marxian thinking was so pervasive that it eventually became a separate and distinct school of economic thought. From 1917 to 1991, communist movements grew to eventually include one-third of the world's population.

In economics today, we clearly distinguish between *Marxist* thinking and *Marxian* thinking. *Marxist thinking* is intended to refer to his revolutionary political ideology, focused on the overthrow of the existing ruling class by a united working class. *Marxian thinking* is intended to refer to his socialist economic ideas and theories, based on equality and social justice.

labour value
Karl Marx's notion that the value of any item is equal to the value of the labour used to produce it.

surplus value
The difference between the value of a good measured in terms of the labour used to produce it, and its higher selling price, a surplus that Karl Marx believed was stolen from labour by capitalists.

Self-Reflect

1 Explain in your own words Adam Smith's concept of the "invisible hand" and how it relates to self-interest and competition as the primary economic motivators.

2 Explain the Malthusian dilemma in your own words. How did the law of diminishing returns contribute to the pessimistic conclusion of Malthus?

3 According to Ricardo, what are the main three classes in any free-enterprise society? How does self-interest result in bitter class conflicts?

4 Do you agree with Marx that all capitalists exploit workers? Support your position by explaining the relationship between surplus value and exploitation.

Thinking like an Economist

Investigating Cause and Consequence Relationships to Support Hypothesis Testing

Parents constantly remind their children that actions (including doing nothing) have consequences. This reality is only magnified in the economic world, which contains many interacting stakeholders with diverse interests. Choices lead to actions (often to protect the interests of decision makers), and these actions or events cause change. The results of an action and the impact (or significance) of an event or happening can be seen as the consequences. These consequences may impact different stakeholders in different ways, causing problems for some and benefits for others. Unbalanced results often trigger a new cycle of economic thinking to prioritize choices and actions to address new problems. (See Figure 5.2.) Serious economic problems are not politically or economically sustainable. Economic thinking must clearly distinguish between causes and consequences.

Economists are sometimes called upon to identify patterns and relationships in a set of data or facts and to use this information to gain insight into an economic problem in need of appropriate attention. To better understand the problem being addressed, economists must identify the consequences most in need of attention. Doing so will reveal evidence of a problem's harmful nature and extent. Next, economic analysis must determine the causes of the problem. Once this cause and consequence relationship is established, options can be hypothesized as potential remedies to improve the situation by addressing the causes.

A **hypothesis** is a speculative theory that requires proof or verification. Supporting evidence is required to confirm a hypothesis as viable. Let's work with some hypotheses to practise the economic thinking

FIGURE 5.2
A cyclical pattern of causes and consequences in economic decision making

As this diagram shows, *choices* are driven by interests, *actions* reflect priorities, *results* are determined by outcomes, and *impact* reflects the significance of consequences.

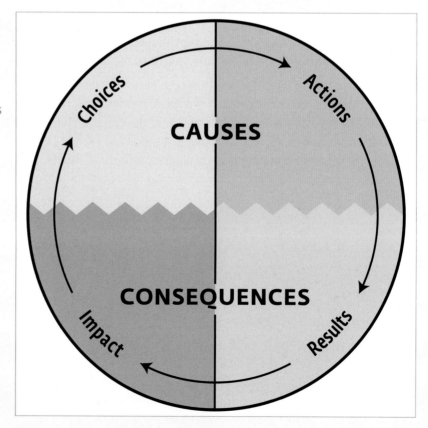

hypothesis
A speculative theory requiring proof or verification.

required. What cause and consequence patterns have you noticed so far in the evolution of economic thought? Use the information in this chapter, and any additional information that you have researched, as supporting evidence to assess each of the following hypotheses:

- **Hypothesis A:** Prosperous times create great economists.

- **Hypothesis B:** The advancement of economic thought reinforces the pattern of economic trade-offs. Very often, solving one economic problem creates another.

- **Hypothesis C:** A great economic thinker is more of a reactionary than a visionary.

APPLYING ECONOMIC THINKING

1   Do the facts about the evolution of economic thought provide sufficient evidence to support Hypothesis A? What is the most important evidence you have to validate or refute this theoretical statement?

2   Do the facts about the evolution of economic thought provide sufficient evidence to support Hypothesis B? What is the most important evidence you have to validate or refute this theoretical statement?

3   Do the facts about the evolution of economic thought provide sufficient evidence to support Hypothesis C? What is the most important evidence you have to validate or refute this theoretical statement?

The colonists of New England loved their tea, consuming some 544 000 kg each year. So why did they raid British ships, disguised as Indigenous Americans, to dump 342 chests (40 800 kg) of fine tea in Boston Harbour on December 16, 1773? This protest became known as the "Boston Tea Party." How did the British parliament respond to this defiance, and what happened in 1775 to change the course of North American history?

Chapter 5
Consolidation Activities

KNOWLEDGE

1   The following four excerpts are taken from Xenophon's *Oeconomicus*, one of the earliest texts on economics. After reading, answer the questions that follow.

   • *A wife who is a good partner in the estate carries just as much weight as her husband in attaining prosperity. Property generally comes into the house through the exertions of the husband, but it is mostly dispensed through the housekeeping of the wife. If these activities are performed well, estates increase, but if they are managed incompetently, estates diminish.*

   • *Land is not wealth for a man who cultivates it in such a way that by its cultivation he incurs loss. . . . Things [including money] . . . can be wealth for the person who knows how to use them, but not wealth for one who does not know. . . . Enemies are wealth to anyone who can benefit from enemies . . . knowing how to use enemies so as to derive benefit from them is a characteristic of a good estate manager.*

   • *The man who is going to be a successful farmer must make his labourers eager and disposed to be obedient. . . . Slaves need some good thing to look forward to no less, in fact, even more than free men so that they will be willing to stay.*

   • *When farming is successful, all other arts prosper, but whenever the earth is forced to lie barren, the other arts, both on earth and sea, are virtually extinguished.*

   According to Xenophon, what is the ultimate proof that an estate farm is properly managed? How did the roles of the estate owner and his wife contribute to this success?

2   Who were the physiocrats, and how did they influence the economic thinking of Adam Smith?

3   According to David Ricardo, why did the British Parliament pass the Corn Laws during a time of food shortages? Why was he an advocate of freer trade?

THINKING & INQUIRY

4   Compare Ricardo's "iron law of wages" with the "reserve army of the unemployed" described by Karl Marx. Who did each thinker identify as the principal hero and villain in society?

5   Answer the following questions about the ideas of Karl Marx and Adam Smith:

   a)   Do you think that Marx would have agreed with Smith that self-interest is the major motivator in a capitalist society? Explain.

   b)   What differences are there in the way that Marx and Smith viewed self-interest?

6   The following three excerpts are taken from Adam Smith's *The Wealth of Nations*, published in 1776. Read each excerpt carefully before answering the questions that follow.

It is not from the benevolence of the butcher, the brewer, or the baker that we expect our dinner, but from their regard to their own interest. We address ourselves, not to their humanity, but to their self-love, and never talk to them of our own necessities, but of their advantages. —Book I, Chapter II

Every individual . . . generally, indeed, neither intends to promote the public interest, nor knows how much he is promoting it. . . . [H]e intends only his own security; and by directing that industry in such a manner as its produce may be of the greatest value, he intends only his own gain, and he is in this, as in many other cases, led by an invisible hand to promote an end which was no part of his intention. —Book IV, Chapter II

According to the system of natural liberty, the sovereign [government] has only three duties to attend to . . . first, the duty of protecting the society from the violence and invasion of other independent societies; secondly, the duty of protecting, so far as possible, every member of the society from the injustice or oppression of every other member of it, or the duty of establishing an exact administration of justice; and, thirdly, the duty of erecting and maintaining certain public works, and certain public institutions, which it can never be for the interest of any individual, or small number of individuals, to erect and maintain. —Book IV, Chapter IX

a) In your own words, explain what Smith believes both motivates and does not motivate producers.

b) Explain the metaphor of "the invisible hand." What does it symbolize?

c) According to Smith, what were the duties of the sovereign or government? How does this view support the notion of laissez-faire capitalism?

COMMUNICATION

7   To organize what you have learned about the economic thinkers presented in this chapter, create a study guide in the form of a summary note.

8   How would you explain the impact of Karl Marx on economic thinking to a schoolmate with no background in economics? Is revolution essential to change the world?

APPLICATION

9   Use Thomas Robert Malthus's ideas to prepare a reasoned argument that supports or challenges additional research into the mass production of genetically modified foods.

10 Who is your favourite of the classical economic thinkers? Explain your choice. Investigate the writings of this economic thinker to find and explain a favourite quote.

11 Marx viewed dictatorship as a temporary necessity in the early stages of communism. Eventually, a spirit of solidarity would prevail and people would govern themselves in a democratic assembly. Some see this view as politically naive. Once a dictatorship is firmly in place, is a return to democracy realistic, without further bloodshed? Explain your own views and use historical examples to support your argument.

6
Modern Economics

INTRODUCTION

Economic thinking continued making significant advances during the twentieth century with the illuminating work of John Maynard Keynes, Joan Robinson, John Kenneth Galbraith, and Milton Friedman. In this chapter, we will explore these modern-era thinkers and the ideas that furthered economic reasoning. We will also look at contemporary economists and their impact on scarcity management as human societies continue to evolve and economic choices become increasingly more complex and challenging.

We encourage you to continue to focus on making meaningful connections between events in the world and the economic ideas that emerged from the great economic thinkers who experienced them. As a budding economist, be sure to distinguish objective and verifiable facts from opinion, inference, and speculation.

LEARNING GOALS

Once you have completed this chapter, you should be able to:

- Understand the major ideas and theories of the following leading economic thinkers: John Maynard Keynes, Joan Robinson, John Kenneth Galbraith, and Milton Friedman

- Understand how economic thinking helps change the world in our own times

- Recognize cause-and-consequence relationships in the thinking of contemporary economists such as Elinor Ostrom, Amartya Sen, Mark Carney, and Dambisa Moyo

- Begin thinking like an economist by distinguishing between fact and conjecture

- Conduct research to locate information from a variety of reliable sources to address the evolution of economic thought, and communicate economic information, research findings, analysis, and conclusions clearly, effectively, and accurately

KEY TERMS

school of economic thought

deferred savings

imperfect competition

monopsony

public goods

monetarist

conjecture

common resources

developmentalist

foreign aid

humanitarian aid

school of economic thought
A group of economists who share and promote common ideas on how economies function.

John Maynard Keynes (1883–1946)

In 1936, John Maynard Keynes published *The General Theory of Employment, Interest, and Money*. In it, he defended the "revolutionary" ideas already being applied by governments in Britain, Canada, and the United States to deal with the era of massive unemployment known as the Great Depression. He also provided a blueprint that explained how government intervention could save a country from widespread unemployment and the economic stagnation that accompanied it. Keynes's book helped to rescue the capitalist system from self-destruction and the spectre of international communism. The approach we have come to call "Keynesian economics" analyzes relationships among demand, production, and unemployment, and focuses on government's role in sustaining economic activity. In time, this way of thinking gained much support and led to the formation of a distinct "Keynesian" **school of economic thought**.

BIOGRAPHY

Keynes was born in Cambridge, England, in the same year that Karl Marx died. In addition to teaching economics at Cambridge University, Keynes served as an economic adviser to the British treasury during both World Wars and attended post-war international peace conferences as a representative of the British government. He was also appointed as director of the Bank of England, Britain's central bank. The tireless Keynes served as editor of a major economics journal, chair of an insurance company, and manager of an extremely successful investment trust. Inspired by his mother, Keynes was an early supporter of the movement that eventually won British women the right to vote.

In 1944, Keynes was the chief British representative at the Bretton Woods Conference, which established the International Monetary Fund and the World Bank. His last major public service was the brilliant negotiation in 1945 of a multi-billion-dollar post-war reconstruction loan from the United States to Great Britain.

THE TIMES

Keynes's career spanned the two World Wars and the period of economic upheaval between them known as the Great Depression. At the end of the First World War, the Allies forced Germany to pay more in reparations than its economy could bear. The result was a severe and long-term depression in Germany that Nazi dictator Adolf Hitler exploited to further his own political agenda.

The Great Depression (1929–1939) was a difficult time in Europe and North America. At the beginning of the Depression, most capitalist governments believed that skyrocketing unemployment rates were only temporary; they thought economic conditions would improve as their market economies reverted to a more balanced state. They called for unemployed workers to tighten their belts, make do with less, be patient, and ride out this period of badly needed correction. Making no attempts to initiate economic improvements, these governments were clearly part of the problem rather than the solution. In fact, government attempts to cut spending and pay back war debts contributed to a decline in the amount of money in circulation.

DID YOU KNOW?

A *school of economic thought* is a collection of thinkers who share a common perspective on how economies work and how governments can support economic growth and stability. Today, critics of the Keynesian school point to his *General Theory* as the leading cause of high inflation rates and massive public debts that Western countries have since accumulated. On the other hand, it is undeniable that national unemployment rates have not returned to the levels witnessed during the 1930s.

IDEAS THAT ADVANCED ECONOMIC THOUGHT

War and Sustainable Peace

As a representative at the peace conference that followed the First World War, Keynes strongly criticized the Treaty of Versailles, which he predicted would ruin the German economy by forcing the country to pay the victorious Allies more than it could afford. He abruptly resigned from the British government.

While serving as a key economic adviser to the British government during the Second World War, Keynes recommended a daring plan that used "**deferred savings**" as the principal means of financing the war effort. A portion of every worker's pay would be automatically invested in government war bonds that could not be cashed until the war had ended. Keynes hypothesized that, during the war, consumer spending would interfere with the war effort; after the war, consumer buying power would help to stimulate investment, permit increased production of consumer goods, and maintain employment levels.

The 1945 peace treaty and post-war reconstruction plan were greatly influenced by Keynes, who argued that, to secure a lasting peace, the defeated enemy should be helped, not punished. As former enemies became business associates, economic co-operation replaced military intervention in Western Europe. With developments such as the European Union, history appears to have proven Keynes correct.

Combatting the Great Depression

In *The General Theory*, Keynes advanced an idea considered unconventional at the time: that governments bore a large part of the responsibility for the high unemployment rates (approaching 20 percent) ushered in by the Great Depression. He believed these rates could be lowered most effectively by government intervention, especially by sponsoring public works projects that would provide jobs to idle workers. By taking control of interest rates and increasing public spending, a government could stimulate consumer spending, raise the demand for consumer goods, and bring more people back into the workforce. As these previously unemployed workers spent their wages, the money would be re-spent by those receiving it. In this way, increased employment would trigger additional rounds of consumption, investment, and employment increases, as the economy continued to put previously idle resources to work. The resulting growth in the economy would have the effect of correcting the problem of high unemployment rates.

Keynes claimed that, since consumers are limited in their spending by the size of their incomes, they are not the source of depressions or any other cyclical business shifts. Business investors and governments are the primary forces behind business cycles. To Keynes, the Great Depression (which was a major downward cycle) was ultimately a problem of too little investment. If investors were given a reason to invest, combined with favourable interest rates, the economy would necessarily recover, but government intervention was required before this could happen.

deferred savings
A policy of bringing foreign peoples under the control of one country for its economic benefit; pursued in the nineteenth and twentieth centuries by European countries over sizable areas of Asia, Africa, and South America.

Joan Robinson (1903–1983)

As a colleague and follower of Keynes, Joan Robinson successfully overcame gender bias and an aversion to mathematics to become one of the most prominent economists of the twentieth century. She is not known primarily for a single idea or focus (unlike many other economists). However, through her diverse writings, she made substantial contributions to various areas of economics.

BIOGRAPHY

Joan Violet Maurice was born in Surrey, England, in 1903. Her controversial father was a major general who publicly accused the British prime minister of misleading Parliament and the entire country during the First World War. Her maternal grandfather was a renowned surgeon and academic. Joan studied economics at Girton College, a women's college in the University of Cambridge. She graduated in 1925 and married fellow economist Austin Robinson the following year. Soon after marriage, the Robinsons moved to Gujarat, India, where Joan became engaged in a research committee studying Anglo-Indian economic relations.

The Robinsons returned to Cambridge in 1928, when Austin was appointed assistant professor of economics at the University of Cambridge. Joan became an assistant lecturer in economics at the university in 1931. As a key member of the "Cambridge School" of economics, she contributed to the fine-tuning and promotion of Keynesian general theory, especially in regard to employment dynamics during the declining production of the Great Depression.

In 1958, Robinson joined the British Academy (a prestigious national funding organization for research projects in the humanities and social sciences). In 1965, she finally assumed the position of full professor and fellow of Girton College at the University of Cambridge. In 1979, just four years before her death, she became the first honorary fellow of King's College at the University of Cambridge.

THE TIMES

Being 20 years younger than Keynes, Joan Robinson experienced the Great Depression, the Second World War, and the period of significant economic growth that followed the war years. She also witnessed the spread and eventual misapplications of Keynesian theory and attempted to revive and redirect this school of economic thought. She did so by promoting the general applicability of Keynesian theory—that it could be applied to matters beyond combatting unemployment—and defending Keynes's ideas against the criticism of mainstream conservative economists who favoured traditional economic restraint.

Robinson witnessed the unionization of workers who fought for fair treatment and wages that would end their exploitation and better reflect their productivity. She also observed a marked disparity between economic growth rates in countries such as the United Kingdom and the United States, compared with struggling countries such as India and China, which she visited and studied.

Before Joan Robinson, economic thinking was a bastion of male dominance. With her sound ideas and prolific writings, she made a significant impact on the

DID YOU KNOW?

Joan Robinson was a leader in moving the Keynesian school of thought forward. Sometimes she is called a *neo-Keynesian*. Given her left-of-centre views later in life, she was also instrumental in revitalizing some of the merits of Marxian economic thinking.

recognition of women as equal contributors. Robinson's early works catapulted her to the forefront of economic thinking. She was an incisive interpreter of the history of economic thought and recognized the discipline as both a means for social control and a vehicle to produce objective scientific knowledge. From Robinson's perspective, this helped to explain the natural tensions in economic thinking.

Robinson was harshly criticized for sympathetic publications (in 1942) about Karl Marx as an important economist and (in 1969) about the successes of China's Cultural Revolution that brought communist leader Mao Zedong to uncontested power. In later life, Robinson's writings reflected a growing pessimism regarding the future of conservative capitalism and a growing appreciation for socialistic (or left-wing) considerations.

IDEAS THAT ADVANCED ECONOMIC THOUGHT

Monopsony and Imperfect Competition

Robinson's early works helped to establish her as a leading economic thinker. In a 1933 publication entitled *The Economics of Imperfect Competition*, she introduced the theory of **imperfect competition** as the more common market occurrence between the extremes of perfect competition (where many sellers interact with many buyers) and monopoly (where one seller interacts with many buyers).

Robinson developed the concept of **monopsony** (the reverse of a monopoly market), where the market is dominated by many sellers (usually workers) and has one buyer (usually an employer). This concept is important in labour economics, where a single employer is buying labour and many workers compete to sell their labour to that employer. Monopsony theory recognizes that employers can exert a large influence over wages: if a sole employer exists in a particular market, that employer can pay workers less than the value of the work they perform. Collective bargaining, where workers negotiate wages as a unit or labour union, is one strategy to address the imbalance of monopsony. Minimum-wage legislation is another way to protect workers from exploitation by employers offering unfair wages. Robinson later used monopsony to help explain the wage discrepancy between male and female workers of equal productivity.

Economic Growth and Development

In 1956, Robinson published what many consider her greatest work, *The Accumulation of Capital*. This work extended Keynesian thinking to address long-term economic growth and prosperity. It reflected on the conditions required for the achievement of a cumulative long-term growth of income and capital, which she referred to as a "golden age." The entire analysis is effectively carried out without the use of mathematics.

In reaction to the exploitation she recognized as coming from the unfair allocation of resources to maximize productivity and the inadequacy of wages to fairly compensate workers, her views sometimes reflected socialistic overtones supporting equity in income distribution. After her time as a researcher in India, Robinson remained keenly interested in the problems faced by underdeveloped countries on the uphill struggle to balanced and sustainable development.

imperfect competition
A common market situation where competition is less than perfect (where many buyers interact with many sellers) but still competitive (unlike monopoly). Samples include monopolistic competition and oligopoly.

monopsony
The reverse of a monopoly market, where there are many sellers (usually workers) but only one buyer (usually an employer).

John Kenneth Galbraith (1908–2006)

Prolific writer and gifted economist John Kenneth Galbraith has been called one of Canada's most notable exports to the United States. When Galbraith published his book *The Affluent Society* in 1958, he coined the term "affluent society," which summed up the remarkable increase in wealth that the United States and Canada had enjoyed since the end of the Second World War. At the same time, the book set out a devastating criticism of government economic policies because they did not pay enough attention to providing and maintaining public services.

BIOGRAPHY

John Kenneth Galbraith was born in Iona Station, Ontario. After graduating in agricultural economics from the University of Toronto in 1931, he earned a doctorate at the University of California at Berkeley in 1934. He taught economics at Harvard and Princeton Universities until the United States entered the Second World War. During the war, Galbraith worked in the federal Office of Price Administration. After the war, he was appointed director of the US Strategic Bombing Survey, which studied the effects of air raids on Japan and Germany.

Galbraith served as editor of *Fortune* magazine from 1943 to 1948 and then returned to Harvard in 1949 to teach economics. He stayed there until his retirement, except for a brief stint as ambassador to India under US President John F. Kennedy. In addition to *The Affluent Society*, his other noted publications include *American Capitalism*, *The New Industrial State*, *Economics and the Public Purpose*, *The Age of Uncertainty*, and *The Nature of Mass Poverty*.

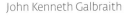
John Kenneth Galbraith

THE TIMES

Galbraith rose to prominence during the period of economic prosperity that followed the Second World War. Despite the Cold War (which pitted the capitalist United States and its allies against the communist USSR and its allies), high levels of employment and consumer spending during this time produced an unparalleled degree of prosperity in Canada and the United States. This affluence, however, did not diminish the amount of poverty in these prosperous societies. At the same time, large international corporations emerged as a new influence in economic decision making.

IDEAS THAT ADVANCED ECONOMIC THOUGHT

Theory of Social Balance

In *The Affluent Society*, Galbraith argued that the United States' post-war emphasis on private-sector production had produced a wealthy private sector and public squalor. Although consumer goods (such as automobiles and televisions) were produced in abundance, **public goods** (such as schools, hospitals, and parks) were neglected or in short supply. Galbraith argued that what society really needed was greater investment in public goods, which serve the common good. He thought national production should be shifted to serve these public priorities.

Galbraith also popularized the view that, in the world of international corporations, corporate managers (not shareholders or consumers) held the real decision-making power in the economy. He believed that more government involvement and regulation of the economy would help improve society.

public goods
Goods produced to serve the greater good, such as schools, highways, hospitals, and parklands.

John Kenneth Galbraith castigated US policy-makers for emphasizing consumerism and for neglecting the common good. How does this photo of Dundas Square in Toronto reflect consumerism?

Milton Friedman (1912–2006)

Whereas Galbraith is regarded as a leading proponent of the liberal economic perspective, Milton Friedman is acknowledged as the most articulate champion of the conservative view and free-enterprise capitalism. He was an influential adviser to Richard Nixon and other US presidents.

BIOGRAPHY

Milton Friedman was born in Brooklyn, New York, in 1912. He enrolled in his first economics course in 1930, a time when the single most important issue facing Western countries was the Great Depression. An accomplished scholar, Friedman studied at Rutgers, Chicago, and Columbia Universities before being appointed a government economist during the Second World War. He joined the faculty of the University of Chicago in 1946, where he remained until 1977.

When he received the 1976 Nobel Prize in Economic Sciences, Friedman was cited for "his achievements in the field of consumption analysis, monetary history and theory, and for his demonstration of the complexity of stabilization policy." Friedman has written many books, the best known of which are *Capitalism and Freedom* and *A Monetary History of the United States, 1867–1960.*

These traders on the floor of the New York Stock Exchange are buying or selling ownership shares for their clients. How would low interest rates affect the volume of trade on these stock exchanges? What effect would high borrowing rates have on investors?

THE TIMES

A contemporary of Galbraith, Friedman was strongly influenced by the amount of unproductive government intervention in the US economy following the end of the Second World War. He believed that government attempts to induce cycles of economic growth and full employment (by increasing spending and reducing taxes) resulted in periods of significant price inflation and a steady increase in the rate of public debt. In addition, Friedman thought government intervention made both the economy and individual citizens increasingly more dependent on government assistance and, therefore, weaker.

IDEAS THAT CHANGED ECONOMIC THOUGHT

Laissez-Faire Capitalism

According to Friedman, free markets will largely resolve their own economic problems more effectively if they are left alone rather than subjected to government intervention. Friedman saw individual self-sufficiency and the preservation of the work ethic as important pillars of productivity and sustained economic growth. For this reason, he advocated a program of guaranteed income (or negative income tax) over centralized social welfare services and the massive, inefficient bureaucracy they require. The abolition of minimum-wage legislation is another laissez-faire strategy that Friedman recommended to free up the marketplace.

Friedman also advocated the application of the free-market principle to the supply of education. Under his plan, parents would annually receive government vouchers equal in value to the cost of a child's education. They could spend the vouchers at the school of their choice. Schools would then be developed to meet the demands of parents (the people who best know the needs of their children). Excellent schools would have no problem attracting students. Schools that did not attract enough numbers would automatically close. The education market could thus take care of itself!

The Importance of Money Supply

Friedman is a leading member of the **monetarist** school of thought, sometimes referred to as the "Chicago school." Monetarists believe that the most effective way for governments to influence the economy is by regulating the money supply in circulation. They maintain that business cycles are determined by the money supply and interest rates, not by levels of taxation and government spending. According to Friedman, governments should raise the money supply by a fixed amount each year. This increase should be equal to the long-term growth rate of the economy, that is, between 3 and 5 percent. Too much money in circulation causes price inflation; too little money reduces investment and employment levels.

monetarist
A school of economic thought based on the belief that the most effective way for government to affect the economy is by regulating the money supply.

DID YOU KNOW?

Faculty from the University of Chicago, including Milton Friedman, have received more Nobel Prizes for economics than any other university. The Chicago school of economic thought favours free-enterprise capitalism and regulation of the money supply to promote economic growth and stability. This monetarist school of thought has been traditionally critical of the Keynesian approach.

Self-Reflect

1 Explain how John Maynard Keynes's "deferred savings" plan would work both during and after war.

2 Explain Joan Robinson's theory of imperfect competition and why it would be a more common market occurrence than perfect competition.

3 Describe in your own words John Kenneth Galbraith's theory of social balance. Do you agree with his assessment that more attention is paid to the private interests than to the public good? Use examples from your own community to support you position.

4 What does Milton Friedman see as the best ways to free up the American economy to maximize the benefits of capitalism?

Thinking like an Economist

Separating Fact from Opinion, Inference, and Conjecture

In economics, like all other sciences, it is extremely important to engage in critical thinking that clearly separates objective and verifiable facts (and fact patterns) from interpretations influenced by opinion, inferences, assumptions, and other forms of guesswork known as **conjecture**. Regrettably, this kind of critical thinking can be as challenging as it is important in making scientific discoveries. Human nature is prone to making opinions, assumptions, and inferences. However, great economists must discipline themselves to see the world as it is, to analyze the factors most responsible (based on observable fact patterns) and to apply corrective measures expressly intended to address these problematic causes.

Try the activity in Figure 6.1 independently to test your own ability to clearly distinguish between statements of fact and conjecture. Your teacher will provide a worksheet for you to record your personal responses. Once you complete the activity, your teacher will provide an answer sheet you can use to assess the effectiveness of your thinking. Discuss your experience with classmates to determine the value of this thinking activity.

APPLYING ECONOMIC THINKING

1 What did working from this story reveal about yourself?

2 What did working from this story reveal about human nature?

3 What did working from this story reveal about disciplined economic thinking?

4 Do you think that economists should never make assumptions or share opinions about facts? Why or why not?

5 Find an economics article in a local newspaper or magazine and make separate lists of the facts and opinions presented?

conjecture
An opinion or guess based on inference or assumption.

FIGURE 6.1
Separating fact from opinion

THE ACTIVITY

The purpose of this activity is to test your ability to separate fact or direct observation from inference or opinion. Read the story and then assess the 10 statements that follow to determine whether each is true or false. If you cannot determine whether a statement is true or false, relative to the facts presented, then mark the statement as "Don't Know." You must not draw any inferences, make unsubstantiated assumptions, or form any opinions.

THE STORY

A storekeeper had just turned off the lights in the store when a man appeared and demanded money. The owner opened a cash register. The contents of the cash register were scooped up, and the man sped away. A member of the police force was notified immediately.

STATEMENTS
(Categorize as *True, False,* or *Don't Know*)

1   A man appeared after the owner had turned off his store lights.

2   The robber was a man.

3   The man did not demand money.

4   The man who opened the cash register was the owner.

5   The store owner scooped up the contents of the cash register and sped away.

6   Someone opened a cash register.

7   After the man who demanded the money scooped up the contents of the cash register, he ran away.

8   While the cash register contained money, the story does not state how much.

9   The story concerns a series of events in which only three persons are referred to: the owner of the store, a man who demanded money, and a member of the police force.

10 The following events were included in the story: someone demanded money, a cash register was opened, its contents were scooped up, and a man sped away.

common resources
Productive resources (such as forests, pasture lands, and fishing waters) that are owned by no single person but are available for use by different people.

Contemporary Economics

THE CONTEMPORARY SCENE

By now, most readers have probably begun to wonder whether economic problems can ever really be solved. Some problems keep reappearing in cycles, and each reappearance makes them seem more complex and difficult to address. At the same time, some new problems appear to be the direct results of theories and strategies intended to fix earlier problems. The concept of trade-offs appears to be key in the development of economic thought. We can address one problem, it seems, only at the expense of aggravating another. Clearly, some of our economic goals are in conflict, and some of our theories need to be rethought in light of changing times. We will now examine the thinking of four contemporary economists, from four different parts of the world, and the problems each has addressed.

ELINOR OSTROM (1933–2012)

In 2009, Indiana University professor Elinor Ostrom became the first woman to be awarded the Nobel Prize in Economic Sciences. She received the prize for her groundbreaking research demonstrating that **common resources** (such as forests, pasture lands, and fishing waters) can be managed more effectively by the people who use them than by governments or private companies. This research helped to disprove the idea long held by economists that "common" resources would be overused and depleted. Conventional wisdom advocated government regulation and privatization. Ostrom's alternative was that key management decisions should be made on site and by the individuals directly involved. Her research showed that, over time, the rules and procedures established in this manner—to care for and use "common" resources—are more economically and ecologically sustainable in the long run. This idea was an important breakthrough in resource management and governance.

Elinor Ostrom

AMARTYA SEN (1933–)

Amartya Sen is a professor at Harvard University and the recipient of the 1998 Nobel Prize in Economic Sciences for his work in famine studies. He is an Indian economist and philosopher who has taught and worked in India, Britain, and the United States. While studying at the University of Cambridge, Sen was influenced by both John Maynard Keynes and Joan Robinson.

As a young boy, Sen became keenly interested in famines after experiencing the Bengal famine of 1943, in which 3 million people died. Sen's studies revealed that in many cases of famine, declining food production is not as critical a factor as poor distribution. In Bengal, for example, while food production was slightly down from previous years, social and economic factors such as lower wages, rising unemployment, panic buying, hoarding, and price gouging led to the maldistribution of available food and, ultimately, to starvation.

In the area of economic development, he stressed the importance of providing capability and opportunity equitably to all citizens. Sen argues that governments should be measured by the tangible capabilities of their citizens. He was also influential in the establishment of the United Nations Human Development Report, an annual publication that ranks countries in terms of the progress they are making on a number of economic and social indicators, such as literacy, income, and health outcomes.

Amartya Sen

DID YOU KNOW?

Originally, the economic world was essentially male-dominated. As economic principles confirm, when half the population is unemployed or underemployed, the production possibilities frontier can never be reached. Since 1950, women have contributed significantly to the development of economic thought. In Canada, economists such as Nuala Beck, Dian Cohen, Sherry Cooper, Judith Maxwell, and Sylvia Ostry have enriched the ongoing advancement of economic thinking.

developmentalist
A school of economic thinkers who believe that economic development makes social and political progress possible.

MARK CARNEY (1965–)

Canadian-born Mark Joseph Carney studied economics at Harvard University before completing his master's and doctoral degrees at the University of Oxford. For 13 years, he worked for Goldman Sachs, a legendary American investment bank with offices in global financial centres including London, New York, Tokyo, and Toronto. He quickly rose up the corporate ranks, and his transfers to offices in different countries provided a wealth of experience in dealing with financial crises. Back in Canada, Carney decided to give up his lucrative private-sector work for a public-service job. He worked for the Bank of Canada (Canada's central bank) and the federal Department of Finance before being appointed governor of the Bank of Canada in 2008. In the same year, the global recession was triggered by the financial meltdown of some major and reckless American banks. Under his stewardship, and low interest rate policy, Canada was not as badly affected by the global economic downturn, and it was one of the first countries to recover. In 2013, Carney became governor of the Bank of England, just three years before Britain's 2016 vote to exit the European Union. This decision sent the British pound plummeting in international money markets. In both cases, Carney acted quickly and decisively, using interest rates to defuse a potentially disastrous situation. This earned him an international reputation as a master central banker.

Mark Carney

DID YOU KNOW?

The **developmentalist** school of economic thought began (around 1960) as a group of economists who believed that economic development drove social and political progress. They believed less-developed countries could best grow their economies through industrialization—by fostering a strong, resource-based domestic market and imposing protective high taxes on imported goods. Over time, their thinking has expanded to include capitalism with a more social conscience so that social justice and government accountability for the welfare of its people are prioritized.

DAMBISA MOYO (1969–)

Zambian-born Dambisa Moyo is an international economist specializing in national economics, international development, and global affairs. She earned her doctorate in economics from the University of Oxford in 2002. In her first book, *Dead Aid* (2009), she argued that ongoing government-to-government assistance has hurt African development and should be stopped because this **foreign aid** has fostered dependency, encouraged corruption, and perpetuated poverty and bad government. It quickly became a bestseller and was translated into many languages. The book suggests that current forms of development assistance actually hinder economic growth and perpetuate poverty. Moyo recommends self-financing ventures (with private-sector investments and free-market solutions) as an alternative to development based on government-to-government aid strategies that have simply not worked for the past 50 years. Moyo's theory draws a big distinction between **humanitarian aid**, which she still sees as being essential, life-saving assistance in times of emergency conditions like famine and drought, and *foreign aid*, which often helps the economy of the contributing country more than the receiving African country.

Two years later, in her second book, *How the West Was Lost*, she analyzed the slow decline of some of the world's economies and concluded that many leading economies are squandering their economic advantage or supremacy. She singled out the United States' flawed decision making and fractured policies around capital, labour, and technology as contributing to the country's steady decline in recent years. A 2012 publication entitled *Winner Take All* explores the implications of China's rush to acquire natural resources around the world to conclude that China is well on the road to gaining a dominant position in the global economy.

foreign aid
Assistance and economic support given from one national government to another to combat poverty and to facilitate economic growth.

humanitarian aid
Life-saving assistance from one country to another in times of emergencies such as famine, drought, earthquakes, tsunamis, and destructive weather storms.

Dambisa Moyo

SUMMING UP

Despite advances in economic thinking, serious problems persist in society. Cynics might say that in some cases, they have gotten worse. The gap between "have" and "have not" countries appears to be widening. Even in prosperous economies, one can find poverty amid affluence. In the United States and Canada, many factories are closed and boarded up. By contrast, in China and Southeast Asia, factories keep springing up to manufacture products once proudly made in North America. Although numerous attempts have been made to help develop the economies of the poorest African countries, progress has been sporadic and limited.

In many ways, today's problems seem to be more complex. Clearly, repeating what has not worked in the past is not a wise choice of action. Some might see it as a sign of insanity! All the more reason to keep taking this course seriously. We will need young, fresh, and perceptive thinkers to address our most persistent problems in new and more effective ways.

Self-Reflect

1 Explain the important breakthrough Elinor Ostrom achieved regarding resource management and governance.

2 What did the theories of Amartya Sen and Dambisa Moyo expose about economic conditions in some of the world's poorest countries?

3 How did Mark Carney choose to stimulate the Canadian economy in 2008 to lessen the impact of the global recession?

Chapter 6
Consolidation Activities

KNOWLEDGE

1 Explain the meaning of school of economic thought by comparing two distinct examples.

2 Explain the monetarist view of the most effective way for governments to stimulate the economy.

3 Explain the difference between foreign aid and humanitarian aid.

THINKING & INQUIRY

4 John Maynard Keynes once wrote that economic slumps and depressions were the result of "upsetting the delicate balance of spontaneous optimism."

  a) Explain the significance of the data presented in Figure 6.2 relative to investor, consumer, and government confidence in Canada between 1929 and 1933. Do the data support Keynes's theory?

  b) Which economic change most contributed to the Great Depression in Canada? Explain your choice.

5 Use the Internet to research a contemporary Canadian economist. Outline the specific contributions this economist has made to the advancement of economic thought. Some examples are Nuala Beck, Dian Cohen, Sherry Cooper, Judith Maxwell, and Sylvia Ostry. Organize your report to resemble one of the profiles in this chapter. Illustrate your report with relevant photos, tables, or graphs.

6 Outline the social and political implications of shifting from John Kenneth Galbraith's model of capitalism to Milton Friedman's model. Which model do you favour? Explain your choice.

FIGURE 6.2
Investment, government spending, and taxation in Canada during the first five years of the Great Depression

Year	Gross Investment Spending (millions of $)	Government Spending (millions of $)	Estimated Government Revenue from Taxes (millions of $)
1929	1 949	1 027	1 085
1930	1 608	1 178	—
1931	1 143	1 160	—
1932	609	1 041	—
1933	462	842	548

Note: All funds are in constant 1949 Canadian dollars. This means that the values have been standardized to 1949 levels as a point of reference. In addition, all data have been rounded to the nearest whole million.

7 Read the following excerpt from Keynes's *General Theory* and answer the questions that follow.

On Reducing Unemployment

If the Treasury [government] were to fill old bottles with banknotes [money], bury them at suitable depths in disused coalmines which are then filled up to the surface with town rubbish, and leave it to private enterprise on well-tried principles of laissez-faire to dig the notes up again (the right to do so being obtained, of course, by tendering for leases of the note-bearing territory), there need be no more unemployment and, with the help of the repercussions, the real income of the community, and its capital wealth also, would probably become a good deal greater than it actually is. It would, indeed, be more sensible to build houses and the like; but if there are political and practical difficulties in the way of this, the above would be better than nothing.

a) What is the most important thing that Keynes is pointing out to political leaders in this excerpt?

b) Keynes proposes the buried treasure as a last resort. What projects could governments finance that would be more beneficial? Give three specific examples.

c) Explain how the government financing of the buried-treasure project can generate increased employment, income, and wealth.

COMMUNICATION

8 Draw a flow chart to explain how governments can effectively combat high unemployment rates, according to Keynes.

9 "Working from within, Galbraith has attempted to give capitalism a social conscience." Prepare a reasoned argument to defend or refute this statement.

10 To organize what you have learned about the economic thinkers presented in this chapter, create a summary chart that you can use as a study guide.

APPLICATION

11 Compare Friedman's view on the best way to stimulate the economy with that of Keynes. Whose views do you think are most correct? Explain why.

12 Explain how, in addressing a specific problem, the ideas or theories of one economist helped create new problems for economists that followed.

13 Who is your favourite contemporary economist? Explain your choice.

Unit 2   Performance Task

Taking a Closer Look at Economic Thinking

Economists use their knowledge and skills to look for patterns in facts and data, and to help make significant connections between causes and consequences of human behaviour. Now that you have explored the evolution of economic thought in this unit, your challenge is to put your knowledge and skills to effective use. The following task presents you with a realistic challenge, very much like the research and reporting presently being carried out by many Canadians with a background in economics.

YOUR TASK

You are a journalist for a national news service. Because of your background in economics, you have been assigned to head up the newly created economics bureau. Your responsibilities are to help build readers' understanding of economics, to establish the significance of economic issues and ideas in people's lives, and to promote economic thinking as a way to address problems more effectively. Your long-term goal is to grow readership and attract advertisers for your articles.

In the short term, you will need to provide readers with sufficient economic background information to help focus their thinking, and to reinforce the importance of economic reasoning. This will help to both inform your readership and establish a loyal base.

To make the new economics bureau viable, the owners of the news service expect to see a demonstrable increase in readership, reader engagement, and advertising revenues every three months.

Your editor, who has many years of experience, has suggested that readers might be better informed if they knew more about the evolution of economic thinking over time. Therefore, your editor suggests a recurring feature article on economics that tackles the following probing questions:

What is the connection between great economic thinkers, their ideas, and the times they lived in? Do troubled or prosperous times create the best economists?

Your editor suggests that the first article be focused on the following:

How my favourite economist helped save the world.

As the lead journalist for the economics bureau, you have been assigned the duty of creating and launching this feature. Your feature can be either a traditional news article or, alternatively, a blog, web page, or a PowerPoint or Prezi presentation for the online edition of the news service.

STEPS AND RECOMMENDATIONS

1   Review the work you have done in this unit to refresh your understanding of related concepts and skills.

2   Use historical analysis to determine the most correct response to the inquiry question asked at the beginning of this unit.

3   Produce an article to launch the recurring feature and introduce the inquiry question in an interesting and informative manner. Be sure to connect specific economic concepts, ideas, and experiences to support your thesis about the link between difficult times and great economic thinkers.

4   Consider both classical and contemporary economists in your article to confirm both historical and current significance.

5   Keep the language and presentation appropriate for your audience.

ADAPTATING THE TASK

Discuss format options for your article with your teacher to select the most appropriate vehicle for you to communicate effectively with your target audience. Remember that many people do not have a background in economics, so this will all be new information for them. Consult examples of traditional news articles, blogs, reports, and presentations to determine how your research and conclusions can best be presented. Share drafts with your teacher, classmates, and parents or guardians to obtain useful feedback about improving your presentation.

ASSESSMENT CRITERIA

The following criteria will be used to assess your work:

- **Knowledge:** accurately using economic concepts, principles, and theories
- **Thinking and Inquiry:** using sound economic thinking to focus analysis and make appropriate connections
- **Communication:** presenting economic information clearly and accurately, and in an appropriate format and style
- **Application:** presenting an interesting account and persuasive argument in response to the question being investigated

Use the rubric provided by your teacher as a coaching tool to help complete this task successfully.

Unit 3
Microeconomics

A defining characteristic of the Canadian economy is that it is composed of many individual markets for the many goods and services we consume. Within each market, large and small, the forces of demand and supply interact to set prices that consumers pay and sellers receive. In this unit, we will examine the factors that determine the demand for and the supply of goods and services that we buy. Some markets—such as the fast food, clothing, and cellphone markets—are highly competitive and vie for consumers' dollars based on price and quality. Other markets—such as the automobile, medical supply, and pharmaceutical markets—are less competitive on price, but invest heavily in research and development to develop the quality of their products.

This unit will also examine how people offering their services in a labour market find that the ever-present forces of demand and supply set their wages too. Finally, we will discuss the characteristics of businesses that operate in Canada—from small businesses to large, multinational corporations—and the price, cost, and profit calculations that all of them must make.

How do markets distribute goods and services to people?

As soon as news came that Pop Star X was on tour and coming to your city, the concert sold out within hours to thousands of quick-acting ticket buyers. Now consider that not everyone who purchased a ticket is a fan, or even plans to attend the show. Instead, these particular buyers plan to resell the tickets they have purchased to fans who didn't manage to buy tickets before they sold out, and they plan to charge a higher price for them. Do you think it is fair that ticket resellers can make high profits by reselling event tickets at higher prices than their original selling prices?

LOOKING AHEAD ──────────▶

The performance task at the end of this unit will require you to investigate the inquiry question above. It provides an opportunity for you to:

- Assume the role of an adviser to the minister of International Trade who is negotiating an important trade deal

- Prepare a cost-benefit analysis on the negotiation issue using the tools and knowledge you have learned from this unit

- Prepare a report, either written or oral, of your analysis of the negotiation issue and your recommendations to the minister on the position that should be taken

- Use a performance task rubric and feedback to prepare a quality report

7

Microeconomics: The Basics

INTRODUCTION

Microeconomics (*micro* = small) is concerned with how consumers and businesses make economic decisions. Consumers must decide what to buy, and businesses must decide what goods and services to sell, how many goods and services to produce, and how much to charge for their goods and services. The operating forces of demand and supply are key to these choices: together, these forces determine the prices for goods and services in each of the many markets that combine to make up our economy.

LEARNING GOALS

Once you have completed this chapter, you should be able to:

- Understand the meaning of demand and supply
- Understand how the forces of demand and supply set prices
- Predict why prices for particular goods or services might change
- Read and construct your own demand and supply graphs
- Calculate price elasticities of demand and supply

KEY TERMS

demand

law of demand

ceteris paribus

demand curve

market demand schedule

supply

law of supply

supply schedule

equilibrium price

non-price factors

substitute goods

complementary goods

perfect (or pure) competition

dynamic pricing

price elasticity of demand (PED)

price inelastic

price elastic

sales revenue

elastic coefficient

unitary coefficient

inelastic coefficient

elasticity of supply

price elasticity of supply (PES)

demand
The quantity of a good or service that buyers will purchase at various prices during a given period of time.

law of demand
A law stating that the quantity demanded of a good or service varies inversely with its price, as long as other things do not change.

Demand and Supply

Who determines the price of goods and services in a market? The answer is that the market itself determines price, based on the interaction of consumers and sellers of a particular good or service. Consumers, for the most part, want the price to be as low as possible, while sellers want the price to be as high as possible. Often, consumers and sellers agree on a price that is somewhere in the middle, but there can be wide fluctuations in the price paid for any good or service. What accounts for the rise and fall of the price of a good or service in a free market? To answer this question, we must start by taking a closer look at the concept of demand.

DEMAND

We can define **demand** as the quantity of a good or service that buyers will purchase at various prices during a given period of time. It is important to understand when it can be said that a person actually has a demand for a particular product—using *demand* in the economic sense.

Picture the following scenario. While walking through a mall, you stop outside the window of a shoe store. Two different pairs of shoes grab your attention. The first is a beautiful pair, made of highly polished leather and showing every sign of craftsmanship. You like these shoes very much but are appalled at the price tag: $300! The second pair of shoes is not as pleasing to the eye as the first. The shoes are made from a lower grade of leather and are not nearly as stylish as the first pair. Nevertheless, they are solidly constructed and comfortable, and the price of $80 is more in line with what you can afford. This is the pair of shoes you actually buy; economists would say you have a "demand" for these shoes.

Whether or not you have a demand for a particular product depends on two factors. One is located in your head or heart, the other in your wallet. In other words, demand exists only for those goods and services that you both want and can afford to buy. If you have both the desire and the financial resources, then it is likely you will make the purchase.

Common sense teaches us another important lesson about demand: the quantity of a product that a consumer will purchase depends on its price. Generally speaking, the higher the price of a product, the less it will be purchased; the lower the price of a product, the more it will be purchased. The trained economist uses more formal language to express the same idea, which is called the **law of demand**:

> *The quantity demanded of a good or service varies inversely with price, as long as other things do not change.*

Thinking like an Economist

Ceteris Paribus

In our discussion of demand, we want to find out what happens to the quantity demanded of a product if only price changes. We do not take into account other factors, such as the number of consumers that might affect the quantity demanded. When economists want to understand the cause-and-effect relationship between two factors, they must assume that all other factors that might affect this relationship remain constant. This assumption is known as **ceteris paribus**, a Latin term meaning "other things being equal" or, as we have stated it, "as long as other things do not change."

As an example, let's suppose that a retail business discovers that when the price of a certain product increases, people buy more of it, not less. This outcome seems to contradict the law of demand. However, economists would point out that several other factors outside of price are probably responsible for the increase in sales. (It is possible that the number of consumers has increased or that consumer tastes for this product have changed.) When economists examine the relationship between the price of the product and the quantity demanded of the product, they hold constant these other external factors. Economists find that, for almost all products, price and quantity demanded are inversely related "as long as other things do not change."

Another way to explain *ceteris paribus* applied to demand involves a simple equation called a *function*. A function represents a relationship between two variables, such as the quantity demanded (Qd) and price. We can write the function equation for these two variables as follows:

$$Qd = Price$$

This equation simply means that the quantity demanded of a product is determined by (or is a function of) its price. However, we know that other factors also determine how much we buy of a particular product. Those factors are our

income (I), the price of a substitute (S), the price of a complementary good (C), the number of consumers (Pop), and taste (T). Including these other factors, our function equation becomes the following:

$$Qd = Price + I + S + C + Pop + T$$

The quantity demanded is affected by all of these factors. However, we want to determine the effect of price *only* on the quantity demanded of a particular product. It follows that we must "freeze," or hold constant, all of those other factors and isolate the effect of price only. In a sense, we pretend that those other factors do not exist when we draw a demand curve, which considers demand and changes in price.

APPLYING ECONOMIC THINKING

Consider the following comment: "It's easy to see why the bagel store is doing well; it's an attractive place, its prices are competitive, it doesn't have much competition, and there's a new office building nearby."

1 How many demand factors are cited here to explain the store's success?

2 Which one(s) would economists want to hold constant? Which one(s) would they vary to determine the quantities of bagels the store could sell?

ceteris paribus
Latin for "other things being equal" or "as long as other things do not change"; an assumption made when economists want to understand the cause-and-effect relationship between any two factors and want other factors affecting that relationship to be held constant.

demand curve
A straight line or curve on a graph illustrating the demand schedule for a product.

Demand Schedule

A demand schedule is one method of portraying the relationship between the price and the quantity demanded of a particular product. It is usually presented as a table showing the quantities demanded at specific prices. Figure 7.1 shows a typical demand schedule that calculates a consumer's demand for T-shirts over a six-month period.

Note that the terms *demand* and *quantity demanded* have distinct meanings. The term *demand* refers to the entire series of price–quantity relationships, as shown in our demand schedule for T-shirts in Figure 7.1. *Quantity demanded* refers to the amount of a product that people are willing to buy at a specific price. For example, in Figure 7.1, if we were to compare the quantities demanded when T-shirts are $24 to when they are $28, we would say that the *quantity demanded* fell by one T-shirt. We would not say that the *demand* fell by one T-shirt.

DID YOU KNOW?

The demand for "normal" goods rises as our incomes rise, while the demand for inferior goods falls when incomes rise. As incomes rise, people may switch from using public transit to buying a car. Can you think of foods that may fall into the category of inferior goods whose demand falls as incomes increase?

As Figure 7.2 shows, on a graph, price is measured on the vertical axis (y-axis), while quantity demanded is measured on the horizontal axis (x-axis). (This way of constructing a graph is standard practice in economics.) The points for both variables are plotted on the graph and joined together. The resulting line, called a **demand curve** (even if it is a straight line), runs downward from top left to bottom right. It runs in this direction for the reason we mentioned earlier: people buy less of a product at higher prices (top left on the graph) and more at lower prices (bottom right). This inverse relationship between price and quantity demanded holds for the majority of goods we buy.

FIGURE 7.1
A demand schedule for one consumer's demand schedule for T-shirts over a six-month period

If the price of T-shirts were . . .	A consumer would buy in a given time period (quantity demanded) . . .
$20	4
$24	3
$28	2
$32	1
$36	0

FIGURE 7.2
One consumer's demand curve for T-shirts over a six-month period

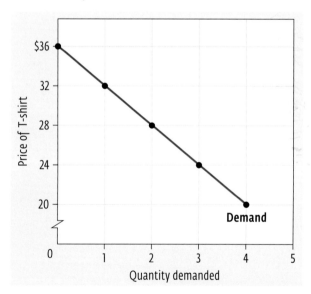

Market Demand

Up to this point, we have discussed the demand for T-shirts by an individual consumer. However, this is not the way the market demand for products is decided. It is the buying habits of thousands of consumers that decide the demand for most products. The sum total of all the consumer demands for a product is called the **market demand schedule**. As an example, let's suppose that there are four consumers with different demands for T-shirts. By examining Figure 7.3, we can see that the market demand is the total of each of the individual demands of the four consumers at each price level. Figure 7.4 illustrates the resulting demand curve for this T-shirt market.

market demand schedule
The sum total of all the consumer demand for a good or service.

FIGURE 7.3
The market demand for T-shirts by multiple consumers

Price of T-shirt	Consumer 1	Consumer 2	Consumer 3	Consumer 4	Total Quantity Demanded
$20	4	3	5	4	16
$24	3	2	4	3	12
$28	2	1	3	2	8
$32	1	0	2	1	4
$36	0	0	0	0	0

FIGURE 7.4
The market demand curve for T-shirts

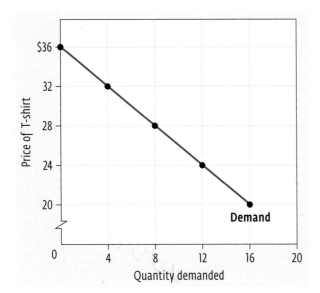

CHECK THIS OUT!

Economist Thorstein Veblen (1857–1929) once argued that some high-priced goods are bought to display an individual's wealth to others, and if their price fell, these people would buy less because the goods were cheaper. What would the demand curve look like if this theory of "Veblen goods" were true? Do you believe it to be true?

supply

The quantities that sellers will offer for sale at various prices during a given period of time.

law of supply

A law stating that the quantity supplied of a good or service will increase if the price increases and fall if the price falls, as long as other things do not change.

SUPPLY

Now let's turn our attention away from the consumers' side of the market to the sellers' (or suppliers') side. **Supply** is defined as the quantities that sellers will offer for sale at various prices during a given period of time. Like consumers, sellers react to price changes but in the opposite way; that is, as the price for a product rises, sellers want to supply more, while consumers, as we learned, want to purchase less. Why is this so?

Sellers are in business to make a profit. If their costs of doing business remain unchanged, their profits will increase as the price of their product rises. Consequently, they want to supply more of their product at higher prices because they can make more money this way. If the price of their product falls, sellers prefer to supply less of it because their profits will fall. Thus, we arrive at the **law of supply**:

> *The quantity supplied of a good or service will increase if the price increases, and it will fall if the price falls, as long as other things do not change.*

In contrast to demand, where there is an *inverse* relationship between price and quantity demanded, quantity supplied is *directly* related to price.

FIGURE 7.5

A supply schedule for T-shirts

If the price of T-shirts were . . .	The seller would like to sell* in a given time period (quantity supplied) . . .
$20	0
$24	4
$28	8
$32	12
$36	16

*The phrase "like to sell" emphasizes the point that "quantity supplied" does not indicate the number of T-shirts the seller will actually sell; rather, it indicates the maximum number the seller is willing to sell at each price. Smaller quantities, but not larger ones, could be sold at any given price.

Supply Schedule

supply schedule
A table showing the quantities of a product supplied at particular prices.

We can get a better idea of the relationship between quantity supplied and price by examining the **supply schedule** for a street vendor of T-shirts, which is displayed in Figure 7.5.

The T-shirt seller's supply schedule has been plotted on the graph in Figure 7.6. By examining this graph, we can see that the same conventions in measuring price and quantity in the demand curve graph (see Figure 7.4) apply here as well. We measure price on the vertical axis and quantity supplied on the horizontal axis. However, the curve is quite different in this case. When the supply figures are plotted on the graph and the points are joined, the supply curve reaches from the bottom left of the graph to the top right. This type of curve illustrates our previous statement that suppliers supply less of a product at lower prices (bottom left) and steadily increase the quantity supplied of a product as its price increases (top right).

As with *demand* and *quantity demanded*, an important distinction exists between the terms *supply* and *quantity supplied*. The term *supply* refers to the entire series of price–quantity relationships, as shown in our supply schedule for T-shirts in Figure 7.5. *Quantity supplied* refers to the amount of a product or service that suppliers are willing to sell at a specific price. For example, in Figure 7.5, if we were to compare the quantities supplied when T-shirts are $24 to when they are $28, we would say that the *quantity supplied* rose by four T-shirts. We would not say that the *supply* increased by four T-shirts.

FIGURE 7.6
The supply curve for one seller of T-shirts

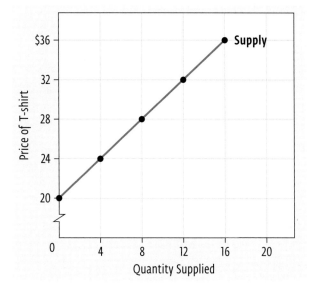

equilibrium price
A price set by the interaction of demand and supply in which the absence of surpluses or shortages in the market means there is no tendency for the price to change.

Market Equilibrium

THE DETERMINATION OF PRICE

At this point, we have the tools we need to examine how the actual prices we pay for a product are determined. You have probably guessed by now that, in the real world, the prices that consumers pay and sellers receive are determined by the interaction of demand and supply. If we combine our two schedules for T-shirts, we can see how this occurs.

By examining Figure 7.7, we can see that only at $28 does the quantity demanded for T-shirts equal the quantity supplied. When the price is set lower than $28, the quantity demanded for T-shirts will exceed the quantity supplied, and a shortage will occur. For example, if the price is set at $24, then 12 T-shirts will be demanded, but the seller will supply only four, creating a shortage of eight T-shirts. In this situation, the seller will then raise the price, since the T-shirts are selling so quickly.

The question becomes: To what level should the price of T-shirts be raised? Suppose that the seller raises the price of T-shirts to $32. The seller wants to sell 12 T-shirts, but consumers are only willing to purchase four. Now there is a surplus of eight T-shirts, and the seller will have to lower the price to persuade consumers to buy. The price of $28 is the only price where no shortage or surplus occurs. Economists call this price the **equilibrium price** because supply equals demand; and when the market for a product or service is at equilibrium, there is no tendency for it to change. The equilibrium price is the only acceptable compromise between consumers who want the lowest prices possible and sellers who want the highest.

FIGURE 7.7
The market for T-shirts

Price of T-shirt	Quantity Demanded	Quantity Supplied
$20	16	0
$24	12	4
$28	8	8
$32	4	12
$36	0	16

A Demand and Supply Graph

We can easily combine the demand and supply data in Figure 7.7 into a graph. In Figure 7.8, we see that the demand curve crosses the supply curve at exactly $28, which we have identified as our equilibrium price. Suppose that we wanted to use this graph to indicate what would happen if the selling price of a T-shirt were set *above* the equilibrium price. In Figure 7.9 a horizontal dashed line is drawn across the graph from the $32 point on the vertical axis. Then vertical lines are drawn downward from the points at which the horizontal line intersects the demand and supply curves. These vertical lines provide us with a pictorial representation of the information in Figure 7.7: at a price of $32, the quantity demanded is four T-shirts and the quantity supplied is 12 T-shirts. In other words, a price of $32 will result in a surplus of eight T-shirts.

In Figure 7.10, we see the opposite situation illustrated, that is, what happens when the selling price of a T-shirt is set *below* the equilibrium price. Here, a horizontal dashed line drawn from the $24 point on the vertical axis will intersect the demand and supply curves in such a way as to indicate a shortage of eight T-shirts. By studying these graphs, we can draw the following general conclusion:

> *A price above the equilibrium price will result in a surplus of goods, while a price below the equilibrium price will result in a shortage of goods, as long as other things do not change.*

CHECK THIS OUT!

Someone asked the nineteenth-century British economist Alfred Marshall whether demand or supply was more important in determining price. Can you understand his reply?

We might as reasonably dispute whether it is the upper or the under blade of a pair of scissors that cuts a piece of paper. . . . It is true that when one blade is held still, and the cutting is effected by moving the other, we may say . . . that the cutting is done by the second; but the statement is not strictly accurate.

FIGURE 7.8
The price and quantity demanded of T-shirts at equilibrium

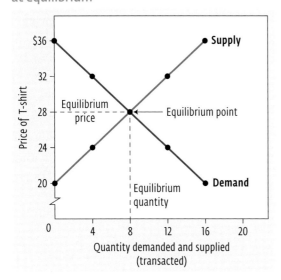

FIGURE 7.9
The price and quantity demanded of T-shirts above equilibrium

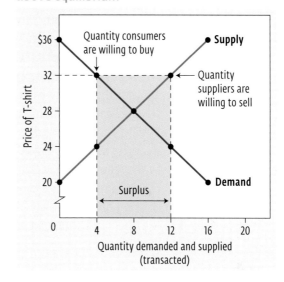

FIGURE 7.10
The price and quantity demanded of T-shirts below equilibrium

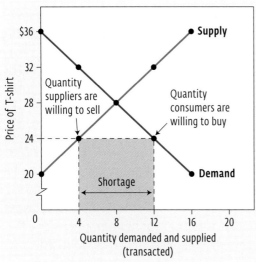

FIGURE 7.11
Data table for Self-Reflect questions

Price of Product	Quantity Demanded (Qd)	Quantity Supplied (Qs)
$2.00	100	190
$1.80	120	180
$1.60	140	170
$1.40	160	160
$1.20	180	150
$1.00	200	140
$0.80	220	130

In our earlier example, we constructed a sample market of four consumers and one seller of T-shirts. It is worth noting that, in the real world, where markets can consist of thousands or millions of consumers and sellers, the laws of demand and supply operate in the same way as we have seen them operate on a small scale. A price set *below* the equilibrium price by sellers will mean that there are many frustrated consumers who are unable to purchase the product in question. Some of these consumers will start to offer to pay more than the stated price. As they try to outbid each other, they will force the price of the product to rise. In contrast, a price set *above* the equilibrium price will result in many unsold products. In this case, the sellers will try to undercut each other by lowering their prices. This process will continue until the quantity demanded equals the quantity supplied; that is, until the market reaches the equilibrium price.

Self-Reflect

1   On graph paper, draw demand and supply curves for the prices and quantities shown in Figure 7.11 (*Qd*, quantity demanded; *Qs*, quantity supplied).

2   Shade in the areas of the graph that represent (a) a surplus; and (b) a shortage if prices higher and lower than the equilibrium price were to be set.

non-price factor

A factor held constant in the relationship between price and quantity demanded and supplied. Non-price factors include, on the demand side, income, population, tastes and preferences, expectations, and prices of substitute and complementary goods; and on the supply side, costs, number of sellers, technology, nature and the environment, and prices of related goods.

CHANGES IN DEMAND

Up to this point, we have assumed that "other things do not change" in our discussion of demand and supply. These "other things" are all various **non-price factors** that we have so far held constant in constructing our demand and supply curves. We emphasized that the *quantity demanded* and the *quantity supplied* changed only because price changed. We saw on the graphs in Figures 7.2 and 7.6 that these changes are represented by movements *along* the curves. Now we shall see that changes in non-price factors cause the *whole curve to shift*, by affecting a product's *demand* or *supply* as opposed to its quantity demanded or quantity supplied. This distinction between movements along a curve and a shift in the whole curve is one of the most important distinctions in the entire field of economics. Before proceeding further, it is crucial that we understand this concept and the way it hinges on the distinction between demand and supply on the one hand and quantity demanded and quantity supplied on the other.

Five non-price factors can affect consumer demand for a product. Changes to any one of these factors can cause the whole demand curve to shift its position on the graph. Let's consider each of these factors in turn.

Income

Staying with our sample T-shirt market, let's consider what would happen if the incomes of the four potential consumers increased substantially. With more income at their disposal, they might be willing to buy more T-shirts at whatever the prevailing market price is. The schedule in Figure 7.12 shows the result of this increase in buying power, and we can see that the quantity demanded increases at all price levels.

Figure 7.13 shows the new demand curve in relation to the old one. The increase in demand shifts the whole demand curve upward and to the right. Since the new quantity demanded at the old equilibrium price of $28 now exceeds the quantity supplied (by four), the equilibrium price must shift upward. It moves to $30, where the quantity supplied is 10. This increase in income has raised the equilibrium price for T-shirts by $2.

Population

Similar to an increase in incomes, an increase in the number of consumers should translate into an increase in demand, shifting the demand curve to the right causing the equilibrium price to increase. Similarly, a decrease in the number of consumers should have the opposite effect, shifting the demand curve to the left and causing the equilibrium price to fall.

FIGURE 7.12
An increase in demand for T-shirts

Price of T-Shirt	Old Quantity Demanded	New Quantity Demanded	Quantity Supplied (Qs)
$20	16	20	0
$24	12	16	4
$28	8	12	8
$32	4	8	12
$36	0	4	16

FIGURE 7.13
An increase in demand for T-shirts

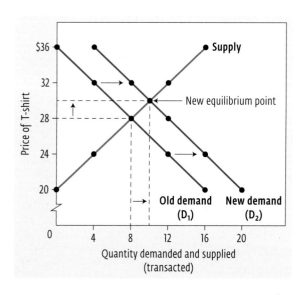

Tastes and Preferences

Changes in taste for a product cause increases or decreases in demand for it. If consumer preferences for T-shirts increase, demand overall will increase, the demand curve shifts up to the right, and the equilibrium price rises.

Expectations

If consumers believe that the price of a particular product is going to rise in the future, they may decide to purchase it immediately, thereby increasing the demand for the product. Thus, the demand curve for a particular product will shift to the right if consumer expectations lead people to believe that price will increase in the future. Increased purchases by consumers create a self-fulfilling prophecy: the price of the product starts to rise almost immediately, driving the demand curve to the right. Conversely, if consumers expect the price of a product to fall in the future, they may delay purchasing that product, which will drive down the demand for it. As a result, consumers end up making the expected lower price of the future a reality in the present.

The Price of Substitute and Complementary Goods

Economists include price changes of **substitute goods** under the non-price factors that can cause the whole demand curve to shift. If the price of good B (a substitute for good A) increases, the demand for good A will increase. Again, the demand curve shifts to the right, and the equilibrium price increases.

Others goods are **complementary goods**: they are interrelated and used together with other goods (for example, tennis rackets and tennis balls). An increase in demand for tennis rackets will increase the demand for tennis balls, shifting the demand curve for tennis balls to the right and driving up their equilibrium price.

In summary, a change in the price of one product that can substitute for another will *directly* increase or decrease the demand for the competing product, thereby shifting its demand curve one way or the other. A change in the price of a product that is associated with a complementary good will *inversely* increase or decrease the demand for the complementary good, thereby shifting its demand curve.

substitute goods
Goods that are similar to other goods and that serve as an alternative if the price of a particular good rises.

complementary goods
Goods that are interrelated and used together (for example, gasoline and automobiles).

A baseball bat, glove, and ball are considered complementary goods. Unlike substitute goods, a change in the price of one complementary good will inversely affect demand for its complements.

CHANGES IN SUPPLY

A shift of the whole supply curve can be caused by a number of factors. Here, we will focus on the five major factors that can cause such a shift. A change in any of these factors will cause the supply curve to move either to the right (to indicate an increase in supply) or to the left (to indicate a decrease in supply).

Costs

An increase or decrease in production costs will affect the quantities that sellers are willing to supply because a change in costs affects profits. Suppose that the cost of cloth for T-shirt manufacturing falls, and the manufacturer passes on this saving to the retailer, in this case our T-shirt seller. Figure 7.14 shows how such a saving might translate into new quantities supplied at each price level, representing an overall change in supply.

The T-shirt seller's increase in supply is illustrated as a movement from S_1 to S_2 in Figure 7.15. Note that consumers will be happy with this increase in supply because it means that the equilibrium price will drop from $28 to $26 per T-shirt. On the other hand, if there were an increase in manufacturing costs, the result would be a decrease in supply. This would be illustrated by a movement of the curve to the left and a corresponding increase in the equilibrium price.

FIGURE 7.14
An increase in supply of T-shirts

Price of T-Shirt	Quantity Demanded	Old Quantity Supplied	New Quantity Supplied
$20	16	0	4
$24	12	4	8
$28	8	8	12
$32	4	12	16
$36	0	16	20

FIGURE 7.15
An increase in supply of T-shirts

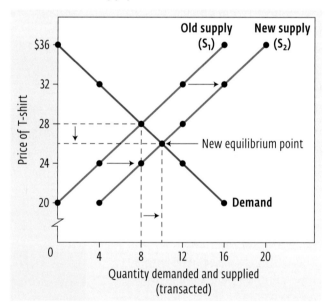

Number of Sellers

The number of sellers may have an effect on the amount of a product that is supplied in a market. If the number of sellers in a market increases, the quantity supplied of a product at any given price will increase, shifting the supply curve to the right. If the number of sellers in a market decreases, and if the remaining sellers do not increase their production, then the quantities supplied of a product at any given price will decrease. The effect will be a shift of the supply curve to the left.

Technology

An improvement in technology will decrease the cost of production, and this, in turn, will enable manufacturers to supply more of a product at any given price. The economic history of the twentieth and twenty-first centuries is largely a story of technological progress of such magnitude that the manufacturing costs have fallen for almost every product we now buy. Technological and productivity improvements have enabled manufacturers to increase the supply of their products, thereby shifting their supply curve to the right, and lowering prices.

The Environment

Something as simple as a change in the weather can have an enormous impact on the supply of certain products, particularly agricultural products. Drought, for instance, can dramatically decrease the quantities of crops that farmers can produce. Similarly, an environmental disaster can affect supply. The collapse of the Atlantic cod stock decreased the quantity of cod supplied to fish retailers, which, in turn, has driven up the price of this particular fish. This decrease in supply has shifted the supply curve for Atlantic cod to the left.

Prices of Related Products

The production of one product may affect the supply of another related product. Farmers may switch from growing oats to growing barley if the market price of barley rises. As a result, the supply of oats will decrease at any given price, shifting its supply curve to the left.

Self-Reflect

1 Which of these four possibilities—a change in quantity demanded, a change in quantity supplied, a shift in demand, or a shift in supply—do each of the following illustrate?

- New steel-making techniques lower steel prices.

- Gold-mining activity picks up as world gold prices increase.

- The price of cellphones falls, and consumers buy more of them.

- An economic downturn lowers incomes affecting consumer purchases of high-end consumer goods.

Thinking like an Economist

Changes in Quantity Demanded or Supplied versus Shifts in Demand or Supply

It is important to understand the distinctions between changes in the quantity demanded or supplied of a product and shifts in the demand or supply of a product. Changes in the quantity demanded or supplied are movements *along* the demand or supply curve caused by price changes of the product itself. Shifts in demand or supply are movements of the *whole* demand or supply curve caused by factors other than price changes of the product.

In Figure 7.16, graph (a) shows a change in the quantity demanded of a product caused by a change in price. It is clearly a movement along the demand curve. When the price of the product rises, the quantity demanded of the product falls; when the price of the product falls, the quantity demanded of the product rises. An inverse relationship exists between price and quantity demanded.

Graph (c) shows a change in the quantity supplied of a product caused by a change in price. It is clearly a movement along the supply curve. When the price of the product rises, the quantity supplied of the product rises; when the price of the product falls, the quantity supplied of the product falls. A direct relationship exists between price and quantity supplied.

Graphs (b) and (d) represent shifts of the whole demand or supply curve. We see in (b) a shift in demand caused by a change in factors other than the product's price. The shift could be caused by factors including a change in consumer incomes, an increase or decrease in the number of potential consumers, a change in the price of substitutes for the product, or a change in the prices of complements of the product. If one or more of these factors increase or change in a positive way, the whole demand curve shifts up to the right. In this context, we would say that demand has increased. And the opposite holds: if one or more factors decrease or change in a negative way, the whole demand curve shifts to the left, and we would say that demand has decreased.

Graph (d) shows shifts in supply. They are caused by changes in factors other than the price of the product itself, such as changes in the cost of production, technology, the number of sellers, or environmental factors. A shift to the left indicates a decrease in supply of the product, which is often caused by an increase in costs. A shift to the right indicates an increase in the supply of the product, which is possibly caused by a decrease in costs, better technology, or (in the case of agriculture) good weather.

APPLYING ECONOMIC THINKING

Which of the four diagrams in Figure 7.16 does each of the following market situations correspond to regarding the market for electric cars?

1 Climate change concerns begin to interest more people in electric cars rather than gas fuelled cars.

2 Electric car manufacturers receive tax breaks from government to encourage production.

3 Consumers receive tax breaks from government to encourage the purchase of electric cars.

4 Governments build more charging stations for electric vehicles.

5 Prices of electric cars start to fall.

FIGURE 7.16

Graphing changes in quantity demanded, demand, quantity supplied, and supply

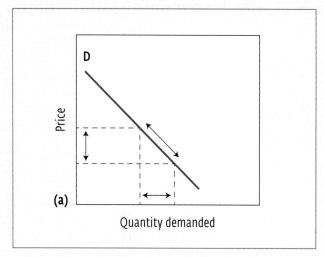

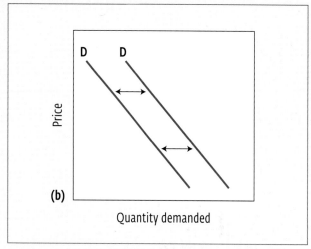

(a) *A change in quantity demanded.* A change in price causes a shift along the demand curve to show a change in the quantity demanded.

(b) *A change in demand.* A non-price change causes the whole curve to shift.

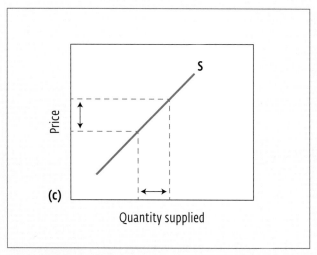

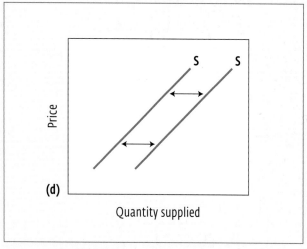

(c) *A change in quantity supplied.* A change in price causes a shift along the supply curve to show a change in the quantity supplied.

(d) *A change in supply.* A non-price change causes the whole curve to shift.

perfect (or pure) competition
A rare market structure characterized by many sellers (selling exactly the same product) and many buyers, no barriers to entry into the market for new firms, and perfect knowledge of prices (so there are no price differences and no individual can influence them).

dynamic pricing
The practice of changing price as demand increases or decreases within a short time frame.

The Determination of Price in a Competitive Market

We can now analyze the way price is actually determined in a *competitive market*—a market that exhibits the following characteristics:

- It has many producers or sellers, with no single seller large enough to dominate the market.

- It has many consumers, with no single consumer large enough to dictate price to sellers.

- Each seller's product is exactly the same as that of the others so that no seller can increase price based on having a higher-quality product than another seller.

- All sellers and consumers know what the prices and conditions are throughout the entire market, thereby eliminating the possibility of any price differences.

This kind of market is called **perfect (or pure) competition**. In a modern economy, it is rare for all of these conditions to be present in a particular market. Nevertheless, perfect competition is an ideal or a model that economists use to compare and evaluate actual markets for the products and services bought and sold in Canada and in other countries that have free-market systems.

For purposes of instruction, let's analyze the retail coffee market in North America. This comes as close as any other market to the perfect competitive market model, and it shows us how changes in demand and supply, with their shifting curves, cause the equilibrium price to rise and fall.

THE COFFEE MARKET IN NORTH AMERICA

- ***An increase in demand*** *will have the following effect:* Suppose that retailers are used to paying a wholesale price of $5 per kilogram for Colombian coffee. Then the spread of coffee houses as social meeting places throughout North America increases the demand for Colombian coffee. In Figure 17A, D_1 and S show coffee at the old equilibrium price of $5 per kilogram. Q_1 shows the quantities demanded and supplied at that price. The increase in demand to D_2 causes an excess demand, or shortage ($Q_2 - Q_1$), to occur. This excess demand will cause the price to rise to $6 at P_2; the quantity demanded and supplied will be equal at Q_3. The new equilibrium price and quantity supplied eliminate the excess demand.

- ***A decrease in demand*** *will have the following effect:* Suppose that a best-selling book raises health concerns about excessive caffeine intake. As a result, many people cut back on the number of cups of coffee they drink per day and turn to other beverages. This reduces the demand for coffee. In Figure 17B, D_1 and S show coffee at the old equilibrium price of $5 per kilogram. Q_1 indicates the quantities demanded and supplied at that price. The decrease in demand to D_2 causes excess in supply, or surplus ($Q_1 - Q_2$), to occur. This excess in supply causes the price to fall to $4 at P_2; the quantity demanded and supplied will be equal at Q_3. The new equilibrium price and quantity supplied eliminate the excess supply.

DID YOU KNOW?

Dynamic pricing is a strategy in which a company's product prices continuously adjust, sometimes in a matter of minutes, in response to real-time supply and demand. It is used with online taxi companies such as Uber, large retailers such as Amazon and Walmart, airlines, and concert ticket sellers.

FIGURE 7.17A
An increase in demand in the coffee market

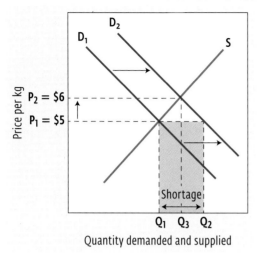

FIGURE 7.17B
A decrease in demand in the coffee market

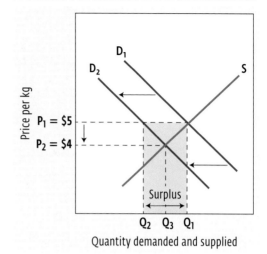

FIGURE 7.17C
An increase in supply in the coffee market

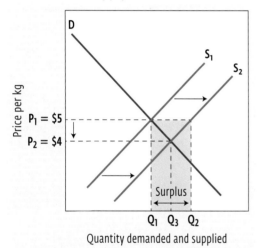

FIGURE 7.17D
A decrease in supply in the coffee market

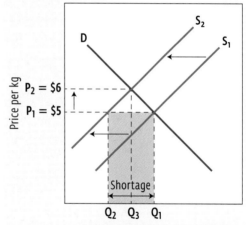

- **An increase in supply** *will have the following effect:* Suppose that scientists discover a way to produce a faster-growing coffee plant through genetic manipulation. In Figure 17C, D and S_1 show coffee at the old equilibrium price of $5 per kilogram. Q_1 indicates the quantities demanded and supplied at that price. The increase in supply (S_2) causes an excess supply, or surplus, ($Q_2 - Q_1$) to occur. This will cause the price to fall to $4 at P_2 and the quantity demanded to rise to Q_3. This movement shifts the supply curve to the right. The new equilibrium price and quantity demanded eliminate the excess supply.

- **A decrease in supply** *will have the following effect:* Suppose that a mildew that strikes coffee plants decimates coffee production in the mountains of Colombia. Supplies of Colombian coffee fall. In Figure 17D, D and S_1 show coffee at the old equilibrium price of $5 per kilogram; Q_1 shows the quantities demanded and supplied at that price. This decrease in supply to S_2 causes an excess demand, or shortage ($Q_1 - Q_2$), to occur. This will cause the price to rise to $6 at P_2; the quantity demanded and supplied will be equal at Q_3. The new equilibrium price and quantity demanded eliminate the excess demand.

Self-Reflect

1 Does price rise or fall with each of the following changes? Draw small, freehand graphs to illustrate:
   a) Demand increases, supply stays the same.
   b) Supply decreases, demand stays the same.
   c) Supply increases, demand stays the same.
   d) Demand decreases, supply stays the same.

price elasticity of demand (PED)

An expression of how much more or less consumers will buy of a product if its price changes.

price inelastic

If the quantity of a good or service bought does not change much when price rises or falls, it is said to be price inelastic.

price elastic

If the quantity of a good or service bought changes a lot when price rises or falls, it is said to be price elastic.

The Elasticity of Demand

We learned that consumers buy more of a product when its price falls and less of it when its price rises. What we did not learn is *how much more* they will buy or *how much less*. You may wonder if it is really possible to calculate such numbers with any precision. As a matter of fact, economists have developed a formula to measure how responsive the quantity bought of a good is to a change in price. This concept is known as the **price elasticity of demand (PED)**, and it is defined as a measurement of how responsive the quantity bought of a good is to a change in price. In general, we find that:

- If the quantity bought of a good *does not* increase or decrease much when price changes, it is said to be **price inelastic**. That is, it is less responsive to price changes.

- If the quantity bought of a good *does* increase or decrease when price changes, it is said to be **price elastic**. That is, it is more responsive to price changes.

We will first learn how to calculate price elasticity. Then, we will look at factors that determine whether a good is likely to be inelastic or elastic.

CALCULATING THE PRICE ELASTICITY OF DEMAND

Economists use coefficients to determine the price elasticity of a product. A coefficient is a number that captures the responsiveness between two variables. Here, the two variables are *quantity demanded* and *price*. The formula that gives us the coefficient for PED is as follows:

$$\text{PED} = \frac{\text{\% change in quantity demanded}}{\text{\% change in price}}$$

Suppose that when the price of a product was increased by 5 percent, the quantity demanded fell by 10 percent. Then,

$$\text{PED} = \frac{-10\%}{+5\%} = -2.0$$

For another product, suppose that when the price was decreased by 3 percent, the quantity demanded rose by 2 percent. Then,

$$\text{PED} = \frac{2\%}{-3\%} = -0.67$$

By convention, we use the absolute value of the PED coefficient, so the minus sign is dropped.

If the PED coefficient is greater than 1.0, then the product is classified as *price elastic*. Thus, the first example above is price elastic because the PED coefficient is 2.0. If the PED coefficient is less than 1.0, then the product is classified as *price inelastic*. Thus, the second example above is price inelastic because its PED coefficient is 0.67. If the PED coefficient is equal to 1.0, then the product is considered to have *unitary* demand elasticity.

THE TOTAL REVENUE APPROACH TO ELASTICITY OF DEMAND

Clearly, it is useful for business people to know whether **sales revenues** will rise or fall if they increase or decrease the price of their goods. PED coefficients help business people figure out how total revenues will react to a change in price. The rules are as follows:

- If demand is elastic, sales revenue will rise as price falls, and fall as price rises.
- If demand is inelastic, sales revenue will fall as price falls, and rise as price rises.
- If demand is unitary, sales revenue will be unaffected by price increases or decreases.

Refer to Figure 7.18. As the price falls from $1.00, the quantity demanded rises. Notice how sales revenue rises too until the price is $0.70, indicating that the **coefficient** is **elastic** until this price. Where sales revenue levels off at a price of $0.60, the **coefficient** is **unitary**. Where sales revenue falls, the **coefficient** is **inelastic**.

sales revenue
A practice of adjusting price according to changing demand in a very short time.

elastic coefficient
A coefficient for a product of more than one, indicating that a given percentage change in price causes a greater percentage change in quantity demanded.

unitary coefficient
A coefficient for a product equal to one, indicating that a given change in price causes an equal percentage change in quantity demanded.

inelastic coefficient
A coefficient for a product of less than one, indicating that a given percentage change in price causes a smaller percentage change in quantity demanded.

FIGURE 7.18
Sales revenue and elasticity

Price	Quantity Demanded	Sales Revenue	Elasticity
$1.00	300	$300	Elastic
$0.90	400	$360	Elastic
$0.80	500	$400	Elastic
$0.70	600	$420	Elastic
$0.60	700	$420	Unitary
$0.50	800	$400	Inelastic
$0.40	900	$360	Inelastic
$0.30	1 000	$300	Inelastic

CHECK THIS OUT!

Economist George Akerlof (1940–) argued that we are suspicious of used-car salespeople because they possess knowledge of a car that we don't. People's fear of buying a "lemon" makes it difficult for used-car salespeople to sell a good car (which Akerlof called a "peach") at a high price. Akerlof proposed that people's willingness to pay only an average price for a used car forced used-car prices down to a midpoint between bad cars (lemons) and good cars (peaches).

Compare the short-term and long-term effects of the cost of gasoline—time being one key factor in the elasticity of demand—on the driving habits and buying choices of drivers.

FACTORS AFFECTING THE ELASTICITY OF DEMAND

Four factors can have a strong effect on the elasticity of demand. Let's consider each of these in turn.

Availability of Substitutes

Goods that have substitutes tend to be more elastic than goods that do not. A single brand of candy, for example, is usually very elastic. Since many other brands of candy are available, consumers will reduce their purchases of a particular candy sharply if the candy manufacturer raises that candy's price. The demand for candy in general is inelastic, however, because there is no close substitute for candy. Consumers will not significantly reduce their expenditures for it if prices rise or significantly increase them if prices fall.

Nature of the Product

Goods that are necessities tend to be more inelastic than goods that are considered luxuries. A necessity such as bread is inelastic; price changes do not significantly change the quantities consumers' purchase. A luxury such as a vacation cruise, on the other hand, is elastic because if prices rise, people can do without this kind of vacation.

Fraction of Income Spent on the Product

Goods that are expensive and, therefore, take up a large part of the household budget, will be elastic. If prices rise for "big-ticket" items such as houses, cars, or furniture, people do without the item entirely, postpone the purchase, or search for substitutes. By contrast, a product that takes up a small percentage of the budget, such as shoelaces, may rise in price without registering a significant decline in the amount purchased. Such a product is classified as inelastic.

Amount of Time Available

Over time, some goods may become more elastic because consumers eventually find substitutes for them. In the short run, however, demand for these same goods can be quite inelastic because consumers may not know what substitutes are available immediately after the price rises. Let's consider gasoline as an example. When the price of gasoline rises, car owners initially may reduce the amount of driving they do, but not significantly. However, if gasoline prices remain high over a long period of time, drivers may switch to smaller cars to reduce their gasoline consumption.

Self-Reflect

1 For which of the following products would demand be elastic? Inelastic? Unitary? Explain why in each case.
   - beef
   - pencils
   - steak
   - housing
   - gasoline
   - public transportation

2 A seller finds out that the PED for the product being sold is 1.5. Would it be better to lower the price or raise the price to gain more sales revenue? How might the seller's sales strategy change if the PED for the product were 0.8?

elasticity of supply
The responsiveness of the quantity supplied by a seller to a rise or fall in its price.

price elasticity of supply (PES)
An expression of how responsive the quantity supplied by a seller is to a rise or fall in the price of a product.

The Elasticity of Supply

The concept of elasticity also applies to the supply, or sellers', side of the market. You will remember that, generally, as the market price for a product rises, suppliers want to supply more of that product because their profits will increase. Can a supplier easily increase the quantity supplied of a product if consumers increase demand? Or, is it more difficult to increase the quantity supplied to take advantage of higher prices? The concept of **elasticity of supply** measures how responsive the quantity supplied by a seller is to a rise or fall in price of a product.

CALCULATING THE PRICE ELASTICITY OF SUPPLY

The formula that gives us the coefficient for **price elasticity of supply (PES)** is as follows:

$$PES = \frac{\% \text{ change in quantity supplied}}{\% \text{ change in price}}$$

Suppose that when the market price of a product was increased by 16 percent, the quantity supplied increased by 18 percent. Then,

$$PES = \frac{18\%}{16\%} = +1.12$$

For another product, suppose that when the market price was increased by 8 percent, the quantity supplied increased by 6 percent. Then,

$$PES = \frac{8\%}{6\%} = +0.75$$

Because the quantity supplied always rises when the price rises, the PES coefficient is always positive (+). If the price falls, the quantity supplied falls too, and the PES coefficient is positive as well. PES, calculated either as $\frac{+}{+}$ = + or $\frac{-}{-}$ = +, will result in positive coefficients whether the price for a product rises or falls. By convention, the positive sign is dropped.

If the PES coefficient is greater than 1.0, then the product is *supply elastic*. Thus, the first example above is supply elastic because its PES coefficient is 1.12. If the PES coefficient is less than 1.0, then the product is *supply inelastic*. Thus, the second example above is supply inelastic because its PES coefficient is 0.75. If the PES coefficient is 1.0, then the product has *unitary supply elasticity*.

FACTORS AFFECTING THE ELASTICITY OF SUPPLY

Three factors can have a strong effect on the elasticity of supply. An understanding of each of these factors will give us a deeper appreciation for the importance of the elasticity of supply.

Time

The longer the time period a seller has to increase production, the more elastic the supply will be. A classic example is a seller of fresh fruits and vegetables. Suppose that the price of tomatoes rises. Tomato growers cannot increase production in one day, or even in one month. Supply, therefore, is inelastic and remains so until more tomatoes can be planted, harvested, and brought to market. In summarizing a situation like this, economists say that in the short term, supply is inelastic, and in the long term, it is elastic.

Ease of Storage

When the price of a product drops, sellers have two options. They can either sell the product at the new low price, or they can put some of their inventory into storage and sell it after the price rises again. The steel industry enjoys high supply elasticity because it is easy to store steel and, therefore, ride out price changes. Agricultural industries have low supply elasticity because it is difficult to store large volumes of their products in a manner that will keep them fresh. This adds to the problems they have in supplying more of a product to the market if prices rise in the short run.

When the price of tomatoes rises, tomato growers cannot increase production immediately. Supply, therefore, is *inelastic in the short term*; that is, until more tomatoes can be planted, harvested, and brought to market.

Cost Factors

Increasing output (supply) may be costly, depending on the industry. Car manufacturers may be able to increase production in the short term by requiring workers to put in more overtime. A permanent increase in production, however, may entail building new factories, which is a far more costly move on the part of the manufacturer. Supply is more elastic in industries that have lower input expenses. CDs, for example, are not costly to manufacture, and their production can be easily expanded if the demand for a particular performer rises.

Self-Reflect

1 Apply the concept of supply elasticity to each of the following products. How elastic or inelastic would each be, and why?
   • a new app
   • cheese
   • cellphone
   • new housing
   • renewable energy

Thinking like an Economist

Elasticity and Slopes of Demand and Supply Curves

Graphs of demand and supply curves provide us with good visual representations of the different kinds of elasticity we have just considered.

In Figure 7.19, an inelastic demand curve, price changes more when compared with the change in the quantity demanded.

In Figure 7.20, an elastic demand curve, price changes less when compared with the change in the quantity demanded.

In Figure 7.21, a unitary demand curve, the quantity demanded changes exactly in proportion to price changes.

In Figure 7.22, an inelastic supply curve, the quantity supplied changes less when compared with the change in price.

In Figure 7.23, an elastic supply curve, the quantity supplied changes more when compared with the change in price.

FIGURE 7.19
An inelastic demand curve

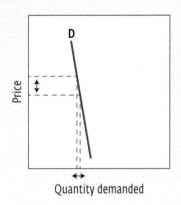

FIGURE 7.20
An elastic demand curve

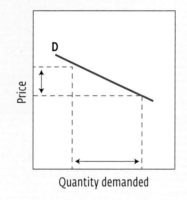

FIGURE 7.21
A unitary demand curve

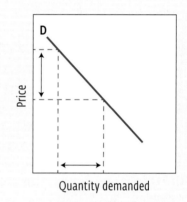

FIGURE 7.22
An inelastic supply curve

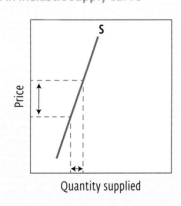

FIGURE 7.23
An elastic supply curve

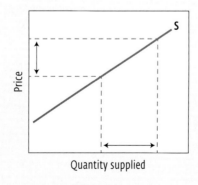

FIGURE 7.24
A unitary supply curve

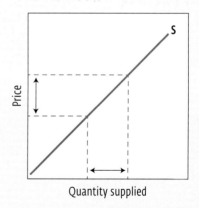

We see that steep demand and supply curves are inelastic, while less steep curves are elastic. We can use demand and supply curves to analyze changes that occur in markets in the economy. For example:

The oil and gas market

- Recent history has shown this market to be especially changeable. Cutbacks in production, particularly in the Middle East, or oil spills and refinery shutdowns cause supply to fall, causing big price swings. Draw a freehand graph similar to Figure 7.19 with a supply curve. Draw another supply curve to indicate a production cutback. Note that it does not take much of a supply decrease to push the price up a lot on an inelastic demand curve.

Cellphones

- The first commercial cellphone was a Motorola device that weighed 1.1 kg, allowed 30 minutes of talk time, and cost US$3 995. Draw a freehand graph similar to Figure 7.20. It illustrates the highly elastic demand for cellphones at that time. Draw one supply curve through a higher price on the demand curve, and draw another supply curve through a lower price on the demand curve. Note how the quantity demanded increases a lot compared with the fall in price, which increases sales revenues. Technology companies knew that if they could reduce prices, their revenues would increase dramatically. The price you pay for your phone today illustrates the success that those technology companies have had in lowering costs, improving quality, and, in the process, becoming some of the world's richest companies.

Skilled labour versus lower-skilled jobs

- Figures 7.22, 7.23, and 7.24 can illustrate labour markets, with wages replacing prices. The Figure 7.22 illustrates the inelastic supply of skilled workers. There are fewer of them, it is more costly and takes more time to train them, and wages must rise considerably to attract them. Notice that a fairly large wage increase brings in a much smaller number of workers. Thus, the supply tends to be inelastic, at least in the short run. Figures 7.23 illustrates the more elastic supply of lower-skilled workers. There is a larger pool available, training takes less time, and wages do not have to rise much to attract more of them. Notice that wages do not have to rise much to attract a larger number of workers. Figure 7.24 illustrates a unitary supply curve, where the quantity supplied of labour changes exactly in proportion to wage changes.

APPLYING ECONOMIC THINKING

For each of the following, determine the elasticity of the good, draw freehand demand and supply graphs to illustrate the market situation, and predict whether sales revenue will rise or fall

1 Restrictions on milk production raise the price of milk for consumers.

2 Producers of generic pharmaceutical drugs enter the market, and the price of generic drugs falls.

3 Advances in agricultural technology result in lower food costs.

4 Airlines reduce the seat size and legroom for non-business class passengers.

Chapter 7
Consolidation Activities

KNOWLEDGE

1   Drawing freehand, create a demand and supply graph for product X. On your graph, show what happens if price is (a) lower than the equilibrium price and (b) higher than the equilibrium price.

2   Consider the following two scenarios:

   a)   For price to rise for product X, what shifts of either demand or supply would have to occur? Illustrate this on a freehand graph.

   b)   For price to fall, what shifts would have to occur? Illustrate this on a freehand graph.

3   Classify the following pairs of goods as either complements or substitutes: (a) hockey sticks, pucks; (b) beef, chicken; (c) public transit, taxi service; (d) printers, toner cartridges; and (e) Coca-Cola, Pepsi.

4   Describe the price elasticity of demand (PED) for each of the following items and give one reason for each answer: (a) clothing, (b) designer jeans, (c) cellphones, (d) post-secondary education, and (e) shoelaces.

5   Describe the price elasticity of supply (PES) for each of the following items and give one reason for each answer: (a) fresh tomatoes, (b) new apps, (c) oil, and (d) automobiles.

THINKING & INQUIRY

6   It's understandable that many of us complain when the price of a good or service rises. What might the price increase indicate about either the demand for, or the supply of, a product? If price were not allowed to rise, what would be the undesirable result?

7   Suppose that a family's income increases. Would its demand for all goods and services rise, or would it rise for some goods and services but fall for others? Explain how a family's demand could change in opposite ways, using two household goods or services as examples.

8   The elasticity of demand for an urban transit company in winter is estimated to be 0.9. In summer, it rises to 1.4. Suggest reasons why the elasticity of demand for transit service differs depending on the season.

9   Sales revenues rise when the price of shoelaces rises 20 percent. Movie ticket revenues fall at the Movielux theatre when ticket prices rise by the same percentage. Explain why this difference exists, using three price elasticity factors to compare the two goods.

COMMUNICATION

10 Draw freehand demand and supply graphs to illustrate each of the following scenarios. Then, in point-form notes, explain how price and quantities change for many consumer goods.

a) The incomes of people in northern Canada increase significantly as a result of the construction of a new pipeline through their land.

b) American restrictions on importing BC lumber cause widespread layoffs in the BC lumber industry.

c) The widespread use of microprocessors lowers the costs of producing many consumer electronic products.

d) Restrictions and delays persist in crossborder transportation of goods and supplies between Canada and the United States.

e) Work in pairs. One partner draws up a list of 10 products believed to have an elastic demand, while the other partner lists products that have an inelastic demand. Then compare lists and justify your choices. Share your findings with the rest of the class, and explain any disagreements or uncertainties.

APPLICATION

11 Think of a product you would like to purchase but are unable to at the moment because the price is too high. Name two things you would like to see happen in each of the following:

a) The demand side, to bring the price down

b) The supply side, to bring the price down

12 How can merchants in a competitive market tell if their prices are too low? How can these same merchants tell if their prices are too high?

13 Review the four conditions that must exist for perfect (or pure) competition to exist. Then, hold three of them constant while you consider the effect of changing one condition. Forecast how prices would be affected, and why. A forecast is included in (a) as an example.

a) The market has many consumers, but only one seller. (The seller would have a monopoly and, with no competitors, would be able to charge a higher price.)

b) The market has many sellers, but only one consumer.

c) Each seller's product is somewhat different from that of the others.

d) Consumers are not well informed about the selling prices of the various suppliers of the product.

14 Copy the table in Figure 7.25 in your notebook, and add two blank columns: one marked *Sales Revenue*, the other marked *Elasticity*.

FIGURE 7.25
A demand schedule for a computer

Price	Quantity Demanded
$3 000	8 000
$2 800	10 000
$2 600	12 000
$2 400	14 000
$2 200	16 000

a) Determine the price elasticity for the computer for each price range.

b) Give two reasons why this product would have this particular elasticity.

c) Because of the costs of manufacturing the computer, it is currently priced at $2 800. As costs fall, should the manufacturer maintain the same price, raise it, or lower it? Explain your reasoning.

d) Suppose that an accessory that most consumers of the computer find useful costs an extra $25. Will this accessory have an inelastic or an elastic demand for the majority of consumers? What would be the best pricing strategy for the seller: to raise, lower, or maintain the price of the accessory? Why?

8

Applications of Demand and Supply

INTRODUCTION

You learned in Chapter 7 how the forces of demand and supply work together to produce the goods and services that Canadian consumers need and want. Business people compete to meet consumer demand for the products they sell. They must use scarce resources efficiently to keep costs down and consumer prices competitive. We may grumble at times about the high price of certain goods, but often that price is the result of increased demand that corrects itself over time. High prices act as a signal for suppliers to produce more, become more efficient, or use technology that increases supply, which lead prices to decline.

These market forces ensure that shortages or wasteful surpluses of goods are infrequent occurrences in our economy. No government or ruler or central planning is necessary to ensure that this happens. It's automatic in a market economy. Adam Smith referred to the self-regulating nature of market forces as an "invisible hand" over 200 years ago (see Chapter 5).

This chapter will deepen your understanding of demand and how people make consumer choices in a rational manner using utility theory. You will find out how this theory explains a famous paradox as to why diamonds are more expensive than the water we drink to maintain life!

We have made a persuasive case for the efficiency of the market process. However, should prices for everything be decided by the workings of demand and supply, especially needs such as wages, rent, or food? You will see in this chapter that governments face pressure to control rental prices, prevent wages from falling, and take action to control the production and prices of some food items. Government intervention to control markets is a highly controversial topic, and you will form your own opinion.

KEY TERMS

marginal utility theory of consumer choice (utility theory)

marginal utility

consumer equilibrium

paradox of value

consumer surplus

ceiling price

black market

floor price

subsidy

quota

marketing board

rent-control program

rent

wage

minimum wage

primary market

secondary market

LEARNING GOALS

Once you have completed this chapter, you should be able to:

- Understand theories of consumer behaviour, such as marginal utility and consumer surplus

- Identify how and why governments intervene in markets and explain whether such actions are beneficial to the economy

- Analyze and graph ceiling prices, floor prices, subsidies, and quotas

- Understand the effects of marketing boards, rent controls, and minimum wages

marginal utility theory of consumer choice (utility theory)

A theory stating that the extra satisfaction that a consumer achieves from consuming successive units of a good diminishes. With two or more items, consumers maximize their satisfaction when they receive the same amount of satisfaction per dollar for each item, a condition called *consumer equilibrium*.

marginal utility

A measure of the extra satisfaction that a consumer achieves from consuming one more unit of a product.

Making Consumption Choices: Utility Theory

What factors determine the demand for the products that each of us buys? Is there a rational way of explaining the decisions we make about buying and consuming? Economist Alfred Marshall (1842–1924), sometimes referred to as "the father of demand and supply," was the first to advance the most widely accepted explanation, known as the **marginal utility theory of consumer choice**, or **utility theory** for short.

To understand Marshall's theory, let's consider an example. Suppose that Lisa, a health-conscious student, is faced with the choice of buying either a veggie burger or frozen yogourt. What factors might influence Lisa in making her choice?

First, she would probably consider how many veggie burgers she has consumed lately. If she has enjoyed several, she might decide that she would gain little *extra* satisfaction from consuming another. The economic term for "satisfaction" or "usefulness" is *utility*; the term used for "extra" is *marginal*. We would say, then, that the **marginal utility** (extra satisfaction) Lisa would receive from yet another veggie burger is low because she has already consumed several recently. However, if she has bought little frozen yogourt in the past week, the extra satisfaction she would gain from buying more yogourt would be higher. Since the marginal utility of buying more yogourt is greater for Lisa than the marginal utility of eating another veggie burger, Lisa would most likely buy the yogourt.

Suppose, however, that Lisa wants both a veggie burger and frozen yogourt. We assume that, like most consumers, she wants to maximize her satisfaction, or utility, for the income she has available to spend on these items. Suppose that Lisa has $20 to spend this week on these two items. The burgers cost $4 each, and a frozen yogourt costs $2. How should she determine how much of each she should buy? We can compare Lisa's choices by using the table in Figure 8.1, which arbitrarily assigns numerical values called utils, or units of satisfaction, to the veggie burgers and frozen yogourt Lisa typically consumes over a week.

We see that the utility Lisa receives from consuming one veggie burger or one frozen yogourt is high. Total utility is 10 utils for one veggie burger and 11 utils for one frozen yogourt. For the first unit of the item in question, the

FIGURE 8.1

Lisa's weekly consumption of veggie burgers and frozen yogourt

Veggie Burgers	Total Utility	Marginal Utility
1	10	10
2	18	8
3	24	6
4	28	4
5	30	2

Frozen Yogourt	Total Utility	Marginal Utility
1	1	11
2	18	7
3	22	4
4	25	3
5	26	1

FIGURE 8.2
Total utility for Lisa's consumption of veggie burgers

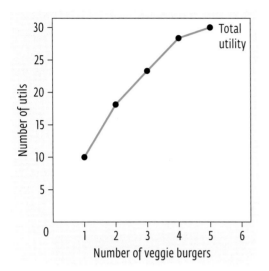

FIGURE 8.3
Marginal utility for Lisa's consumption of veggie burgers

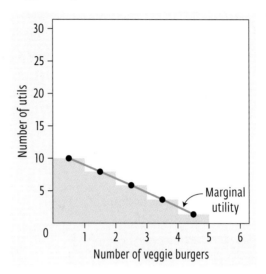

The unusual placement of values here reflects the fact that marginal utility involves the satisfaction between one unit and the next.

marginal utility is always the same as total utility. Lisa is gaining 10 utils of extra satisfaction by consuming one veggie burger instead of none and, similarly, 11 utils of extra satisfaction by consuming one frozen yogourt instead of none. If Lisa buys a second veggie burger or a second frozen yogourt, the extra satisfaction she experiences drops slightly to 8 utils for the second burger and 7 for the second frozen yogourt. Her total satisfaction is now 18 utils for two veggie burgers and is also 18 utils for two frozen yogourts—a total of 36 utils for the two different items. We see the same pattern through a third and fourth veggie burger or frozen yogourt: marginal utility steadily falls as Lisa consumes one more of either product. Total utility continues to rise as more is consumed, but not as quickly.

Figures 8.2 and 8.3 illustrate how to plot this information on a graph. In Figure 8.2, total utility rises steadily as Lisa consumes more veggie burgers, but in Figure 8.3, we see that marginal utility steadily falls. The same patterns would hold true for her consumption of frozen yogourt.

If Lisa's budget were unlimited, she could maximize her utility by consuming five veggie burgers and five frozen yogourts. Since she has limited herself to $20, however, Lisa must find another combination that will yield her the highest satisfaction, or total utility, possible.

The formula that yields the answer for her best combination is the utility maximization formula:

$$\frac{MU}{\text{price of product A}} = \frac{MU}{\text{price of product B}}$$

where MU = marginal utility. $\frac{MU}{\text{price}}$ signifies the amount of satisfaction received per dollar. Figure 8.4 shows the calculations we need to perform to determine the $\frac{MU}{\text{price}}$.

CHECK THIS OUT!

Can marginal utility be applied to other things in life? Does your attention and satisfaction (utils) decline the longer you listen to a speech? Or music? Can you think of other areas of life where it does or does not apply?

consumer equilibrium

The state of satisfaction a consumer reaches when the marginal utility divided by price is equal for two or more products bought by that consumer.

We can now determine Lisa's best combination for maximizing her satisfaction. She will do so by purchasing three veggie burgers and four frozen yogourts because, at these positions, the $\frac{MU}{price}$ is equal for both items. Since Lisa is receiving the same amount of satisfaction per dollar for each item, she has no reason to buy more of one and less of another. An economist would say the Lisa is in a condition of **consumer equilibrium**. She has spent 3 × $4 = $12 on veggie burgers and 4 × $2 = $8 on frozen yogourt for a total of $20. More importantly, she has maximized her total utility by amassing 49 utils. No other combination will give her more total utils within her $20 budget limit. Using the tables in Figures 8.1 and 8.4, try other combinations to prove this to yourself.

FIGURE 8.4

Lisa's $\frac{marginal\ utility}{price}$ for veggie burgers and frozen yogourt

Veggie Burgers	Marginal Utility	MU / Price
1	10	$^{10}/_{\$4}$ = $2.50
2	8	$^{8}/_{\$4}$ = $2.00
3	6	$^{6}/_{\$4}$ = $1.50
4	4	$^{4}/_{\$4}$ = $1.00
5	2	$^{2}/_{\$4}$ = $0.50

Frozen Yogourt	Marginal Utility	MU / Price
1	11	$^{11}/_{\$2}$ = $5.50
2	7	$^{7}/_{\$2}$ = $3.50
3	4	$^{4}/_{\$2}$ = $2.00
4	3	$^{3}/_{\$2}$ = $1.50
5	1	$^{1}/_{\$2}$ = $0.50

DID YOU KNOW?

Economist Richard Thaler (1945–) won the Nobel Prize in Economic Sciences for developing a new field called *behavioural economics* that combines economics and psychology. One of his ideas is called the "nudge," which is an action that gently motivates people to make good choices. For example, to encourage healthy eating, displaying fruits and vegetables in stores in prominent places works better than calorie counts!

APPLICATIONS OF UTILITY THEORY

Let's look at the application of utility theory as it relates to the demand curve, Adam Smith's paradox, and consumer surplus.

The Demand Curve

We have seen that the demand curve slopes downward from top left to bottom right because consumers will buy more only if price falls. The theory of marginal utility supports this idea because it tells us that as people consume more, the extra satisfaction they receive declines. If people receive less satisfaction as they consume more of a product, then, obviously, they will want to pay less (not more) for that product the more they buy it.

Adam Smith's Paradox

Adam Smith wrestled with an economic problem he was never able to solve, one he called the **paradox of value**. Why, he wondered, are diamonds more costly than water, when water is essential to human life and diamonds are not? Smith could not understand why the demand for a necessity should not be high enough to assure that its price is as high as the price for luxury items. This paradox remained unsolved until the development of utility theory.

The key to unlocking the paradox lies in the difference between the total and marginal utility for water and diamonds. Clearly, water has infinitely greater total utility (usefulness) than diamonds, which, in comparison, could vanish from the earth with no harm to the human race. However, diamonds are scarce compared with water. Few are bought; thus, the satisfaction one receives from a diamond is extremely high. The marginal utility, or extra satisfaction, consumers receive from purchasing a diamond once or twice in a lifetime means they are willing to pay a high price for something that, in reality, has little total utility.

In comparison, the very abundance of water means that most people can consume so much of it that its marginal utility is pushed very low. If a product's marginal utility is low, people are not willing to pay a high price for it, not even for something as vital, and with such great total utility, as water.

paradox of value
A seeming contradiction in the economy in which the demand for necessities needed for survival is not high enough to ensure that their prices at least match the prices of luxury items, which are unnecessary for survival.

Utility theory answers the question: Why are diamonds more expensive than water, when water is essential to life and diamonds are mere luxury?

consumer surplus
The difference between what consumers are willing to pay for an item and what they actually pay.

Consumer Surplus

If we examine the concept of marginal utility closely enough, we shall come to a surprising conclusion: we get a bargain on everything we buy! Economists call this result a **consumer surplus**, which we will define after working through an example using Lisa's purchases of a different product—her favourite brand of bottled water.

Let's suppose that we asked Lisa how many cases of bottled water she would buy at different prices. She provides us with the answers shown in Figure 8.5, which we can identify as Lisa's bottled water demand schedule. This table shows that Lisa would buy only one case of bottled water if the price per case were $9. However, if after consuming this one case the price dropped to $8, she would buy another case, for a total of two cases in one month and a total cost of $17. Lisa would continue to buy one more case of water each time the price fell further, until, by the time the price per case reached $6, she would have bought four cases. The results summarized in Figure 8.5 are a perfect illustration of marginal utility because they demonstrate that Lisa would buy more cases of water only if the price fell.

In reality, however, the sellers of bottled water do not drop their prices throughout the month to encourage Lisa to buy more of their product. They charge a constant price, say $6 a case. The happy result is that Lisa actually receives a surplus for the first three cases of bottled water she buys. The third column in Figure 8.5 shows that this surplus is calculated by subtracting the amount she *would* have paid for each case of water from the amount she actually paid. Lisa would be willing to pay $30 for the four cases of bottled water she buys each month ($9 + $8 + $7 + $6 = $30). In reality, she pays only $24 ($6 × 4 = $24) for four cases, achieving a total consumer surplus of $6 ($3 + $2 + $1 + $0 = $6). We can best define this concept as the difference between what we are willing to pay for an item and what we actually pay.

Follow Lisa's story to see how the different prices for cases of bottled water help to illustrate the idea of consumer surplus.

Figure 8.6 provides an illustration of this concept. It shows Lisa's demand curve (D) for bottled water. Lisa actually pays the amount represented by blue shaded area for the four cases of bottled water she buys each month. However, the total value to her of the four cases is the entire shaded area (both blue *and* yellow). Thus, the consumer surplus she receives is the yellow area.

FIGURE 8.5
Lisa's consumer surplus for bottled water

Price	Number of Cases of Water	Consumer Surplus
$9	1	$9 – $6 = $3
$8	2	$8 – $6 = $2
$7	3	$7 – $6 = $1
$6	4	$6 – $6 = $0

FIGURE 8.6
Lisa's consumer surplus for bottled water

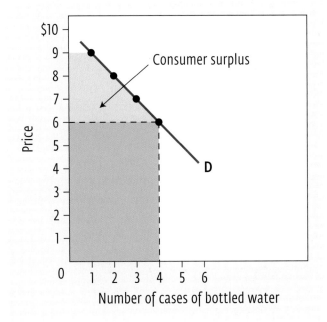

Number of cases of bottled water

Self-Reflect

1 Explain the difference between total utility and marginal utility using as an example a person drinking cans of soft drinks.

2 Consider the following scenario.

a) Stefan is willing to go to one movie a month if the price is $10, two if the price drops to $8, and three if the price drops further to $6. If the price of a movie is set at $8, what is Stefan's consumer surplus?

b) Draw a graph of Stefan's demand curve for movies, and shade in the area of his consumer surplus.

ceiling price
A restriction imposed by a government to prevent the price of a product from rising above a certain level.

Government Intervention in Markets

Former US President Ronald Reagan once used the phrase "the magic of the marketplace" to explain the buoyant state of the American economy during his terms in office (1981–1985, 1985–1989). His brief description of a market economy was accurate in many ways. The market engines of demand and supply automatically produce the vast range of goods and services consumers want and then distribute these goods and services with a minimum of waste or shortages. All of this happens without the benefit of any individual or group providing direction for the economy.

Governments do, however, intervene extensively in markets. Why do they do this? Are they threatening the "magic of the marketplace" by intervening? To answer these questions, we will look at three examples of controversial government actions:

1 If the government believes that people are paying too high a price for a product, it will introduce a *ceiling price* as a solution.

2 If the government believes that sellers are receiving too low a price for a product, it will introduce a *floor price* as a solution.

3 If the government believes that it must intervene in a market for social or environmental reasons, it will introduce a *subsidy* or a *quota* as a solution.

CEILING PRICES

A **ceiling price** is a restriction placed by a government to prevent the price of a product from rising above a certain level. If the ceiling price is set below the equilibrium price, a shortage will result. Consider the market for gasoline illustrated in Figure 8.7. Suppose that an international crisis has interfered with oil supplies to such an extent that gasoline prices start to climb. The government, concerned by the hardship these price increases have caused for motorists, places a price ceiling (PC) on gasoline. The equilibrium price was $1.35 per litre, with 100 million litres per month demanded and supplied. The price ceiling prohibits prices from rising above $1.25 per litre. At this price, 110 million litres (QD_1) are demanded, and 90 million litres (QS_1) are supplied. The result is a shortage of 20 million litres of gasoline ($QD_1 - QS_1$).

There are three possible outcomes of price ceilings. First, the shortages can cause long lineups for the product. This problem occurred in 1974 in the United States when American motorists pressured their government to restrict the rising price of gasoline. This price ceiling led to gasoline shortages and long lineups that snaked for blocks around gas stations until the

FIGURE 8.7
The gasoline market
The effect of a ceiling price is a shortage.

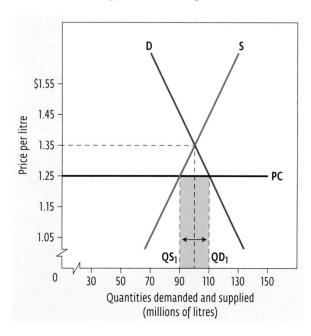

ceilings were lifted to allow the price of gasoline to rise and bring demand and supply into equilibrium.

Second, price ceilings may create a **black market** for certain goods. This happens when a shortage of a product encourages some people to buy up as much of it as they can at the ceiling price, stockpile it, and then sell it at a higher price to people who cannot get enough for their own use. This happened in Canada during the Second World War when the government rationed several basic food items.

Third, price ceilings may cause the quality of a product to suffer if sellers try to reduce their costs to make more money. This situation is less likely to occur with natural resource products such as gasoline or foods, but it occurs more frequently when the government places a ceiling on a product such as rental accommodations.

black market

The illegal exchange of goods in short supply, as when some people buy up as much of a good as possible, stockpile it, and sell it at a higher price.

floor price

A restriction that prevents a price from falling below a certain level.

FLOOR PRICES

A **floor price** is a restriction that prevents a price from falling below a certain level. If the floor price is set above the equilibrium price, it will cause a surplus. Suppose that the government believes that milk producers are making too little profit on milk, which is priced at $1.50 per litre. The government may set a floor price (FP) of $1.60 per litre, below which prices are not allowed to fall. The result can be seen in Figure 8.8.

The line labelled "FP" is the floor price of $1.60 per litre. At that price, 10 million litres will be supplied, which is more than the 9 million litres that would have been supplied at the equilibrium price of $1.50 per litre. The higher floor price cuts the quantity demanded to 8 million litres, less than would be demanded at the equilibrium price. The result is a surplus of 2 million litres of milk ($QD_1 - QS_1$).

Maintaining this floor price causes two problems. One problem is what to do with the surplus. To keep the floor price at $1.60 per litre, the government must buy the surplus of milk (using taxpayers' money) with little chance that the surplus will generate a return. It cannot be sold within the country at prices below the floor price without undercutting the floor price. Sometimes, surpluses can be sold on the world market or donated to less-developed countries. Otherwise, since milk is perishable, it must be turned into products that can be stored, such as powdered milk, butter, and cheese.

The second problem is that consumers on the whole pay a higher price for the product and receive less. In Figure 8.8, we can see that consumers in an unregulated market would probably have paid the equilibrium price of $1.50 per litre and would have received 9 million litres of milk. With the floor price set by the government, consumers pay $1.60 per litre and receive 8 million litres of milk.

FIGURE 8.8
The milk market
The effect of a floor price is a surplus.

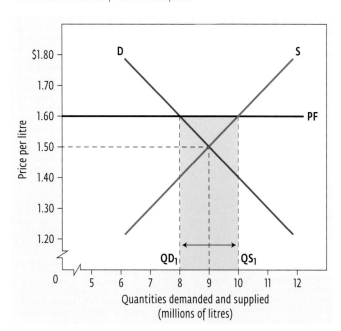

subsidy
A grant of money from a government to a producer to achieve some desired outcome, such as the installation of pollution-control equipment.

SUBSIDIES AND QUOTAS

Both price ceilings and price floors share a common problem: less of the product is actually exchanged between sellers and consumers when the price is forced away from its equilibrium price by government policies. (Look again at Figures 8.7 and 8.8 to verify this important point.) To avoid this problem, governments sometimes provide subsidies. A **subsidy** is a grant of money from a government to a particular industry to achieve some desired outcome, such as lowering the financial burden placed on an industry.

Let's look at Figure 8.9 to see how the milk market will be affected by a subsidy of $0.10 per litre. The immediate impact is that the supply curve increases by the amount of the subsidy, since producers supply more milk because they are receiving an extra $0.10 per litre. The result is that the new equilibrium price of $1.45 is lower than the old equilibrium price of $1.50, and the quantity of milk sold is increased by 3 million litres (from Q_1 to Q_2).

Subsidies benefit consumers with lower prices and sellers with extra revenue. They also lead to an increase in the exchange of products between consumers and sellers. However, subsidies have a couple of drawbacks. Since taxpayers pay for subsidy programs, some critics charge that subsidies keep inefficient producers in business. In the global economy, subsidies are often seen as barriers to fair trade.

FIGURE 8.9
The effect of a subsidy is to increase the quantity supplied

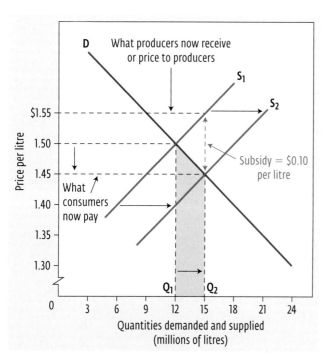

FIGURE 8.10
The effect of a quota is to increase the income of suppliers by raising the price of a product

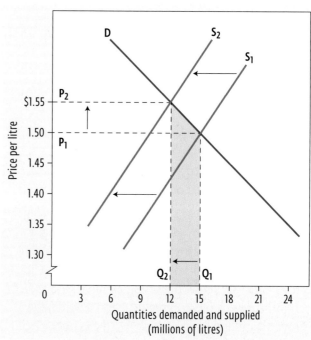

Quotas are another means of helping producers. A **quota** is a restriction placed on the amount of a product that individual producers are allowed to produce. These restrictions are administered by organizations called **marketing boards**, composed of representatives from the government and from the industry. As one example, milk marketing boards operate in every province in Canada.

Figure 8.10 illustrates what happens when a provincial marketing board enforces a reduced quota of 3 million litres on all milk producers in the province. S2 shows the shift of the supply curve to the left. P2 at $1.55 is the new, higher price, and Q2 at 12 million litres is the new, smaller amount of milk that is actually sold.

Quotas set by marketing boards raise farmers' incomes mainly because food is an inelastic commodity. Remember that when prices rise on an inelastic product, sales revenue also rises because the quantity demanded does not fall by much.

Farmers were given the authority to establish marketing boards years ago because governments believed that their incomes were, on average, too low. Farmers are producing an essential commodity, and if too many of them go out of business, so the argument goes, Canadians will wind up paying more for their food. Critics reply that marketing boards raise prices above the equilibrium point, with the result that less of the product is actually produced and exchanged. Whatever the argument, the fact remains that most of the Canadian meat, vegetable, and dairy products we buy in supermarkets are sold to the stores by marketing boards.

quota
A restriction placed on the amount of product that domestic producers are allowed to produce; also, a limit on the total quantity of goods imported into a country.

marketing board
An agricultural organization established to administer quotas and market the products of its producers.

rent-control program
A government program that limits the amount landlords can increase rents.

rent
The price people pay for accommodation, determined by demand and supply for rental accommodation.

Rent Controls

A **rent-control program** is a good example of a price ceiling. Most Canadian provinces and many American states have enacted such programs, and the controversy that surrounds them never seems to end. Let's use the tools of supply and demand to examine the rental market and the effects that controls have on it.

Rent is the price paid for accommodation and, like any other market price, it is determined by demand and supply. Figure 8.11 shows the rent the market sets for the quantity of apartments demanded and supplied in a particular building. At $1 500 for a one-bedroom apartment, the owner will supply 50 apartments. We have made the supply curve vertical because the owner cannot increase supply immediately (because that would involve building more units). In other words, the supply of apartments is fixed, or *perfectly inelastic*, in the short term.

FIGURE 8.11
How apartment rents are set

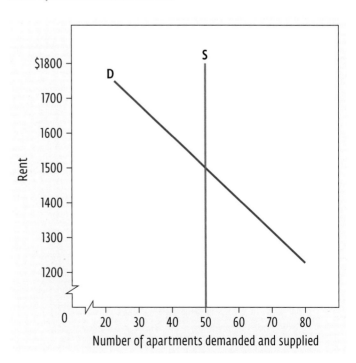

Number of apartments demanded and supplied

wage

The price a worker receives for supplying labour to a business with a demand for it.

minimum wage

A government-established wage, higher than one set by the demand for, and supply of, workers.

Suppose that an increase in renters occurs, shifting the demand curve upward. This change encourages owners to raise rents to $1 600 a month. This increase in rent has two effects: those who can afford the higher rent will stay and pay, while those who cannot will have to find less expensive accommodation elsewhere.

Higher rents mean higher profits for the owner, who is therefore encouraged to build more units. Figure 8.12 illustrates the effect of this long-term decision to construct another apartment building: the supply curve shifts to the right. This long-run supply curve, with greater elasticity, also has beneficial effects for renters, as we can see from the graph. The supply of apartments increases, and the rental price, at least in theory, falls to $1 550. This is the way a free rental market tends to work, and both renters and apartment owners appear to win in the long run.

Now suppose that, in response to the increase in demand that caused rents to rise to $1 600 in the short term, the government comes under pressure to alleviate the economic hardship renters are experiencing. The government introduces a rent-control program: a law that freezes, reduces, or controls the amount of rent that owners can charge. We will simplify the discussion at this point, and assume that a freeze on rent for one-bedroom apartments will be fixed at $1 500. Figure 8.13 shows that if demand continues to rise to D2, there will be a shortage of supply of 10 units.

If this kind of shortage is repeated in buildings all over the city, people will have great difficulty finding essential accommodation. Those who are looking for an apartment will be tempted to offer building owners more money "under the table" in hopes of beating others to a vacancy. Owners, with no incentive to keep their buildings in good repair to attract new tenants, may stop making essential repairs and renovations. With rental prices fixed, they will also be disinclined to build more units.

The problems with rent controls have not prevented many cities throughout the world from using them.

FIGURE 8.12

What happens to the rent of apartments when demand increases

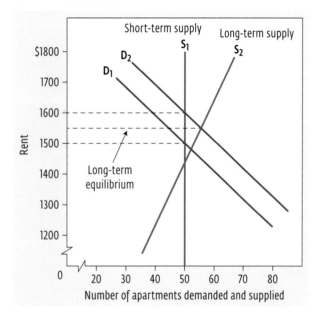

FIGURE 8.13

Rent controls and their effects

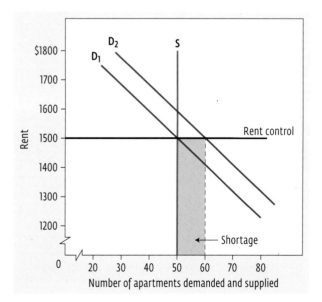

FIGURE 8.14
The labour market before minimum wage

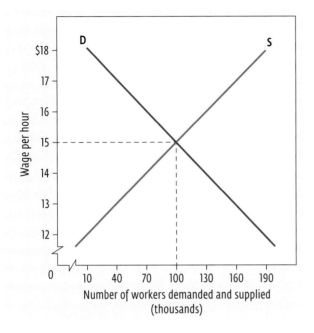

FIGURE 8.15
The labour market after the government sets a minimum wage

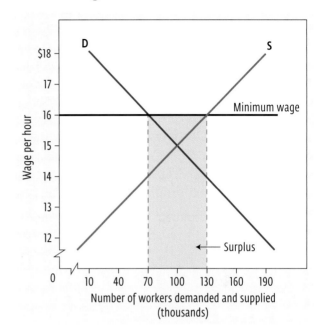

Minimum Wages

Rent controls are an example of how governments intervene in markets to establish a ceiling price when they think the price that sellers are receiving for their product is too high. As we stated before, governments also intervene to establish floor prices when they believe the price sellers are receiving is too low. A **wage** is the price a worker receives for supplying labour to a business with a demand for it. In Figure 8.14, we see that 100 000 workers are receiving wages of $15 an hour. Suppose that the government responds to public pressure to raise the low wages of these workers by setting a **minimum wage**, a wage that is higher than the one set by the forces of demand and supply.

We can see the results of the government's move in Figure 8.15. The minimum wage is set at $16 an hour. Businesses adjust to this by employing only 70 000 workers, 30 000 fewer than at the old wage rate of $15 an hour. Furthermore, the higher wage rate attracts an additional 30 000 workers into the labour market, for a total of 130 000 workers who are willing to work for $16 an hour. If businesses are willing to hire only 70 000 workers, this means the minimum wage has created an unemployment problem: 60 000 workers who cannot find jobs.

As noted earlier, floor prices tend to create surpluses. In the case of minimum wages, they create surpluses of potential workers who cannot find jobs. On the other hand, the minimum wage increases the wages of thousands of people at the low end of the wage scale. These people receive a more substantial paycheque than they would have if wages had been set solely by supply and demand.

Self-Reflect

1 Define and state the purpose of a ceiling price. What problems can it cause?

2 Define and state the purpose of a floor price. What problems can it cause?

3 What effects do subsidies and quotas have on the market for a good?

4 What kind of government intervention is a rent-control program? What effect might it have on the rental market?

5 What kind of government intervention is a minimum-wage law? What effect might it have on the labour market?

Thinking like an Economist

The Economics of Ticket Reselling

Have you ever been to a concert or sporting event and witnessed individuals reselling tickets to the event? Have you ever seen tickets available to purchase online at a cost that exceeds the original price? Often referred to as "scalping" or "ticket brokering," the act of reselling event tickets is controversial. Many believe that ticket resellers are profiting at the expense of the event organizers, the artists, and fans.

How do economists analyze this practice? They use the same demand and supply tools you have learned in this chapter to understand the issues that ticket resale raises.

Tickets for a concert or sporting event are sold in what is called a **primary market**. Fans buy their tickets online, over the phone, or in person. Figure 8.16 shows the demand and supply of tickets for a concert by a top performer. Suppose that the top performer can easily fill a 2 000-seat concert hall. (Notice that the supply curve is vertical because there is only one performer.) The concert organizers price tickets at $75 apiece.

FIGURE 8.16
Demand for, and supply of, concert tickets
The result? Ticket resale.

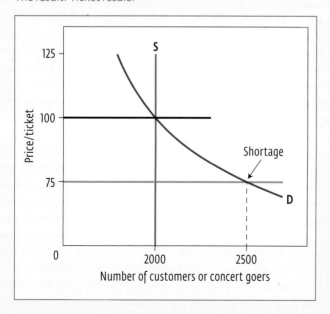

If the ticket price is $75, a full 2 500 fans would purchase tickets, but the hall holds only 2 000 people. Clearly, the price is too low, causing a shortage of 500 tickets. If the price per ticket were $100, demand would equal supply, and no shortage would occur.

The opportunity to make a profit comes because those tickets are underpriced and undersupplied in relation to the demand for them. Ticket resellers, through various means, buy up tickets in the primary market and resell them at a higher price to people who want to attend, but have missed out on buying a ticket. Economists say that the transactions between resellers and ticket buyers occur in a **secondary market**.

If the problem is that the price per ticket is too low, then why don't event organizers raise prices to eliminate shortages? One theory is that event organizers believe that attendees enjoy the concert or sporting event more when the hall or stadium is full. Higher prices might discourage fans and leave empty seats. Another theory is that some artists, out of a sense of fairness, want average-income fans to be able to afford to attend their concerts. These theories are possibilities, but a little research indicates that Bruce Springsteen, Adele, Taylor Swift, and Radiohead, among many others, are very vocal in their dislike of ticket reselling. There may be self-interest in not alienating average people who listen to their music—by charging more and thereby reducing reselling. This is a debatable issue for sure. Event organizers also know that if prices are too high, fans have less to spend on profitable refreshments and merchandise sold at the event.

primary market
The first time a ticket is sold for an event by an event organizer such as Ticketmaster.

secondary market
The reselling of tickets bought from buyers in the primary market at a higher price than the stated ticket price.

Four approaches to the ticket reselling issue are worth considering:

1   Recognize that reselling often occurs because of faulty pricing. If tickets are priced high enough, shortages won't occur. Reselling "helps" people who missed out in the primary market fulfill their demand — albeit for a higher price.

2   Limit the profits resellers can make by setting a fixed percentage limit above the ticket price (say 50 percent) resellers can charge.

3   Try to prevent ticket reselling by printing the names and birth dates of ticket buyers on all tickets sold.

4   Forbid reselling and secondary markets in tickets.

APPLYING ECONOMIC THINKING

1   What might performers do on the supply side to reduce ticket reselling?

2   Who wins or loses from raising average ticket prices at events?

3   Which of the four approaches do you support?

DID YOU KNOW?

"Scalping bots" are computer programs that facilitate the rapid purchase of large numbers of tickets from event sites such as Ticketmaster before other people can buy them. They are illegal in Canada and in many US states, but it is hard to stop bots from being used in other countries, such as Panama and Gibraltar, although at the time of writing, class-action lawsuits were being initiated in both Canada and the United States.

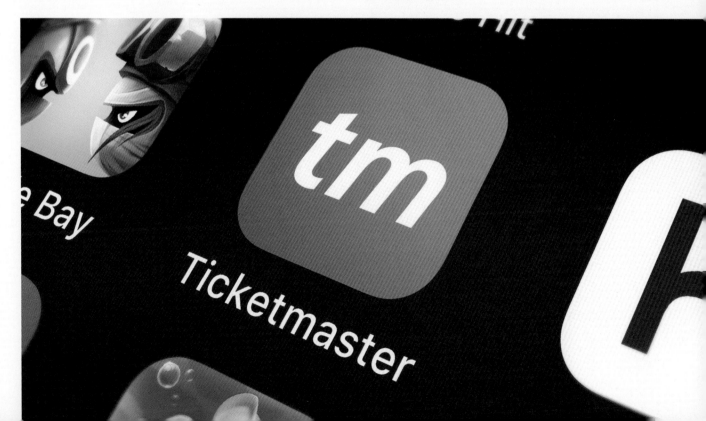

Chapter 8
Consolidation Activities

KNOWLEDGE

1 In a sentence, define the difference between total utility and marginal utility. For most goods, which of the two increases, and which decreases? For a rational consumer buying two items for a meal, what does the theory suggest about the best way to maximize income and satisfaction?

2 How does marginal utility support the idea of a downward slope of a demand curve?

3 What common problem do both price ceilings and price floors share? How does a subsidy eliminate that problem, but cause another? How do quotas help suppliers, but hurt consumers?

THINKING & INQUIRY

4 A demand curve normally slopes down from left to right. What does this indicate about consumer behaviour with regard to price and quantity demanded? How does marginal utility help to explain this consumer behaviour and, thus, the direction of the demand curve?

5 Using the example of your favourite type of drink, explain how your demand for it can be derived from the utility you receive from its consumption.

6 Although parking meters may yield little revenue because of the costs of installation and the employees who check and maintain them, most cities still regard them as essential for proper traffic flow. Explain why this is so using the concepts of demand, supply, and price.

COMMUNICATION

7 Organize a debate around this issue: "In the interests of fairness and reducing poverty, the minimum wage should be boosted immediately to $16 per hour for all employees, young and old."

APPLICATION

8 Suppose that a certain city has a demand for two-bedroom apartments, as shown in Figure 8.17:

FIGURE 8.17
A demand schedule for two-bedroom apartments

Rent	Quantity Demanded
$1 300	1 000
$1 200	2 000
$1 100	3 000
$1 000	4 000
$900	5 000
$800	6 000

a) Plot demand and supply curves for this schedule, assuming that there are 3 000 apartments. What is the equilibrium rent? Is the supply elastic or perfectly inelastic in the short term?

b) Assume that demand for apartments in the city increases, rising by 1 000 at each rental price. What happens to the equilibrium price?

c) Suppose that the city council steps in and freezes rent at the original equilibrium rent. Graph the results of such a rent-control law.

9 Assume that a province's demand and supply for milk is as indicated in Figure 8.18.

FIGURE 8.18
A hypothetical demand and supply schedule for milk in a Canadian province

Price per Litre	Quantity Demanded (million litres)	Quantity Supplied (million litres)
$1.20	10	4
$1.40	9	5
$1.60	8	6
$1.80	7	7
$2.00	6	7
$2.20	5	9
$2.40	4	10

a) Graph the information in Figure 8.18. In a free market, what is the price for a litre of milk?

b) Suppose that the government sets a floor price of $1.00 per litre. How would the market be affected? Show the results on your graph.

c) Suppose that, instead of a floor price, a marketing board establishes a quota that cuts production by 1 million litres at all possible prices. Graph this restriction on a new graph, and determine what the new price of milk per litre would be.

d) Suppose that the marketing board launches a successful advertising campaign that raises milk consumption by 1 million litres at each price level. On your second graph, indicate what the results would be if this advertising campaign were used along with the quota referred to in part (c), and determine what the price would be.

9
Labour Economics

INTRODUCTION

In Chapter 3, we examined the productive resources in the economy—land, labour, capital, and entrepreneurship. One of these resources—labour—should be of particular interest to you, because soon enough you will be an active participant in the labour market. Over the next few years, you will make a series of important decisions about how best to prepare yourself for the labour market. It is not enough to say, "I want to become a dentist because I know that people will always have teeth and, therefore, there will always be a demand for dentists." The labour market is a complex system of interrelated factors based on supply and demand, just like the market for many other goods and services. The difference in this market, however, is that households are the suppliers, business firms are the consumers, and the price is the wage rate.

LEARNING GOALS

Once you have completed this chapter, you should be able to:

- Understand the forces that influence the market demand for labour and the market supply of labour
- Explain how wage rates are determined in a perfectly competitive market and why different wage rates exist for different types of labour
- Describe the "Essential Skills" people require for today's job market
- Understand the rights of workers and the role of unions and the government in protecting these rights
- Explain how technology and globalization have influenced labour markets in Canada

KEY TERMS

direct demand
derived demand
marginal revenue product of labour (MRPL)
marginal product
labour demand curve
labour supply curve
wage differentials
human capital
Essential Skills
labour union
trade unions (or craft unions)
industrial unions
public sector unions
collective bargaining
collective agreement
union dues
open shop
closed shop
union shop
Rand Formula
conciliation (or mediation)
voluntary arbitration
compulsory arbitration
strike
lockout
rotating strike
work-to-rule
boycott
Canadian Labour Congress
public policy issue
outsourcing
offshoring
gig economy

direct demand

Consumer demand for goods and services that directly determines the kind and quantity produced.

derived demand

Demand for resources (such as labour) that is dependent on, or derived from, the direct demand of consumers for the goods and services being produced.

marginal revenue product of labour (MRPL)

The amount of additional, or marginal, revenue that is generated for a firm as a result of adding one more worker to the production process.

marginal product

The change in output that occurs from adding an additional unit of input.

Demand for Labour

The concept of demand for labour is very similar to the concept of demand for goods and services; both relate to a quantity that is demanded at a given price—the price of labour being the wage rate. However, there is a significant difference in the origin of the demand. The demand for goods and services is known as **direct demand** because consumers determine it directly using their dollars to indicate the value they place on the utility of a good or service at various price levels. The demand for resources, including labour, is known as **derived demand** because it is dependent on, or derived from, the consumer demand for the good or service being produced. The greater the quantity demanded of a good or service, the greater the quantity of labour demanded to produce it.

The demand for labour depends on more than just the demand for the product. It is also influenced by how much each worker can produce in a period of time; a concept known as *productivity*. It is this productivity, tied to both the price of the good or service and the wage rate, that determines the demand for labour.

The **marginal revenue product of labour (MRPL)** is a concept that explains how the demand for labour is derived. The MRPL is directly related to the concept of **marginal product**. As an additional unit of labour is added to a firm's productive process, the extra output created is known as the *marginal product*. The MRPL is the amount of *additional revenue* generated by this marginal product.

BUSINESS DEMAND FOR LABOUR

For a firm operating in a perfectly competitive market, the MRPL equals the price of the good multiplied by the marginal product, because each new unit produced is sold at the market equilibrium price. For example, Figure 9.1 displays the production schedule for a firm known as Paolo's Pizza Place. It demonstrates what happens as the firm adds additional workers to its productive process. To simplify the explanation, we will assume that the only cost incurred by the firm is the cost associated with labour input.

FIGURE 9.1

Worker productivity and production schedule for Paolo's Pizza Place

Units of Labour (# of workers)	Total Product (TP) (pizzas/day)	Marginal Product (MP) (pizzas/day)	Marginal Revenue Product of Labour (MRPL)
4	180		
5	244	64	$640
6	276	32	$320
7	292	16	$160
8	300	8	$80
9	304	4	$40
10	306	2	$20

When Paolo has four employees, his firm produces an output of 180 pizzas per day. When an additional worker is hired, the marginal product of this fifth worker is 64 pizzas per day because the addition of that worker increases total production from 180 pizzas to 244 pizzas. If the equilibrium price for pizzas is $10, the MRPL is 64 pizzas × $10, or $640. This is the additional revenue that is generated by adding the fifth worker. As the schedule shows, adding more workers increases output, but at a decreasing rate. The sixth worker adds only 32 pizzas and has an MRPL of $320. The decreasing MRPL is due to the law of diminishing marginal returns—each new worker contributes less marginal product and, therefore, less MRPL.

The number of workers demanded will depend on the wage rate in relation to the MRPL. Assume that the wage rate is $40 per day. Would it make sense for the firm to hire the fifth worker? The additional cost to the firm is $40, but the additional revenue is $640. Therefore, the firm would be wise to hire the fifth worker. What about the sixth worker? The additional cost is again $40 and the MRPL is $320, so the firm would again hire another worker. Looking at the schedule in Figure 9.1, you may safely conclude that this firm will continue to add workers up to and including the ninth worker, who contributes as much revenue as costs. This worker would cost the firm $40 and generate an additional $40 in revenue. Any additional worker leading up to that ninth worker adds more revenue than they cost. If the 8.9th worker adds $40.01 in revenue, that worker still contributes more revenue than she or he costs. Thus, firms will hire additional workers as long as the MRPL they provide is greater than the wage rate, leading to an equilibrium where MRPL is equal to the wage rate.

What if the wage rate were to change? If the wage rate rises to $80, the firm would hire eight workers. If it were $160, it would hire seven workers. As the price of labour goes up, the quantity of workers demanded by the firm decreases. Plotting the quantity of workers demanded by the firm against the different possible wage rates results in the individual firm's demand curve for labour, which is graphed in Figure 9.2.

FIGURE 9.2
One firm's demand curve for pizza labour
This curve shows the number of workers demanded by a firm at each possible wage rate.

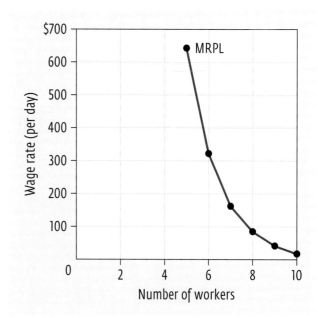

labour demand curve
A graphical representation of
the relationship between the
quantity of labour demanded
and the wage rate.

MARKET DEMAND FOR LABOUR

To derive the market demand curve for "pizza labour," it is necessary to add
together the quantity of labour demanded by each firm in the pizza industry at
each of the possible wage rates. Assuming that there are 20 identical pizza firms
in the industry, we have constructed the market demand schedule for pizza
labour in Figure 9.3. When graphed, this schedule reflects the market demand
curve for pizza labour (see Figure 9.4). It shows the total number of workers that
would be demanded at each wage rate. The market **labour demand curve**, then, is
the quantity of labour demanded by all firms in an industry for a particular type
of labour at each of the possible wage rates.

FIGURE 9.4
Market demand curve for pizza labour
This curve shows the number of workers demanded in the
industry at each possible wage rate.

FIGURE 9.3
Market demand schedule for pizza labour if the
market had 20 identical firms

Wage Rate (per day)	Firms 1–20: Units of Labour (per firm)	Total Units of Labour Demanded (# of workers)
$640	5 × 20	100
$320	6 × 20	120
$160	7 × 20	140
$80	8 × 20	160
$40	9 × 20	180
$20	10 × 20	200

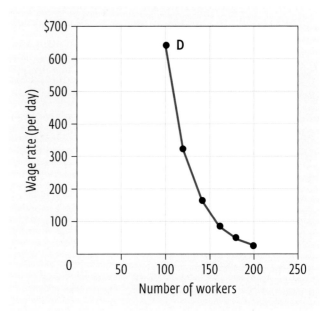

CHANGES IN LABOUR DEMAND

The labour demand curve illustrates the change in quantity demanded as the price of labour changes, *ceteris paribus* ("other things being equal"). As other factors in the market change, however, the labour demand curve is subject to shifts. The labour demand curve shifts primarily as a result of the three factors discussed next.

A Change in the Demand for the Product of Labour

Because the demand for labour is derived from the demand for the product the labour is producing, it makes sense that a shift in the demand curve for the product will lead to a shift in the demand curve for workers involved in its production. If the demand for automobiles increases, a corresponding increase occurs in the demand for automobile workers. This occurs because an increase in demand for a product leads to a higher equilibrium price for that product. The higher equilibrium price for the product means that the same output now has a higher MRPL. The result is a shift to the right of the labour demand curve because firms will hire more workers at each wage rate. Conversely, a decrease in the demand for automobiles will result in a decrease in the demand for automobile workers.

A Change in the Price of Related Productive Resources

In the construction of our demand curve for labour at Paolo's Pizza Place, we assumed that there were no other inputs. In reality, however, most products require inputs from land, labour, and capital. Capital is usually considered to be a substitute for labour. For example, an automobile manufacturer might choose to produce automobiles primarily using capital goods (such as robotic equipment) or manual labour. If the price of robotic equipment increases relative to the price of labour, the demand for labour will increase. Because labour is now relatively cheaper when compared with capital goods, it will be substituted in the production process. On the other hand, as the price of capital goods decreases, the demand for labour decreases. The price of land inputs (or raw materials) can be considered complementary to labour. If the price of raw materials increases, production costs will go up. If production costs increase, less output is produced, and the demand for labour will see a decrease. On the other hand, a decrease in the price of raw materials will lead to an increase in the demand for labour.

A Change in Worker Productivity

As workers become more productive—in other words, as they increase their marginal product of labour—the demand for labour will increase. This occurs because as each worker produces more output, his or her MRPL is higher. An increase in productivity can come from a number of sources. The introduction of more or better capital goods will help workers become more efficient, producing more output per worker. Better worker training and improved worker management both have the potential to increase worker productivity and, therefore, the demand for labour. Once again, the opposite effect is also possible. A decrease in worker productivity leads to a decrease in the demand for labour.

Self-Reflect

1 Explain the difference between direct demand and derived demand.

2 How is marginal product related to the hiring of workers?

3 Why does a firm seek to equate its marginal revenue product of labour with the market wage rate?

4 Explain what the term *productivity* means and why an improvement in productivity shifts the labour demand curve.

5 List the three factors that shift the labour demand curve and provide an example of each.

labour supply curve
A graphical representation of the relationship between the wage rate and the number of people willing to offer their services in the form of labour.

Market Supply of Labour

The market **labour supply curve** shows the number of people willing to offer their services to firms in an industry at each of the possible wage rates. The opportunity cost of working is the value of what individuals could have earned doing something else in the same time, or the value they place on their leisure time. As the wage rate increases and becomes greater than the opportunity cost for more individuals, more of these individuals are willing to offer their services in the labour market. Therefore, at higher wage rates, the quantity of labour supplied is greater, and, as a result, the labour supply curve is upward sloping.

Other factors influence the labour supply curve. The specific skills needed for certain jobs restrict some people from offering their services for labour in some markets. For example, most people cannot offer their services as a medical doctor because special skills must be learned before one can practise medicine. On the other hand, few special skills are necessary to stock grocery store shelves, so more individuals can offer their services at any given wage rate.

The geographical location of a market is also a factor. Labour markets that are in large population centres tend to have a greater quantity of labour supplied at each wage rate than those that are in more isolated areas. Jobs that are deemed unpleasant, distasteful, or dangerous also tend to have fewer people willing to offer their services. For this reason, it must be understood that when we talk about labour markets, we are really talking about many different markets. These markets are influenced by the specific characteristics of the job, the skills necessary for performing the job, and the location in which the job is to be performed.

CHANGES IN LABOUR SUPPLY

The factors discussed in the preceding section tend to be relatively stable over time. Changes in these factors will shift the labour supply curve. However, oil drilling tends to occur in markets that are away from large population centres, and firefighting is dangerous—these characteristics are *unlikely* to change. The basic nature of these jobs means that the labour supply curve is farther to the left than in markets where these restrictions do not exist. Several other variables do cause shifts in the labour supply curve, as the following sections indicate.

Factors that influence the supply of labour for high-voltage-wire workers include the fact that the job requires special skills and is dangerous.

Changes in Income Tax Rates

An increase in income tax rates means that the government takes away a greater proportion of wages earned; the effect is the same as if the employer were to pay a lower wage rate. This increase leads to a reduction in the supply of labour, shifting the supply curve to the left. Likewise, a decrease in income tax rates leads to an increase in the supply of labour, shifting the supply curve to the right.

Changes in the Size and Composition of the Population

As the population increases or decreases, the relative number of people available to offer their services at a given wage rate also increases or decreases. The amount of immigration can shift the supply of labour in many job markets. Supply can also be influenced by the age distribution of the population. In the early twenty-first century, concerns arose about the aging workforce and the fact that, as people retire, there will not be enough skilled workers to replace them—effectively decreasing the supply of labour. An increase in the workforce, then, shifts the labour supply curve to the right, and a decrease in the workforce shifts the curve to the left.

Changes in the Price of Complementary Goods and Services

Sometimes, additional costs are associated with supplying labour to the market. In deciding whether to work, people consider factors such as the cost of child care, household maintenance, and transportation. If, for example, the cost of child care increases, it becomes more expensive to participate in the labour market, and some people will withdraw from the market, reducing the labour supply.

Change in Barriers to Entry

Barriers to entry are costs or other obstacles that make it difficult to enter a particular market. For example, if new licensing requirements are introduced in a market, the supply of labour in that market will be affected. Imagine that new legislation requires transport truck drivers to complete extensive and expensive mandatory training to be able to obtain a licence. Some will view the training as a barrier and choose another career path. As a result, the supply of labour in this job market will decrease.

Changes in Attitudes about Roles

Another factor that has tended to increase the supply of labour over time is changing attitudes about roles in society. For a long time, the role of women was seen to be in the household and not in the labour force. Over the past 120 years, these attitudes have steadily changed. According to Status of Women Canada, a federal government agency, in 1901, women made up 15 percent of the labour force. A century later, in 1999, this figure had risen to 46 percent. This change has shifted the labour supply curve to the right. Conversely, in the late nineteenth century and early twentieth century, child labour was frequently used in manufacturing. As attitudes changed and laws were created that applied age restrictions to the use of labour, the labour supply was decreased, shifting the labour supply curve to the left.

Self-Reflect

1 What is the opportunity cost of someone offering his or her labour skills in the workplace?

2 What factors tend to restrict labour supply?

3 Why does a change in income tax rates shift the labour supply curve?

4 How has the changing role of women in Canadian society over the last 120 years affected labour supply?

Wage Determination

Equilibrium in the labour market is attained when the amount of labour supplied by households is equal to the quantity of labour demanded by firms. If the wage rate is too low, a shortage of labour occurs because the quantity demanded exceeds the quantity supplied. Firms will tend to offer higher wages to attract workers, pushing the wage rate higher and encouraging a greater quantity of labour to be supplied. If the wage rate is too high, a surplus occurs because the quantity of labour supplied exceeds the quantity demanded. In this case, workers who are willing to offer their services for less will tend to drive down the wage rate. The rate tends to stabilize at a wage rate for which there is no shortage or surplus, and the market is therefore in equilibrium. In Figure 9.5, the market for pizza labour is in equilibrium when the wage rate is $160 per day and 140 workers are employed. Because Paolo's Pizza Place is only one small firm in a perfectly competitive market, it must accept the wage rate that is set by the labour market—$160 per day. As a result, according to its labour demand curve in Figure 9.1, Paolo will hire seven workers.

FIGURE 9.5

Market equilibrium in the pizza labour market

The equilibrium wage rate is established by the intersection of the labour demand curve (D) and the labour supply curve (S). In the market for pizza labour, firms will hire a total of 140 workers at a wage rate of $160 per day.

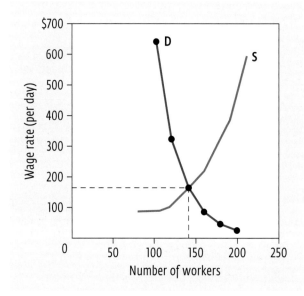

WAGE DIFFERENTIALS

Wage differentials, or differences in wage rates among different labour markets, are a function of labour supply and demand. All the factors mentioned previously that determine supply and demand influence the wage rates in individual labour markets. Non-monetary benefits in certain jobs influence supply and demand as well. Factors such as length of vacations, hours of work, and working conditions must be factored into individual labour markets. Other "monetary" benefits such as availability of extended health care, sick leave, child-care provisions, and contributions to pension plans also need to be considered. This makes labour market analysis very complex, and a comparison of wages or salaries alone will not provide you with a complete picture. As we continue the analysis of wage differentials, it is important to consider that when talking about a "wage rate," we are actually considering all the forms of remuneration that are described above.

wage differentials
Differences in wage rates among different labour markets.

To simplify analysis of the labour market, jobs are often described as being "high skilled" or "low skilled." The reason for this distinction is that a significant factor in determining wage rates is often the level of training that a worker has received.

As Figure 9.6 shows, the supply curve for high-skilled labour (SHSL) is above that for low-skilled labour (SLSL). The vertical distance between the two curves is the difference in the wage rate required to compensate the high-skilled worker for obtaining the higher skill (often achieved through some post-secondary education or apprenticeship). The demand curve for high-skilled labour (DHSL) is also above the demand curve for low-skilled labour (DLSL), reflecting the higher marginal revenue product (or productivity) of high-skilled labour. This results in higher equilibrium wage rates for high-skilled workers. The impact on earnings from investing in education can be seen in Figure 9.7.

FIGURE 9.6
The equilibrium wage rate for high-skilled labour is higher than that for low-skilled labour
The vertical difference between the low-skilled and high-skilled curves is due to the value that is placed on attaining the skill.

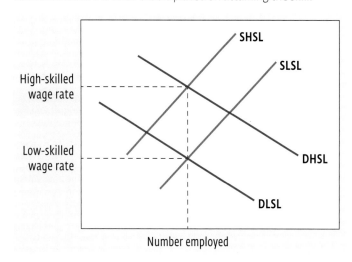

FIGURE 9.7
Average annual earnings by highest level of education completed in Canada (2015)

Level of Study Completed	Average Full-Time Earnings (2015)
No certificate, diploma, or degree	$25 345
High school diploma or equivalence certificate	$33 830
Certificate of apprenticeship or qualification	$54 060
College, CEGEP, or other non-university certificate or diploma	$45 652
Bachelor's degree	$62 363
University certificate, diploma, or degree above bachelor level	$79 010
Canadian Average	**$46 057**

human capital

The knowledge, skills, and talents possessed by workers.

Essential Skills

Skills defined by Employment and Social Development Canada that people require if they are to learn, work, and live.

HUMAN CAPITAL

Human capital refers to the knowledge, skills, and talents that workers have, either through education or by nature. Education is an investment in human capital, just as purchasing a computer is an investment in capital goods. Both help to improve efficiency and output in the productive process.

Employment and Social Development Canada (ESDC) provides useful information for those who want to be adequately prepared for today's job market. Knowledge about the kinds of skills that employers will be looking for, as well as where to obtain these skills, is invaluable because the rules that applied even just a decade ago are much different from those that apply today.

ESDC identifies a set of "**Essential Skills**" that people require if they are to learn, work, and live (see Figure 9.8). Note that many of these skills are interconnected and reflect the speed with which both technology and information change in today's economy. Adaptability and willingness to integrate new information and technology are vital in the economy of the twenty-first century. Radical changes in elementary, secondary, and post-secondary education have been occurring all over North America and very closely reflect the change in the skills that are required for success in the modern workplace.

FIGURE 9.8

Skills considered essential in the modern workplace

Skill	Description
Reading Text	The ability to scan, read, and understand complex sentences and paragraphs in the form of notes, letters, memos, manuals, specifications, regulations, books, reports, or journals.
Document Use	The ability to interpret and understand documents that include information in a variety of forms, including words, numbers, icons, graphics, tables, lists, graphs, and schematics.
Writing	The ability to communicate using words, numbers, and symbols in forms, such as memos, letters, notes, and reports; this also includes using tools for writing, such as computers.
Numeracy	The ability to use numbers for numerical calculation and estimation in money, measurement, budgeting, scheduling, and analysis of data.
Oral Communication	The ability to use speech to exchange thoughts and information in complex ways and through a variety of modes, such as greeting people, persuading, and speeches and presentations, in both small and large groups.
Thinking Skills	The ability to conduct independent cognitive skills, such as problem solving, decision making, critical thinking, task planning and organizing, use of memory, and researching information.
Working with Others	The ability to work with others in carrying out tasks, the self-discipline to meet targets while working independently, and the ability to participate in supervisory or leadership activities.
Computer Use	The ability to use computers and other forms of technology to complete workplace tasks.
Continuous Learning	The ability to learn, to understand one's own learning style, and to gain access to a variety of materials and learning opportunities to continually upgrade skills and knowledge about your occupation.

DID YOU KNOW?

According to the Organisation for Economic Co-operation and Development's *Education at a Glance 2017* report, in 2014 Canadian university graduates with a bachelor's degree earned $1.41 for every $1.00 earned by those with only a high school diploma.

FIGURE 9.9

The story of two students graduating from high school in the same year

Max enters the workforce, while Ashley enrols in an engineering program. The rate of return on investing in an education as an electrical engineer estimates the annual monetary return on the cost of the investment.

	Ashley	Max
Educational/work choice	Ashley goes to university to become an electrical engineer.	Max has a high school diploma. The average income for a worker (15 to 24 years old) with a high school diploma (if full-time work can be found) is $29 455. (The average income for all workers of all ages in this group is $13 708.)
Annual costs	Annual costs are $61 564: $32 109 for tuition, books, and living expenses plus earnings lost by not entering the labour market (that is, $29 455). The total "cost" of a four-year honours degree in engineering is $246 256 ($61 564 × 4 years).	Annual costs: Living expenses.
Total lifetime income	As an electrical engineer, Ashley is expected to earn on average $85 000 per year or $3 655 000 over her 43-year working life, from age 23 to 65.	As a high school graduate, Max is expected to earn $1 938 951 over his 46-year working life, from age 19 to 65 (average income for group age 25 to 65 is $42 981).
Net benefit	Ashley will earn $1 716 049 more in lifetime employment income than Max.	
Rate of return on post-secondary education*	Ashley invested $246 256 and earned an additional $1 716 049—a 16.2% annual rate of return.	None.

* Net benefit ÷ Cost ÷ Years Working × 100

FIGURE 9.10

Unemployment rate by level of education completed in Canada (2016)

Level of Study Completed	Unemployment Rate (%) (2015)
No certificate, diploma, or degree	13.0
High school diploma or equivalence certificate	9.0
Certificate of apprenticeship or qualification	6.6
College, CEGEP, or other non-university certificate or diploma	5.7
Bachelor's degree	5.4
University certificate, diploma, or degree above bachelor level	5.0
Canadian Average	**7.1**

Individuals invest in their own education in the hopes of making themselves more marketable in the future. They want to be able to offer their services in a specific area of the labour market where the demand for labour is high, while the supply of labour is low, and thereby obtain a higher wage rate. Firms also invest in human capital through on-the-job training, in-service training, and supporting further formal education for their employees in the hopes of raising productivity and thereby improving the marginal physical product of labour. Governments invest in human capital through subsidizing public education, some post-secondary education, and numerous job-training programs because improved efficiency expands the productive capacity of the economy and promotes economic growth. The impact of investing in one's own human capital can be seen in both its influence on lifetime employment earnings (see Figure 9.9) and the likelihood of being able to find a job (see Figure 9.10).

Self-Reflect

1 Why does a labour shortage tend to push wages higher?

2 Besides wages, what forms of compensation need to be considered as part of labour-market analysis?

3 Explain why the labour supply curve for high-skilled labour is above that of low-skilled labour.

4 Provide three examples of investing in human capital.

labour union

A workers' organization that negotiates with employers and promotes the interests of its members.

trade unions (or craft unions)

Unions that represent workers in a single occupation.

industrial unions

Unions that represent all workers in a given industry, regardless of the type of job they do.

public sector unions

Unions representing workers employed by governments.

collective bargaining

A process whereby a union negotiates wages and working conditions with the employer on behalf of all members of the union.

collective agreement

A contract lasting a specific period of time, negotiated by a union with the employer through the process of collective bargaining.

DID YOU KNOW?

Over the last 30 years, unionization rates have tended to fall in most industrialized countries. Between 1985 and 2015, Canada's rate fell from 36 to 29 percent; France, from 13 to 8 percent; Germany, from 34 to 18 percent; United Kingdom, from 45 to 24 percent; and the United States, from 17 to 10 percent. Canada's higher unionization rate is associated with the high rate of unionization in the public sector.

Labour Unions

A chapter on labour economics would not be complete without addressing the role of labour unions in the labour market. Approximately 28 percent of workers in Canada were members of labour unions in 2017. A **labour union** is an organization of workers that collectively promotes the interests of its members and negotiates with their employers. While it is true that one role it plays affects the wage rate of union members, a union does much more than this. Unions have been responsible for shaping labour relations, laws, and working conditions in Canada over the past 170 years.

The three most common types of unions are trade unions, industrial unions, and public sector unions.

Trade unions, also known as **craft unions**, represent workers in a single occupation, regardless of where they work. An example of a trade union is the International Brotherhood of Electrical Workers. Trade unions are very common in the construction industry.

Industrial unions represent all workers in an industry, regardless of the job that they perform. Historically, an example of an industrial union was the Canadian Auto Workers (CAW), which represented workers in the automobile industry, whether they were on the assembly line or sweeping the shop floor. Like many industrial unions, the CAW expanded its membership outside the original industry in which it was established. In 2013, it merged with the Communications, Energy and Paperworkers Union of Canada, giving birth to Unifor. Unifor represents over 300 000 workers across Canada in communication, transportation, manufacturing, resource, and service industries.

Finally, **public sector unions** represent workers who are employed by any of the levels of government in Canada. Two of the biggest unions in Canada are public sector unions: the Public Service Alliance of Canada (PSAC) and the Canadian Union of Public Employees (CUPE). Public sector unions began to develop throughout the 1960s as the services provided by government began to grow.

COLLECTIVE BARGAINING

In 1943, the federal government passed legislation that restricted when unions could strike in exchange for the legal requirement that employers must negotiate an agreement on wages and working conditions with a union, if a majority of workers voluntarily agreed to have the union represent them. Prior to this, the role of unions in the workplace was often volatile. Strikes occurred for all sorts of reasons: day-to-day disputes with management, perceived mistreatment of individual workers, and general strikes against employers.

The process of reaching an agreement is known as **collective bargaining**, and the contract that is negotiated is known as the **collective agreement**, which usually lasts for a period of one to three years. This agreement outlines the responsibility of both employees and employers concerning wages, vacations, job safety, fringe benefits, training, job security, hours of work, and grievance procedures (the process by which alleged violations of the collective agreement are settled between a company and its workers).

Another element that is negotiated in the collective agreement is the union's security clause. The union seeks to enrol as many workers as possible from each workplace. Not only is there strength in numbers, but members also give the union a source of revenue—union dues—with which to finance its operations. **Union dues** are an amount of money that each member of the union pays to support the union's activities. The three most common types of union security clauses in Canada are the open shop, closed shop, and union shop.

In an **open shop**, union membership is voluntary. In a **closed shop**, the employer may only hire workers who are already members of the union. This is more common in trade unions, where there is an element of skilled-trade training, such as apprenticeship, controlled by the union. A **union shop** is somewhere between an open shop and a closed shop. In a union shop, an employer may hire whomever it wishes, but after some sort of probationary period, the employee is required to join the union. Almost half of collective agreements in Canada involve a union shop.

A breakthrough for unions and their security came in a 1945 arbitration decision resolving a dispute between Ford Motor Company of Canada and its workers. Mr. Justice Ivan Rand ruled that all workers in the workplace were required to pay union dues whether or not they were members of the union. The company was responsible for deducting these dues and remitting them to the union. This was because all workers, union members or not, benefited from the collective-bargaining activities of the union. As a result, most Canadian industries now use some version of what is known as the **Rand Formula**.

Labour law is generally a provincial matter, so regulations vary from province to province, but all provinces have regulations that govern the process of collective bargaining. Most of the time, the union and the employer begin to negotiate a new collective agreement well before the old one has expired. If an agreement is not reached between the two parties, the old agreement continues to remain in force while further attempts are made to reach a new agreement. If an agreement cannot be reached, there are several options.

Conciliation (or mediation) occurs when a third party is brought in to help both parties find a middle ground. Usually, some form of conciliation or mediation is required before a strike or lockout can occur. If conciliation or mediation fails, the parties may submit their dispute for voluntary arbitration. In **voluntary arbitration,** both sides agree to have a third party, who acts as a judge, decide which position is fairer. The arbitrator does not seek a compromise but chooses only one side in an effort to get both parties to submit their most realistic proposals. Both parties must then abide by the decision. Occasionally, parties are forced to submit to **compulsory arbitration**, in which the government orders the two parties to submit their disputes to an arbitrator. This action is sometimes taken when a strike would be so disruptive to the general public that the government considers it undesirable.

union dues
The amount of money that each member of a union pays to support its activities.

open shop
A clause in the collective agreement between a union and an employer that allows union membership to be voluntary.

closed shop
A clause in the collective agreement between a union and an employer stipulating that the employer may hire only union members.

union shop
A workplace where all employees, upon being hired, must become union members.

Rand Formula
A 1945 ruling stating that all workers in a workplace in which a union exists and bargains for all workers must pay union dues, even if they are not union members.

conciliaton (or mediation)
A process in which a third party helps a union and an employer reach an agreement.

voluntary arbitration
A process during a labour dispute in which the parties agree to submit proposals to a third party who is given the power to decide which proposal, the union's or the employer's, is fairer.

compulsory arbitration
A process in which a government forces both sides in a labour dispute to accept the decision of a third party.

strike

A temporary work stoppage by employees to force their employer to accept the union's contract demands.

lockout

The shutting down of the workplace by an employer to force the union to accept the employer's contract offer.

rotating strike

A union strategy, used when an employer has several workplaces, of withdrawing services for a short time from each workplace on a rotating basis.

work-to-rule

A union tactic of performing only the duties required in the contract, and not extra work carried out voluntarily or after hours.

boycott

A union tactic of bringing pressure upon an employer by encouraging the public not to purchase the employer's product.

Canadian Labour Congress

A federation of Canadian unions, which lobbies the federal government on labour legislation and other social and economic policies affecting workers.

DID YOU KNOW?

The 1919 Winnipeg General Strike was the largest general strike in Canadian history. Employees across a wide variety of sectors, including tradesmen, factory workers, police, firefighters, and telephone operators walked off their jobs demanding collective bargaining, improved wages, and better working conditions. A month into the strike, intervention by government troops trying to end the work stoppage led to 30 casualties and one death in an event known as "Bloody Saturday."

JOB ACTIONS

Contrary to popular belief, the majority of collective agreements are settled without a strike or lockout. In the period between 1984 and 2014, over 90 percent of collective agreements in Canada were achieved without a strike or lockout. Sometimes, however, the union and the employer are unable to find common ground, and each side uses the tools at their disposal in an attempt to force the other's hand.

Probably the most well-known tool is the union's use of a strike. A **strike** is a temporary work stoppage by employees, designed to force an employer to meet the union's contractual demands. A strike can occur only after a majority of workers have approved of this action and only after certain conditions have been met, such as the expiry of the old collective agreement and the use of conciliation or mediation. An equivalent tool from the perspective of the employer is the lockout. A **lockout** occurs when an employer shuts down the place of employment to force workers to accept its contract offer. The use of either strike or lockout is uncommon, but the threat of both provides incentive for the two parties to conduct successful negotiations.

The costs of both strategies are high. As well as direct costs, such as the lost wages employees suffer and the lost output resulting in lost sales and profits for the employer, there are indirect costs. Other related industries are often affected by strikes. For example, a strike at an auto parts manufacturing company may force an independent automobile producer that relies on these parts to lay off workers because it is unable to obtain materials to continue its own production. Another indirect cost is that borne by consumers, who are unable to obtain a good or service that they desire because a strike or lockout has stopped production. As a result, unions often use several other strategies before a strike is considered.

One such strategy is a **rotating strike**, which is usually used when the employer has several different work sites. Instead of having all workers withdraw their services, the union organizes the withdrawal of services at individual work sites on a rotating basis, usually for a period of a day or two. The advantage to this strategy is that it causes disruption to the employer but limits the impact on union members in terms of lost pay.

Another strategy is the use of **work-to-rule**, where employees perform only the duties specifically stated in their contracts. This tool is particularly effective when employees find that they perform a lot of work after hours or in other situations (for example, when employee goodwill in the past has resulted in workers taking on many duties not specifically stated in the collective agreement).

Finally, a union may encourage a **boycott** of the employer's product by the members of other unions and the public. In a boycott, people are asked not to purchase the product produced by the employer. In so doing, the union is hoping to lower sales to a point that lost revenues encourage the employer to reconsider its position.

INFLUENCE OF UNIONS

Unionization in Canada peaked at 36 percent of workers in 1985 and fell to 28 percent in 2017. The decline of union membership in Canada over the past several decades is due to many factors. Among them, Canada has shifted from a manufacturing economy to an information economy with more professional services that tend to be less unionized. The perception of non-unionized stakeholders also plays a role. There is often resentment when a labour disruption inconveniences people for the benefit of what appears to be a small segment of workers in the economy. There is also the perception that unions protect bad workers and hamper business productivity. Finally, there is a broader perception that many things unions used to fight for—safe working conditions, minimum wages, and reasonable work hours—are now legislated, and therefore the need for unions has disappeared.

Many of the current labour laws that we take for granted are in place largely because of the role of unions in achieving them. Minimum wages, parental leaves, pensions, workplace sexual harassment laws, health and safety standards, statutory holidays, worker injury compensation, and laws preventing unjust dismissal are the result of the actions of organized labour and likely would not exist without them. Much of this general activity has been pursued by large federations of unions working together, such as the **Canadian Labour Congress**, which lobbies the federal government, and the Newfoundland and Labrador Federation of Labour and the Ontario Federation of Labour, which lobby their respective provincial governments.

Unions continue to evolve in the face of a changing economy. This evolution has led to a more co-operative role with employers in improving workplace productivity and solving workplace problems. They also fight to maintain many of the gains described above and to address the continued problem of working-class poverty at the margins of Canadian society. Studies have demonstrated that higher rates of unionization tend to reduce poverty in both unionized and non-unionized households, further demonstrating the spillover effect that union achievements tend to have for many in the economy.

This quilt by Laurie Swim, *Breaking Ground, The Hogg's Hollow Disaster*, 1960, commemorates the tragic events of 1960, when five Italian immigrant workers in Toronto were killed while digging a subway tunnel that collapsed. This tragedy spurred unions to fight for reforms to occupational health and safety in Ontario and led to the passage of the Industrial Safety Act, which was the foundation for the occupational health and safety part of the Canada Labour Code.

Self-Reflect

1 Explain the difference between a trade union and an industrial union.

2 List the items that are negotiated through collective bargaining.

3 What is the Rand Formula, and why is it important to unions?

4 What kind of help is available to unions and employers if they cannot reach a collective agreement on their own?

5 Besides a strike, what tools are available to a union to place pressure on an employer when negotiating a collective agreement?

Thinking like an Economist

Analyzing a Public Policy Issue: Conflicting Stakeholder Views on Unions

A lot of debate surrounds the role that unions play and whether they benefit society. Because the role of unions is defined by government legislation, their existence is a public policy issue. A **public policy issue** is a matter that impacts members of a society that the government oversees through its positions, actions, and laws.

To analyze a public policy issue, economists use a decision-making model like that used by an individual (see the *Thinking like an Economist* feature in Chapter 1). They assess the costs and benefits of different choices. The major difference is that a public policy issue has costs and benefits that affect a significant proportion of the population, either directly or indirectly. In this kind of analysis, each stakeholder needs to be identified, and the relative value of the costs and benefits of each choice must be considered for each stakeholder.

The steps that follow are taken in the analysis.

❶ Define the Issue

Should unions exist to protect the needs and interests of workers?

❷ Identify the Stakeholder Groups and Criteria

Workers

- Health and safety
- Wages and benefits
- Job security

Producers

- Economic freedom
- Allocative efficiency and freedom
- Impact on profit
- Long-term planning

Consumers

- Cost of goods and services
- Impact on delivery of goods and services

❸ Analyze the Choices

Two options are presented in Figure 9.12 and Figure 9.13, respectively. The figures detail the costs and benefits of each option. Refer to the assessment scale in Figure 9.11 to assess the costs and benefits of each option.

❹ Conclusion

Unions should continue to be used to protect the needs and interests of workers, as the score of +4 is higher than the score of +1 for allowing a free market to operate.

APPLYING ECONOMIC THINKING

1   Review the cost-benefit analysis shown here. Do you agree with the weighting of the criteria? Explain your opinion. If you do not agree, re-weight the criteria. How does this re-weighting affect the final decision?

2   Should other stakeholders or criteria be considered? If so, factor this new information into the cost-benefit analysis.

3   Consider a third option: "Eliminate unions and allow the government to take on the role of unions as another 'social welfare' responsibility." You now need to add another stakeholder, establish the criteria for this stakeholder, and re-evaluate the decision.

FIGURE 9.11
An assessment scale for cost-benefit analysis

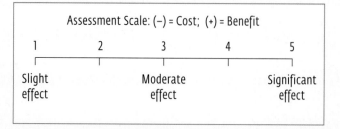

FIGURE 9.12

An example of a cost-benefit analysis

Option 1: Allow unions to operate in labour markets.

	Workers	Producers	Consumers
Costs	• Jobs lost as higher wages are negotiated (–4) • Individual freedom to seek better pay from employer is limited (–4) • Have to pay union dues (–2)	• Reduced profit levels may decrease sustainability of enterprise (–5) • Tough to replace or discipline less productive workers (–5) • Adversarial process may promote hostility instead of co-operation (–3)	• Price inflation triggered as a result of increased operating expenses being passed on to consumers (–3) • Work stoppages disrupt delivery of goods and services (–2)
Benefits	• More equitable income distribution (+5) • Healthier and safer working conditions (+5) • Seniority rights provide workers with greater job security (+3) • Provides guaranteed advocate and clear rules (+5)	• Because of wage increases, some workers command more goods and services, which increases demand (+4) • Long-term contracts allow for long-term planning (+3) • Provides clear rules and formal dispute process (+5)	• Higher wages for unionized workers have spillover effect raising wages for non-union workers—ability to consume more (+2)
Total	+8	–1	–3
Overall Total	+4		

FIGURE 9.13

An example of a cost-benefit analysis

Option 2: Allow the free market to work without outside interference of unions.

	Workers	Producers	Consumers
Costs	• Current regulations protect workers, but there would be no force in place to assure regulations remain (–4) • Income differentials between high- and low-skilled labour will increase (–4) • Employer may terminate an employee without just cause (–5)	• Unpredictable job action by workers could interfere with efficient production (–4)	• Work stoppages could still disrupt goods and services and would be more unpredictable (–4) • Lower wages in general leads to less ability to purchase goods and services (–3)
Benefits	• Increased employee freedom in negotiating (+4) • Individual performance may have greater influence on wage and promotions (+3)	• Ability to terminate workers who are not efficient (+5) • Long-term planning of wage costs is more reliable (+4) • More control over wage costs could lead to higher profit (+5)	• Impact of wage inflation would be limited by market forces (+1) • Prices of goods may decrease with lower associated wage costs (+3)
Total	–6	+10	–3
Overall Total	+1		

outsourcing
The practice of moving some internal business operations to third-party firms to save on costs.

offshoring
A geographical business activity that takes advantage of lower costs of production in other countries by outsourcing parts of the production process.

Changing Labour Markets and Economics

Earlier in this chapter, we examined how different factors affect individual labour markets through the labour supply and demand curves. Some changes are the result of trends in globalization and technology, and these trends have a general impact on the labour market as a whole. Two of these trends are outsourcing and the development of the "gig economy."

OUTSOURCING

Outsourcing describes the practice of moving some internal business operations to a third-party firm. These segments of the business may be either operational, such as manufacturing, or supportive of operations, such as accounting services.

Companies engage in outsourcing because it allows them to focus on parts of the business at which they are relatively more efficient, while having another firm provide support in its area of specialization. Outsourcing provides cost savings that lead to higher profits.

By itself, the practice of outsourcing has a limited effect on overall employment in a country. Because the cost savings are often the result of higher productivity, in theory the task that is being performed leads to higher wages for workers because there is a higher marginal revenue product of labour. There is a rightward shift of the labour demand curve, as described on page 157. This shift increases both the wages and the number of workers demanded in that labour market. The savings for the company comes in the form of increased output per worker. The cheaper per-unit cost of the "outsourced" good or service leads to a higher quantity demanded for that good or service, which creates more employment opportunities in the labour market.

Offshoring

As international trade barriers decreased over the 1960s and 1970s, outsourcing was combined with relocating certain business processes offshore. **Offshoring** is a geographical business activity that takes advantage of lower costs of production in other countries. The cost savings come in many forms. Lower expenses in the form of taxes, land costs, and the cost of complying with local environmental and labour regulations play a role, as do lower labour costs. Originally, offshoring focused on manufacturing as companies tapped into big pools of labour in countries such as China, India, and Mexico that had large populations and low wages.

In essence, the businesses doing the offshoring add to the labour supply curve by "importing" a huge pool of workers to engage in part of the production process. However, offshoring creates downward pressure on wages and a loss of employment in the country doing the offshoring. This effect is reflected in the offshoring of manufacturing operations by Canada and the United States in the 1980s and 1990s. Offshoring led to depressed wages in manufacturing in both countries, a shift to more service-oriented economies, and the movement of workers to different sectors of employment.

Technological improvements in telecommunications in the 1990s and 2000s have made service industry work more mobile: the transportation costs for information have fallen to almost zero. This has led to the offshoring of business services such as email servers, payroll, marketing, and accounting. The provision of some customer-service operations, such as call centres and customer support lines, has also seen an increase in offshoring, as has the diagnostic interpretation of medical imaging, such as X-rays and magnetic resonance imaging (MRI) scans, and the transcribing of legal and medical documents.

Concerns about Offshoring

Criticism of offshoring comes in different forms. The first is the concern about depressed wages and the loss of jobs that occur in the country that outsources production. While there is some legitimacy to this concern, studies indicate that these effects are mitigated by several factors:

- *An increase in productivity in the home country:* A study published by the London School of Economics' Centre for Economic Performance concluded that job losses in the home country as a result of offshoring are offset by job increases in the home country due to improvements in productivity that lead to a bigger domestic "economic pie." However, these job increases are not necessarily spread equally among industries, so one sector might see significant job losses, while others might see significant job growth. This is why a flexible workforce that knows how to learn and adapt is so important.

- *International market expansion:* The process of offshoring can also strengthen relationships between countries and, therefore, provide a bigger foreign market for goods produced by businesses. The product being produced offshore is not limited to sale within the home country of the business doing the offshoring. It is also sold in international markets, which can increase the workforce in parts of the business that are not offshored (for example, sales and marketing).

- *Lower wage differentials over time:* As the demand for workers increases in offshore labour markets, there is a corresponding increase in their wage rates. Therefore, wage differentials between countries do not produce the same cost savings for businesses that they used to, making offshoring less attractive.

A second and significant criticism is that offshoring causes harm to the environment and workers in the countries where offshored work is done. It is believed that many businesses use offshoring to save on the costs associated with laws that protect the environment and working conditions in their home country. In countries where offshored work is done, typically environmental and labour laws are not as stringent in comparison with those of the home country.

Around the world, several incidents related to worker health and safety prompted companies to rethink their use of offshoring. A 2012 factory fire in Bangladesh that killed 117 workers was linked to Walmart through a subcontractor that used the factory to manufacture clothes without Walmart's knowledge. The factory had been cited numerous times for safety concerns, including the absence of a fire-suppression system. This event was followed by a building collapse in

DID YOU KNOW?

Offshoring is sometimes called "global labour arbitrage." In economics and finance, *arbitrage* is the term used to describe the practice of buying and selling currency or commodities in different markets to take advantage of the price differences that exist between two markets.

gig economy
A shift in the labour market that sees firms using more freelance workers and independent contractors instead of full-time employees.

2013 that killed over 1 100 workers, also in Bangladesh, where it was discovered that clothes with the "Joe Fresh" label were being produced for Loblaws by a subcontractor. In both cases, the third-party subcontractors were in violation of standards set by the parent company, but the negative publicity associated with their brand was a problem for Walmart and Loblaws. As these examples demonstrate, significant issues can exist when outsourcing parts of a company's production process to another country.

Many businesses are beginning to "re-shore" some of their previously offshored processes. As savings in labour costs as a result of offshoring become less significant, and consumers hold businesses more accountable for ensuring that their products are produced using acceptable safety standards and fair wage practices internationally, offshoring becomes less desirable.

THE GIG ECONOMY

The "**gig economy**" refers to a labour market in which firms are using more freelance workers and independent contractors instead of full-time employees. "Gigs" have a beginning and an end that are defined by a task over a period of time. They may exist for a few years, months, weeks, or even minutes. As a result, workers are faced with a market that includes more temporary jobs, a situation often referred to as "precarious employment."

As an economic issue, the existence of the gig economy is not so much that it is new as how it is changing. Contract work in many forms has existed for a long time. Tradespeople hired for a specific building project is one example; a wedding photographer hired for that special day is another; and contract instructors hired by the semester as enrolment numbers at colleges and universities change from year to year is yet another.

The difference today is that contract hiring is expanding as a means of achieving a more agile workforce without providing full-time wages and benefits to employees. For example, a 2017 labour dispute between Ontario colleges and their faculty resulted in a five-week strike that was centred around the use of part-time contract instructors who had grown to represent 70 percent of the instructional workforce.

The Internet and the Gig Economy

The gig economy is also expanding into new areas, as Internet-based firms offer services using employees that work on a gig basis. The most well-known of these firms is Uber. Uber is a ride-sharing service that arranges rides-for-hire using a smartphone app. Each ride is a "gig." Uber drivers are not considered employees of the firm. As such, the firm pays them no salary or benefits. The driver is also responsible for all the expenses related to providing rides. Uber provides the technological infrastructure for customers and drivers to match up and receives a percentage of the price of the ride. As of 2017, Uber had 16 000 permanent employees internationally, but the rest of its "workforce" consists of 3 million drivers who are not considered employees.

Many new "Uber-type" companies deliver services over the Internet. Examples include TaskRabbit (a company that connects people for the completion of specific tasks, such as mowing the lawn, shopping, assembling furniture, or packing to move), Postmates (a delivery service for dry cleaning, groceries, meals, or anything else you can think of), and HelloTech (a company that installs, sets up, and repairs electronics and computers). Other companies provide ways for traditional firms to find short-term labour, such as Freelancer (a website that allows independent service providers to bid on projects) and Wonolo (an app where employers can seek workers to fill hourly or daily jobs, referred to as "on-demand staffing").

Impact on the Workforce

The gig economy has a number of benefits. Gig workers have a considerable amount of independence, because they have more freedom and flexibility regarding when and how they work. Many feel that they are in a better position to pick and choose assignments, in contrast to being told what to do by a permanent employer. This economy also provides young workers with opportunities to discover what kind of jobs interest them and to experiment and gain experience with different people and companies. In addition, it makes it easier for older workers to transition into retirement by moving to more casual work. Many gig workers report that they feel more ownership over their work because they are not closely supervised, and they achieve more personal satisfaction from their work.

The gig economy also has a number of drawbacks, however. A lot of potential gig opportunities exist, but finding work stability is a challenge because many workers compete regularly for the same gigs. Moreover, the jobs workers are able to do may not always be available. Worker selection for gigs is often based on Internet reviews provided by previous customers. This means that workers are constantly worried about maintaining ratings. The precarious nature of the gig economy has a serious impact on the mental health of those in the labour market, with many reporting feelings of depression and anxiety. The lack of regular contact with other workers, as is found in most traditional workplaces, can make these workers feel isolated and without guidance when they need to make decisions. Gig workers don't have sick leave, a dental plan, or pension benefits. Gaps between gigs can lead to periods without income and make it difficult to qualify for traditional financing sources, such as mortgages. The inconsistent income can also make it difficult to plan for the future.

The degree to which the gig economy impacts the labour market is tough to assess, because it operates largely outside of traditional measures for the labour market. Estimates suggest that between 10 and 30 percent of the labour force are involved in freelance work of some sort. Some pushback is occurring. For example, the question of whether Uber drivers should be classified as "employees" has given rise to considerable debate. When people are not employees, companies do not collect employment insurance premiums or provide legal benefits such as maternity leave or minimum wages. One of the challenges for governments is how to respond to the gig economy in areas such as tax collection and labour laws (which include health and safety regulations).

This Uber Eats courier is an example of the gig economy in action.

Self-Reflect

1 Explain the difference between outsourcing and offshoring and how the two terms are related.

2 How does offshoring impact the labour supply curve?

3 Why have many firms begun to "re-shore" some of their business arrangements?

4 What is the "gig economy," and how has the Internet had a role in shaping it?

5 Describe some of the drawbacks associated with the gig economy.

Chapter 9
Consolidation Activities

KNOWLEDGE

1 What evidence has been provided in this chapter to suggest that the level of education you attain plays a significant role in your ability to make a living in the twenty-first century?

2 List some of the benefits available to all Canadian workers due, in part, to the role of unions.

3 What advice would you give a friend who wants to have a high-paying occupation in the future? Provide your friend with several different options based on your knowledge of labour markets.

4 Describe the three different kinds of union security clauses that exist in a collective agreement and explain which you think is preferable to the union and which is preferable to the employer.

THINKING & INQUIRY

5 Lawyers receive a higher hourly wage rate than retail store workers. What factors contribute to this higher wage rate? Explain your answer using supply and demand curve analysis.

6 The right to strike is a controversial one. Many people believe that some workers are "essential" and, therefore, should not have the right to strike.

   a) Make a list of occupations that you believe are essential and should, therefore, not have the right to strike. For each occupation, state why you believe it is essential.

   b) How do you think these essential workers should resolve differences they have with their employers when negotiating a collective agreement? Can you see any issues of unfairness that might exist in your solution? Explain.

   c) Use the Internet to research the ministry responsible for labour in your province. What services does the ministry list as essential? What mechanisms does it have in place to help workers reach fair collective agreements?

7 Refer to Figure 9.8 and make a table with two columns. In the left column list the Essential Skills identified by Employment and Social Development Canada. Choose a course that you are currently taking in school. In the right column, beside each of the Essential Skills that you identified, list an assignment or activity from your course that is encouraging you to develop the skill and explain how it is developing the skill.

8 Use the Internet to find out the meaning of "right-to-work" legislation, which exists in many states in the United States. How does it relate to the Rand Formula in Canada? What impact does "right-to-work" have on wage levels and union membership? Are right-to-work laws fair? Take a position and list some arguments in support of your position.

9 Choose a service that is available through an app on a smartphone. Create a brief profile of the company. Your profile should describe the platform of the app, explaining the service and how it matches sellers and consumers. List the benefits and drawbacks of becoming a service provider through the app. Would you consider using the app to offer your services? Explain why.

COMMUNICATION

10 Consult the website of the ministry responsible for labour in your province. From this site, choose an element of the labour market that the government regulates. Write an information brochure for the public that explains the purpose of the government's involvement, the regulation(s), the impact that it has on workers, and what workers should do if they feel they are not being treated fairly. Include a list of definitions, if appropriate. Here are some suggested topics: minimum

wage; parental/pregnancy leave; public holidays; termination and severance pay; vacations; sexual harassment; hours of work and overtime; a particular health and safety measure; a regulation governing unions, such as how to unionize a workplace; and student workers.

11 Choose a specific union or federation of labour. Investigate its website to examine one

of its current policy goals. Complete a cost-benefit analysis that evaluates the impact of implementing the policy. You need to identify the stakeholders and criteria against which to judge the impact of the policy. Write a one-page report that explains this concern and your opinion as to whether or not its achievement is a desirable outcome.

APPLICATION

12 Figure 9.14 displays the production schedule for Risa's Silk Shirt Company. If Risa's shirts sell for $25 each and the workers can be hired in a competitive labour market for $100 each per day, how many workers should be hired? What if the wage rate in the market were to rise to $200 per day due to a decrease in the supply of workers? Clearly explain your answers.

FIGURE 9.14
Production schedule, Risa's Silk Shirt Company

Number of Workers	Total Shirts per Day
0	0
1	10
2	18
3	24
4	28
5	30
6	32

13 Using supply and demand curves, explain the impact of each of the following events on the wage rate in the labour market for landscape workers:

a) The federal government lowers personal income tax rates.

b) A new trend for "natural gardens" that require no maintenance is promoted by gardening magazines.

c) New innovations in leaf blowers and lawn mowers allow workers to become more efficient.

d) A new high-tech automated robotic lawn mower is introduced. Its cost is cheaper than that of labour.

e) The cost of gasoline, disposal bags, and rakes rises.

f) The government increases the minimum age for employment from 16 to 18 years.

15 Refer to Figure 9.15 and answer the following questions.

FIGURE 9.15
Supply and demand for taxi drivers

Number of Drivers Demanded	Hourly Wage	Number of Drivers Supplied
1 000	$15.00	300
900	$16.00	400
800	$17.00	500
700	$18.00	600
600	$19.00	700
500	$20.00	800
400	$21.00	900
300	$22.00	1 000

a) Graph the supply and demand curves for taxi drivers.

b) What is the equilibrium wage, and how many workers would be hired at this wage?

c) Explain two factors that might shift the labour demand curve to the right. What would be the impact on the wage rate?

d) Explain two factors that might shift the labour supply curve to the right. What would be the impact on the wage rate?

e) If the government instituted a minimum wage of $20 per hour, how would this change the employment situation in the taxi driver labour market?

16 It is sometimes argued that labour unions, by demanding wages higher than the market equilibrium wage rate, sometimes hurt their members more than they help them. Using labour supply and demand curves, explain this reasoning.

10

Production, Firms, and the Market

INTRODUCTION

One key function of any economic system is to provide goods and services to satisfy wants and needs. In Chapter 3, we learned that all economic systems must answer three basic questions to achieve this goal: What to produce? How to produce? and For whom to produce? In a market economy, largely determined by free competition among businesses, private companies play a very large role in the production and sale of goods and services. In Canada's mixed market economy, the government also takes part by providing some goods and services funded by tax dollars. In this chapter, we will investigate the *theory of the firm* to understand how businesses determine what they will produce and sell, as well as how they will produce it. We will explore this thinking by considering diverse market conditions and different types of markets with varying degrees of competition.

LEARNING GOALS

Once you have completed this chapter, you should be able to:

- Determine how much to produce of a product and the best way to do it
- Explain the importance of the role profit plays in production decisions
- Understand the nature and importance of productivity and efficiency
- Identify the importance and nature of competition in different markets
- Understand the economic thinking behind a firm's plan to maximize profit

KEY TERMS

explicit costs

implicit costs

economic profit

firm

efficiency

cost per unit

unit labour cost

gross domestic product (GDP)

labour-intensive production

capital-intensive production

technology-intensive production

economies of scale

collusion

social (third-party) costs

regulation

accounting profit

theory of the firm

total revenue

total cost

fixed costs

variable costs

short run

long run

marginal cost

marginal revenue

non-price competition

black market

perfect competition

monopolistic competition

product differentiation

oligopoly

monopoly

copyright law

patent law

natural monopoly

deregulation

privatization

Production Choices and Issues

THE IMPORTANCE OF PROFIT: HOW FIRMS THINK

Businesses use production to process and transform economic resources into goods and/or services with economic value. The resources used in production (land, labour, capital, and entrepreneurship) are called *inputs*. These inputs are processed to produce *outputs*; the quantity of a good or service that results from the production process. Society depends on these goods and services that are produced by firms. The firm is a business that sells its goods or services for a profit, and its main objective is to maximize its profit. What is profit? Profit is the difference between the amount of revenue gained by a business over the expenses, costs, and taxes of operating the business. The profit formula is as follows:

$$\text{Total profit} = \text{Total revenue} - \text{Total costs}$$

Since the goal for the firm is to maximize profit, it can do so by maximizing its total revenue and minimizing its total costs. The greater the difference between total revenue and total costs, the greater the profit.

It is important to note that economists view profit differently from accountants. Take for example the following situation: After graduating from school, you decide to invest all of your savings, $20 000, to start your own business. In your first year of business, you sold $100 000 worth of goods and incurred $75 000 in total costs. Was your business profitable? Accountants would say that you earned a profit. Why?

$$\text{Accounting profit} = \text{Total revenue} - \text{Total costs}$$
$$= \$100\,000 - \$75\,000$$
$$= \$25\,000$$

Accountants would say that you earned a profit of $25 000 in your first year because they consider only the **explicit costs** of your business (costs that appear on a business's accounting statements, such as payment for material, machines, rent, utilities, and taxes).

Economists, however, would disagree. Why? Remember the concept of opportunity cost in Chapter 2? Opportunity cost is the sum of what is lost in making one decision over another. Economists consider these **implicit costs** (costs not included among expenses on the income statement of a business firm), such as the amount of an owner's time spent devoted to his or her business and the money invested in the business that could have earned interest if invested somewhere else.

In this case, what was the opportunity cost for running your own business? What could you have earned working elsewhere? Perhaps you could have worked full time for another business earning $40 000 a year. How about that money you invested in your business? You could have invested your savings in a bond, for example, at 5 percent interest and earned $1 000 on your savings.

Economists consider opportunity cost when calculating profit and, more specifically, implicit costs. In this case, your **economic profit** would be as follows:

$$\text{Economic profit} = \text{Total revenue} - (\text{Explicit costs} + \text{Implicit costs})$$
$$= \$100\ 000 - (\$75\ 000 + \$40\ 000 + 1\ 000)$$
$$= \$100\ 000 - \$116\ 000$$
$$= -\$16\ 000$$

As you can see, economists would say that you were not profitable in your first year because of your implicit costs—that is, the opportunity cost of what you could have earned in working for another company and the interest you gave up on your savings that were invested in the business. Therefore, in comparing accounting profit to economic profit, we see that economists consider implicit costs, or opportunity costs, when calculating profit.

$$\text{Accounting profit} = \text{Total revenue} - \text{Explicit costs}$$

$$\text{Economic profit} = \text{Total revenue} - (\text{Explicit costs} + \text{Implicit costs})$$

By considering explicit and implicit costs, you are thinking like an economist when calculating the profitability of a business.

PRODUCTION CHOICES

Controlling the Costs of Production

Consumer demand, as we have learned, plays a major role in determining market price and total sales—the two factors that determine total revenue for a business enterprise. Since many businesses have little control over the total revenue they receive in a market, they focus their efforts on controlling production costs. The company, business, or **firm** that is able to produce the desired product at the lowest possible cost has the best chance of maximizing profits. This is why *productivity* (maximizing the output from the resources used) and **efficiency** (producing at the lowest possible cost) are of such importance to a firm. Competition in the marketplace contributes to uncertainty. For this reason, some businesses try to limit competition.

Output per worker is the most common measure of productivity. A great many factors influence productivity. The skills, education, and experience of the workforce are important; so are the quantity and quality of the resources with which labour works. A factory with machinery that is continually breaking down will produce less than a factory with state-of-the-art machinery. How the work is organized is also important. When a firm improves its productivity (but does not increase its costs), it can produce more goods and services for the same cost. Consequently, it can offer its goods or services at a lower price, making the firm more competitive. The same equation applies to an economy. When an economy becomes more productive, it can produce more for the same cost and can, therefore, offer its goods and services to other countries for a lower price. Increased productivity results in increased competitiveness.

economic profit
The excess of a business's revenue over its economic costs (implicit and explicit costs).

firm
A privately owned organization engaged in business activities.

efficiency
A firm's ability to produce at the lowest possible cost, measured by either its cost per unit or its unit labour cost.

cost per unit

A measure of a firm's efficiency, obtained by dividing total costs by the number of units produced.

unit labour cost

A measure of a firm's efficiency, obtained by dividing its total labour costs by the number of units it produces.

gross domestic product (GDP)

The total market value of all final goods and services produced by an economy in a given year.

The cost per unit of production and unit labour cost are the most common measures of efficiency when applied to either a firm or an economy. **Cost per unit** takes into account all costs incurred in creating a product. **Unit labour cost** measures only the cost of labour involved in producing one unit.

If the efficiency of a firm decreases—or if the efficiency of its competitors improves—the firm will be at a competitive disadvantage. Many Canadian businesses compete in a global marketplace. If unit labour costs in other countries decrease faster than they do in Canada—or at least increase at a slower rate—then Canada will be less competitive internationally and will lose both sales and profits.

Gross domestic product (GDP) per hour worked is a measure of labour productivity. It measures how efficiently labour input is combined with other factors of production and used in the production process. It is intended to give an overall view of measuring productivity between countries. For example, in Figure 10.1, Canada's GDP per hour worked is compared with that of the other G7 countries (a group of seven advanced democracies that meet annually to discuss and address global issues).

Competitiveness is ultimately determined market by market and company by company. Bombardier, a Canadian aerospace and transportation company, is one of the largest producers of transportation vehicles in the world. It would be in trouble if its competitors' production efficiency improved more rapidly than its own. Its international sales and profits would slump if its competitors' unit labour costs decreased more, or increased less, than its own.

Choosing Production Methods

With the goal of keeping production costs to a minimum, firms will try to produce goods or services in a way that makes the most productive use of available resources. Available resources will vary among countries, regions, industries, and individual firms. Firms will choose a mix of resources that will result in the most efficient method of production. For example, producers may use parts supplied by another company instead of producing all the parts themselves. This practice is very common in cellphone and automobile production.

FIGURE 10.1
GDP per hour worked for G7 countries (in 2010 USD)
How does Canada compare to other G7 members? What does this indicate about Canada's competitiveness?

Country	2012	2013	2014	2015	2016	2017
Canada	$101.60	$102.80	$105.40	$105.20	$105.90	$107.70
France	$101.09	$102.46	$103.43	$104.23	$104.27	$105.29
Japan	$101.17	$103.26	$103.34	$104.89	$105.18	—
Germany	$102.69	$103.49	$104.55	$105.16	$106.65	$107.60
Italy	$100.17	$101.09	$101.27	$101.52	$100.68	$101.15
United Kingdom	$99.79	$100.04	$100.21	$101.88	$101.32	$102.02
United States	$100.45	$100.67	$101.23	$101.97	$102.16	—

Many factors influence the choices made. In markets where labour is abundant and relatively inexpensive, some manufacturers may choose a **labour-intensive production** strategy (in which most work is conducted by hand). This traditional approach dates back to medieval times. Current examples include office-cleaning and house-painting businesses. In modern times, many firms have elected to employ the **capital-intensive production** of a mechanized factory system to produce their goods. Investors acquire production equipment and technology to automate and expedite the production process (for example, in automobile and electronics assembly industries). Some businesses in today's information age use **technology-intensive production** to specialize in high-tech products and services. Specific examples include medical research and pharmaceutical laboratories, such as Teva, and information technology software design and engineering facilities, such as Google.

Labour-intensive production gave way to the capital-intensive production of the factory system. This development made good economic sense because the capital investment in buildings and machinery made the labour force more productive and the production process more efficient. The drawback of switching to capital-intensive production was a sharp increase in fixed costs relative to variable costs. It became difficult to increase production in a boom or to decrease costs in bad times. Financial risks grew, but so did the potential for profit, thanks to economies of scale.

The concept of **economies of scale** refers to the greater efficiency that some firms can achieve when they produce a very large amount of output. While some firms may become less efficient owing to the law of diminishing returns (see Figure 2.7 on page 27), others may see their cost per unit drop sharply as output increases. This is particularly true of firms that produce in a capital-intensive way. This method of production has high fixed costs and lower variable costs. Increasing output allows a firm to spread its fixed costs over the increasing number of units produced, which rapidly reduces cost per unit produced. (For example, consider a firm that produces 200 units per month. If it pays $2 000 per month to rent its premises, the rental cost per unit is $10. If the company could increase production to 400 units per month, the rental cost per unit would drop to $5.) Other benefits are derived from the greater specialization of labour that is possible with large staff. Large firms also have more market power to negotiate better prices from their suppliers.

Firms in the private sector largely determine the economic question of "How to produce?" in a market economy. The decision-making process involves the artful acquisition and balancing of economic resources whose prices have been determined by resource markets. Resources must be blended and organized to avoid diminishing returns and maximize productivity at the lowest possible cost. To see how you can compare the costs of various production alternatives, see *Thinking like an Economist* on page 196.

labour-intensive production
Industry in which labour, rather than machinery, dominates the production process.

capital-intensive production
Production in which machinery rather than labour dominates the process, characteristic of the factory system.

technology-intensive production
Manufacturing goods or providing services that involve the extensive use of highly specialized technology, such as medical research laboratories and computer software design and engineering facilities.

economies of scale
The greater efficiency a firm can achieve when it produces very large amounts of output.

Quality-control workers inspect cookies on an automated assembly line. Compare the number of workers visible in this photo to the capital investment by the firm to determine the type of production being used. What issues might a government inspector raise?

collusion
An illegal agreement among competing firms to set prices, limit output, divide the market, or exclude other competitors.

social (third-party) costs
Production costs that are not paid by either the product's producer or consumer but passed on to others; for example, environmental pollution, garbage disposal, and resource depletion.

PRODUCTION ISSUES

What is the best way to produce goods and services to satisfy our needs? Should we rely on firms competing for profit in the market? What matters of public interest can we entrust to the marketplace? Should we depend on government to oversee matters? Are there other options?

Is Bigger Always Better?

In his book *The Wealth of Nations*, Adam Smith expressed his reservations about leaving things to competitors in private markets:

> *People of the same trade seldom meet together, even for merriment and diversion, but the conversation ends in a conspiracy against the public, or in some contrivance to raise prices.*—Book I, Chapter X

Smith is referring to the temptation of **collusion** among businesses, where firms conspire to influence market prices and sales in their favour. Smith would have had particular concerns about the production methods of modern industry. Capital-intensive production can be more efficient but also results in fewer, very large producers competing. As the number of competitors in a marketplace drops, Smith's "conspiracy . . . to raise prices" is more easily achieved. The benefits of efficient production and the economies of scale are more likely to go to the producer in the form of higher profits than to the consumer in the form of lower prices. When a few very large firms are involved, normal market behaviour may result in less competition, and without the pressure of competition to keep prices down, they can more easily float upward.

Third-Party Costs

Markets have flourished under capitalism, but that does not make them perfect. Even a market with many small, privately owned firms will not necessarily ensure that economic resources will be used efficiently. Profit-seeking producers try to reduce their costs of production to a minimum. Markets are not always good at internalizing or passing on all the costs of production to those who consume the product. Pollution is an example. When the wastes of production are released into the water, air, or soil rather than being properly treated as part of the production process, firms effectively pass on the environmental costs of production to others. These non-monetary costs are called **social costs** or **third-party costs**. The existence of these costs reflects a shortcoming of efficiency as a production objective. Achieving production efficiency by reducing the costs of production can lead to the destruction of scarce resources rather than their efficient use.

The Public–Private Balance

The Canadian government has also been found wanting as an efficient provider of goods and services. During the three decades after 1960, it expanded its role as a producer, particularly as a provider of essential services such as education and health care. Its enhanced role occurred partly in response to a growing population. It also stemmed partly from a widespread belief that government was able to satisfy essential needs better than markets and the private sector. By

1990, however, government spending seemed out of control. Annual deficits grew at alarming rates, and our accumulated public debt threatened the well-being of present and future generations.

During the 1990s and 2000s, the Canadian government cut its spending, its payroll, and its services. It downsized, privatized, and deregulated markets. It also cut its levels of social spending faster than the government of any other developed nation. In its haste, the Canadian government made mistakes.

Do governments make the right choices? Should governments invite more participation of private companies in the delivery of social programs such as health care? Should we be wary of transferring cherished social programs into the hands of firms, whose primary goal is profit?

Is Regulation the Answer?

Markets cannot exist without **regulations** that define contracts, protect private property and competition, and require certain production standards. Regulations must be effectively enforced. If markets don't work (for example, because of collusion), it may be because they are poorly regulated. If we are worried about involving more private business in the delivery of health care, perhaps regulation of the industry would help control the profit motive. If competition is not working or production is polluting, perhaps it is the regulations that need to change, not who is doing the producing. The Competition Act (1985) and other statutes control competition.

In Canada, regulation is a matter of public policy and decided by public debate. That debate should be based on the values we think are most important. Why might we regulate an industry? How best can our governments balance the need to make the business environment attractive (for example, with low taxes, low utility rates, and low safety or environmental standards) against the needs of citizens? We should also ask ourselves if the ways in which we produce goods and services can be better regulated to serve the ultimate needs of society.

Even with the perfect set of regulations, however, we should not expect the market to do more than it can. We want an economy that responds to our needs, but markets can only respond to demands. The difference between a need and a demand is the ability to pay the market's price. Only those who can pay will get a need satisfied by a market. Only money guarantees a choice.

If we don't like the idea that only wealthy people may be able to afford an education or health care—or a comfortable lifestyle—it is not an issue of production. It is an issue of distribution. The question to ask is not "How to produce?" but rather "For whom to produce?" Considerations of equity rather than efficiency may be more important. To what extent should production be distributed according to need rather than the ability to pay? Who should get what is provided, regardless of whether government or the private sector produces it? Organizing our scarce resources to provide goods and services that are efficiently produced and equitably consumed is a matter of public debate and regulation to which we can all contribute. It is our economic responsibility, as citizens, to address this issue, because we will enjoy the benefits or bear the costs that result.

regulation
Government rules that oversee, standardize, and control markets, industries, and business practices.

Self-Reflect

1 What is the best measure of a firm's competitiveness? Explain your answer.

2 Explain the difference between labour-intensive, capital-intensive, and technology-intensive production.

3 Define *implicit costs* and *explicit costs*. Provide two examples of each.

4 How does accounting profit differ from economic profit?

accounting profit
The excess of a firm's
revenues over its costs.

Firms

HOW FIRMS THINK: THE IMPORTANCE AND CALCULATION OF PROFIT

Key people within firms (owners, directors, managers) make the economic decisions about what and how much to produce, as well as about how to do it, all with the principal goal of helping the firm make a profit. In a small firm, one person may make all the decisions. In a large firm, decision making is delegated to a small group of executive managers with specialized training and experience. For example, one manager may handle suppliers, while another oversees the delivery of finished goods. This example illustrates Adam Smith's *division of labour* (see Chapter 5) in the realm of decision making, leading to better decisions and greater productivity.

Firms may make decisions for a wide variety of reasons, but all decisions should take into account what is commonly called "the bottom line." This expression originally referred to the last line of an accounting sheet, which shows whether a firm is taking a loss or earning an accounting profit. **Accounting profit** is what we usually think of and refer to simply as profit (that is, the excess of revenues over costs). This concept is important for decision makers in a firm because it tells them whether they can stay in business. Most firms attempt to maximize profit. Ultimately, all must at least break even; that is, they must cover their costs of production or cease to exist.

Profits are beneficial to a business's success for many reasons. For producers, profits act as an incentive and a reward for the work they do and the risks they take. Further, profits are the producer's least expensive source of money for expanding or improving production. Producers also use profits to evaluate how well their firm is doing by comparing their profits with those of their competitors.

Producers pay close attention to which of their product lines are selling the most and making the most profit. Depending on their assessment, they may shift resources to increase the production of goods and services that clearly meet the most urgent demands. Consequently, consumer choice improves, as does the company's profitability.

High profits also allow privately owned companies to pay dividends to their shareholders. Many shares in companies are owned by pension funds, insurance companies (which invest premiums for eventual payment on claims), and individuals purchasing stocks or mutual funds through their retirement savings plans. Therefore, when companies make profits, many people within the community benefit because their incomes grow.

THEORY OF THE FIRM

To understand how firms make decisions, we must analyze the relationship that exists between profits, revenues, and costs—a relationship sometimes referred to as the **theory of the firm**. The theory of the firm assumes that producers are all profit maximizers. Adam Smith's concept of the "invisible hand" of self-interest leads producers to increase their revenues and decrease their costs to increase their profits.

This theory may seem simple. Fortunately, a good deal of it is common sense that you already possess and intuitively use. All you have to do to understand the theory of the firm is to start thinking like a producer instead of as a consumer. The theory of the firm—the economic relationship that connects total profit, revenues, and costs—can be expressed in the simple equation of accounting profit:

$$\text{Total profit} = \text{Total revenue} - \text{Total costs}$$

Total Revenue

Total revenue refers to the money a firm receives from its sales. Only two factors influence how much that will be: the price you decide to charge and the quantity you can sell at that price. In other words, if you can sell 20 cookies for a dollar each, your total revenue will be $20. In greater detail, then, the economic formula that relates profit, revenue, and costs is as follows:

$$\text{Total profit} = (\text{Price} \times \text{Quantity sold}) - \text{Total costs}$$

To be profitable, a firm must be able to maximize its revenues. Before launching a new product, a firm's economic decision makers gather information from markets about how many people would probably purchase the potential product and at what price. In other words, they must determine—or estimate as accurately as possible—the demand for the product. Analyzing past spending patterns and predicting the impact of currently changing circumstances can help to determine consumer demand with reasonable accuracy.

Total Costs

The economic world is not always transparent. You might expect your firm to generate more revenue by specializing in selling higher-priced products. However, products with a high price don't necessarily mean greater profit. A high price may simply reflect a higher cost of production, or it may discourage sales. To determine profitability, firms must gather information about production costs.

A firm's **total cost** of production refers to the money the firm spends to purchase the productive resources it needs to produce its good or service. This money includes all payments a firm must make to its suppliers, employees, landlords, bankers, and so on.

When economists analyze the production decisions of firms, they divide cost into two basic categories: fixed costs and variable costs. **Fixed costs** are those that remain the same at all levels of output. They must be paid whether or not the firm produces. Fixed costs include rent, property taxes, insurance premiums, and interest on loans. For example, a bakery has to pay off the loan for a new gas oven, no matter how many sales it makes. Fixed costs are difficult to adjust in the short term. They are often referred to as *overhead costs*.

theory of the firm
The relationships that exist between a firm's revenues, costs, and profits.

total revenue
The price of a product multiplied by the quantity demanded of the product.

total cost
The total of a firm's fixed and variable costs, which includes all the purchases made by a firm for productive resources to produce a good or service.

fixed costs
Costs (such as rent and property taxes) that remain the same at all levels of output and must be paid whether the firm produces or not.

variable costs
Costs that change or vary with the level of output, such as labour and raw materials.

short run
A time period in which the firm's maximum capacity is fixed by the shortage of at least one resource.

long run
A time period in which the firm can adjust both its fixed and variable costs to increase its maximum capacity.

Variable costs, such as those associated with labour, fuel, raw materials, and power, are relatively flexible. They change with the level of production. As production increases, it becomes necessary to employ more resources, such as labour and raw materials, so these costs tend to rise as production rises. The bakery with the new gas oven will have a higher gas bill as its level of production increases. Variable costs are often targets for "emergency" cutbacks. For example, should sales at the bakery drop suddenly, the baker might think of laying off a part-time counter person. The baker might have to work longer hours on Saturday afternoon, but at least the loan payment for the gas oven is paid. (For more examples of fixed and variable costs, see Figure 10.2.)

Thus, our equation showing the economic relationship among profit, revenue, and costs develops as follows:

$$\text{Total profit} = (\text{Price} \times \text{Quantity sold}) - (\text{Fixed costs} + \text{Variable costs})$$

After determining both revenue and costs, we can calculate potential profits. As a rule, the potential for profits is highest when selling prices are most favourable and combined costs are relatively low. Since firms cannot always count on influencing the market price upward, they must focus their profitability on the reduction of production costs.

FIGURE 10.2
Fixed and variable costs
What types of business would have higher fixed costs? Which would have higher variable costs?

Fixed Costs
Fixed costs must be paid and remain the same, whether or not production occurs.
Fixed costs are items such as: • Lease payments or rent for premises • Loan payments to a bank or lending institution • Property taxes • Payment of insurance premiums • Cost of security

Variable Costs
Variable costs are those that vary with the level of production; they tend to rise with an increase in production and fall with a decrease in production.
Variable costs are items such as: • Wages or salaries paid to labour • Costs of raw materials or inventory • Cost of electricity used for productive purposes • Costs of fuel, power, and transportation

The Short Run and the Long Run

Economists consider two different time periods when assessing the overall costs of a business: the short run and the long run. The **short run** is a period over which the firm's maximum capacity becomes fixed because of a shortage of at least one resource. The costs of some resources, such as labour, fuel, and raw materials, are relatively flexible and can be quickly adjusted. For example, assume that a printing company has purchased enough paper to keep its printing presses running at 80 percent capacity. Suddenly, it gets a new contract that requires it to expand production immediately. If it is able to quickly acquire the additional paper it needs, the paper is a short-run, or variable, cost and does not limit the firm's ability to expand production.

Some resources, however, cannot be quickly increased. For example, if the same printing company in the example above gets a new contract that far exceeds its current capacity. In this case, the printing company might have to build an addition to its factory to handle it. This addition would likely take months, if not years to complete. In this example, the **long run** refers to a period when all costs become variable, including plant capacity. Over the long run, a firm will be able to adjust not only labour, fuel, raw materials, and so on, but also its plant or factory facilities. In a firm's long run, there are no fixed costs of production. All costs become variable, from staffing to location. The long run is considered the planning period when the firm has enough time to enlarge its productive capacity, shift production to generate other goods or services, or, if necessary, shut down completely.

Marginal Revenue and Marginal Cost

When considering how to maximize profits, economists spend a lot of energy trying to determine the exact production level that will result in the most profit. These detailed calculations nearly always involve a consideration of the costs and benefits of making small changes in production. Marginal thinking involves thinking about producing one more or fewer product each time. Despite the detailed nature of the work, thinking "at the margin" is very important in a firm's profit calculations and, hence, its business strategy.

If a firm wishes to maximize its profit, it should always produce up to the point at which there is no added benefit (that is, profit) from producing any more. In other words, it should keep producing to the point at which the **marginal cost** (that is, additional cost) of producing one more unit equals the **marginal revenue** (that is, additional revenue) received from the unit's sale. At the point when the marginal cost *exceeds* the marginal revenue that results from producing one more unit, the firm would waste resources and reduce its profit.

Let's consider a dairy that specializes in goat cheese. The dairy is located near a dozen goat farmers, who regularly supply it with the goats' milk it requires to make cheese. Should the dairy decide to increase production, it would have to transport the additional milk from another area, requiring a sharp increase in transportation costs. If the additional revenue to be had from producing more goat cheese did not exceed the additional costs, the dairy would have no incentive to produce more.

A firm will maximize its profit (that is, make the most profit) by producing up to the point at which its marginal revenue equals its marginal cost. In highly competitive markets, marginal revenue is equal to the market price. The following equation sums up the concept:

Profits are maximized at a production level when
Marginal revenue = Marginal cost

marginal cost
The additional cost for a firm of producing one more unit of its product.

marginal revenue
The additional revenue gained by a firm from producing one more unit of its product.

Self-Reflect

1 List five reasons why profits are important.

2 Explain three factors that influence the amount of profit a firm can make in a market.

3 Use specific examples to distinguish between labour-intensive, capital-intensive, and technology-intensive production.

4 In your own words, distinguish between fixed and variable production costs and long- and short-run planning periods.

non-price competition
Competition among firms in areas other than price (for example, quality of product).

Firms, Competition, and the Market

Firms in the private sector consider many factors when determining the business strategies that will best serve their self-interest. Financial considerations related to profitability motivate all firms. As we learned earlier in this chapter, however, the ultimate purpose of all economic activity is not the profit of individual firms but the satisfaction of consumer needs. In this larger picture, both firms and profits are means to an end, not ends in themselves.

In Canada, we rely mainly on private firms operating in markets to produce the goods and services we need. A *market* is a group of buyers and sellers of a particular good or service. For example, the energy market consists of all firms that supply energy and all the individuals or companies to whom they sell energy. We rely on competition among producers to create choices for consumers and to keep prices down within markets. *Competition*, then, is the primary mechanism that ensures firms remain accountable to consumers as well as to their managers and owners.

Firms compete against one another in many ways. Price is one of the most obvious and significant areas of competition. A lower price will increase the sale of most products. Firms also engage in **non-price competition**—competition that involves changing anything but price. For example, firms compete on the basis of quality. Firms can compete by offering the best-built product, the latest style, or by delivering the most complete warranty and timely service. The competition for customers among firms in the market encourages the supply of good products at low prices. It also encourages firms to use their resources to produce new and better products and to do so more efficiently. However, not all markets are the same. In some, there is little competition or choice for consumers.

MARKET STRUCTURE

What factors influence the production decisions of large corporations such as Bell Canada, the Royal Bank, and Air Canada? Do the same factors affect the decisions of a small restaurant in rural Ontario? Clearly, a large corporation and a rural restaurant operate within different market structures. In every case, the structure of the industry or market in which a firm operates influences its decisions regarding price and output. The five factors that help to determine market structure are as follows:

1   The number (and size) of firms in the market

2   The degree to which competitors' products are similar

3   A firm's control over price

4   The ease with which firms can enter or leave the market

5   The amount of non-price competition

Most markets and industries can be classified into one of four basic market structures: perfect competition, monopolistic competition, oligopoly, and monopoly. Of these, perfect competition and monopoly represent opposite ends of the market spectrum. The other two structures represent benchmarks along this spectrum and characterize the conditions faced by most firms in the Canadian economy. This simple spectrum is illustrated in Figure 10.3. For a summary of the characteristics of these four types of market structures, see Figure 10.4.

Today, a growing number of Canadians participate in a **black market**. This term refers to market activities conducted within Canada's underground or hidden economy. People often do this to make business and personal transactions private and confidential or to avoid government interference, regulation, and taxation. For example, until the legalization of marijuana, many Canadians were forced to buy recreational marijuana from illegal suppliers in the underground economy. A few years before legalization, medical marijuana became available in licensed dispensaries, where product quality could be controlled for patients seeking relief from pain and seizures. This was done to create a "grey market" period to transition to legalization.

black market

The illegal exchange of goods in short supply, as when some people buy up as much of a good as possible, stockpile it, and sell it at a higher price.

FIGURE 10.3
Types of market structure

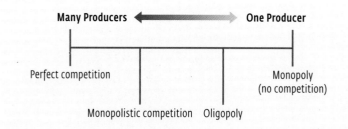

FIGURE 10.4
Characteristics of market structures

Characteristics	Perfect Competition	Monopolistic Competition	Oligopoly	Monopoly
Number and size of firms in the market	Large number of firms, but small in size	Many firms, but not large in size	Few firms, but large in size	One large firm
Degree of product similarity in the market	Identical products in the market	Product differentiation in the market (in quality, packaging, marketing, etc.)	Some product differentiation in the market	Unique product in the market
A firm's control over price	No control; a price taker	Some control; a price influencer	Significant control; informal collective pricing	Total control; a price maker
Ease with which firms can enter the market	No barriers to market	Some barriers to market	Many barriers to market	Almost total exclusion
Amount of non-price competition	Little (location sometimes)	Some (product quality, advertising, packaging)	Considerable (packaging, advertising, brand name)	Not much (public relations, advertising needed when close substitutes exist)

Perfect Competition

Perfect competition is characterized by many producers and a uniform product. For example, suppliers of agricultural goods operate within such a market. Farmers' markets are often used as the closest example of a perfectly competitive economic environment. The main characteristics of a perfectly competitive market are as follows:

1   There are many buyers and sellers in the market. There are so many sellers that individual firms have no control over total market supply or price.

2   All the firms sell a standardized product. Imagine a very long country road along which every second farmer has a stand selling the same produce: corn, peaches, and apples.

3   Producers must accept the market equilibrium price for their product. They can sell as much or as little as they choose at that price without changing it. They are price takers—they must take the market price—because individually they have no impact on total supply.

4   It is relatively easy to enter and exit the market. The start-up costs or the costs of leaving are not so great as to prevent firms from doing either one.

5   Because all firms sell the same product and each firm can sell as much or as little as it wants at the market price, there is little non-price competition among them.

The success of a firm in a perfectly competitive market depends entirely on how well it manages its costs. Decision making focuses entirely on reducing the cost per unit of production. Because the firm has no influence on price or total quantity sold, profitability depends entirely on making efficient use of the economy's scarce resources. Those firms that are the most efficient (that is, those that can maintain low costs) will be rewarded with profit. Achieving very low costs can work against a firm, however, because the large profits will attract more producers who, collectively, will increase supply and drive market prices and profits down. Such competitive pressure guarantees the lowest price to consumers with just enough profit for producers to keep them producing.

In reality, the perfectly competitive market does not exist, primarily because there are always some start-up costs and some use of non-price competition. The classic example of a group of producers that comes closest to being perfect competitors are wheat farmers. They produce an identical product, have no influence over the market price, and do not participate in non-price competition. Nonetheless, wheat farmers need huge amounts of capital to start up a new business, so there is a barrier to entering the market in a large way.

Monopolistic Competition

In most markets, some sellers compete with one another in different ways and with varying degrees of intensity. **Monopolistic competition** is characterized by many producers that can differentiate their products. The main characteristics of monopolistic competition are as follows:

1   A substantial number of firms compete in the market.

2   Firms sell a similar but not identical product.

3   Individual firms are large enough to influence total supply, and so they have some influence over price.

4   It is relatively easy for a new firm to start up.

5   Non-price competition is significant.

In the Canadian economy, monopolistically competitive markets are most prevalent in the service and retail sectors. As consumers, we shop in them frequently. Think of your favourite pizza parlour. It competes with several other pizza parlours. The competition might come in the form of a price war if each store attempts to increase its market share by offering lower prices and special deals. Competition might also include non-price factors. For example, each pizza parlour might try to differentiate itself from the rest by offering different benefits, such as guaranteed 15-minute delivery, gourmet toppings, thin-crust or deep-dish pizzas, and 24-hour service. Each pizza parlour might expand its product line or advertise its goods in various media. The drawback to such initiatives is that they have to be factored into the firm's production costs.

Monopolistically competitive markets are also relatively easy to enter and exit. Generally, the firms are fairly small. Economies of scale and capital requirements are limited. Firms must still distinguish their products from those of their competitors, which creates some financial barriers.

In monopolistically competitive markets (and in oligopolistic markets, about which you will read more in the next section), firms seek to distinguish their product or service from those of their competitors in some desirable way. They use a number of techniques to accomplish this **product differentiation**, as you can see in Figure 10.5.

When product differentiation is successful, it leads to something marketers call *brand loyalty*, a situation in which consumers become attached to a product and will pay more to satisfy that preference. Because of brand loyalty, successful firms in a monopolistically competitive market do have some control over price. Some consumers willingly pay more for jeans from a favourite designer or label. Are you one of them?

monopolistic competition
A market structure in which many small to medium-sized firms sell a differentiated product, each having some control over price.

product differentiation
The attempt by competing firms to distinguish their product in some desirable way from that of their competitors to gain greater control over price.

FIGURE 10.5
Approaches to product differentiation
Firms know that in a competitive market, they must somehow differentiate their goods or services from those of their competitors. What examples of product differentiation have you noticed?

Product Differentiation
❶ **Product quality:** Firms attempt to create physical or qualitative differences. Examples:
• Tender versus tough meat (at restaurants) • High-end computer hardware (in the home-computer business)
❷ **Services:** Firms offer special follow-up services surrounding the sale of a product. Examples:
• "Delivery in 15 minutes or your pizza's free!" • An extended warranty for a new automobile
❸ **Location and accessibility:** Firms choose locations convenient to their customers or stay open long hours. Examples:
• 24-hour stores • Locating a gas station on a busy highway rather than a rural route
❹ **Promotion and packaging:** Firms attempt to differentiate their products by packaging them in different ways or by advertising them. Examples:
• Glitzy packaging • Advertising with a celebrity endorsement

oligopoly

A market structure characterized by a few large firms, selling an identical or differentiated product, each with some to substantial control over price.

Oligopoly

If you made a list of the 10 best-known brand-name companies in Canada, you might mention Air Canada, Indigo, CIBC, Bell Canada, Petro-Canada, and Loblaws. All of these companies are oligopolists. They operate as huge firms in each of their respective markets. CIBC, for example, shares the market for financial services with just a few other chartered banks. The main characteristics of an **oligopoly** are as follows:

1 It is dominated by a few, very large firms.

2 Competing firms may produce products as similar as steel or as different as automobiles.

3 The firm's freedom to set price varies from slight to substantial.

4 Significant financial and other barriers exist to enter this industry.

5 Non-price competition can be intense.

Many consumers become frustrated as they watch competition play out among firms in an oligopoly. Their frustration comes from a sense of helplessness because oligopolies seem to raise and lower prices at will. Prices do move up or down, but competitors' prices all seem to move in exactly the same way at exactly the same time. Gasoline prices are an excellent example: they all go up at about the same time and then go down at about the same time. On occasion, observers suspect that a price conspiracy exists, and they demand that gasoline firms be investigated for illegal activity.

Further suspicion arises because prices for products in an oligopoly tend to stay within a particular range. For example, the service charges on your bank account will be pretty similar, no matter which bank you decide to trust with your savings. Similarly, all banks charge about the same rate of interest on funds borrowed on a credit card. Again, is there a conspiracy going on? Not necessarily. By shopping around for the lowest price, consumers push firms to compete on the basis of price. In a free-market economy, firms have the right to set prices at any level they see fit. A firm that sticks with a slightly higher price can lose a lot of business.

Nonetheless, a common pricing strategy among oligopolists may occur. Since there are few competitors, they may engage in collusion. It is illegal in Canada and the United States for firms to collude. One recent example occurred in the Canadian gasoline industry. Irving Oil owns more than 800 gas stations in Atlantic Canada, Quebec, and New England (in the United States). In 2012, Irving Oil and several other companies were charged with fixing gasoline prices in Victoriaville, Sherbrooke, and Thetford Mines, Quebec. In the end, 7 companies and 27 individuals pleaded guilty, paying a total of $3 million in fines and receiving a total of 54 months in jail time. Corporate giant Irving Oil maintained that it was unaware of the illegal activities.

Have you ever noticed that gasoline always seems more expensive just before a long weekend? Is it collusion, or is it just a consequence of high demand?

monopoly
A market structure in which one firm has complete control over supply, allowing it to set a profit-maximizing price.

copyright law
A law that protects the intellectual property rights of writers and the creative works of artists.

patent law
Laws that protect the rights of product inventors and developers by giving them the sole right to benefit from product sales for a set period of time.

Monopoly

The word *monopoly* comes from the Greek words *monos polein*, which mean "alone to sell." In a **monopoly**, one firm or organization enjoys complete control of the marketplace. The main characteristics of a monopoly are as follows:

1   It is a market completely dominated by a single firm having complete control over total supply.

2   The firm produces a unique product for which there are no close substitutes.

3   The firm is a price maker; that is, by changing supply it can set whatever price will maximize profits.

4   Major barriers to entry prevent other firms from entering the market.

5   Because there are no direct competitors, non-price competition is unnecessary.

A firm may establish a monopoly by gaining legal control of its product and the exclusive right to benefit from its sale. **Copyright law** gives writers control of the work they produce. **Patent law** protects the inventors and developers of a new product or technology by giving them the sole right to benefit from its sale for a period of time. Many a private firm owes its birth, growth, and profitability to patent protection.

NHL team owners in Toronto and Buffalo, for example, have a territorial monopoly on the game, and would not want a new team to be created in a neighbouring city.

Governments may also create at least a local monopoly by awarding the sole right to provide a product or service to one particular firm. The Canadian Radio-television and Telecommunications Commission (CRTC) awards exclusive rights of service to cable television providers in specific areas of Canada. Each provider then holds a monopoly in its area. (For example, Cogeco holds the right to service Kingston, but Rogers holds the right to service Ottawa.) In most cases, the CRTC must approve any price changes by cable television providers.

In a few cases, producers themselves may create a monopoly by selling exclusive franchises. Professional sports leagues are an example. Residents in the Hamilton, Ontario, area would probably love to have an NHL team in their city, but team owners in Toronto and especially Buffalo, New York, oppose such a move as an infringement to their territorial monopoly.

Monopolists are better able to produce large quantities of output. They have the financial resources and market exclusivity to assume the costs and risks of capital-intensive production and can achieve the efficiencies that come from economies of scale.

Some products, particularly those with high fixed costs, are more efficiently produced by a monopoly than by a few, or many, smaller producers. This type of monopoly is referred to as a **natural monopoly**. It is found most often in the field of public utilities (such as the generation, supply, and delivery of natural gas or electricity; local public transit; and water and sewer supply), where having more than one supplier would be impractical and wasteful. Imagine how wasteful it would be to have six different hydroelectricity lines available for your house to choose a service provider. With the high infrastructure costs of building six independent power lines, it is doubtful that the customer would see lower prices despite the increased competition.

Some markets that were once considered more efficient as natural monopolies are now being opened up for market competition through deregulation or privatization. **Deregulation** involves legally opening a market to more competition. This may be accomplished in a variety of ways. **Privatization** refers to one method of deregulation that involves, among other things, the sale of public assets to private firms.

Are monopolists better at producing goods at lower prices than perfect competitors? Check out *Thinking like an Economist*, which takes a close look at this question.

natural monopoly
A field with high fixed costs (such as public utilities) in which greater efficiencies result when one firm supplies the product or service.

deregulation
The opening of a market to more competition by eliminating government regulations originally put in place to limit competition.

privatization
The sale of public assets in a government enterprise to private firms.

Self-Reflect

1 Using Figure 10.4 as a guide, identify specific examples of firms in your local community that compete in each type of market structure.

2 Make a list of the ways firms engage in non-price competition.

3 Explain the differences between a firm that is a "price taker" and one that is a "price maker."

4 Monopolistic competition and oligopoly are often referred to as "imperfect competition." Compare and contrast the features of these two "imperfect" markets.

Thinking like an Economist

According to most economists, society is best served when the maximum number of goods is produced at the lowest possible prices. Which type of market structure, perfect competition or monopoly, is most likely to do this? Let's think through this question.

Maximizing Profit in Perfect Competition

Given the steady demand for organic eggs in your region, you have decided to enter the egg business. The regular price for a 10-dozen box of Grade A organic eggs is $50. This price has remained constant for the past five years, so you can count on receiving $50 for every box of eggs you bring to market. You can produce as much or as little as you choose at that price. Figure 10.6 presents your costs and revenues for producing different quantities of eggs.

Under these conditions, and assuming that you are a profit maximizer, you would probably want to determine how many eggs you should produce to make the most profit. In other words, you would like to determine when the marginal revenue equals the marginal cost, as described on page 187. Remember that in the case of perfect competition, the price you charge for the item stays constant at $50 per box. Therefore, your marginal revenue is fixed at $50.

FIGURE 10.6
The monthly cost of producing organic eggs

Level of Output (number of boxes produced)	Total Production Costs	Marginal Cost (for last extra box produced)	Total Revenue (boxes sold × $50)	Marginal Revenue (from last extra box produced)	Profit (total revenue − total costs)
0	$40	—	$0	—	$0 − $40 = −$40
1	$70	$30	$50	$50	$50 − $70 = −$20
2	$95	$25	$100	$50	$100 − $95 = $5
3	$125	$30	$150	$50	$150 − $125 = $25
4	$160	$35	$200	$50	$200 − $160 = $40
5	$200	$40	$250	$50	$250 − $200 = $50
6	$245	$45	$300	$50	$300 − $245 = $55
7	$300	$55	$350	$50	$350 − $300 = $50
8	$365	$65	$400	$50	$400 − $365 = $35
9	$440	$75	$450	$50	$450 − $440 = $10
10	$520	$80	$500	$50	$500 − $520 = −$20

APPLYING ECONOMIC THINKING

1   At what level of monthly production would you maximize your profit?

2   How does marginal revenue compare with marginal cost at this maximum profit point? In comparing these marginal figures, why would it not make sense to continue increasing production? Why would it not make sense to stop production before six boxes?

3   Study the graph in Figure 10.7 for the same data to identify the exact point where the marginal cost (MC) and marginal revenue (MR) curves meet. Why is MR$_1$ a straight, horizontal line?

The graph in Figure 10.7 presents the organic egg market from the point of view of the perfect competitor. Since the marginal revenue (MR$_1$) curve remains the same as the price, regardless of the amount produced, it is a straight, horizontal line marking the $50 market price. The marginal revenue curve cuts the marginal cost (MC) curve between the sixth and seventh unit of output at point A. This graph clearly demonstrates that the marginal cost of producing the seventh unit would be greater (by $5) than the additional revenue that could be earned. Producing more than Q$_1$, which is the quantity produced at the production level at point A, will reduce total profit, so there is no incentive to produce it.

FIGURE 10.7
The point of profit maximization for a perfect competitor
Under perfect competition, marginal revenue is equal to the market price.

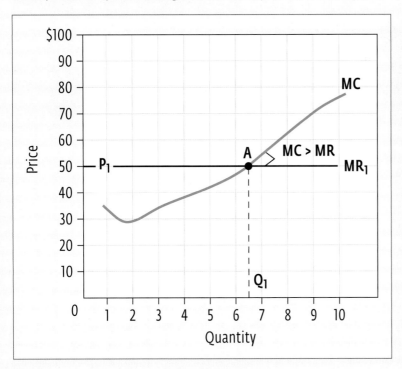

Thinking like an Economist

Maximizing Profit in Monopoly

Now, let's assume that you are the only licensed producer of organic eggs in Canada. In this situation, you are a monopoly. The consumers' interest and ability to pay will determine demand, and the price you can charge will vary depending on demand. Assume that the table in Figure 10.8 represents the consumer demand for organic eggs. We will keep numbers small to make them more manageable. Your production costs remain the same as in the previous example.

APPLYING ECONOMIC THINKING

1   Under these conditions, as a profit maximizer, how many boxes of eggs would you choose to produce to make the most profit possible in this monopoly market?

2   Does it pay to increase production beyond four boxes of eggs?

3   Compare Q_1 (the quantity transacted in the perfectly competitive market represented by Figure 10.7) with Q_2 in this monopoly graph (Figure 10.9). Which market provided the most goods for the lowest price? Compare the data tables in Figures 10.6 and 10.8 to determine which market provides the highest profits for producers.

FIGURE 10.8

The market demand, cost, and revenue data for the organic egg monopoly
As you lower the price you charge for a box of eggs, the quantity you sell increases because you attract more buyers.

Price Charged	Quantity Demanded (boxes)	Total Production Costs	Marginal Cost (for last extra box produced)	Total Revenue (boxes sold × selling price)	Marginal Revenue (from last extra box produced)	Profit (total revenue – total costs)
$100	1	$70	—	1 × $100 = $100	—	$100 – $70 = $30
$90	2	$95	$25	2 × $90 = $180	$80	$180 – $95 = $85
$80	3	$125	$30	3 × $80 = $240	$60	$240 – $125 = $115
$70	4	$160	$35	4 × $70 = $280	$40	$280 – $160 = $120
$60	5	$200	$40	5 × $60 = $300	$20	$300 – $200 = $100
$50	6	$245	$45	6 × $50 = $300	$0	$300 – $245 = $55
$40	7	$300	$55	7 × $40 = $280	–$20	$280 – $300 = –$20
$30	8	$365	$65	8 × 30 = $240	–$40	$240 – $365 = –$125
$20	9	$440	$75	9 × $20 = $180	–$60	$180 – $440 = –$260
$10	10	$520	$80	10 × $10 = $100	–$80	$100 – $520 = –$420

The graph in Figure 10.9 illustrates the difference between production in a perfectly competitive market and production in a monopoly market. The MC curve remains the same, but the new marginal revenue curve, MR_2, slopes downward and is closely related to the demand curve (red). This new MR_2 cuts the MC curve at a lower production level (at point B) at or near the fourth unit of output. Producing more than Q_2, which is the quantity produced at the production level at point B, would mean that marginal cost would exceed marginal revenue, thereby reducing total profit. The demand curve (D) has been added to illustrate how the reduction in quantity supplied will lead to a higher selling price, P_2.

Our investigations of maximizing profit in perfect competition and in monopoly confirm that, subject to certain conditions, perfect competition results in the highest efficiency. Intense competition forces firms to produce as much as possible and to offer these goods or services at the lowest possible price. However, the assumption that both types of producers have identical cost structures is rarely true.

FIGURE 10.9
The point of profit maximization for a monopoly compared with a perfectly competitive market

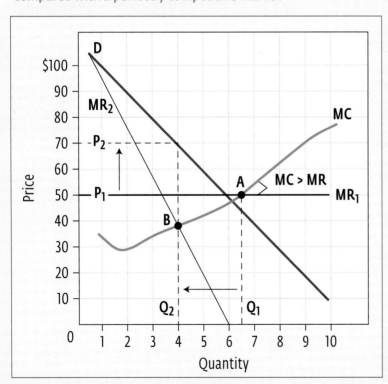

Chapter 10
Consolidation Activities

KNOWLEDGE

1 A firm's total revenue depends on the price it charges and the quantity it sells. However, the most profitable firm is not necessarily the one that charges the highest price or makes the most sales. Explain why.

2 Classify each of the following industries by type of market structure:

   a) Natural gas distribution

   b) Local telephone service

   c) Long-distance telephone service

   d) Internet service providers in large cities

   e) Internet service providers in small towns

   f) The garment industry

   g) Fast-food restaurants

   h) Nuclear-generated electricity

   i) Gold mining

   j) Wheat production

   k) Automobile manufacturing

   l) Steel production

3 Describe how firms use marginal analysis to determine how much of a product to produce, or how much of a service to provide.

THINKING & INQUIRY

4 Explain how competition holds firms and the managers who run them accountable to both the firm's owners (shareholders) and its customers.

5 Under what conditions would a firm continue producing in the short run even if it were experiencing a loss?

6 ABC Inc. is a bakery business that sells cakes online. Last year, the company sold 40 000 cakes at a price of $5 per unit. The total costs for the year consisted of $30 000 in rent, $50 000 in labour, $20 000 in materials, and $10 000 in miscellaneous costs. The owner of ABC Inc. gave up her job working at another company for $90 000 a year. She also invested her retirement savings in the business, which she believes could have earned $10 000 in interest during the year if it had been invested. Calculate ABC Inc.'s total revenue, accounting profit, and economic profit. Should the owner of ABC Inc. stay in business or go back to her previous job?

COMMUNICATION

7 Every firm is subject to significant government regulation. Interview a business operator in your community.

   a) Identify the different ways in which the particular business is regulated.

   b) Determine which regulations the operator would like changed and why.

   c) Identify any new or different regulations the operator wishes that government would introduce.

8 Select an interesting business in your community or region. Assume that you wished to start your own business to compete with it.

   a) Describe the barriers to entry that would make it challenging for you to get started.

   b) What argument would you use to persuade a friend to partner with you?

9 Create a concise study sheet to summarize the most important information about the *theory of the firm* to review prior to a test or exam.

10 Consider the question of whether oil companies are gouging Canadian consumers in today's market. Research newspaper and magazine articles online. Then write a concise opinion piece that answers the question, based on your analysis of research findings.

APPLICATION

11 Figure 10.10 illustrates a firm's cost schedule for its production of portable speakers.

FIGURE 10.10
A firm's cost schedule for production of portable speakers

Quantity Produced	Total Cost
0	$35
1	$59
2	$74
3	$96
4	$120
5	$155
6	$199
7	$245

a) What are this competitor's fixed costs of production?

b) Calculate the total variable costs of producing four portable speakers.

c) At which level of output is the firm operating most efficiently?

d) Why might a firm not always choose to produce portable speakers at the point that is most efficient?

e) What problem does the firm face? What would you recommend the firm do to overcome this problem?

f) What production decisions should this firm make if it could sell its portable speakers at each of the following price levels: (1) $40, (2) $30, and (3) $20? Explain your reasoning in each case.

12 Advertising is a form of non-price competition. Assume that the provincial milk marketing board conducts an expensive but successful "Milk Is Beautiful" campaign. How would such a campaign affect the market for milk in the province? Analyze its effect on demand and supply as well as *elasticity* (how sensitive quantity demanded and quantity supplied are to a change in price), and forecast the resulting change in market price and the quantity of milk consumed.

13 Select two or more competing firms at which you might shop in your community.

a) Describe the ways in which they compete against each other, and try to differentiate their goods or services.

b) Rank order the ways in which they compete, according to their effectiveness in influencing your buying decisions.

14 Typically, roads in Canada are built, maintained, and operated at public expense. Highway 407 north of Toronto was sold to a private firm, which now charges motorists a toll to use it. Should more roads be privatized and operated in this way? Assess the benefits and costs of this privatization and prepare a persuasive argument to support your position.

15 Some economists argue that product differentiation brings both an element of competition and an element of monopoly into a marketplace. From your experience, evaluate the validity of this claim.

11

Business Organization and Finance

INTRODUCTION

Large multinational corporations (companies with business ventures in various countries) have emerged as one of the most creative and powerful international institutions of the twentieth century. In this chapter, we will investigate corporations and other ways of organizing and financing business enterprises in Canada. Although some critics suggest that multinational corporations use their power and size to secure greater returns on their investments, others claim that their self-interest is no different from the behaviour of most other forms of business enterprise in the free-market system. Do you know of any multinational corporations? In what businesses are they engaged? What do you know about their corporate image?

LEARNING GOALS

Once you have completed this chapter, you should be able to:

- Describe the four types of industrial activity
- Describe the evolution of Canadian industry and the increasing concentration of corporate power in Canada
- Identify patterns in data to explain economic relationships
- Compare the different forms of business organization and finance (private and public) in Canada
- Explain the function of securities and commodities markets
- Conduct research to locate information from a variety of reliable sources to assess supply management strategies in Canadian agriculture and communicate recommendations clearly, effectively, and accurately

KEY TERMS

primary, secondary, tertiary, and quaternary industrial activity

high-tech industries

staple

firm

sole proprietorship

unlimited personal liability

progressive tax

partnership

partnership agreement

corporation

private corporation

public corporation

articles of incorporation

shares

shareholders

proxy

dividend

co-operative

patronage

government enterprise

privatize

Crown corporation

non-profit/charitable organization

merger

acquisition

horizontal integration

horizontal merger

vertical integration

holding company

conglomerate

corporate alliance

subsidiary

multinational corporation (MNC)

branch plant

bond

principal

asset value

book value

market value

stock market

stock exchange

Nasdaq

Nasdaq Composite Index

stockbroker

mutual fund

commodity

spot market

futures market

Dow Jones Industrial Average

blue-chip stock

S&P/TSX Composite Index

bear market

bull market

primary, secondary, tertiary, and quaternary industrial activity
Primary industries are those enterprises concerned with the harvesting or extraction of natural resources. Secondary industries are concerned with the manufacturing of marketable products. Tertiary industries are concerned with providing a marketable service. Quaternary industries are concerned with providing extremely specialized and high-tech services.

Types of Industrial Activity

All human industrial activity can be classified into one of four types, based on the nature of the activity, as demonstrated in Figure 11.1. **Primary industrial activity** involves harvesting or extracting natural resources (or raw materials). **Secondary industrial activity** (often called *manufacturing*) involves the processing of raw materials into final or semi-processed goods. **Tertiary industrial activity** involves the provision of services to businesses, institutions, households, or individuals to serve economic needs.

   Quaternary industrial activity consists of high-tech services provided to people, firms, and institutions. At one time, economists considered the high-tech sector part of tertiary industrial activity. However, as high-tech services expanded and became more complex and important, a special category was created for them. The importance of the quaternary sector has continued to grow in today's "information economy." Since industrial activity in this sector is so expensive and highly specialized, its presence, especially in less-developed countries, remains limited.

   All five examples of primary industrial activity are listed in Figure 11.1; for all other types, the examples provided are not intended to be a complete listing.

FIGURE 11.1
The four types of industrial activity

Industrial Activity	Description	Examples
Goods-Producing Industries		
Primary	Resource extraction	Farming, fishing, forestry, mining, hunting
Secondary	Manufacturing	Steel mills, paper mills, automobile assembly plants, breweries, furniture and appliance factories
Services-Producing Industries		
Tertiary	Provision of services	Wholesale and retail outlets, medical clinics, legal offices, schools
Quaternary	Provision of highly specialized and expensive technology support services	Research and development laboratories, information technology design, applied nuclear technology

THE HISTORICAL DEVELOPMENT OF CANADIAN INDUSTRY

Historically, an economy begins by first developing its natural resources, then its manufacturing activities, then its service sector, and, finally, its **high-tech industries**. In other words, a linear progression is usually evident in the development of a country's economy from the primary through to the quaternary sectors. This is not to say that service industries emerge only after all primary and secondary industries have been fully developed. In fact, some tertiary industries are developed immediately to serve people engaged in primary and secondary industrial activities. Figure 11.2 outlines the growth sequence of some of Canada's main industries.

high-tech industries
Industries that develop, provide, or use highly complex technology.

staple
Products requiring little processing that become the main exports and economic building blocks for a national economy; from the sixteenth century to the nineteenth century, Canada's main staples were fish, fur, and lumber.

FIGURE 11.2
Canadian labour force data by industrial sector, 1881–2015
What evidence do you notice indicating the expansion of oil production in Canada since 2000?

Industrial Activity	1881 (%)	1921 (%)	1955 (%)	1975 (%)	1990 (%)	1999 (%)	2015 (%)
Primary (resource extraction)	51.3	36.6	19.8	7.6	5.8	4.7	5.6
Secondary (manufacturing)	29.4	26.5	32.5	26.7	23.0	21.4	16.0
Services (tertiary from 1881 to 1975; tertiary and quaternary from 1990 to 2015)	19.3	36.9	47.7	65.7	71.2	73.9	78.4

Primary Industries

Canada's economy first emerged and grew in response to the demands in Europe for Canadian natural resources. During the sixteenth, seventeenth, and eighteenth centuries, fish, fur, and lumber were the export **staples** that gave the new economy the largest part of its income. These abundant resources attracted labour and capital from Great Britain and France. Primary industries were, therefore, the first type of industrial activity to develop in Canada on a significant scale. Since Canadian fish, fur, and lumber could be sold in European markets for gold and silver, the British and French governments carefully controlled the expansion of these industries.

Canadian colonists served as an additional market for European manufactured goods. The early colonists had few manufacturing industries of their own. As settlement in Canada increased and moved westward, first wheat, then iron, nickel, gold, copper, and other metals were added to the growing list of export staples. This attracted more specialized labour and capital into the economy, and Canadians began to manufacture locally some of the expensive consumer goods that had previously been available only from Europe. This local production meant that manufactured goods became cheaper for Canadians to buy.

CHECK THIS OUT!

Cod fish attracted large numbers of fishers to Canada's Atlantic shores as early as the sixteenth century. Beaver pelts attracted hunters and settlers into the Canadian interior. By the beginning of the nineteenth century, timber became the dominant staple. Conduct a word search to investigate and assess the importance of these three staples in the economic development of Canada.

The Stelco steel plant in Hamilton, Ontario is an example of a secondary industry in operation. Large quantities of iron ore, coal, limestone and scrap metal are brought in to manufacture Canadian steel.

Secondary Industries

The Industrial Revolution that started in Britain around 1780 changed the way manufactured goods were produced. After about 1850, the development of fast steam-powered trains and ships affected the trade of goods between countries. As more labour and capital moved to secondary industrial activities in Canada, the national infrastructure slowly changed to focus more on manufacturing and distribution than on resource extraction. After Confederation in 1867, the federal government imposed protective taxes called *tariffs* on Canada's young industries to develop sustained markets for their goods.

The transcontinental railway, the large-scale infrastructure project included in the National Policy of 1879, was built to complement the existing canals and waterways and to help increase the population of Western Canada. Around this same time, manufacturers began to build coal-powered steam generators and, later, hydroelectric generators as inexpensive power sources to run the machinery required to make consumer goods in large quantities. This automation in factories meant that fewer workers were needed to produce manufactured goods.

Services Industries

The resulting surplus of production workers encouraged a shift of labour and capital from export staple production to specialized services, such as transportation and warehousing, finance and insurance, retail and wholesale trade, health and education, entertainment, and personal grooming. As primary and secondary industries continued to develop and expand in Canada, the base of staple goods for domestic and foreign markets was strengthened. By the middle of the twentieth century, Canada had become an industrial country and had achieved a more balanced economy with strong primary, secondary, and tertiary sectors. At the same time, Canada's prosperity and growth remained dependent on its ability to find export markets for foodstuffs, raw materials, and manufactured goods. In any economy, the development of a large service—or tertiary—sector is supported by goods-producing industrial sectors that have a strong base of staple goods for export and establish a steady flow of money into the economy.

Employment growth in the service sector intensified during the economic boom that followed the Second World War and continues today. The level of service specialization has increased significantly over the last 25 years, as Canada has developed its quaternary industries. Today, Canada is a major exporter of fibre optic technology, nuclear power generation technology, satellite-sensing technology, and other high-tech applications.

Self-Reflect

1 Identify the category of industrial activity represented by each of the following examples: barber shop, pig farm, gold mine, steel mill, automobile assembly, and nuclear energy research laboratory.

2 Prepare a summary note to explain how Canadian industrial activity evolved over time.

3 Why has a distinction been made (since 1990) to subdivide the services sector?

Thinking like an Economist

Detecting Patterns in Data to Explain Economic Relationships

Economists often use data to explain economic relationships. Sometimes bar graphs are visually helpful when comparing the size of important components. Figure 11.3 shows the percentage of the labour force in 15 different countries that was employed in each industrial sector at the end of the last millennium, an important historical benchmark. Since the full bar represents 100 percent of each country's economy, the colour-coded segments depict the relative size of each industrial sector.

For most countries, the largest employer of labour in the primary sector is agriculture. *Gross domestic product (GDP) per capita* compares the value of all goods and services produced in a year with national population data. It is sometimes referred to as the "standard-of-living" statistic because it reports the value of goods and services available per person living in a country. The more industrially developed countries achieve a significantly higher GDP per capita rate than is possible for less-developed countries. For example, Niger can be identified as the poorest economy being compared in this graph. We will examine GDP per capita in more detail in Unit 4. For now, use Figure 11.3 to look for patterns and relationships in the data across the national economies being reported.

FIGURE 11.3
Percentage of labour force in primary, secondary, and service sectors, 1999

Nation (GDP per capita)	% in primary industry	% in secondary industry	% in service industry
Examples of more-developed countries			
United States* ($31 500)	4	23	73
Japan* ($23 100)	7	33	60
France* ($22 600)	7	31	62
Canada ($22 400)	5	21	74
United Kingdom ($21 200)	3	25	72
Examples of less-developed countries			
Mexico ($8300)	25	20	55
China ($3600)	65	20	15
Morocco ($3200)	50	21	29
Mozambique ($3200)	46	25	29
Indonesia ($2800)	54	10	36
Nicaragua ($2500)	47	16	37
Cameroon ($2000)	74	5	21
Vietnam ($1770)	66	12	22
India ($1720)	63	11	26
Niger ($970)	85	3	12

*When sector data were not reported for a nation in the 2001 *Almanac*, data from earlier editions were used.

APPLYING ECONOMIC THINKING

1   Which industrial sector do most less-developed countries depend on to employ much of the labour force? How does this compare to the employment patterns reported by more-developed countries such as Canada?

2   What relationship exists between GDP per capita and the percentage of the labour force employed in primary industrial activity? Why are the majority of people in poorer countries engaged in agriculture?

3   Applying what you have learned about the development of the Canadian economy, forecast how the labour force will change as less developed countries continue their economic development.

4   Research current data for the 15 countries in Figure 11.3 to test your hypothesis about labour force changes in developing countries.

5   What can you do to confirm that the patterns and relationships reflected in Figure 11.3 are not exclusive to these 15 countries?

A small market on the outskirts of Niamey, Niger, is compared to a typical Canadian produce market in Ottawa, Ontario. What economic differences do these images reveal?

firm
A privately owned organization engaged in business activities.

sole proprietorship
A business owned and operated by one person.

unlimited personal liability
When the owner or owners of a business are personally responsible for all debts incurred by the business.

progressive tax
A tax (such as income tax) in which the tax rate increases as an individual's income increases.

partnership
A business or firm owned by two or more people that is bound by the terms of a signed agreement.

partnership agreement
The legal agreement between individuals in a partnership.

Forms of Business Organization

In Chapter 10, we learned that to engage in business activities in any sector of the Canadian economy, people organize their funds and abilities into enterprises called **firms**. Firms are usually designed to achieve maximum profits by providing goods and services for which customers are willing and able to pay. Business ventures can be set up in one of the following ways: sole proprietorship, partnership, corporation, co-operative, government enterprise, or non-profit or charitable organization.

THE SOLE PROPRIETORSHIP

As the name suggests, a **sole proprietorship** is a business owned and operated by one person. This is the most uncomplicated way to do business today. Even though proprietors may employ other people, they make all the business decisions. Proprietors are solely responsible for all of the firm's debts and solely entitled to all of the firm's profits.

Advantages and Disadvantages

This usually small-scale form of business organization appeals to those people who prefer to be their own bosses and who prefer to keep their financial affairs, business dealings, and production processes confidential. Most businesses are required to have a municipal licence or a provincial vendor's permit. The name and business particulars of the firm have to be registered with the provincial government only when a name other than the real name of the proprietor is being used.

The biggest disadvantage of a sole proprietorship is the **unlimited personal liability** of the owner. This means that the proprietor's personal assets can be seized to pay off outstanding business debts. In addition, the sole proprietor usually has no one else to rely on to run the business or raise needed funds. Sole proprietors often find it difficult and expensive to obtain business loans. Since ownership is personal and income tax is **progressive** (the more one earns, the higher the percentage rate of income tax one must pay), sole proprietors may pay more income tax than they would if set up as a corporation. In addition, because sole proprietorships are owned and operated by one person, they do not have a long duration because succession planning is often difficult. For example, a sole proprietor's children may not be interested in or able to continue the business. Despite these disadvantages, sole proprietorships are very common in Canada today.

THE PARTNERSHIP

A **partnership** is a firm owned by two or more people and bound by the terms of a legal document known as a **partnership agreement**. This document governs the business conduct of all partners and outlines their rights and obligations. A partnership agreement can establish either a general or a limited partnership. In a *general partnership*, all partners take part in the management of the firm and have unlimited personal liability for business losses. In a *limited partnership*, there are limited partners and at least one general partner. Limited partners are not permitted to take part in the management of the business and, in turn, are personally liable for business debts only up to the amount of their original investment. No additional personal assets can be seized to pay off partnership debts.

Advantages and Disadvantages

The advantages of a partnership include the pooling of talent and capital, high personal motivation, and relatively few legal expenses and restrictions. Partnerships appeal to people who prefer not to assume all the risks of business operation on their own. In addition to the pride of ownership and the satisfaction that comes from being self-employed, partners share all after-tax profits according to the distribution formula specified in the partnership agreement.

Since a partnership pools the funds of a number of people, it can attract more capital (money or other assets to invest in the business). It is usually easier for a partnership to obtain credit from suppliers or to borrow money from banks because more people are personally responsible for repayment. Since banks consider these loans more secure, they often set a slightly lower interest rate for them than for the loans they make to sole proprietors. In view of these advantages, professional firms of lawyers, architects, and accountants are often organized as partnerships.

Unfortunately, general partners must assume unlimited personal liability. Similar to sole proprietorships, the personal assets of general partners can be seized to pay the balance of business debts once all business assets have been used up. In the case of general partnerships, if the other partners fail to pay their share of the debt, one or more partners may be required to pay all remaining debts.

Similar to a sole proprietor, partners have to pay a progressive personal income tax, so the percentage of tax they pay increases as their revenues go up. Another drawback is that it is not easy for partners to sell their share in the firm. Most partnership agreements require that a partner obtain the approval of the other partners before ownership can be transferred to a new partner. The other partners often have the right to buy out a retiring partner rather than allow a new partner into the group. To complicate matters further, partnerships can obtain investment funds only from within the existing partnership. Partners must use personal savings or take out mortgages on personal assets to raise money for the partnership. For this reason, partnerships usually cannot attract large amounts of capital.

Since all the general partners are involved in the daily management of the firm, disputes may arise over time. Personality clashes and disagreements on what is best for the firm cause many partnerships to end. A partnership legally ends if one of the general partners dies, becomes mentally incapacitated, becomes financially insolvent, or commits a breach of the partnership by acting against the best interests of the firm. Thus, partnerships often do not last for a long period of time.

A family-owned cheese shop in Toronto's Kensington Market neighbourhood. Why do you think that proprietorships are a popular form of small business in Canada today?

corporation

A business firm recognized legally as a separate entity in its own right.

private corporation

A company that privately controls all sales of its ownership shares, instead of publicly trading in a stock market.

public corporation

A firm or company that freely trades its ownership shares in a stock market, subject to government supervision.

articles of incorporation

A legal document, filed with the government, that incorporates a business.

shares

Corporate assets divided into equal parts that are sold to buyers, giving them ownership and a share of the corporation's profits.

shareholders

The owners of the shares of a corporation; they are entitled to voting rights and a share of the corporation's profits.

proxy

A document signed by a shareholder appointing another person to vote on behalf of that shareholder.

dividend

Corporation profits distributed to shareholders on a per-share basis.

THE CORPORATION

A **corporation** (or *limited company*, as it was once called) is a business firm recognized legally as a separate entity in its own right. Corporations can be either public or private. The shares of a **private corporation** are privately traded; that is, their transfer or sale must be approved and carried out by the corporation's board of directors. Shares of a **public corporation** can be freely traded among the general public, subject to the supervision of the provincial securities commission.

A corporation can be established only through government authorization. A document known as the **articles of incorporation** must be filed with either the federal government (if the corporation intends to conduct business in more than one province) or with the provincial government (if business is to be conducted in one province only).

Corporate assets are divided, with government authorization, into equal parts called **shares**. These ownership shares are made available to prospective buyers and can be quickly re-sold through a stockbroker. The owners of a corporation are known as **shareholders**, and any given corporation can have just a few or thousands of shareholders. At an annual general meeting, shareholders elect a board of directors to run the company. These directors hire professional managers to make all day-to-day operating decisions. The fact that investors do not assume personal responsibility for the day-to-day operation of companies that could provide them with a financial return makes investing in those companies attractive.

Generally, corporations can offer two types of ownership shares to investors: *common shares*, which provide a shareholder with voting rights, and *preferred shares*, which give a shareholder a preferential position in regard to profits and assets but do not provide voting rights. Shareholders can vote on decisions at the annual general meeting in person or by **proxy**. A proxy is a document signed by a shareholder appointing another person to vote on behalf of that shareholder.

Advantages and Disadvantages

One attractive feature of the corporation is its method of profit distribution. At the end of the fiscal year, the majority of shareholders may vote to reinvest a portion of corporate profits into the firm. This provides an internal source of additional investment capital. Because of their size and scale of operations, many large corporations have become self-financing, no longer requiring bank loans to finance corporate expansion. The promise of even greater profits in the future is usually all the incentive it takes to persuade shareholders to forgo a portion of their current profits. Profits that are not reinvested into the firm are distributed to shareholders in the form of **dividends** and are paid on a per-share basis. Holders of preferred shares collect their guaranteed dividends first, then the remaining profits are divided up among the common shareholders on a per-share basis.

Once a corporation is legally established, it can sue and be sued, enter into contracts, own property, and incur debts and other obligations in the same way as any adult person. Any obligations incurred are generally the legal responsibility of the corporation, but not of the individual owners. Corporate shareholders have the advantage of *limited personal liability*. This means that the risk of the owners is restricted to the amount they have invested in the business. Creditors cannot claim the shareholder's other possessions (such as houses, cars, and personal savings) if the corporation goes bankrupt.

Clearly, the risks of investing in a corporation are substantially less than those of a partnership or sole proprietorship. Corporations can, therefore, attract a much wider pool of investors and a larger amount of investment capital. As a result, corporations can operate on an extremely large scale. In addition, when a shareholder dies or wishes to leave the firm, the corporation is not dissolved. The shares can be transferred to others easily while the corporation carries on its usual business; longevity is another advantage of firms established as corporations. Finally, corporations generally pay lower rates of income tax than sole proprietorships and partnerships. Dividends received by shareholders are also taxed at a lower rate.

Nevertheless, corporations do have their disadvantages. First of all, the legal and government fees for establishing a corporation are significantly higher than those for sole proprietorships and partnerships. Second, corporations are more closely regulated by the government. They must keep a set of books that lists their shareholders, directors, assets, and business dealings. They must also hold annual general meetings, produce an annual financial statement, and file annual corporate tax returns. (Since the corporation is legally recognized as an artificial person, like any other person earning an income, it must file an annual tax return.) Executives of many firms believe that these public disclosures can adversely affect the corporation's level of privacy by providing important information to competitors. However, the government requires the disclosure of this information to protect investors.

A final disadvantage is the reduced personal incentive that can be present in large corporations. With professional managers in place, investors are not able to exercise the same hands-on control that sole proprietors and general partners can exercise. Although they may have great personal ambition and dedication to the business, professional managers rarely have the same incentive and loyalty as owners. This disadvantage is addressed in some firms by offering managers stock options, profit sharing, and performance bonuses.

Roots Canada is an example of a public corporation, operating over 200 shops in Canada, the United States, and Asia.

co-operative
A business owned equally by its members who have a common relationship, goal, or economic purpose.

patronage
Profits made by a co-operative enterprise that are paid out to co-operative members based on the individual member's activity as a customer.

THE CO-OPERATIVE

A **co-operative** is a business owned equally by its various members. Members of a particular co-operative must have a common relationship, goal, or economic purpose. *Retail co-operatives* are formed to provide goods to members at reduced prices. *Marketing co-operatives* are created to sell the produce of members at the best prices possible. *Financial co-operatives* are formed to arrange savings and loans for members at better rates than those available at local banks. *Service co-operatives* are created to provide members with special services, such as housing, medical insurance, and equipment rentals.

Many co-operatives incorporate themselves under their provincial corporations act. Doing so allows co-operatives to secure limited personal liability for their members while maintaining all the other privileges of membership.

In any co-operative enterprise, for the purposes of collective decision making, each member (regardless of the amount invested) is entitled to a single vote, and a majority vote is required to carry any decision. To facilitate the day-to-day operation of the co-op, members elect a board of directors annually. Officers generally assume their roles on a voluntary basis. Co-operatives are generally most popular in Western Canada and in rural parts of Eastern Canada.

Credit unions, known as *caisses populaires* in Quebec, are well-known examples of financial co-operatives. Members can obtain many of the same services (chequing and savings accounts, and loans) available from banks but at more favourable interest rates. Unlike banks, credit unions can only accept deposits from, and arrange loans and mortgages for, members.

Advantages and Disadvantages

The one-vote-per-member rule allows each member an equal say in all management decisions. As well, co-operatives are not adversely affected by the death, insolvency, or incapacity of individual members. Members can obtain goods or services through the co-operative or sell their products at better prices than they could otherwise. In addition, members can enjoy limited personal liability for the debts incurred by the co-op. Finally, any profits made by the co-op that are not reinvested into the business are paid out to the members in the form of **patronage** returns. These payments are based on the amount of business transacted by each individual member. In other words, if a member is responsible for buying 1 percent of the goods sold by a retail co-operative, then that member is entitled to 1 percent of the profits for the same period.

The disadvantages of co-operative enterprises are linked to management, capital, and transaction issues. First, the decision-making process can be problematic when many equal members have radically different ideas. Second, the voluntary and therefore unpaid nature of the officers' positions may discourage some capable people from offering their management expertise to the group. Third, since co-operatives are able to raise investment funds only from existing members, they have a limited ability to raise capital when needed. Fourth, co-ops are restricted to conducting business with existing members.

This restriction limits the number of customers and, ultimately, the volume of business transactions. Co-operatives are designed primarily to serve members rather than to generate substantial profits.

THE GOVERNMENT ENTERPRISE

Some businesses in Canada are owned by the federal, provincial, or municipal government. These **government enterprises** generally provide services that the private sector won't offer because the profits generated are low relative to the amount of capital invested. The government may establish an enterprise to provide competition in industries dominated by a single firm or to prevent the total private control of key industries. The government may also set up one of these companies to increase employment or to centralize and standardize services. More government enterprise exists in the Canadian economy than in the United States. However, Western European countries such as Austria, Britain, France, and Germany have an even higher degree of state ownership.

In recent years, the federal government and some provinces have made a concerted effort to **privatize** all or part of some government enterprises. During the 1980s in Canada, the federal government privatized a number of Crown corporations, including Canadair, de Havilland Canada, Teleglobe Canada (all three of which are no longer in business), and Air Canada. In 1990, the government embarked on a plan to sell Petro-Canada; by 1999, 80 percent of Petro-Canada shares were privately owned.

The provincial governments of Ontario, Quebec, Saskatchewan, Alberta, and British Columbia have also privatized a number of government enterprises. The phased sale of Hydro One (2015–2017), resulted in private investors assuming control (minimum 51 percent ownership) of the Crown Corporation that formerly owned Ontario's electricity transmission system. This move was intended to improve long-term performance of the utility and reduce the government's budget deficit. As a private corporation, Hydro One is no longer required to comply with freedom of information laws regarding management decisions and salaries.

Most businesses owned by the federal government are operated as **Crown corporations**, which, like all other corporations, have the status of distinct legal persons. The federal government, rather than private individuals, holds all or most of the ownership shares of these corporations. Examples of Crown corporations include Canada Post, the CBC, Via Rail, and Atomic Energy of Canada.

At the provincial and municipal levels, government enterprises take various forms:

- Public utilities supply electricity and water.
- Provincial control boards sell liquor.
- Housing corporations provide affordable shelter.
- Transit commissions provide affordable public transportation.

Government enterprises are meant to operate in the best interests of the community rather than to generate profits for shareholders. The government usually covers operating expenses and business losses through grants, subsidies, or annual operating budgets.

government enterprise
A business that provides services owned by the federal, provincial, or municipal government.

privatize
To turn over ownership and operation of a government enterprise to the private sector.

Crown corporation
A business owned by the federal government.

Canada Post is an example of a Crown corporation, which is owned and controlled by the federal government. If Canada Post were privatized, what would happen?

Canadians continue to debate the merits of government enterprise relative to private enterprise. Some argue that private enterprise is more efficient and productive. Yet, at some point, all political parties have supported the government takeover of certain firms or industries for the common good. Different provinces have come to different conclusions in regard to certain industries. For example, only private companies in Ontario and Quebec provide telecommunications services, while in Saskatchewan these same services are also provided by the provincial Crown corporation SaskTel. Each method seems to work well for the respective provinces. The federal government created Petro-Canada to establish a state watchdog company in a petroleum industry dominated by large foreign corporations. Canadian National Railway and Air Canada were Crown corporations created to provide competition in the transportation industries that would otherwise lack it. Economists often argue that the level of efficiency in a specific industry is determined by the level of competition present.

Certain enterprises that have a major impact on the public good (such as postal services, power companies, and railways) are state-owned in many countries because they seem to operate best without competition. These enterprises are sometimes referred to as *natural monopolies*. However, at times the public favours privatizing government enterprises to reduce the size and cost of their government. Over time, if the public concludes that private interests are not serving the common good adequately, it will pressure government to take over formerly state-owned enterprises again. The Canadian mixed-market economy will continue to exhibit both capitalistic and socialistic tendencies as it searches for the most effective balance between the two.

NON-PROFIT AND CHARITABLE ORGANIZATIONS

Some organizations are government registered (either federally or provincially) as **non-profit/charitable organizations**. These private institutions are not permitted to generate profits; in return, their activities are income-tax exempt. Many of these institutions raise money to cover operating expenses from donations, grants, and fundraising activities. Examples of private non-profit charitable organizations include the Canadian Cancer Society, the Canadian National Institute for the Blind, and local food banks. District school boards are examples of public non-profit organizations. These enterprises are managed by a board of directors or elected trustees and operate through the work of both hired staff and volunteers. Organizations such as Save the Children Canada, World Vision Canada, and Development and Peace are actively involved in collecting funds and recruiting volunteers to help people in less-developed countries around the world.

non-profit/charitable organization
A government-registered form of business created not for profit but to provide a service or to organize and perform works of charity.

Self-Reflect

1 Which form of business organization would be most appropriate in each of the following cases?
   a) A three-person law firm
   b) A corner convenience store
   c) A savings-and-loan organization for school-district employees only
   d) A chain of 12 restaurants with 60 owners
   e) An enterprise providing affordable public transportation to the residents of a community
   f) An enterprise raising money to build wells for clean water in developing countries

2 Explain the difference between the following pairs of terms:
   • *General partner* and *limited partner*
   • *Public corporation* and *private corporation*
   • *Dividends* and *patronage*
   • *Crown corporation* and *non-profit organization*

Small and Big Businesses

Given the wide range of businesses in Canada, there is no general definition of a small or large business. Both Statistics Canada and Innovation, Science and Economic Development Canada often use number of employees as an indicator of the size of a business. Figure 11.4 reports the number of firms in each general size category in 2015.

Small businesses, by virtue of their numbers, constitute the engine that fuels the Canadian economy. The smallest of all business, often called *micro-enterprises*, constitutes the largest portion of the small business group. Big businesses, each of which employs thousands of Canadians, have a great deal of political influence. Think of them as the wheel that steers the national economy in a given direction.

SMALL BUSINESSES

Small businesses are generally limited in the size and scope of their operations. In addition, they face intense competition from numerous other small firms. This level of competition keeps small businesses operating efficiently.

Many small businesses maintain their competitive advantage by limiting their operations to one specialized field or process. For example, a garage may repair only vintage automobiles. Because they are limited in revenue and focused on one area of specialization, small businesses are usually very sensitive to changes in their niche market.

The most successful small businesses are usually those that best anticipate market conditions or that best respond to market changes. Therefore, successful small businesses tend to be aggressively innovative and tend to maximize profits at the expense of weaker competitors. Over time, the most productive and effectively managed businesses force their weaker rivals out of business or buy them out. In the process, these successful small businesses grow larger.

BIG BUSINESSES

Big businesses account for almost half of the private sector (non-government) jobs in Canada (see Figure 11.5). These large enterprises generally benefit from economies of scale and from the accumulation and concentration of their employees' expertise. Big businesses can acquire the latest technology by purchasing control of smaller companies that have pioneered technological innovations in very competitive markets. Large-scale enterprises can assume greater risks and accumulate the investment capital required to initiate expensive and complex projects.

Often, along with size comes power. Large enterprises that have limited competition could attempt to manipulate the marketplace to maximize profits and harm competitors. As a result, governments have competition legislation to prevent large enterprises from engaging in anti-competitive practices in the marketplace. We will look more closely at the government's role in protecting competition in Unit 5.

DID YOU KNOW?

The Canadian Federation of Independent Business (CFIB) was formed in 1971 to raise government awareness of the benefits and needs of small business in Canada. At the time, the federal government was considering raising taxes on small businesses. Within 40 years, this special-interest (or *lobby*) group exceeded 110 000 members, becoming the most influential group representing small business in Canada.

FIGURE 11.4
Classifying Canadian Enterprises by number of employees, 2015
By far, most Canadian businesses are small.

General Size	Number of Employees	Number of Firms	Percentage of Total
Small (micro)	1–4	705 358	56.4
Small	5–19	383 831	30.7
Small	20–49	104 028	8.3
Medium	50–99	32 910	2.6
Medium	100–199	14 488	1.2
Medium	200–499	7 242	0.6
Large	500+	2 965	0.2
Total	—	1 250 822	100.0

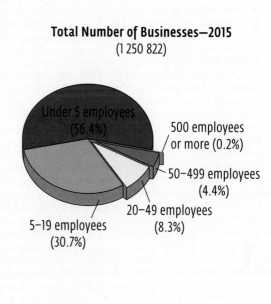

Total Number of Businesses—2015
(1 250 822)

FIGURE 11.5
Private-sector employment in Canada
By 2015, small and medium-sized businesses employed slightly more than
half of all Canadians working in the private sector.

General Size	Number of Employees	Total Employed	Percentage of Total
Small (micro)	1–4	1 043 605	6.7
Small	5–19	2 097 629	13.5
Small	20–49	1 721 240	11.1
Medium	50–99	1 310 314	8.4
Medium	100–199	1 699 855	11.0
Medium	200–499	681 800	4.4
Large	500+	6 963 951	44.9
Total	—	15 518 393	100.0

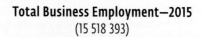
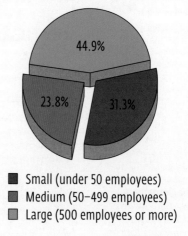

Total Business Employment—2015
(15 518 393)

- Small (under 50 employees)
- Medium (50–499 employees)
- Large (500 employees or more)

merger
The joining together of two firms or companies to operate more effectively as one.

acquisition
The purchase of controlling interests in one company by another.

horizontal integration
The joining together of two firms that produce the same product or service to operate as one firm.

horizontal merger
A consolidation of two firms producing the same product or service.

vertical integration
The merging of two firms involved in different stages of the production process of a good or service.

holding company
An enterprise that holds shares in other producing companies.

conglomerate
A group of companies involved in different industries, but controlled by a central management group.

Mergers, Acquisitions, and Corporate Integration

Successful firms frequently use profits to expand production by purchasing their competitors. Through **mergers** (the combination of two firms into one) and **acquisitions** (the buying of one firm by another), firms reduce the risks of competition by controlling it. For example, after taking over a competing firm, the new firm can cease production of any goods or reduce any service that the competing firm supplies, thereby eliminating unwanted competition. In the late 1990s, several of Canada's major banks sought to merge to achieve the size they felt was necessary to compete in global markets. Federal regulations blocked these mergers because of concerns that it would reduce competition and the availability of banking services in Canada.

HORIZONTAL INTEGRATION

Smaller firms often grow larger through a process known as **horizontal integration**, which takes place when one firm purchases another that produces the same product or provides the same service. Horizontal integration can create economies of scale in production processes and reduce duplication of effort. For example, if two companies merge and consolidate their research and development (R&D) departments, a substantial amount of money in employee salaries can be saved. By increasing the size and efficiency of operations, larger Canadian firms can compete more effectively on a global scale.

This sort of **horizontal merger**, or consolidating acquisition, can also give the larger firm better access to both domestic and foreign markets. In 1998, Sobeys Canada Inc. of Stellarton, Nova Scotia (through its corporate parent Empire Co. Ltd.) acquired the Oshawa Group to become one of Canada's largest supermarket chains. In 2016, Enbridge Inc. acquired Spectra Energy Corporation, a Texas-based natural gas and crude oil pipeline company, to create the largest energy infrastructure company in North America. These are two examples of friendly mergers, but corporate takeovers can also be hostile if forced by an aggressive buyer.

VERTICAL INTEGRATION

When companies involved in successive stages of the production (or consumption) process combine into a single firm, the result is **vertical integration**. Examples of vertical integration happen when a major publishing house purchases a chain of bookstores or when a broadcaster (such as Rogers Communications) buys a sports franchise (such as the Toronto Blue Jays).

Vertical integration can diversify and extend the scope of a firm's operations by helping it to establish ready markets for its products and to secure sources of supplies for the intermediate goods required in the production process. When Rogers bought the Blue Jays, the team provided the company with hours of sports programming for its Sportsnet television network. Vertical integration can also enable a firm to assume more control over the quality, quantity, and prices of required goods. For example, Blue Jays games are now only available through

DID YOU KNOW?

Holding companies are enterprises that are not engaged in any form of industrial activity. Instead, their sole purpose is to acquire large blocks of ownership shares in other companies to influence or control them. Through the systematic acquisition of common shares, holding companies are able to create corporate **conglomerates**, a group of companies involved in different industries but controlled, to varying degrees, by a central management group, often the directors of the holding company.

Sportsnet. In addition, a large and diversified corporation may not be as adversely affected by a decline in one industry. For example, if Acme Corp. manufactures cars, computers, and beer, a decline in car sales will not hurt overall profits as much as if the firm only produced cars.

CORPORATE ALLIANCES

Firms can also choose to strategically collaborate on specific projects with competitors or suppliers—without triggering the ownership struggles and investment anxieties that mergers and acquisitions often bring. A growing number of firms, especially in Europe and Asia, are agreeing to collaborate in strategic corporate alliances in the pursuit of mutual benefits. A **corporate alliance** is a group of companies that agree to form a business network that, in turn, operates like a co-ordinated mega-company.

Individual members might bring different assets to this strategic alliance, including products, capital equipment, specialized technology or expertise, distribution channels, manufacturing capability, and intellectual property, with the intent to benefit from the synergies of collaboration.

In 1999, International Business Machines Corp. (IBM), which ranked second in worldwide computer sales at the time, entered into a strategic alliance with Dell Computer Corp., which ranked third in worldwide sales. The seven-year agreement allowed the sharing of patented technology between the companies as well as joint development of new technologies. IBM supplied component parts and technology to Dell; and Dell engineers integrated and refined IBM technology in new products. This example illustrates how joining forces can be profitable for each ally. In 2014, IBM entered into a strategic alliance with arch rival Apple Inc. to share technology and develop new applications. If present trends continue, the traditional business landscape will be significantly redefined by the growing number of corporate collaborations.

CORPORATE CONCENTRATION

A large amount of business activity is concentrated in a handful of corporations. Some of these corporations are, in turn, controlled by a few wealthy individuals. Over time, this concentration appears to be increasing. In 1999, the 50 largest corporations in Canada (ranked by sales revenues) controlled close to half of all corporate assets in Canada and accounted for one-third of all business revenues. The 100 largest companies (representing well below 1 percent of Canada's business enterprises) accounted for 40 percent of corporate revenues. According to the *2016 CSCA Retail 100* report by Ryerson University's Centre for the Study of Commercial Activity, the 100 largest retail companies in Canada accounted for 76 percent of all retail sales (excluding autos). Moreover, the top 10 largest retail companies alone accounted for half of all retail sales.

Since corporate size can generate market influence, large companies can make substantial profits in their respective markets. Given that some of these large companies are owned and controlled by a handful of wealthy individuals, this dynamic greatly affects the distribution of wealth in Canada.

corporate alliance
A group of companies that agree to operate as a single company while retaining separate ownership.

CHECK IT OUT!

Another example of a strategic corporate alliance occured in 1997, with the formation of Star Alliance, which was created by United Airlines, Scandinavian Airlines, Thai Airways, Lufthansa, and Air Canada. In time, other airlines joined to create a 27-member alliance operating a co-ordinated fleet of over 4 500 aircraft, serving more than 1 330 airports in some 190 countries around the world, with a common rewards program for customers.

subsidiary
A branch plant of a multinational corporation.

multinational corporation (MNC)
A firm that operates in more than one country; a corporation with a global production and selling strategy, having headquarters in one country and branch plants in several other countries.

branch plant
A firm or factory owned by a multinational corporation that operates in another country.

The Multinational Corporation in the Global Economy

As part of their natural growth and expansion, many firms sell a portion of their output abroad, license foreign companies to use their manufacturing processes, or even establish their own branch plants (or **subsidiaries**) abroad. Once this involvement in other countries becomes substantial, corporate managers begin to base their financial, production, and marketing decisions on global (rather than on domestic or national) concerns. Any company registered in one country that conducts business in two or more countries is called a **multinational corporation (MNC)**. Firms that are successful in their home country become MNCs to enter international markets and prosper on a global scale.

Numerous multinationals operate in the Canadian economy today. For example, the Canadian automobile industry includes large MNCs from the United States, Japan, South Korea, and Germany. Numerous American multinationals (such as Apple Corp. and General Motors Company) have chosen to operate subsidiaries in Canada because of Canada's geographical proximity, political stability, abundance of natural resources, and well-developed markets. These subsidiaries are often wholly owned and operated by the parent company. Sometimes, Canadian communities compete to attract foreign multinationals to open facilities locally, in the hope of attracting investment dollars and jobs. Many successful Canadian companies have expanded to include branch plants in other countries; they have become MNCs with their headquarters in Canada. Figure 11.6 lists some of the largest examples.

One reason corporations prefer to operate as multinationals is to improve their profitability. Foreign **branch plants** provide free access to new markets and the increased revenues these markets represent. In addition, having offices and factories abroad can give the parent company direct access to comparatively cheap raw materials and labour, effectively reducing its operating costs. Foreign governments, eager to attract industrial activity, often provide tax concessions or development grants to companies willing to operate subsidiaries in their country. In turn, the financial stability of a company is greatly enhanced by geographical diversification. For example, market fluctuations and political upheaval in one country may be effectively offset by stability and growth in others. Today, a substantial portion of international trade is conducted between multinationals and their foreign subsidiaries.

Large multinationals can negotiate favourable terms when dealing with suppliers, governments, and trade unions by playing off one community against another. In terms of raw economic power, some MNCs control corporate assets comparable to (if not greater than) the assets of the governments with which they deal. Since their activities cross political borders, MNCs can effectively operate beyond the control of any one national government. For this reason, they are sometimes referred to as *transnational companies*.

DID YOU KNOW?

General Motors Corporation was the world's largest automobile manufacturer from 1931 to 2007. It collapsed during the Great Recession of the late 2000s, declaring bankruptcy in 2009. With the financial aid of the US government, it was reborn as General Motors Company. The US government invested $50 billion in General Motors to protect 1.2 million jobs and $35 billion in tax revenue. When the government sold its interests in the company in 2013, it got back most of its investment. Together, the governments of Canada and Ontario bailed out the Canadian subsidiary of General Motors in 2009, spending $10.5 billion.

FIGURE 11.6
Large Canadian multinational companies, circa 2016

Name (Headquarters)	Main Activities	Size (circa 2016)	Total Revenues (2016)
Magna International Inc. (Aurora, Ontario)	Automobile parts design, testing, and manufacturing	159 000 employees in 29 countries	US$45.77 billion
BCE Inc. (formerly Bell Canada Enterprises) (Montreal, Quebec)	Fixed-line and mobile phone services, telecommunications, and broadcasting	48 000 employees	CDN$21 billion
Bombardier Inc. (Montreal, Quebec)	Aerospace and transportation equipment, including planes and mass-transit vehicles	66 000 employees in 28 countries	CDN$20 billion
Celestica Inc. (Toronto, Ontario)	Electronics manufacturing services, including computer hardware	25 000 employees in 11 countries	CDN$7.5 billion
Four Seasons Hotels Ltd. (Toronto, Ontario)	Luxury hospitality company, including hotels and resorts	30 000+ employees around the world	CDN$5.5 billion
Lululemon Athletica Inc. (Vancouver, British Columbia)	Retailer of active wear, including workout and yoga apparel	2 860 employees in 3 countries	CDN$2.3 billion

Their wealth and mobility give MNCs a strong political influence in many of their host countries, which sometimes raises ethical questions. For instance, if an MNC is operating in a country with strict environmental laws, it may react in one of two ways. It may simply shut down its operations in that country and move them to another where the environmental laws are not as strict. It could also influence the politicians in the first country to change their environmental laws or to grant special exemptions. Either way, critics could accuse this MNC with putting concern for its profits ahead of concern for the environment.

One wonders whether the economic development game can ever be a level playing field, especially when so many country's economies are seeking to increase industry and employment. It could be argued that large transnational corporations are the modern-day versions of exploitative nineteenth-century colonial empires of the Age of Imperialism. By contrast, it could also be argued that multinationals provide capital, employment, and access to a wider choice of goods and services to the host countries in which they have operations.

Public debate about MNCs will heat up from time to time, especially when their behaviour is seen to fall short of good corporate citizenship. Attempts by the Organisation for Economic Co-operation and Development (OECD) to work out a Multilateral Agreement on Investment (1995–1998) failed to establish international rules for MNCs because the final draft was seen as providing too much power and freedom to multinationals. Meanwhile, multinationals have continued to conduct their businesses in the most profitable manner possible, often with little regard for the economic, environmental, and social impact on host countries. We will investigate international economic issues in Unit 6.

Self-Reflect

1 Prepare a comparison organizer to summarize the advantages and disadvantages of small and big business ventures.

2 Explain the differences among horizontal integration, vertical integration, and strategic alliance.

3 List the positive and negative attributes of multinational corporations.

bond

A financial asset that represents a debt owed by a corporation to the holder, on which interest is paid by the corporation to the holder.

principal

The original amount a corporation borrows with a bond, repayable to the bondholder, and on which interest is paid.

asset value

A corporate share's portion of the corporation's net worth, represented by its assets minus its liabilities.

book value

The value of a share when it was first issued; also known as *face value*.

market value

The actual price at which a share will sell on the stock market.

Financing Corporate Expansion

In Canada today, the majority of business enterprises are corporations. For example, in the manufacturing sector alone, more than 95 percent of the enterprises are corporations. Like sole proprietorships and partnerships, corporations can obtain the funds needed to finance expansion by borrowing from banks and by reinvesting profits in their growing businesses. In addition, because of their legal status, corporations can also raise investment capital by selling bonds and additional ownership shares.

DIFFERENT FORMS OF SECURITIES

Corporate **bonds** are issued by corporations to raise money to run or expand their operations. Corporate bonds represent a fixed debt: a corporation that sells these bonds must pay back buyers at some fixed future date, usually 10 or more years after the date of issue. The buyer, or bondholder, will receive periodic interest payments, usually at six-month intervals and at a fixed interest rate. On the maturity date, the bondholder will receive the full amount of the original loan, known as the **principal**.

The interest rate the bond pays must be competitive with rates available to investors elsewhere. As a general rule, the longer the loan period, the higher the interest rate required to persuade investors to tie up their funds for the longer period. The bondholder can resell the bond at whatever price the market will bear. Sometimes, bonds are discounted by the seller to complete a transaction. A bond with a face value of $100 000 may sell for $90 000 if the seller cannot find a buyer willing to pay more. The new buyer assumes all existing conditions of the bond, including the interest rate and date of maturity.

It is important to note that the bondholder is not a part owner of the corporation but merely a creditor who is entitled to receive payment prior to the shareholders if the corporation closes down.

Corporations can also raise money by issuing and selling additional ownership shares. These shares (common or preferred) represent additional part ownership of a corporation's capital. Since the corporation often uses the funds raised to acquire additional assets, the **asset value** of each share may not be adversely affected; the asset value is each share's portion of the corporation's net worth (assets minus liabilities). The **book value** of a share is the value at which it was originally issued. Usually, shares in a publicly traded corporation are sold through a stockbroker. However, no guarantee exists that the stockholder will receive either the asset value or book value of the shares. The actual price or value of any share at any particular time is what it will fetch in the stock market (known as the **market value**). The market value of a share can vary significantly over time.

SECURITIES MARKETS AND TRADING

Shares in a publicly traded company can be conveniently bought and sold in the **stock market** in which that particular company is listed. The **stock exchange** is the actual building where publicly held shares are traded. The ease with which stocks can be traded through a formal stock exchange encourages individuals and institutions to invest in the stock market, which raises capital for corporations.

The first stock exchange in Canada opened in Toronto in 1852; the Montréal Exchange opened 11 years later. Today, the Canadian cities of Vancouver, Calgary, and Winnipeg also have stock exchanges. The Toronto Stock Exchange (TSX) is the largest stock exchange in the country, accounting for well over 90 percent of total shares traded in the country, based on the number of transactions and their dollar value. On a global scale, the largest stock exchanges (in terms of the value of stocks traded) are those of New York, Tokyo, and London.

Since it was founded in 1971, the **National Association of Securities Dealers Automated Quotation System (Nasdaq)** has grown to become one of the largest stock markets in the world. Nasdaq was traditionally the place for smaller and new-technology companies to list their stock. However, with the rapid expansion of the technology sector, Nasdaq has grown in importance. By 2018, its market capitalization was valued at US$10 trillion. Unlike other stock markets, Nasdaq has no central location for trading. Instead, brokers acting on behalf of clients place orders with Nasdaq market brokers, called *market makers*, who concentrate on trading specific stocks. Trades are made directly between brokers and market makers by telephone or through the Internet. The **Nasdaq Composite Index** is considered an important indicator of overall performance and current trends for this stock market and, by extension, for the global economy.

Suppose you decide to invest in a company listed on the Toronto Stock Exchange. First, you have to contact a brokerage firm with a seat on the TSX. A **stockbroker** acts as your agent for all transactions. Trading is done directly by computer through a series of networks linking member brokerage firms to TSX computers. Member brokers of the TSX must pay an annual fee for their trading privileges, which buys them a seat at the exchange. In turn, brokers charge their clients a commission based on the dollar value of all transactions completed on their behalf.

Direct computer links to the TSX allow online brokerage firms to execute trade orders quickly and, sometimes, at discounted rates. As online trading technology continues to advance and as trading rules become more relaxed, major investors may eventually be able to bypass stock exchanges altogether.

Mutual funds were developed for people who prefer a more passive investment. They want to own stocks, but prefer not to be bothered with the details of buying and selling. For a fee, expert fund managers lump together the investment dollars of many clients, amass a diversified portfolio of investments, and then manage the fund on behalf of their clients.

The price of a company's stock may fluctuate greatly in response to changes in the *supply* (the amount of shares offered for sale) and the *demand* (the number of shares being sought for purchase) for shares. Factors influencing the demand

---

stock market
Either a physical place or an electronic network through which shares can be bought or sold.

stock exchange
The actual building in which shares are traded.

Nasdaq
Commonly used acronym for the National Association of Securities Dealers Automated Quotation, one of the largest stock markets in the world. It is an electronic network that functions as a stock market for over 4 100 companies, including many technology companies.

Nasdaq Composite Index
The indicator used by Nasdaq to monitor and summarize its daily trading activities and to report general or overall changes in the market value of the many stocks listed on this exchange.

stockbroker
An agent who buys and sells shares on the stock market for individuals and companies.

mutual fund
A fund comprising the investments of many clients; it is invested in the shares of other companies and managed by professional managers.

commodity
A raw or semi-processed good (such as minerals, lumber, or grain) that is often sold in bulk.

spot market
A market (such as the Ontario Food Terminal) for commodities that are bought and sold for immediate delivery.

futures market
A market for commodities that are bought and sold for future delivery.

for shares include the current profits and dividend shares of the corporation, the degree of confidence in the corporate management team, trends in the industry to which the firm belongs, and the general economic climate and outlook. Generally speaking, the rule that David Ricardo discovered over 200 years ago still applies: investors react to bad news by undervaluing certain stocks and to good news by overvaluing them. Clearly, when investing in the stock market, one must have a calm disposition, a long-term strategy, and a willingness to stay the course.

COMMODITIES MARKETS

A commodity market is a place or an institution through which **commodities** (standardized raw or semi-processed goods resulting from primary industrial activity) are traded in bulk. Soft commodities include agricultural products such as wheat, corn, sugar, coffee, soybeans, orange juice, and pork bellies. Hard commodities include mined semi-processed materials such as gold, aluminum, heating oil, gasoline, and copper.

Non-standardized commodities that require physical inspection prior to trading, such as fish and fresh vegetables, are often still traded in regular markets. The Ontario Food Terminal in Toronto, where farmers bring their produce to sell to merchants, restaurateurs, and retailers, is one such example.

The traditional physical marketplace is being replaced by a network of telephone and computer links designed to facilitate instant commodities trading. Commodities markets include both **spot markets** (where goods are traded for immediate delivery) and **futures markets** (where prices are agreed to in advance, for delivery on a specified future date). In a futures market, speculators invest in crops that are yet to be harvested or minerals that are yet to be mined. If the market price of the commodity changes, the speculators that predicted the market price correctly will realize a profit. To facilitate transactions, futures are generally traded through a stock exchange.

Most participants in commodity futures do not intend to receive delivery of the actual commodity they invest in. Therefore, futures markets deal in the trading of futures contracts, or *options*. These contracts commit both parties to buy and sell commodities at a fixed price on a set date. A *call option* is a contract giving the holder the right to buy a commodity at a prearranged date and price. A *put option* is a contract giving the right to sell a commodity at a prearranged date and price. Options are usually purchased for large quantities of a commodity. The difference between the contract price and the market price, on the day the contract matures, is paid by one party to the futures market. The futures market will then transfer this amount into the account of the other party to satisfy the contract.

Futures markets are highly speculative and, therefore, full of risk. For example, if you are confident that oil-producing countries are about to cut production to improve the market price for crude oil, and if you are confident that the following winter will be cold, you may decide to buy heating oil futures at today's market prices, with the hope of realizing a profit from any increases in market price. As a general rule, if the market price is above the contract price, the futures buyer profits and the futures seller loses money. If the market price is below the contract price, the futures seller profits and the futures buyer loses money.

UNDERSTANDING STOCK MARKET INDICATORS

The **Dow Jones Industrial Average** (often called "the Dow") is the most widely quoted indicator of general stock market trends in the United States. It is calculated daily, based on the closing prices of 30 **blue-chip** (or safe and stable) US corporations traded on the New York Stock Exchange. These companies are carefully chosen to represent all key sectors of the US economy. The Dow is considered a mirror of the stock market as a whole. If it goes up 5 percent, it is projected that the entire New York Exchange is up, on average, by the same amount. The Dow can be used over a period of time to track patterns in stock price changes on the New York Stock Exchange.

Canada's leading stock market indicator is the **S&P/TSX Composite Index**. This indicator is based on approximately 250 key stocks representing the Canadian economy. Changes in this index are believed to mirror what is happening in the entire Toronto Stock Exchange and, by extension, in the Canadian economy. Instead of being based on a set number of companies, this index uses two main criteria for inclusion: company size and trading activity on the TSX. This index also incorporates the Standard & Poor's Global Industry Classification Standard, giving investors an accurate comparison of the performance of Canadian indices with those around the world.

Regardless of the indicator being used, stock market prices can be elevated by investor confidence and shaken by evidence of economic contractions, such as declining retail sales and increasing unemployment. By shaking investor confidence, bad economic news can adversely affect stock prices. These conditions can create a **bear market**—a stock market under the influence of traders who expect prices to fall. Traders may attempt to sell off stock, hoping to buy it back after the price has fallen. When a large number of investors are like-minded, the actions of these traders, known as "bears," tend to be self-fulfilling. The abrupt stock market decline that followed the terrorist attacks of September 11, 2001, is a good example of the bear mentality at work.

Traders who expect stock prices to rise are called "bulls." They will buy stock, speculating that they will profit by owning the stock while it appreciates in value. By increasing the demand for shares, the actions of bulls can also be self-fulfilling. A market influenced by a large number of investors expecting price increases is called a **bull market**.

Dow Jones Industrial Average
The most widely known indicator of stock market activity based upon the daily closing prices of 30 blue-chip US corporations.

blue-chip stock
Shares of large corporations that are commonly regarded as safe and stable investments.

S&P/TSX Composite Index
The indicator of stock market activity used in Canada.

bear market
A stock market under the influence of traders expecting prices to fall, an expectation that is usually self-fulfilling.

bull market
A market influenced by investors expecting prices to rise, an expectation that is usually self-fulfilling.

Self-Reflect

1 Explain the difference between the market value, book value, and asset value of a corporate stock. Which value is most important? Explain why.

2 Explain how the laws of supply and demand lead to fluctuations in the market value of corporate stock.

3 Explain the difference between the following pairs of market terms:
- *commodities market* and *stock market*
- *futures market* and *spot market*
- *bull market* and *bear market*

Chapter 11
Consolidation Activities

KNOWLEDGE

1   Describe the four types of industrial activity and outline the importance of each type for the Canadian economy.

2   Prepare a comparison chart to summarize what you know about the different forms of business. Use the following criteria for your comparison: ownership, size, decision making, investor liability, profit distribution, and factors attracting investors and capital.

3   Corporations have different ways of securing the funds they need to finance expansion. Each method has its costs or drawbacks. Create a summary chart to explain and compare these costs.

THINKING & INQUIRY

4   Refer to the labour force data in Figure 11.2 (on page 205).

   a)   Applying the development theory presented in this chapter, what pattern would you expect to exist in the labour force data for 1800? Explain your reasoning.

   b)   Using the Internet, find the most recent employment-by-industry data compiled by Statistics Canada. Copy the table in Figure 11.2 in your notebook and add one more column to present the data that you found. Graph the table data to establish trend curves for each industrial sector. Use a vertical scale of 5 percent employment per large square and a horizontal scale of 5 years per large square. After you have determined trend curves for each industrial sector, project what percentage each sector will employ by the year 2050.

5   Research one of Canada's non-profit charitable organizations and present an oral report on its various activities and how it contributes to Canadian society.

6   Research the activities of two multinational corporations to assess their impact.

7   Analyze the costs and benefits of a merger from the point of view of (a) the producer and (b) the consumer.

8   Over the next month, graph the changes in the S&P/TSX Composite Index, the Dow Jones Industrial Average, or the Nasdaq Composite Index. Explain the changes in the index over this time. Compare your graph and explanation with those of your classmates to determine which stock market experienced the most change during the month.

COMMUNICATION

9 Which form of business would you prefer to use if you were starting your own business? Justify your selection in a short speech or blog post.

10 What constitutes good corporate citizenship in your opinion? Provide specific examples to support your hypothesis.

11 Do conglomerates and the concentration of corporate power in Canada pose a threat to Canadian society? Prepare a reasoned economic argument to support your position on this question.

APPLICATION

12 Use supply and demand curves to explain how stock prices might fluctuate as a result of one of the following headlines.

a) Bombardier lands jet-plane order for $2.1 billion with US airline company

b) Stelco projected to lose $50 million in fourth quarter as steel costs soar and foreign steel producers flood the market.

c) Intel to develop a microchip that boosts the capacity of Bell's fibre optic networks.

d) Fiat Chrysler announces production cuts and temporary plant closings as sales decline and vehicle inventory rises.

e) Transition Metals reports high-grade finds of platinum near Thunder Bay, Ontario.

13 "Profit sharing for corporate executives is a smart application of capitalist principles."

a) Do you agree with this statement? Explain.

b) Do you think a profit-sharing plan would make sense for employees who are not at the executive level? Explain.

14 Will small businesses become more important or less important in the Canadian economy in the future? Prepare a reasoned economic argument to support your position on this question.

Unit 3   Performance Task

Assessing Canada's Supply Management System

Canada has a supply management system for producers of milk, cheese, poultry, and eggs that guarantees a selling price higher than production costs and ensures a profit. Each farmer purchases a quota that limits production of these food items so that, overall, supply matches the estimated Canadian demand for these foods, and a price is set. High tariffs against foreign dairy and poultry ensure that Canadian prices are not undercut by cheaper imports. Is this system worth preserving?

YOUR TASK

You are chief adviser to the minister of international trade diversification who is engaged in negotiations with several countries that oppose Canada's supply management system. These countries offer to give Canada concessions in trade negotiations if this system is abolished. Prepare a report to the minister and her colleagues, making a persuasive recommendation to either abolish or retain Canada's supply management system.

STEPS AND RECOMMENDATIONS

1   Read the two contrasting positions on supply management to get started. Do additional Internet research to gather more facts on the pros and cons of the issue.

2   Work through the critical-thinking questions to help understand some of the economics of agriculture. Use the diagrams in your written or oral report.

3   Prepare a cost-benefit analysis using the steps presented in Figure 4.3 in Chapter 4.

4   Prepare a report, either written or oral, to present to the minister.

CRITICAL THINKING QUESTIONS

1   Why is demand for food inelastic? What is the impact upon price when supply shifts up or down? Draw freehand graphs to help you see the effects of supply shifts on an inelastic demand curve.

2   Would these supply shifts cause prices to shift more or less if the demand line were elastic? Again, draw graphs to illustrate.

3   What kind of market structure do farmers operate in? Check Chapter 10 to answer this question. Consider the similarity of their products, and their numbers.

4   If farmers understand the effects of overproduction on the prices they receive, why don't they voluntarily cut back?

5   Draw a freehand graph to illustrate supply management, carefully noting the impact upon price.

ADAPTING THE TASK

You may organize your report in a written, oral, or video report. A written report should be about 2 000 words. An oral or video report with diagrams should be about five minutes long. If you choose an oral report, encourage questions from your audience. In any format, diagrams are essential to clarify the concepts.

ARGUMENTS FOR PRESERVATION

Supply management corrects a problem that is common to farmers everywhere: large swings in production that cause big changes in price. The problem lies in the nature of demand and supply for agricultural products. Demand for food in general is quite inelastic. Therefore, shifts in supply due to weather or subsidized production cause significant changes in price. Individual farmers tend to produce as much as possible, contributing to overproduction that pushes prices down below production costs so that they are unable to make a profit.

When farmers are limited by a quota on how much they can produce, supply will be controlled, and prices can be set at a reasonable level to match demand. Smaller family farms are kept in business, producing just enough for domestic consumption, with the added benefit of keeping rural communities in Canada alive.

One of the benefits of supply management is quality control. The steroids and antibiotics used by farmers invariably end up in the milk, meat, and eggs being produced. Imported milk and eggs may not meet the same quality standards.

ARGUMENTS FOR ABOLITION

Supply management has created a closed Canadian market protected by a wall of tariffs that prevent cheaper imports from being sold to Canadians.

Farms in the United States, New Zealand, and Australia operate without limits on production, and, as a result, are bigger and more productive, with lower costs per unit of product.

As a result of supply management, the average Canadian family pays about $600 more per year for food. These extra costs are particularly hard on low-income families.

Ending supply management and opening up the market would force Canadian farmers to become more competitive and produce more, and it would encourage them to seek markets abroad.

ASSESSMENT CRITERIA

The following criteria will be used to assess your work:

- **Knowledge:** accurately using economic terms, concepts, and diagrams related to the economics of this issue
- **Thinking and Inquiry:** researching relevant evidence, and applying it in a sound manner
- **Communication:** presenting economic evidence in a written or oral report clearly; for an oral report, engaging the audience in an appropriate manner
- **Application:** presenting a persuasive argument to inform government decision makers

Use the rubric provided by your teacher as a coaching tool to help complete this task successfully.

Unit 4
Macroeconomics

Over the last 100 years, Canadians have increasingly come to expect the government to play a role in managing the economy. When the economy experiences trouble, such as increased unemployment or a rapid increase in the price of goods and services, Canadians often hold the government accountable for these problems and look to the government for solutions. In this unit, we will explore how the government sets economic policies in its attempts to live up to these expectations.

We will begin by looking at the main economic indicators that the government uses to determine current economic conditions and concerns, exploring their purpose and their limitations. We will examine how the economy tends to move in cycles and what factors influence these cycles. We will then consider how the government attempts to stabilize the economy through the use of spending and taxation policies. In conclusion, we will look at how the Bank of Canada, a Crown corporation of the federal government, uses the tools at its disposal to stabilize the economy.

How do governments determine economic policy?

If you are using this resource, there is a pretty good chance that you are either newly eligible to vote or very close. Election campaigns are often filled with a variety of platform positions related to economic policy that can be very confusing. Often these promises involve trade-offs—they hurt some stakeholders and help others. Making decisions about which party to support can have significant implications for you, your family, your community, and your country. After reading the four chapters in this unit, you will be more prepared to understand language related to economic policy, know what to ask candidates, voice informed opinions about policy proposals, and decide how to vote. Economics is the study of making choices about the best use of limited resources, and it is important that you seriously consider who will make those economic decisions on your behalf.

LOOKING AHEAD ⟶

The performance task at the end of this unit will require you to investigate the inquiry question above. It provides an opportunity for you to:

- Assume the role of a policy adviser for the Department of Finance in your provincial government

- Apply economic knowledge and skills to assess the economic conditions and recommend a course of action regarding appropriate fiscal and monetary policy

- Prepare and present a formal policy recommendation to the provincial minister of finance

- Use a performance task rubric and feedback to prepare a high-quality report

12
Macroeconomics:
The Basics

INTRODUCTION

An understanding of some of the key measures of overall economic performance of the national economy is important in investigating macroeconomic issues. Why is measuring national economic performance important?

- Governments use this information to understand the effect of their economic policies on meeting economic goals.
- Governments use this information to decide on tax policies and spending priorities.
- Unions and wage earners use this information in contract negotiations.
- Investors and businesses use this information to help them make investment decisions.
- Economists use this information to compare how the performance of our economy compares with that of economies of other countries.
- Economists use this information to look at the role and impact of specific industries on the whole economy.

When using a macroeconomic measure, it is important to consider the following:

- What does it assess?
- How is it calculated?
- What are its limitations?
- How do people use it?

While there are many different macroeconomic measures, we will focus on the three that receive the most attention in our economy: the consumer price index (which measures price stability), gross domestic product (which measures a country's output), and the unemployment rate (which measures the state of employment).

LEARNING GOALS

Once you have completed this chapter, you should be able to:

- Understand what *macroeconomics* means
- Describe the components included in the consumer price index (CPI), and explain how the CPI is used to adjust for the effects of inflation
- Describe the components included in gross domestic product (GDP)
- Understand why unemployment occurs, how the unemployment rate is calculated, and the impact of unemployment on the economy and citizens of a country
- Describe the strengths and weaknesses of GDP, the CPI, and the unemployment rate as macroeconomic indicators

KEY TERMS

microeconomics

macroeconomics

inflation

consumer price index (CPI)

inflation rate

indexing

hyperinflation

gross domestic product (GDP)

expenditure approach

income approach

consumption

investment

imports

exports

economic growth

standard of living

GDP per capita

nominal GDP

real GDP

underground economy

unemployment rate

labour force

full employment

GDP gap

potential GDP

Okun's law

microeconomics
The branch of economics that studies the behaviour of individuals and firms in the economy.

macroeconomics
The study of the economy as a whole.

inflation
A general rise in the price levels of an economy.

consumer price index (CPI)
A price index that measures changes in the level of prices of consumer goods and services.

Defining Macroeconomics

So far in this book, we have focused on issues related to **microeconomics**, the branch of economics that studies the behaviour of individuals and firms in the economy. Among other topics, we looked at individual markets and how they operate, and we concerned ourselves with the ideal output for firms and the characteristics of the industries in which they operate. However, this kind of analysis does not tell us much about the economy as a whole. For example, the medical technology industry may be thriving, while the auto industry is laying off large numbers of workers. Based on this information, what can we say about the economy in general? Is it in good shape or not? The study of the economy as a whole is known as **macroeconomics**.

Measuring Price Stability: The Consumer Price Index

One of the main economic goals of the federal government has been to maintain price stability. If the prices of goods and services are allowed to rise and consumers' incomes stay the same, it is as if consumers have less income. For example, if you earn $1 per day, and the only item that you ever buy is a chocolate bar that is priced at $1, you would be shocked if one day you went to the store and the bar was $2. Not only would you be shocked, you would be hungry because you could not afford to buy the bar. Even though your actual income has not changed, the price change makes it appear as if your income has decreased.

The term **inflation** is used to describe the persistent rise in the general level of prices in a country. Every year, prices tend to increase a little for a variety of reasons, which include increased consumer demand and increases in the prices of productive resources.

THE INFLATION RATE

DID YOU KNOW?

Microeconomics is rather like the pixels on an LCD screen. Individually, one can look at a pixel and say that it is "red" or "blue." To understand the complete picture, one must look at all of the thousands of pixels together. The manner in which these pixels combine gives us the picture on the screen. This complete picture is like macroeconomics. All the markets—consumers, workers, and firms together—create the "big picture" of our economy.

In Canada the responsibility of collecting data about the Canadian economy and its people lies with an organization known as Statistics Canada. To track inflation, Statistics Canada uses a tool known as the **consumer price index (CPI)**. The CPI is a price index that measures the changes in the level of prices of consumer goods and services.

It would be nearly impossible to monitor every single good and service used by every single Canadian throughout a given year. Consequently, Statistics Canada uses a type of "representative basket" of goods and services. Think of this representative basket like a shopping cart. If the typical Canadian household buys a dozen eggs and one tube of toothpaste in a month, then these items go into the shopping cart. The shopping cart that Statistics Canada uses has over 600 goods and services in it that remain constant from month to month. Each of these goods and services are put into one of eight broad categories and then "weighted" to reflect how important they are in a typical household's "shopping cart." This

FIGURE 12.1
The consumer price index (CPI)

CPI weights by major index component for Canada, 2015, expressed in percentages.

inflation rate
The annual percentage by
which the CPI has risen.

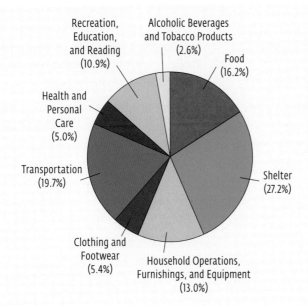

weighting is based on the proportion of the budget the typical household tends to spend in each category. Figure 12.1 presents these eight categories in a pie chart. As the chart indicates, the typical Canadian household tends to spend 27.2 percent of its consumption expenditures on costs associated with providing shelter, so the "price" of shelter is weighted at 27.2 percent in the CPI basket. Every month, employees of Statistics Canada total up the value of the shopping cart to see how much it would cost to buy the goods and services in the cart, given the price changes that occurred during the month.

To establish a basis for comparison of prices from year to year, Statistics Canada sets a base year for which it fixes the representative basket value at 100 (or 100 percent, but without the percent sign). The value of the representative basket is then totalled for each succeeding year and expressed as a percentage in terms of the base year. If the value of the representative basket is $234 in the base year (for which the CPI would be 100) and one year later it costs $249 to purchase that same basket, the CPI at the end of that year would be 106.4 ($\frac{\$249}{\$234} \times 100$).

The CPI is used primarily to calculate the **inflation rate**, which is the annual percentage by which the CPI has risen. Any two back-to-back years can be used to calculate an inflation rate. The equation for the inflation rate is as follows:

$$\text{Inflation rate} = \frac{(\text{CPI year 2} - \text{CPI year 1})}{\text{CPI year 1}} \times 100$$

For example, in June 2017 the Canadian CPI was 130.4, and in June 2018 it had risen to 133.6. Therefore, the inflation rate over that period was as follows:

$$\frac{(133.6 - 130.4)}{130.4} \times 100 = 2.5\%$$

This inflation rate tells us that over that one-year period, the general level of consumer prices rose 2.5 percent.

DID YOU KNOW?

Statistics Canada conducts an annual survey called the "Survey of Household Spending" that is used to help create the CPI "representative basket." Interviews of 17 590 households are conducted to discover their household expenditures. Fifty percent of those households then complete a spending diary for a two-week period following the interview.

indexing
An adjustment made to some wages and pension payments to offset year-to-year price increases, using the CPI as a guide.

hyperinflation
A particularly serious period of price inflation when the inflation rate exceeds 50 percent per month.

PRICE STABILITY: WHY IS IT A GOAL?

Stable prices are a sign of a healthy and well-managed economy. In Canada, the Bank of Canada is responsible for policies that try to maintain an inflation rate target of between 1 and 3 percent. When prices fluctuate above or below that range, it makes planning for consumers, producers, investors, and governments very difficult for a variety of reasons. The history of the inflation rate in Canada from 1915 to 2017 is presented in Figure 12.2.

When the general level of prices increases, consumers tend to spend money relatively quickly because they believe it will not hold its value. Think back to the example of the $1 chocolate bar described at the beginning of this chapter. If you expect the price of this chocolate bar to rise to $2 in the not too distant future, you are likely to purchase it fairly quickly so that you can actually afford to buy the bar. The same holds true for overall consumer incomes in the face of rising prices throughout the economy. As you learned in Chapter 7, this increased demand for individual goods and services can put upward pressure on prices in all individual markets, causing further inflation in the economy.

Inflation also erodes the value of savings, as money saved now is unable to purchase the same quantity of goods and services in the future. In a similar way, inflation also erodes wages. If you negotiate a wage rate to take effect right now, a high inflation rate means the wage you earn today is unable to provide the same amount of goods and services for you in the future. For this reason, unions and wage earners negotiating contracts often use the CPI to establish how future wages should be adjusted to offset year-to-year price increases. This practice is known as **indexing**. These adjustments can remove the entire effect of a price increase by increasing wages at the same rate as the CPI change (fully indexed), or they can minimize the effect of a price increase by increasing wages by a rate that is smaller than the full CPI change (partially indexed). Indexing is also sometimes used to adjust pension payments for people who are retired.

Moreover, inflation increases the cost of borrowing. It leads lenders to seek to protect the value of their loaned funds with higher interest rates to ensure that, when they are paid back, the loans maintain their original value. As a result, inflation can have a negative impact on consumers by making the cost of home mortgages higher. As well, it can slow business investment that contributes to economic growth.

FIGURE 12.2

Canada's annual inflation rate, 1915–2017

Using the labels on the graph, in addition to other knowledge that you may have about Canadian history, make some judgements about what factors have influenced the inflation rate in Canada.

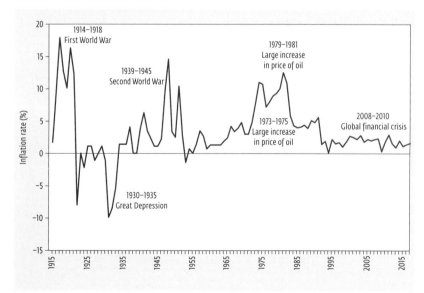

A particularly serious kind of price instability is **hyperinflation**. It occurs when inflation exceeds 50 percent in any month. When hyperinflation arises, the problem is so serious that people lose confidence in the value of their local currency and try to exchange it for a more stable foreign currency. Hyperinflation is often caused by a government printing money to support government spending while the total production of consumer goods and services remains fairly stable. The large amount of money in circulation reduces the value of each monetary unit, and it takes increasingly more of the currency to buy goods and services.

Zimbabwe experienced hyperinflation between the early 2000s and 2008. At its peak, hyperinflation was almost 100 percent per day, meaning that prices roughly doubled every 24 hours. Venezuela has also experienced hyperinflation: in 2016, the inflation rate hit 800 percent, and in 2017, it climbed to 2 400 percent. According to the International Monetary Fund, the annual inflation rate in Venezuela was projected to reach 1 million percent by the end of 2018.

LIMITATIONS OF THE CONSUMER PRICE INDEX

No economic measure is without its limitations, and the CPI is no exception. A couple of issues that need to be considered are the weighting of the categories shown in Figure 12.1 and the items included in these categories. While Statistics Canada goes to great lengths to ensure that the categories represent the spending habits of the typical Canadian household, not every household's spending habits reflect the index weights of the CPI. Some households may spend no money on tobacco and alcohol, but an above-average amount on housing. In addition, as prices change, consumers will substitute less expensive goods (such as chicken for beef) that are different than the weightings assigned by Statistics Canada. An increase in the CPI due to a price increase in these goods would disproportionately affect these households.

Another problem is changes in individual items in the representative basket. A smartphone sold today is very different in its quality, price, and composition than a smartphone sold two years ago. In addition, people may switch their purchases to entirely new products; for example, an increasing number of Canadians have "cut the cord" by switching from cable to streaming devices to watch TV. Statistics Canada tries to address some of these weaknesses by updating the spending patterns of Canadians and revising the weights of the items in the CPI basket every two years.

Cultural diversity is also an important area of concern. Some areas in Canada are very multicultural, while others have little cultural diversity. Consumption patterns are often culturally unique because housing, recreation, food, and clothing all take on varying degrees of importance in the domestic budgets of different cultures. For a family that maintains its cultural traditions, the CPI may not be a true measure of the impact that price changes have on households. This limitation is of special concern if the CPI is being used to index wages and pensions. A family may find that the CPI "understates" the impact of price increases on its budget, which would mean that its indexed income increases are not enough to cover the higher cost of living.

DID YOU KNOW?

Some individuals in Venezuela turned to "gold farming" to deal with hyperinflation. They played online video games earning virtual game coins, points, and special characters that they then sold online to international buyers in exchange for foreign currencies or cryptocurrencies such as bitcoin. Former engineers, computer programmers, and brick layers, among others, were better able to support their families than many salaried workers by earning money in a currency that was more able to retain its value.

DID YOU KNOW?

When Statistics Canada updated the CPI representative basket in 2011, smartphones, tablets, and memberships to retail clubs such as Costco were added for the first time.

Self-Reflect

1 How does Statistics Canada measure the change in the level of prices in Canada?

2 How is the inflation rate related to the CPI?

3 Explain how hyperinflation is different from regular inflation.

4 What is indexing, and why is it an important use of the CPI?

5 Why can it be said that the CPI is a good indicator for the country but not a very good indicator for individuals?

gross domestic product (GDP)

The total market value of all final goods and services produced by an economy in a given year.

expenditure approach

A calculation of GDP that totals all that the economy spends on final goods and services in one year.

income approach

A calculation of GDP that totals all the incomes earned by the different factors of production in producing all final goods and services in one year.

consumption

Household spending on goods and services.

Measuring Output: Gross Domestic Product

The most commonly used measure of a country's output is **gross domestic product (GDP)**. GDP is the total market value of all final goods and services produced within a country in one year. GDP can be calculated in two ways. The first is to add up the total that is spent on all final goods and services in one year—the **expenditure approach**. The second is to add up all the income that is earned by the different factors of production (wages, rent, interest, profit) in producing the final goods and services.—the **income approach**. In each case, GDP should be the same (that is, an expenditure for one person in the economy is an income for someone else).

Consider the purchase of an automobile. If the entire economic activity for one country were the selling of one automobile for $50 000, the expenditure approach would say that the value of GDP was the money that was spent to purchase the car—$50 000. Conversely, the income approach would measure the income earned by those who sold the car—also $50 000.

Of course, even in a one-car economy, the money flows would be a little more complicated than this. What about all the components that went into producing the car, such as the tires, the engine, the seats, and the windshield? This is why GDP measures only the *final* value of goods and services that an economy produces. Using the final value avoids what is known as *multiple counting*. The cost of these components is included in the final price of the car. If the components were counted when they were sold to the company that built the car and then counted again when the car was sold to the consumer, they would be counted twice, which would make the output of an economy appear higher than it actually is. To get an accurate measure of the value of an economy's total output, the only goods and services included are the ones purchased for final use. In other words, they are goods and services that will not be resold.

THE GDP EQUATION

To understand the coming chapters on fiscal and monetary policy, it is important to develop the concept of the expenditure approach a little further. To calculate GDP using the expenditure approach, the final value of goods and services produced in Canada is calculated by Statistics Canada by gathering expenditure information on a nationwide basis and then using a complex process to arrive at GDP. This process can be simplified to the following equation:

$$\text{GDP} = C + G + I + (X - M)$$

In the equation, the letter C represents **consumption**, or what households spend on goods and services. It is the total spent on durable goods (goods that last a long time, such as cars and household appliances), semi-durable goods (goods such as clothing that last a reasonable amount of time but not as long as durable goods), non-durable goods (goods that are used up very quickly, such as food and gasoline), and services (services such as haircuts, car tune-ups, and eating out at restaurants). It also includes money spent by non-profit institutions on supporting households.

The letter *G* represents government spending. This component is the value of expenditures on goods and services by all levels of government and includes spending on wages to employees, office supplies, and public capital goods (such as schools, highways, and hospitals).

The letter *I* represents **investment**. In economics, investment refers to the purchase of new capital goods for use in the production process, the construction of new buildings, and changes in business inventories. Statistics Canada refers to the first two components as "fixed capital formation." Another component—changes in business inventories—is included because it is output that has been produced in the time period and has value, but has not yet been sold.

Finally, *(X − M)* represents the value of net exports in Canada. In considering consumption, investment, and government spending, Statistics Canada includes purchases of all items, some of which are produced outside Canada. These items, bought by Canadian stakeholders from abroad, are known as **imports** (M). They must be subtracted from GDP because they do not represent Canadian production. On the other hand, there is also production that originated in Canada but is purchased by consumers, businesses, and governments in other countries. These items are known as **exports** (X) and must be added to GDP because they are part of Canadian output.

A breakdown of Statistics Canada's expenditure approach to calculating GDP in 2017 can be seen in Figure 12.3.

investment
A business's purchase of capital goods, construction of new buildings, or changes to inventories, with a view to increasing production and profit.

import
A good or service that is purchased by consumers, businesses, or governments that was produced in another country.

export
A good or service that is produced in one country, but sold to consumers, businesses, or governments in another country.

FIGURE 12.3
Components of Canada's gross domestic product (GDP), 2017: The expenditure approach

Component	2017 Amount (at 2007 constant prices, in $ billions)	Percentage of GDP
Consumption expenditures:		
Durable goods	165.2	8.9
Semi-durable goods	89.8	4.8
Non-durable goods	244	13.1
Services	586.3	31.5
Non-profit institutions serving households	25.1	1.3
Total consumption expenditures (C)	**1 110.4**	**59.7**
Government expenditures:		
Total government expenditures (G)	**433.3**	**23.3**
Investment expenditures:		
Fixed capital formation	343.2	18.4
Inventory change	15.5	0.8
Total investment expenditures (I)	**358.7**	**19.3**
Exports and imports:		
Exports of goods and services (X)	582.9	31.3
Less: imports of goods and services (M)	623.2	33.5
Net exports (X − M)	**−40.3**	**−2.2**
Statistical discrepancy	-1.3	-0.1
Total GDP	**1 860.8**	**100.0**

economic growth

An increase in an economy's total production of goods and services.

standard of living

The quantity and quality of goods and services that people are able to obtain to accommodate their needs and wants.

GDP per capita

The total value of a country's annual production of goods and services divided by its population; also called *per capita GDP*.

nominal GDP

The total value of GDP before it is adjusted for price increases; also called *current dollar GDP* or *money GDP*.

WHY IS ECONOMIC GROWTH A GOAL?

Economic growth is an increase in an economy's total production of goods and services. When economic output increases, the amount and quality of goods and services available to a country's citizens rises, which tends to raise the average **standard of living**. Usually, improvements in health, education, and general well-being accompany economic growth. In addition, economic growth is fuelled by maximizing a country's use of its resources, which means that during periods of economic growth, citizens are more likely to be employed.

Historically, economic growth has been an important goal for most countries. In Canada, successful economic growth is generally considered to occur when real GDP increases between 2 and 4 percent annually. The equation to calculate the GDP growth rate is as follows:

$$\text{Real GDP growth rate} = \frac{(\text{Real GDP year 2} - \text{Real GDP year 1})}{\text{Real GDP year 1}} \times 100$$

Increasingly, the idea that the goal of economies should be endless economic growth has been placed into question. Evidence exists that economic growth has some side effects that can negatively affect quality of life. As a result, many people advocate for countries to strive for *sustainable* economic growth that considers social justice, ecological justice, and economic justice, providing a goal that goes beyond increasing GDP. Some proposed alternative measures will be explored further in Chapter 22.

LIMITATIONS OF GDP

When using GDP, it is important to be aware of its limitations as a measure of output, its purpose according to Statistics Canada, and its limitations as a measure of well-being.

Limitations of GDP as a Measure of Output

As a measure of output, GDP has limitations due to a number of factors:

- *Population size:* Comparing GDP for different years may be misleading if the population of the country has changed significantly. A country where GDP has grown by 5 percent may seem to have had substantial growth, but if the population has grown by 7 percent, there is actually less output per person. Dividing a country's GDP by its population reveals its **GDP per capita**. This measure accounts for the effect of a population change on GDP.

- *Inflation:* If total GDP in one year is valued at $300 million and in the next year it is measured at $320 million, what can we say about the increase in output? On the surface, it appears to have increased by 6.7 percent, but some of that change is because of an increase in prices due to inflation and some of that change is due to an actual increase in the amount produced. If prices increased by 2 percent, then the "real" GDP growth would be 4.7 percent. **Nominal GDP** (also known as *current dollar GDP* or *money GDP*) is the total value of the output of an economy before the effect of price increases is removed. In our example, that would be $320 million. Once the effects of inflation are removed, the **real GDP** (also known as *constant-dollar GDP*) is revealed to be $314 million.

- **Non-market production:** GDP does not count output that has no dollar value attached to it. This means, for example, that the contributions of people who create output by renovating their own homes, the productive services of homemakers, and voluntary services to charitable organizations are not counted. This omission seriously weakens GDP as an accurate measure of a country's output.

- **Underground economy:** Another type of economic activity that GDP does not measure is transactions for which no "paper trail" exists. Illegal activities such as selling drugs are included in this category, as are "under-the-table" transactions that occur so that parties can avoid paying taxes. Statistics Canada studies estimate that the value of these **underground economy** activities is between 2 and 3 percent of the value of GDP.

Limitations of GDP as a Measure of Well-Being

As a measure of well-being, GDP has limitations due to a number of factors:

- **Types of goods produced:** The inclusion of all types of goods and services that are produced weakens GDP as a measure of well-being. Many goods and services produced create harm to people when used in certain ways. For example, while some drugs provide a benefit when treating a medical condition, they create harm when used illegally. Some would argue that the production of drugs that harm people and the production of weapons that wound or kill people do very little to improve society's well-being.

- **Leisure:** Theoretically, GDP could grow significantly if all workers began to work 24 hours a day, seven days a week, but few would argue that a society with this workload had a higher standard of living than one in which its workers had at least some free time. An effective measure of well-being would take leisure time into account (something GDP does not do).

- **Environmental degradation:** GDP does not consider the negative environmental effects of our economic production. Water pollution, air pollution, and solid waste disposal do not make us better off, yet the production of the goods and services that create these problems add to our GDP. In an ironic twist, environmental disasters, such as oil and chemical spills, actually increase GDP because money is spent to clean them up.

- **Distribution of income:** GDP does not consider how evenly the income in a country is distributed among citizens. A country can have significant economic growth and the appearance of rising living standards for its population, but if the growth is so unevenly distributed that a very small segment of the population is reaping most of the rewards, it cannot be said that the standard of living has actually risen for most of the citizens in that country.

real GDP
The total value of all goods and services produced in a country in a given year, adjusted for price changes; also called *constant dollar GDP*.

underground economy
Economic activity for which no paper trail exists because it is illegal or conducted "under the table" to avoid following regulations or paying taxes on the transaction.

Some stakeholders use increases in GDP as an indicator of a nation's well-being. A train derailment has many costs associated with it that could hardly be described as improving well-being. Rescue costs, healthcare costs for those who are injured, costs to replace damaged infrastructure, costs associated with mitigating environmental damage all add to the GDP, but can we really say that society is better off than if the accident had never occurred?

Noting the limitations of GDP does not necessarily make GDP a useless measurement tool. GDP remains an important measure of the vitality of an economy. However, anyone using statistics, economic or otherwise, should understand that all measures have their limitations. When using measures, it is essential to identify these limitations and understand their impact on any conclusions reached.

US Senator Robert F. Kennedy once summed up the drawbacks of measures of output such as GDP in this way:

> [GDP] . . . counts air pollution and cigarette advertising, and ambulances to clear our highways of carnage. It counts special locks for our doors and the jails for those who break them. It counts the destruction of our redwoods. Yet the gross [domestic] product does not allow for the health of our children, the quality of their education, or the joy of their play. It does not include the beauty of our poetry or the strength of our marriages . . . it measures everything, in short, except that which makes life worthwhile.

DID YOU KNOW?

In the early 1990s, Chilean economist Manfred Max-Neef proposed a "threshold hypothesis" for GDP growth. It stated that "for every society there seems to be a period in which economic growth (as conventionally measured) brings about an improvement in the quality of life, but only up to a point—the threshold point—beyond which, if there is more economic growth, quality of life may begin to deteriorate."

Self-Reflect

1 Why is it important that only the final value of goods and services is measured when calculating GDP?

2 Describe the components of the equation used to calculate GDP using the expenditure approach.

3 What is the difference between nominal GDP and real GDP?

4 What is the difference between non-market production and underground economic activity? How do they impact GDP as a measure of output?

unemployment rate
The percentage of the labour force that is not working at any given time; the total number of unemployed people divided by the total labour force.

labour force
The total of all people holding jobs plus all of those actively seeking work.

Measuring the State of Employment: The Unemployment Rate

The unemployment rate is likely the economic measure that receives the most attention in Canada. This is due to the personal and easily observed nature of unemployment. Most of us have had to look for a job at one time or another, and the impact of not finding a job is easy to imagine. It is also obvious that if someone is not working, that person is not contributing to economic output, so a high unemployment rate is a clear sign that the economy is not using all of its resources efficiently.

The **unemployment rate** is the percentage of the labour force not working at any given time. Statistics Canada calculates this figure once per month. It starts by conducting a nationwide Labour Force Survey of 100 000 individuals in 56 000 households across Canada, asking a series of questions about all members of the household and their role in the economy.

The population is then grouped into a number of categories. The first category includes those under the age of 15 and those who are institutionalized (for example, in a prison)—in other words, those who are not legally eligible for the workforce. The second category is people who are eligible to be part of the workforce but have chosen not to participate. Some examples would include homemakers, students older than 16 years of age and in school full-time, and those who are retired. The third category is the **labour force**: people who are either employed or who are willing and able to work and actively seeking employment. Those who are unemployed, then, are those members of the labour force who are without work and seeking work. The equation for the unemployment rate, therefore, is as follows:

$$\text{Unemployment rate} = \frac{\text{Number unemployed}}{\text{Labour force}} \times 100$$

TYPES OF UNEMPLOYMENT

The reasons for unemployment are varied and can be classified into several types:

- *Structural unemployment:* It occurs when the skills or location of workers no longer matches the patterns of labour demand in the economy. Subclasses of structural unemployment include technological unemployment and replacement unemployment.

  - *Technological unemployment:* It results from industries using more technology in the production process and thus reducing the need for workers. Increased automation in industries such as the automobile industry leads to technological unemployment.

  - *Replacement unemployment:* It results as firms move labour-intensive production to other countries where labour costs are cheaper, such as China and Mexico. This type of unemployment has taken place in manufacturing industries across Canada. Workers producing in another country replace the local Canadian labour.

- **Geographical unemployment:** It results when unemployment affects a specific region of a country (it is also known as *regional unemployment*). This type of unemployment occurred in the 1990s in Atlantic Canada when cod fisheries shut down due to declining fish stocks. Geographical unemployment is part of the reason for differences in the unemployment rates listed in Figure 12.4.

FIGURE 12.4

Average annual unemployment rate by province, 2017

The differences in provincial unemployment rates demonstrate the existence of geographical unemployment in the economy.

Province	Unemployment Rate (%)
Newfoundland and Labrador	14.7
Prince Edward Island	9.9
Nova Scotia	8.4
New Brunswick	8.1
Quebec	6.0
Ontario	6.0
Manitoba	5.4
Saskatchewan	6.3
Alberta	7.8
British Columbia	5.1
Canada	**6.3**
*All sexes; 15 years of age and over	

- **Frictional unemployment:** It results from people moving between jobs. It includes both students who are graduating from school and looking for jobs, and workers who have made a choice to move from one job to another. A certain amount of frictional unemployment is natural in an economy.

- **Cyclical unemployment:** It results from a reduction in overall consumer spending. As overall demand for goods and services declines in all industries, fewer workers are needed in all industries. This type of unemployment was predominant in the Great Depression of the 1930s.

- **Seasonal unemployment:** It is caused by seasonal variations in climate over the year. Fishing, farming, construction, and recreational camps are all examples of industries that see a decline in employment over the winter months. Statistics Canada adjusts for this type of unemployment when it calculates its "seasonally adjusted" unemployment rate.

- **Classical unemployment:** It is sometimes called "real wage" unemployment. This type of unemployment occurs when wages are driven too high (above the natural equilibrium wage rate in the labour market), thereby causing a surplus of workers. Governments have been accused of causing this type of unemployment by setting minimum-wage rates above the equilibrium rate. In addition, labour unions have also been accused of causing this type of unemployment through strong collective bargaining.

full employment
The lowest possible rate of unemployment, seasonally adjusted, after allowing for frictional and structural unemployment.

WHY IS FULL EMPLOYMENT A GOAL?

Having the goal of full employment is important for a number of reasons. First, it helps to maximize the efficient use of the productive input of labour. When workers are sitting idle, the economy by definition must be falling below its potential output levels. Second, a high unemployment rate also burdens the government with the financial cost of programs like Employment Insurance (EI), which help alleviate the problem of unemployment. The financial cost to the government is compounded by lost taxation revenues due to lower incomes and decreased spending on goods and services. Third, significant social costs are associated with unemployment. People who suffer from unemployment face a loss of self-esteem, a loss of job skills, and an increase in family tension. Periods of high unemployment have also been linked to periods of social unrest, higher crime rates, poorer physical and mental health, and political upheaval.

One would think that full employment means an unemployment rate of zero, but that is not necessarily the case. Most economists believe that, in an active and free economy, at least some structural and frictional unemployment will always exist. Indeed, the only way to eliminate frictional unemployment is for the government to decide where and when workers can move from job to job. Figure 12.5 indicates that over the past few decades, even when the economy has been in a period of significant growth, the unemployment rate has been no lower than in the range of 6 to 7 percent. Workers tend to feel more confident about leaving their positions and seeking better employment opportunities when the economy is doing well, and, therefore, the amount of frictional unemployment during this time is probably at its maximum. Other types of unemployment are minimized because the economy is doing very well. As a result, **full employment** in Canada is considered by many to be when the unemployment rate is in the range of 6 to 7 percent. This is also known as the *natural rate of unemployment*.

FIGURE 12.5
Seasonally adjusted unemployment rate for Canada, 1976–2017

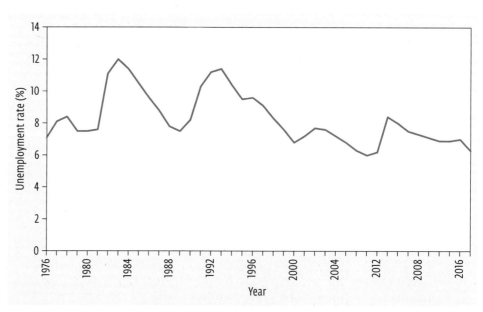

LIMITATIONS OF THE UNEMPLOYMENT RATE

The definition of the *labour force* used by Statistics Canada to calculate the unemployment rate has led some to question the accuracy of this measure of unemployment. First, the *labour force* is defined as anyone with a wage-earning job, 15 years old and over. Yet many workers are part-time; they want to be employed in full-time jobs, but must accept part-time jobs to get by. In reality, part-time workers are only partially employed, but for the purposes of the unemployment rate, they are counted as if they were fully employed. Second, the *labour force* does not include those workers who have been looking for a job for so long that they have just "given up," believing that no suitable work is available for them. Statistics Canada calls these people "discouraged workers." People who are not actively looking for work are not counted as part of the labour force and, therefore, are not considered in the unemployment rate. In addition, Indigenous people living on reserves are not counted in the labour force due to the difficulty in collecting data on them. All of these factors contribute to the understatement of the unemployment rate. In other words, the actual unemployment rate is higher than the official figure suggests. For example, while the official unemployment rate in 2017 was 6.3 percent, a supplementary unemployment rate calculated by Statistics Canada that includes discouraged workers and involuntary part-timers was estimated to be 9.1 percent.

The unemployment rate also falls short as a means to estimate whether the resource of labour is "fully employed." Many people accept jobs for which they are overqualified; for example, a recently graduated teacher who can only find work as an educational assistant. These people are said to be "underemployed" because their skills are not being fully utilized. Underemployment means the economy is falling short of its full productive capacity. Some people who are not counted as part of the labour force because they are "discouraged workers" may actually be involved in black market activity known as "off-the-books employment," where they are paid in cash and not actually recorded as an employee. Moreover, those involved in unpaid housework and volunteer work are not counted as part of the labour force, but their labour is certainly "employed" in productive output in the economy.

In closing, it is important to note that, even with its shortcomings, the unemployment rate is still a useful measure (like the CPI and GDP) for tracking the performance of the Canadian economy and comparing its performance to that of other countries. Statistics Canada follows international methodology guidelines set by the United Nations Statistics Division (UNSD) in an effort to standardize measures. Therefore, Canada uses the same definitions and calculations as other countries that follow the statistical methods prescribed by the UNSD.

Self-Reflect

1 Explain how Statistics Canada determines the unemployment rate.

2 Outline the social and economic costs of unemployment.

3 What is the natural rate of unemployment considered to be in Canada?

4 Why is zero percent unemployment not considered full employment?

5 Describe the limitations of the method used by Statistics Canada for calculating the unemployment rate.

Thinking like an Economist

Okun's Law

GDP gap

The cost of unemployment to the economy, measured by the difference between the actual GDP produced and the potential GDP that could be produced if the unemployment rate equalled the natural rate of unemployment.

potential GDP

The output that the economy can produce if the unemployment rate is equal to the natural unemployment rate.

Okun's law

A formula that states that for every percentage point that the actual unemployment rate exceeds the natural employment rate, a GDP gap of 2 percent occurs.

A level of unemployment that is above the natural rate of unemployment has both financial and social costs associated with it. One of the financial costs of unemployment is the lost output that results from the labour resources that are sitting idle. Think back to what you learned about the production possibilities curve in Chapter 2. Now, have a look at Figure 12.6. At point A (inside the production possibilities curve), the economy falls short of what it is actually able to produce because of unemployed resources. With respect to unemployed labour, this lost output is known as the **GDP gap**. It is the difference between the actual GDP produced by the economy and the **potential GDP** that could have been produced if the unemployment rate were equal to the natural rate of unemployment (point B).

In the 1960s, American economist Arthur Okun studied the relationship between GDP and unemployment. **Okun's law** states that for every percentage point by which the actual unemployment rate exceeds the natural rate of unemployment, a GDP gap of 2 percent occurs. The GDP gap equation is as follows:

$$\text{GDP gap} = \text{Actual GDP} \times \frac{\text{Unemployment rate} - \text{Natural rate of unemployment} \times 2}{100}$$

FIGURE 12.6

The GDP gap and its impact as demonstrated by a production possibilities curve (PPC)

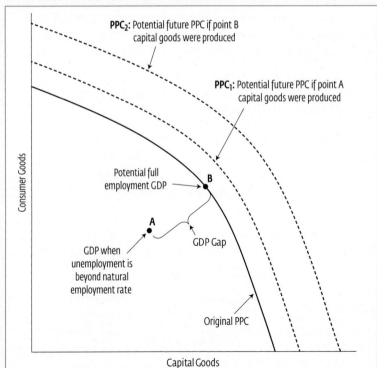

In Canada in 2009, during the economic recession, the unemployment rate was 8.4 percent. If the natural rate of unemployment is assumed to be 6.5 percent, then the real unemployment rate exceeded the natural rate by 1.9 percent (8.4 minus 6.5). This means that GDP could have been 3.8 percent higher (1.9 percent times 2). The actual real GDP during the economic downturn in 2009 was $1 549.8 billion, but it could have been 3.8 percent higher, or $58.9 billion more, in terms of dollars ($1 549.8 × 0.038). This figure represents the GDP gap. The potential GDP of the Canadian economy in 2009 was $1 608.7 billion— if only it had been able to achieve full employment.

This GDP gap can have a compounding effect over time. In Figure 12.6, the significance of labelling the two axes "Capital Goods" and "Consumer Goods" lies in the fact that, if the economy were fully utilizing its resources, the potential for producing more capital goods, without sacrificing any consumer goods, exists. The production of more capital goods in the present would translate into an outward shift of the production possibilities curve in the future because more capital goods would be available as inputs for the production process. If a country produces at point A, its future production possibilities curve (PPC) only shifts to PPC_1 because of the relatively smaller amount of capital goods it is adding to the productive resource base compared with point B. If that same country were to produce at point B, its future PPC curve shifts to PPC_2 instead because it has added relatively more capital goods for use in production without sacrificing any consumer good production. In future years, this "loss" of capital goods would continue to hold PPC curves to levels below what they could have been. This means that the GDP gap in the present has a significant long-term impact in the future—the loss of potential growth.

APPLYING ECONOMIC THINKING

1   In 2016, Canada's GDP was $1 803.3 billion, and the unemployment rate was 7.0 percent. If the natural rate of unemployment is 6.5 percent, what was Canada's GDP gap in 2016?

2   The data in the table below are from the Organisation for Economic Co-operation and Development (OECD). The "natural rate of unemployment" in the OECD table is called the Non-Accelerating Inflation Rate of Unemployment (NAIRU). Calculate the GDP gap for each country presented in the table.

Country	2015 Nominal GDP ($ billions)	2015 Unemployment Rate (%)	NAIRU (Natural Unemployment Rate) (%)
Australia	1 638.1 (AUD)	6.1	5.6
Canada	1 995.0 (CAD)	6.9	6.6
Greece	176.0 (EURO)	24.9	16.0
Korea	1 486 076.4 (WON)	3.6	3.4
Spain	1 080.0 (EURO)	22.0	15.5
United States	18 120.7 (USD)	5.3	4.5

Chapter 12
Consolidation Activities

KNOWLEDGE

1. Develop your own analogy to explain the difference between microeconomics and macroeconomics.

2. "Not all Canadians feel the impact of inflation equally." Explain this statement, referring to the limitations of the CPI.

3. Why should one be cautious in using per capita GDP as a means of comparing standards of living?

4. Calculate the unemployment rate for each of the countries in the following table.

Country	Labour Force (2017)	Number Employed (2017)
Brazil	103 743 000	90 495 000
Philippines	42 776 000	40 355 000
Portugal	5 219 000	4 756 000
South Africa	22 289 000	16 169 000
Turkey	30 952 000	27 582 000

THINKING & INQUIRY

5. What type of unemployment is each of the following scenarios contributing to?
   a) Jacob is laid off by Olubuyide Motors as it brings new automation to its assembly line.
   b) Yixuan is a lift operator laid off from a ski resort for the summer.
   c) Katie graduates from university and is searching for her first job.
   d) Anusha loses her job when Hoyt Enterprises, a hockey stick manufacturing company, closes its plant in Canada, preferring to manufacture its sticks in Sweden and import them.
   e) Andrew is laid off by Chang Incorporated, a doughnut company, because consumers have shown a tendency to eat more bagels than doughnuts.
   f) Parnia is one of many workers dismissed by a large number of companies because of a general decline in demand for goods and services.
   g) Daniel is laid off by Zappone Farms when a drought in the province destroys many of the crops.

6. Suggest one course of action that could be used to ease or eliminate each of the types of unemployment listed on page 247.

7. Which of the following transactions are counted as part of GDP, and to which component of expenditure GDP does each belong?
   a) The purchase of building materials by Pietersen Designs, a contractor who is working on remodelling your kitchen
   b) The purchase of building materials by you for the basement renovation project that you are completing
   c) The sale of a dozen ears of corn in the supermarket
   d) The provision of tutoring services to you in exchange for your accountant mother's help in completing the tutor's tax return
   e) The building of a new factory by Waterston Inc. for its stained-glass manufacturing
   f) The purchase by Rojina of a Swiss-made watch

8. Use the Internet to determine the real GDP growth rate, unemployment rate, and inflation rate in Canada for the last two years. Double-check your answers by comparing the data from two different sources. Some suggested sites are Statistics Canada, the Organisation for Economic Co-operation and Development (OECD), the International Monetary Fund (IMF), and the World Bank. If there are discrepancies between the data, investigate possible reasons for the discrepancy.

COMMUNICATION

9   Choose any one of the three economic measures explored in this chapter. Imagine that you are a communications officer for Statistics Canada. Create a public information brochure designed to communicate to the general public the significance of the economic indicator. Some points to consider include the following: How is it measured and calculated? What does the indicator reveal about the economy? Why is it important? What are its weaknesses and limitations?

10 Collect two or three articles from newspapers, magazines, or online databases that you believe relate to the concepts taught in this unit. For each of the articles, write a brief summary and explain how the article relates to what you learned in this chapter.

11 Many economic measures other than those described in this chapter are useful in macroeconomics. Choose a source such as Statistics Canada, the OECD, the IMF, the World Bank, or back issues of newspapers to find two other macroeconomic measures. Write a brief report to explain what they measure and how they might help you assess the state of the economy.

12 Create a "mind map" with GDP as the central concept. Use separate branches to demonstrate the components of GDP (expenditure approach) and further sub-branches to provide examples of each component. Feel free to use any combination of images, symbols, or words to create your mind map.

13 Either on your own or with a partner, consult one of the following websites: OECD, IMF, or the World Bank. Collect and compare the data regarding the three main economic measures described in this chapter for any five countries and Canada (ensure that the data for each country are from the same year). Create one set of bar graphs for each measure that displays the results of your research. Examine the graphs for similarities and differences between countries. Conduct further research to determine why any differences occur. Write a summary of your findings.

APPLICATION

14 a) The fictional economy of Timla measures its GDP at $540 billion in a year when its actual unemployment rate is 9.3 percent. Economists estimate the natural unemployment rate as 4 percent. What is the GDP gap of Timla?

    b) Timla government economists estimate that if the Ministry of Labour had spent $10 billion on programs to create employment, the unemployment rate would have gone down to 7 percent. From a financial point of view, would it have been wise for the ministry to go ahead with these programs? Explain your answer.

15 Which is most likely to have a bigger impact on the CPI? A 10 percent increase in the price of gasoline or a 10 percent increase in the price of clothing? Explain your reasoning.

16 Koskins Inc. has negotiated a collective agreement with its workers that fully protects them against the effects of inflation by fully indexing wages to the CPI. If the wage rate for workers in the first year of their contract was $15.75 per hour when the CPI was 127, what would be the wage rate at the end of the third year of the contract when the CPI is 145?

17 The federal government decides to give a tax deduction (income that a person is not required to pay tax on) for the purchase of educational books. In the year 2015, the deduction is valued at $1 000, and in 2018, the deduction is valued at $1 100. The CPI in 2015 is 128, and in 2018, it is 145. Is the deduction fully or partially indexed? Explain your answer.

18 You sometimes hear politicians tout tax cuts for consumers as a way to stimulate economic output. Use Figure 12.3 to help explain this claim.

13

Business Cycles and Fiscal Policy

INTRODUCTION

Chapter 12 introduced critical macroeconomic indicators such as the unemployment rate, the inflation rate (measured as an annual percentage change in the consumer price index [CPI]), and economic growth (measured as an annual percentage change in gross domestic product [GDP]). In Chapter 2, we examined how the production possibilities curve helps describe the choices that an economy faces and the potential that exists if all of its resources are used to maximum efficiency. In other chapters, we also explored how equilibrium is determined in the product, labour, and capital markets. These concepts form the foundation necessary to understand how the macroeconomy works.

In this chapter, based on this knowledge, we will examine models of macroeconomic supply and demand, and how these models are used to explain what a healthy economy looks like. As well, we will explore the business cycle and its phases, and what they indicate about the state of the economy. Finally, we will examine how the government seeks to ensure economic stability through something called *fiscal policy*.

LEARNING GOALS

Once you have completed this chapter, you should be able to:

- Explain the macroeconomy through aggregate demand and supply analysis
- Demonstrate an understanding of the fluctuations of the economy as explained by the business cycle
- Use an aggregate supply and demand model to analyze how government fiscal policy can be used to achieve economic goals
- Explain how fiscal policies influence the economic decisions of individuals and organizations, and analyze the consequences of these policies
- Analyze the factors that influence fiscal policy decisions in Canada
- Describe the challenges of using fiscal policy to manage the economy

KEY TERMS

aggregate demand (AD)

aggregate supply (AS)

full-employment equilibrium

recessionary gap

inflationary gap

business cycle

prosperity cycle

recession

depression

circular flow of income

leakage

injection

stabilization policies

fiscal policy

expansionary fiscal policy

contractionary fiscal policy

automatic stabilizers

progressive tax

discretionary fiscal policy

infrastructure

multiplier effect

marginal propensity to consume (MPC)

marginal propensity to withdraw (MPW)

deficit budget

surplus budget

balanced budget

debt

cyclical deficit

structural deficit

recognition lag

decision lag

implementation lag

impact lag

crowding out

aggregate demand (AD)
The total demand for all goods and services produced in an economy.

Aggregate Demand and Supply

In previous chapters, we looked at supply and demand to explain how equilibrium is established in individual markets. Our explanation of equilibrium at the macro level begins with a similar analysis. If we could add up all consumer demand, at all the various price levels, for all markets, we should be able to determine the total demand schedule for an economy. Similarly, if we could add up all that producers are willing to supply, at all the various price levels, for all markets, we should be able to determine the total supply schedule for an economy. When we combine all markets' goods and services in society, we are looking at the aggregate, or total, for the entire economy.

AGGREGATE DEMAND

DID YOU KNOW?

The GDP deflator is an index that measures price levels against a base year, much like the consumer price index. The main difference is that the CPI measures only consumer prices, while the GDP deflator accounts for price changes in all components of the GDP.

Aggregate demand (AD) is the total demand for all goods and services in an economy. In constructing the AD schedule, instead of examining individual prices (as in the microeconomic concept of demand) we will use the GDP deflator. The AD schedule in Figure 13.1 presents the total amount of output that would be demanded at each of the GDP deflator price levels that might exist in an economy. The graph of its AD curve is displayed next to it. Note that the AD curve looks very similar to the market demand curve studied in microeconomics—as price levels rise, the aggregate quantity demanded falls.

Finally, notice that the aggregate demand at each of the price levels is equivalent to the real GDP that would occur at that price level, or the sum of all consumption (C), investment (I), government spending (G), and net exports (X – M) in the economy. In Chapter 12, we defined the GDP equation as follows:

$$GDP = C + I + G + (X - M)$$

For real economic growth to occur, real GDP must grow—in other words, the aggregate quantity demanded must increase at each of the price levels. This means that one or more of the variables in the GDP equation must increase in value.

FIGURE 13.1
Aggregate demand schedule
This table shows the total amount of goods and services that would be demanded at each of the price levels in an economy. Beside it is its accompanying aggregate demand curve.

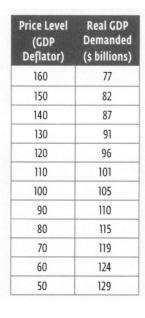

Price Level (GDP Deflator)	Real GDP Demanded ($ billions)
160	77
150	82
140	87
130	91
120	96
110	101
100	105
90	110
80	115
70	119
60	124
50	129

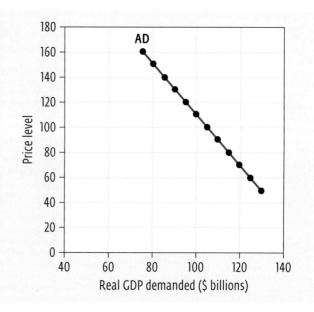

AGGREGATE SUPPLY

Aggregate supply (AS) is the total supply of all goods and services produced in an economy. The AS curve displays the total amount of goods and services that would be supplied at each price level, as measured by the GDP deflator, in an economy. Figure 13.2 presents an AS schedule for an economy. The AS curve is displayed beside it.

While similar in shape to the supply curve in microeconomic supply and demand analysis, the AS curve features some important differences. It is very elastic, or flat, at low output levels. At very low output, most of a society's resources are idle and their prices low. For example, when many people are unemployed, little competition exists for workers, keeping the costs of labour low. Therefore, there is little increase in the costs of production when new workers are hired to increase output. Price levels would consequently stay low even as output increases. However, as output increases further, more competition occurs among producers for limited amounts of land, labour, and capital inputs. As a result, input prices go up and put upward pressure on the prices of all goods and services.

At higher output levels, prices tend to rise more rapidly. At some point, the economy would run out of resources altogether. Then, any attempted increase in output would simply result in producers pushing input prices to higher levels without producing any more output. The aggregate supply curve becomes perfectly inelastic, or vertical, at this level of output. In theory, an economy producing at that level of output is producing at a point on its production possibilities curve—it cannot physically produce more output without improvements in technology or the discovery of new physical inputs.

aggregate supply (AS)
The total supply of all goods and services produced in an economy.

Price Level (GDP Deflator)	Real GDP Supplied ($ billions)
160	140.0
150	140.0
140	139.5
130	137.5
120	134.0
100	123.0
90	110.0
85	80.0
84	60.0
83	40.0

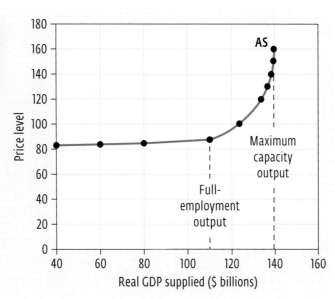

FIGURE 13.2
Aggregate supply schedule
This table shows the total amount of goods and services that would be supplied at each of the price levels in an economy. Beside it is its accompanying aggregate supply curve.

full-employment equilibrium

The intersection of aggregate demand and supply, at which full employment is reached and prices have just started to rise.

recessionary gap

The gap between aggregate demand and full-employment equilibrium, characterized by high unemployment, low inflation, and low GDP growth.

inflationary gap

The gap between aggregate demand and full employment equilibrium; characterized by high inflation, low unemployment, and high GDP growth.

EQUILIBRIUM OUTPUT AND PRICE

The point at which the AD curve intersects the AS curve is the equilibrium level of price and output for the economy (see Figure 13.3). When the economy is at **full-employment equilibrium**, the two curves intersect at a point on the AS curve where prices start to rise more rapidly, but the curve is not yet vertical. As the economy approaches full employment, competition for scarce resources starts to push price levels up. The economy still has room for further increases in real GDP because of frictional unemployment and the possibility of increasing output beyond the full-employment level (by having employees work overtime). However, at some point the curve would become vertical as an absolute capacity is reached. Therefore, full-employment equilibrium is the point at which price levels start to rise more quickly but below the absolute capacity of the economy.

Two other possibilities exist for an economy. Below full employment, equilibrium occurs when the AD curve intersects the AS curve to the left of full-employment equilibrium. At this point, real GDP is lower, and price levels are rising very slowly. The low level of output leads to higher unemployment levels and what is known as a **recessionary gap**. This situation is characterized by high unemployment, low inflation, and low GDP growth. Above full employment, equilibrium occurs when the AD curve intersects the AS curve to the right of full-employment equilibrium. At this point, real GDP growth is high, and unemployment low, but price levels are rising very rapidly. This gap is known as an **inflationary gap**. It is characterized by high inflation, low unemployment levels, and high levels of GDP growth.

FIGURE 13.3

Full-employment equilibrium occurs when the aggregate demand (AD₁) intersects aggregate supply (AS) at full-employment output (FE)

If aggregate demand (AD₂) intersects below full-employment output, a recessionary gap exists with high unemployment levels, low output levels, and low inflation. If aggregate demand (AD₃) intersects above full-employment output, an inflationary gap exists with high inflation, higher output levels, and low unemployment.

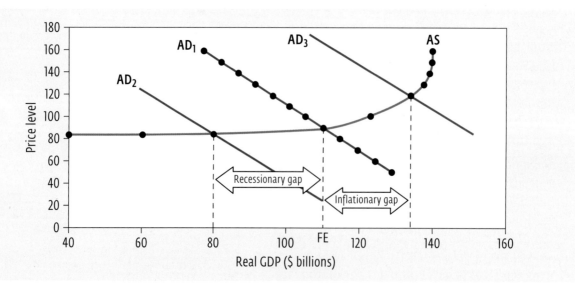

CHANGES IN AGGREGATE SUPPLY

Just as the supply curve can shift in microeconomics, the AS curve can shift in macroeconomics. There are three basic reasons why the AS curve might shift: a change in the price of any of the basic inputs (land, labour, and capital), a change in the amount of basic inputs available, or a change in the efficiency of the production process.

Changes in Price of Inputs

If the prices for land, labour, or capital increase, firms will be able to produce less at each price level. As a result, the AS curve will shift upward and to the left at all points to the left of its perfectly inelastic section (see Figure 13.4[a]). The perfectly inelastic section of the curve will not move because, while prices are higher, the maximum amount of inputs available are still the same. Therefore, the maximum real GDP possible is the same as it was before the price increases. Decreases in the price of inputs will have the opposite effect on the AS curve.

Changes in the Amount of Inputs Available

If new resources are discovered, more capital goods are made available, or the workforce grows, then more inputs are available for use. Because these changes shift the production possibilities curve outward, they increase the maximum capacity of the economy. The availability of more resources also reduces competition for them, pushing down the costs of inputs. The effect on the AS curve is to shift the relatively elastic, horizontal portion downward, reflecting decreased input prices, while shifting the vertical portion to the right, reflecting the increased capacity of the economy (see Figure 13.4[b]).

Changes in Efficiency

Improvements in technology make the workforce more productive. As the workforce becomes more efficient, it can produce more output with the same resources. The resulting impact on the AS curve is the same as increasing the amount of resources available. The curve shifts downward, with the vertical portion moving farther to the right (see Figure 13.4[b]).

FIGURE 13.4
Summary of aggregate supply curve shifts

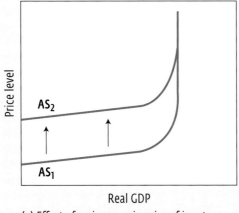

(a) Effect of an increase in price of inputs

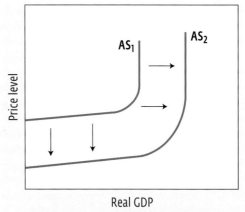

(b) Effect of an improvement in technology or the availability of more inputs

CHANGES IN AGGREGATE DEMAND

Just as events in the marketplace can shift the AS curve, the AD curve is subject to movements as well. Shifts in the AD curve can be attributed directly to changes in the variables that make up the GDP: consumption (C), investment (I), government spending (G), and the balance of foreign trade (X – M).

Changes in Consumption

Consumer income can be used in four ways. It can be used for consumption, paid to the government in the form of taxes, saved for future use, or spent on imports. In terms of the impact on aggregate demand, we are most concerned about the consumption component because it makes up almost 60 percent of GDP. The amount that is available for consumption is whatever is left over after the other three components are considered. As a result, an increase in aggregate demand will occur when consumption increases. This result may be due to either an increase in the level of income or a decrease in one or more of savings, taxes, and import spending. Such an increase in consumption is represented by a rightward shift of the AD curve because, at each price level, a higher level of real GDP is demanded.

In Figure 13.5(a), a move of the AD curve from AD_1 to AD_2 reflects an increase in aggregate demand. The result is an increase in the equilibrium level of prices, real GDP, and employment. By contrast, a decrease in consumption (or an increase in savings, taxes, and import spending) will decrease aggregate demand, shifting the curve in Figure 13.5(b) to the left from AD_1 to AD_2, decreasing price levels and real GDP, and increasing unemployment.

FIGURE 13.5
Summary of aggregate demand curve shifts

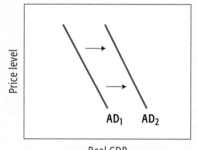

(a) An increase in aggregate demand

Caused by any one or all of these:
- increase in consumption
- decrease in taxes
- decrease in savings
- decrease in import spending
- increase in investment
- increase in government spending
- increase in exports

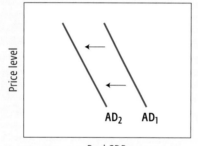

(b) A decrease in aggregate demand

Caused by any one or all of these:
- decrease in consumption
- increase in taxes
- increase in savings
- increase in import spending
- decrease in investment
- decrease in government spending
- decrease in exports

Changes in Investment

Since profits are equal to revenue minus costs, expected profits are equal to expected revenue minus expected costs. The overall level of investment spending is related, then, to the expectation of future profits. For instance, if business profits are expected to increase and the economic climate looks strong, investment will increase, and the AD curve will shift to the right. However, if businesses foresee a downturn in their profits, investment will decrease, and the AD curve will shift to the left.

These movements are also closely tied to interest rates. Because most investment necessitates the borrowing of funds, if interest rates go up, the costs associated with the investment also go up (which would reduce the potential for profit). Therefore, increases in interest rates also tend to reduce investment spending, which decreases aggregate demand and shifts the AD curve to the left. Decreases in interest rates have the opposite effect.

Changes in Government Spending

If a government increases its spending, aggregate demand will increase. As a result, the AD curve will shift to the right by acting on the G component of the GDP equation. If a government reduces its spending, the AD curve will shift to the left. These changes are at the heart of fiscal policy, which will be discussed in greater detail later in the chapter.

Changes in Trade

Three major factors influence demand for Canadian-produced exports: the domestic rate of inflation, the relative levels of income in other countries, and the value of the Canadian dollar. Domestic inflation affects the prices of domestic goods and services only; it doesn't affect the prices of foreign goods and services. Therefore, a general increase in the price of Canadian goods and services makes them relatively more expensive than foreign-made goods and services. A rapid rise in inflation will reduce export demand because foreign consumers will purchase fewer Canadian products. Conversely, a decline in the rate of inflation in Canada will make Canadian goods and services relatively less expensive and thus increase export demand.

A similar effect is felt when the income levels rise for consumers in countries that are trading partners. Their demand for goods and services will increase, and, as a result, Canadian exports to these countries will rise. The opposite would be true for a decrease in the level of foreign incomes.

An increase in the value of the Canadian dollar will increase the cost of Canadian products for those buying them in other countries, making them less attractive to foreign buyers. An increase in the value of the Canadian dollar can translate into a decrease in aggregate demand because Canadians end up exporting fewer products. On the other hand, a decrease in the value of the Canadian dollar will make the relative price of Canadian products more attractive to foreign consumers, thus increasing aggregate demand.

Any factors that increase the demand for Canadian exports relative to imports will increase aggregate demand, shifting the AD curve to the right, while factors that decrease the demand for Canadian exports relative to imports will decrease aggregate demand, shifting the AD curve to the left.

Self-Reflect

1 How are aggregate demand and supply similar to the microeconomic concepts of demand and supply?

2 What are the components of aggregate demand?

3 Why is the AS curve elastic at low levels of output and inelastic at high levels of output?

4 Describe the characteristics of an economy suffering from a recessionary gap.

5 Explain why decreases in income taxes, savings, and import spending all increase aggregate demand.

business cycle

A rise and fall in national economic performance characterized by four phases: peak, contraction, trough, and expansion.

Business Cycles

To understand the purpose of fiscal policy, we must first understand what a business cycle is. A **business cycle** is a period of swings in national economic performance as measured by changes in real GDP. It is characterized by four distinct phases: expansion, peak, contraction, and trough. A business cycle represents the ups and downs of the economy. The duration of a business cycle and its size (in loss or gain of real GDP) vary from one cycle to the next and are very difficult to predict. Some expansionary (or growth) periods are extended, while others are not. Some contractionary periods can last a long time, becoming recessions, while others seem to disappear before we notice them. In Canada, since the Second World War, recessions have averaged 13 months in length, while expansionary periods have averaged 6 years, although the two expansionary periods prior to 2018 both lasted more than 10 years.

A business cycle occurs because of the fluctuations (expansion and contraction) that economies experience over time. Earlier in this chapter, we explained such changes as shifts of the AD and AS curves. Business cycles, then, are at the heart of macroeconomics.

Economists try to determine how well the economy is doing and, more importantly, where it is heading. Forecasting patterns in the business cycle allows economists to advise political and business leaders on how to deal with possible adverse future economic events. When the economy is heading in an undesirable direction, economists may advise a country's leaders to apply policies to try and alter the course of the economy.

FIGURE 13.6

An economic business cycle is a time period of alternating expansion and contraction

In this figure, the horizontal axis measures time, while the vertical axis yields the real GDP growth rate. While the cycle appears to be even and regular, it is drawn this way only for simplicity. Actual business cycles vary in length and slope.

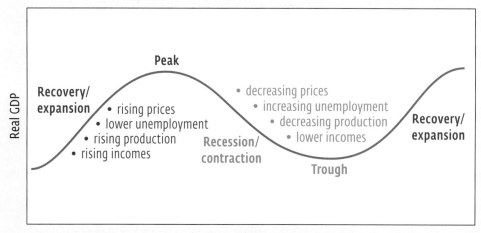

EXPANSION

The causes of fluctuations in economic activity are varied. The cyclical nature of the marketplace is dynamic, and it is not possible to detail all the reasons for cyclical fluctuations in the economy. Here we will look at two examples to illustrate how a simple macroeconomic model works.

An expansion period begins when consumer spending increases and production increases. As Figure 13.6 shows, expansion is represented by an upward trend in the business cycle. Let's assume that the Canadian economy is on an upswing—that is, unemployment is declining, business activity is increasing, and there is increased production. Generally, increased production leads to more workers being hired. New employment leads to a general rise in consumer incomes, which, in turn, generates increased levels of consumption spending. Consumer psychology that is influenced by positive economic news can also contribute to increased spending. Increased spending translates into an increase in the demand for goods and services. As we described earlier in this chapter, an increase in aggregate demand leads to higher levels of output and employment as well as higher prices. This higher demand leads to increased production, more workers being hired, and so on. As Figure 13.7 shows, this **prosperity cycle** is the result of aggregate demand feeding itself.

At first glance, it would appear that, as long as resources are available, this trend for greater and greater economic expansion should continue, which is part of the psychology that drives expansionary periods to their peak. However, at some point economic expansion inevitably ends. The economy will peak, and then the trend will begin to reverse. The reasons for the turnaround at the peak of a business cycle are varied, and therefore difficult to predict. Although economists invest a lot of time in trying to discover patterns and clues, there is no surefire way to be certain when a contraction will begin.

prosperity cycle
An increase in aggregate demand leading to a cycle of higher production, more jobs, increased income, and greater consumption, resulting in even higher aggregate demand.

FIGURE 13.7
The prosperity cycle

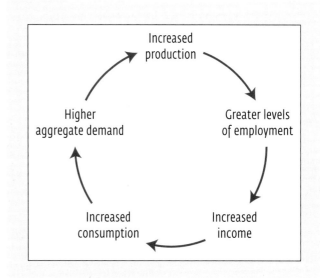

CONTRACTION

The contraction begins as the business cycle passes its peak (see Figure 13.6). Consumers may simply have exhausted the purchasing patterns that pushed up aggregate demand. After all, many of the expensive durable goods (such as automobiles, appliances, and new homes) that drive a booming economy do not need to be replaced very often. Demand begins to decrease when many consumers' wants are satisfied.

Sometimes, the turnaround is linked to an event, called a "shock," such as the stock market crash that occurred on October 29, 1929. When this event was combined with restrictive trade policies, the dependence of the Canadian economy on the market for natural resources, and reduced investment and government spending, the result was a huge drop in aggregate demand.

Frequently, peaks are created by "bubbles." A bubble is characterized by a rapid increase in the value of assets such as stocks, bonds, precious metals, or land. These bubbles are often caused by irrational expectations that an increase in asset values will continue. A surge in asset values often makes people feel wealthy, so they increase consumption. The United States' recession of 2008–2009 was blamed in part on a "housing bubble" that saw house prices rise significantly. A lot of consumer spending was supported by credit attached to the price of houses that were overvalued. When house prices dropped in a "correction," many people were unable to pay back their debts and lost their homes as a result, which triggered a contraction.

A contraction can also be the result of producers competing for capital funds to support business expansion, which tends to put upward pressure on interest rates. When interest rates rise, consumers are less likely to buy goods for which they need to borrow money—the durable goods that make up almost 10 percent of our GDP.

Finally, if the AD curve shifts too far to the right, it will exceed the economy's capacity to produce. At this point, according to aggregate supply and demand analysis, more severe inflation begins to occur. As prices rise, higher inflation levels have the effect of reducing the real income of consumers. As a result, aggregate demand begins to decline. Together, these factors have the effect of reversing the direction of shift of the AD curve. Instead of moving to the right, as it did while the economy was expanding, it now begins to shift to the left. This trend is reflected in the contractionary part of the business cycle, which has a negative slope.

In a reverse of the prosperity cycle, reduced demand for domestic goods leads to an accumulation of business inventories, and firms tend to be overstocked with goods. An increase in business inventories indicates to firms that they should cut back production. Production cutbacks lead to worker layoffs, which in turn lead to lower incomes.

Decreased incomes lead to a decrease in consumer demand for goods and services, shifting the AD curve to the left. If a decrease in aggregate demand occurs, the revenues of firms will tend to decline. Some firms will be forced to cut

DID YOU KNOW?

The CPI, real GDP growth rate, and the unemployment rate are all "lagging indicators." They provide information about economic conditions after contractions are underway. Economic forecasters try and identify "leading indicators" that can predict when a contraction will occur. This goal is notoriously difficult because every contraction is unique. Some leading indicators include factory orders for goods, the issue of building permits, and changes in commodity prices.

back production to control costs, while others may lay off workers, and firms that cannot reduce their costs may go out of business. When this type of downward spiral in economic activity occurs, it is referred to as a *recessionary trend*. It is generally agreed that a **recession** occurs when real GDP growth is negative, or declines, for two consecutive quarters (two consecutive three-month periods). The recessionary, or contractionary, part of the business cycle is characterized by increasing levels of unemployment, low (or negative) levels of real GDP growth, and low levels of inflation or even falling prices (deflation).

The contractionary period is often influenced heavily by consumer psychology. As media reports of layoffs (and the threat of more layoffs) occur, those who still have jobs reduce their levels of consumption spending. Sometimes individuals begin to save to provide a "cushion" in case they should find themselves out of work—an increasingly likely prospect, according to the news reports. Others may cut back on the purchase of "big-ticket" durable goods, fearing to increase their debt load at a time when wage increases are unlikely, and loss of income is possible. These changes in the level of consumption spending make the contractionary period worse as they tend to pull the AD curve farther to the left. If a recessionary period becomes prolonged, with very high unemployment and very low output levels, it is known as a **depression**.

At some point, events will occur that will stop the downturn in economic activity and will generate increases in consumer spending. For instance, prices may fall to a point where consumers start to spend again, and the upward movement of the business cycle resumes. Also, consumers can postpone the purchase of some items only for a certain length of time. A new automobile or refrigerator is bought when it is no longer worthwhile to repair it. Clothes wear out. As consumer purchases grow, the inventory of firms begins to dwindle, and, in most cases, firms increase production again.

While these regular fluctuations of economic activity can vary in duration and intensity, over time the level of business activity in an economy tends to increase steadily (see Figure 13.8).

recession

A contraction of the economy in which real GDP declines for a minimum of two consecutive business quarters (six months).

depression

A prolonged recession characterized by falling GDP, very high unemployment, and price deflation.

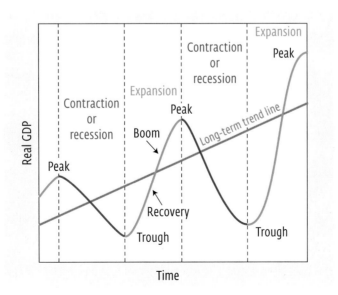

FIGURE 13.8
The phases of the business cycle can vary in intensity and duration
Over time, however, a steady upward growth trend is apparent.

circular flow of income
A model of the economy that sees GDP as a total of all the money payments made to businesses and individuals.

leakage
Any use of income (such as saving, paying taxes, and spending on imports) that causes money to be taken out of the income–expenditure stream of the economy.

injection
Any expenditure (such as investment, government spending, and exports) that causes money to be put into the income–expenditure stream of the economy.

CIRCULAR FLOW OF INCOME

A business cycle can also be explained by focusing on the money payments that flow through the economy. This **circular flow of income** represents the GDP as a total of all money payments flowing in the economy in one year. Businesses pay individuals from households in exchange for their labour, and pay individuals money through interest payments on the capital that they borrow for expansion. Individuals, in turn, spend the money they earn on the goods and services that businesses produce. This simplified circular flow of income appears in green in Figure 13.9.

Changes in the level of aggregate demand occur because of leakages and injections in the circular flow of income, as demonstrated in Figure 13.9. The term **leakages** describes any payments that lead to money being taken out of the central income–expenditure stream of the economy. Due to the role of the government, financial intermediaries such as banks, and foreign markets, the money flowing between businesses and households is subject to three leakages as it circulates. These leakages are taxes (T), savings (S), and imports (M). Taxes levied by the government on financial transactions must be paid, some of the income generated by production will be saved by both households and businesses, and some of the money flow will be used to buy imported goods.

Each of these leakages in the circular flow of income has a counterpart. **Injections** are defined as any expenditure that leads to money returning to the central income–expenditure stream. The three major injections into the economy are government spending (G), investment (I), and exports (X). Note that consumption is not considered an injection; however, it is hidden in the leakages

FIGURE 13.9
The circular flow of income
The circular flow of income (shown in green) with leakages (shown in red) and injections (shown in blue).

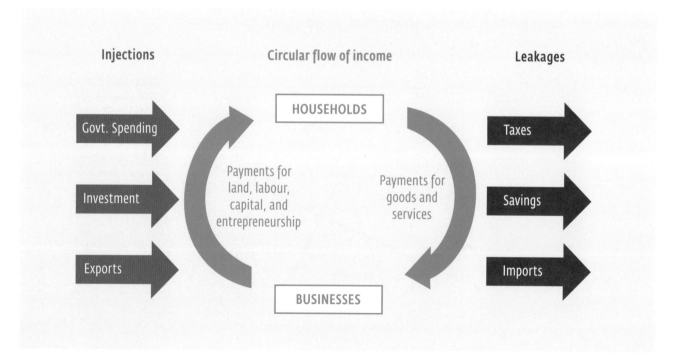

and injections model. Consumption is the "payments for goods and services" in the central part of the circular flow model. Since consumer incomes are disposed of through some combination of consumption, taxes, savings, and import spending, if leakages go up, consumers generally reduce consumption spending; if leakages go down, consumers generally increase consumption spending.

The total amounts of leakages and injections are not likely to be the same. For instance, governments might spend more or less than the amount they receive in tax revenues. Other countries' export earnings might be used to purchase imports, but there is no guarantee that trade will be balanced or that people in other countries will purchase Canadian goods. The money we save might be borrowed for business investment inside Canada, but then again, it might not.

The relationship between the three leakages and three injections determine whether overall demand is growing or shrinking. If the total of the leakages is greater than the total of the injections, aggregate demand will shrink. However, it will not shrink forever. As production falls, consumers will pay fewer taxes, save less, and buy fewer imported goods. When the total of the leakages falls to the level of the total injections, the economy generally stops shrinking. At this point, the economy is in equilibrium. The equilibrium level may be below full employment (a recessionary gap), at full employment, or above it (an inflationary gap).

When the total of the injections is larger than the total of the leakages, the economy will grow as aggregate demand increases. However, as production and incomes rise, so do taxes, savings, and imports. When the three leakages are, together, as large as the injections, growth will generally stop. Once again, this may be at, above, or below full-employment equilibrium.

Some have likened this model to filling a bathtub. If the amount of water coming in (the injection) is greater than the amount going down the drain (the leakage), the bathtub fills up (GDP gets bigger). If the amount of water coming in is less than the amount that is leaking out, the bathtub empties (GDP shrinks). Finally, if the water coming in and the water leaking out are equal, the amount of water in the tub remains the same (equilibrium).

Self-Reflect

1 List the four phases of the business cycle.

2 Explain why an expansionary phase tends to "feed itself."

3 Identify the characteristics of (a) a contractionary phase and (b) an expansionary phase of the business cycle.

4 When does a contraction become a recession?

5 List the three leakages and the three injections that exist in an economy and explain how they affect the circular flow of income.

stabilization policies
Government intervention in the economy to try to stabilize it, using fiscal and monetary policies.

fiscal policy
Government taxation, spending, and borrowing policies used to try to stabilize the economy.

expansionary fiscal policy
A government policy to increase aggregate demand through tax cuts, increased spending, or both.

Fiscal Policy

Most mixed economies go through upheavals caused by the ups and downs of the business cycle. Should the government intervene in these economic booms and contractions, or should it let the market make its own adjustments? As you learned in Chapter 6, economist John Maynard Keynes believed that government intervention can help stabilize the economy. He proposed that the business cycle could be managed, and advocated for some government involvement through fiscal and monetary **stabilization policies**.

KEYNESIAN ECONOMICS

By examining the relationships among the various forms of demand and income, Keynes was able to explain the Great Depression in a way that economists from the "classical school" could not. When the economic downturn started in 1929, businesses reduced investment and laid off employees, which decreased income and consumption. Trade was halted by high tariffs, as countries attempted to protect their economies by increasing domestic demand for their products. Governments decreased spending and raised taxes to balance their budgets. Together, these actions had the effect of shrinking the circular flow of income.

During the Great Depression, economists from the classical school advocated for minimal government involvement in the economy. They believed that government involvement hindered the efficient allocation of resources and should occur only in areas of the economy in which the private sector could not or would not effectively deliver goods and services. Taxes should be collected only to cover the yearly level of government expenditure. The classical school predicted that prices, wages, and interest rates would eventually adjust. For example, prices would fall to low enough levels that people could afford to buy goods again, and wages would fall to low enough levels that businesses would begin to hire workers. This would eventually pull the economy out of the recession cycle. However, prices, wages, and interest rates did not adjust. They stabilized at very low levels for an extended period, while unemployment remained high for a prolonged period. Keynes claimed that when traditional market mechanisms fail to work, government policy could influence the size of leakages and injections, and aggregate demand could be managed.

EXPANSIONARY FISCAL POLICY

Fiscal policy is the use by a government of its powers of expenditure, taxation, and borrowing to stabilize the economy. When the economy is in a recession, aggregate demand is too low. Unemployment is high, and there is little, or even negative, growth in output. The government could increase aggregate demand by using an **expansionary fiscal policy**. This type of fiscal policy involves decreasing taxes, increasing government spending, or both to stimulate economic growth and lower unemployment rates. Figure 13.10 illustrates how this mechanism would work.

By cutting taxes (a leakage), the government would increase the disposable income of consumers, increasing the aggregate demand in the economy through

DID YOU KNOW?

While Keynes's theories have been challenged by many, during times of extreme economic downturns, governments continue to turn to them, and the application of his ideas continues to influence economic thought in the twenty-first century. The rapid application of Keynesian-style stabilization policies in the United States and Canada during the recession of 2008–2009 is largely credited for limiting the severity and length of that economic downturn.

the consumption (C) portion of the GDP equation. The increase in aggregate demand from AD_1 to AD_2 would lead to both an increase in employment levels and an increase in GDP as the equilibrium moves closer to full-employment (FE) output. There would be little increase in the general level of prices if the equilibrium remained below full-employment equilibrium.

The same stimulation of the aggregate demand curve would occur if the government decided to enact an expansionary fiscal policy through an increase in the level of government spending; an injection in the circular flow of income. As one of the four components of GDP, an increase in government spending would directly shift the AD curve to the right through the government (G) portion of the GDP equation. A reduction in the level of taxes encourages consumers to follow through by spending their increase in income on domestic production, as opposed to saving it or spending on imports. If consumers choose not to increase consumption, aggregate demand will not increase. Because an increase in government spending acts directly on aggregate demand, there is no risk that the policy will not have some effect.

Finally, if the government wanted to maximize the effect of expansionary fiscal policy, it would both cut taxes and increase spending to stimulate aggregate demand.

CONTRACTIONARY FISCAL POLICY

When the economy is suffering from inflation, aggregate demand is too high. Employment is high, and there is high output growth. In this context, the government may wish to decrease aggregate demand by using a **contractionary fiscal policy**. This type of policy involves increasing taxes, decreasing government spending, or both to reduce upward pressure on prices. Figure 13.11 illustrates how this mechanism would work.

By increasing taxes, the government would decrease the disposable income of consumers, decreasing the aggregate demand in the economy through the consumption (C) portion of the GDP equation. The decrease in aggregate demand from AD_1 to AD_2 would lead to a decrease in the inflation rate. However, the decrease would also have the trade-off of lowering GDP and employment levels as equilibrium moved back toward full-employment (FE) output.

The government could also address this problem by altering its spending. A reduction in government spending would reduce aggregate demand. As in expansionary fiscal policy, the use of both tax and government-spending tools would increase the overall effect.

contractionary fiscal policy
Government policies to decrease aggregate demand through tax increases and/or decreased spending.

FIGURE 13.10
The effect of an expansionary fiscal policy on aggregate demand

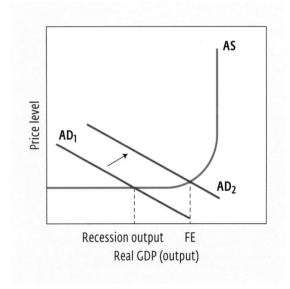

FIGURE 13.11
The effect of a contractionary fiscal policy on aggregate demand

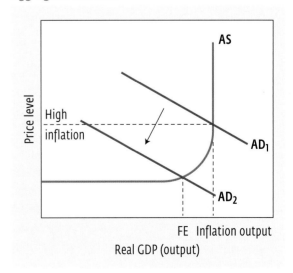

The goal of these fiscal stabilization policies is to smooth out the ups and downs of the business cycle, as Figure 13.12 indicates.

FIGURE 13.12
The effect of fiscal policy on the business cycle
A well-managed fiscal policy reduces the wide variations between the peaks and troughs of the business cycle, making the economy relatively more stable while encouraging steady growth.

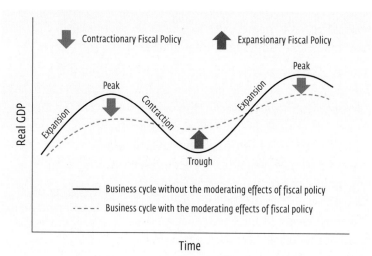

FIGURE 13.12
The effect of fiscal policy on the business cycle
A well-managed fiscal policy reduces the wide variations between the peaks and troughs of the business cycle, making the economy relatively more stable while encouraging steady growth.

automatic stabilizers
Mechanisms built into the economy that help to stabilize it by automatically increasing or decreasing aggregate demand, such as Employment Insurance, welfare programs, and progressive taxes; often contrasted with discretionary fiscal policy.

progressive tax
A tax (such as income tax) in which the tax rate increases as an individual's income increases.

AUTOMATIC STABILIZERS

What are the tools that a government has at its disposal to enact fiscal policy? Some of the key tools are known as **automatic stabilizers**. These are government-spending and taxation policies that are already in place and are acting on aggregate demand before a recession or inflationary trend fully takes hold. These stabilizers are mechanisms built into the economy that automatically stimulate aggregate demand during economic downturns and slow aggregate demand when the economy is too inflationary. They require absolutely no direct action or legislation by policy-makers because they are already legislated.

Employment Insurance (EI) and social assistance programs are two examples of automatic stabilizers. During periods of economic downturn, EI payments increase as more people become unemployed. Since unemployment increases during contractionary periods, EI payments help maintain people's incomes and, thus, the consumption (C) portion of GDP. If the contraction period is prolonged, the number of people on social assistance also increases. The purpose of social assistance programs is to ensure that people have a level of income that enables them to survive, but these payments also help increase consumption so that downward pressure on aggregate demand is somewhat cushioned. These automatic stabilizer payments either slow the leftward shift of the AD curve or begin to increase the rightward shift of the AD curve.

Another example of an automatic stabilizer is the tax rate, which varies with the level of income. A **progressive tax** acts as a stabilizer in that the percentage of income taken in taxes rises as incomes rise and has the effect of increasing a leakage as incomes grow. At lower levels of income, the income tax rate may be 20 percent, but as a person's income rises and they move to a "higher tax bracket," the rate may rise to 30 percent. This approach to taxation slows down the growth in consumption and, therefore, stops the AD curve from shifting too quickly to the right, which could lead to inflation.

Any built-in mechanism that increases or decreases government spending or taxation as the business cycle fluctuates is considered an automatic stabilizer. It is important to note that there are also discretionary elements to automatic stabilizers. At any time, the government may decide to change the level of EI payments or taxation levels. These actions are considered to be discretionary fiscal measures.

DISCRETIONARY POLICY

When the government takes deliberate actions through legislation to alter spending or taxation policies to influence the level of spending and taxation, it is using **discretionary fiscal policy**.

Changes in Spending

If the government wants to stimulate the economy, it can increase general spending in all areas of its normal budgetary programs—health and welfare, culture, education, and so on. The difficulty in increasing the budgets in these areas is that it is tough to decrease them once the economy turns around. Another way to increase spending is to undertake infrastructure programs. **Infrastructure** is the underlying foundation of goods and services that allows an economy and society to operate. These projects might include the building of roads, hospitals, schools, transit systems, and communications systems. The advantage to increased spending on infrastructure is that it can be temporary in nature by limiting it to specific projects; once the project is built, the spending ends. Moreover, spending on infrastructure adds to the stock of an economy's capital goods and, therefore, promotes the outward shift of the production possibilities curve in the future.

Changes in Taxation

To restrain or stimulate economic activity, the government can also use discretionary fiscal policy to change the amount of tax that it collects. It has several options that it may consider in pursuing this policy.

The government could raise or lower personal income taxes, corporate income taxes, or sales taxes, thus changing the amount of money leaking out of the circular flow of income during economic transactions.

Another possibility is to alter tax deductions or tax credits. Examples of tax deductions include Registered Retirement Savings Plan (RRSP) contributions, child care expenses, and payments of union dues. Examples of tax credits include EI premiums and education expenses. Tax deductions and credits are both effectively portions of income on which you are not required to pay taxes. Changing what is considered a deduction or credit would alter the amount of leakages in the circular flow of income.

The government may also provide special tax incentives for business investment, such as larger capital cost allowances on new buildings and equipment; this would influence aggregate demand through the investment (I) portion of the GDP equation.

discretionary fiscal policy
Deliberate government action taken to stabilize the economy in the form of taxation or spending policies; often contrasted with automatic stabilizers.

infrastructure
The foundation of goods and services (such as roads, power grids, transit systems, communications systems, schools, and hospitals) that allows an economy to operate efficiently.

Self-Reflect

1 How was Keynesian economics a radical departure from the classical school of economics?

2 What is the difference between discretionary fiscal policy and automatic stabilizers?

3 Under what conditions would expansionary fiscal policy be used? Contractionary fiscal policy?

4 What three options are available to a government pursuing a discretionary fiscal policy?

5 What is infrastructure, and how is spending on it beneficial in both the short and long terms?

Thinking like an Economist

The Multiplier Effect

Increasing government spending or changing taxes to help boost economic output seems rather like trying to fill an ocean with an eyedropper. In a country with a real GDP that is close to $2 trillion, how much of an effect could an increase in government spending or a decrease in taxes have? Even if government spending increased by $5 billion, that amount is only a small fraction of GDP.

This concern is mitigated by the **multiplier effect**, which describes how changes made in government spending or taxation influence the circular flow of income. The multiplier effect is the cumulative impact on GDP that occurs due to a change in people's incomes. When people have more income, they spend more, which increases the consumption of goods and services. Ultimately, the initial injection of government spending (or a tax cut) leads to a much greater increase in GDP.

The **marginal propensity to consumer (MPC)** and the **marginal propensity to withdraw (MPW)** are the foundation of the multiplier effect. These terms refer to a person's likelihood to spend extra income on domestically produced goods and services or to withdraw extra income from the circular flow of income in the form of savings, taxes, or imports.

The MPC measures the change in consumption spending that occurs with a rise or fall in income. By measuring how consumption changes in response to a rise in income levels, economists can make predictions about how an increase in incomes will affect the economy as a whole.

The MPC is calculated as follows:

$$\frac{\Delta \text{ consumption}}{\Delta \text{ income}} = \text{MPC}$$

The symbol "Δ" is read as "change in." This can be calculated by subtracting the old value of consumption and income from the new value. For example: (income in year 2 – income in year 1).

The MPW measures the change in withdrawals due to savings, taxes, and buying of imports that occurs with a rise or fall in income. The MPW is calculated as follows:

$$\frac{\Delta \text{ withdrawals}}{\Delta \text{ income}} = \text{MPW}$$

Now we will try a simple numerical example. Let's say that a household's income rises by $10 000, and the family chooses to spend $8 000 of the increase on domestic consumer items and $1 500 on imports, and it saves the last $500. In this example, the MPC would be 0.8 and the MPW would be 0.2. These values are calculated as follows:

$$\frac{\Delta \text{ consumption}}{\Delta \text{ income}} = \frac{\$8\ 000}{\$10\ 000} = 0.8$$

$$\frac{\Delta \text{ withdrawals}}{\Delta \text{ income}} = \frac{\$2\ 000}{\$10\ 000} = 0.2$$

The family in this example spent 80 percent of the increase in their income on consumption. If all families in the economy did this, there would be a cumulative impact. For example, Family 1 spent $8 000 of their increase in income. This $8 000 represents an increase in income to whomever received it (Family 2). Family 2 would then spend 80 percent of this sum, or $6 400. This amount would be

---

multiplier effect

The multiplied effect upon GDP that results from a change in people's income.

marginal propensity to consume (MPC)

A measurement of the tendency to spend a change in income on consumption, calculated by dividing the change in consumption by the change in income.

marginal propensity to withdraw (MPW)

A measurement of the change in withdrawals from national income due to savings, taxes, and buying of imports divided by a change in income.

received by Family 3, who would spend 80 percent of it, or $5 120. This re-spending would continue until the fraction becomes so small that the increase in income is finally exhausted.

If one were to add up all the re-spending in the economy that came from the initial increase in income, it would be possible to estimate the final increase in the GDP. The factor by which it increases is known as the *multiplier*. The magnitude of the multiplier depends on the size of the leakages from the circular flow of income. The equation to determine the multiplier is as follows:

$$\frac{1}{MPW} = \text{Multiplier}$$

It can also be expressed in this way:

$$\frac{1}{1 - MPC} = \text{Multiplier}$$

The multiplier in this example is as follows:

$$\frac{1}{0.2} = \frac{1}{1 - 0.8} = 5$$

This means that if all the rounds of spending were added together, the GDP would increase by a total of five times the initial increase in income. For our example, that would mean an increase in GDP of $5 \times \$10\ 000$, or a total of $50 000. As for the $5-billion increase in government spending that was indicated at the beginning of this feature, the multiplier would turn this amount into a $25-billion increase in GDP. This is why the use of fiscal policy is sometimes referred to as "priming the pump." When a pump is used to get water out of the ground, it needs to have a little water poured into the top to generate the suction that will pull water from the bottom of the well. A little bit of water to prime the pump results in a lot of water being pumped out. In the case of fiscal policy, a little bit of government spending leads to a larger increase in GDP.

The multiplier in Canada has been estimated at between 1.4 and 2, largely because of the leakage role that taxes play on increased incomes. This means that reductions in taxation levels could have a significant impact on GDP. Tax reductions not only increase disposable income for consumption spending but also decrease the MPW, which would increase the multiplier.

As a final note, just as increases in government spending and decreases in taxation have relatively large impacts on the growth of GDP through the multiplier, the reverse can also be true. Cuts in government spending and increases in taxes have a "reverse multiplier effect" with respect to how much the GDP will shrink.

APPLYING ECONOMIC THINKING

1   The Lam family has an income of $75 000 and uses $60 000 of it for consumption. They receive an increase in income to $100 000 and now spend $77 500 on consumption. What is their marginal propensity to consume?

2   If the scenario in the preceding question held true for all individuals in the economy, and the source of the increase in income was a $250-million rise in government spending, by how much would the GDP increase after the full effect of the multiplier?

deficit budget

The situation that occurs when the government spends more than it collects in taxes, causing a shortfall (or deficit), which it must cover through borrowing.

surplus budget

The situation that occurs when a government spends less than it collects in taxes, causing it to have money left over (a surplus).

balanced budget

The situation that occurs when a government spends an equal amount to what it has collected in tax revenue.

debt

The total amount that a government owes on money it has borrowed to fund deficit budgets in the past.

The Challenges of Using Fiscal Policy

While the application of fiscal policy as an economic tool has existed since the Second World War, its use is still controversial. There are many challenges in using it that need to be considered.

GOVERNMENT BUDGETS

Governments in Canada usually announce their changes in revenue and spending plans in the spring by outlining the coming year's budget. Prior to the Second World War, the only purpose of government budgets was to finance government. Today, government budgets are incredibly complicated documents drafted for both political and economic purposes. They contain economic forecasts, macroeconomic goals, and social policy objectives. In establishing its budget, a government can end up with one of three scenarios:

- A **deficit budget**, which occurs when the government spends more than it collects in tax revenue. It must borrow money to cover the shortfall.

- A **surplus budget**, which occurs when the government collects more in tax revenue than it spends. Consequently, it has money left over.

- A **balanced budget**, which results when the government spends an amount equal to what it collects in tax revenue.

A term related to deficit budgets is *debt*. The **debt** is the total amount that a government owes on money it has borrowed to fund budget deficits. For instance, if a government spends $150 billion in year 1 but takes in only $130 billion in revenues, it has a shortfall (or deficit) of $20 billion. To make up that shortfall, it must borrow $20 billion. In year 2, the government spends another $150 billion (including interest on the debt incurred in the previous year) and takes in $140 billion in revenues. Thus, in year 2, it has a deficit of $10 billion and an accumulated debt of $30 billion ($20 billion from year 1 plus $10 billion from year 2).

This cover from the 2018 federal government budget demonstrates how government fiscal documents serve both political and economic purposes.

VIEWS ABOUT GOVERNMENT BUDGETS

Over the past century, economists have been divided as to how fiscal policy should be used; when the government should have deficit, surplus, and balanced budgets; and why these decisions should be made. Part of the issue lies in the difficulty of predicting the actual output gap. Because recessions are incredibly hard to predict, little general agreement exists on when fiscal policy is needed, how much to apply, when it should be applied, and when it should be removed. Both expansionary and contractionary parts of business cycles are driven, in part, by irrational behaviour by consumers and investors, and it is very hard to predict this kind of behaviour.

Annually Balanced Budget

Until the Second World War, the primary aim of fiscal policy in Canada was to ensure that government expenditure each year did not exceed revenue—in other words, to balance the budget annually. During the Great Depression, the problem with a strict annually balanced budget policy—that it could exacerbate an existing problem in the economy—became obvious. If the government seeks to balance the budget during recessionary periods, it must either cut back spending or increase taxes. Both policies serve to intensify the effects of the recession by holding back aggregate demand. By cutting back spending, the government spending (G) portion of GDP is reduced. By increasing taxes, the government reduces incomes due to increased tax leakages, which would reduce the consumption (C) portion of GDP. Either way, the current economic problem is intensified—the recession is made worse. Conversely, during inflationary periods, tax revenues rise, and the government is forced to increase spending or lower the tax rate to balance the budget. Either way, more income is put back into the circular flow of income, causing upward pressure on aggregate demand and subsequently causing further inflation.

Cyclically Balanced Budget

Classical economists believed that the economy was self-correcting, but if the periods of downturn are prolonged and painful, is it worthwhile to wait, when the government could intervene and achieve economic infrastructure goals while at the same time alleviating the unemployment problem? According to Keynesian economists, governments should use their fiscal policy to achieve a high, stable level of national income with neither unemployment nor inflation. If an economic recession begins, the government should start to spend more than it receives in tax revenues. Such a policy is centred on altering fiscal decisions according to changes in the business cycle. During a recessionary phase, the government should run deficits by increasing government spending, decreasing taxes, or both. During an inflationary phase, the government should run surpluses by decreasing government spending, increasing taxes, or both. During weak economic times, the government should work to stimulate the economy; during expansionary and peak periods of economic activity, the government should work to slow the economy. Over the whole cycle, the deficits and surpluses should balance. The government's role, then, is to act as a stabilizer.

Deficit and Surplus Budgets as Necessary

The goal of having a cyclically balanced fiscal policy was criticized for not recognizing that the economy can sink into long periods of economic recession (as was the case in the 1930s), while subsequent expansionary phases may be relatively short. As a result, the budget may not be able to be balanced over the business cycle. An extension of Keynesian theory held that fiscal budgets could be managed from the perspective of running deficits or surpluses when necessary. A deficit budget would be used only when the economy needed a boost. If a debt was accumulated as a result, so be it. The general health of the economy was more important than the balancing of budgets over the business cycle.

Full-Employment Budget

Yet another belief is that governments should achieve a non-inflationary, full-employment level of output. That is, they should intervene with fiscal policy only when the economy falls below its full-employment targets. Inflation control because of economic expansion should be left to the Bank of Canada through tools of monetary policy (which you will discover over the next two chapters). Full employment in Canada is generally considered to be achieved when the unemployment rate is in the range of 6 to 7 percent. A full-employment budget would entail using just the right amount of government spending and taxation, combined with the multiplier effect, to shift the AD curve so that it intersects the AS curve at full-employment equilibrium.

Supply-Side Economics

Keynesian views on fiscal policy are not universal. Other schools of thought argue that government budgets should not be used to manage aggregate demand. One such school is known as *supply-side economics*. Economists of this school believe that government policies should encourage the growth of aggregate supply. Increased private investment will lead to an increase in aggregate supply, and incentives such as tax cuts should be used to encourage savings and investment for this purpose. They also believe that aggregate demand will take care of itself, as more people become employed through the increase in aggregate supply.

Critics of supply-side economics call it "trickle-down economics." They believe that tax cuts generally focus on helping corporations and those who are wealthy, and that the benefits proposed by "supply siders" are supposed to eventually "trickle down" to everyone else. They are quick to point out that such tax cuts may be held on to by the wealthy and treated as a form of additional income, never trickling down to the rest of society. Part of the problem is that investment will only occur if businesses believe the economy will be robust enough to make investment worthwhile, which is unlikely in a downturn. Increased savings also further reduces consumption, which means that investment is less likely. This scenario has been called the "paradox of thrift." While savings may be good for an individual in an economy, if everyone saves too much and consumes less, aggregate demand falls, unemployment increases, incomes fall, and everyone has less opportunity to save.

SIZE OF THE GOVERNMENT DEBT

The size of the government debt can limit the use of fiscal policy as an effective tool. The higher the government debt, the higher the amount of government spending that must be devoted to servicing the debt. (Recall that interest payments must be made on the funds borrowed as well.) Moreover, if an expansionary fiscal policy is required due to economic conditions, the government would have little room to increase spending and cut taxes without further additions to the debt.

Just how much government debt is too much? Many economists believe that the size of the debt itself is not as important as its size relative to the GDP. In Canada, between 1967 and 1997, the federal government posted a deficit budget in 30 of 31 years. Many of these years were periods of economic boom when, according to the "budget as necessary" theory, there should have been budget surpluses. The deficit budgets led to a significant accumulation of government debt. Figure 13.13 illustrates the history of Canada's net federal debt-to-GDP ratio from 1967 to 2017. In 1995, this ratio peaked at 66.8 percent. Concern about how high that ratio had grown led successive governments to run 11 straight years of surpluses, driving the ratio down to 28.1 percent. The economic downturn of 2008–2009 saw the government implement another deficit budget. Continued annual deficit budgets have occurred through 2017, driving the ratio up to 30.4 percent—still well below levels of the mid-1990s.

cyclical deficit
The part of a deficit that is incurred when the government is trying to pull an economy out of a recession.

structural deficit
The deficit that would exist even if the economy were at full employment due to the structure of government spending and taxation policies and not current economic conditions.

FIGURE 13.13
Canada's net federal debt-to-GDP ratio, 1967–2017

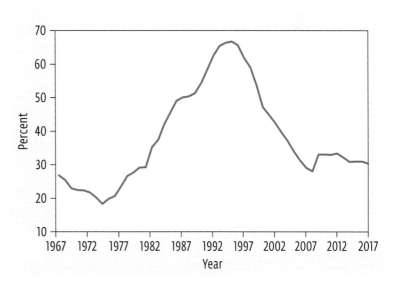

Budget deficits have two components: a cyclical deficit and a structural deficit. The **cyclical deficit** is that part of the deficit that is incurred in trying to pull an economy out of a recession. It would include spending on infrastructure projects and programs that invest in human capital, such as job retraining or the upgrading of skills. In a perfect world, the cyclical deficit would be just enough to put the economy at full-employment equilibrium.

The **structural deficit** is the deficit that would exist even if the economy were at full employment due to the structure of government spending and taxation policies and not current economic conditions. Many economists consider the presence of a structural deficit to be a sign of financial mismanagement, and an unnecessary addition to government debt.

DID YOU KNOW?

President Harry Truman of the United States is famously associated with a quote regarding his frustration with economic advisers who were unable to agree on economic projections and recommended courses of action. He is purported to have said, "Give me a one-handed economist! All my economists say, 'on the one hand . . . but on the other hand . . .'

recognition lag
The time it takes a government to recognize a problem in the economy that requires an appropriate fiscal policy to correct.

decision lag
The time required for a government to decide on an appropriate fiscal policy after recognizing that an economic problem exists.

implementation lag
The time required to implement an appropriate fiscal policy after making the decision to carry it out.

impact lag
The time required for a fiscal policy to bring about a change in the economy.

TIME LAGS

The time lags that exist in utilizing fiscal policy can be problematic. Initially, there is the **recognition lag**, or the time it takes for the government to recognize there is a problem in the economy. Once a problem is identified, there is a **decision lag**. This is the time required for the government to determine the most appropriate spending and taxation actions to implement the desired fiscal policy. Following this period, there is an **implementation lag**. Once the decision has been made, various government departments have to figure out how to implement the new directives regarding government spending and taxation. Finally, there is the **impact lag**. Once the policy is in place, time is required before its full effects can be felt through the multiplier effect. The total time lag may amount to years. This delay leads to the potential for an "overcorrection." If an expansionary fiscal policy is enacted, but the market self-corrects, the fiscal policy could actually create an undesired inflationary period. Conversely, a contractionary fiscal policy could cause a recession. The time lags are why it is important for a government to have good automatic stabilizers in place, as they help to minimize the challenges associated with these lags. Because they are already in place, automatic stabilizers only face an impact lag.

ELECTION CYCLES

Since the Great Depression, the expansionary periods have been longer than the contractionary periods, so a large debt should not be an issue. But by the year 2017, Canada had a federal debt of $714 billion. What happened? One theory is that there is a conflict between election cycles in Canada and the business cycle.

It is hard for governments to make budget cuts and raise taxes in general, but it is even harder when they are thinking about being re-elected. Generally, in the first two years of their mandate, governments make the toughest spending cuts—long before voters must cast a ballot. The nearer the time for an election, the harder it is to make spending cuts. In fact, a government that wants to be re-elected is more likely to increase spending and decrease taxes, running a budget deficit even when the economy does not need it.

It is also difficult to convince the electorate that the government should collect more in taxes than it spends, which is necessary to run a surplus budget to pay down the debt. People seem to want government help when times turn tough, but object to being "overtaxed" when the expansion years arrive.

REGIONAL VARIATIONS

Regional variations may exist that interfere with the implementation of fiscal policy. If part of the country is doing well while another region is suffering from a slowdown, what policy should be used? An expansionary fiscal policy would likely cause inflation in the region doing well, yet a contractionary fiscal policy would make the recession worse in the part of the country suffering a slowdown. Targeting fiscal policy to a specific region does not work very well. While initial government spending and taxation policies could be targeted at a specific region, it is likely that the impact of the fiscal policy would be spread well beyond the specific region once the multiplier effect is fully felt.

Additionally, conflict between the various levels of government regarding the appropriate fiscal policy might limit its effectiveness. If the federal government is reducing spending and increasing taxes in an effort to slow down economic growth, and a powerful provincial government is increasing spending and cutting taxes to gain political support, the two policies would be at odds, limiting the desired impact on economic conditions.

IMPACT ON INVESTMENT

Another potential concern about the use of fiscal policy is that a **crowding out** of private investment may occur when the government competes with the private sector to borrow funds to finance the debt. Some economists argue that expansionary fiscal policy drives up interest rates as the government competes in the market for loanable funds and, subsequently, reduces the amount of funds available for private investment. As a result, private investment in capital goods decreases and the rate of economic growth slows. In this case, the government is simply replacing government spending for investment spending with no net impact on GDP.

INCOME EQUITY

Deficits redistribute income from all taxpayers to bondholders. In a sense, the deficit creates a debt that we owe in large part to ourselves. The government sells bonds and treasury bills to finance some of that debt. These financial instruments are known as *marketable debt*. Department of Finance Canada estimated in 2017 that approximately 70 percent of the federal marketable debt was in the hands of Canadians, while 30 percent was held by foreign investors. However, only some Canadian citizens are the government's creditors. The government pays interest on the debt, but does so with tax dollars. The people who hold bonds are receiving a portion of the tax dollars paid by all Canadians. Most government bondholders are corporations or those with above-average incomes. Creating debt and financing it through bonds redistributes income from the poor to the rich in society—because most income earners pay taxes, but the interest payments go only to bondholders.

BURDEN ON FUTURE GENERATIONS

Finally, there is a concern that deficits impose a net burden on future generations because citizens at some point in the future will have to pay that money back, or at least maintain the interest payments, in the form of taxes. This concern largely depends on what the deficit is used to finance. If the money is spent on economic infrastructure, such as roads or buildings, then future generations will get the benefit of using those expenditures. However, if the deficit is generated by funding current expenditures, such as employee salaries or EI payments, then future generations will derive no net benefit from the debt that is created.

crowding out
The theory that government borrowing drives up interest rates and reduces the amount of loanable funds, thereby making it more difficult for businesses to borrow.

Self-Reflect

1 Describe the three types of government budgets.
2 How is the "debt" different from the "deficit"?
3 How does an annually balanced budget differ from a cyclically balanced budget?
4 Why is a structural deficit considered a sign of financial mismanagement in the application of fiscal policy?
5 How do automatic stabilizers help deal with the problem of time lags in fiscal policy?

Chapter 13
Consolidation Activities

KNOWLEDGE

1   Explain the three reasons an AS curve might shift.

2   Why is a shift of the AS curve to the right like an outward shift of the production possibilities curve?

3   How does a change in the interest rate influence the AD curve?

4   If the value of the Canadian dollar increases, what is the likely impact on aggregate demand?

5   Explain how the media can play a role in influencing the business cycle.

THINKING & INQUIRY

6   In a situation of declining GDP, rising unemployment, and a budget that already has a small deficit, explain the effect that each of the following government actions would have on the economy, the current year's budget, and the national debt:

   a)   A reduction in personal income taxes

   b)   A reduction in social assistance payments

   c)   An increase in spending to deal with a backlog of school building repairs

   d)   An increase in corporate taxes

7   Identify the type of fiscal policy and explain the impact on economic output, employment, and price levels, using aggregate supply and demand analysis:

   a)   Increase government expenditures and leave tax revenues unchanged when the economy is in a recession.

   b)   Increase tax revenues and leave government expenditures unchanged when the economy is suffering from inflation.

   c)   Increase government expenditures and increase tax revenues when the economy is in a recession.

8   Suppose that an economy is operating at full-employment equilibrium. Identify the type of "gap" that will occur and what will happen to output, employment, and price levels in the face of each of the following events.

   a)   A cut in income taxes

   b)   A decrease in business investment

   c)   Introduction of new technology that improves productivity

   d)   An increase in Canadians' level of saving

9   Conduct research into two economic indicators that change with the business cycle. What is the relationship between changes in these indicators and the business cycle? Assess whether these indicators could be used to predict changes in the business cycle before they occur.

10 Analyze the data presented in Figure 12.2 (Canada's annual inflation rate, 1915–2017) (page 238) and Figure 12.5 (Seasonally adjusted unemployment rate for Canada, 1976–2017) (page 248), and sketch a business cycle that is consistent with the data. For each of your "peaks" and "troughs," record the unemployment rate and/or inflation rate.

COMMUNICATION

11 Use the Government of Canada's website to locate information about the current year's budget. Write a summary of the main points in the minister of finance's latest budget statement. You may want to look for a summary document, sometimes called "Budget in Brief," to make your task easier. Identify the spending and taxing priorities in the budget. What kind of fiscal policy do you think is being followed? Assess the impact these policies will have on the national debt.

12 Figure 13.7 (page 263) displays the prosperity cycle that occurs when there is a boom. Create a flow chart that shows what a stagnation cycle would look like when a contraction is occurring.

13 Imagine that the country is suffering from a recessionary phase in the business cycle, and the federal government is carrying out an expansionary fiscal policy. The government of one of the more populous provinces is increasing taxes and decreasing government spending to get its provincial debt under control. As the minister of finance, write a letter to the premier of this province, explaining the problem with this situation. Use AS and AD curves to further your argument. How might you convince the premier that following a slightly expansionary fiscal policy could help the provincial government achieve its goal?

14 Draw a diagram illustrating leakages and injections and their relationship to GDP using the "bathtub" analogy (or create your own analogy).

15 Write a newspaper editorial to accompany the headline "Stats Canada Reports 4% Growth in Real GDP, Inflation Feared." In your editorial, explain the connection between the "report" and the "fear." In addition, include a recommendation for government action.

APPLICATION

16 One of the dangers of using expansionary fiscal policy is that it can cause inflation. Under what circumstances is an expansionary fiscal policy likely to cause inflation?

17 A fiscal policy is introduced because a recession seems to be starting. Describe what would happen to aggregate supply and demand and the three main economic measures (CPI, GDP, and the unemployment rate), if time lags cause the fiscal policy to take hold after the recession has already corrected itself.

18 Use aggregate demand and supply analysis to explain why a significant increase in the price of inputs is such a serious problem that even the application of fiscal policy may fail to address it.

19 On a trip to the East Coast, Koji discovers that the local economy has been depressed because of restrictions on fishing. He spends over $5 000 on hotels, restaurants, and entertainment. What factors will influence the actual amount by which total GDP rises in the region because of his expenditures?

20 If the marginal propensity to consume is 0.6 and the government wants to raise GDP by a total of $300 million, by how much must it increase government spending?

14
Money and Banking

INTRODUCTION

In the previous chapter, we learned how government fiscal policy attempts to stabilize the economy by influencing our spending on goods and services. We use money to pay for these goods and services, which is to say that we use money to make purchases from individuals or businesses. In this chapter, we will examine the origin and development of money from very early times to the present. We will see that banks began first as storehouses to safeguard gold and silver coins. Later, banks discovered that they could create a new type of money, known as bank deposits, which now comprise almost all of our economy's money supply.

Money and banking continue to evolve as our economy changes. With plastic credit and debit cards, we can easily draw down our deposits stored as data in bank computers to pay for goods and services. The history of money indicates that, as our economies advanced, the form that money took became less physical and more abstract. **Currency**—coins and bills—are used less and less as digital devices replace them more and more. Banks are changing from locations we visit to websites that we log on to.

LEARNING GOALS

Once you have completed this chapter, you should be able to:

- Understand the purpose, history, and functions of money in an economy
- Explain how the Canadian money supply is measured
- Identify the differences between the Canadian and US banking systems
- Recognize how banks create money through lending
- Describe how the nature of banking and money is changing

KEY TERMS

currency

double coincidence of wants

money

commodity money

fractional reserve banking

gold standard

fiat money

legal tender

bank deposit money

medium of exchange

measure of value (or standard unit of account)

store of value

liquidity

money supply

near money

demand deposit

chequing account

current account

savings account

term deposit

notice account

money market mutual fund

M1

M2

M2++

M3

near bank

branch banking system

chartered bank

monopoly bank

balance sheet

asset

liability

reserve ratio

excess reserves

cash drain

deposit (or money) multiplier

currency
Coins and notes that compose the money supply of an economy.

double coincidence of wants
The problem of barter: for a trade to occur, both parties must want what the other is willing to trade.

The History of Money

Money was not invented at one time or in one place. As societies progressed from producing a few goods that sustained life to producing many goods that also enriched life, money became a necessity. Thousands of years ago, small groups dependent on hunting and gathering spent most of their time trying to provide themselves with enough food, shelter, and clothing simply to survive. Few goods were produced, and any exchanges of goods between people were carried out through barter. The value of a good was determined in relation to another good, usually in terms of weight. For example, it might be agreed that two goats were equal to one cow or to a given amount of wheat. Although it worked well enough for exchanges between these hunter gatherers, barter still faced the **double coincidence of wants** problem. This meant that if a person wanted to exchange wheat in return for goats, that person had to find someone who had goats and wanted wheat. This is a key problem in the system of barter—one that led people to invent money.

As far as we know, cattle were the first type of money. Initially bartered for other goods, cattle came to be the *measure of value* for all other goods and, eventually, the *medium of exchange*, a type of money that was used to buy a good from a seller. No longer did a person have to offer what another wanted and want what the other offered.

As societies of hunters and gatherers evolved into agricultural economies, settling in the great river valleys of the Middle East, India, and China, farmers were able to produce surpluses of food. These surpluses allowed people to shift their energies from working the land to taking on other occupations. They became artisans, merchants, soldiers, government officials, priests, and so on. These specialists needed a way to obtain food, shelter, and clothing. For example, it was difficult for someone who produced metal agricultural tools to barter or to obtain cattle (which could then be used as a form of money to purchase necessities). Thus, money became vital to acquiring the growing number of goods that these more developed economies produced. As societies continued to advance, money took on different forms.

The ancient Lydians are credited as the first to make the leap from using metals as commodity money by minting the first coins. The coin seen here (back and front sides) dates from the sixth century BCE, though they had minted coins as early as the seventh century BCE.

THE EVOLUTION OF CURRENCY

Commodities

Money can be defined as anything that is generally acceptable in purchasing goods or settling debts. We are most familiar with coins and notes, but cattle, oxen, wheat, shells, salt, amber—and even whisky—have all served as money in various societies. These items are called **commodity money** because they have value in themselves. Although cattle were most commonly used as money in early agricultural societies, they were not practical for small transactions because they are not divisible while still alive! As societies discovered metals, cattle were usually replaced by smaller commodities, such as metal picks, hoes, and fish hooks.

About 5 000 years ago, gold, silver, and copper were introduced as commodity money. They were first used in the form of ornaments or jewellery and then were given value by weight and made into ingots, usually oblong pieces of metal. By 3 000 BCE, Babylonia used silver as money, measuring it by units of weight (known as *shekels* and *talents*) that were originally used for grain measurement. Today, the shekel is the principal unit of money in Israel. The British pound dates from the time when precious metals were circulated by weight. The pound was originally an amount of silver that weighed a pound; in 1816, Britain switched to the gold standard, a concept we will explore later in the chapter.

Coinage

The next stage was to mint the metals into coinage. The use of gold and silver as money, which merchants measured using grain on their scales, began to supersede their use as commodities. The ancient Lydians, people who lived in modern-day Turkey, are credited with minting the first coins in the seventh century BCE. The Greeks copied the Lydian idea and produced their own coinage, spreading it throughout their Mediterranean trading empire.

After Alexander the Great amassed his empire, the custom began of imprinting the head of the ruler on coinage as a guarantee of the purity and weight of the metal. However, even these coins could not deter the ruler's subjects—or even the ruler—from the temptation to cheat. Small slivers of gold or silver were collected by shaving the edges of coins, a process called *clipping*. *Sweating* was another method of collecting gold or silver slivers and dust, done by shaking the coins vigorously in a bag. The slivers and dust were then melted down and either formed into new coins or sold to make jewellery.

Rulers often *debased* the coins they issued by reducing their stated gold or silver content. They would then mint new coins that indicated the same stated value but that actually contained a smaller portion of gold or silver to provide extra revenue for themselves.

Paper

Paper money was the next stage in the evolution of money. The Chinese were the first people to develop paper money and did so in the seventh century CE. From the seventh to the eleventh centuries CE, paper receipts were issued by Christian

money
Anything generally acceptable in an economy to purchase goods and services.

commodity money
Money that has value in itself; for example, cattle, wheat, or salt.

fractional reserve banking

The discovery made by goldsmiths that they could lend much of the gold deposited with them for safe keeping because only a fraction of it was usually withdrawn by the depositors.

monastic orders for coinage deposited for safekeeping in monasteries and churches. By the thirteenth century, Italian merchants in Venice, Genoa, and Florence had taken over this role and operated as merchant bankers. The paper receipts were used to transfer ownership of coinage from one person to another. However, it was not until the seventeenth century that goldsmiths in England introduced paper receipts as a form of money that could be used to purchase goods.

Travelling merchants and people who held large numbers of coins or precious metals in bulk found it safer to deposit their money with a local goldsmith and accept a receipt for the amount deposited. These receipts then could be transferred to another person as payment for a good or service, with the assumption that, at any time, the holder could redeem the receipt for the metals stored safely in the goldsmith's vault. As long as the goldsmith was reliable, the receipts were "as good as gold." By the seventeenth century, the idea that paper could represent monetary value was accepted in England and then in continental Europe. It was a short step from paper receipts to paper currency, which promised the holder gold on demand.

The Origins of Banking and Money Creation

The goldsmiths discovered that the holders of their receipts seldom returned for payment of the full amount of gold or silver because the receipts themselves were safer and easier to use as a form of money. While small amounts of the precious metals or coins might be withdrawn, generally, the store of valuable metals in the vaults continued to pile up. A wonderful opportunity to make money now presented itself.

A goldsmith could make a loan from the untouched coinage or metals in the vault and charge the borrower interest on it. The goldsmith would insist that the borrower secure the loan by pledging property or other valuable assets that would be surrendered if the loan was not repaid. The loan itself would be granted in the form of a simple notation in the goldsmith's account books. Borrowers might use a loan for a good or service by transferring some or all of it to the account of another customer of the goldsmith. They might also take the loan in the form of paper certificates that promised payment in gold or coinage and use these certificates for payment.

Goldsmiths felt secure in the knowledge that borrowers, like the original depositors of the coinage, tended to leave most of the coinage to which their paper certificates entitled them untouched and idle in the vaults. Now there was more paper in circulation than there was coinage and metal to back it up. With the creation of paper currency, along with the notations in their account books, goldsmiths had, in reality, created money.

In their lending and deposit-accepting roles, goldsmiths had also created banking, based on the discovery that only a *fraction* of the total amount of money deposited for safekeeping needed to be kept on reserve. The rest could be lent in the form of paper. Thus, **fractional reserve banking** was born, ushering in a change in the nature of money. We will learn more about this system later in the chapter when we look at Canadian banking.

DID YOU KNOW?

In 1685, the governor of New France was unable to pay his soldiers because of a shortage of coins in the colony. He called in all the playing cards used in the colony, divided them into three denominations, signed them, and used them to pay the soldiers. The cards proved to be popular in the colony, and circulated until 1717. They were Canada's first paper money.

Central Banks

There is no doubt that if the holders of the goldsmiths' paper receipts or the borrowers with notations in the account books had all wanted to cash in at the same time, there would have been insufficient coins and metals to pay them. Indeed, this situation has occurred in every country at one time or another. When a financial crisis developed—as the result, possibly, of a war or a poor harvest—a "run on the banks" took place as note holders demanded payment in "hard money." The banks, unable to pay all the holders of their notes, were forced to close their doors and declare bankruptcy. During the nineteenth and early twentieth centuries, many banks collapsed in Europe, Canada, and the United States, taking with them the savings of their depositors. Between 1867 and 1900, for example, there were 51 banks in Canada; by 1900, 17 had failed or had been stripped of their charters.

The collapse of these banks, along with the problems associated with coinage and paper money, led to demands for governments to establish central banks and regulate the issue of coins and paper money. The Bank of England, founded in 1694, was one of the first central banks to be established with the support of its national government. Canada's central bank, the Bank of Canada, was established in 1934. By the twentieth century, most countries had central banks to regulate private banks, provide security for depositors, and issue currency. Paper currency, once issued by the private banks, was now issued by the central banks.

Like the goldsmiths' paper receipts, most national currencies were convertible into gold, until the 1930s. Countries that promised to pay gold on demand for their notes were said to be on the **gold standard**. Central banks counted on the fact that all the national currency would not be presented for payment in gold at the same time. Thus, like the goldsmiths, they could issue more currency than the amount of gold held in reserve—within limits. However, with the Great Depression of the 1930s, most countries "unhooked" their currencies from gold, abandoning the gold standard. The terrible insecurity of the Depression had undermined people's confidence in the soundness of their currency. Governments feared that their citizens might suddenly demand gold for their currency—gold that governments did not have in sufficient quantity to meet demand. Currencies became known as **fiat money**—in other words, money that is accepted not because it can be exchanged for gold but because governments declare that it is **legal tender** and, therefore, must be accepted for all payments.

Bank Deposit Money

So far in our description of money, we have concentrated primarily on currency—coins and paper. Although currency is the most visible type of money that we use, it is not the most important. In fact, currency comprises only about 7 to 8 percent of the total money supply in developed countries. The rest of the supply is called **bank deposit money**, most of which is created by the banks when they grant loans (in the same way the goldsmiths did in earlier times). Today, we use plastic bank credit or debit cards for most purchases that draw down our own bank deposits. We will discover how bank deposit money is created when we examine the Canadian banking system.

---

gold standard
A promise by a government that it will exchange gold for the national currency on demand.

fiat money
Money that represents value because governments have declared it to be legal tender, not because it is valuable in itself or exchangeable for gold.

legal tender
Money that a government has declared must be accepted within the national economy as payment for goods and services.

bank deposit money
Money composed of people's deposits and loans granted by the banks, exchangeable by cheque or electronic transfer.

Self-Reflect

1 What is the major problem with barter as a method for exchanging goods? How does money in any form solve barter's problems?

2 Why were people willing to accept paper receipts instead of gold or silver?

3 Why could goldsmiths lend more money than they had in their vaults? What risks were involved?

4 Why would people be more confident in central bank money than that issued by individual banks?

medium of exchange
The main function of money, allowing the exchange of goods and services.

measure of value (or standard unit of account)
A function of money that allows comparisons of the value of various goods and services.

What Is Money?

We have defined money as anything that is generally acceptable as payment for goods and services. Our study of the history of money reveals that, as money evolves, it becomes steadily more abstract. From being acceptable only as a valuable commodity in itself, money progressed to coins and paper backed by gold and silver, to fiat money representing value, to notations in bank accounts. Today, we are in another stage where money exists in digital form stored on bank computers.

THE FUNCTIONS OF MONEY

It is said that "money is what money does." People will accept anything as money as long as it performs the three functions for which it is designed. We will examine each of these functions in turn, starting with the most important.

A Medium of Exchange

Barter, as you will recall, requires a double coincidence of wants. Your desire for a good or service held by someone else must be matched by the other person wanting the good or service you possess. It would require much time and effort to find someone who wanted what you have and who also had what you wanted—time that both of you could be using for some other productive activity. Using money as a **medium of exchange**, you save time: you can sell your good or service to any willing buyer and then use the money to buy what you want from any seller.

The time and effort wasted in barter force people to try to become as self-sufficient as possible because they cannot be assured of obtaining through trade the goods they may need. However, money gives people the freedom to specialize in the goods and services they produce because they can then obtain the other goods they need through purchase. When people specialize, they become more skilled and productive at what they do, contributing to an increase in their community's total wealth.

As a medium of exchange, cash is legal tender in Canada. Strictly speaking, bank deposits that are exchangeable by cheque or debit card are not legal tender because they may not be accepted for all payments. Their acceptance depends on people's confidence that deposits can be converted into cash.

DID YOU KNOW?

Canadian banks issued their own currency, in various dollar denominations, until 1935 when the new Bank of Canada began to print and mint a national currency. The banks were given 10 years to phase out the use of their own notes. All notes featured portraits of members of the British Royal family.

A Measure of Value

As a **measure of value**, or **standard unit of account**, money allows us to compare the value of various goods in our economy. In the barter system, the value of any good would be expressed in terms of many other goods; for example, a loaf of bread would be worth so many eggs, so much milk, and so forth. In a money system, a unit of currency serves as a standard against which we can measure the value of a good or service and compare its value with that of another good or service. For example, if the cost of a trip to a beautiful Caribbean island is equal to the cost of a certain make of used car, money makes the comparison easy because the items are the same price.

A Store of Value

Money also serves as a **store of value**, or an instrument for storing purchasing power for the future. With barter, some good must be accepted in exchange for another; with money, a good can be sold today, and the money received for that good can be stored until it is needed. While other items known as assets (jewellery, rare paintings, antiques, real estate, stocks, and bonds) can store value as well, money is the asset that allows us to pay most easily for a good or service. The term **liquidity** refers to the relative ease with which an asset can be used to make a payment. Money is the most liquid of assets. Other assets are less liquid because, although they have value, they are not so easily exchanged for goods since they must first be sold to obtain money.

THE CHARACTERISTICS OF MONEY

In order for money to serve as a medium of exchange, it must above all be generally acceptable. Several other characteristics enhance money's acceptability, particularly when we examine coins and bills:

- Since we use money on a daily basis, it should be portable and easy to use. Heavy, cumbersome coins or large-sized bills that are difficult to pocket will not be popular.

- Money must be durable because it is passed from hand to hand countless times, stored in wallets and purses, and used in vending machines.

- Money must be easily divided into units to facilitate both small and large purchases.

- The various units of coins and bills should be readily recognizable by shape and colour to avoid mistakes during monetary transactions.

- Money must be hard to falsify. Counterfeiting is a universal problem in money systems. In the past, counterfeiters needed considerable skills to design the metal plates used in offset printers to produce counterfeit bills. The development of computer technology and high-resolution photocopiers has made the process easier, and criminals have been counterfeiting large-denomination bills. Designers of currency try to create designs and use materials that are difficult to duplicate.

- Most important, a money system composed of currency and deposits must retain its value over time. Each unit of money loses its value when prices rise in an economy because more of each unit must be exchanged to purchase a good or service. As we learned in Chapter 4, this rise in the general level of prices is known as *inflation*, and it has the potential to undermine the acceptability of money in a short time. The Bank of Canada is vigilant about inflation and is quick to warn the public and politicians of its impending appearance.

store of value
A function of money that allows value to be stored for the future, allowing it to be used in the purchase of goods and services.

liquidity
The relative ease with which an asset can be used to make a payment. Money is the most liquid asset.

Self-Reflect

1 Of the three functions of money, which one do you regard as most essential? Why?

2 Which of the three functions of money does a rise in inflation undermine most severely?

3 What is meant by *liquidity*? Rank the following assets in terms of their liquidity: a rare painting, gold jewellery, shares in a large corporation, a diamond ring, a tax return cheque.

Measuring Canada's Money Supply

money supply
The total amount of cash in circulation plus bank deposits.

near money
Deposits or assets that can act as a store of value and can be converted into a medium of exchange but are not themselves a medium of exchange.

demand deposit
A bank deposit (such as a chequing account) that can be used to make immediate payment.

chequing account
An account that serves primarily as a medium of exchange, paying little or no interest.

current account
A bank account for a business that operates like a chequing account, paying little or no interest and serving as a medium of exchange; also, part of a balance of payments account that records totals for three components: goods, services, and investment income.

savings account
A bank account that allows holders to earn interest on saved money.

term deposit
Bank accounts in which the holder agrees to deposit a fixed amount of money for a fixed period of time for a fixed interest rate.

notice account
A deposit that requires the depositor to give some notice to the bank before withdrawal of funds.

money market mutual fund
Mutual funds specializing in short-term governmental and corporate securities.

We have defined money as anything that is generally acceptable to people as payment for goods and services. The total **money supply** of a modern economy is defined as the total amount of cash in circulation outside the banks plus bank deposits. As well as fulfilling the essential *medium of exchange* function described before, money also serves to measure and store value. Currency serves all these functions at the same time, but what about all the various types of bank deposits? If they don't perform the *medium of exchange* function, should they be included in the money supply?

People now hold different types of bank deposits, along with other financial assets. This variety makes it difficult to put forward an exact definition of what should be included in the money supply. The term **near money** is used to define these other types of deposits or assets that act as a store of value and can be converted into a medium of exchange but are not themselves a medium of exchange. To understand the problem of measuring the money supply, we need to define the main types of deposits and financial assets.

COMPONENTS OF THE MONEY SUPPLY

Banks offer different types of bank deposits to their customers. Some are used for immediate, day-to-day payments by individuals and businesses, others for saving money for future use. These are the main types of bank deposits:

- **Demand deposits** can be held by individuals, businesses, and governments and allow holders to transfer money immediately, or "on demand," by cheque or debit card. The following are three types of demand deposits:
    - **Chequing accounts** pay little or no interest and are usually subject to service fees. They are used primarily as a medium of exchange.
    - **Current accounts** are set up for businesses but operate in much the same way as chequing accounts, and are also used as a medium of exchange.
    - **Savings accounts** allow holders to save money for the future and earn interest. They are not generally used for making immediate payments, although some savings accounts have chequing privileges. Banks reserve the right to require notice of withdrawal on these deposits but, in practice, allow people to make withdrawals at any time.
- **Term deposits** are accounts in which the customer agrees to deposit a fixed amount of money for a fixed period of time (usually ranging from one month to several years) in return for a higher rate of interest, which is surrendered if the deposit is cashed in. An example of a term deposit is a guaranteed income certificate (GIC).
- **Notice accounts** require the depositor to give notice to the bank before withdrawal. These accounts pay some interest and are used primarily by businesses, in which case they are called *non-personal accounts*.
- **Money market mutual funds** are mutual funds specializing in short-term (less than a year) securities issued by governments (for example, treasury bills) and corporations (for example, bonds).

DEFINITIONS OF THE MONEY SUPPLY

The Bank of Canada has broken down the money supply into several categories ranging from a narrow definition to a very broad one:

1 **M1** is the narrowest definition of the money supply. It is money that is used primarily as a medium of exchange to make payments. It includes all currency in circulation outside the banks as well as demand deposits held in chequing and current accounts. Currency that is out of circulation and held in bank vaults or automated teller machines (ATMs) is excluded because when this currency is deposited, it becomes a bank deposit. If M1 included the currency held by banks in vaults or ATMs, as well as bank deposits, the money would be counted twice.

2 **M2** is a larger measure of the money supply. It includes all M1 plus personal savings accounts, including chequing and savings accounts, term deposits, and non-personal notice deposits. This is a broader definition because it includes two types of deposits—term deposits and non-personal notice deposits—not generally used for making immediate payments. These deposits are examples of near money.

3 **M2++** includes all M2 as well as deposits at non-bank deposit-taking institutions (for example, credit unions, trust companies, and caisses populaires), money market mutual funds, and individual annuities at life insurance companies. These assets are used primarily as a store of value but typically can be turned into cash in one to two business days.

4 **M3** comprises M2++ as well as large term deposits held by businesses and foreign currencies held by Canadians. Although both types of deposits are used primarily as a store of value, they can be converted into cash.

The composition of the money supply in Canada for January 2017 and January 2018 appears in Figure 14.1. As we will see in Chapter 15, the Bank of Canada must have an accurate measurement of the money supply that is actually being used for transactions in the economy. Based on this measurement, it adjusts policies (such as the level of interest rates) to support our economy's growth. The problem for economists revolves around the question of what account or asset can be used for immediate payment by most people.

Should the money supply include only M1, the narrowest definition? M1 includes currency about which there is no argument because it is legal tender that must be accepted for payment. M1 also includes chequing accounts, which people use for payment as readily as they do currency with the advent of debit cards. However, there is a strong argument for including M2 in the money supply, especially because most people now use ATMs as well as telephone and Internet banking. These systems allow easy transfer of funds between the various accounts—from savings to chequing, for example. Does the fact that systems are in place to facilitate immediate payment encourage people to ignore the divisions between different accounts and assets? If so, a broader definition of the money supply—M2 or even M3—is most accurate.

M1
The narrowest measurement of the money supply, comprising cash in circulation along with chequing and current accounts.

M2
A larger measurement of the money supply than M1, comprising M1 plus all types of personal savings accounts, term deposits, and non-personal notice deposits.

M2++
A larger measurement of the money supply than M2, comprising M2 plus deposits at non-bank deposit-taking institutions, money market mutual funds, and annuities.

M3
A larger measurement of the money supply than M2++, comprising M2++ plus foreign currencies held by Canadians and large term deposits held by businesses.

FIGURE 14.1
The composition of the official money supply in January 2017 and January 2018 (in CAD millions)

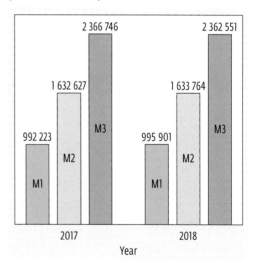

Self-Reflect

1 Which of the following assets serve as a medium of exchange: coins and bills, a term account, a savings account, a chequing account, a money market mutual fund? Which serve as a store of value?

2 Should a $50 bill found stuffed in a mattress be counted as a part of M1?

near bank
Financial institutions (such as credit unions, caisse populaires, trust, and mortgage companies) that perform several functions similar to those of chartered banks, but that do not have the power to expand or contract the money supply as the chartered banks are able to do.

Canada's Financial System

Up to this point in the chapter, we have examined money and its association mainly with banks. However, as important as they are, banks are actually part of a larger financial system in Canada that includes banks, trust companies, credit unions, insurance companies, and brokerages. These institutions used to be restricted to carrying out specific functions. For example, banks could not sell insurance, and trust companies could not sell shares of corporations, because those were the functions of brokerages. By 1992, these barriers had been removed; today, financial institutions offer several services.

While financial institutions can be divided into three broad categories, keep in mind that they cross over to perform other functions. The three broad categories are as follows:

- *Deposit-taking and lending institutions:* These include chartered banks as well as **near banks**, which comprise trust companies, mortgage companies, and credit unions. Chartered banks have a close association with the Bank of Canada; we will learn more about them shortly. The near banks now closely resemble the chartered banks in their operations, but they are not allowed to use the word *bank* in their names. In addition to accepting deposits, trust companies administer estates and trusts, mortgage companies invest depositors' assets in real estate, and credit unions are co-operatives that offer banking services to their members.

- *Insurance companies and pension funds:* Insurance companies cover individuals and businesses against fire, damage, automobile accidents, and other risks. Pension funds are pools of capital invested in financial assets, such as shares, bonds, and real estate, to provide retirement income for contributing members.

- *Investment dealers, and sales and finance companies:* Investment dealers sell new issues of company shares to the public and act as brokers for investors in the stock market. Sales, finance, and consumer loan companies lend money to businesses and individuals.

Since the chartered banks are the largest of these financial institutions, we will focus on the banking system. Its lending activities create the money necessary to purchase the goods and services produced by our economy.

DID YOU KNOW?

The worst bank failure out of the three Canada had in the last 100 years was the Home Bank in 1923. With 71 branches across the country, the bankruptcy wiped out the savings of 60 000 depositors, mostly farmers, plus large numbers of Toronto's Catholic community. Ten of the bank's executives were arrested on fraud and other charges, with the young president unable to testify due to a nervous breakdown. He died in October of the same year.

THE CANADIAN BANKING SYSTEM

Two types of banking systems operate in modern economies. The *unit banking system* allows many independent banks to exist, but limits the branches each bank can establish. The **branch banking system** restricts the number of banks that can operate, but allows these banks to establish as many branches as they want. The United States used to be an example of a unit banking system until changes made in the 1990s allowed branches to be established. Canada, on the other hand, follows the British model and has a branch banking system with few banks but many branches.

The advantage of a branch banking system is one of security for depositors. If one bank branch faced an unexpected withdrawal that could lead to a "run on the bank" by customers fearful of losing their deposits, the other branches could supply the necessary cash and restore confidence. If a bank in a unit banking system faced the same situation, it might collapse because it would have no branches to support it.

For much of the twentieth century, the Canadian branch banking system held up well in comparison to the US unit banking system. Only three banks failed in Canada between 1923 and the present. No Canadian banks failed during the Great Depression of the 1930s, or in the 2008–2009 financial crisis. In contrast, 2 200 US banks failed in 1932 alone, along with 465 during the 2008–2009 financial crisis.

The Canadian banking system may be safe, but it has been criticized for being too concentrated among a few large banks in comparison with the highly competitive US banking system. In 1998, four of the largest Canadian banks attempted to win approval to merge into two large banks, claiming they needed to be larger to compete internationally. The government turned down the proposal, sensing the public was against further concentration. Instead, the government moved ahead in 2001 with plans to stimulate further competition in Canadian banking (as we will see shortly).

branch banking system
A banking system, such as Canada's, that restricts the number of banks that can operate, but allows them to have as many branches as they want.

The six largest chartered banks in Canada, which together hold over 90 percent of all Canadian banking assets: Toronto-Dominion, Royal Bank of Canada, Bank of Nova Scotia, Bank of Montreal, Canadian Imperial Bank of Commerce, and National Bank of Canada.

chartered bank
A bank established by a charter passed by the Canadian federal government.

The Chartered Banks

At present, Canada has 28 **chartered banks**, or banks established by a charter passed by the federal Parliament. Non-residents of Canada cannot own them. Six of these banks—with over 90 percent of Canadian banking assets and about 8 000 branches across the country—dominate the Canadian banking system (see Figure 14.2).

The other chartered banks are small local banks with a few branches. One of these, the First Nations Bank of Canada, started as a joint venture between the Toronto-Dominion Bank and the Federation of Saskatchewan Indians. It is now over 80 percent owned by various Canadian Indigenous organizations.

The top six banks have numerous international branches, particularly in the United States, South America, the Caribbean, and Asia. These foreign operations are an important source of revenue for these banks: they earn up to 40 percent of the banks' total profits.

FIGURE 14.2
The top six banks in Canada by total assets, October 31, 2017

Bank	Assets ($ billions)
Toronto-Dominion	1 276
Royal Bank of Canada	1 121
The Bank of Nova Scotia	973
Bank of Montreal	727
Canadian Imperial Bank of Canada	566
National Bank of Canada	251

The First Nations Bank of Canada started as a small chartered bank in Saskatchewan in 1996. Since then, it has expanded operations across several provinces and is now over 80 percent owned and controlled by Indigenous shareholders from Alberta, Saskatchewan, Manitoba, Yukon, Northwest Territories, Nunavut, and Quebec.

FOREIGN BANKS IN CANADA

For most of Canada's history, our federal government has ensured that, by law, ownership of Canadian banks was restricted to Canadian investors. Government regulations also ensured that bank shares were widely held by Canadian investors to avoid one investor, or a small group, from controlling a bank. Canadian laws also prevented foreign banks from establishing branches or subsidiaries in Canada. However, under legislation (Bill C-8) passed in 2001, foreign banks can establish either full-service or lending branches in Canada. Fifty foreign banks now operate in Canada.

To further encourage more competition in Canada and to reduce the amount of concentrated control by the top six banks, other changes came into effect as a result of Bill C-8. The law divides Canadian chartered banks into three categories based on their size. Each category stipulates certain ownership regulations. The top six fall into the large-size category; the others into the small- and medium-sized categories. These ownership regulations allow for the creation of community-based banks (such as the First Nations Bank of Canada), with services tailored to the needs of a specific clientele. They also permit commercial enterprises with a significant retail presence to own a bank. Canadian Tire Corporation, for example, owns Canadian Tire Financial in partnership with the Bank of Nova Scotia. Other banks such as Rogers Bank exist only online with no physical location. The future will likely see more small- and medium-sized Canadian banks being established, which, along with the foreign banks, should give Canadians a reasonable amount of choice for their banking needs.

Self-Reflect

1 Contrast the branch banking system with the unit banking system. Which do you think was more desirable in the past? Which is more desirable today? Why?

2 What changes were made in 2001 to make banking in Canada more competitive?

monopoly bank

A hypothetical example of a single bank with no competitors.

balance sheet

A snapshot of the financial health of a business such as a bank, recording its assets and liabilities.

asset

Anything that is owned by a business, company, or government.

liability

Anything owed by an individual, a business, or a government.

reserve ratio

The ratio between the reserves a bank keeps on hand and the amount it has on deposit.

excess reserves

The amount of cash over and above what is needed to meet demand from depositors and so can be lent.

How Banks "Create" Money

To understand how bank deposit money is created in a banking system, we will begin by looking at the operations of a fictitious bank serving an isolated community. We will assume that no other banks are operating in this community, so residents who want to deposit money or obtain loans must deal with this **monopoly bank**. First, we have to understand how to read its books.

As with other businesses, a bank maintains a **balance sheet**, which is a snapshot of its financial health. A balance sheet is divided into two columns: assets appear in the left column and liabilities in the right column. An **asset** is something the bank *owns* or is *owed*. A **liability** is something the bank owes. Figure 14.3 shows the balance sheet of our monopoly bank. A customer who has $10 000 in cash wants to deposit it in the bank for safekeeping. The bank now has $10 000 in cash; in other words, it now owns an asset. When the customer handed over the $10 000, the bank credited the customer by creating a bank deposit, so the deposit is also a liability for the bank because it owes $10 000 to the customer. In other words, a deposit of cash creates both an asset and a liability for the bank and is recorded as such on the balance sheet.

The bank realizes that the depositor will likely withdraw only a fraction of the deposit in cash. The rest of the cash to which the depositor is entitled will not be withdrawn. Thus, the bank needs to keep only a fractional reserve against the deposit. The depositor will likely spend the new deposit by writing cheques or using a debit card. Since it is a monopoly bank, cheques will be redeposited in the bank, and the amounts will be simply transferred to the account of another bank customer. If the depositor uses a debit card, the bank will again transfer the amount from the depositor's account to another account.

Fractional reserves allow the bank to make loans and create new money. Let's suppose that the bank normally keeps 10 percent of a cash deposit as a reserve. This means that the monopoly bank keeps $1 of reserves for every $10 of deposits, a concept known as a **reserve ratio**. In this way, it can expand its deposits to *10 times* the original amount of cash deposited. How is this possible?

The bank created a deposit of $10 000 for the initial depositor of cash. Through experience, it realizes that the depositor will withdraw only 10 percent of the $10 000, or $1 000, in cash. The bank has $9 000 in cash left in the vault as **excess reserves**—that is, the amount of cash over and above what is needed to meet normal demands from the depositors. Suppose that a credit-worthy customer wants a large loan. How much could the bank lend? It could lend up to $90 000 in the form of a new deposit for this customer because the bank's experience is that borrowers will, at the most, withdraw only 10 percent in cash from their deposits. Ten percent of a $90 000 deposit is $9 000 in cash. Thus, the total cash withdrawn ($1 000 + $9 000 = $10 000) equals the total amount originally deposited. As a safety net, the bank also has cash deposited by other customers.

FIGURE 14.3

Initial balance sheet of the monopoly bank

Assets		Liabilities	
Cash	+$10 000	Deposit	+$10 000

Let's check the balance sheet after the loan by examining Figure 14.4. The loan is recorded as an asset because the borrower has signed a contract, usually called a *promissory note*, backed by collateral—something of value (for example, real estate, bonds, or stocks) that the bank would take if the loan were not repaid. At the same time, because the loan has been granted to the borrower in the form of a new deposit, it is recorded as a liability because the bank owes the amount to the borrower.

It may seem that some sort of numerical trick has been performed because the amount of money created by the loan is so much greater than the amount of "real money" the bank has in its vault. However, there are three key points to keep in mind:

- The loan is in the form of a bank deposit—a figure (noted in an account book in the past, imprinted on a chip in the bank's computer system today) that is money. It is considered money because it can be exchanged for goods by writing a cheque or by using a debit card. In the case of our monopoly bank, none of this money leaks out to another bank. All of it returns in the form of cheques or credits to other accounts in the same bank.

- Generally, people demand little cash relative to the size of their deposits. In a sense, the bank can "get away" with creating loans much larger than its cash reserves. The loans, in turn, create the bank deposits that compose the greatest part of the economy's money supply.

- The bank has a constant flow of incoming cash deposits that give it a safety hedge of cash against occasional customers who draw out more than 10 percent of their deposits in cash.

Modern economies have many banks, making the process of money creation more complicated, but the result is still the same: a given amount of reserves can support a much greater expansion of the money supply measured in newly created bank deposits. Before we turn to a modern multibank system to see how this is accomplished, we have to make two assumptions. First, each bank lends the fullest possible amount from its reserves. Second, each borrower uses the total amount of a loan to repay a debt, and the amount is immediately redeposited by the person who has been repaid.

We will go through the process of money creation in the banking system by looking at a series of transactions. Let's begin with Bank A, which has the same balance sheet as our monopoly bank and the same reserve requirement—10 percent. It has $9 000 in excess reserves (see Figure 14.5).

Bank A is now in a position to use its excess reserves to make a loan of $9 000 to Ms. Yeung. It grants the loan in the form of a new bank deposit in the borrower's (Ms. Yeung's) chequing account (see Figure 14.6).

FIGURE 14.4
Balance sheet of the monopoly bank following a loan

Assets		Liabilities	
Cash reserves	$10 000	Initial deposit	$10 000
Loan	+$90 000	New deposit	+$90 000
Total	$100 000	**Total**	$100 000

FIGURE 14.5
Bank A's balance sheet
It now has excess reserves that it can use to make a loan.

BANK A			
Assets		Liabilities	
Cash	+$10 000	Initial deposit	+$10 000
Required reserves	$1 000		
Excess reserves	-$9 000		
Total	$10 000	**Total**	$10 000

FIGURE 14.6
Bank A makes a loan of $9 000 from its excess reserves to Ms. Yeung

BANK A			
Assets		Liabilities	
Cash reserves	$10 000	Initial deposit	$10 000
Loan (owed by Ms Yeung)	+$9 000	New deposit (owed to Ms Yeung)	+$9 000
Total	$19 000	**Total**	$19 000

Ms. Yeung spends the loan by writing a cheque or using a debit card. Let's assume that she buys new furniture and writes a cheque to a furniture store for the full amount of the loan. The store's account is with another bank, Bank B, where the cheque is deposited. Bank A must pay Bank B $9 000. Figures 14.7 and 14.8 show the new balance sheets for Banks A and B.

Bank A's reserves and deposits have been reduced by $9 000, but Bank B now has a new deposit of $9 000. When it allows 10 percent (or $900) for its required reserves, it will have $8 100 in excess reserves. Suppose that Bank B then lends all of the excess to another customer, Mr. Papas.

Mr. Papas writes a cheque for the full amount of the $8 100 loan to another person, Ms. Bray, who deposits it in Bank C. Setting aside 10 percent of the new deposit for required reserves, Bank C has $7 290 in excess reserves that it can lend to another customer, Mr. Khan (see Figure 14.9).

Mr. Khan then writes a cheque for the full amount to another person who, in turn, deposits it in Bank D. Once again, Bank D will keep 10 percent of the deposit on hand as a reserve and lend the rest. Thus, the process of lending and deposit creation will continue through other banks.

Banks A, B, and C created new deposits totalling $27 100 ($10 000 + $9 000 + $8 100). As the process continues through the rest of the banks in the system, more deposits will be created. How much in total will be created if we trace the process through Banks D, E, F, G, and so on? The monopoly bank will have created $100 000 in new deposits from a $10 000 cash deposit. We have already noted that the result of a multibank lending process will be exactly the same. With a 10 percent cash reserve ratio and the same initial cash deposit, a modern banking system will create $100 000 in new deposits from a $10 000 cash deposit. If we subtract the initial $10 000 in cash that was already circulating in the economy, the banks have created $90 000 ($100 000 − $10 000) in new money. In the *Thinking like an Economist* feature on page 300, we will learn the formula for calculating the total amount of new deposits that could be created by a multibank banking system.

FIGURE 14.7
When Ms. Yeung spends her $9 000 loan, Bank A's cash reserves and deposits fall by $9 000

BANK A			
Assets		**Liabilities**	
Cash reserves	$1 000	Initial deposit	$10 000
Loan	$9 000		
Total	$10 000	**Total**	$10 000

FIGURE 14.8
The furniture store's deposit has increased the excess reserves of Bank B, allowing the bank to give Mr. Papas a loan of $8 100

BANK B			
Assets		**Liabilities**	
Cash reserves	+$9 000	Initial deposit	+$9 000
Required reserves	$900	New deposit (owed	+$8 100
Excess reserves	$8 100	to Mr Papas)	
Loan (owed by Mr Papas)	+$8 100		
Total	$17 100	**Total**	$17 100

FIGURE 14.9
Ms. Bray's deposit has increased the excess reserves of Bank C, allowing it to lend $7 290 to Mr. Khan

BANK C			
Assets		**Liabilities**	
Cash reserves	+$8 100	Initial deposit	+$8 100
Required reserves	$810	New deposit (owed	+$7 290
Excess reserves	$7 290	to Mr Khan)	
Loan (owed by Mr Khan)	+$7 290		
Total	$15 390	**Total**	$15 390

THE REALITIES OF MONEY CREATION

Before we traced the process of deposit creation, we made two rather extreme assumptions: first, that each bank lent all its excess reserves, and, second, that all borrowers immediately withdrew and spent the total amount of the deposits created for them. At this point, we need to withdraw these assumptions and consider a more realistic situation for the banks and the borrowers by examining the following two limitations: excess reserves and cash drains.

EXCESS RESERVES

If banks do not lend all their excess reserves, the total amount of new deposits that can be created is reduced. There are two reasons all reserves might not be loaned. First, there must be a sufficient number of people borrowing from the banks in order for their excess reserves to be fully lent. However, there is no guarantee that this will happen. The economy could be suffering job losses, declining retail sales, and uncertain economic forecasts, all of which discourage people from borrowing money. The banks may want people to borrow, but people cannot be forced to do so!

Second, banks may not be willing to lend up to their maximum in excess reserves if they perceive that the risk of borrowers defaulting on repayment of their loans is too great. This reluctance on the banks' part is understandable, since the loans they grant are obtained from other people's money. Bank managers are very aware that they must safeguard the deposits of their customers. Banks must be prudent in their lending practices, particularly when economic conditions are not favourable. Individuals who lose their jobs are likely to default on repayment of their loans. Businesses that borrow when times are good may not be able to repay their loans if economic conditions reverse and their sales decline.

CASH DRAIN

Not all people hold money in bank deposits. If our original depositor, Ms. Yeung, had kept a portion of her $9 000 in cash on her person or at home, the amount of her deposit would have been reduced. Bank A would have less in excess reserves to lend, which, in turn, would reduce the reserves, loans, and deposits of all the other banks. Similarly, if other borrowers down the line drew a portion of their loans out in cash, the banking system's lending potential would be decreased. These **cash drains** limit the banks' capacity to create new deposits.

These two limitations mean that the ability of the banking system to create deposits is somewhat more restricted than in our example of the process of money creation in the banking system. However, a multibank system can still expand bank deposits—and thus the money supply—many times more than the amount of currency issued.

cash drain
The proportion of a bank deposit that a person chooses to hold in cash outside the bank, reducing the bank's excess reserves and, thus, its ability to lend.

Thinking like an Economist

The Deposit (or Money) Multiplier

A simple formula can be used to determine the total amount of new deposits that can be created from an initial deposit. The **deposit (or money) multiplier** is the amount by which a change in the monetary base is multiplied to determine the resulting change in the money supply. The deposit multiplier is calculated as follows:

deposit (or money) multiplier
The amount by which a change in the monetary base is multiplied to determine the resulting change in the money supply.

$$\text{Change in deposits (D)} = \frac{1}{\text{reserve ratio (R)}} = \text{Change in reserves (C)}$$

Example 1

If $100 is deposited in a bank that is part of a multibank system with a reserve ratio of 10 percent, how much will total deposits increase?

$$D = \frac{1}{0.10} \times \$100 = \$1\,000$$

Total deposits will increase by $1 000.

Example 2

If $500 is deposited in a bank that is part of a multibank system with a reserve ratio of 5 percent, how much will total deposits increase?

$$D = \frac{1}{0.05} \times \$500 = \$10\,000$$

Total deposits will increase by $10 000.

What is the total amount of new money that has been created in both examples? Remember that the money supply is defined as cash in circulation plus bank deposits. When cash is deposited, it is subtracted from the money supply because it is no longer in circulation. Keep in mind that the bank credits the cash depositor with a bank deposit. Thus, we subtract the initial cash deposit from the total of bank deposits created to determine the total addition to the money supply:

Total increase in money supply = Total new deposits – Initial cash deposit

Example 1 (continued)

Total new deposits	= $1 000
Initial cash deposit	= $100
Total increase in money supply	= $1 000 – $100
	= $900

Example 2 (continued)

Total new deposits	= $10 000
Initial cash deposit	= $500
Total increase in money supply	= $10 000 – $500
	= $9 500

APPLYING ECONOMIC THINKING

1   If $5 000 in cash is deposited in a bank that is part of a multibank system with a reserve ratio of 10 percent, how much could be created in (a) new deposits and (b) new money?

2   If $10 000 in cash is deposited in a bank that is part of a multibank system with a reserve ratio of 8 percent, how much could be created in (a) new deposits and (b) new money?

3   Suppose that a person withdraws $1 000 in cash from an account. How much would total deposits decrease if the reserve ratio is 20 percent?

4   Create a balance sheet for Bank A and Bank B showing the effect of a $10 000 withdrawal on deposits and the money supply.

How Banks "Destroy" Money

A banking system can "destroy" money by contracting (decreasing) deposits and, therefore, the money supply. Let's return to Bank A to see how this happens. Suppose that the original depositor withdraws the $10 000 from the bank. Bank A has $1 000 in its reserves, but the person withdrawing the deposit demands $10 000. The bank is now short $9 000. How would Bank A make up the shortfall in its reserves?

First, Bank A would cease lending money until new deposits of cash replenished its reserves. Second, it would count on its cash reserves being replenished from existing loans that are in the process of being repaid. Its borrowers would probably make withdrawals from other banks in the system to make loan payments. For instance, if Bank B, loses $9 000 to withdrawals that a borrower makes to repay Bank A, then Bank B must cease its lending and count on its loans being repaid to replenish its reserves. Since Bank B has $900 in reserves, the withdrawals leave it with a $8 100 shortfall. In turn, Bank B's borrowers would repay their loans by drawing on Bank C, and so the chain of withdrawals would continue, contracting deposits and reducing the money supply. Figure 14.10 shows how the balance sheet of Bank A would be affected. The balance sheets of the other banks would be affected in a similar way.

Balance sheet (a) shows a $10 000 withdrawal, which causes required reserves to fall by $1 000, while actual reserves drop by $10 000. Thus, excess reserves are short by $9 000. Balance sheet (b) shows a loan reduction of $9 000, which increases cash reserves by $9 000. The loan would be repaid through a withdrawal from Bank B, which would experience similar effects on its balance sheet. This process would continue through the other banks, reducing deposits and thus contracting the money supply.

FIGURE 14.10
Bank A's balance sheets, showing contraction of deposits

BANK A					
(a) Loss of Deposit			**(b) Reduction in Loans**		
Assets		**Liabilities**	**Assets**		**Liabilities**
Cash reserves	−$10 000	Deposits −$10 000	Loans	−$9 000	
Changes in reserves:			Cash reserves	+$9 000	
Actual reserves	−$10 000		*Changes in reserves:*		
Required reserves	−$1 000		Actual reserves	+$9 000	
Excess reserves	−$9 000		Required reserves	—	
			Excess reserves	+$9 000	
Total	−$10 000	**Total** −$10 000	**Total** (no change)	—	**Total** (no change) —

Self-Reflect

1 You deposited $10 000 in cash at a bank that is part of a multi-bank system. Why does it become both an asset and a liability for the bank?

2 What tendency among its depositors does a bank count on so that the bank can lend its excess reserves?

3 If the bank retains 5% of deposits as cash reserves, how much of the $10 000 deposit can it lend?

Chapter 14
Consolidation Activities

KNOWLEDGE

1. a) What is the major problem that a barter system poses for a society?

    (b) Explain how money, in one form or another, solved the problems of a barter system.

2. a) Why did paper receipts come to be used more than gold or silver to make payments?

    b) What did early goldsmiths discover they could do with gold and silver stored with them by merchants, and why did they do it?

    c) In what sense do modern banks operate in the same way as the goldsmiths?

THINKING & INQUIRY

3. How strongly does a country identify with its currency? Is there a sense of identity derived from distinctive coins and bills that digital forms of money might undermine? What is your opinion?

4. "Money has steadily become more abstract." Explain this statement with reference to the past, present, and future of money.

COMMUNICATION

5. Using the Internet, research several of Canada's newer banks and report on how they are attempting to distinguish themselves from the larger established banks.

6. "Canada's banking system is stable because it stresses security over competitiveness." Do you agree? Debate this statement in a small group.

APPLICATION

7. Draw up four balance sheets representing four banks. Assume that a person deposits $4 000 in the first bank. Each bank lends all its excess reserves, and the reserve ratio is 10 percent.

    a) How much in new deposits will be created by the four banks? How much will be created in new money?

    b) Using the deposit multiplier, determine how much would ultimately be created in new deposits and new money if the process continued through other banks in the system.

8. Suppose that an economy uses barter to trade 100 goods. Each good could be priced in terms of 99 other goods. For example, a baseball glove could be measured as being worth 12 baseballs, or two baseball bats, or 100 packs of sunflower seeds, or any number of the other 96 goods that the economy trades. How many different price combinations where one good is measured in terms of another would there be? Use the following formula to figure it out:

    $$\frac{n(n-1)}{2}$$ (where n is the number of goods)

    In contrast, how many prices would there be in a money system?

Launched in stages from 2011 to 2013, Canada's "Frontier Series" of banknotes are made of polymer (instead of cotton) and contain several security features in their design, significantly reducing the number of counterfeit notes in circulation.

15
Monetary Policy

INTRODUCTION

We learned in the previous chapter how the banking system, through its bank deposits, bank reserves, and lending practices, actually creates money beyond paper and coin currency. The size of this money supply is vitally important to the economy. An increase in the money supply without an increase in an economy's output does not make people better off. Instead, it inflates the prices everyone must pay for goods and services and inflicts real hardship on those people whose incomes do not increase. A situation in which too little money is created can also cause problems. If the economy does produce more output, and the money supply is not allowed to grow, people may not purchase the total output. Prices will fall, and the economy will enter a painful period of deflation.

To ensure that Canada's economy has just the right amount of money to purchase goods and services without causing inflation or deflation, the government uses monetary policy to adjust **interest rates** (the "price" charged for borrowing money) and thereby the size of the money supply. We can define **monetary policy** as a process by which the government affects the economy by influencing the expansion of money and credit. The agency through which these policies are delivered is our central bank, the Bank of Canada.

LEARNING GOALS

Once you have completed this chapter, you should be able to:

- Define and understand the general purpose of monetary policy
- Understand the purpose and organization of the Bank of Canada
- Explain the difference between easy money and tight money monetary policies
- Appreciate the importance of interest rates to the economy, and understand how they are set
- Conduct research to locate information from a variety of reliable sources to assess current economic conditions and communicate recommendations for a stabilization policy clearly, effectively, and accurately

KEY TERMS

interest rate

monetary policy

bank note

foreign exchange
    reserve

easy money policy

tight money policy

rate of return

prime rate

bank rate

inflation premium

nominal interest rate

real rate of interest

overnight rate target

operating band

overnight rate

bond

interest rate
The price charged for borrowing money.

monetary policy
A process by which the government affects the economy by influencing the expansion of money and credit.

bank note
Paper currency issued by a country's central bank.

The Bank of Canada

A SHORT HISTORY

The Bank of Canada was founded by Parliament in 1934 at the height of the Great Depression for the purpose of stabilizing the Canadian economy and providing security for the banking system. It was believed that the banks had allowed too many people to build up too much credit during the 1920s, leading to the 1929 crash that ushered in the Great Depression of the 1930s. Banks throughout the Western world were unstable; several thousand US banks suffered runs on their deposits by panicked customers who lost their life savings when the banks had insufficient cash reserves to pay them all.

Canadians hoped that a government-run central bank could prevent the mistakes that had been made previously and maintain confidence in the Canadian banking system. Examples of other countries' central banks were close at hand: Britain's Bank of England had been operating since the eighteenth century while, in the United States, the Federal Reserve System (an association of 12 regional central banks) had been established in 1904.

At first, there was considerable opposition from the chartered banks to the Bank of Canada. These banks feared that politicians would use a government-run central bank to manipulate them. To calm these concerns, the Bank of Canada was set up as a private corporation that sold shares to the public, with limits placed on the number of shares one individual could own. The only connection to the government would be the deputy minister of finance, who sat on the corporation's board as a non-voting member. By 1938, however, the government of Prime Minister Mackenzie King bought all the shares to make the Bank of Canada a Crown corporation. Nonetheless, the corporation has always maintained the original intention of operating at arm's length from the government.

The chartered banks had a second reason to resist the formation of a central bank. Every chartered bank had the power to issue its own **bank notes** (paper money), a function that had been a profitable part of their business and a significant source of prestige. Bank notes looked just like the currency issued by the federal government, called *Dominion notes*. Once formed, the new central bank moved swiftly to control Canada's currency. The day the Bank of Canada began its operations (March 11, 1935), it replaced Dominion notes with notes of its own. The Bank of Canada also moved to phase out the right of the chartered banks to issue their own bank notes, all of which finally went out of circulation in 1945.

THE BANK OF CANADA'S ORIGINAL MANDATE

The Bank of Canada was given a broad and ambitious role in the Canadian economy as outlined in the Bank Act, passed in 1934. The Bank of Canada was expected to "regulate credit and currency in the best interests of the economic life of the country, to control and protect the external value of the national monetary unit [the Canadian dollar] and to mitigate [reduce] by its influence fluctuations [changes] in the general level of production, trade, prices, and employment" (The Canadian Bank Act, 1934, Chapter B-2).

At the time these words were written, Canada's production, foreign trade, prices, and employment had all fallen to their lowest levels in the century. Much faith was placed in the new central bank; everyone from economists and politicians to ordinary people hoped that the Bank of Canada would be able to achieve the targets outlined in the Bank Act and pull Canada out of the Depression. This expectation was probably unreasonable considering that John Maynard Keynes's theories—the ones you studied in Chapter 6—were not known at this time. These theories would have explained how depressions could be ended through appropriate fiscal policies. Nonetheless, the new central bank, which many Canadians wanted, was at least a beginning in the battle to haul the country out of economic depression.

foreign exchange reserve
The store of foreign currencies and gold held by the central bank, used at times to intervene in the foreign exchange market.

THE FUNCTIONS OF THE BANK OF CANADA

Today, the Bank of Canada performs four functions in the economy:

- *Director of monetary policy.* First and foremost, the Bank of Canada is responsible for controlling the growth of the money supply in Canada by regulating credit, currency, and interest rates. Later in this chapter, we will examine how it carries out this primary function.

- *Banker to the chartered banks.* Just as people and businesses have deposit accounts with the chartered banks, chartered banks have deposit accounts with the central bank. The chartered banks use their accounts at the Bank of Canada to settle debts among themselves. The Bank of Canada also lends money to the chartered banks for short periods of time for investment purposes. If a chartered bank is threatened by a loss of confidence—in which case many depositors may attempt to withdraw all their money at once—the central bank can support it with cash advances.

- *Banker to the federal government.* The federal government's revenues are on deposit in two locations: the Bank of Canada and the chartered banks. These deposits are regularly shifted between the two locations, as we shall see when we examine monetary policy. The central bank also buys and sells federal government bonds and makes interest payments on them to bondholders. Finally, the Bank of Canada handles **foreign exchange reserves**—holdings of foreign currencies such as the US dollar—and uses them when it intervenes in the foreign exchange market to manage the Canadian dollar, a topic we will examine in Chapter 21.

- *Issuer of currency.* The Bank of Canada is responsible for the issue of paper currency. It decides on the design of the notes, gauges the amount required at various times of the year (Christmas time requires more notes than other times), and tries to eliminate the problem of counterfeiting. Coinage is the responsibility of another Crown corporation, the Royal Canadian Mint.

Regarding the deposits of its customers, it is also important to note that if a chartered bank faces a run on its deposits, depositors are guaranteed up to $100 000 per person. Strictly speaking, this function is carried out by an allied Crown corporation called the Canadian Deposit Insurance Corporation (CDIC).

THE BANK OF CANADA'S ORGANIZATION

CHECK IT OUT!

James Coyne, Bank of Canada governor in 1961, became involved in a bitter dispute with the government led by Prime Minister John Diefenbaker over the Bank of Canada's monetary policy of tight money. Coyne resigned before the government began the process to force him out.

The Bank of Canada is run by a board of directors appointed by the government. The board appoints a governor and deputy governor for a seven-year term with the approval of the federal government. (The signatures of these two officials are on every bank note.) These officials cannot be removed from their posts without a special act of Parliament passed by both the House of Commons and the Senate. The question arises: How independent from government and democratic control is the governor and the Bank of Canada? Some critics believe that the Bank of Canada has too much power.

On the one hand, it is desirable to have a central bank that functions independently of government so that it can control the country's money supply without political interference. History has numerous examples of governments that paid their bills by literally "running the printing presses" to create money. Germany did this in the early 1920s, triggering a massive inflation that caused the currency to lose so much value that it eventually became worthless. In 1920, one US dollar was worth about 50 German marks. By 1923, one US dollar was worth about 4 200 billion marks. An independent central bank protects the value of money by separating the power to spend money—held by government—from the power to create money, a power held by the central bank and the banking system.

The governor of the Bank of Canada, as powerful as the governor is within Canada's financial system, is ultimately responsible to the federal government. The governor meets regularly with the federal finance minister to co-ordinate the Bank of Canada's monetary policy with the government's fiscal policy.

The Bank of Canada's main office is situated in Ottawa.

THE BANK OF CANADA'S OBJECTIVES

In Chapter 13, you were introduced to the idea of the business cycle. The diagram in Figure 15.1 shows the business cycle as it revolves through expansion, recession, and expansion once again. Let's suppose that the Canadian economy is on an upswing in the business cycle, as illustrated by the rising line on the left-hand side of the diagram. With the higher incomes and increased number of jobs that accompany an upswing, Canadians will want to borrow more to buy a house, new appliances, or a new car. Businesses will want to borrow to expand their facilities, build a new plant, or buy more stock to cash in on the increased demand by consumers for their goods. The chartered banks will be only too happy to lend money to credit-worthy consumers and businesses. As we learned in the previous chapter, the result is that the money supply expands as more bank deposit money is created to support the desire of individuals and businesses to spend more.

However, economic good times always carry a price—higher prices in this case—as inflation begins to creep into the economy. At this point, the Bank of Canada must play the "spoiler of the party" by raising interest rates to restrain borrowing and slow the growth of the money supply. Otherwise, consumers and businesses will fuel the demand for goods and services so much that price increases will accelerate throughout the economy, causing serious inflation. However, the Bank of Canada must be careful; too much restraint, badly timed, and the economy could be thrown back into a recession. Its goal is to slow growth, not to end it.

Let's now suppose that the Canadian economy is on a downswing in the business cycle, as illustrated by the dropping line at the centre of the diagram in Figure 15.1. Such a recession brings falling levels of production, consumption, and investment, and it brings high levels of unemployment. At such a time, the Bank of Canada will attempt to increase spending by lowering interest rates to encourage borrowing by consumers and businesses.

The term used to describe a monetary policy of low interest rates, easy availability of credit, and growth of the money supply is **easy money**. Easy money policies are used to curb recessions. The term used to describe a monetary policy of high interest rates, more difficult availability of credit, and a decrease in the money supply is **tight money**. Tight money policies are used to restrain the economy in times of expansion. The diagram in Figure 15.1 indicates where easy and tight money policies should be applied. Later, we will explain in more detail how the Bank of Canada brings about easy or tight money policies. First, though, we have to understand more about interest rates.

easy money policy
A monetary policy of low interest rates, easy availability of credit, and growth of the money supply.

tight money policy
A monetary policy of high interest rates, more difficult availability of credit, and a decrease in the money supply.

FIGURE 15.1
The business cycle

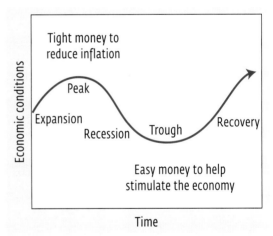

Self-Reflect

1 Why do the federal government and the chartered banks both need accounts at the Bank of Canada?

2 In what ways does the Bank of Canada provide security to the banking system?

3 Why must the power to spend money be kept separate from the power to create money?

rate of return
The amount of extra revenue an investment by a business in new machinery, new technology, or a new plant will bring in.

Interest Rates

Interest rates play a key role in the economy because they affect our decisions as consumers about both saving money and borrowing money. The higher interest rates are, the less likely we are to borrow, and the more likely we are to save. Interest rates influence the decisions made by businesses to invest by purchasing new machinery, expanding, or building a new plant. They also influence the value of the Canadian dollar internationally, as higher interest rates attract more foreign investors and, therefore, increase the demand for Canadian dollars. The budgets of governments are affected because the more they spend on interest on their debts, the less money they have available for social or other programs.

DEMAND FOR LOANABLE FUNDS

Interest is a price paid for a loan. We can use a simple demand and supply graph, like the one in Figure 15.2, to examine how interest rates are set.

The demand for loanable funds comes from three sources: consumers, businesses, and government. The downward sloping demand curve in Figure 15.2 shows that as interest rates decrease, more loanable funds are borrowed; as rates rise, the demand for loanable funds decreases. The following three examples show how interest rates can affect various purchases:

- Many consumers considering major purchases, such as a house, an automobile, appliances, and furniture, have to borrow money. Lower interest rates mean that they pay less for these goods than they would if rates were higher. When rates rise, major purchases cost more, and consumers postpone their purchases if they can.

- Businesses considering a new investment must take into account how much more they will earn with new machinery or an expanded plant. If they estimate the **rate of return**—the amount of extra revenue the investment will bring in—as 7 percent and the interest rate on the loan as 4 percent, they may well go forward with their plans. If interest rates rise to, say, 7 percent and the rate of return remains the same as without the investment, investment plans become problematic.

- Governments borrow money as well, but their decisions are not usually affected by interest rates. However, higher or lower rates mean higher or lower interest costs for the government, an expense paid ultimately by taxpayers.

SUPPLY OF LOANABLE FUNDS

The supply of loanable funds comes from individuals, businesses, and chartered banks. The upward sloping supply curve in Figure 15.2 indicates that, as interest rates rise, more loanable funds are supplied; as rates fall, the supply of loanable funds decreases. How does the amount of loanable funds increase or decrease? Let's look at the situation for each of the three suppliers of loanable funds:

- Individuals affect the amount of loanable funds by increasing or decreasing the amount of money in their deposit accounts. The higher the amount of money in deposit accounts, the more money the bank has to lend. Individuals save for a variety of reasons. They may save to spend at a later date, thereby avoiding the costs of borrowing. They may simply have no major purchase to make at the present time. Others save because they expect a downturn in the economy that may adversely affect their income or employment status. The upward-sloping curve indicates that, when interest rates rise, people are encouraged to save more; when rates fall, they save less.

- Businesses affect the amount of loanable funds in the same way that individuals do—by increasing or decreasing the amount of money in their deposit accounts. Businesses tend to save money to cover future expenses, such as the cost of replacing machinery that wears out. Instead of distributing all their profits to shareholders, businesses may save a portion for future expansion. They, too, tend to save more money during periods of high rates.

- Banks, as we learned previously, are the agents that use the money deposited by consumers and businesses to lend to individuals and to businesses that want to borrow. Through this process, banks create new money. If interest rates rise, chartered banks, as lenders, will want to supply more so they can increase their interest income.

WHAT CHANGES INTEREST RATES?

While interest rates can affect both the supply of and demand for loanable funds, the inverse applies as well: the supply and demand for loanable funds can affect interest rates. The demand for loans can increase when employment levels are high, incomes are rising, and people want to purchase goods immediately. Businesses may believe that the investment climate is favourable and will therefore increase their demand for loans. As indicated in Figure 15.3, this eagerness to borrow will shift the demand curve to the right (D_1 to D_2 or D_3 to D_1), increasing the rate of interest. At another time, when the economy is in a recession or the economy's future looks uncertain, both individuals and businesses will lower their demand for loans, causing the demand curve to shift to the left (D_1 to D_3 or D_2 to D_1) and the interest rate to fall.

FIGURE 15.2
How interest rates are set
Borrowers demand funds, while savers supply funds.

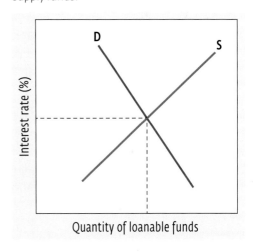

FIGURE 15.3
Change in demand for loanable funds
Demand falls in recessionary times (to D_3) and rises in expansionary times (to D_2).

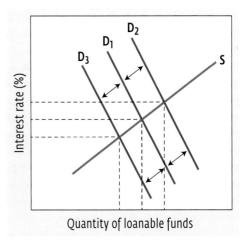

prime rate
The lowest rate of interest a financial institution offers to its best customers, such as large corporations.

bank rate
The rate of interest charged by the Bank of Canada to the chartered banks, which serves as a benchmark for the interest rates charged by financial institutions to their customers.

inflation premium
An allowance for inflation that is built into all interest rates.

The supply of loanable money can increase or decrease as well. If the economy is doing well, with rising employment and incomes, people tend to spend more but also save more. Similarly, higher profits for business will encourage them to save a greater percentage of their profits. Changes such as these increase the amount of funds available to chartered banks for lending. Therefore, as in Figure 15.4, the supply curve shifts to the right (S_1 to S_2 or S_3 to S_1) causing the interest rate to fall. Alternatively, a recession causing unemployment and falling incomes means individuals and businesses are unable to save as much as they could when times were good. Many withdraw funds from their deposit accounts, decreasing the amount that chartered banks have available for loan. This causes the supply curve to shift to the left (S_1 to S_3 or S_2 to S_1), causing the interest rate to rise.

DIFFERENT TYPES OF INTEREST RATES

Different types of interest rates exist, serving a variety of purposes. It is important to grasp that savings rates and lending rates all tend to rise and fall together over the long run. You might be familiar with the interest rate charged on credit cards. Another important lending rate is the **prime rate**, which is the lowest rate of interest a financial institution offers to its best customers (such as large corporations). The prime rate serves as a benchmark for the other lending rates that the institution offers to its other customers. If approved for a loan, a customer will be offered an interest rate that is a certain number of points "above prime," a number that varies depending on the customer's credit-worthiness, the amount of the loan, the term of the loan, and the amount of other business that the individual does with the institution.

Another type of interest rate is the **bank rate**. This is the rate of interest charged by the Bank of Canada for loans made to the chartered banks and other financial institutions. If the bank rate rises, financial institutions will usually raise the rates they charge their borrowers; if it falls, they lower the rates. The bank rate is set at 0.25 percent above the overnight rate target (a tool of the central bank that you will learn about in the next section on the tools of monetary policy).

FIGURE 15.4
Change in supply for loanable funds
Supply falls in recessionary times (to S_3) and rises in expansionary times (to S_2).

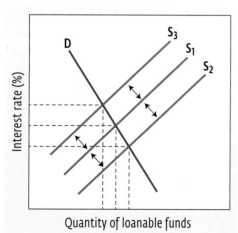

Quantity of loanable funds

One of the most important factors built into all interest rates is the allowance for inflation, called the **inflation premium**. Let's examine how this works. Suppose that you borrow $1 000 from your friend with the understanding that you will repay the loan in one year. During that year, Canada's general price level rises 4 percent. This means that the $1 000 you borrowed is worth 4 percent less when you repay the loan, or $960 ($1 000 – [$1 000 × 4%] = $960). Your friend receives dollars that are worth less in purchasing power than they were when you were granted the loan. You have benefited because you are repaying dollars worth less than when you borrowed them. Inflation hurts lenders—your friend, in this case—and benefits creditors. The only way to avoid the effects of inflation is to set the interest rate at a level that compensates for the loss of purchasing power.

If, for example, your friend was aware of inflation's damaging effect, you would have been charged a rate of interest that would cover the loss in purchasing power—an inflation premium of 4 percent. You would be required to repay $1 040 ($1 000 + [$1 000 × 4%] = $1 040). Your friend, however, does not know for sure that inflation will raise prices by 4 percent. If it stands at only 2 percent, your friend would come out ahead. However, if it stands at 5 percent, your friend would lose.

Financial institutions that lend money build an inflation premium, based on future inflation estimates, into all the rates they charge borrowers. The interest rate that includes an inflation premium plus an allowance for risk and credit-worthiness is called the **nominal interest rate**. If the expected rate of inflation is subtracted from it, we have the **real rate of interest** on the loan. Here is a simple formula demonstrating the relationship:

Real rate of interest = Nominal rate of interest – Expected rate of inflation

If you borrow from a chartered bank and it allows 2 percent for the risk of granting you a loan plus 4 percent for inflation, the nominal rate would be 6 percent. If the rate of inflation for the year ended up matching the predicted 4 percent, the real rate of interest for the bank would be 2 percent. We see, then, that inflation raises interest rates, making borrowing more expensive. When inflation rates are low, Canadian interest rates are low as well. Remembering that both lending rates and savings rates rise and fall together, low inflation means low interest rates for savers as well as borrowers.

nominal interest rate
An interest rate that includes an inflation premium, an allowance for risk, and credit worthiness.

real rate of interest
The nominal rate of interest minus the expected rate of inflation.

Self-Reflect

1 Refer to Figure 15.2. Why is the demand curve for loanable funds downward sloping and the supply curve for loanable funds upward sloping?

2 Refer to Figure 15.3. What causes the demand curve for loanable funds to shift right? To shift left? What happens to the interest rate in each case?

3 Refer to Figure 15.4. What causes the supply curve for loanable funds to shift left? To shift right? What happens to the interest rate in each case?

4 A bank offers a one-year loan at "3 points above prime." Prime is 4 percent.

a) What is the nominal interest rate?

b) If the expected inflation rate is 3 percent for next year, what is the real rate of interest?

overnight rate target
A monetary tool used by the Bank of Canada to control the overnight rate; it is set by the Bank of Canada at the midpoint of the operating band.

operating band
The range of 0.5 percent between the bank rate charged by the Bank of Canada and the interest it pays on deposits; the overnight rate target is set at its midpoint.

overnight rate
The rate of interest, controlled by the Bank of Canada, that is charged by financial institutions on short-term loans made between them; it is set within the operating band.

bond
A financial asset that represents a debt owed by a corporation to the holder, on which interest is paid by the corporation to the holder.

Tools of Monetary Policy

The Bank of Canada has repeatedly stated that it considers price stability—a consistently low inflation rate—as its primary goal. The Bank of Canada's goal is to keep it within a 1 to 3 percent band, never allowing it to fall or rise below or above the band. If it falls close to 1 percent, the Bank of Canada decreases short-term interest rates to nudge inflation up a bit with an easy money policy. If it rises close to 3 percent, the Bank of Canada raises rates to pull inflation down with a tight money policy.

OVERNIGHT RATE

The main tool used by the Bank of Canada to control the inflation rate is the ability to change its **overnight rate target**, which is an indispensable tool of monetary policy. Financial institutions know that they can always borrow money from the Bank of Canada at the bank rate. The rate at which the Bank of Canada pays interest on its deposits is half a percentage point lower than the bank rate. The 0.5 percent range between these two rates is called the **operating band**. The overnight rate target always lies at the midpoint within the operating band. For example, if the central bank sets the overnight rate target at 3.75 percent, it will charge a bank rate of 4.0 percent for loans and pay 3.5 percent for interest on deposits. The operating band would be between 3.5 and 4 percent.

Chartered banks and other financial institutions pay a rate within the operating band when they borrow money from one another for very brief periods. The actual rate they charge one another becomes the **overnight rate**, which the Bank of Canada attempts to control by stating its overnight rate target. It makes no sense for financial institutions to lend funds to each other outside of the operating band because they know they could get a better deal with the Bank of Canada.

By changing the overnight rate target, the Bank of Canada tells the chartered banks and other financial institutions the direction that it wishes monetary policy to take. An increase in this target usually encourages chartered banks to increase their own interest rates to higher levels.

Part of the reason for this increase is the bank rate, which moves whenever the overnight rate target is moved. To lend money to customers, the chartered banks often need to borrow money at the bank rate from the Bank of Canada. To make a profit, the interest rate they charge their customers must be higher than the bank rate. Thus, if the bank rate rises, the banks raise their interest rates starting with their prime rate, which then leads to a rise in other rates. In this manner, the Bank of Canada effectively controls interest rates and, indirectly, the size of the money supply. You can see the effect that a change in the overnight rate target can have on the economy in Figures 15.5 and 15.6.

CHECK IT OUT!

Interest rate changes affect the exchange value of the Canadian dollar. When interest rates rise, the dollar's exchange rate rises; when they fall, the dollar's exchange rate falls. Find out more in Chapter 21.

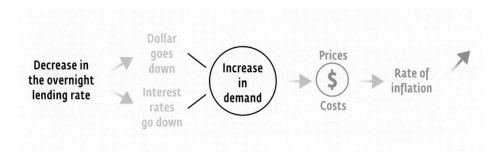

FIGURE 15.5
Easy money policy
This is how the Bank of Canada keeps the rate of inflation above 1 percent. How does decreasing the overnight rate target affect the economy?

FIGURE 15.6
Tight money policy
This is how the Bank of Canada keeps the rate of inflation below 3 percent. How does increasing the overnight rate target affect the economy?

THE BANK'S BALANCE SHEET

Just as the chartered banks have a balance sheet (as we saw in the Chapter 14), so does the Bank of Canada. The central bank's balance sheet consists of three types of assets and three types of liabilities, as you can see in Figure 15.7. Together, they constitute tools of monetary policy, as outlined below.

Assets:

1   ***Government of Canada bonds.*** A **bond** is an IOU issued by a borrower to repay a certain amount of money by a fixed date. The lender receives interest on the loan from the borrower. Sometimes the Canadian government sells bonds to the Bank of Canada. When this happens, the central bank is the lender and the Canadian government is the borrower because the Canadian government receives money in exchange for the bonds, which are a promise to pay back the Bank of Canada. Through the Bank of Canada, the government also sells bonds to Canadian individuals, businesses, chartered banks, financial institutions, and foreign buyers.

2   ***Foreign exchange.*** This is the stock of foreign currencies used to defend the Canadian dollar on international money markets. Consisting mainly of US dollars and some gold holdings, these currencies are used on occasion to purchase Canadian dollars, an action that props up the dollar's price.

3   ***Advances to the chartered banks.*** The Bank of Canada lends money to chartered banks and other financial institutions for their investment purposes. It charges interest—the bank rate—to all such borrowers.

Liabilities:

4   ***Currency outstanding.*** This item consists of the bank notes issued by the Bank of Canada. All paper money in circulation in Canada is really a liability to the Bank of Canada because it is an asset to you.

FIGURE 15.7
Balance sheet of the Bank of Canada

Assets
1   Government of Canada bonds
2   Foreign exchange
3   Advances to the chartered banks

Liabilities
4   Currency outstanding
5   Deposits of the chartered banks
6   Deposits of the federal government

5 ***Deposits of the chartered banks.*** These are balances held by the chartered banks at the Bank of Canada to settle debts among them and to act as reserves for them. The Bank of Canada pays interest on these deposits.

6 ***Deposits of the federal government.*** This item constitutes the "chequing account" of the federal government. The government deposits its revenues here and makes payments from this account for expenses such as paying its employees and employment insurance claimants.

By shifting deposits and by buying or selling bonds, the Bank of Canada can lower or raise short-term interest rates and speed up or slow down the growth of the money supply.

Monetary Policy at Work in the Economy

HOW MONETARY POLICY WORKS

We will use a model you studied in Chapter 13—the aggregate (or total) demand (AD) and aggregate supply (AS) model—to see how monetary policy, properly used, can help the economy. Let's suppose the Canadian economy is in a recession, as illustrated in Figure 15.8. Aggregate demand is at AD_1, below the full-employment (FE) equilibrium. The minister of finance will use various fiscal tools, such as increased government spending and tax cuts, to try to move AD_1 to AD_2. You will remember that increasing aggregate demand increases real gross domestic product (GDP) and encourages employment levels closer to full employment. Acting in concert with the government's actions, the Bank of Canada will engage in an easy money policy, by lowering interest rates and increasing money supply growth.

Ideally, the easy money policy of the Bank of Canada will put into action a series of four consequences that conclude with an end to the recession:

- ***Stage 1.*** The Bank of Canada lowers the overnight lending rate as a signal to the banks that all lending and savings rates should fall. It shifts its government deposits to the accounts of the chartered banks, thereby increasing their reserves. With extra reserves, the chartered banks are able to lend more. To attract potential borrowers of these extra reserves, the banks lower their interest rates.

- ***Stage 2.*** Lower interest rates encourage consumers to borrow for large purchases such as houses, appliances, and cars. Businesses respond to increased consumer spending by borrowing more to invest in new stock, equipment, and plants.

- ***Stage 3.*** New borrowing by consumers and businesses increases money supply growth (through increased bank deposits and reserves), allowing the increased output to be purchased throughout the economy.

FIGURE 15.8
Aggregate demand and aggregate supply model illustrating a recession

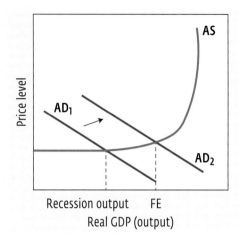

FIGURE 15.9
Aggregate demand and aggregate supply model illustrating a period of inflation

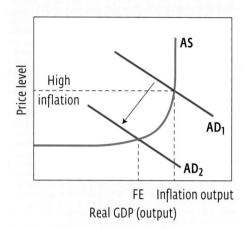

- **Stage 4.** The increased spending by consumers and businesses pushes AD_1 to AD_2, increasing GDP and thereby ending the recession and leading to full employment at FE.

Now let's suppose that the economy is experiencing a period of high inflation, as illustrated in Figure 15.9. Aggregate demand is at AD_1. The minister of finance will use fiscal measures such as tax increases and lower government spending to try to move AD_1 down to AD_2. Acting in concert with the government's fiscal policies, the Bank of Canada will use a tight money policy by raising interest rates and reducing the rate of money growth.

Ideally, the tight money policy of the Bank of Canada will put into action a series of four consequences that conclude with an end to high inflation:

- **Stage 1.** The Bank of Canada raises the overnight rate as a signal that lending and savings rates should rise. It shifts government deposits from the government accounts at the chartered banks back to the government account with the Bank of Canada. With reserve levels down, the chartered banks do not have as much money to lend out to potential customers. With the decreased supply, banks can raise interest rates for the money they do lend out and still maintain the level of customers they need.

- **Stage 2.** Higher interest rates discourage consumers from borrowing for large purchases. Businesses respond to both the higher interest rates and the fall in consumer spending by cutting investment in new stock, machinery, and plants.

- **Stage 3.** Less borrowing by consumers and businesses decreases the money supply growth as chartered banks find it more difficult to lend based on their reserves, a situation that contributes toward the desired fall in spending.

- **Stage 4.** Decreased spending by consumers and businesses pushes AD_1 down to AD_2; prices decline, thereby ending the period of high inflation.

Self-Reflect

1 What interest rate policy does the Bank of Canada use to keep inflation within a range of 1 to 3 percent?

2 Explain the relationship among the overnight rate target, the operating band, and the overnight rate.

3 Which assets and liabilities of the Bank of Canada's balance sheet act as tools of monetary policy?

Thinking like an Economist

How the Bank of Canada Develops Monetary Policy

Bank of Canada economists use theory, computer models, and a wide range of statistics to develop an appropriate monetary policy. Monetary policy actions take six to eight months to have an impact on the economy, so trying to forecast future economic changes in Canada's economy plays a major role in determining the best monetary policy.

Figure 15.10 shows some of the indicators that were studied by Bank of Canada economists in 2017 to develop the monetary policy for that year and the next three years. Data for the first nine indicators represent percentage changes in the indicator from the previous year. For example, consumption in 2017 increased by 1.9 percent from the year before. For 2018 to 2020, percentage changes in indicators are based on economic growth forecasts. Data for the last three indicators represent projected dollar values and rates.

FIGURE 15.10
Major economic indicators: Growth forecasts
Data for the first nine indicators represent percentage changes in the indicator from the previous year. Data for the last three indicators represent projected dollar values and rates.

Indicator	2017 (%)	2018 (%)	2019 (%)	2020 (%)
Consumption	1.9%	1.3%	1.3%	1.2%
Housing	0.2%	0.1%	0.0%	-0.1%
Government	0.6%	0.7%	0.3%	0.4%
Business investment	0.3%	0.7%	0.2%	0.2%
Exports	0.3%	0.5%	0.8%	0.8%
Imports	1.2%	1.2%	0.4%	0.6%
GDP	3.0%	2.0%	2.2%	1.9%
Domestic income	4.0%	2.6%	2.3%	2.0%
CPI inflation	1.6%	2.4%	2.2%	2.1%
Dollar, US/CDN	$1.30	$1.29	$1.31	$1.34
Unemployment rate	5.9%	5.9%	6.0%	6.7%
Interest rate	1.5%	1.75%	2.0%	2.25%

What is the overall picture of the Canadian economy, both in 2017 and as it proceeds to 2020? Let's take a closer look at the five major indicators highlighted in bold in Figure 15.10:

- **GDP:** GDP growth from 2017 to 2020 shows a steady decline, except for one increase predicted for 2019, because the growth rates of most of the GDP's components (that is, consumption, housing, government spending, and business investment) fall. The only GDP component to offset these declines is exports, which expand vigorously.

- **CPI inflation:** Consumer price index (CPI) inflation shows a very gradual decline after 2018.

- **Dollar, US/CDN:** The value of the Canadian dollar shows a slight decline in its exchange value up to 2020.

- **Unemployment rate:** It is projected to increase.

- **Interest rate:** It continues to increase.

What could economists interpret from these figures?

- GDP's declining growth rate causes unemployment rates to increase and domestic income growth to slow down.

- The increase in exports prevents GDP and domestic income growth from falling even more.

- CPI inflation appears to be under control, staying at around 2 percent, which is the middle of the Bank of Canada's 1 to 3 percent inflation range, possibly due to increases in interest rates or the general decline in the GDP and income growth rates.

- Interest rate increases reduce the effective demand and prices for housing because the cost of mortgages increases.

What would economists not be able to interpret from these figures?

- The reasons for the slowdown in consumption and business investment and, thus, GDP, are not evident.

- The reason for the slowdown in the growth of government spending is not evident. Why government spending is predicted to fall comes under fiscal policy and may be the result of political decisions.

- The reason for slight decrease in the Canadian dollar is not evident because increases in interest rates usually increase the dollar's exchange value. However, lower Canadian dollar values do encourage exports, which are growing.

What conclusions might economists draw about the Bank of Canada's monetary policy?

- The Bank of Canada is sticking to a steady increase in interest rates to keep inflation in check. They are not lowering rates to stem the falling growth rates in consumption, investment, GDP, and rising unemployment. There is no simple monetary policy to restore GDP growth and lower unemployment. The Bank of Canada is concerned about rising housing prices, which push inflation up. Higher interest rates charged by the Bank of Canada result in higher mortgage rates. In turn, this change lowers the demand for houses, and the increase in the price of houses levels off.

APPLYING ECONOMIC THINKING

1 Explain the relationship between falling growth in GDP and rising unemployment.

2 Select two indicators whose movement best explains the fall in personal income growth.

3 Referring to the business cycle in Figure 15.1, answer the following questions:

   a) Determine from the numbers forecasted in Figure 15.10 where on the cycle the Bank of Canada believes the economy is positioned.

   b) What type of monetary policy is the Bank of Canada pursuing?

   c) Does this monetary policy align with the general mandate of the Bank of Canada?

   d) Do you agree with the emphasis the Bank of Canada places on this monetary policy?

Chapter 15
Consolidation Activities

KNOWLEDGE

1   Why does a modern economy need a central bank such as the Bank of Canada?.

2   What economic conditions would move the Bank of Canada to introduce (a) an easy money policy or (b) a tight money policy?

THINKING & INQUIRY

3   Inflation must be taken into account when parties lend or borrow money.

　　a) Why does inflation tend to benefit the borrower and penalize the lender?

　　b) How does inflation affect interest rates?

　　c) Why is inflation particularly unwelcome to the financial community?

4   Visit the Bank of Canada's website to find answers to the following questions:

　　a) How does the Bank of Canada set the overnight interest rate?

　　b) What is the monetary conditions index, and how is it used?

　　c) How does the Bank of Canada define *core inflation* and the *consumer price index*?

5   A political power struggle between the government and a governor of the Bank of Canada highlighted the need to establish who controls monetary policy. Research the events of 1961 involving James Coyne and his struggle with Parliament.

COMMUNICATION

6   In groups of five, assign each member the role of one of the individuals listed here, and answer the following:

　　What would be your attitude toward (a) a tight money policy and (b) an easy money policy? Explain to the others in your group why you would either support or oppose each policy.

　　• A real estate agent
　　• A retired person living on a fixed pension plus a modest level of savings invested in term deposits
　　• An automobile salesperson
　　• A construction worker
　　• A banker

APPLICATION

7   It is often said that easy money policies are like "pushing on a string" in their ability to encourage people to borrow and spend. Explain this saying. In contrast, tight money policies are likened to "pulling on a string." Explain.

8   Suppose that you are considering buying a guaranteed investment certificate (GIC) that will pay a set amount of interest per year. If the GIC is cashed in before its term, the interest is forfeited, meaning that you only get back the principal—what you originally invested. You have to decide whether to buy a GIC for a two- or three-year term. What factors about inflation and interest rates would you consider before your purchase? Explain how these factors would affect your decision.

Housing prices have risen sharply across Canada in recent years. Interest rate increases are designed to slow the growth in housing prices by raising the cost of mortgages.

Unit 4   Performance Task

Examining Economic Conditions and Proposing a Stabilization Policy

Throughout this unit, we have explored the dynamic nature of the Canadian economy, and how the interaction of various stakeholders influences the ups and downs of economic activity. We have also looked at the government's role in influencing this economic activity. It is now time to examine the current state of your province's economy and then propose an appropriate stabilization policy.

YOUR TASK

You are a policy adviser in your provincial government's Department of Finance. Your employer has asked you to assess the current economic trends in your province using the principle economic measures. Once you have completed your assessment, you will produce a report outlining your policy recommendations to the minister of finance, who will then deliver these recommendations to the premier and the Cabinet.

STEPS AND RECOMMENDATIONS

1   Research the three principal economic measures (the real GDP growth rate, the unemployment rate, and the inflation rate) and their fluctuations over the past three years. Some possible sources of information include the websites of the federal or provincial Departments of Finance, Statistics Canada, and/ or the Conference Board of Canada.

2   Using the business cycle and aggregate supply and demand analysis, explain the direction in which the economy is moving and suggest the dangers that lie ahead if it should continue to move in the same direction.

3   Identify the appropriate fiscal and/or monetary policies that should be used to deal with the current economic climate.

4   Outline the appropriate economic tools to implement your policy, applying the economic language you learned in this unit.

5   Provide specific, appropriate, and reasonable examples of how your policy recommendations could be achieved, addressing the impact (both positive and negative) on all economic stakeholders—consumers, producers, government, investors, exporters, and importers.

6   Present your findings in a well-organized written report addressed to the minister of finance.

CRITICAL THINKING QUESTIONS

1   How do the current values of the three principle economic measures compare to government targets? Which of the three principle economic measures are of most concern to you based on the targets? What do these measures suggest about aggregate supply and aggregate demand? Draw freehand graphs to help explain your conclusions.

2   How are automatic stabilizers already addressing economic conditions? What type of fiscal policy would best address the current economic conditions? What specific spending and taxation actions could the government take to implement this fiscal policy?

3   How would these fiscal policy actions influence the circular flow of income and aggregate demand? What role will the multiplier effect have on these actions?

4   What drawbacks might these fiscal policy actions have? What time lags need to be considered when implementing this fiscal policy?

5   What actions could the Bank of Canada take to supplement the fiscal policy you are recommending? How would these actions influence the circular flow of income and aggregate demand? Draw freehand graphs to help illustrate the impact on the economy.

ADAPTING THE TASK

You may choose to act as an adviser to the federal minister of finance, creating a policy recommendation to guide the prime minster. Instead of a written report, you may organize your findings in an audio-visual, multimedia report, or a PowerPoint or Prezi presentation, which could then be presented to Cabinet. Discuss the selection of a format for your report with your teacher.

ASSESSMENT CRITERIA

The following criteria will be used to assess your work:

- **Knowledge:** appropriately and accurately using terminology related to macroeconomics and fiscal and monetary policy

- **Thinking and Inquiry:** researching relevant evidence and interpreting it effectively; applying sound economic reasoning

- **Communication:** clearly presenting and communicating your recommendations to the intended audience, using an appropriate tone and language

- **Application:** stating the appropriate conclusions regarding economic policy; planning a clear course of action for the government

Use the rubric provided by your teacher as a coaching tool to help complete this task successfully.

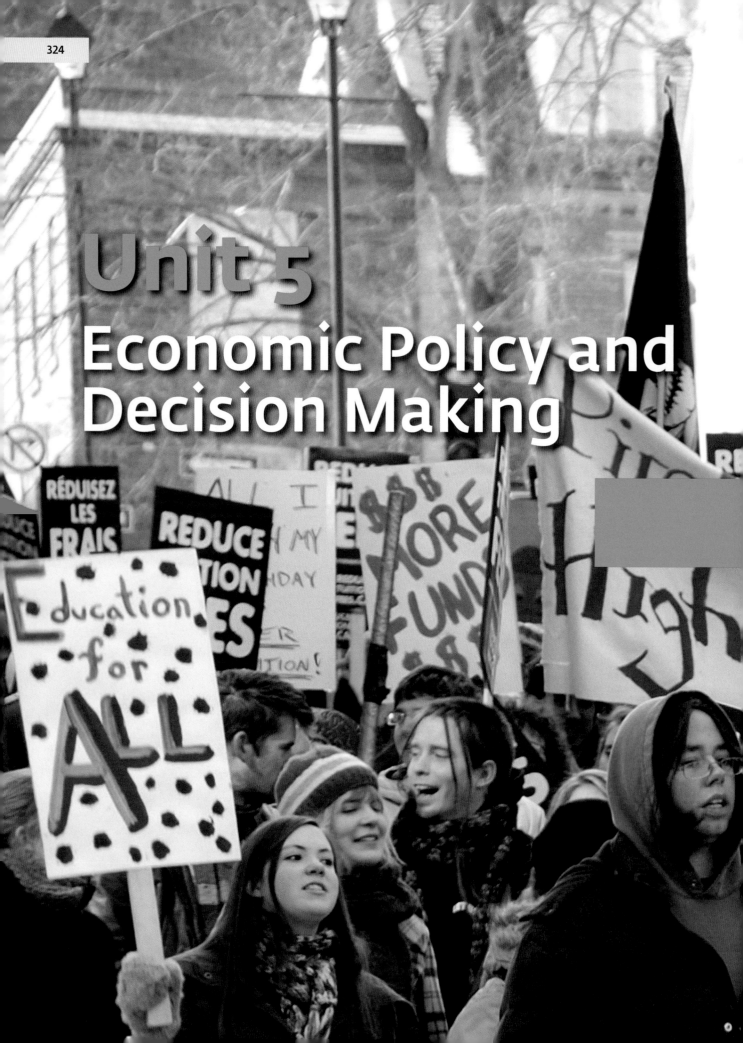

324

Unit 5
Economic Policy and Decision Making

In this unit, we focus our attention on collective decision making to understand how the Canadian economy works and why a balance between self-interest and the common good is necessary. We will explore public policy issues arising from the diverse and sometimes conflicting economic interests and goals of different stakeholders. Even when goals are complementary, there are conflicting views about the best course of action to achieve them.

First, we will examine the role of government in the Canadian mixed-market economy. Then, we will consider the relationships between aggregate national production, unemployment, and price inflation to develop a better sense of employment issues and prospects. Next, we will turn our attention to the economic goal of equity to investigate government strategies to redistribute incomes and combat poverty. Finally, we will explore how economists explain the impact of economic activity on the environment and how this impact must be addressed by both the public and private sectors to enable sustainable practices.

What role should government play in the Canadian economy? Is society best served when government involvement in the economy is maximized or minimized?

As a voter and taxpayer, you will soon have to make difficult choices about the policies, decisions, and priority setting you expect from your government, as the institution charged with the responsibility of collective decision making. Canadians have been debating the role government should play in the economy since Confederation in 1867. With limited resources and conflicting interests and goals, each choice has consequences. You may prefer to see the government more heavily involved in the economy, especially in the areas of health care and education. Conversely, you may prefer to see less government intervention, with individuals assuming more responsibility for their personal well-being. Alternatively, you might catch yourself going back and forth on this subject.

When confronted with higher taxes and bureaucratic inefficiency, you might resent government intrusion in your economic life. When you feel that you have been ripped off by your giant cellular service provider, you might favour more government intervention to protect consumer rights. Economic thinking involves careful analysis of available options to make a sound decision. With diverse stakeholder views, collective decision making and priority setting are often difficult and value-laden activities.

LOOKING AHEAD ———→

The performance task at the end of this unit will require you to investigate the inquiry question above. It provides an opportunity for you to:

- Assume the role of social advocate
- Apply economic knowledge and skills to outline the most appropriate role of government in the Canadian economy today
- Prepare and present a persuasive argument
- Use a performance task rubric and feedback to prepare a high-quality product

16
The Role of Government

INTRODUCTION

As Canada celebrated its 150th anniversary of Confederation, the issue of government involvement in the economy continued to attract controversy. Since the 1990s, federal and provincial governments in Canada have reduced their spending and scaled back their involvement in the economy. Social critics lament the systematic dismantling of the social welfare safety net that had distinguished Canada among industrialized countries. Today, some Canadians embrace a more "Americanized" model of government that features less government and reduced taxes. As government becomes less involved in economic matters, individuals and groups assume more economic freedom, but they must also assume more social responsibilities.

Fundamental questions are asked continually. How can the common good prevail in an environment driven by individual self-interest? Can an economy correct itself sufficiently and quickly enough to eliminate the need for government involvement? What is the appropriate amount of government involvement in an economy? Should government involvement be limited to certain areas and methods of intervention? Current attitudes range from a strong advocacy of laissez-faire to unqualified support for substantial government involvement to ensure economic stability and a fair distribution of wealth. In this chapter, we shall look at the role of government in the Canadian economy.

KEY TERMS

welfare state

social welfare safety net

Unemployment Insurance (UI)

Employment Insurance (EI)

Family Allowance

Child Tax Credit

Old Age Security (OAS)

Guaranteed Income Supplement (GIS)

Canada Assistance Plan (CAP)

Canada Pension Plan (CPP)

Quebec Pension Plan (QPP)

medicare

transfer payments

marginal tax rate

universality

means testing

bureaucracy

progressive tax

regressive tax

proportional tax

direct tax

indirect tax

personal income tax

corporate income tax

sales tax

Provincial Sales Tax (PST)

Goods and Services Tax (GST)

Harmonized Sales Tax (HST)

excise tax

custom duty

property tax

mill rate

brain drain

Combines Investigation Act (1889)

Competition Act (1986)

Competition Bureau Canada

Competition Tribunal

American antitrust law

Swedish Competition Authority (Konkurrensverket)

cartel

LEARNING GOALS

Once you have completed this chapter, you should be able to

- Explain the different roles that government performs in the Canadian economy: as a provider of goods and services, a supplier of infrastructure (roads, schools, etc.), an employer of resources, a regulator of competition and aggregate demand, and a redistributor of income

- Evaluate the effectiveness of government programs designed to increase the economic security and welfare of Canadians

- Identify the most important sources of local, provincial, and federal government revenues and classify government spending by purpose

- Use supply and demand curves to explain the impact of taxation on different markets

- Identify the economic benefits of competition and explain how the Canadian government seeks to regulate competition and business practices compared with other countries

The Canadian Welfare State

CANADA'S SOCIAL WELFARE SAFETY NET

welfare state
A philosophy that government should intervene to help people who are poor, sick, or unemployed as well as provide equal access to education, health care, and social services.

social welfare safety net
Government programs, such as Employment Insurance and the Child Tax Credit, established to help vulnerable members of the population.

Among industrialized countries, few human tragedies parallel the pain and suffering inflicted by the Great Depression of the 1930s. Between 1929 and 1933, production in the United States dropped an estimated 42 percent. Approximately 85 000 businesses failed, and some 5 000 banks closed. Unemployment, which had been 3 percent prior to the stock market crash of October 29, 1929, rose to an alarming 25 percent. In Canada, unemployment soared to a record level of 20 percent as national production levels dropped an estimated 37 percent.

The frightening thing was that the "classical" economic answers were no longer valid. Prices had dramatically declined, but so too had national production and employment levels. These economic responses were unexpected because falling prices, lower wages, and lower interest rates were supposed to return the national economy to its normal state of full employment and production. Any glitches in the economy were supposed to be short-lived and self-correcting. However, by 1933, it became apparent that something radically different had to be done. John Maynard Keynes was one of the first economists to propose that governments had to spend their way out of the Depression by hiring unemployed workers in major public works projects. At first, Keynes's views were considered heretical, but as governments experimented with his new theory, economic activity eventually began to pick up. The government spending and private investment that resulted from the Second World War returned the Canadian economy to full employment.

Since there was no formal welfare system during the Great Depression, federal and provincial governments were not obliged to provide financial help to those in need. It was usually left to local governments to help residents faced with unemployment and severe financial hardships. However, in provinces such as Saskatchewan, where a lot of people needed assistance, the provincial governments had to provide organized relief services. As economic conditions worsened and millions of Canadians became unemployed, governments in Canada began to spend more on relief programs or social assistance to needy individuals and families.

From the 1930s to the 1970s, the role of government (especially the federal government) in attending to the socio-economic welfare of its citizens continued to expand. During the second half of the twentieth century, Canada transformed itself into a **welfare state**. In a welfare state, the government plays a significant role in attempting to ensure the economic well-being of its residents. The welfare state represents a radical departure from the laissez-faire capitalism supported by the more traditional schools of economics. Figure 16.1 outlines the principal components of Canada's **social welfare safety net** today, where government spending on social services, health care, and education represent the three main pillars of the Canadian social welfare system. Government spending on these social pillars continues to increase annually, often leading to budget deficits and increased borrowing to absorb these rising costs.

FIGURE 16.1
Canada's social welfare safety net

Component	Description
Social Services	
Unemployment Insurance (UI) /Employment Insurance (EI)	The federal **Unemployment Insurance (UI)** program began in 1942. This program provides temporary assistance to Canadians who have paid benefits for at least one year and who now find themselves out of work because of job loss, illness, or the birth or adoption of a child. All working Canadians and their employers pay compulsory premiums to build up the fund. Any shortfalls are made up by the federal government. In 1996, the program was updated and renamed **Employment Insurance (EI)** to reflect a more positive outlook. Premiums were increased and benefits were decreased to keep the program sustainable. Critics of EI claim that reduced premiums will enable employers to create more jobs.
Family Allowance	The **Family Allowance** was introduced in 1945 to provide families with a standard amount of monetary support for each child under 18 years of age. Also known as the "baby bonus," this was a universal benefit paid to all families, regardless of income. In 1978, the federal government restructured the program and established a **Child Tax Credit** that was available only to low-income households.
Old Age Security (OAS)	The **Old Age Security (OAS)** was introduced in 1952 to provide monthly benefits to all residents of Canada once they reach the age of 65. These benefits are considered taxable income. The **Guaranteed Income Supplement (GIS)** was introduced in 1966 to help boost the monthly income of older Canadians whose primary source of income is OAS.
Canada Assistance Plan (CAP) / Canada Social Transfer (CST)	In 1965, the federal government introduced the **Canada Assistance Plan (CAP)**, a cost-sharing program to help fund the welfare services provided by provincial, territorial, and local governments to individuals and households that cannot support themselves. By 2004, it was renamed and expanded to include post-secondary education, social assistance, social services, early childhood development and daycare.
Canada Pension Plan (CPP)	The **Canada Pension Plan (CPP)** and the **Quebec Pension Plan (QPP)** began in 1966 to provide monthly payments to retired workers who made regular contributions to the plan during their working years. Employers and employees pay an equal share of CPP premiums.
Health Care	
Medicare	In the **medicare** program, launched in 1968, the cost of medical services for Canadians is shared by the federal and provincial governments, instead of being paid directly by the individuals receiving the service. Through medicare, Canadians receive quality medical services without the burden of large, unexpected bills. Despite escalating healthcare spending, many Canadians are still concerned about the quality of socialized health care. Reports of hospital emergency wards with patients being treated in hallways, because of a lack of beds and staff, often generate heated discussions about private healthcare alternatives.
Education	
Publicly funded education	Primary and secondary education are financed entirely by tax revenues. Despite rising tuition fees, post-secondary education is heavily subsidized by both federal and provincial governments. This support is generally accepted on two grounds. First, this investment in "human capital" is necessary in an increasingly complex and competitive world. Second, public funding provides greater equality of opportunity for Canadians who might not otherwise be able to afford the costs of higher education. Canada has traditionally spent more on public education (as a percentage of gross domestic product) than most other developed countries.

Unemployment Insurance (UI)
A federal program started in 1942 to assist those temporarily out of work due to job loss, illness, or birth or adoption of a child; it was renamed *Employment Insurance* (EI) in 1996.

Employment Insurance (EI)
A federal program to assist those temporarily out of work due to job loss, illness, or birth or adoption of a child.

Family Allowance
A program of monetary support, started in 1942, for all Canadian households with children under 18; replaced by Child Tax Credit in 1978.

Child Tax Credit
A federal payment to low-income households with children under 18 years.

Old Age Security (OAS)
A program whereby all Canadians are paid a monthly benefit after the age of 65.

Guaranteed Income Supplement (GIS)
A program of extra support for older Canadians whose primary income source is Old Age Security (OAS).

Canada Assistance Plan (CAP)
A federal transfer of money to the provinces to help fund welfare programs for Canadians.

Canada Pension Plan (CPP)
A pension paid to all retired workers who have made compulsory payments to the plan during their working years.

Quebec Pension Plan (QPP)
The pension plan similar to the Canada Pension Plan (CPP), but administered by the Quebec government.

medicare
Canada's national health care program, which is administered by the provinces and territories. It covers all Canadians and is funded by taxation.

transfer payments
Direct payments from governments to other governments or to individuals; a mechanism for providing social security, income support, and alleviation of regional disparities.

marginal tax rate
The tax rate paid on an increase in an individual's income.

A demonstration during the International Day for the Eradication of Poverty in Halifax, 2006. These demonstrators were part of a women's solidarity march that walked through Spring Garden to the legislature to voice their concerns about homelessness and support for the poor.

A Critical Look at the Welfare State

After the 1970s, government spending in Canada increased much faster than tax revenues. This spending led to annual budget deficits and increased borrowing to support growing social welfare programs. By the 1990s, it was clear that neither the Canadian economy nor the Canadian government could continue to absorb these rising costs. During the "nasty 90s," many Canadians began to fear the systematic dismantling of the social welfare safety net as a means of reducing huge government deficits. Champions of free-enterprise capitalism welcomed the return to more fiscally responsible government. As a general rule, Liberal and NDP governments tend to favour more government, while Conservative governments favour the opposite.

Critics of the welfare state and of **transfer payments**—the transfer of monies primarily from the federal government to the provinces to help fund health care and programs for disadvantaged individuals and households—generally point to three main problems, as outlined below:

- *Incentive to work.* One major criticism of Canada's social welfare programs is that they often reduce an individual's incentive to work and, therefore, to be self-supporting. For every dollar that a welfare recipient earns by working, welfare benefits are reduced. Although the purpose of this policy is to provide finite government assistance where it is most needed, it also has the unintended effect of discouraging some recipients from finding full- or part-time jobs. The **marginal tax rate**, or the tax rate paid on any increases in income, also acts as a disincentive. Since, as a general rule, welfare recipients are low-income earners, they pay very little income tax. Many welfare recipients gain little from taking on work because they have to pay a relatively high marginal tax rate. As much as 80 percent of their extra income can be lost to taxes. In comparison, the highest income earners in Canada pay a marginal tax rate of close to 50 percent.

  To escape this high rate of marginal tax, welfare recipients must move beyond the low-income levels. Unfortunately, it is difficult for untrained and inexperienced persons to get well-paying jobs. The self-interest that drives most Canadians to improve their economic circumstances through hard work offers little motivation for the poorest citizens.

Canada's Employment Insurance (EI) program has been criticized for actually contributing to unemployment by allowing repeated claims for benefits after a brief work period. This can reduce the incentive to find more permanent employment in a different industry or region of Canada. In addition, employers' EI contributions increase each time an additional worker is hired—a factor, supporters of free-enterprise capitalism argue, that may discourage employers from increasing their workforce.

- **Inequities, abuses, and inefficiencies.** The welfare system is designed to redistribute income from higher-income Canadians to lower-income Canadians. However, under the present system, some disadvantaged Canadians fail to receive enough assistance while billions of dollars of benefits are paid out, instead, to less disadvantaged people. This outcome is a direct result of **universality**, a long-standing principle of the Canadian welfare system. It recognizes that some benefits, such as EI, Old Age Security (OAS), and medicare, should be available to all Canadians, regardless of income. In recent years, to combat the escalating cost of social welfare programs, there has been a move toward **means testing**. Under means testing, transfer payments vary according to each recipient's income. Examples of means-tested programs include the Guaranteed Income Supplement (GIS) for seniors and the Child Tax Credit for parents.

  Advocates for low-income groups challenge the use of means testing because, by raising the requirements, many Canadians who need social assistance are disqualified from receiving full benefits. On the other hand, critics often point to program abuses. For example, the cost of medicare is greatly increased by systemic abuses linked to the fraudulent use of health cards and the charging of unnecessary expenses and procedures. EI can be abused by people who work the minimum time required and then claim all benefits possible before returning to work.

  It is generally agreed that Canada's social welfare system is too complex and inefficient; there are too many programs with too many levels of government administering them. Critics point to the uncertainty about the benefits to which individuals and households should be entitled, to program overlaps and costly duplication, and to the levels of expensive government **bureaucracy** (or administrative structure) as proof of systemic inefficiency.

- **Effectiveness and cost.** Despite the spending of billions of dollars annually on social welfare programs, the distribution of income in Canada has remained virtually unchanged, even as the welfare system has expanded over the past 40 years. Many Canadians still live in poverty, with the poorest segment (20 percent) of the population continuing to receive about 4 percent of all income. Critics conclude that the present system has been relatively ineffective as a tool to redistribute income. Pointing to evidence such as the increased number of homeless people since 1995, social advocates suggest that lower income levels would drop even further if existing programs were scaled back.

universality
A principle of the Canadian welfare state specifying that some benefits, such as health care, should be available to all citizens, regardless of income.

means testing
An income test applied to an individual as a prerequisite to receiving social welfare programs such as the Child Tax Credit or Guaranteed Income Supplement.

bureaucracy
The administrative structure of government responsible for delivering programs such as Employment Insurance and medicare.

Self-Reflect

1 How did government relief programs during the Great Depression set the foundation for the Canadian welfare state?

2 Identify and explain the three main pillars of the Canadian welfare state.

3 Compare the principles of universality and means testing.

4 What are the main problems with Canada's social welfare system? What reforms have been introduced to address these concerns?

A Personal Lesson from the Great Depression

HOW THE GREAT DEPRESSION RUINED DANIEL WYE

CHECK IT OUT!

Daniel Wye's story is a composite of the difficult experiences encountered by thousands of Canadians living in cities during the Great Depression. Research different accounts to identify similarities and differences. The experiences of prairie farmers in Western Canada were made even more difficult by drought, insect infestations and bank foreclosures when farmers were no longer able to pay back their loans. Many lost their farms.

In 1920, Daniel Wye was hired to work in the shipping department of the Timothy Eaton Catalogue Company. His salary was $10 per week. In 1922, based on advice from his manager, Mr. Wye decided to buy shares in Allied Canadian, a successful chemical company. He bought 100 shares at $0.50 each, for a total investment of $50. By 1925, Allied Canadian was prospering, and its shares were now selling on the Toronto Stock Exchange at $2.50 per share. On paper, Mr. Wye's stock holdings represented half a year's wages. He borrowed $500 from the bank and bought 200 additional shares of Allied Canadian at $2.50 per share. He intended to pay off the loan with his profits.

By October 1929, rumours began to surface that stock prices had climbed too high and the bubble was about to burst. Allied Canadian was still holding firm at $3 per share. A large number of investors decided that it was time to sell before stock prices began to fall. More and more investors followed suit as they saw others getting rid of their stock. To find someone willing to buy the stock, stockholders had to settle for a much lower selling price. On Thursday, October 24, 1929, an avalanche of sales flooded the New York Stock Exchange as prices plummeted. The Toronto market followed this rapid decline. Bankers and stockbrokers began to insist that investors pay back the money they had borrowed to buy stock. The panic continued as investors rushed to sell their shares before the price dropped further. On Tuesday, October 29, 1929 ("Black Tuesday"), the New York stock market crashed. In Toronto, similar panic unfolded. Mr. Wye sold all of his shares for $0.20 each, making only $60 on the transaction. The $500 he had borrowed was lost. Like many other Canadian investors, Mr. Wye suddenly found himself without savings and deeply in debt. He owed the bank a year's wages. The economy had shifted from boom to bust.

FIGURE 16.2
A vicious circle
With each repetition of this downward spiral, the economies of Canada and the United States lapsed deeper into economic depression.

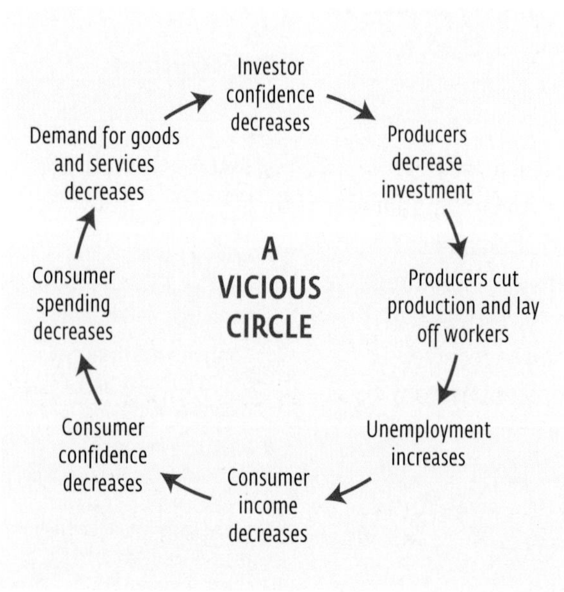

As individuals like Mr. Wye failed to repay their loans, large chartered banks began to seize personal property to recover as much money as possible. Many small banks in the United States folded because people failed to repay their loans. Those who had accounts in these banks lost their life savings. Consumers in both Canada and the United States became very worried about their economic prospects, and, as a result, consumer spending declined. In addition, investment declined sharply as firms became concerned about declining sales. Like many others, Mr. Wye found himself out of work by 1930. The company promised to hire him back as soon as catalogue sales picked up, but as more workers were laid off each month, consumer spending declined even further, creating a vicious circle (see Figure 16.2). Mr. Wye could not find steady work for almost 10 years.

Taxation and Government Spending

TAXATION

The main purposes of taxation are as follows:

- To finance state activity (such as national security and social welfare)
- To promote income equity
- To influence conditions in specific markets

The taxes collected by all three levels of government in Canada have increased significantly over the past decades, relative to national production figures. While taxes represented close to 10 percent of gross national production in 1926, this ratio had increased to approximately 38 percent by the end of the century, and decreased to 32 percent by 2016.

The principles of benefits received (as applied to gasoline consumption taxes) and ability to pay (as applied to income taxes) are generally used to determine how the burden of tax is distributed to taxpayers.

Taxes are related to income in one of three possible ways (Figure 16.3). In each of the three taxes outlined, the amount of tax paid by the person earning $40 000 is greater than the tax paid by the person earning $10 000, but the difference varies greatly between each tax. A **progressive tax** generally provides the greatest proportional difference between what high- and low-income earners will pay. By contrast, a **regressive tax** takes a proportionately lower percentage of income from those with higher incomes, while a **proportional tax** takes the same percentage of income from all earners. Progressive taxes are politically popular because they are based on the principle of ability to pay.

When a government tax is imposed, the individual or firm for whom the tax is intended may actually assume the burden of payment. However, in some cases, the burden of payment can be passed on to others. When the burden of payment is considered, economists recognize two different forms of taxation. With **direct taxes**, the real burden of payment falls directly on the individual or firm immediately responsible for payment and cannot be passed on to others. Taxes collected on the income earned by individuals and firms are an example of direct taxes. With **indirect taxes**, the real burden of payment is added to the selling price and is, therefore, passed on to the buyer. Taxes on goods and services are an example of indirect taxes. In this case, producers may prepay the tax and then recover all or part of this payment from their customers.

progressive tax
A tax (such as income tax) in which the tax rate increases as an individual's income increases.

regressive tax
A tax rate that takes a proportionally lower percentage from higher-income earners.

proportional tax
A tax that takes a constant percentage for all income earners.

direct tax
A tax (such as income tax) whose burden cannot be passed on to others by the taxpayer.

indirect tax
A tax (such as sales taxes) whose burden is passed on by the seller to the buyer of the good.

FIGURE 16.3
Taxes (progressive, regressive, and proportional) and income

Economic Concept	Progressive Tax		Regressive Tax		Proportional Tax	
Taxable income	$10 000	$40 000	$10 000	$40 000	$10 000	$40 000
Tax rate	10%	20%	10%	5%	10%	10%
Tax payable	$1 000	$8 000	$1 000	$2 000	$1 000	$4 000
Relationship between tax and income	Tax rate takes a proportionately higher percentage from higher income earners.		Tax rate takes a proportionately lower percentage from higher income earners.		Tax rate takes a constant percentage from all income earners.	

personal income tax

A tax paid to the federal and provincial governments by individuals on their income.

corporate income tax

A tax paid to the federal and provincial governments by corporations as a percentage of their profits.

sales tax

A tax (such as the Goods and Services Tax or the Provincial Sales Tax) paid to the federal and provincial governments on the purchase and consumption of goods and services by the end user.

Provincial Sales Tax (PST)

A Canadian provincial government sales tax levied on a range of goods and services.

Goods and Services Tax (GST)

A Canadian federal government sales tax levied on a range of goods and services.

Harmonized Sales Tax (HST)

A single tax that blends together the federal goods and services tax with the provincial sales tax.

excise tax

A tax paid to the federal and provincial governments, as a set dollar amount per unit, on items such as liquor, gasoline, and tobacco.

custom duty

A tax charged on foreign goods entering the country; also called *tariff*.

property tax

A tax paid to local governments (such as cities and towns) by holders of houses and commercial properties.

mill rate

The property tax rate; a percentage of the value of a property as assessed by the local tax authorities.

TYPES OF TAXES

Canadian governments use five main types of taxes to generate revenues:

- **Personal income taxes** are payable to both federal and provincial governments on the income individuals earn from wages and salaries, interest (from savings certificates deposited in financial institutions), dividends (from profits earned by stock holdings), capital gains (from the difference between the purchase and selling prices of assets such as land, property, and stock), and transfer payments (from governments for social assistance). Generally speaking, Canadians earning higher incomes pay higher percentage rates of income tax. Therefore, income taxes are considered to be progressive taxes.

- **Corporate income taxes** are directly payable to federal and provincial governments as a percentage of a company's annual profits after all available deductions have been applied. Corporations, as we learned in Chapter 11, are treated as distinct persons under Canadian law.

- **Sales taxes** are payable to both federal and provincial governments on the purchase and consumption of goods and services by the end user. **Provincial Sales Tax (PST)** is charged by provincial governments on a wide range of goods and services as a set percentage of the selling price. **Goods and Services Tax (GST)** is charged by the federal government on a wide range of goods and services as a set percentage of the selling price. These taxes are harmonized into one **Harmonized Sales Tax (HST)** in some provinces.

- **Excise taxes** are payable to federal and provincial governments as a set dollar amount per unit on particular products, such as gasoline, liquor, and tobacco. **Custom duties** (or tariffs) charged by the federal government on foreign goods entering Canada are a special type of excise tax used to protect Canadian producers. Tariffs will be explained more fully in Chapter 20. Excise taxes are a good example of an indirect tax because they are ultimately added to the selling price and paid by consumers.

- **Property taxes** are payable to local governments on the value of buildings and land. First, these holdings are assessed to establish a set value, intended to approximate the market value at a specific time. Then, each year, the local government establishes a **mill rate** that represents the property tax rate as a fraction of the assessed value. For example, if the mill rate is set at 0.0123 for every $100 000 of assessed property value, the owner will be charged $1 230 (0.0123 × $100 000) in property taxes. Property taxes are affected by changes in the assessed value as well as by changes in the mill rate. In most communities across Canada, property taxes tend to increase as the operating expenses of local government grow.

A CLOSER LOOK AT GOVERNMENT REVENUES AND EXPENDITURES

Main Sources of Revenue for Governments in Canada

Figure 16.4 presents the main sources of revenue for all levels of government in Canada, combined. Figure 16.5 presents the main sources of revenue broken down by each level of government.

FIGURE 16.4
Consolidated revenues for all levels of government in Canada, 2000 and 2016
What changes are evident over time?

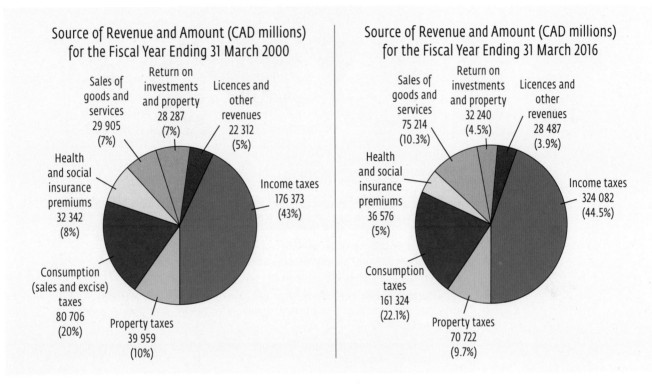

FIGURE 16.5
Revenues by level of government for the fiscal year ending March 31, 2016
What revenue patterns does this table reveal?

| | Level of Government | | | | | |
| | Federal | | Provincial / Territorial | | Local | |
Source of Revenue	In $ millions	%	In $ millions	%	In $ millions	%
Income taxes	194 770	67.5	129 312	38.8	0	0.0
Property taxes	0	0.0	11 565	3.5	59 157	55.5
Consumption (sales and excise) taxes	56 561	19.6	102 949	30.8	1 814	1.7
Health and social insurance premiums	22 954	8.0	13 622	4.1	0	0.0
Sales of goods and services	8 676	3.0	41 133	12.3	25 405	23.8
Return on investments and property	4 426	1.5	24 689	7.4	3 125	3.0
Licences and other revenues	1 139	0.4	10 284	3.1	17 064	16.0
Total	**288 526**	**100.0**	**333 554**	**100.0**	**106 565**	**100.0**

FIGURE 16.6
Consolidated spending by all levels of government in Canada in 2016

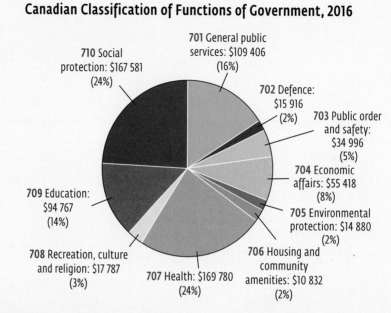

Canadian Classification of Functions of Government, 2016

710 Social protection: $167 581 (24%)

701 General public services: $109 406 (16%)

702 Defence: $15 916 (2%)

703 Public order and safety: $34 996 (5%)

704 Economic affairs: $55 418 (8%)

705 Environmental protection: $14 880 (2%)

709 Education: $94 767 (14%)

708 Recreation, culture and religion: $17 787 (3%)

707 Health: $169 780 (24%)

706 Housing and community amenities: $10 832 (2%)

Note: Dollar amounts are in $ millions.

Canadian Classification of Functions of Government

701   **General public services:** spending on public debt charges (interest on government loans); government operations including supervision of financial, fiscal, and foreign affairs

702   **Defence:** spending on military forces, civil defence, and military aid to foreign countries; research and development of military technology; intelligence gathering and personnel

703   **Public order and safety:** spending on police services and fire protection services, law courts, and prisons

704   **Economic affairs:** transportation support spending (roads, waterways, railways, airports, and pipelines); activities supporting economic well-being of the country including citizenship and immigration, agriculture, communication, energy, manufacturing, construction, etc.

705   **Environmental protection:** spending on solid waste and waste water management, pollution abatement, and technological research

706   **Housing and community amenities:** spending on housing, community development, street lighting, and water supply, purity, and quality control

707   **Health:** providing health services and management (including hospitals and outpatient services) and supporting research into illness prevention and treatment

708   **Recreation, culture and religion:** operation and support of facilities such as community centres, pools, skating rinks, libraries, museums and historical sites; operation of public spaces such as parks, beaches, and campgrounds; support of cultural events; regulation and support of broadcasting and publishing

709   **Education:** administration and operation of primary and secondary schools; support of college and university education

710   **Social protection:** social assistance for the welfare of needy citizens (including the ill, disabled, unemployed, elderly, children, homeless, and victims of crime)

How Tax Dollars Are Spent

Figure 16.6 uses the Canadian Classification of Functions of Government (CCOFOG) reporting system to outline consolidated spending by all levels of government in Canada in 2016. You will note that the "three pillars" of social services ("social protection"), health care ("health"), and education account for 62 percent of all government spending. Government spending in these areas was 57 percent (or 5 percent lower) in 2000.

When considering the spending patterns for different levels of government, consolidated figures are the most appropriate because they are carefully adjusted to avoid counting the same dollars more than once. For example, if the federal government transfers $5 million to a province to support the expansion of affordable daycare programs, and the province then transfers these funds to its five largest cities to spend on their daycare programs, the total consolidated spending on this social assistance program is $5 million and not $10 million (that is, $5 million federal spending plus $5 million municipal spending). General spending data can be slightly higher than consolidated data when double counting is not corrected. If consolidated data are not available, general data can still be used for meaningful comparisons between levels of government (see Figure 16.7).

FIGURE 16.7
Spending by different levels of government in Canada in 2016
What four spending priorities can be generally identified for each level of government?

Canadian Classification of Functions of Government (CCOFOG)		Federal		Provincial / Territorial		Local	
		In $ millions	%	In $ millions	%	In $ millions	%
701	General public services	84 301	29%	55 146	14%	13 330	17%
702	Defence	16 230	6%	0	0%	0	0%
703	Public order and safety	10 734	4%	12 670	3%	15 322	20%
704	Economic affairs	14 993	5%	35 702	9%	13 813	18%
705	Environmental protection	3 698	1%	4 594	1%	7 591	10%
706	Housing and community amenities	3 525	1%	3 796	1%	7 109	9%
707	Health	40 884	14%	150 349	37%	2 155	3%
708	Recreation, culture and religion	5 224	2%	4 588	1%	9 015	12%
709	Education	5 169	2%	74 521	18%	255	0%
710	Social protection	108 842	37%	64 213	16%	9 559	12%
Total spending		**293 600**	**100%**	**405 579**	**100%**	**78 149**	**100%**

brain drain
Emigration of highly skilled Canadian workers to the United States and other countries.

TAXATION REFORM AND DEFICIT REDUCTION

Generally speaking, when governments generate revenues by taxing incomes, assets, and spending, there are economic costs. High income taxes can be a disincentive to work, save, and invest and can, therefore, have an adverse effect on national production levels. Personal income tax was introduced in Canada during the First World War as a temporary means of raising funds. By the end of the century, well over half of federal government revenues came from personal income tax.

Property taxes discriminate against those who hold property assets instead of other assets. Since property taxes consume a larger portion of the income earned by lower-income residents, property taxes are considered to be regressive taxes. Sales taxes are also more burdensome on low-income households, taking up a higher percentage of disposable income. For this reason, economists also consider sales taxes to be regressive taxes.

To avoid taxes, a growing number of Canadians choose to become active in Canada's underground economy. By paying cash for services and not requiring a receipt, a transaction can become invisible and avoid any associated taxes. These savings can then be shared by buyer and seller. The problem is that government revenues needed to help support social programs and infrastructure maintenance are lost. Governments must often borrow money to make up the shortfall.

Taxes collected by all three levels of government in Canada increased steadily during the twentieth century relative to the size of the national economy. Where total taxes represented approximately 12 percent of gross domestic product (GDP) in 1926, by the end of the century, they represented closer to 40 percent of GDP. This increase was needed to build and administer the social welfare safety net that Canadians wanted from their governments.

Toward the end of the last century, Canadians also became increasingly more concerned about overtaxation relative to their American neighbours and trading partners. Critics often identify high taxation as one main reason for the **brain drain**, or exodus of highly educated and talented Canadians (for example in the field of medicine) to lucrative jobs in the United States. Many Canadians are prepared to pay current tax levels to preserve their quality of life. However, according to recent public opinion polls, most Canadians would like to see a reduction in what they perceive to be wasteful spending by government. Every year, for example, the federal Auditor General's report outlines examples of the inefficient or wasteful use of public funds.

The last comprehensive review of the Canadian tax system was carried out in the 1960s. Since the late 1980s, the federal government has introduced a series of reforms intended to focus on three important aspects of taxation:

- Marginal tax rates on personal incomes were reduced so that if Canadians earned extra income, they could keep more of it to spend, save, or invest.

- Tax credits were increased for lower-income earners to help offset the regressive effects of sales and property taxes and reduce the tax burden on low-income Canadians.

- The GST, a broadly based 7 percent tax on consumption when it was introduced in 1991, replaced the Federal Sales Tax (FST) on manufactured goods.

The GST is different and more complicated to administer than other sales taxes because producers do not have to pay GST on the materials needed for production. GST payments made on the purchase of production materials are refunded to manufacturers when they sell their final products. Therefore, unlike the old FST, there is no increase in production costs and no reduction in global competitiveness. The GST is ultimately paid by the consumers of goods and services at the point of purchase. To help offset the regressive nature of this tax, a GST tax credit plan was introduced. Under this plan, low-income households receive GST rebates four times a year—in advance of actually paying the GST on their purchases.

A 1998 research study comparing tax rates in Ontario to those in neighbouring New York State revealed that the difference in tax rates is relatively small. In fact, at lower income levels, tax rates were relatively lower in Canada. For moderate income levels, the rates on both sides of the border seem comparable. Only at higher income levels do US households experience lower rates of taxation. Similar global comparisons conducted after 2000 indicate that taxation rates in Canada compare favourably to those of most other G7 countries.

Reducing tax rates is seen by economists as a good way to stimulate consumption, production, investment, and employment. With government spending generally exceeding revenues each year, governments in Canada had to borrow increasingly larger sums of money to finance their spending programs. As annual deficits grew, the proportion of government spending required to make interest payments on the total accumulated debt continued to climb. Critics of deficit budgeting link inflation (general price increases) to unrealistic levels of government spending. Advocates of deficit budgeting are quick to point out that, as the Canadian economy continues to grow, the accumulated public debt will remain manageable and slowly lose significance relative to the volume of national production. As government deficits started growing rapidly after 2015, many young Canadians began to question the feasibility of expecting steady economic growth to reduce the significance of growing public debt. In addition, they began to question the morality of imposing substantial debts on future generations of Canadians. Many Canadians remain convinced that increasing public debt to fund social programs, as was the case during the second half of the twentieth century, may no longer be a viable option.

Self-Reflect

1 Explain the difference between benefits received and ability to pay as principles of taxation. Which is most fair? Explain.

2 For each of the five main types of taxes collected by governments in Canada, determine whether each is an example of direct or indirect taxation and whether each is progressive or regressive.

3 List the economic and political advantages of using each of the following methods to increase government revenues: personal income taxes, corporate income taxes, gasoline excise taxes, tobacco excise taxes, and consumption/sales taxes.

Thinking like an Economist

Analyzing the Effects of Taxation on the Marketplace

When the government imposes a new tax on a product, who actually ends up paying this tax? A cynic might suggest that the poor consumer always pays in the end. A moralist might suggest that the tax is shared equally by buyers and sellers. A romantic soul might conclude that the tax is paid by socially conscious producers and sellers. Economists carefully use supply and demand theory to determine the effects of direct taxation on market conditions for specific goods or services.

The graphs in Figure 16.8 help to illustrate the specific effects of taxation on the market price and the quantity transacted for pork (representing goods with an elastic demand) and gasoline (representing goods with an inelastic demand). Review the concept of elasticity of demand in Chapter 7 to help you understand the elasticity of demand for each sample commodity.

Let's assume that the federal government imposes a special excise tax amounting to $1.00 per kilogram on pork and $0.50 per litre on gasoline. Figure 16.8 demonstrates that the effect of indirect taxes depends on the elasticity of demand for the good or service being taxed. In the case of the pork market, the new tax acts as a tax on production and may seriously affect the ability of some pork producers to stay in business. In the case of the gasoline market, the new tax acts as a tax on consumption and may affect both driving habits and the sale of more energy-efficient vehicles. Which of these two taxes is the Canadian government more likely to impose?

Anyone operating a motor vehicle today will quickly recognize that the excise taxes already imposed on gasoline account for one-third of the per-litre price paid by Canadian consumers at the pump. Governments prefer to impose these indirect taxes on goods such as tobacco, gasoline, and alcohol to generate steady revenue streams and to tax and regulate consumption. Some of the revenues generated from gasoline excise taxes can then be used by governments to build and maintain the infrastructure of roads and bridges needed by both individuals and industry.

As you think your way through this comparison table you will gain a more functional understanding of the impact of taxation on different markets.

APPLYING ECONOMIC THINKING

1 Why would an excise tax on pork be a much more dangerous economic decision for government than a tax on gasoline?

2 How might an excise tax on gasoline be used to help reduce carbon emissions?

FIGURE 16.8
Market comparison table for gasoline and pork

	Effect of a $0.50 Tax on the Gasoline Market	Effect of a $1.00 Tax on the Pork Market
Elasticity of demand	The demand for gasoline is relatively insensitive to price changes because gasoline is an essential source of fuel for automobiles, with very few substitutes readily available.	The demand for pork is sensitive to price changes because pork is a non-essential source of protein, with substitutes such as beef, fish, and poultry readily available.
	Required reduction in quantity transacted so that the difference between what buyers pay and what sellers receive is the exact amount of the tax collected by government ▢ Proportion of tax burden assumed by buyers/consumers (70% or $0.35) ▢ Proportion of tax burden assumed by suppliers/producers (30% or $0.15)	Required reduction in quantity transacted so that the difference between what buyers pay and what sellers receive is the exact amount of the tax collected by government ▢ Proportion of tax burden assumed by buyers/consumers (25% or $0.25) ▢ Proportion of tax burden assumed by suppliers/producers (75% or $0.75)
Pre-tax market conditions	The market is at equilibrium when 140 000 L of gasoline are being transacted at a price of $0.70/L.	The market is at equilibrium when 140 000 kg of pork are being transacted at a price of $3.50/kg.
Applying the new tax	With the tax in place, the price that buyers actually pay ($1.05) and the price that suppliers actually receive ($0.55) must differ by the exact amount of the tax ($0.50) to keep the market in balance.	With the tax in place, the price that buyers actually pay ($3.75) and the price that suppliers actually receive ($2.75) must differ by the exact amount of the tax ($1.00) to keep the market in balance.
Effect of tax	As a direct result of the tax, the price to consumers has increased by $0.35, and the quantity transacted and consumed has decreased by 30 000 L.	As a direct result of the tax, the price to consumers has increased by $0.25, and the quantity transacted and consumed has decreased by 30 000 kg.
Tax burden	Given the insensitivity of this commodity to changes in price, most of the tax burden (%) has been passed on to the buyers/consumers.	Given the sensitivity of this commodity to changes in price, most of the tax burden (75%) has been assumed by the sellers.

Regulation of Competition in the Economy

In Canada, government regulation is also useful for maintaining safe drinking water, for inspecting and grading agricultural produce intended for human consumption, for maintaining the quality of hospitals and schools, and for providing healthy levels of competition in the economy.

Competition is seen as a positive factor in a market economy for the following reasons:

- **Competition increases consumer choice.** In a competitive market, both the quantity and the variety of goods available to consumers are increased. By choosing among the products available, consumers determine whether firms succeed or fail. For example, styles, models, and optional features of automobiles provide consumers with ample choice at different price levels. Unpopular models are quickly discontinued and replaced by manufacturers.

- **Competition increases entrepreneurial freedom.** In a competitive marketplace, few obstacles bar producers from getting into an industry. Entrepreneurs will be attracted to industries where profit potential is seen to be relatively high. For example, many entrepreneurs have chosen to enter the growing field of information technology by developing and marketing specialized computer and mobile applications software.

- **Competition encourages investment and growth**. When there is healthy competition in an industry, products and services often improve. Improvements and innovations in the production process are rapidly implemented across the industry to maintain competitiveness, as firms are motivated to invest in and develop new technology. For example, in recent years, Ontario winemakers have invested heavily in new varieties of grapes and production processes that have led to the development of ice wine and other award-winning products.

- **Competition keeps prices down and product quality high.** In a competitive environment, there is increased pressure on firms to provide high-quality products at competitive prices. Firms have less ability to manipulate prices upward because doing so will drive buyers to other competitors. For example, as a result of increased competition, today you can make an overseas phone call for a fraction of what it would have cost you in 1980.

- **Competition improves resource allocation and efficiency.** The efficient use of productive resources allows firms to generate profits in a competitive environment. Available resources are allocated based on market demand, and production shortages and surpluses are immediately corrected. For example, an automobile manufacturer can respond to high consumer demand for popular vehicles by converting assembly lines to manufacture popular models instead of less popular models (which also reduces waiting times for buyers).

COMPETITION LEGISLATION

When one or more firms are able to influence the marketplace by using misleading advertisements, fixing prices, limiting production, or controlling distribution to limit competition to the detriment of consumers, they are engaging in "restraint of trade." The **Combines Investigation Act** was passed in 1889 to prevent firms from taking actions that would "unduly lessen competition." This legislation was largely ineffective because it failed to define clearly what was meant by "unduly lessening" competition. Furthermore, since the Combines Investigation Act was based on criminal law, proof beyond a reasonable doubt was needed to secure a conviction. Very few cases were successfully prosecuted under the act because agreements to lessen trade were rarely put in writing. In addition, absolute physical proof that actions were "detrimental to the public interest" was required.

Prior to 1986, competition legislation was based on the premise that large corporations were able to exercise unfair influence on the domestic marketplace. With the evolution of freer global trade, especially during the 1970s and 1980s, the focus of attention gradually shifted to a consideration of whether Canadian firms were actually large enough to compete effectively in global markets. Large foreign firms were also recognized as sources of increased competition for Canadian companies. Some smaller Canadian companies could better compete in the global economy if they were allowed to join forces or merge with their competitors. With a steady decrease in trade tariffs, the competitive balance would be maintained by opening Canadian markets to large foreign corporations.

In 1986, the Combines Investigation Act was replaced by the **Competition Act**. The purpose of this new legislation was to encourage competition in Canada while promoting economic efficiency and the ability of Canadian firms to compete effectively in larger global markets. The three main goals of the act are as follows:

- To expand opportunities for Canadian firms to compete in global markets while recognizing the role of foreign competition in Canada

- To ensure that small and medium-sized businesses have an opportunity to participate fairly in the Canadian economy

- To provide consumers with competitive prices and quality product choices

The act is administered by **Competition Bureau Canada**, which is attached to Innovation, Science and Economic Development Canada. The process created by this act was designed so that matters could be addressed outside the criminal courts. Most concerns are dealt with through negotiations between the Bureau and the corporations involved. When the parties are unable to reach an agreement, the matter is taken to the **Competition Tribunal**. Tribunal decisions may be appealed to the Federal Court of Canada.

Of the 340 merger deals that the Competition Bureau was required to examine during its first three years in operation, most were accepted without challenge. In nine cases, the Bureau negotiated a restructured proposal with the merging companies. In 19 cases, the Bureau decided to monitor market conditions after

Combines Investigation Act (1889)
Canada's first act to prevent firms from fixing prices or lessening competition to the detriment of consumers; replaced in 1986 by the Competition Act.

Competition Act (1986)
The act that replaced the old Combines Investigation Act to address problems caused by business mergers, acquisitions, and price fixing.

Competition Bureau Canada
Government agency that administers the Competition Act.

Competition Tribunal
The board empowered to make decisions on disputes between corporations and Competition Bureau Canada that cannot be decided through negotiation.

American antitrust law
Federal laws to protect competition and to prevent a company or enterprise from becoming too powerful or dominant in the marketplace.

approving the merger. In seven cases, the proposed mergers were voluntarily abandoned as a result of the objections raised by the Bureau. Only four cases were forwarded to the Competition Tribunal for a formal ruling.

Between 2007 and 2011, the Competition Bureau noted that Bell Canada unfairly misled consumers about its pricing. Bell was advertising a set monthly fee for landline, Internet, and wireless services. Bell used "disclaimers" in its fine print to hide extra fees amounting to a 15 percent price increase. In 2011, Bell agreed to change its ads and pay a record $10 million fine. Major competitors Rogers and TELUS also paid smaller fines for similarly misleading customers. As a result of this case and others like it, many economists have concluded that the Competition Act is more effective than its predecessor as a competition watchdog.

BUSINESS REGULATION IN DIFFERENT COUNTRIES

The American Antitrust Model

Motivated by the laissez-faire spirit, Americans have been historically indisposed to interfere in an enterprise's freedom to conduct business. **American antitrust law** is a collection of federal and state laws that collectively regulate the conduct and organization of businesses in the United States. The Sherman Act of 1890, the Clayton Act of 1914, and the Federal Trade Commission Act of 1914 are the three main pieces of legislation. These acts prohibit the following actions, which constitute exploitative abuses of corporate freedoms:

- Collusion and the creation of any groups restraining trade to the detriment of consumers
- Any mergers and acquisitions that substantially lessen competition
- Monopoly creation and the abuse of power by monopolies

The Federal Trade Commission, the U.S. Department of Justice, state governments, and exploited private parties may all bring actions in American courts to enforce antitrust laws. Generally speaking, American laws and penalties are strict and firm, once the freedoms afforded to corporations have been confirmed to have been abused in detriment to the public interest. Public interest is often defined in the United States as protecting consumers and competitors from market manipulation (including price fixing, bid rigging, anti-competitive mergers, and monopolization) stemming from corporate greed.

As an example, in 1974 the U.S. Department of Justice filed an antitrust lawsuit against AT&T. At the time, this large and powerful company was the sole provider of telephone service throughout most of the United States. In addition, most telephone equipment was produced by its subsidiary, Western Electric. This vertical integration gave monopolistic control to AT&T over communication technology. By 1982, feeling that it was about to lose the lawsuit, AT&T agreed to break up its vast operations into several independent regional enterprises.

By 2016, the climate in the United States had changed regarding giant businesses, which were now sometimes seen as necessary to create economies of scale. In this new climate, AT&T attempted a $85 billion acquisition of media giant Time Warner. Given the media/communication giant that it would create, the acquisition was quickly taken to court. In June 2018, after a six-week trial, U.S. District Court judge Richard Leon ruled (in a 172-page decision) that the government had failed to prove that the deal violated antitrust laws. The U.S. Department of Justice quickly appealed the decision claiming that the judge ignored "mainstream economics."

The Swedish Competition Authority (Konkurrensverket)

The Swedish Competition Act (2008) and some articles from the Treaty on the Functioning of the European Union (TFEU) are the main tools used by the **Swedish Competition Authority (Konkurrensverket)** to regulate competition and fair business practices. Laws are intended to prevent and deal with the abuse of a dominant position in the marketplace. Market dominance is defined as holding 40 percent or more of market share. Surprisingly, Swedish competition law may also apply to foreign companies operating in other countries when their behaviour or decisions adversely affect competition in Sweden. Mergers and acquisitions creating market-dominating companies are not allowed. Penalties for violations of the Swedish Competition Act include fines, orders imposing corrections, damages paid to victims, and prohibitions from conducting additional business. There are no jail terms for violators.

Anti-competitive behaviour includes the following:

- Directly or indirectly fixing prices or other trading conditions

- Limiting output to the detriment of consumers (for example, controlling production, markets, technological development, or investment)

- Dividing markets or sources of supply

- Discrimination (for example, by applying dissimilar conditions to equivalent transactions with other parties, thereby placing them at a competitive disadvantage)

- Tie-ins (for example, making the conclusion of contracts subject to acceptance of extra obligations that have no connection to the subject of the contracts)

In 2001, acting on a tip, the Swedish Competition Authority uncovered a large asphalt cartel that had been operating since 1997. A **cartel** is a group of companies conspiring together to exploit the marketplace. In this case, the construction companies involved used bid rigging to secure better job contracts for cartel members. Instead of submitting competing bids, other cartel members would receive secret kickbacks from the successful bidder, after submitting inflated bids or refusing to bid on specific paving jobs. They would each take turns being the successful bidder. The paving of roads is an expensive infrastructure cost, especially in cold weather countries where freezing and thawing occur regularly. In 2007, the five companies involved were issued a total of 1.2 billion kronor (US$175 million) in fines. At the time, this was the largest cartel case in Swedish history.

Swedish Competition Authority (Konkurrensverket)
An agency of the Swedish government assigned the responsibility to regulate competition and to ensure fair business practices, especially by companies holding a dominant position (40 percent or more of a market share) in the marketplace.

cartel
A group of competitors collaborating together to limit competition or to increase profits.

Self-Reflect

1 List the benefits of competition to consumers by order of importance. Justify your ranking.

2 How effective has the Competition Act been in dealing with mergers, acquisitions, price fixing, and misleading advertising in Canada?

3 How does the American antitrust model compare with Canadian competition legislation?

4 How does the Swedish approach compare with Canadian competition legislation?

Chapter 16
Consolidation Activities

KNOWLEDGE

1   Summarize three main arguments for and against Canada's social welfare system.

2   Explain why governments in Canada, Sweden, and the United States all seek to ensure healthy competition in their domestic economies. Note any similarities and differences in their approaches.

THINKING & INQUIRY

3   Research the current state of the healthcare system in your province. Prepare a report on the economic realities affecting the demand for nurses and doctors, as well as the supply of services, under the current fee structure. Draw a supply and demand graph to help explain the current market for healthcare services.

4   Each fiscal year, federal and provincial finance ministers present a budget summarizing the government's revenues and expenditures for the past year and outlining their plans for the coming fiscal year. Research a current budget to prepare an oral report that addresses the following topics:

   a)   Revenue sources and amounts recorded for the past year and projected for the next year,

   b)   Expenditures and amounts recorded for the past year and projected for the next year,

   c)   New budget initiatives and a rationale for their adoption,

   d)   Assessments from critics and supporters, and

   e)   Your overall assessment of the budget

5   Visit the reference section of your local public library to find a recent copy of the Public Accounts of Canada, published annually by the Auditor General of Canada. Research specific examples of questionable spending, then prepare a written report outlining the examples you found and recommending actions to prevent future occurrences.

6   It has been widely speculated that baby boomers (Canadians born between 1946 and 1966) will exhaust social welfare programs such as medicare and the Canada Pension Plan as they age in large numbers. Research this topic to produce a position paper recommending a specific course of action to the Government of Canada and to aging baby boomers.

COMMUNICATION

7 Write a one-page position paper or a letter to the editor that advocates either universality or means testing to best allocate Canada's limited social assistance funds.

8 Draw a causation cycle diagram, similar to the one in Figure 16.2 (page 332), to explain the effect of a general reduction in taxes on GDP in Canada. Explain the trade-offs, or opportunity costs, involved in achieving the benefits as shown in your diagram.

9 Right-wing advocates of free-enterprise capitalism are generally less sympathetic to people with low incomes, believing that they should do more to help themselves and that, unless they do so, the help that others provide is of limited benefit. Use economic reasoning to defend or refute this position.

10 Prepare a video news report outlining how and why the role of government in Canada changed during the second half of the twentieth century. Assess the increased role of the public (government) sector in the Canadian economy since 1966.

11 a) Complete a cost-benefit chart, identifying benefits (advantages) and costs (drawbacks) for each of the following ways to use government surpluses:

   • Pay down debt
   • Increase social spending
   • Cut taxes
   • Increase spending on security

   b) Prepare an argument for the most effective use of government surpluses from the perspective of one of the following stakeholders: unemployed student, stock market investor, worker permanently disabled by a workplace accident, bank manager, social worker, or small-business entrepreneur. Share your argument with classmates to compare the views of different stakeholders.

APPLICATION

12 You are a politician faced with a budget deficit. Would you choose to reduce spending, increase taxes, or increase borrowing to maintain the deficit? In defending your choice, explain the economic costs of each strategy.

13 Assume that Canadian hog producers are experiencing economic hardships, and many are going bankrupt. To protect the supply of pork to Canadian consumers, the government decides to provide a $1-per-kilogram support payment, or subsidy, to hog producers. Use the pork market graph in Figure 16.8 (page 341) to determine the effect of this government subsidy program on the pork market. Who receives most of this subsidy? Explain why. Draw a market graph to confirm your reasoning.

14 Some economists argue that there should be more rather than fewer mergers and acquisitions in the Canadian economy. Use economic reasoning to support or refute this position.

15 In the United States, property owners can deduct mortgage payments from their taxable income. Who would benefit most from this deduction? Who would benefit least? What specific effects would this deduction have on the housing market? In your opinion, should Canada adopt a similar plan? Explain.

16 During the 1980s, taxes on cigarettes were increased as part of the government's anti-smoking program. In February 1994, taxes were slashed by Ottawa (in concert with Ontario, Quebec, Nova Scotia, New Brunswick, and Prince Edward Island) in a bid to halt cigarette smuggling. Draw a market graph to help explain the effect of the self-interest of cigarette smugglers, operating in the "underground economy," on the supply of cigarettes to Canadian consumers, on the market price, on profits of organized crime, and, ultimately, on the effectiveness of the government's anti-smoking program.

17

Employment, Recession, and Recovery

INTRODUCTION

In this chapter, we will investigate the relationships among aggregate national production, unemployment, and price inflation. Although employment indicators may not be perfect, they are standardized "best guesses" that are useful for comparisons over time and space. This chapter will also examine the personal, social, and national costs of unemployment.

A closer look at fluctuations in the Canadian economy will reveal a continuously alternating pattern of economic slowdown, recovery, and expansion that creates distinct business cycles. The traditional inverse relationship between unemployment rates and inflation rates will be examined to better understand the economic factors that led to the stagflation experienced in Canada from 1973 to 1982. As well, the phenomenon of a "jobless" recovery after an economic recession will be examined to determine whether it is best considered as the new normal or a temporary adjustment.

Later in this chapter, we will examine government policies and programs in Newfoundland and Labrador that have focused on addressing the region's economic disparity and its diversification after the collapse of the North Atlantic cod fisheries in 1992. Finally, we will explore the complexities of assessing and prioritizing diverse economic interests when seeking to develop policies intended to serve the common good.

LEARNING GOALS

Once you have completed this chapter, you should be able to:

- Identify the types, causes, and effects of inflation, deflation, and unemployment
- Describe the characteristics and causes of instability in each phase of the business cycle
- Explain the causes and consequences of the stagflation experienced in the Canadian economy from 1973 to 1982
- Apply economic thinking to assess and compare employment and production indicators
- Analyze public policy issues related to unemployment, inflation, and recession

KEY TERMS

labour force

employment rate

seasonally adjusted unemployment rate

participation rate

underemployment

discouraged workers

hidden unemployed

frictional unemployment

seasonal unemployment

structural unemployment

technological unemployment

replacement unemployment

geographical unemployment

cyclical unemployment

inadequate demand unemployment

full employment

potential output

actual output

Okun's law

business cycle

recession

recovery

demand-pull inflation

cost-push inflation

Phillips curve

stagflation

"jobless" recovery

downsize

rightsize

common good

sustainability

The Atlantic Groundfish Strategy (TAGS)

aquaculture

labour force
The total of all Canadians
holding jobs plus all of those
actively seeking work.

employment rate
The total number of
employed divided by
the total labour force.

**seasonally adjusted
unemployment rate**
An unemployment rate
adjusted to eliminate
recurring and unavoidable
unemployment due to
seasonal factors.

Tracking Employment Data

Keeping track of economic activity on a national scale is a very complicated
business. Aggregate economic indicators are used to compare changes from
one reporting period to the next. In Chapter 12, the **labour force** was defined as
people who are either employed or who are willing and able to work and actively
seeking employment. Through its Labour Force Survey, Statistics Canada keeps
track of fluctuations in the labour force by surveying a random sample of 56 000
representative households each month.

National figures are computer projected, based on the survey data collected.
Interviewers gather employment information on all household members who are
15 years of age and older. Those individuals who did any part-time or full-time
work during the month are considered to be employed. All those who had jobs
but did not work because of labour disputes, vacations, or illness are also included
in the employed category. Labour force figures are used to determine various
employment data including the employment rate, the unemployment rate
(introduced in Chapter 12), and the participation rate.

THE EMPLOYMENT RATE

In 2016, the total number of employed Canadians was over 18.2 million, and the
total Canadian labour force was over 19.5 million people. The following formula is
used to calculate the **employment rate**:

$$\text{Employment rate} = \frac{\text{Number employed}}{\text{Labour force}} \times 100$$

$$= \frac{18\,225\,000}{19\,575\,700} \times 100 = 93.1\%$$

Thus, the employment rate in Canada in 2016 was 93.1 percent.

THE UNEMPLOYMENT RATE

The unemployed group consists of all those who are not working but who are
actively seeking and presently available for work. Workers who are on temporary
layoff are also included in this category. In 2016, the total number of unemployed
Canadians was over 1.3 million. Applying the formula used to calculate the
unemployment rate (see Chapter 12, page 246):

$$\text{Unemployment rate} = \frac{\text{Number unemployed}}{\text{Labour force}} \times 100$$

$$= \frac{1\,350\,700}{19\,575\,700} \times 100 = 6.9\%$$

Thus, the unemployment rate in Canada in 2016 was 6.9 percent.

Statistics Canada calculates two unemployment rates: an actual
unemployment rate and a seasonally adjusted rate. The **seasonally adjusted
unemployment rate** eliminates short-term or seasonal fluctuations, such as the
noticeable rise in unemployment each winter when many employed in farming,
fishing, construction, and other seasonal industries are temporarily out of work.

THE PARTICIPATION RATE

The total labour force includes both the employed and the unemployed, with the exception of full-time military personnel, inmates of penal institutions, full-time students, retired workers, and homemakers. As noted earlier, the Canadian labour force consisted of over 19.5 million people in 2016. When the labour force is expressed as a percentage of the total employable population (all those 15 years of age and over), that percentage is known as the **participation rate**. The equation for the participation rate is as follows:

$$\text{Participation rate} = \frac{\text{Total labour force}}{\text{Total employable population}} \times 100$$

Thus, the participation rate in Canada in 2016 is calculated as follows:

$$= \frac{19\ 575\ 700}{29\ 841\ 000} \times 100 = 65.6\%$$

The higher the participation rate, the higher the proportion of available human resources actually employed and contributing to a country's aggregate production. The inclusion of all individuals 15 years of age and older in the participation rate is challenged by some who believe that those 65 and older should not be included. Do you agree?

THE LIMITATIONS OF EMPLOYMENT DATA

As with gross domestic product (GDP) data, it is important to realize that the accuracy of national employment figures can be at issue because of the way they are calculated. Critics often cite the three factors of underemployment, discouraged workers, and dishonesty when they question the accuracy of employment data.

Unemployment figures may understate the true level of unemployment because part-time workers are recorded as fully employed workers. Although some people work part-time by choice, others would prefer full-time work but cannot find it. They are statistically recorded as fully employed, but they are, in fact, only partially employed. Furthermore, during tough economic times, some workers may have to work at jobs that do not fully utilize their skills and education. In both examples, **underemployment** is evident.

Discouraged workers are those who would like to work but have stopped looking because they believe nothing is available for them. Since they are not actively seeking employment, these discouraged workers are not considered part of the labour force and not included among the unemployed.

Some economists have suggested that the numbers of underemployed and discouraged workers, sometimes referred to as the **hidden unemployed**, would increase the official unemployment rate in Canada by more than half. If accurate, this would mean that during the great economic recession that peaked in 1992, the true unemployment figure would have been closer to 14 percent rather than the 9.3 percent reported by Statistics Canada.

participation rate
The labour force expressed as a percentage of the total employable population.

underemployment
A situation in which workers hold jobs that do not fully utilize their skills or that employ them only part time when they would prefer to work full time.

discouraged workers
Those who would like to work but have stopped looking because they believe nothing is available for them.

hidden unemployed
The total of all underemployed workers plus all discouraged workers, a number not included in calculating the official unemployment rate.

frictional unemployment
Unemployment caused by workers who are between jobs or who are entering or re-entering the labour force.

seasonal unemployment
Unemployment caused by recurring climatic factors, such as the impact of winter on construction, tourism, farming, and so on.

structural unemployment
Unemployment caused by long-term changes in the economy, such as shifts from goods production to services, or the introduction of technology that replaces labour.

technological unemployment
Unemployment caused by replacement of workers with more capital-intensive production methods; a type of structural unemployment.

replacement unemployment
Unemployment caused by the movement of firms with labour-intensive production to foreign countries in which labour rates are lower.

Dishonesty can also be a problem for Statistics Canada. Respondents to the monthly Labour Force Survey may claim to be actively seeking work when, in fact, they are not. It is extremely difficult to verify how seriously respondents are actually looking for work or to check whether they have unreported jobs in the underground economy.

Considering these three factors, it can safely be concluded that national and regional unemployment figures are "best estimates" and, thus, not absolutely accurate. However, since these figures are recorded in the same manner each month, they provide useful comparative data.

UNDERSTANDING UNEMPLOYMENT

The eight types of unemployment introduced in Chapter 12 (see pages 246–47) describe the reasons for unemployment in Canada. Economists use these unemployment terms to help clarify the causes and impact of unemployment.

Frictional unemployment refers to the short-term unemployment of those workers who are presently between jobs or who are entering or re-entering the labour market. Since workers are free to change jobs, some 3 percent of the labour market may be between jobs at any time. Given its short-term nature, this type of unemployment is considered the least serious.

Seasonal unemployment is the result of climatic changes that may leave workers unemployed for specific periods each year. As a result of Canada's climate, the construction, lumbering, fishing, farming, and tourism industries all experience seasonal fluctuations in employment. These fluctuations are less significant today than they were in the past. Today, a smaller proportion of the Canadian labour force is employed in seasonally affected primary industries, and technological advances now permit increased construction activity in winter. As mentioned earlier, to minimize seasonal fluctuations in unemployment data, Statistics Canada calculates a seasonally adjusted unemployment rate.

Structural unemployment is the direct result of structural changes in the economy. As the Canadian economy evolves, some industries grow while others decline and even disappear. For example, the depletion of natural resources may cause miners to lose their jobs permanently. It may also become profitable for a firm to employ more capital-intensive methods of production, replacing workers with automation technology. This type of structural unemployment is often classified as **technological unemployment** to identify the cause.

Some structural unemployment is created when workers permanently lose their jobs because of competition from lower-priced foreign imports. As firms move labour-intensive production to countries where labour rates are cheaper, workers in another country effectively replace Canadian labour. This type of structural unemployment, referred to as **replacement unemployment**, is one of the costs that Canada and other industrial countries face in the global economy. However, as we will learn in Unit 6, the global economy also offers considerable benefits.

When the skills and location of available workers do not match the skill requirements and location of employment opportunities, a structural type of unemployment called **geographical unemployment** (or *regional unemployment*) occurs. For example, many fish-processing workers who lost their jobs in Newfoundland and Labrador because of the collapse of the North Atlantic cod fisheries required retraining and had to relocate to find new employment. Learning new skills, moving elsewhere to find work, and developing new industries in a region where the traditional industries are in decline all take time. As a result, structural types of unemployment can persist for long periods.

Market economies typically experience periodic upswings and downturns known as *business cycles*. **Cyclical unemployment** is caused by reduced employment opportunities during periods of economic decline. As overall consumer confidence and spending decrease, the aggregate demand for goods and services declines, and fewer workers are needed in most industries. As we learned in Chapter 16, during the Great Depression of the 1930s, unemployment levels in Canada reached 20 percent. During the subsequent recessions of 1982–1984 and 1990–1994, unemployment levels reached over 10 percent.

Cyclical unemployment is largely the result of declining demand during periods of economic downturn. In periods of high consumer demand, auto workers may work overtime, but in periods of low demand for new cars, they may be laid off by their employers. For this reason, cyclical job losses are sometimes referred to as **inadequate demand unemployment**. Government policy can contribute to cyclical unemployment. If the Bank of Canada restricts the money supply and raises interest rates to combat inflation, the level of consumer demand is adversely affected, investment is discouraged, and unemployment may increase. If legislation is passed to raise the minimum wage, employers may not be able to afford as many workers and a surplus supply of labour may be created.

geographical unemployment

Unemployment created in specific parts or geographical regions of a country due to a weak economy in the area that is overly reliant on one or two struggling industries. Ultimately, this unemployment is caused when the skills and location of available workers do not match or support the limited economic opportunities that exist in the region.

cyclical unemployment

Unemployment caused by a downturn in the business cycle.

inadequate demand unemployment

Unemployment caused by declining aggregate demand; another term for cyclical unemployment.

Landscaping and construction are two industries that experience seasonal unemployment across Canada due to climate restrictions.

full employment
The lowest possible rate of unemployment, seasonally adjusted, after allowing for frictional and structural unemployment.

FULL EMPLOYMENT

From what we have learned about the nature of unemployment in Canada, it is unreasonable to expect 100 percent employment. Economists believe that structural, seasonal, and frictional unemployment are inevitable. For economists, then, **full employment** is the lowest possible rate of unemployment, making allowances for the portion of unemployment that is inevitable and necessary to keep the rate of price inflation from accelerating.

In effect, full employment is the highest reasonable expectation of employment, sometimes referred to as the *natural employment rate*. The full-employment rate traditionally includes frictional and structural unemployment and excludes cyclical and seasonal unemployment. Cyclical unemployment is excluded because this type of unemployment can be effectively controlled by stabilizing the downturns and upswings of the business cycle. Cyclical unemployment is neither inevitable nor necessary. Seasonal unemployment is automatically excluded from all seasonally adjusted data.

Thousands of demonstrators from unions across the country staged this action on Parliament Hill, Ottawa, in 2007. The "job loss cemetery" was a poignant expression of significant job losses in manufacturing and other sectors.

The full-employment rate has been adjusted over time. In the 1960s, the Economic Council of Canada concluded that a 3 percent rate of unemployment was reasonable. This goal was almost reached in 1966, when unemployment in Canada reached 3.4 percent. By 1980, the full-employment rate was doubled to 6 percent to reflect increases in frictional and structural unemployment. By 2000, most definitions of full employment included a natural unemployment rate of almost 7 percent, with frictional unemployment alone now estimated to create 3 percent unemployment at any given time.

THE COSTS OF UNEMPLOYMENT

Chronic unemployment can hurt both individuals and the Canadian economy as a whole. Human and economic costs are associated with joblessness, especially unemployment lasting for extended periods of time. Unemployment can create stress, financial hardship, discouragement, and low self-esteem for jobless workers and their families. Chronically high unemployment rates can lead to social unrest and produce negative attitudes toward the government in power and toward immigration policy. Some unemployed Canadians believe that immigrants take jobs away from them. Even though economists have demonstrated that immigration creates additional job opportunities, during periods of high unemployment, the call for reduced immigration can still be heard.

Although these human and social costs are difficult to calculate in dollar terms, they must be carefully considered in any assessment of the full impact of unemployment. Too often the emphasis is placed on costs that affect the economy as a whole rather than on individual well-being. We will investigate these human costs in Chapter 18.

The cost of unemployment for the entire economy is reflected by the GDP gap (see Chapter 12). The GDP gap is the amount by which the **potential output** (associated with full employment) exceeds the **actual output**, measured in dollars. The greater the GDP gap, the greater the value of national production lost because of the underemployment of labour resources. To recap **Okun's law**:

> *For every 1 percent that the actual unemployment rate exceeds the full-employment rate (the natural rate of unemployment), there is a 2 percent gap in GDP.*

During the major recession of 1983, unemployment reached 11.8 percent while the GDP was determined to be $439.5 billion, based on 1986 dollar values. Assuming a 7 percent full employment rate, we can estimate the GDP gap during that recession by using Okun's law:

$$\text{GDP gap} = \$439.5 \text{ billion} \times \frac{(11.8 - 7) \times 2}{100}$$

$$= \$42.19 \text{ billion}$$

Therefore, the lost national production that resulted from the unemployment of labour resources in 1983 amounted to $42.19 billion, or $1 700 in lost income for every single Canadian. Unfortunately, since the costs of unemployment are not shared equally in Canada, the losses suffered by some individuals and families in 1983 were far greater.

potential output
The GDP that the economy could produce with full employment.

actual output
The GDP that the economy actually produces, which may be lower than its potential GDP.

Okun's law
A formula that states that for every percentage point that the actual unemployment rate exceeds the natural employment rate, a GDP gap of 2 percent occurs.

Self-Reflect

1 Explain how the Statistics Canada Labour Force Survey determines the status of employed, unemployed, and those not officially in the labour force. Explain the age requirements to be considered as part of the labour force.

2 Explain how unemployment types are all cause based. List the different types of unemployment. Identify the most important types in your community, and explain why.

3 What is meant by the term *hidden unemployed*? What effect do they have on unemployment data?

4 Identify and explain three important costs of unemployment.

Economic Instability: Business Cycles and Employment Patterns

CANADIAN UNEMPLOYMENT PATTERNS, 1976–2017

Despite its limitations, the annual unemployment rate is often used as an indicator of general economic health. Furthermore, comparing rates from one year to the next provides a relative indication of how effectively the economy is creating new jobs for Canadian workers. In net terms, new jobs require growth or expansion in economic activity. Therefore, periods of relatively low unemployment (that is, relative to the years that precede or follow) identify intervals when the economy has been able to create more new jobs than it lost. These are considered periods of economic expansion or recovery, even if the impact is only modest.

Figure 17.1 clearly presents the fluctuations in the average annual unemployment rates in Canada (and, therefore, the general health of the Canadian economy) from 1976 to 2017. Over this 40-year period, changes in the level of unemployment seem to follow a cyclical pattern of peaks and valleys. Unemployment rates averaged about 4 percent during the late 1960s and climbed above 11 percent during the early 1980s and 1990s, before beginning a slow downward trend. The following are some of the reasons offered to explain this gradual escalation of the unemployment rate:

- Globalization has led to increased replacement unemployment as manufacturing jobs continue to migrate to countries with cheaper labour costs.

- High employment insurance benefits act as a disincentive to permanent employment.

- Automation has created technological unemployment as workers continue to be replaced by machines.

- Greater economic freedom and worker mobility have resulted in an increased number of Canadians who are between jobs during any reporting period.

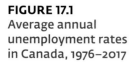

FIGURE 17.1
Average annual unemployment rates in Canada, 1976–2017

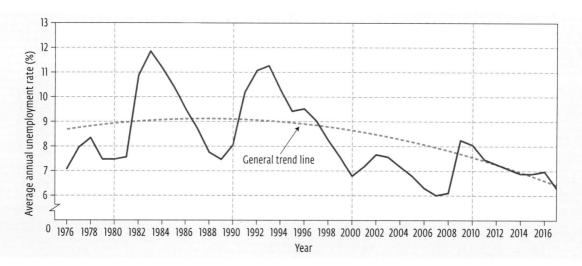

Periods of relatively high unemployment (1978, 1983, 1992, and 2009) are noticeable in Figure 17.1 as peaks, or upward bulges. Periods of relatively low unemployment (1979, 1989, and 2015) appear on the graph as troughs, or downward bulges. These downward bulges correspond with peaks in the GDP, identifying periods of relative economic growth or expansion. In absolute terms, the lowest unemployment rate during this period was observed in 2007; the highest rate was observed in 1983. By extending the general trend line, a reasonable forecast can be made about future unemployment rates in Canada. What would you expect the unemployment rate to be in 10 years?

FLUCTUATIONS IN THE CANADIAN ECONOMY

Expansion and Contraction

Since the Canadian government began to collect economic performance data in 1926, national production records reveal a continuously alternating pattern of economic slowdown, recovery, and expansion. These fluctuations are generally referred to as **business cycles**. Figure 13.6 (see page 262) illustrated the four general phases present in each cycle: expansion, peak, contraction, and trough. Business cycles may vary significantly in severity and duration.

As we have learned, the most significant economic downturn since 1926 occurred during the Great Depression of the 1930s. In Canada, between 1929 and 1933, unemployment approached 20 percent, and real GDP declined by 30 percent. This was a period of significant economic contraction in Canada and abroad. As the economy declines, workers are laid off in response to the decreasing demand for the goods and services being produced. Therefore, unemployment rates climb sharply during a period of contraction. If this contraction is seen to last longer than six consecutive months (two business quarters), the economy is said to be in **recession**. A recession is a pronounced contraction, as was the case circa 1982, 1992, and 2009. A *depression* is a severe and lengthy recession.

Periods of expansion (increasing national production) generally follow recessionary periods. During the first part of an expansionary period, the economy is said to be in **recovery** mode. Since expansion phases represent periods of sustained increases in real aggregate output, generally speaking, employment rates increase as the economy expands. A direct relationship exists between GDP and employment. By contrast, an inverse relationship exists between GDP and unemployment. You will notice in comparing the patterns shown in Figure 17.1 that peak unemployment occurs during the same years that GDP growth bottoms out. Unemployment bottoms out as aggregate production peaks.

Inflation and Employment

In his analysis of business cycles, John Maynard Keynes also linked employment to price inflation. According to Keynesian theory, the business cycle model implies that fluctuations in aggregate production levels will cause economies to alternate between periods of inflation or unemployment. During a recession, levels of unemployment are relatively high. With more workers unemployed, consumer spending is adversely affected. Both the amount of money in circulation (*money supply*) and the rate at which money changes hands through

business cycle
A rise and fall in national economic performance characterized by four phases: peak, contraction, trough, and expansion.

recession
A contraction of the economy in which real GDP declines for a minimum of two consecutive business quarters (six months).

recovery
The first part of an expansionary period following a downturn in the economy.

demand-pull inflation
Inflation caused by excessive increases in consumer demand relative to available production.

cost-push inflation
Inflation caused by the passing down of increased production costs to consumer goods and services.

Phillips curve
A diagram demonstrating an inverse relationship between inflation and unemployment rates.

business transactions (*velocity of money*) are also adversely affected. All of these economic adjustments act to reduce aggregate demand and inflationary pressures in the economy; thus, prices generally stabilize.

During periods of economic expansion, levels of unemployment are reduced because more of the labour force is able to find work. With more workers employed, the demand for consumer goods increases. As economic activity increases, both the supply and the velocity of money increase. If the production side of the economy does not keep pace with this increased demand, prices will rise as more dollars attempt to chase after available goods and services. Economic expansion can produce inflationary pressures in the economy.

Two distinct types of inflation are identified by economists. **Demand-pull inflation** results from excessive increases in consumer demand, relative to available aggregate production. **Cost-push inflation** results from the passing down of increased operating costs from producer to consumer. Thus, rapid expansion is synonymous with inflation, and recession is synonymous with unemployment. Price deflation is usually synonymous with a depression.

Continuing in the Keynesian tradition, in the early 1960s, at the London School of Economics in Britain, economist A. W. Phillips researched the link between inflation and unemployment rates. What eventually evolved from these studies was a diagram, known as the **Phillips curve**, showing a stable and predictable inverse relationship between inflation and unemployment rates.

This curve presumes a natural trade-off between inflation and unemployment: the lower the inflation rate, the higher the unemployment rate, and vice versa. In Figure 17.2, as the inflation rate rises from 2 to 4 percent, reflected in a movement from point A to point B, unemployment decreases from 10 to 6 percent.

When an economy adopts an *easy money policy* (low interest rates) and an *expansionary fiscal policy* (cutting taxes while increasing government spending) to combat unemployment, it must accept a higher rate of inflation as a consequence. The converse can also be forecasted. A *tight money policy* and a *contractionary fiscal policy* (raising taxes while cutting government spending) will combat inflation at the cost of increased unemployment. This trade-off between inflation and unemployment exists in both the short and the long terms.

FIGURE 17.2
The Phillips curve

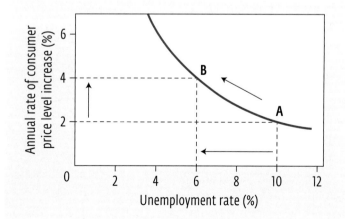

Until the 1970s, many economists agreed that Keynes and Phillips had provided an accurate model of how a market economy fluctuates. However, by the mid-1970s, an interesting economic phenomenon occurred. Although inflation and unemployment were previously seen as opposites, the Canadian economy began to experience simultaneous increases in unemployment and inflation. These periods of economic stagnation, where aggregate production slows down and both unemployment and inflation rates increase, became known as **stagflation**. This particular period of stagflation was caused by aggregate supply not being able to keep pace with increases in aggregate demand. Figure 17.3 outlines some of the principal causes of the stagflation that occurred during the 1970s in Canada, as well as their effects.

stagflation
A period of slow growth when both unemployment and inflation increase, as seen from 1973 to 1982 in Canada.

FIGURE 17.3
Factors that caused stagflation in Canada from 1973 to 1982
Most point to a downward shift in the aggregate supply curve.

Factor	Effect on Production/ Supply	Effect on Unemployment	Effect on Inflation
Sharp increases in global oil prices. The price of crude oil was more than 10 times higher in 1982 than it was in 1972 as a result of the actions of the Organization of the Petroleum Exporting Countries (OPEC), a cartel that includes many of the world's major oil producers.	Since oil is an important resource to many industries and a fuel for transportation and heating, production costs increased significantly. Many firms responded by decreasing their output.	Fewer workers were needed when firms cut production.	Prices were increased to cover increases in production costs (i.e., cost-push inflation).
Poor harvests in Eurasia. Climatic and technological problems resulted in poor harvests in China and the Soviet Union in the 1970s.	The global food supply decreased as a result of low crop yields. Canadian production levels remained constant.	The percentage of the Canadian labour force employed in agriculture continued to decline.	Prices of agricultural products increased as the global food supply decreased.
Devaluation of the Canadian dollar. The value of the Canadian dollar decreased in foreign money markets.	Prices of foreign supplies and materials increased, raising production costs and adversely affecting production levels.	Fewer workers were needed when firms cut production.	Prices of foreign goods increased as a result of a weaker dollar.
Push for higher wages by Canadian labour. With inflation rates climbing and expected to continue to climb, workers began to push for higher wages and cost-of-living adjustments in labour negotiations.	Wage increases were not based on increased worker productivity but rather on keeping up with inflation. Rising wages increased operating costs. Many firms responded by cutting production.	Higher labour costs meant that firms made do with fewer workers. As a result, unemployment increased.	Firms raised prices to recover their increased labour costs and protect their profit margins.
Government policy. Regulations (e.g., minimum-wage legislation, mandatory vacation pay, and worker's compensation) increased production costs. Policies protecting declining enterprises led to reduced productivity.	Aggregate supply did not reach maximum potential as producers sought to reduce labour costs and declining enterprises operated at reduced efficiency.	Employers made do with fewer workers as labour costs increased. Jobs in declining industries and depressed economic communities were protected.	Increased labour costs and decreased efficiency in declining industries caused prices to increase.
Bank of Canada interest policies. High interest rate policies were designed to control consumer spending and reduce inflationary pressures.	High interest rates discouraged investment and adversely affected productivity.	With less investment spending, fewer new jobs were created for Canada's growing labour force.	Demand-pull inflation was reduced slightly, but cost-push inflation and inflation imported from other countries continued to grow.

CHECK IT OUT!

The highest interest rates in Canadian history occurred in 1981 when banks were charging slightly over 21 percent interest on five-year mortgage loans for home buyers. By comparison, the same mortgage in 2018 would cost slightly over 3 percent interest. Compare the monthly payments a family would have to make in 1981 and 2018 on a $300 000 home mortgage. What lifestyle changes might 1981 and 2018 mortgage rates cause?

Self-Reflect

1 Explain the relationship that exists between national unemployment levels and GDP.

2 Why does the business cycle occur? Compare an economic contraction to a recession and a depression.

3 Explain the difference between cost-push inflation and demand-pull inflation and give two examples of each.

4 Explain the relationship between unemployment and inflation. How well does the Phillips curve help visualize this relationship?

Thinking like an Economist

Working with Indicators

Although indicators are often best estimates, economists use them to make comparisons and detect patterns and trends over time. In Figure 17.4, the employment indicators that we examined in previous chapters are used to track important changes and detect significant employment and production patterns from 1990 to 2000. This decade was chosen because it represents a period when the Canadian economy fluctuated greatly, from a major economic recession to a strong recovery. These data were compiled from various Statistics Canada publications.

APPLYING ECONOMIC THINKING

1. Explain the relationship between the employment and unemployment rate for any given year. Use a pie chart to illustrate this relationship.

2. Calculate the number of "Total unemployed" Canadians from 1990 to 1998.

3. Calculate the "Participation rate" for 1992 to 1998. Compare the usefulness of this indicator to the employment rate indicator. In 1996, the employment rate increased while the participation rate actually decreased. Explain how this is possible.

4. Explain the relationship between unemployment and education.

5. Explain the changes in the labour market between 1990 and 2000 by referring to the percentage of workers working longer hours, the percentage of workers employed in temporary or contract positions, and the percentage of unionized workers. Research current figures to determine if these changes have improved or deteriorated since then.

6. When was the unemployment rate highest from 1990 to 2000? Based on the reported changes to GDP figures at this time, explain what happened to the Canadian economy in the early 1990s and in the late 1990s.

FIGURE 17.4
Employment and production indicators

	1990	1992	1994	1996	1998	2000
Population (15+ years)	21 223 547	21 860 274	22 433 589	23 028 593	23 683 103	24 277 997
Labour force	14 241 000	14 362 200	14 626 700	14 899 500	15 417 700	15 999 200
Participation rate	67.1	?	?	?	?	65.9
Total employed	**13 084 000**	**12 760 000**	**13 111 700**	**13 462 600**	**14 140 400**	**14 909 700**
Employment rate (%)	**91.9**	**88.8**	**89.6**	**90.4**	**91.7**	**93.2**
Self-employed workers (%)	—	15.0	15.5	16.1	17.2	16.2
Temporary/contract workers (%)	—	—	—	11.2	11.8	12.5
Those working 40+ hrs/week (%)	—	20.3	21.7	21.2	18.9	18.0
Unionized workers (%)	34.7	34.9	34.5	33.9	31.8	29.0
Total unemployed	**?**	**?**	**?**	**?**	**?**	**1 089 500**
Unemployment rate (UR) (%)	**8.1**	**11.2**	**10.4**	**9.6**	**8.3**	**6.8**
UR among those aged 15–24 (%)	12.4	17.1	15.8	15.3	15.1	12.6
UR among those aged 25–54 (%)	7.1	9.9	9.2	8.5	7.0	5.7
UR among those with high school education or less (%)	12.2	14.0	13.1	12.4	11.1	9.3
UR among those with post-secondary certificate or diploma (%)	6.4	9.3	8.9	8.1	6.5	5.2
UR among those with university degrees (%)	3.8	5.5	5.4	5.2	4.4	3.9
Consumer price index (% increase)	4.8	1.5	0.2	1.6	0.9	2.7
Gross domestic product (in billions of 1992 dollars)	609.2	604.3	645.9	672.8	721.9	786.9
GDP (annual % change)	0.3	0.7	4.5	1.5	3.1	4.5

"jobless" recovery
A phenomenon, not fully understood, of a rise in GDP unaccompanied by a fall in unemployment.

"Jobless" Recovery: Short-Term Adjustment or Long-Term Reality?

THE PARADOX OF COLLECTIVE BARGAINING

During the 1990s, inflationary pressures were effectively reduced. However, unemployment proved far more difficult to remedy. This phenomenon is described as a **"jobless" recovery**. Surprisingly, one of the reasons for this persistently high unemployment was the effectiveness of labour unions in the collective bargaining process. In this section, we will use a supply and demand graph to explain the effect that collective bargaining (see Chapter 9) had on the labour market during the 1970s and 1980s.

In the 1970s and 1980s, most labour unions focused their collective bargaining efforts on securing better wages, working conditions, and benefits (such as cost-of-living allowances as protection against continued inflation) for their members. However, the laws of supply and demand acted to create an additional, unintended effect. As Figure 17.5 illustrates, as wages improve from $12 to $16 per hour, two changes take place. First, given the nature of the supply curve for labour, there is an increase (E to B along the supply curve) in the number of workers willing and able to supply labour at the higher wage level. At the same time, the quantity of labour demanded at this higher wage is naturally reduced. As labour becomes more expensive, employers will find methods of production that involve fewer workers. The increase in the quantity of labour supplied, coupled with a simultaneous decrease in the quantity of labour demanded (from E to A), produces 7 000 unemployed or surplus workers in our example.

FIGURE 17.5
The effect of collective bargaining on the labour market during the 1970s and 1980s

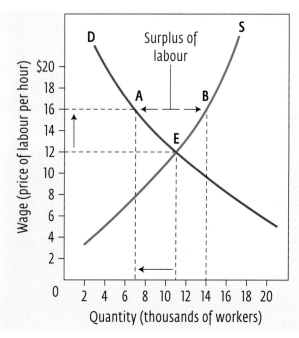

This example illustrates an interesting paradox for labour unions. As unions collectively negotiate higher wages for members, they may inadvertently negotiate a reduction in their own membership. While wage rates were set at $12 per hour, 11 000 union members were employed. As wages were increased to $16 per hour, only 7 000 union members remained employed. In this example, union negotiators did achieve higher wages but at the cost of lost jobs for their membership. This economic phenomenon happens when workers are being paid more without producing more. When worker productivity increases, the higher cost of labour can be offset by the higher revenues resulting from this increased production. To keep an economy healthy, negotiated wage increases should be proportional to actual or aggregate increases in productivity. When wage increases exceed productivity increases, price inflation can occur.

During the 1990s, as labour costs continued to be quite high, many firms began to **downsize** their workforce. Through incentive packages, veteran workers were encouraged to take early retirement. Retired workers were not replaced, and surplus workers were laid off. Generally speaking, those who remained found that their workload had increased. Another trend involved **rightsizing**, which meant reviewing the size of operations to correct any previous overuse of labour. Rightsizing, it was argued, was necessary to keep operations viable in an increasingly competitive global economy. Some unions reluctantly agreed to take wage reductions and to give up negotiated benefits to protect jobs. Labour advocates have pointed out that, in some cases, rightsizing produced short-term benefits, such as increased profitability and higher corporate stock prices, but also produced longer-term costs, such as declines in product quality and customer service. To save labour costs, some firms have chosen to hire workers on temporary contracts, instead of hiring them as full-time employees entitled to additional benefits. Sometimes these work contracts are renewed for long periods of time.

downsize
Reduce the number of employees in a company to lower production costs.

rightsize
Review the size of a company's workforce to correct the previous overuse of labour.

AUTOMATION AND INCREASED INDUSTRIAL PRODUCTIVITY

Beginning in the 1990s, many firms decided to reduce their labour force and trim their payroll to protect or improve profits. In competitive enterprises, this was accomplished by increasing industrial productivity. Through computer-assisted technological advancements, many low-skill tasks previously performed by workers were assumed by machines. As labour became increasingly more expensive (as a result of collectively negotiated wage increases and increases in the minimum wage set by governments), there was added incentive to invest more money in industrial technology.

Furthermore, in an environment where traditional low-technology jobs were becoming more and more difficult to find, it became easier to motivate grateful employees to work harder. Since 2000, the workplace has become a generally "leaner" environment. To organized labour, and many other Canadians, increases in productivity have become synonymous with forcing more work out of fewer employees.

Spurred on by increases in industrial productivity, and using a smaller, better-trained, and better-equipped workforce, firms have been able to maintain and sometimes increase production levels. This practice has generally had a positive effect on profit levels. Unfortunately, in the Canadian economy, increases in domestic productivity have not always kept pace with productivity increases in the United States and in the economies of other major trading partners. This discrepancy has prompted many economists to focus attention on comparative productivity levels. They argue that economic prosperity and the recovery of the weak Canadian dollar in foreign money markets will require substantial growth in domestic productivity. Canadian productivity has improved somewhat since 2000.

Increased productivity of labour can act to increase the demand for labour. If aggregate demand grows with aggregate supply, the demand for labour will increase to pursue this growing aggregate demand. If aggregate demand does not increase, as would be the case during a recessionary period, then productivity gains may serve to reduce the number of workers actually needed. This reduction in the demand for labour will be felt most in the low-skill, low-experience (youth) segment of the labour force, where productivity is more difficult to improve.

As aggregate production recovers from a period of economic downturn, employment levels may no longer recover to the same extent that they did in the past because of the effects of technological innovation and increased productivity. Technological innovation replaces low-skill jobs but creates high-skill jobs. Unfortunately, displaced workers may not have the training required to compete for the new technological jobs that have been created. The result is that some new jobs remain unfilled. By 2000, many Canadian employers were concerned about not being able to find the skilled workers that their enterprises required.

EMPLOYMENT PATTERNS IN THE GLOBAL ECONOMY

Another factor in persistently high unemployment levels during the recovery phase of recent business cycles has been the steady movement toward greater economic globalization. As national borders continue to lose their economic significance, some corporate decisions that are based on profit maximization will have adverse effects on unemployment rates in Canada and other industrialized countries. Some unemployment in industrialized countries can be traced to the loss of manufacturing jobs to less-developed countries, where wage levels, working conditions, and environmental protection legislation are conducive to increased corporate profits.

As a result of the North American Free Trade Agreement (NAFTA), some US firms decided to reduce costs by scaling down their Canadian operations and supplying Canadian customers from the closest US plant. Other firms, previously based in Canada, relocated to Mexico to take advantage of lower wage rates and less stringent environmental regulations. We shall explore this trend in detail in Chapter 20, when we investigate international trade patterns. Although there have also been some job gains as a result of globalization, unemployment levels in Canada have remained generally higher, perhaps partially because of the manufacturing jobs lost as a result of globalization.

The mechanical engineers seen here, inspecting a gas turbine engine in Airdrie, Alberta, are an example of high-skilled labour in Canada's growing industries.

THE EFFECTS OF TAXATION

High levels of corporate and business taxation can act to discourage investment and corporate expansion. Where consumer and investor confidence is high, lower levels of corporate taxation (relative to the rates paid in countries that are major trading partners) help to create a business climate conducive to expansion and greater employment opportunities.

Levels of personal taxation affect both the disposable income left to consumers and investors and the government's ability to finance the infrastructure improvements necessary to promote increased productivity and economic activity. For example, in Canada, complex and expensive communication and transportation networks have been developed (and are being improved) to link the country together. In addition, government spending on education and health contributes significantly to national productivity.

High taxes can have adverse effects on employment levels. Unless the decreases in disposable income (caused by tax increases) are offset by increases in government spending, taxation can reduce aggregate demand. Decreases in aggregate demand or in consumer confidence prompt firms to cut employment to protect profit levels in a declining marketplace.

THE EFFECTS OF DEMOGRAPHIC CHANGES

The unemployment rate may remain high even though jobs are actually being created, if the labour force increases faster than the economy's ability to create jobs. For example, as employment prospects increase in an expanding economy, people who had previously given up looking for work may return to the labour force. Since 2000, as average family size continues to decrease and the average age of Canadians continues to increase, senior citizens will require more government services while contributing less to national production. Some economists have suggested that monitoring the number of employed Canadians is a truer indicator of job creation than monitoring changes in the unemployment rate. Any thorough analysis of whether a recovery period is actually jobless should involve the monitoring of both indicators.

TAKING STOCK

Several reasons have been advanced to explain the phenomenon of a "jobless" recovery. The question that remains, however, is an extremely important one for you. Is a "jobless" recovery a short-term economic correction or a long-term economic reality? On this issue, the Canadian economic community is clearly divided, and it appears that only time will tell. By the time you write your own economics textbook, you will be able to provide historical documentation to explain the longevity of the "jobless" recovery phenomenon.

Self-Reflect

1 Summarize the main theories used to explain the phenomenon of "jobless" recovery. Which do you consider to be most important?

2 Use the data in Figure 17.4 to determine whether the period between 1992 and 2000 should be considered a period of jobless recovery. Justify your decision.

3 Explain the impact of increased globalization and trade on the market for labour in Canadian manufacturing industries. Using Figure 17.5 as a model, draw a graph to show this effect on the Canadian labour market.

4 Explain how technological innovation can create both employment and unemployment.

common good
The well-being of society at large, sometimes referred to as *the most good for the greatest number.*

sustainability
Practices and conditions that can be expected to continue safely for the long term because they minimize waste and inefficiency of resources, environmental damage, and the unfair treatment of vulnerable stakeholders.

Public Policy Issues and Implications

DEFINING AND SERVING THE COMMON GOOD

Recent, current, and projected unemployment levels are a constant source of concern for many Canadians. Many socio-political implications arise from prolonged unemployment. Armed with trend graphs and economic theories, first to explain and then to project unemployment levels to the next quarter and beyond, many economists and politicians seek to influence public policy to better serve the common good. This **common good** can be defined as the well-being of Canadian society at large, or as an aggregate. Social activists constantly remind us that this "common" good must also extend to the poor and marginalized members of society.

Some economists have long attempted to isolate themselves from this political decision-making arena, claiming that their role is apolitical and informative rather than partisan and normative (that is, values based and policy oriented). There are problems with this notion. First, in attempting to steer a "values-neutral" course, the science of economics can become relatively academic, dry, and soulless. Second, as we discovered in Chapter 1, the political and economic systems of any country are usually interconnected. Given the complex multi-interest nature of political decisions, the trade-off realities of the economic world (driven by scarcity and choice), and human nature's dependency on positive values, very few politico-economic decisions can ever be "values neutral."

The principal task is not to neutralize values but, rather, to recognize the values inherent in every perspective on a particular social or policy issue. This recognition will facilitate the recognition of values that serve and that run counter to the common or greater good. It will allow for the analysis of values-driven benefits and costs to assess policy alternatives. Ultimately, this process will result in better informed and balanced decisions—decisions that take account of trade-offs and address the consequences. These consequences are the price we collectively pay for the alternatives we choose, and the trade-offs we make, to secure priorities.

PROMOTING SUSTAINABLE CHOICES

In theory, all public policy choices seek to promote growth and stability. In practice, this may not always be the case in our finite economic world. All wise economic choices must be sustainable or designed to last with minimal side effects. All **sustainability** is rooted in economy, ecology, and equity (see Figure 17.6). This means that waste, inefficiency, environmental damage, and unfair treatment must be kept to an absolute minimum.

FIGURE 17.6
The recipe for sustainability

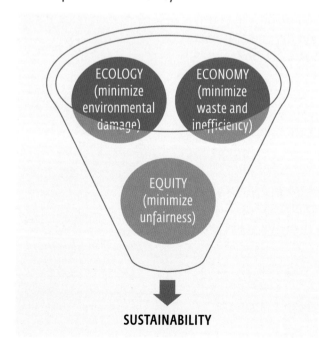

With conflicting stakeholder interests and views, this recipe for sustainability may prove difficult to achieve. For example, environmental protection can be forced to the periphery when many jobs are on the line. In the forestry industry, allowing trees to be harvested at a faster rate than they can be regrown is clearly not a sustainable practice in the long run. Government policy can direct economic activity toward sustainable practices such as conservation, reforestation, and recycling to help counterbalance the push for profit maximization by private enterprise.

REGIONAL ECONOMIC DIVERSIFICATION: NEWFOUNDLAND AND LABRADOR'S RESPONSE

Economic diversification is considered a wise policy, both nationally and regionally. At the national level, for years the Canadian government has negotiated trade agreements with new trading partners to lessen Canada's overall dependency on the American economy. To avoid overdependence on a single industry or resource, different regions in Canada have sought to diversify their local economies. Once diversified, the impact of a prolonged setback in one industry can be softened by growth or stability in other industries. One of the best examples of diversification policy can be found in Newfoundland and Labrador, one of the regions in Canada that has traditionally experienced relatively high unemployment.

Since 1497, when John Cabot found fish that were so plentiful they could be scooped from the water in baskets, cod became the catalyst for the settlement and economic development of Newfoundland and Labrador. In 1992, after years of government reductions in the "Total Allowable Catch," the northern cod fisheries were still the biggest group of fisheries on the East Coast, contributing $700 million to the Canadian economy. However, by 1994, two years after the federal government placed a moratorium (ban) on northern cod fishing, the cod had been fished to "commercial extinction" according to the Food and Agriculture Organization of the United Nations. Some of the possible causes of the cod stock's collapse include the following: overfishing and mismanagement; climatic change that resulted in changes in temperature and aquatic life; an increase in the fish-eating seal population; the use of dragnets, which destroy fish eggs and other marine life; the use of electronic technology to locate schools of fish; and the use of large automated factory trawlers with built-in filleting and freezing equipment.

Virtually every community in the province depended on the cod fisheries. When they collapsed, approximately 31 000 people lost their jobs, most of which were in Newfoundland and Labrador. The cod moratorium represented the largest layoff in Canadian history. The laid-off workers received a $1.9 billion aid package from Ottawa known as **The Atlantic Groundfish Strategy (TAGS)**. This program, which ran from 1994 to 1998, temporarily helped to provide the necessities of life. However, an economic blow such as the collapse of the cod fisheries—a major source of employment—had to be met with substantive structural changes to the provincial economy. A summary of the economic diversification strategy follows.

The Atlantic Groundfish Strategy (TAGS)
A $1.9 billion federal aid program from 1994 to 1998 for the 31 000 people who lost their livelihood with the collapse of the North Atlantic cod fisheries.

Developing the Hibernia Oil Field

Discovered in 1979, the Hibernia oil field is 315 km east-southeast of St. John's, in 80 m of water. The $6 billion drilling-production platform was installed (by a consortium of large oil companies) in 1997 after six years of design, engineering, and construction work. The Canadian Association of Petroleum Producers (CAPP) estimated that the site contained 615 million barrels of recoverable oil, with another 4.6 billion barrels in the Grand Banks. However, the high-risk offshore oil industry required far too much capital for small enterprises to get involved. Being near Iceberg Alley provided additional expensive challenges.

Directly and indirectly, Hibernia operation was expected to create 3 100 new jobs, representing 1.6 percent of the provincial total. In its first full year of production (1998), the Hibernia operation and its indirect impacts (including suppliers and service providers) produced a GDP increase of $626 million, representing 5.7 percent of the province's total GDP. Since many of the Hibernia jobs pay well, personal income in Newfoundland and Labrador was $168 million higher in 1998, which led to a $124 million increase in consumer spending. The total population grew by 5 000 as a result of reduced out-migration and increased in-migration.

The Hibernia oil platform with a ship ready to tug icebergs out of harm's way. A 15-metre thick ice belt was also designed to protect the platform.

By the end of 2016, a total of 1 billion barrels of crude oil had been harvested at the Hibernia oil field, and most recent estimates indicate that it has another 15 to 20 years of profitable oil recovery remaining. The market value of all oil production at Hibernia to the end of 2016 was estimated to be $65 billion.

Aquaculture

Some in the province have turned to **aquaculture**, the breeding and raising of marine life in tanks, ponds, and reservoirs. To date, aquaculture (also known as *fish farming*) in the province has focused on the production of Blue Mussels, Steelhead Trout, Atlantic Salmon, and Atlantic Cod. By 2016, the industry produced a record $276 million for the provincial economy and employed over 1 000 people. Both federal and provincial governments are promoting this industry aggressively as part of the Canada/Newfoundland Agreement on Economic Renewal. Research into more ecological methods of aquaculture is being carried out.

Information Technology

The province's information technology (IT) sector has experienced considerable growth since the collapse of the cod fisheries. Funded by the Canada/Newfoundland Agreement on Economic Renewal in 1996, Operation ONLINE is a non-profit organization created to promote growth in the very competitive IT sector. Of the over 200 high-technology companies (which employ over 8 000 workers in the province), 163 are IT companies. Seventy percent are located in the St. John's Census Metropolitan Area.

These IT companies experienced substantial and steady annual growth between 1992 and 2002, adding an additional 7.5 percent annually to the provincial GDP. The contribution IT makes to the provincial economy is important from two perspectives. First, it generates employment and income for those working in the sector. Second, and perhaps more important, it has an enabling effect on other parts of the economy by enhancing productivity and performance.

Tourism

In recent years, there has been a concerted effort to attract more non-resident tourism to the province to create employment in the hospitality and service industries. In 1997, the province celebrated the 500th anniversary of John Cabot's historic voyage from England to Newfoundland. This highly publicized celebration produced a 22 percent increase in automobile and air visits from the previous year. In 1999, the province celebrated its 50th anniversary of Confederation, which brought an increase of 8 percent from the previous year in auto, air, and cruise-ship visits.

In 2000, celebrations surrounding the Viking explorers saw a 3 percent increase in auto, air, and cruise visits over the previous year. The 100th anniversary of Marconi's trans-Atlantic wireless radio transmission from Newfoundland was celebrated in 2001. According to the provincial Department of Finance, by the end of 2010, the growing tourism industry accounted for $288 million, or 1.1 percent of the provincial GDP. This contribution ranked higher than logging (0.3 percent), fish-harvesting (0.6 percent), and fish-processing (1.0 percent) industries. Job opportunities and incomes in the hospitality and tourism sector continue to grow.

aquaculture
The breeding and raising of marine life in tanks, ponds, and reservoirs; also known as fish farming.

Filmmaking

The film industry in Newfoundland and Labrador has produced more than 100 films over the past 40 years. Since the 1990s, there has been a steady increase in more ambitious projects involving documentaries, feature films, and television programs. Between 1990 and 1996, film projects valued at $14 million were produced in the province. From 1997 to 2017, the total of all production activity in the province was $399 million.

Film and television productions are labour intensive, with approximately 60 percent of a film project's budget being spent on salaries and fees for creative and technical workers. A typical feature film crew can employ 50 to 60 full-time cast and crew members. The film industry is recognized as a very efficient job creator. Independent production companies create one job for every $36 000 received in gross revenues, compared with one job for every $144 000 for most dominant industrial sectors.

There are also sizable spinoff benefits for communities where productions are actually filmed, in the form of goods and services purchased from local businesses. Statistics Canada estimates that for every dollar spent directly on film and video productions, an additional dollar is generated in spinoff benefits.

To attract increased filmmaking activity, the provincial government has instituted a corporate income tax credit administered by the Newfoundland and Labrador Film Development Corporation (NLFDC). The program provides incentives for the development, training, and hiring of local film personnel in all aspects of the production process. It provides incentives to production companies to create economic growth in the province.

Not to be confused with *aquaculture* (the breeding and raising of marine life), the film *Aquaman* (2018), pictured here, was filmed in part in Newfoundland and Labrador. The fim industry stimulates economic growth in the province, both by creating jobs and through sizable spinoff benefits.

Economic Diversification and Growth Enterprises

The province's Economic Diversification and Growth Enterprises (EDGE) is an incentive program that was launched in 1995 to attract business investment and create jobs in the province. It features a 10-year "tax holiday" from provincial corporate income tax and health and payroll taxes. Forty-five municipalities have joined with the province to extend the tax holiday to municipal property and business taxes. With incentives like these, the cost of doing business in Newfoundland and Labrador has been significantly reduced. By 2001, 60 companies had filed business plans for acceptance into the EDGE program, representing an investment of $730 million and the creation of 2 437 jobs. By the end of 2004, a report by the provincial auditor general confirmed that 57 percent of these business plans had materialized. It has proven challenging to attract sustainable business ventures to the province, but the EDGE project has continued.

Figure 17.7 summarizes the multifaceted approach to diversifying the province's economy. Overall, great strides have been made since it was developed, and in 2001, Newfoundland and Labrador recorded the strongest employment growth rate of any province. Regrettably, this growth rate proved to be economically unsustainable.

FIGURE 17.7
A multifaceted approach to diversifying a provincial economy after the collapse of the North Atlantic cod fisheries

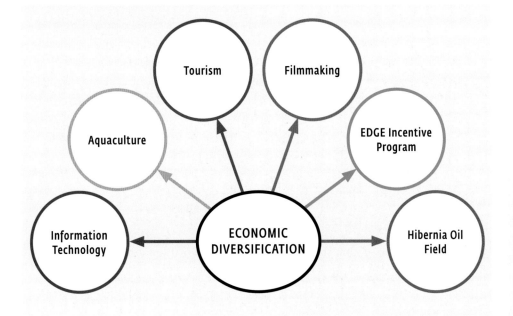

Self-Reflect

1 Explain what is meant by the *common good*.

2 Why are politico-economic decisions rarely "values neutral"?

3 Explain what is required to make something sustainable.

4 Explain four examples of how the economy of Newfoundland and Labrador was diversified after the collapse of the cod fisheries in 1992.

Thinking like an Economist

Analyzing Conflicting Interests and Values to Determine the Common Good

For each of the five employment-related issues presented here, a brief outline of conflicting perspectives is included to focus economic analysis. As only three economic arguments are provided to support each position, additional arguments might arise from personal reflection and class discussion.

For an economist, the task at hand is to recognize the assumptions, interests, and priorities inherent in each statement, as the *values* being expressed. Once recognized, these *values* must be assessed to determine both benefits and costs for each perspective. This should help to identify the viewpoint that best supports the common or greater good for each employment issue. It might be useful to review the

section in Chapter 4 on establishing economic goals (pages 52–55) prior to beginning this issues analysis/decision-making activity. Be warned: The common good may prove as elusive as "common" sense!

APPLYING ECONOMIC THINKING

1   Conduct a cost-benefit analysis for each of the five issues presented here to identify whether arguments for or against best support the common good.

2   Compare the cost-benefit analyses conducted by other students to reach consensus for each employment issue discussed.

ISSUE 1: Should governments pursue debt reduction during periods of high unemployment?

Arguments For	Arguments Against
• Carrying charges on public debt limits government spending on social assistance programs for disadvantaged people. • Government borrowing to carry public debt forces interest rates to climb, adversely affecting both investment and consumer spending. • The present generation does not have a moral right to incur debts that future generations must pay.	• Cutting government spending and raising taxes to reduce the public debt has an adverse effect on aggregate demand and will increase unemployment. • Cutting government spending to balance budgets affects disadvantaged Canadians most. • Debt reduction can be reserved for expansionary phases of the business cycle, where it helps to reduce inflation.

ISSUE 2: Should corporate taxes be reduced in Canada to stimulate job creation?

Arguments For	Arguments Against
• Lower taxes make Canadian firms more competitive with their foreign counterparts. • Lower taxes attract business investment and create new jobs. • New jobs promote increases in consumer spending and aggregate demand.	• Canadian corporations are not presently paying their fair share of taxes in light of the tax supported infrastructure on which these firms rely. • Since corporations have the same rights as individuals, corporate income should be treated the same as personal income. • Corporate expansion is driven by confidence and retained profits, not by tax reductions.

ISSUE 3: Should the powers of large labour unions be reduced?

Arguments For	Arguments Against
• By negotiating wage increases, labour unions contribute to higher unemployment. • Negotiated wage increases that are not based on productivity increases are inflationary when supply cannot keep pace with demand. • Strikes and other labour disputes affect aggregate production adversely.	• Unions protect the rights and working conditions of workers. • Unions are needed to balance the growing powers of large corporations. • Unions help to secure a larger portion of gross domestic product (GDP) for the working class, and, therefore, a more equitable distribution of wealth through income.

ISSUE 4: Should minimum wage and employment insurance (EI) benefits be increased?

Arguments For	Arguments Against
• Both would increase the disposable income of low-income Canadians, providing a more equitable distribution of wealth. • Both would lead to an increase in consumer spending and generate an increase in aggregate demand (i.e., additional labour would be needed to increase production to meet demand). • By increasing EI, the exploitation of low-skilled labour is reduced (better pay and opportunities to find better jobs).	• By increasing EI, there is less incentive for unemployed workers to fill available job vacancies. • By increasing EI, there is less incentive for unemployed workers to retrain so that they qualify for better-paying jobs (greater dependency on government assistance). • An increase in the minimum wage means that the cost of labour rises and fewer workers will be required by employers.

ISSUE 5: Should companies pay taxes for the workers they displace as a result of automation?

Arguments For	Arguments Against
• Unemployed workers pay less tax to government, but they require more assistance from government. • Firms increase their profitability by automating production processes and replacing workers, so they have the money to contribute. • Firms should assume some responsibility for the unemployment they create in pursuit of greater profit.	• Placing a tax on technological innovation and capital investment would have an adverse effect on productivity and aggregate production. • No other structural economic changes causing the displacement of workers are presently taxed; these changes are inevitable and, in the long run, beneficial. • Ultimately, such taxes would be passed on to the consumer in the form of higher prices.

Chapter 17
Consolidation Activities

KNOWLEDGE

1   What is the labour force status (employed, unemployed, or officially not in the labour force) for each of the following individuals? Explain why in each case.

   a)   A university graduate who is seeking her first job

   b)   A male homemaker who stays home full-time to care for three children and an ailing parent

   c)   A mechanical engineer who has left her job to look for a better position

   d)   A computer programmer who has a job but is too ill to work

   e)   An unemployed fisheries worker who has given up looking for work after 10 frustrating months trying to find a job

   f)   A new Canadian with a PhD in microbiology who has to drive a cab to make a living

2   Draw a diagram to explain the four phases of a typical business cycle.

3   Explain the main causes of the stagflation experienced in Canada from 1973 to 1982.

4   Identify the type of unemployment represented by the following examples. Explain your choice.

   a)   Declining salmon stocks in the Pacific Northwest have reduced the number of people working in the fishing industry in British Columbia

   b)   Employees tired of working for an unreasonable boss quit to seek better jobs.

   c)   Foreign automobiles have increased their market share in Canada since 1990. As a result, some Canadian auto workers have lost their jobs.

   d)   Retailers who hire extra staff for the Christmas period lay off these workers after the Boxing Week sales.

   e)   As labour unions secure higher wages for their members, it becomes more attractive for manufacturers to use machines instead of unionized workers. As a result, some workers are laid off.

   f)   Increases in interest rates cause mortgage rates on new homes to climb. As a result, consumer demand for new houses decreases and some construction workers are laid off.

THINKING & INQUIRY

5   Research data to compare Canadian unemployment rate figures with those of other industrialized countries, such as Japan, Germany, the United States, Britain, France, and Italy. How did Canadian unemployment rates compare in the 1990s? in the 2000s? in the 2010s?

6   "Full employment is reached when cyclical unemployment is zero." Do you agree with this statement? Explain.

7   Referring to the data in Figure 17.4 (page 361), develop a theory to explain the relatively high unemployment rate among 15- to 24-year-olds.

8   A seesaw is an effective metaphor for the traditional relationship between unemployment and inflation represented by the Phillips curve. Explain this traditional relationship. Research Statistics Canada data to find out what happened to this relationship during the 1980s and the 1990s. In your opinion, is the Phillips curve still relevant? Explain.

COMMUNICATION

9 a) Create an organizer to explain what generally happens to these 10 economic variables during each phase of the business cycle:

- Unemployment
- Inflation
- Consumer confidence and spending
- Household savings
- Aggregate demand
- Investor confidence in future profits
- Interest rates
- Stock market prices
- Utilization of factories and production equipment
- Aggregate production (or total national output)

Use symbols to denote increase ($\uparrow$), decrease ($\downarrow$), and no significant change ($\leftrightarrow$) for each variable.

b) For each variable, explain why the changes in the recession and expansion phases occur.

10 Explain the terms *stagflation* and *"jobless" recovery* in a way that would make sense to people with no background in economics.

APPLICATION

11 Some critics claim that unemployment statistics hide some types of unemployment. What limitations do you see with the way labour force numbers, unemployment rates, and participation rates are determined? Should the participation rate replace the unemployment rate as an indicator of economic health? Explain your position.

12 Are "jobless" recoveries short-term adjustments or long-term realities? What economic facts or theories can you use to support your conclusion? Explain.

13 Suppose that full employment in the fictional kingdom of Pandora is defined as 7 percent unemployment. Last year, the actual unemployment rate was 9 percent and GDP was US$500 billion. The population of the kingdom is 25 million. Apply Okun's law to calculate the following:

a) Potential aggregate output

b) The GDP gap

c) Per capita lost income as a result of the underemployment of labour resources

14 In July 2008, the world price of crude oil reached a record high of US$147 per barrel, fuelled by an ever-increasing demand from a booming global economy. However, by late December 2008, the world price of crude oil dropped suddenly to US$32 per barrel. The global price of oil is greatly affected by the massive quantities being produced by low-cost, high-volume producers such as the 14 member countries of the Organization of the Petroleum Exporting Countries (OPEC) cartel and Russia. When the global economy suddenly sank into severe recession, after a series of financial crises and scandals, volume producers such as OPEC and Russia refused to cut production. This oil glut caused the global price to collapse. Research the economic effects of this global reduction in the price of oil on the oil-dependent economies of Alberta and Newfoundland and Labrador. Present your findings in a written, oral, or video report.

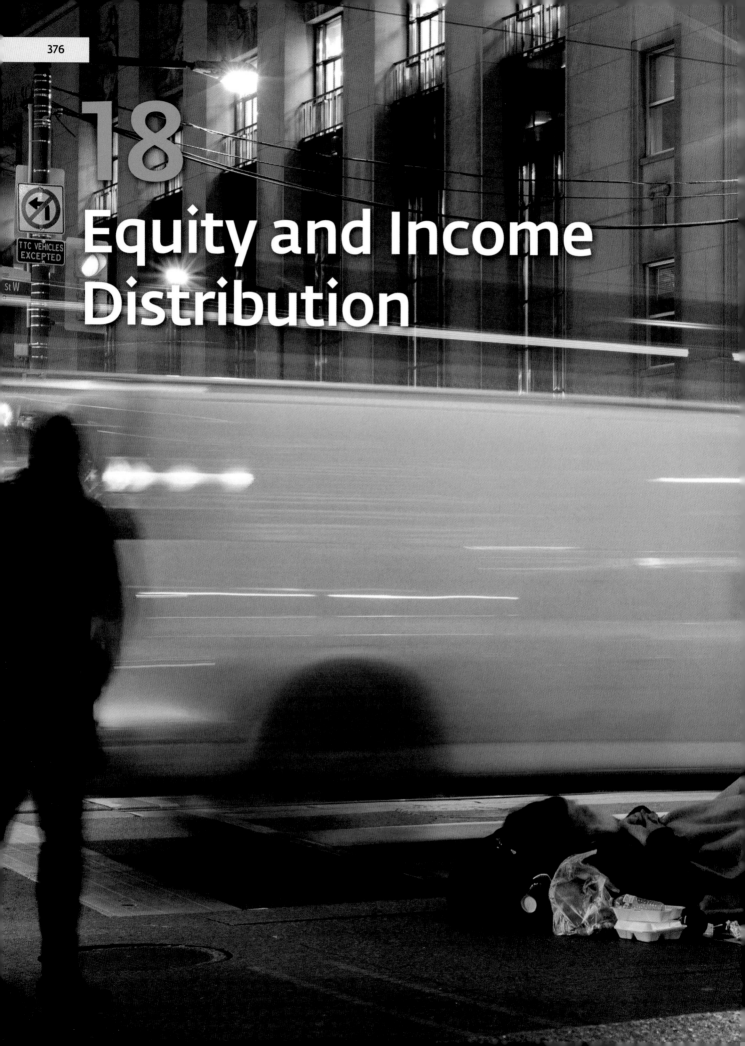

18 Equity and Income Distribution

INTRODUCTION

As we learned in Chapter 16, Canada's social welfare safety net has undergone significant "downsizing" since the 1990s as various levels of government attempted to eliminate their substantial budget deficits. Some critics of Canada's safety net justify this policy change because the Canadian model had clearly become unsustainable. Other Canadians believe these cutbacks were necessary to "harmonize" Canadian practices with those of our dominant economic partner, the United States.

Yet, other Canadians see the deterioration of Canada's social safety net as problematic. The Canadian system has been designed to effect a fairer distribution of income and, ultimately, national wealth—a goal many Canadians value. Many believe that the Canadian system for maintaining the well-being of its citizens has been fundamental in establishing Canada's international reputation as one of the best countries in which to live and that further downsizing threatens that hard-earned reputation. This complex public debate continues.

LEARNING GOALS

Once you have completed this chapter, you should be able to:

- Explain how tools such as the Human Development Index (HDI), the Lorenz curve, and low-income cut-offs (LICOs), or "poverty lines," can be used as indicators of socio-economic well-being

- Distinguish between absolute and relative poverty, and structural and relief strategies to address poverty

- Explain how government is involved in the Canadian economy as a redistributor of income

- Evaluate the effectiveness of government programs designed to ensure greater equity and economic security for Canadians

- Apply economic inquiry skills to analyze public policy issues focused on income inequality and redistribution

KEY TERMS

equity

inequity

Human Development Index (HDI)

mean average income

median income

quintile

Lorenz curve

risk premium

cohort

asset income

absolute poverty

relative poverty

low-income cut-off (LICO)

before-tax income

after-tax income

poverty line

deprivation

exclusion

working poor

welfare poor

residential school

welfare state

progressive tax system

wealth

structural strategy

relief strategy

equity

Fair and just distribution of income within an economy.

inequity

A condition or privilege that benefits some to the detriment of others because fairness and distributive justice have been overlooked.

Human Development Index (HDI)

Established by the United Nations, a measurement of a country's achievements in three aspects of human development: life expectancy, literacy and education levels, and GDP per capita. In 2018, Canada ranked 12th among the 189 countries included in the HDI.

Equity: A Canadian Perspective

COMING TO TERMS WITH EQUITY AND HUMAN DEVELOPMENT

Equity is often presented as a key economic goal, but what exactly does *equity* mean? How does equity relate to concepts such as equality, fairness, and distributive justice? The term **equity**, when used in economics, refers specifically to a distribution that is just and fair. Equity as fairness or distributive justice can have different meanings. Sometimes equity is intended to mean equality. Sometimes it is meant to suggest that rewards be proportionate with differences in the effort or workload that is required. Sometimes the term is used to mean that reasonable expectations are not disappointed.

These different interpretations of equity can sometimes conflict. For example, we can apply these concepts of equity to retirement pensions. If equity means equality, it implies that all employees will receive pensions of about equal value. If equity means matching rewards to effort, it implies that hard and responsible work will earn a higher pension than work that is lacking or casual. If equity means conforming to expectations, it implies that workers will not be disappointed relative to the pension they have been led to expect.

You will remember from Chapter 3 that one of the three main production questions an economic system must address is For whom to produce?; that is, How will total output be shared among the different members of society? This production question is undoubtedly the most controversial of the three. Karl Marx attempted to answer this question. Marx believed that all of society's problems are caused by inequality of income. He theorized that an economic system that shares goods on a basis of equality would bring out the best in people. This theory contrasted with capitalism, which is built on free enterprise driven by self-interest and the accumulation of personal wealth.

Capitalism appears to have prevailed in almost every country in the world, and income **inequities** are now the norm. Although earnings are only part of the picture when we consider income, they do give us some idea of the disparities within our society. Figure 18.1 shows some of the highest-paying and lowest-paying jobs in Canada.

Despite the vast differences in earnings among various professions, Canada's efforts to redistribute income to make life better for all Canadians have resulted in a society that is recognized around the world as a good place to live. As Canadians, we may not wave our national flag at every opportunity, but most of us consider ourselves fortunate to be living in Canada. Since 1992, this feeling has been confirmed by the United Nations **Human Development Index (HDI)**. This annual index uses education, standard of living, and life expectancy data to rank 189 countries in terms of human development, or "quality of life." Canada placed first overall from 1992 to 2000. By 2018, Canada had dropped to a still very respectable 12th place. Despite this achievement, there is growing evidence that income inequality is increasing within Canada. The issue of equity, or what is a fair distribution of national production, income, and wealth, remains with us still.

FIGURE 18.1
Some highest- and lowest-paying occupations in Canada
The data collected in the 2016 census reveal interesting income patterns. What patterns can you identify in the data? What pattern is most significant in relation to equity?

Occupation	2016 Census Average Earnings ($)		
	All sexes	Men	Women
All occupations	**48 930**	**54 369**	**39 372**
Ten of the highest-paying occupations			
Judges	228 381	225 476	233 409
Senior managers—financial, communications, and business services	215 911	237 639	153 013
Senior managers—goods production, utilities, transportation, and construction	190 444	199 566	134 943
Petroleum engineers	174 528	182 383	136 416
Specialist physicians	162 208	176 637	140 148
Lawyers and Quebec notaries	140 230	164 436	110 226
Senior managers—insurance, real estate, and financial brokerage	134 031	170 461	88 425
Geoscientists and oceanographers	130 026	140 940	97 013
General practitioners and family physicians	120 334	131 082	108 558
Dentists	118 488	130 742	99 593
Ten of the lowest-paying occupations			
Industrial sewing machine operators	22 271	24 594	22 063
Artisans and craftspersons	18 950	24 208	15 585
Taxi drivers	17 313	17 247	18 321
Service station attendants	17 404	17 682	16 680
Bartenders	17 120	18 910	15 939
Harvesting labourers	15 683	17 011	14 739
Child-care providers—baby-sitters, nannies, and parents' helpers	15 635	16 690	15 591
Food and beverage servers	15 076	17 575	14 406
Food service counter attendants, kitchen helpers, and food preparers	13 886	12 509	14 714
Cashiers	12 813	11 967	12 999

AVERAGE INCOMES IN CANADA: A SNAPSHOT

Per capita income is one of the factors used to calculate the HDI because the more income people have, the more likely they are to be able to support themselves and their families in a comfortable lifestyle.

Canadians earn high incomes, though not the highest among the more developed countries. In the 1996 census, the average income in Canada was reported as $25 196. Through a combination of economic growth and price inflation, by 2016 this amount had become $48 930. This average, which is calculated by dividing Canada's total income by the total population, is called **mean average income**. Mean averages are useful and easy to calculate, but they tend to be pulled off the centre by either very low figures or very high ones.

Another kind of average income is the **median income**, which is the middle income dividing Canada's range of incomes into two equal halves. The number of people earning more than the median income is the same as the number of people earning less. Medians provide a good idea of the central tendency in a range of figures. Averages are a generalization of a set of figures to determine one representative value.

In the 2016 census, Canada's median income was $36 693, indicating that substantially fewer Canadians earned more than the mean average income and that the majority of Canadians earned significantly less. The mean average figures were distorted by the extremely high incomes earned by a few Canadians.

Mean and median averages are useful for comparing income changes from one year to another and for comparing the present standard of living with that of the past or that of other countries. Generally speaking, when mean and median calculations differ significantly, a disproportionate number of very low or very high figures have pulled the mean average off the centre point. Yet, when mean and median calculations are close, the data are said to be more evenly distributed. How would this statistical rule apply to the distribution of marks in an economics class?

DID YOU KNOW?

Did you know that in the 2016 census, Canadian athletes reported an average income of $145 584 but a median income of only $17 181. This means that the average value was badly skewed by a handful of professional athletes earning huge six-figure salaries, while the vast majority of athletes earned closer to $17 000 annually or less. This example shows how averages can be deceiving.

Income Distribution

To examine income distribution, economists divide Canadian income earners into groups called *quintiles*. A **quintile** is one-fifth (or 20 percent) of the total number of earners. Suppose that the incomes of all family households in Canada were placed in order from the lowest to the highest. If there were 10 million households in Canada, the first quintile would consist of the 2 million families earning the lowest incomes, the second quintile would be the next 2 million, and so on until the fifth quintile was grouped together representing the incomes of the 2 million households earning the highest incomes. The incomes of each of the five quintiles are totalled and represented as a percentage of the total income of all the quintiles. The results for Canada for 2000 and 2017 are shown in Figure 18.2.

An examination of Figure 18.2 shows that income is not distributed equally in Canada; the lowest quintile received only 6.7 percent of the total national income in 2017. In 2000, this same quintile received only 4.4 percent of total national income. In comparison, the highest quintile received 41.4 percent of the total income in 2017 and 45.3 percent in 2000. If the income of the lowest three quintiles is totalled, we can see that 60 percent of Canadian households received only 30 percent of the total income in 2000 and almost 36 percent in 2017. However, the top 40 percent received the rest (70 to 64 percent) of national after-tax or "disposable" income. This gap represents a considerable disparity between Canadian households, but it seems to be closing slowly. Economists try to see patterns in quintile data by making use of graphs such as the **Lorenz curve** described in this chapter's *Thinking like an Economist* feature.

quintile
One-fifth (or 20 percent) of the total number of income earners in an economy; it is used to examine income distribution.

Lorenz curve
A graph used to show the degree of inequality that exists among groups of income receivers of the same size.

FIGURE 18.2

Shares of Canadians' after-tax income in 2000 and 2017
How does this distribution pattern help shed light on the distribution of disposable incomes in Canada?

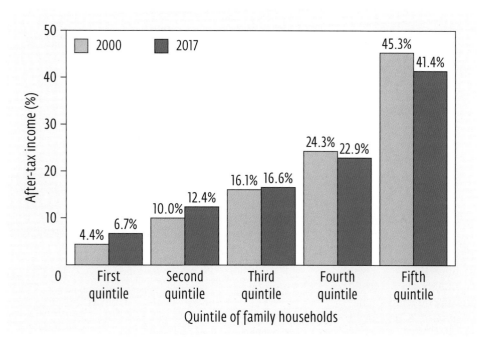

Self-Reflect

1 Assess the three interpretations of equity in reference to the establishment of a breakfast program in your school. Which interpretations are most appropriate for achieving distributive justice? Justify your choices.

2 Why is the Human Development Index considered a useful measure of "quality of life" by the United Nations?

3 In what occupations are women paid substantially less than their male counterparts? What do these data suggest about gender equity in Canada?

4 Define a *quintile* and explain how quintiles help analyze the distribution of income in Canada, both for one year and over time.

Thinking like an Economist

Reading and Creating Lorenz Curves

The distribution of income represented by Figure 18.2 (page 381), can be easily visualized by converting it into a **Lorenz curve**. Unlike the bar graph in the figure, which shows the income for each quintile individually, a Lorenz curve shows cumulative income. That means that the income shown for the second quintile indicates the income for the second quintile plus the income for the first quintile. To make a Lorenz curve of the data in Figure 18.2, we must first make the calculations in Figure 18.3 to determine cumulative shares.

On a Lorenz curve, the horizontal axis represents households divided into quintiles, and the vertical axis represents income. To make the curve, we plot the cumulative incomes for the five quintiles on the graph. You can see these as points A, B, C, D, and E on the graph in Figure 18.4. To complete the graph, we join these points together in a smooth curve.

You will notice on this graph that a 45-degree line bisects the horizontal and vertical axes. Any point on that line is an equal distance from either axis, representing a perfectly equal distribution of income. In the hypothetical society that would match that line of equal distribution, 20 percent of households would receive exactly 20 percent of total income, 60 percent of families would receive exactly 60 percent of total income, and so on.

However, the actual distribution of income in virtually all societies creates not a straight line but a curved line that bows out to the right. The greater the distance the line bows out from the complete equality line, the greater the degree of inequality. That the Lorenz curve for Canada bows out from the complete equality line shows that Canadian incomes are not equally distributed. Lorenz curves can be compared to understand changes over time. A very slight improvement can be noted from 2000 to 2017. Figure 18.5 reveals that income distribution in Canada has changed very little since 1951.

Lorenz curves can also be used to compare income distribution in different countries to determine the relative degree of income inequality in different political economies. These curves will provide an indication of how income distribution in Canada compares to its trading partners, as well as other economically developed and developing countries. Data from Figure 18.6 are used to create the Lorenz curves in Figure 18.7.

APPLYING ECONOMIC THINKING

1 Ten individuals work in a dry-cleaning plant. The total wage bill is $100 000 per year. Some employees work part-time while others work full-time. Here are the 10 annual salaries:

   Individual A = $1 000; B = $6 000; C = $12 000; D = $8 000; E = $10 000; F = $11 000; G = $20 000; H = $14 000; I = $16 000; J = $2 000.

   a) What is the mean average salary?

   b) What is the median salary?

   c) Group the salaries into quintiles, with the first quintile including the two lowest-paid workers, and so on.

   d) Determine the percentage each quintile receives of the total wages paid by the plant.

   e) Construct a Lorenz curve to illustrate the income distribution in the dry-cleaning plant. What does this curve indicate about income distribution?

2 Reproduce the Lorenz curve shown in Figure 18.4. Using the information provided by Figure 18.5, construct a set of colour-coded Lorenz curves (1951 to 2017) to assess whether or not income distribution in Canada has improved since the middle of the twentieth century.

3 Use Figure 18.7 to compare income inequality in selected countries. How does Canada compare with developing countries like Brazil, Mexico, and South Africa? How does Canada compare with other economically developed countries?

FIGURE 18.3
Cumulative shares of Canadians' after-tax income, 2000 and 2017

Cumulative % of Families (lowest- to highest-income earners)		Share of Cumulative After-Tax Income (% in 2000)	Share of Cumulative After-Tax Income (% in 2017)
A	First 20%	4.4	6.7
B	First 40%	4.4 + 10.0 = 14.4	6.7 + 12.4 = 19.1
C	First 60%	14.4 + 16.1 = 30.5	19.1 + 16.6 = 35.7
D	First 80%	30.5 + 24.3 = 54.8	35.7 + 22.9 = 58.6
E	100%	54.8 + 45.3 = 100	58.6 + 41.4 = 100

FIGURE 18.4
Lorenz curve of income distribution in Canada, 2000 and 2017
Compare this method of presenting data with the bar graph in Figure 18.2.

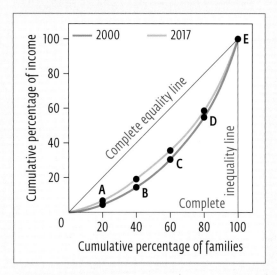

FIGURE 18.7
Lorenz curves of income distribution in different countries, circa 2015
How do these curves, based on the data in Figure 18.6, help to identify countries with more and less equitable distributions of national incomes?

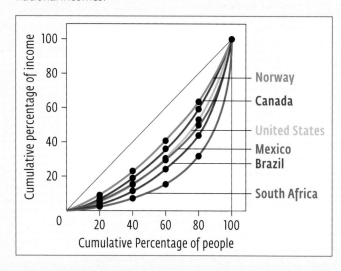

FIGURE 18.5
Distribution of family income in Canada, 1951–2017

How do you think the Lorenz curves for these historical data would compare with the recent curves in Figure 18.4?

	Total Income Received by Each Quintile of the Population (%)						
	1951	1961	1971	1981	1990	2010	2017
Lowest income quintile of families	6.1	6.6	5.6	6.4	6.5	6.7	6.7
Second quintile	12.9	13.4	12.7	12.8	12.6	12.4	12.4
Third quintile	17.4	18.2	18.0	18.3	17.8	16.9	16.6
Fourth quintile	22.5	23.4	23.7	24.1	23.8	22.8	22.9
Highest income quintile	41.1	38.4	40.0	38.4	39.3	41.2	41.4
All families	100.0	100.0	100.0	100.0	100.0	100.0	100.0

FIGURE 18.6
Distribution of family income in various countries, circa 2015

Which country had the most equitable income distribution for this time period? The most inequitable?

	Share of Income Received by Families in Each Quintile (%)				
Country	Lowest 20%	Second 20%	Third 20%	Fourth 20%	Highest 20%
Canada	6.6	12.4	17.0	23.2	40.8
United States	5.0	10.2	15.3	22.6	46.9
Norway	9.0	14.1	17.7	22.7	36.5
Mexico	5.7	9.8	14.0	20.4	50.1
Brazil	3.6	7.9	12.7	19.7	56.1
South Africa	2.4	4.8	8.2	16.4	68.2

Reasons for Income Inequality

Karl Marx grudgingly recognized capitalism's ability to produce goods and services efficiently. However, he was correct in his main criticism that capitalism breeds income inequality. Inequality in the distribution of wealth, income, and production is inevitable in capitalism because of the very efficiency of the market mechanism in rewarding "success" and punishing "failure"! People can get their income from many different sources within the capitalist system, including wages and salaries, rent, capital gains, dividends, interest, profits, and government transfers. Some people have several sources of income while others have few.

When competition is effectively limited, large producers can influence the marketplace to great advantage. For example, a sole employer in a one-industry town can pay low wages. Should another major employer come to town, wages will rise. Producers of goods and services who are able to meet and satisfy consumer demands are rewarded handsomely by the market. The producer could be a new performer hitting the top of the music charts, an entrepreneur developing a new product, or even a person entering an occupation that is currently in high demand. Because consumers "vote" for the goods and services they want with their purchases, the singer, the entrepreneur, and the employee have every chance of doing well.

Consumers are equally harsh in punishing those sellers who do not meet their demands. Eventually, listeners may tire of a singer's songs, buyers may switch to a competitor's "new and improved" product, and the demand for a particular occupational field may decline. In these cases, the singer, entrepreneur, and skilled employee will find that the flow of income that once gave them a good living has shrunk. They will have to adapt accordingly. There is nothing inherent in the market system that guarantees a "fair" or equitable income for anyone, however that is defined. Consumers change their tastes, often very quickly; innovative competitors are free to enter a market; demands for occupations change.

These high school students in New York City ask two fundamental questions during a 2015 demonstration for greater income equality and a higher minimum wage.

Some reasons for inequality in income in a free-market system are as follows:

1   ***People have different physical and mental abilities.*** All of us can learn to throw a ball or shoot a puck, but few of us can do so as well as a professional baseball or hockey player. These elite athletes are rewarded highly for their level of skill. Not all of us are as scientifically minded as doctors or research scientists or have the facility with finance and numerical calculation that accountants possess. A limited supply of these people combined with a heavy demand for their services means they can demand high incomes. Abilities can make one worker far more productive and valuable than another.

2   ***People differ in the degree of education and training that they receive.*** Trained graduates often represent a more valuable asset to potential employers. A decision to obtain postsecondary education instead of entering the job market entails a direct cost for tuition, books, and possibly accommodation. Students also pay an opportunity cost in terms of the income they give up while attending institutions of higher learning. Individuals expect that their future earnings will compensate them for these added costs with higher incomes.

3   ***Some people are willing and able to work longer and harder than others.*** Even within the same occupation, some people work more overtime and take on more tasks, clients, patients, or customers to earn higher incomes than their peers. Individuals differ in the value they place on income and leisure, and people are free to substitute one for the other.

4   ***People who take on extra risk and responsibility are usually rewarded.*** The entrepreneur who borrows money and mortgages her home to develop a new product or a new service may earn higher-than-normal profits if successful. The quick infusion of capital might allow the fledgling company to get into a new market before a competitor that chose to take the slow and safe approach. An economist would say that individuals who take these big risks receive a "**risk premium**" over and above their normal profits. The high-rise construction worker, the oil rigger, and people in other dangerous occupations must also be compensated with a risk premium. Most often, the assumption of additional responsibilities receives compensation for the extra workload and stress.

5   ***Luck and health can affect income.*** A person may inherit money, marry into it, or even win a lottery. On the other side of the coin, a person may be injured unexpectedly, become ill, or suddenly lose a job when a company goes bankrupt or shifts operations. Being at the right place, at the right time, with the right idea and skills may be as much a result of luck as it is of careful planning. Often through no fault of their own, the stamina to work long and hard is one asset that some people cannot count on. Others may be able to work a double shift without issue.

6   ***Family background can affect future earnings.*** Children from high-income families certainly benefit from inherited money. Previous capital accumulation and present holdings and investments can provide additional personal income in the forms of interest, profit, dividends, capital gains,

risk premium
An additional bonus or compensation paid to individuals for the risks voluntarily assumed and handled responsibly as part of their work. For example, fire fighters and other first responders are paid a premium for having to risk their lives to save others. High-rise construction workers and oil riggers are also paid a bonus for the dangerous work they do.

and rent. In a market economy, accumulated wealth (if properly managed) serves to create more wealth. Children from high-income families enjoy other benefits as well, such as connections for getting good jobs. Increasing statistical proof suggests that children from better-off families earn more, on average, over a lifetime. The findings of the Statistics Canada study on page 389 provide reasons and evidence for this theory. A sociologist might suggest that poverty can be hereditary.

7 ***Market power means higher income.*** Before becoming a world-class philanthropist in his retirement years, American billionaire Bill Gates once dominated the computer software market with his company's Microsoft programs. This high-profile entrepreneur acquired so much market power that he was forced to fight a lengthy legal battle to preserve his company from anti-monopoly prosecution in the United States and Europe. Larger companies, such as McDonald's Restaurants, often have an advantage over smaller companies in the marketplace owing to their massive advertising campaigns and the public's instant recognition of their brand. Workers, too, may gain some market power as sellers of their labour by belonging to a union or an association that can negotiate collectively for higher wages.

8 ***Discrimination has a negative effect on incomes.*** Age, gender, ethnicity, race, and disability have been widely noted as factors causing differences in average incomes. Figure 18.1 (page 379) clearly shows that women report lower average incomes than men in almost every field listed. With the advent of improved antidiscrimination laws, with numerous successful appeals to the Canadian Charter of Rights and Freedoms and the provincial Human Rights Codes, and with shifts in the attitudes of society, discrimination may not affect people's chances at earning a high income as decisively as it once did, but it remains a significant factor.

A number of studies confirm that the adverse effects of discrimination are still being felt by some groups. For example, Professor James L. Torczyner of McGill University conducted a study about racism in the workplace in 1997. He found that, with comparable levels of education, African Canadians tended to have a much higher rate of unemployment than the average Canadian (15 percent versus 10 percent). They also tended to earn 15 percent less. In addition, more than three out of ten African Canadians lived below the poverty line, while only 16 percent of Canadians did so in the same year. Another study in 2010 showed that Indigenous people in Canada were unemployed at twice the national rate and earned a median income of only $20 701 compared with $30 195 for the general population. The 2016 census confirmed that visible minorities in Canada earn only 81.2 percent of what non-visible minorities earn, and this gap has actually widened by 2.6 percent since 2000. Clearly, eradicating these inequalities will require a more concerted effort going forward.

9 **Regional economic disparities contribute to income differences.** Some parts
   of Canada, depending on the makeup of their regional economy, historically
   report lower average income levels (see Figure 18.8). Income levels in these
   communities may be affected by chronic unemployment and other adverse
   economic conditions. In communities dependent on few resources and
   industries, setbacks in these major sources of employment may have severe
   economic repercussions for many years. For example, the collapse of cod
   fisheries in the North Atlantic has had significant impact on the income
   of many residents of Atlantic Canada, especially in Newfoundland and
   Labrador. Lumber disputes with the United States have depressed incomes
   in British Columbia, for example, where forestry is a main employer.

FIGURE 18.8
**Median (after-tax) family income and incidence of low income,
by province, 2016**
According to this table, how is income distributed across Canada? What is the
relationship between median (after-tax) income and incidence of low income?

Province	Median (After-Tax) Family Income, 2016 ($)	Incidence of Low Income (% of total population)
Newfoundland and Labrador	72 100	15.6
Prince Edward Island	70 300	14.4
Nova Scotia	68 900	16.1
New Brunswick	65 400	14.7
Quebec	70 300	14.0
Ontario	80 800	13.7
Manitoba	74 600	13.3
Saskatchewan	82 400	11.6
Alberta	92 800	8.1
British Columbia	82 100	12.9
Canada	**78 400**	**13.0**

A CLOSER LOOK AT PROVINCIAL DISPARITIES

Historically, the economies of Canada's four Atlantic provinces have lagged behind the rest of the country. The closure of the North Atlantic cod fisheries in 1992 represented the largest industrial layoff in Canadian history. These four economies are overly dependent on primary industries (farming, fishing, forestry, and oil and mineral extraction) and are therefore prone to slow and sluggish growth given this lack of economic diversification. Low population growth and an aging population further complicate matters.

Ontario and Quebec have traditionally benefited from their central location, skilled labour force, proximity to large American markets, and a diversified economic base, including a healthy manufacturing sector. Canada's Prairie provinces (Manitoba and Saskatchewan) have a primarily agricultural economy based on wheat production. Being Canada's largest oil-producing province, Alberta's economy is greatly affected by fluctuations in the global price of oil. For example, between 2015 and 2016 alone, some 64 000 workers were laid off as the price of oil dropped drastically. British Columbia's economy is also based on its rich endowment of mineral and forest resources. In addition, the port of Vancouver has become an important hub for international trade.

A cedar lumber stockpile in British Columbia. Lumber, wood pulp, biofuels, and other wood products make a significant contribution to this province's economy.

A CLOSER LOOK AT HOW FAMILY BACKGROUND CAN AFFECT FUTURE EARNINGS

The following findings are taken from a Statistics Canada study, based on income tax information reported by a **cohort** (a group with similar statistical characteristics) of 285 000 young adult Canadians aged 28 to 31. Their total income was compared with the income of their parents 12 years earlier, when the cohort was between the ages of 16 and 19 and still living at home. To eliminate some variables, this study excluded families headed by single mothers and families not residing in urban communities.

- The sources of a parent's income (especially the father's income) and the community that the family lives in significantly influence the employment outcomes of their grown-up children.

- A parent's integrity, responsibility, work ethic, and encouragement of the pursuit of higher income tend to have a positive impact on the income levels of their adult children.

- Adult children (especially sons) had substantially higher incomes if their fathers had some **asset income** (income in the form of interest, dividends, or rent). The actual amount of the father's asset income does not matter as much as its presence.

- Adult children (especially sons) had higher incomes if their fathers had self-employed income.

- Adult children (especially sons) were more likely to have low adult incomes if their fathers had received Employment Insurance benefits.

- The affluence of the neighbourhood in which children (especially sons) spend their teens is positively associated with their incomes as adults. Affluent neighbourhoods offer a better-developed physical infrastructure— higher-quality schools, recreational facilities, and social institutions—as well as social standards that help reinforce parents' goals for their children.

- The adult children of families who moved once during their teen years earned about $550 less than those whose families stayed in the same neighbourhood. Children whose families moved three or more times earned about $2 000 less.

- Thirty percent of the sons and 25 percent of the daughters of low-income fathers also had low incomes. Only 15 percent of the sons and 13 percent of the daughters of high-income fathers had low incomes.

- Thirty-five percent of the children of high-income fathers also had high incomes. Only 14 percent of the children of high-income fathers had low incomes.

- Sons and daughters whose very-low-income fathers had self-employed incomes or some asset income did better than those whose fathers did not.

cohort

A group with similar statistical characteristics, such as all Canadians between 18 and 25 years of age.

asset income

Income received by an individual in the form of interest, dividends, or rent.

Self-Reflect

1. Explain and assess each of the nine reasons for inequality in income to determine whether each is of moderate or high importance. Explain your reasoning.

2. For each occupation listed in Figure 18.1, use the nine reasons for inequality in income to explain why the occupations command the incomes that they do. Are the income differences justified?

3. Use Figure 18.8 to create a summary chart identifying the provinces at, above, and below the national median (after-tax) family income. Explain the significance of your chart. Do the same for the incidence of low-income data and compare your results?

relative poverty
Poverty defined as lacking the conditions of life enjoyed by most people in the same economy.

low-income cut-off (LICO)
A Statistics Canada measurement of low income, defined as any household spending more than 55 percent of its before-tax income on food, shelter, and clothing.

before-tax income
Total annual income before federal and provincial taxes are deducted.

after-tax income
Total annual income after federal and provincial taxes are deducted.

poverty line
The unofficial term used for the Statistics Canada low-income cut-off.

Poverty in Canada

What does it mean to be poor in Canada? Most would agree that poverty involves substandard housing, poor nutrition, limited social opportunities, difficulties in financing post-secondary schooling, and problems in providing for children. Where people disagree, however, is in how we should determine who is poor, why people become poor, and what measures we should take to reduce poverty.

MEASURING POVERTY

How many Canadians are poor? We cannot determine the answer to this question until we decide on a poverty level. There are two opposing schools of thought on where to set this "poverty line," depending on whether poverty is considered to be a relative condition or an absolute condition. Television images of poorly clothed children with swollen bellies reflect a desperate condition often referred to as **absolute poverty**—a state of utter destitution. Thanks in part to Canada's complex social welfare safety net, the incidence of this extreme form of poverty is rare in Canada. However, in comparing the relative abilities of Canadians to command necessary goods and services, it quickly becomes evident that the gap between the "haves" and "have nots" in Canadian society is widening.

Proponents of poverty as a relative condition claim that to be poor means to lack the conditions of material life that most other people in Canada have. A poor Canadian, then, does not necessarily lack food, safe water, shelter, and clothing as many millions of people in some other countries so visibly do. Nonetheless, this Canadian feels poor, and we see this person as poor, compared with—or relative to—the rest of us. This form of relative poverty is an important policy issue for governments in Canada. Although no Canadians are known to be starving, a growing number are relying on food banks to make ends meet. This **relative poverty** is most disturbing, perhaps, because it is found in the midst of affluence.

Since 1968, Statistics Canada has attempted to identify Canadian families that are relatively worse off than other Canadian families by examining income and spending patterns. This statistical measure is based on the establishment of a **low-income cut-off (LICO)** to identify income levels below which a household is statistically classified as being in a relatively limited income situation. Statistically, the average Canadian household spends 35 percent of its before-tax income (or 44 percent of its after-tax income) on food, clothing, and shelter. Statistics Canada defines as relatively worse off any household that spends more than 20 percentage points above the national average on the three necessities of food, clothing, and shelter.

Separate LICO tables are calculated for **before-tax income** and **after-tax income** (total annual income before federal and provincial taxes are deducted and after, respectively). Although before-tax income levels are less complicated and, therefore, easier to calculate, after-tax LICOs have become more common because all purchases of necessities are made with after-tax dollars. Although Statistics Canada's LICOs are commonly referred to in the media as **poverty lines**, they have no officially recognized status, and Statistics Canada does not use this term in relation to LICOs. Nonetheless, in the absence of a more accepted definition, many analysts use a LICO as an indication of poverty. Figure 18.9 outlines how LICOs are influenced by the number of members in a household and the size of the community in which the household is located. Using this indicator, 12 percent of Canadians were living in poverty in 1999 and 13 percent in 2015.

Many analysts consider any household with an after-tax income below the amount stipulated by this table to be poor. For example, a family of four living in a city of 450 000 residents with a combined after-tax income of $33 060 would be considered poor. Note that if that same family had lived in a rural area, their income would have been above the statistical "poverty line."

Canada's Fraser Institute has long contended that governments exaggerate measures of poverty by not adhering to a more absolute definition that focuses on "real" hunger, **deprivation**, and hardship and ignores the absence of non-essentials. Their longstanding position has been that no Canadian should be considered poor if they can meet "basic needs."

The Organisation for Economic Co-operation and Development (OECD) argues that absolute poverty measures have little meaning in advanced industrialized societies. The OECD prefers to view poverty more as "**exclusion**" than deprivation. It notes: "in order to participate fully in the social life of a community, individuals may need a level of resources that is not too inferior to the norm in that community." What do you think?

deprivation

A term associated with the idea of absolute poverty; that is, income so low that an individual cannot afford the basic necessities of life.

exclusion

A term associated with the idea of relative poverty; that is, income so low that an individual cannot enjoy the standard of living of the majority of society.

FIGURE 18.9
After-tax low-income cut-offs (LICOs) for Canadian households, based on the size of the community where the household is located, 2016

Family Size	Urban Areas				Rural Areas
	500 000 and over	100 000 to 49 999	30 000 to 99 999	Less than 30 000	
1 person	$20 675	$17 485	$17 267	$15 478	$13 525
2 persons	$25 163	$21 281	$21 016	$18 840	$16 461
3 persons	$31 334	$26 499	$26 169	$23 457	$20 498
4 persons	$39 092	$33 060	$32 649	$29 266	$25 571
5 persons	$44 514	$37 646	$37 178	$33 326	$29 119
6 persons	$49 367	$41 750	$41 232	$36 959	$32 294
7 or more	$54 220	$45 854	$45 284	$40 593	$35 469

working poor
People who work for low wages and are defined as poor.

welfare poor
Non-working people who are poor because they are ill, disabled, elderly, or single parents, or for other reasons.

CANADA'S MARGINALIZED

Having looked at various ways of measuring the level of poverty, we can now look at those most likely to face poverty in Canada today.

A good indicator of the prevalence of poverty is the number of people who need to use a food bank to supplement their incomes. Food bank use in Canada is increasing. In the Greater Toronto Area, for example, 799 320 visits were made to food banks in 2001 compared with 905 970 visits in 2016, according to the Daily Bread Food Bank, Canada's largest food relief agency. Although many people using food banks are temporary users experiencing such temporary hardships as being laid off, others have become habitual users because their stagnant income is consistently insufficient to cover the cost of all necessities.

The poor include people who work for low wages—the **working poor**. The market power of employers, particularly in the absence of organized labour, can force wages down to levels that do not keep workers out of poverty. People in households whose heads are not in the labour force constitute Canada's non-working poor, or **welfare poor**. These are the people left behind by our economic system—individuals who are elderly, have an illness or a disability, or are the head of a single-parent family (usually the mother) with young children. "Deadbeat" parents who avoid paying support to their former spouses for the care of their children contribute to the poverty in many single-parent households. Poor physical and mental health contribute to the poverty, probably because the ability of these people to support themselves is limited. The incidence of poverty among senior citizens who live alone is significantly higher than for those who live with families. Differences in wage rates paid to men and women contribute to a higher incidence of poverty among women and single-parent households led by women.

According to census data, about one in six children in Canada (17 percent of all Canadian children) lived in poverty in 2015. This percentage represents a modest improvement from 1998, when 18.8 percent of children in Canada lived in poverty. However, since in 1989, the Canadian government had voted unanimously to work toward eliminating child poverty in Canada by 2000, this improvement is disappointing. Figure 18.10 compares child and adult poverty rates in 2015.

A full 1.2 million Canadian children lived in low-income households in 2015. This number represents one-quarter of the 4.8 million Canadians living in poverty. The percentage of children living in low-income households was especially high in single-parent households, at 40 percent. In addition, Indigenous children in Canada are twice as likely to experience

FIGURE 18.10
Low-income rates for children and adults by province, 2015
Which four provinces dealt with the highest rates of child poverty in 2015? In what four provinces was adult poverty the lowest? How can you explain these patterns?

Province	Children (%)	Adults (%)
British Columbia	18.5	14.9
Alberta	12.8	8.2
Saskatchewan	17.8	11.4
Manitoba	21.9	13.5
Ontario	18.4	13.4
Quebec	14.3	14.7
New Brunswick	22.2	16.0
Nova Scotia	22.2	16.2
Prince Edward Island	21.7	15.7
Newfoundland and Labrador	17.8	14.9
Canada	**17.0**	**13.4**

poverty than non-Indigenous children. In relative terms, Canada's child poverty rate is significantly higher (more than double) the rate experienced in the Nordic countries of Denmark, Sweden, Norway, and Finland, and many other industrially developed countries.

ADDRESSING POVERTY

Why do many people find it difficult or impossible to climb out of poverty? Many people live in regions of the country where jobs are scarce. Others lack the marketable skills (education and training) to earn incomes large enough to lift them out of poverty. Children who are born into poor families are at a distinct disadvantage relative to their counterparts in comfortable families. Children born poor tend to be undernourished and to do less well in school. They are also less likely to move on to post-secondary education. Thus, their chances of experiencing poverty as adults are higher than for the rest of the population. Lack of self-esteem, motivation, hope, and incentive can act to perpetuate poverty if they are passed down from parents to children.

Social advocates often suggest that addressing the causes of poverty is the best way to combat poverty. Given the nature of the problem, most recommend long-term remedies such as the following:

- Improving the availability of affordable and quality child care to enable more parents to work regular hours

- Increasing minimum wage rates to help the working poor earn a wage that allows them to live above the poverty line

- Building more affordable housing for people living in poverty so that they can have a decent place to live and more money for basic needs such as food and clothing

- Improving access to education and training to increase the employability of workers (including people with disabilities) and their ability to earn higher incomes

- Providing better access to health care (including mental health care) to improve the employability and productivity of workers

Where transfer payments from governments to needy individuals and households allow for immediate relief from hunger, homelessness, and deprivation, the five remedies above will slowly improve the ability of marginalized Canadians to participate in and benefit from the Canadian economy more fully. For example, note the effect of higher education on the incidence of poverty in Figure 18.11.

FIGURE 18.11
Low income in Canada, by education level, 1999 and 2015
Use the statistical pattern that exists between the level of education and the incidence of poverty in Canada to explain the economic benefits of investing tax dollars in educating and training the Canadian workforce.

Level of Education	Percentage of Group Living in Poverty, 1999	Percentage of Group Living in Poverty, 2015
Up to eight years of schooling	28.8	26.5
Secondary school graduates	22.4	18.7
Post-secondary certificate and diploma holders	17.9	13.3
University graduates	11.0	9.2

Self-Reflect

1 Explain the difference between absolute and relative definitions of poverty. Which does Statistics Canada use to measure poverty? Do you agree? Explain.

2 Distinguish between the working poor and the welfare poor.

3 List five factors that contribute to poverty in Canada.

4 Identify the groups most likely to be poor and explain why.

Indigenous Poverty: Traditional Economies Turned Upside Down

Some of the most severe and sustained poverty in Canada can be found on remote First Nations reserves. These impoverished communities struggle with the following recurring issues and their severe economic consequences:

- Residents face serious health problems including diabetes, heart disease, respiratory problems, and infectious diseases at much higher rates than the general population.

- Formal education (including health education) is limited. The 2011 census confirmed that only 22.8 percent of Indigenous people completed their secondary school education. The 2016 census reported that rates of both secondary and post-secondary school completion reflected significant improvement since 2011.

- Housing, living quarters, and the quality of drinking water are inadequate for many residents. Since wood is often burned for heating, house fires are common, and houses rarely qualify for insurance because of their condition.

- Income levels are significantly lower than the general population, and unemployment rates are significantly higher. The 2011 census reported an average unemployment rate of 15 percent in Indigenous communities, double the Canadian average of 7.5 percent.

- Higher rates of alcoholism, substance abuse, and suicide are observed compared with the rest of Canada. Often the victims are children, who are often unsupervised, ignored, and seemingly uncared for by parents living with serious problems of their own.

The causes of poverty are not difficult to identify. Indigenous people constitute the fastest-growing segment of the Canadian population. This relatively higher birth rate results in a housing shortage and overcrowding. Overcrowding in inadequately constructed and poorly maintained living quarters can lead to health problems. The lack of employment opportunity can have a debilitating effect on self-esteem, mental health, and attitude toward life.

Residential school survivor Lorna Standingready is comforted by a fellow survivor in the audience during the closing ceremony of the Indian Residential Schools Truth and Reconciliation Commission, in Ottawa on June 3, 2015.

The forced **residential school** experience of an estimated 150 000 Indigenous youth between 1880 and 1996 is recognized as a cause of personal and social issues in First Nations communities. The residential school system was a government-sponsored attempt to assimilate Indigenous youth into the dominant "white" culture and strip them of their links to traditional beliefs and values. Many former residents of these schools became broken adults for the balance of their lives, and many are still living out the consequences of this experience. Intergenerational trauma—how the trauma experienced by one generation is passed down and experienced in some form by the generations that follow—can also have devastating effects on families affected by this program.

Today, in certain Indigenous communities, a lack of educational, recreational, and vocational opportunities and support networks have led a number of Indigenous youth to feel helpless, hopeless, and in some cases suicidal. The case studies that follow will help explain the causes, impact, and extent of poverty in two Indigenous communities: the Mushuau Innu of Davis Inlet and the Cree of Attawapiskat.

residential school
A government-sponsored system that was established to assimilate Indigenous children into the dominant "white" Canadian culture. The residential school system ran from 1880 to 1996.

THE MUSHUAU INNU OF DAVIS INLET

In 1993, a video of six Innu children in Davis Inlet, Labrador, sniffing gasoline and screaming that they wanted to die became international news. A report released in 1999 by Survival for Tribal Peoples International, a charity that works with Indigenous peoples around the world, blamed Ottawa for the gradual deterioration of the Innu community and its high suicide rate. The Innu of Labrador's Davis Inlet were labelled "the most suicide-ridden people of the world." Indeed, the suicide rate in Davis Inlet was 13 times higher than the overall rate in Canada, with nearly one-third of the Innu population of Davis Inlet having attempted suicide. With 80 percent of the adult population suffering from alcoholism, Innu children and teenagers were especially vulnerable. Where did things go so terribly wrong?

The Mushuau Innu were a nomadic people, travelling through a yearly cycle to follow wild game on the vast barrens of Labrador and Quebec. The traditional economy of the Innu worked well, with smaller groups harvesting the resources of the land over a widely dispersed area.

In 1967, the federal government decided to consolidate the people of Davis Inlet and move them to a new island location. Government officials viewed bringing small groups of people together and concentrating their populations into permanent communities as the most cost-effective way of providing services, such as education, health care, and social assistance. The underlying assumption was that the traditional subsistence lifestyle of the Innu was impractical and outdated in the modern industrialized era.

The move to Davis Inlet made government administration easier, but for the Innu, the move had serious repercussions for their community and way of life. In Davis Inlet, Innu hunters could no longer freely follow the wild caribou herds because the community was now on an island. Since the Innu could not hunt during the breakup of the ice each spring (prime hunting season), their traditional economy was severely impaired.

DID YOU KNOW?

Since being forcibly relocated in 1926, the Mi'kmaq community of Membertou in Cape Breton Island, Nova Scotia, have worked hard to build a diversified economic base to support their community of some 810 members on the reserve and 480 living off the reserve. A hotel, business park, convention and trade centre, community radio station, and (most recently) sports and wellness centre have been built to employ some 700 people and to bring money into the community.

In addition, the transition to a settled industrialized society did not generate sufficient employment opportunities to provide steady income streams for the majority of households in the permanent settlement. As a result, residents became increasingly more dependent on government assistance and increasingly pessimistic about their future. Instead of living a self-sufficient life according to ancient traditions, the Innu were forced to become dependent on government handouts. Because the Innu identified so closely with their land, relocation affected not only their way of life but also their identity as a people. They were used to living in small family hunting camps. Having to live in a larger community, with people from different tribes and clans, was a difficult social adjustment.

In time, the Innu of Davis Inlet lived in absolute poverty. Most people shared two-room homes with five or six others. The community had no roads, no sewers, and no running water. The nearest hospital was a two-hour journey by bush plane. The long-ago promised amenities, such as running water and good schools, did not materialize. The children had to shower in school on Tuesdays and Thursdays. Human waste was often thrown out onto snowbanks.

Living in this environment, many people turned to alcohol. Some of the children turned to glue and gasoline sniffing. Innu Chief Simeon Tshakapesh suggested that anger was at the root of the substance abuse. "They told our people they would have running water, good schools, and everything. They took away our cultural, spiritual values and tried to turn us into modern Canadians. We were told we would be lawyers, doctors, nurses. Instead, our people fell apart."

After the 1993 video appeared, the Canadian government was pressured into taking drastic action. It spent $152 million to relocate the 600 Innu of Davis Inlet to a new 133-home community on the mainland, just 15 km west of Davis Inlet, in 2002. This site, chosen by the Innu, is in a traditional hunting area known as *Natuashish*. Homes were built with running water, bedrooms, and windows made of glass. The new community includes a new school, a band office, and other public buildings. But 15 years after the move, alcoholism and substance abuse persisted in the community of 1 000.

An aerial view of the town of Natuashish, on the coast of Labrador, in 2014.

THE CREE OF ATTAWAPISKAT

The Attawapiskat First Nation, a community of about 2 000 residents, is located at the mouth of the Attawapiskat River on James Bay, in a remote part of Northern Ontario. This community began as a settlement of temporary dwellings (tents and teepees) in the early 1950s and transitioned to log cabins and, finally, wood-frame buildings by the early 1970s. The culture and identity of these Indigenous people were greatly influenced by their traditional economy, which is based on fishing, fur trapping, and hunting caribou and goose.

Housing conditions in the Attawapiskat First Nation reserve in Northern Ontario, 2016.

For decades, this community has been plagued by housing crises, substance abuse, and suicides. In 2012, Chief Theresa Spence went on a liquids-only hunger strike to draw attention to the plight of her people. Given the high birth rate experienced in the community, the supply of houses could not keep up with the growing demand. After receiving international condemnation, the federal government was forced to provide more homes. However, although there was a waiting list of 300 families, only 50 new houses were constructed by 2018.

The most troubling suicide epidemic in Attawapiskat started in the fall of 2015 when an alarming number of residents (including many youths) tried to kill themselves. With almost 30 suicide attempts in March 2016, Chief Bruce Shisheesh declared a state of emergency, forcing federal and provincial governments and First Nations crisis response units to mobilize.

Responding to local requests, the federal government promised to build a youth centre where young people could work with families and elders on cultural and wellness programs. Provincial government funding has provided an interim youth centre in anticipation of Ottawa's permanent structure. As also promised, the federal government spent $180 000 on a trailer to house two mental health clinicians, but finding appropriate staff has proven difficult. Indigenous Services Canada provides $1.25 million a year for youth mental health to Attawapiskat and the regional tribal council.

Substance abuse and suicide attempts continue as many residents still see themselves as a "broken" people. Without rebuilding this self-image, and effectively addressing these social, housing, and health issues, economic growth and improved quality of life will remain elusive.

Self-Reflect

1 How did the residential school experience of Indigenous youth contribute to their conditions today?

2 Explain why the consolidation plan for the Innu of Davis Inlet failed both socially and economically. What makes the recovery period long and difficult?

3 What factors led to the decline of the Attawapiskat First Nation community? What was done to address the community's problems?

welfare state
A philosophy that government should intervene to help people who are poor, sick, or unemployed as well as provide equal access to education, health care, and social services.

The Redistribution of Income in Canada

REFLECTING ON EQUALITY, EQUITY, AND GENERAL WELFARE

In the first section of this chapter, we saw that income levels vary dramatically among Canadians. Most of us would agree that some of the reasons for higher incomes are justifiable, while others are not. Canadian society accepts some unjustifiably higher incomes. This is the trade-off that we must make between equality and efficiency, with *efficiency* being defined as the economy's capacity to get the most out of its productive resources. Entrepreneurs, for example, are allowed to reap the benefits of success because they serve a useful function by taking risks that make the economy grow.

Let's suppose a country attempted to bring about complete equality, with all individuals receiving equal incomes. Individuals would be less inclined to work harder, take risks, and study harder and longer if they knew they would end up earning as much as their neighbours, who made less effort. Efficiency would fall, and with it, the economy's ability to increase its production of goods and services. For a capitalist society to work, unequal incomes are essential.

Should incomes be determined solely by the market? Some of the reasons for higher incomes are not justified by efficiency. Income streams that are the direct result of inheritance, for example, may have little to do with efficiency. Income streams that are reduced by gender, age, ethnicity, and racial discrimination have more to do with biased attitudes than efficiencies. Further, all societies feel some compulsion to help those whose earning power may be weakened by sickness, accident, age, or other circumstances. This inclination is rooted in fundamental values with which a majority of people generally agree.

The quandary faced by all societies is this: How do we ensure people's economic rights and reduce inequality—particularly poverty—without "killing the goose that laid the golden egg"? What good is equity if it leads to a decline in economic efficiency, productivity, and, ultimately, the country's ability to compete in the global economy?

The Welfare State Compromise

Is there too much inequality in Canada? Do we need to ensure the economic rights of all citizens? Certainly, governments of all political persuasions would answer in the affirmative. Early in the twentieth century, Canada established a **welfare state** to reduce the inequalities in people's incomes and personal circumstances, differences that became especially evident during the Great Depression of the 1930s. A welfare state reflects a philosophy that governments should use social programs and transfers, financed out of taxation, to help people who are poor, suffer illness, or are otherwise disadvantaged. In addition, the Canadian welfare state attempts to provide universally the social programs and services required for the well-being of all its citizens. All Canadians, both rich and poor, are supposed to have equal, free access to such services as public education, health care, and social services (such as recreational centres and libraries).

TAXATION AND REDISTRIBUTION FOR THE COMMON GOOD

The first goal of the welfare state is to allow lower-income earners to keep most of whatever earnings they have. Thus, the Canadian income tax system is a **progressive tax system**, one designed to reduce income inequality and to help finance social spending. Such a system taxes higher-income earners at a higher percentage rate than lower-income earners, leaving lower-income earners with a greater percentage of their income. This system not only allows poorer people to live independently but also benefits the economy, particularly because it increases the ability of lower-income earners to participate as consumers. Therefore, the welfare state attempts to grant people their economic rights without taking away too much of their income.

Redistribution of income takes place in many ways in Canada. Our examination of the role of government in Chapter 16 identified the three main pillars of Canada's social welfare safety net: social services, health care, and education. This spending, funded principally by tax dollars (collected on an ability-to-pay basis), provides valuable services to all Canadians. Schools, libraries, recreational and cultural centres, transportation networks, hospitals, national security, and law enforcement are just a few examples of how governments redistribute income in ways that benefit all Canadians. As well, it offers support for scientific research and development, environmental initiatives, and the maintenance of our national and provincial parks. This tendency to value the *common good*, or the collective interest over individual interests, is one clear distinction between Canadian society and American society, in which the individual is expected to be more self-reliant.

Many Canadians see the redistribution of wealth as an opportunity to benefit the whole country. At a high level, we can see this redistribution going on, from region to region, in the federal transfer payments made from regions of generally higher income to regions of generally lower income. Over time, higher incomes usually result in higher accumulation of **wealth**, which can be defined as the accumulated assets of individuals and families less total debts. Sometimes this idea is also referred to as *net worth*. We can see in Figure 18.12 that individual wealth tends to vary from region to region. It can also be seen to vary significantly with family composition.

Across Canada, significant regional differences appear in wealth accumulation. Median family wealth increases as you travel east to west. In 2016, British Columbia reported the highest median wealth at $429 400. In this same year, the median wealth reported in New Brunswick was only $158 400. The two main reasons for this disparity are the diversified and healthy nature of the economy of British Columbia and the extremely high property values in its largest city, Vancouver. Real estate holdings constitute the largest component of accumulated wealth for most Canadians, and property prices have been rising significantly in most Canadian cities. By consulting the "Total Net Worth, 2016" column, you will see why the provinces of Ontario, Quebec, British Columbia, and Alberta are considered Canada's "have" provinces. Every year, a portion of the federal taxes

progressive tax system
A taxation system that taxes higher incomes at a higher percentage rate than lower incomes; it is designed to reduce income inequalities and finance social spending.

wealth
Accumulated assets of individuals and families less their total debts.

collected in these provinces is transferred to the other provinces to help finance very costly but essential services such as health care.

On further examination of Figure 18.12, you will notice that family composition is another factor influencing wealth accumulation. The median wealth of families consisting of seniors (age 65 and older) is substantially higher than all other types of families, especially for lone-parent families, which are reportedly 13.3 times less wealthy. Non-seniors living alone are 20 times less wealthy. Most seniors live off their life savings or accumulated wealth during their retirement years.

Wealth distribution in Canada is further complicated by the fact that the top 20 percent of income earners account for 67.3 percent of the country's wealth, or almost $7 trillion. By comparison, the lowest 40 percent of income earners account for only 2.3 percent of the country's wealth. The top 20 percent (highest quintile) also hold 74.6 percent of all financial assets (such as stocks, bonds, and bank deposits). The median wealth among the poorest 10 percent of Canadian families is represented by negative figures across Canada, indicating that their debts are higher than their assets. Collectively, Canada's poorest families are more than $1.5 billion in debt. Personal debt is a serious problem for a large number of Canadians, and not just for those from the poorest families. These data reinforce the longstanding concern of social policy groups, such as the Canadian Centre for Policy Alternatives, about the extent of economic inequality in Canadian society. They also reveal the tenuous financial position of a significant portion of Canadians, and the need for greater financial literacy.

FIGURE 18.12
Differences in wealth (accumulated net worth) of Canadians, 2016

	Total Net Worth, 2016 ($ millions)	Median Net Worth, 2016
All Canadians	$10 272 540*	$295 100
Economic families	$8 510 473	$478 600
Senior families	$2 149 110	$762 900
Couples-only families	$2 199 546	$456 200
Couples with children	$2 074 458	$361 400
Lone-parent families	$175 934	$57 200
Persons living alone	$1 762 067	$77 200
Seniors living alone	$830 000	$277 000
Non-seniors living alone	$932 017	$37 700
All Canadians by province		
Newfoundland and Labrador	$101 683	$211 800
Prince Edward Island	$30 919	$204 000
Nova Scotia	$199 473	$225 200
New Brunswick	$136 765	$158 400
Quebec	$1 886 065	$208 900
Ontario	$4 229 651	$365 700
Manitoba	$299 876	$320 800
Saskatchewan	$317 141	$293 500
Alberta	$1 243 063	$290 500
British Columbia	$1 827 905	$429 400
*Represents a value of $10.27 trillion.		

ATTACKING POVERTY

In addition to investing in the common good, governments in Canada also redistribute income and share wealth in ways that are intended to address the inequalities and inequities experienced by the poorest citizens.

Programs to combat poverty can be divided into two broad but overlapping categories: structural and relief strategies. **Structural strategies** are programs that attempt to eliminate the causes of poverty. They focus on long-term economic adjustments that are needed to reduce income disparities. Initiatives intended to reduce the incidence of poverty and break its self-perpetuating cycle include worker education and retraining programs, worker relocation programs, and programs that help build self-esteem and motivation. Structural programs of this nature are extremely important if Canada is to improve its distribution of national wealth, its productivity, and, in turn, its ability to compete in global markets. Structural strategies often involve long-term, gradual systemic changes that combat the root causes of poverty.

Relief strategies are programs that attempt to reduce the symptoms of poverty. They focus on providing immediate support for needy Canadians. Community food banks and government transfer payments to individual households are two examples of relief strategies. Because these remedies do not address the causes of poverty—and, therefore, do not help people emerge from poverty—critics sometimes refer to them as "band-aid solutions." However, it must be recognized that these solutions have ensured that few Canadians find themselves in a state of absolute poverty. If Canadians become destitute, they receive some form of government help.

Structural Strategies to Combat the Causes of Poverty

1   ***Education.*** All evidence points to a direct link between educational level and incomes. Governments have provided universal elementary and secondary education for the better part of a century and have expanded access to post-secondary education enormously since the 1960s. Both federal and provincial governments subsidize colleges and universities heavily, with students paying only part of the cost in tuition fees. Some programs are designed to help lower-income students with post-secondary costs, but recent increases in tuition costs have been criticized as discriminating against poorer students. These students often end up with huge student debts that take many years to pay off. Nonetheless, by funding all of the cost of elementary and secondary education and much of the cost of post-secondary education, Canadian governments go a long way to providing students from low-income families with equal opportunities to become educated, productive members of society. Public investment in the development of human capital is one important way to reduce the incidence of poverty in Canada. In addition, educational programs improving financial literacy will help more Canadians to make sound decisions regarding their financial affairs.

structural strategy
A long-term program to reduce poverty, such as retraining and relocating workers.

relief strategy
An anti-poverty program that provides immediate relief for poor Canadians, such as government transfer payments and community food banks.

2 **Day care.** Because of the high incidence of poverty in single-parent homes, free or subsidized day care is important because it can allow more parents to attend school or work. The programs are provincially run. One model held in high regard is Quebec's universal daycare program. Anti-poverty activists have lobbied for many years for a universal, national daycare program modelled after the generous European programs. Despite promises, a comparable universal program is yet to emerge in the rest of Canada.

3 **Increasing employability and employment.** Workers with limited skills who lose their jobs have every chance of falling below the poverty line. Governments try to increase employment opportunities by funding training intended to teach marketable skills and by sponsoring relocation programs to assist unemployed workers in moving to communities with better job opportunities for their skill set. To date, these programs have helped some Canadians improve their economic conditions, but they don't work in all cases. These programs are more successful when individuals are motivated to seek retraining and relocation. During the 1970s, the federal government (through the former Department of Regional Economic Expansion [DREE]) attempted to create employment by attracting industry to economically depressed areas. This program met with limited success and, in time, the free market was seen as the better source of sustainable job creation. Government efforts focused instead on supporting business expansion.

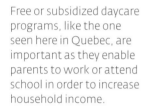

Free or subsidized daycare programs, like the one seen here in Quebec, are important as they enable parents to work or attend school in order to increase household income.

4 **Minimum wage legislation.** Working Canadians should all be able to live on the wages earned. With the decline of labour unions and organizations promoting workers' rights, some wages have not kept up with the rising cost of living over the years. In addition, some employers have been able to hold Canadian wages down by outsourcing work to developing countries where labour costs are a fraction of Canadian costs. Governments legislate minimum wage amounts to protect workers and ensure living wages.

5 **Affordable housing.** A growing number of desperate and marginalized Canadians join the ranks of the homeless each year. In addition, many working poor spend a disproportionate amount of their modest incomes on accommodations. Often, this leaves insufficient money for food, clothing, and other basic necessities. By supporting the construction of affordable housing, governments help improve the living conditions of the working poor. Affordable housing has become an increasing concern as property prices and rents continue to climb in many Canadian cities.

6 ***Comprehensive health care.*** By providing access to quality health care, including mental health care, governments can improve the employability and productivity of individuals presently facing the hardships of disproportionately low income. Many of Canada's chronically poor citizens have complex health issues that impede their abilities to function effectively in the Canadian economy. For those Canadians that have been mentally or spiritually broken by a traumatic experience, rebuilding self-esteem may enable them to become productive members of their communities.

Relief Strategies to Combat the Symptoms of Poverty

1 ***Welfare benefits.*** Welfare is the social safety net of last resort, administered by the provinces with money both from the federal government under the Canada Assistance Plan and from provincial budgets. The specific amount received is usually set provincially, and it depends on the circumstances of the individual or family.

2 ***Seniors' benefits.*** The Old Age Security plan and the Guaranteed Income Supplement (GIS) provide pension benefits to all Canadian senior citizens. GIS payments are made only when reported incomes do not meet established minimums.

3 ***Canada Pension Plan (CPP).*** CPP is a compulsory pension plan for all working Canadians. The amount received on retirement depends on income and contributions made during the individual's working years. It may be received in full at age 65 or partially at age 60. Canadians who are medically identified as no longer able to work as a result of a permanent disability receive a disability pension until they qualify for CPP.

4 ***Employment Insurance.*** This national plan pays a percentage of the unemployed person's former income level, depending on the number of weeks worked previous to the period of unemployment. All employed Canadians contribute to this compulsory plan. They then receive benefits while temporarily out of work.

5 ***Child Tax Credit.*** Replacing the universal family allowance program, this newer approach gives only lower-income families a tax credit to help support each child.

6 ***Compensation for work-related disability.*** Workers injured on the job risk falling into the low-income category. Medicare and provincial workers' compensation boards, such as Ontario's Workplace Safety and Insurance Board, help facilitate workers' recovery and return to work.

7 ***Charitable and community-based relief.*** Many non-profit charitable organizations, such as the Salvation Army and the Daily Bread Food Bank, seek to provide relief with dignity to needy individuals and families. In 2015, food banks were active in 450 Canadian communities. Food Banks Canada estimated that, as of 2018, more than 860 000 Canadians needed help from a food bank every month. This figure represents a threefold increase in the number of people who used this service in 2000.

Self-Reflect

1 How does the nature of capitalism simultaneously lead to both production efficiency and in-come inequality?

2 In what ways does the income tax system used in Canada help address income inequality?

3 Refer to Figure 18.8 (page 387) and Figure 18.12 (page 400). Explain the difference between income and wealth. How does the distribution of wealth compare with the distribution of income in Canada?

4 Explain the difference between structural and relief strategies to combat poverty. Provide three important examples of each strategy type.

Chapter 18
Consolidation Activities

KNOWLEDGE

1   Canadians have long valued equity, yet several inequities continue to result in the unfair economic treatment of citizens. Identify and explain the inequities you consider most unfair in the Canadian economy.

2   Why are Statistics Canada's low-income cut-offs (LICOs) influenced by family size and community size? Explain why LICOs are an indicator of relative poverty.

3   In light of what you have learned about the incidence of poverty in Canada, what would you identify as the principal causes? Why has combatting poverty proven to be so difficult? What three specific recommendations would you make to governments regarding effective long-term solutions?

THINKING & INQUIRY

4   Prepare a brief report on key Employment Insurance (EI) topics, such as eligibility, regular benefits, claim period, special benefits, and premiums. Explain how the EI program helps redistribute income in Canada. You can find information in the Employment Insurance Act of 1996 and at the Government of Canada website.

5   In 1989, the House of Commons unanimously passed a resolution "to seek to achieve the goal of eliminating poverty among Canadian children by the year 2000." Visit the website of Campaign 2000, a coalition of many organizations wanting to end child poverty in Canada. Use the information you find to produce a newsletter or poster to promote one specific policy initiative or strategy to address child poverty.

6   Consult the most recent Human Development Index (HDI) data available through an Internet search. Between 1992 and 2000, Canada occupied the top position on the HDI.

   a)   What has happened to Canada's ranking since 2000?

   b)   Make a list of Canada's current ranking for each statistic used in the HDI. For which statistics does Canada receive its highest and lowest rankings? What message does this send to policy-makers and others reflecting on normative economics?

COMMUNICATION

7 Prepare an argument to debate one of the following public policy statements:

   a) "For the sake of distributive justice, wealthy individuals and corporations should be taxed more to pay their fair share of taxes."

   b) "For the sake of distributive justice, Canada should introduce an inheritance tax."

   c) "For the sake of distributive justice, Canada would be best served by a public policy focus on income equality as opposed to income equity."

8 Write a letter to the editor as an advocate for homeless people. Explain how the factors affecting income distribution help to cause poverty in Canada and suggest what governments, businesses, social agencies, and concerned citizens can do to address this growing problem.

9 Suppose that you are a doctor. How would you argue, using the economic concepts learned in this chapter, that your relatively high income is justified?

10 Many analysts see the Human Development Index as a better indicator of quality of life than per capita income, average income, or median income. Defend or refute this claim by explaining the economic significance of each of these indicators.

11 "Women are more likely to be poor than men in Canada." Cite four examples of data in tables in this unit either to support or to refute this claim. Compare your findings with a classmate.

APPLICATION

12 What is the absolute minimum you would need to live on as a single person? Using flyers from grocery stores, classified sections from newspapers for apartment rentals (or apartment rental websites), and other information, design a budget for yourself.

   a) Compare your total with the low-income cut-off (LICOs) figures for the size of your community, as a "relative poverty line."

   b) Compare your calculation of basic needs with the welfare payments for a single individual living in your region.

13 Right-wing advocates of free-enterprise capitalism are generally less sympathetic to poor people, believing that they should do more to help themselves and that, unless they begin to help themselves, the help that others provide is of limited use. Use economic reasoning to defend or refute this position.

14 Refer to Figure 18.8 (page 387), showing differences in median income and incidence of low income among the provinces in Canada.

   a) Which parts of Canada reported the highest income levels in 2016?

   b) Which parts reported the lowest income levels

   c) Compare the incidence of low incomes (or "poverty") in Atlantic Canada, Ontario, the Prairie provinces, and British Columbia. Which parts of Canada report income levels above and below the national average? Explain the significance of this comparison.

15 Use the contents of this chapter and the additional information that you have researched to support or refute the argument that poverty is passed on from parents to children.

19

The Environment and Sustainable Development

INTRODUCTION

In Chapter 1, the study of economics was introduced as a social science that examines how we make decisions about utilizing the scarce resources available to us. These resources include the air, water, land, and animals that surround us. An economic system that utilizes these resources such that they will not be available for future use is an economic system that is bound to fail. While privately owned resources tend to be taken care of, resources that citizens of the earth share in common are often found to be in trouble: oceans depleted of fish stocks, extinction of species, pollution of drinking water, pollution of air, and a vast island of plastic floating in the Pacific Ocean. Many of the shared resources used by the world as a community are in trouble. This chapter will explore how economists attempt to explain the impact of economic activity on our environment and how resources might be allocated in a way that better protects these commonly owned resources.

LEARNING GOALS

Once you have completed this chapter, you should be able to:

- Understand the pressures on the environment related to economic growth and how these pressures threaten sustainable development

- Identify positive and negative externalities

- Apply the concept of externalities to economic decision making through marginal social cost and marginal benefit analysis

- Analyze how different stakeholders view the trade-off between economic growth and concerns for the environment

- Explain and assess a variety of responses used to address the impact of negative externalities on the environment

- Conduct research using a variety of reliable sources (such as media, institutions, businesses, and interest groups) to address an inquiry question, and communicate economic information, research findings, analysis, and conclusions clearly, effectively, and accurately

KEY TERMS

carrying capacity

drawing down

sustainable development

externality

negative externality

positive externality

spillover costs (or neighbourhood effects)

tragedy of the commons

marginal social cost (MSC)

marginal benefit (MB)

marginal private cost (MPC)

greenhouse gases (GHGs)

climate change

Coase theorem

tort law

class-action lawsuit

subsidy

Pigouvian tax

United Nations Framework Convention on Climate Change (UNFCCC)

Kyoto Protocol

Paris Agreement

carbon pricing

carrying capacity

Environmental term referring to the number of people that the earth's resources can support indefinitely if those resources are managed effectively.

drawing down

An environmental term referring to the process of using up resources (such as minerals or forests) or abusing ones (such as fresh water or air) in the present that should be available for future generations.

sustainable development

Economic development that considers how current production and consumption patterns affect the ability of future generations to meet their needs with respect to economic prosperity, social justice, and environmental sustainability.

Including the Environment in Economic Decisions

In his book *The David Suzuki Reader*, Canadian scientist David Suzuki calls for ecologists and economists to unite. He begins one of his essays by comparing the root words of the two disciplines:

> *The words* ecology *and* economics *derive from the same Greek word,* oikos*, meaning "household" or "home." So ecology* (logos *meaning "study") is the study of home, and economics* (nomics *meaning "management") is home management. These two fields should be companion disciplines, and yet with few exceptions there is little communication between them.*

Suzuki goes on to point out that all the natural resources of our world are really the "fundamental capital that all countries depend on" and that the actions of many of the participants in our economic system do not always consider our best interests in using these resources. Our natural resources provide benefits that exist beyond the dollar values that they contribute to economic output; yet these benefits—or the destruction thereof—are not factored into the output decisions made in the economy. Suzuki concludes the essay by stating that "economists cannot afford any longer to ignore their companion discipline of ecology."

SUSTAINABLE DEVELOPMENT

Concerns about the relationship between economics and the environment relate to our initial introduction to the study of economics and the underlying economic problem—scarcity. The resources that sustain our world are finite. Some will regenerate given time and effective management, some are used up in the production of goods, and others can be recycled. If our world is to continue and the human race to thrive, these resources must be managed carefully.

In 1982, sociologist William Catton wrote about the concept of carrying capacity in his book *Overshoot: The Ecological Basis of Revolutionary Change*. He defined **carrying capacity** as the number of people that the earth's resources can support indefinitely if managed effectively. In other words, resources must be used in a way that sees the environment is not harmed to the extent that it cannot continue to support its human population.

Over time, concern has grown that economic activity is consuming resources at a pace beyond the earth's carrying capacity. Catton referred to this idea as the **drawing down** of resources—the process of using up resources in the present that should be available for future generations. Many people interpret this statement as applying only to the overconsumption of non-renewable resources, such as minerals and fossil fuels, but it goes well beyond this. Poor management of renewable resources (such as forests, fish, fresh water, and even air) must also be included.

In discussions about the balance between economic development and its impact on the environment, the term *sustainable development* is frequently used. The United Nations' World Commission on Environment and Development introduced the concept of **sustainable development** in its 1987 report titled

Our Common Future. It stated that "sustainable development is development that meets the needs of the present without compromising the ability of future generations to meet their own needs." In other words, a sustainable society is one that considers the impact of current production and consumption patterns on the economic viability of future generations. Since 1987, the term *sustainable development* has grown beyond its application to the environment to include three pillars: economic prosperity, social justice, and environmental sustainability. To achieve sustainability, affluent societies must adjust how they consume and change how they interact with the environment. Paying the full economic and social cost of the resources that they use would be a place to start.

EXTERNALITIES

The conflict between economic and environmental concerns can be explained by the existence of a market inefficiency that is known as an *externality*. An **externality** is a side effect of the productive process that is experienced by a third party who does not participate, as either a buyer or a seller, in an actual market transaction related to the good.

For example, a pulp and paper company produces paper that is sold to a printing company. During the manufacturing process, the pulp and paper company dumps liquid waste (known as *effluent*) into a river, which causes fish to die. People who catch fish from the river now suffer from the side effect of fewer fish to catch. They are not engaged in the economic transaction, yet suffer a cost. This is a **negative externality**—a cost (such as pollution or some other annoyance) that is imposed on a third party as the result of an economic transaction. Other examples of negative externalities include the consequences of oil spills, traffic congestion, toxic-waste dumping, greenhouse gas (GHG) emissions, solid-waste disposal, and noise generated by a factory near a residential area.

An opposing externality also exists. A **positive externality** is a benefit to a third party as the result of an economic transaction. Examples include an increase in the property values of surrounding homes owing to the construction of a new subway and the recreational use of an area that is developed for resource extraction due to the building of roads that allows access for other purposes.

Externalities are really sources of economic inefficiency because market forces do not account for all the costs and benefits associated with making an economic decision. In fact, the primary costs and benefits considered are monetary measurements associated with the parties directly involved, while the external costs borne by other parties are ignored. For this reason, externalities are also called **spillover costs** and **neighbourhood effects**. If the market does not require decision makers to consider these costs, there is no incentive for producers to limit their harmful effects.

A solution to the problem of externalities requires producers to consider spillover costs as part of their inputs. Remember that an input is any factor used in the production process. A producer who uses river or coastal waters to discharge effluent, or the air to expel emissions, is really using water and air as inputs. The consumption of these inputs must be considered as factors in decision making if the outcome is to be considered economically efficient.

externality
A side effect of production, either positive or negative, experienced by a third party who is neither a producer nor a consumer of the product.

negative externality
A cost suffered by a third party as the result of production or consumption.

positive externality
A benefit to a third party as the result of an economic transaction; for example, an increase in the property values of homes near the construction of a new subway.

spillover costs (or neighbourhood effects)
Costs (such as those associated with cleaning up pollution) that are borne by a third party instead of the producers and consumers of the product.

DID YOU KNOW?
Kate Raworth presented an alternative model to "endless growth economics" in a 2018 TED talk. Her "doughnut model" focuses on balance instead of growth. Use of resources to address 12 dimensions of social foundation (such as health and education) radiates out of the "hole" toward a balanced "regenerative and distributive" economic "sweet spot" that is the doughnut. The doughnut edge is the ecological ceiling that, once breached, leads to environmental damage such as climate change and biodiversity loss.

TRAGEDY OF THE COMMONS

The **tragedy of the commons** is a situation in which a shared resource is depleted or destroyed by individual self-interest acting contrary to what is good for society as a whole. The concept was first developed by British economist William Foster Lloyd and comes from the shared use of common grazing land. If a society has a shared public pasture for use by its farmers, and all farmers graze a responsible amount of cattle on this common land, the pasture can thrive and all can benefit from its use. The tragedy of the commons arises because it is a free resource. If some farmers decide they want to increase the number of their cattle grazing on the land, at no additional cost to them because the land is free, the pasture can find itself overused and trampled, thereby leaving it unsuitable to feed cattle anymore. The tragedy of the commons revolves around the concept of incentives. Private ownership of a resource provides an incentive to properly manage the resource so that it is available for future production, as the cost of using it is borne by the owner. Public ownership of a resource provides an incentive to overuse the land, spreading costs to everyone else in society.

DID YOU KNOW?

The studies of Nobel Prize winning economist Elinor Ostrom (see page 96) confirmed that common resources like pasture lands and fishing waters can be more effectively managed by responsible users than by governments and private companies. Do you agree with William Foster Lloyd, that private ownership (and interests) best protect common resources?

The reality is that many external costs are associated with natural elements that are used as factors of production and have no clear right of ownership. If someone owns the land that a forestry company uses to harvest trees, it is easy to see who should be reimbursed for the cost of the trees. However, what about the air? No one owns it, so how can a value be placed on the oxygen that the tree no longer produces? If no one owns the river polluted by oil leaking from the logging machines, how can a cost be determined for the fish that die as a result? Because no individual owns these elements, it is very difficult to ensure their well-being.

MARGINAL SOCIAL COSTS AND MARGINAL BENEFITS

If no one owns the river polluted by oil from a neighbouring industrial plant, how can a cost be determined for the fish and vegetation that die as a result?

The transaction inefficiencies that result in pollution occur because of externalities. An economic explanation for these inefficiencies emerges from an analysis of marginal costs and marginal benefits. This approach is very different

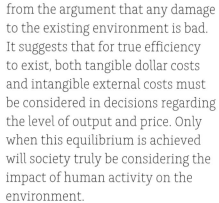

from the argument that any damage to the existing environment is bad. It suggests that for true efficiency to exist, both tangible dollar costs and intangible external costs must be considered in decisions regarding the level of output and price. Only when this equilibrium is achieved will society truly be considering the impact of human activity on the environment.

In Chapter 10, you learned about marginal cost–revenue analysis. Because it explains the "most profitable" level of output for a firm,

such analysis indicates the most efficient allocation of a firm's resources. The firm will be naturally guided to achieve a level of output at which the marginal cost is equal to the marginal revenue. In essence, the model states that as long as the added benefits (marginal revenue) exceed the added costs (marginal cost), it makes sense to produce an additional unit of output. This model can also be used to determine the most efficient level of output if the environmental costs are included, as demonstrated in the following example.

The production of whizbangs results in the discharge of toxic chemicals into a lake. In Figure 19.1, the **marginal social cost (MSC)** reflects the additional cost to society (from increased levels of pollution) of an increase in the level of production of whizbangs: the more whizbangs the firm produces, the higher the marginal social cost. The **marginal benefit (MB)** reflects the firm's demand for the use of the externality. This marginal benefit is the additional revenue that is generated as additional units are produced. The curve is downward sloping because of the law of diminishing marginal returns. Every additional unit that is produced results in smaller increases in the total benefit to the firm. At some point, the additional benefit falls to zero.

As in marginal cost–revenue analysis for the firm, the most efficient level of output occurs at the point at which the marginal benefit equals the marginal social cost. In our example, this would mean a marginal social cost and marginal benefit of $50 per tonne and an amount of discharged waste of 25 tonnes per week. However, the firm actually produces a total of 50 tonnes of waste per week. The reason? Because the firm does not own the lake, it bears none of the burden of the marginal social cost. This cost is borne by the residents around the lake who draw their drinking water from it or the people fishing who may no longer catch healthy fish in the lake. The firm, therefore, produces at the level where it receives its greatest benefit (when marginal benefit falls to zero), while the residents pick up the marginal social cost of $100 per tonne. Although the firm's level of output is its most efficient, that same level of output is higher than what is most efficient for society. By this analysis, then, the firm's level of output is inefficient.

marginal social cost (MSC)

Part of a process to assess the impact of production decisions, marginal social cost is the additional cost to society in terms of an increase in externalities caused by an increase in production.

marginal benefit (MB)

The additional revenue generated by a firm as additional units are produced, thereby increasing the use of an externality, such as a lake for dumping waste.

FIGURE 19.1

Inefficiency due to an externality
An "inefficient" level of waste occurs because the firm bears none of the social costs of pollution. These costs are fully borne by the residents around the polluted lake.

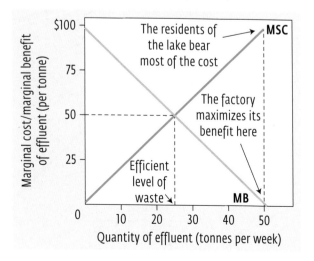

DID YOU KNOW?

The global climate has always seen temperature variations through warming periods and ice ages. However, changes over the last 50 years have been more rapid than at any other time and appear to directly correspond to the increase in global population and industrialization. The average temperature of the earth's surface has risen by 0.8°C in the last 100 years, with 0.6°C of this increase occurring over the last 30 years.

marginal private cost (MPC)

Part of a process to assess the impact of production decisions, marginal private cost is the additional production cost incurred privately by a firm as it increases units of output. It does not take into account the cost of negative externalities.

ACCOUNTING FOR MARGINAL SOCIAL COSTS

What is the impact on price and output of not including the social costs of pollution? By not accounting for these externalities, the actual cost fails to include the value that members of society place on the damage incurred in the environment. Therefore, the price charged is lower than the actual value of the product. The low price is the result of a failure in the pricing system because the actual costs are not passed on to the consumer.

We will conduct our analysis based on the assumption that a firm is operating in a perfectly competitive market, but the model works equally well for the other three market types (see Chapter 10). Figure 19.2 displays the marginal cost and revenue curves for a typical firm in the fictional "whizbangs" market. The marginal cost curve has been labelled **MPC (marginal private cost)** instead of MC because it includes only the private costs incurred by the firm and ignores the externalities. The firm receives the current market price for each unit, so the marginal revenue (MR) is equal to the price for each additional unit. Using marginal cost–revenue analysis, the firm's most efficient output would be 1 000 units (where price = MPC = MR). However, if marginal cost is to include *all* costs, it must account for external costs too. For each additional unit added, the external costs increase. This shifts the MPC curve to the left. This new curve is now labelled MSC (marginal social cost). Notice that this new curve intersects the MR curve at a point farther to the left, indicating that a lower output (500 whizbangs) is now the more efficient level of output. Because each firm is producing less, the total market supply curve shifts to the left, as indicated in Figure 19.3. The result is a lower quantity of whizbangs exchanged at a higher price because consumers are now paying the real cost of the good or service, and therefore a lower quantity is demanded.

FIGURE 19.2
Output for a typical whizbang firm, considering external costs
When this firm is forced to consider external costs, its most efficient level of output is reduced from 1 000 units to 500 units.

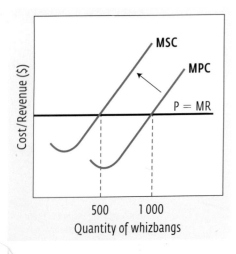

FIGURE 19.3
Effect on the whizbang market if external costs are included
With each firm producing less at any given market price, the market supply curve is shifted to the left, leading to higher prices and a lower quantity demanded.

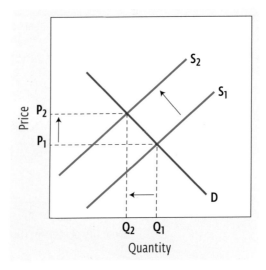

CLIMATE CHANGE AND EXTERNALITIES

The greenhouse effect is a natural phenomenon that creates the conditions necessary for life to exist on earth. Heat is trapped in the earth's atmosphere by **greenhouse gases (GHGs)**, raising temperatures to a life-supporting level. GHGs include carbon dioxide (CO_2), methane, and nitrous oxide, with CO_2 representing approximately 75 percent of the total. The excessive increase in these gases caused by human activity is responsible for an increase in global warming that goes beyond what is considered natural.

Global warming is caused by the emission of GHGs, mostly from burning fossil fuels such as coal, oil, and natural gas, as well as the destruction of natural mechanisms that remove GHGs from the atmosphere, such as forests. Carbon dioxide levels are believed to be higher now than at any time in the past. These levels are measured in parts per million (ppm), and, once in the atmosphere, GHGs circulate for centuries. In 1960, CO_2 levels measured approximately 317 ppm; they rose to 370 ppm in 2000 and 403 ppm in 2016.

The consequences of rising global temperatures, which many refer to as **climate change**, are divergent and confusing. Global awareness of climate change was raised in 2006 by the documentary *An Inconvenient Truth*, which is about former US Vice President Al Gore's campaign to educate people about the issue of global warming.

The effects of climate change are a perfect example of externalities in economics. The emission of GHGs in electricity production, manufacturing, and transportation are not included as "costs of production"; therefore, the third parties that bear the costs of these emissions are subject to the external costs. The effects of climate change include rising sea levels leading to coastal flooding, disrupted food production, extreme weather events, an increase in diseases such as malaria, changes in rainfall patterns leading to both floods and droughts, and plant and animal extinctions.

The external costs related to climate change include funds spent to prevent the above events, such as the building of dykes to prevent flooding. They also include the costs of dealing with the impact of climate-change events, such as rescue efforts during flooding, and insurance compensation for those who lose property.

The overall costs of climate change are difficult to calculate for many reasons. First, it is challenging to assess which costs are "natural"—after all, flooding from storms has always occurred—and which costs are the result of bigger and worse storms due to rising global temperatures. Second, the costs will continue to accrue into the future, and models predicting these costs vary considerably. Some models predict multiple trillions of dollars of associated costs worldwide by 2025 alone.

greenhouse gases (GHGs)

Gases such as carbon dioxide, methane, and nitrous oxide released by the burning of fossil fuels that are contributing to global warming and climate change.

climate change

The varied consequences of global warming, including excessive rainfall and drought, and other extreme weather events, linked to the release of greenhouse gases.

Self-Reflect

1 What does David Suzuki mean when he says that the natural resources of the world are really the "fundamental capital that all countries depend on"? How is this statement linked to the concept of sustainable development?

2 How are the concepts of sustainable development, carrying capacity, and drawing down related?

3 Explain the difference between a positive and a negative externality.

4 An efficient level of output is defined as the point at which marginal cost is equal to marginal benefit. Explain why output is inefficient when external costs are not considered.

5 What is the greenhouse effect, and how does it relate to the concept of externalities?

Coase theorem
Theory of economist Robert Coase, which states that in some circumstances private negotiations are more efficient than government intervention in dealing with negative externalities such as pollution.

Toward Sustainable Development

How can these market forces be addressed in a way that supports sustainable development? All stakeholders have a role. The entire responsibility for the impact of externalities cannot be placed at the feet of firms and industry. First, calculation of the precise financial costs of externalities is inexact and debatable. Second, a socially conscious firm that seeks to internalize all costs faces a much worse cost structure than its polluting competitors, making competition based on price very difficult. In many cases, the fact that a firm takes an ethical position is not enough to persuade consumers to pay a higher price for its product. Often, then, the reward for the pollution-conscious firm is a clear conscience, a declining market for its product, and diminished profits. Therefore, to create meaningful change in the reduction of environmentally harmful externalities, different courses of action need to be considered.

COASE THEOREM

In 1960, economist Ronald Coase proposed a theorem that suggested externalities can be solved by market forces in some circumstances. The **Coase theorem** states that private transactions can be efficient, accounting for externalities through bargaining and negotiation, under the following conditions:

- The property rights are clearly defined.
- The number of firms, people, or parties involved is limited to a few.
- The level of cost is low and easily negotiable.
- The issue is simple and clearly understood.

Coase argued that, when the above criteria are in place, the role of government is to act as a facilitator, encouraging bargaining between the affected stakeholders. Those who create the externality should work together with those who are affected by the externality so that they may find an acceptable solution to the problem. Establishing clearly defined property rights allows a price tag to be placed on the use of the property. Clear property rights and ownership provides incentive for the owner of the externally affected property to act, because it includes the right to exclude others from using the property and the right to sue for damages to the property caused by others. It also allows an owner to seek compensation for any nuisance or other socially unacceptable consequences. In some cases, this ownership can extend to common property rights (for example, common-pool resources such as farmer-managed irrigation systems, user-managed groundwater systems, or club-owned recreational facilities).

In a sense, the Coase theorem relates to a complex analysis of opportunity cost into which all costs—both internal and external—are factored. Logging in wilderness areas that also attract tourists provides an example of an instance where the Coase theorem can be utilized. If the owner of a large parcel of forest near an area where tour operators conduct their business is considering whether to allow a large logging company to harvest her forest, the local tour operators face a problem. The tour operators want to have a pristine wilderness to attract tourist dollars. The logging company, on the other hand, wants to log the area using the most cost-effective means possible—clear-cutting. Although relatively cost effective, clear-cutting is environmentally devastating. Furthermore, clear-cutting in a wilderness area that also attracts tourist dollars hurts the tourist industry. In this situation, if the landowner and the tour operators were brought together to establish clear costs and benefits, perhaps a compromise might be reached between the two parties that would consider the external costs.

As long as one of the parties in the dispute has clear property rights with respect to the issue, there is an incentive for both parties to negotiate a mutually acceptable settlement. The owner of the forest holds the property rights for the potential logging land, and the tour operators have an incentive to negotiate with the landowner because excessive logging in the area will seriously affect their operations. The question then arises, what incentive does the owner of the land have to negotiate with the tour operators?

Here we must look at opportunity cost. In a sense, if the owner of the land allows a logging company to clear-cut her trees, she gives up the payment the tour operators would be willing to make to stop the logging. She also gives up the enjoyment derived from pristine wilderness (a non-monetary but relevant cost). The tour operators should be willing to buy the forested land, or at least make user payments at a price that will prevent the logging. These costs can be spread over several years since the value of this use is ongoing. Logging, on the other hand, is a one-time, lump-sum payment. In this case, if the tour operators were willing to negotiate a set of payments that met or exceeded the opportunity cost of not logging the land, the Coase theorem would predict a negotiated settlement that ends without clear-cutting. Here, private bargaining and negotiation lead to an efficient solution to an externality, because a monetary value is assigned to the external cost.

TORT LAW

While the Coase theorem suggests that a negotiated settlement may occur under certain circumstances, cases where there are many people affected by the externality, or where property rights are not so clear, may be settled using tort law. **Tort law** is the body of law that allows a person who is injured by the actions of others to seek compensation from the parties who caused the injury by suing them. It also allows a group of people to seek compensation through a **class-action lawsuit**. In a class-action lawsuit, one or more parties file a complaint on behalf of themselves and all other people who are "similarly situated" or suffering from the same problem. This type of lawsuit is often used when many people have similar claims or when individual property rights cannot be determined (which means the Coase theorem does not apply).

Class-action lawsuits in response to the effects of environmental externalities were popularized in the late 1990s through films such as *A Civil Action* and *Erin Brockovich*. In both films, based on true stories, compensation was awarded due to the impact of a contaminated water supply on the health of residents. An example of a class-action lawsuit related to environmental externalities in Canada is *St. Lawrence Cement Inc. v. Barrette* in 2013. Neighbours of a cement plant in Quebec were awarded $15 million in damages related to "abnormal" dust, noise, and odour created by the factory.

tort law
The body of law that allows a person injured by another to seek compensation by suing; it is used as a basis for class-action lawsuits against companies causing environmental externalities.

class-action lawsuit
A lawsuit brought by one or more persons who file a complaint on behalf of themselves and others affected by a problem, such as pollution caused by a firm's activities.

DID YOU KNOW?

According to the National Oceanic and Atmospheric Administration, as of 2017 the top five costliest US hurricanes on record (adjusted for inflation) have all occurred since 2005: Katrina in 2015 ($161 billion), Harvey in 2017 ($125 billion), Maria in 2017 ($90 billion), Sandy in 2012 ($71 billion), and Irma in 2017 ($50 billion). In many cases, the damage was caused less by the ferocity of the storm than by the amount of rainfall and storm surge flooding that accompanied it.

While, in general, a class-action lawsuit addresses the externality after it occurs, the possibility of this type of legal action can also serve to prevent the externality in the first place if it raises the fear that compensatory damages may have to be paid to those affected.

SUBSIDIES

The government might provide a subsidy to firms or consumers to encourage them to take external costs into account. A **subsidy** is a payment made by the government to producers or consumers on the condition of a desired outcome. For example, if the government wants to reduce the amount of water pollution created in the production of whizbangs, it could ask the company to install technology that removes pollutants from the factory effluent. To achieve this objective, they might offer to subsidize all or part of the cost of the technology necessary to remove the pollutants. The introduction of a subsidy increases supply, causing a reduction in the market price of the good or service in question, as well as an increase in the market quantity exchanged. Examples include subsidies for upgrading windows (as demonstrated in Figure 19.4), insulation, or smart thermostats to make a home more energy efficient, thereby reducing GHG emissions. A major complaint regarding this strategy is that the producer and consumer of the product are not held accountable for the external cost; rather, the general public pays through the collection of the tax revenue necessary to pay the subsidy.

TAXES

Another method that can be used to limit spillover costs is to tax the transaction. A **Pigouvian tax** (named after Arthur Cecil Pigou, the British founder of welfare economics) may be levied on production that causes a negative environmental externality. Its purpose is to force producers and consumers to consider the external environmental costs. Instead of forcing society as a whole to pay for pollution costs, the producer is forced to "internalize the externality." The effect of the tax is to shift the supply curve in the market to the left, as shown in Figure 19.5, as producers must now receive a higher price to maintain the same level of production. As a result, the equilibrium price in the market rises, and a smaller quantity is bought and sold. The smaller quantity exchanged should also be reflected in a decrease in the environmental damage that is of concern.

Using taxes to internalize externalities results in a market price that reflects the true social costs of production

FIGURE 19.4

The effects of a government subsidy on the energy-efficient window market

The introduction of a government subsidy in this market will lead to an increase in supply, causing a decrease in price and an increase in the quantity of energy-efficient windows demanded. A more energy-efficient home will reduce the release of greenhouse gases.

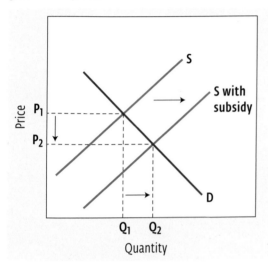

FIGURE 19.5

Passing on the cost of externalities to consumers through a Pigouvian tax

The tax shifts the supply curve to the left, resulting in an increase in price from P to P_t (price with tax) and less pollution, as the quantity exchanged decreases from Q to Q_t (quantity with tax).

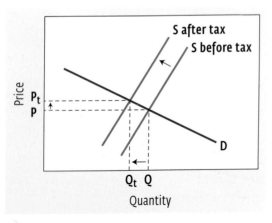

and forces firms and consumers to bear the full social cost of their economic activities. However, these methods have attracted some criticism. First, the money raised through taxes does not actually go toward compensating those who are affected by the externality. For example, the lake that is being polluted in the production of whizbangs is still being polluted—albeit to a lesser degree—but the residents who are not able to draw their drinking water from the lake are not receiving any of the tax revenue to compensate them for their loss. Instead, the compensation goes to the government in the form of tax revenue.

Second, it is difficult for the government to set a tax that makes up for the difference between the marginal cost and the marginal social cost. The best strategy for a government to take is to set a tax rate that slowly creeps upward, called a "ratchetting mechanism," until the pollution is reduced to an acceptable level. Note that this does not mean that the level of pollution will necessarily fall to where marginal social cost is equal to marginal benefit. Political concerns may limit the shift of the marginal cost curve.

Third, pollution still occurs. The only difference is that the new level of pollution is efficient, as long as the Pigouvian tax shifts the marginal cost curve so that it is equal to the marginal social cost curve. One advantage of the Pigouvian tax is that it may cause some producers to adopt a technology that reduces external costs. Firms with cleanup costs that fall below the level of the tax will implement the required technology to avoid the tax.

In 2004, France implemented a Pigouvian noise tax on airplanes taking off from its nine busiest airports. The tax is set at 2 to 35 euros per departure depending on the plane's size, the amount of noise the plane makes, and the time of the departure. The revenue is dedicated to soundproofing homes around the airports.

REGULATION

The federal and provincial governments may use direct regulations to limit externalities. Regulation is usually necessary when the production of a good or service results in a highly toxic or dangerous by-product. For instance, the use of chlorine in bleaching pulp for paper production results in a waste by-product that contains dioxins and furans. These highly toxic compounds have been associated with reduced reproductive capabilities in fish-eating birds that live around the Great Lakes. Therefore, it is necessary for the government to regulate the allowable levels or amounts of these substances permitted to enter the environment. Many environmentalists argue that no dioxins or furans should be allowed from industrial sources. On the other hand, industry advocates argue that there are safe levels that the environment can absorb. For extremely dangerous pollutants, the government has little choice but to use regulation to protect the public interest. Regulation 347 of Ontario's Environmental Protection Act of 1990, which governs rules related to hazardous waste, is an example of direct regulation of harmful externalities.

The government might also use regulations to protect renewable resources such as fish and lumber. Quotas—such as restrictions on the amount of fish that can be caught within territorial waters—are designed to help manage public resources that would otherwise be overused. Critics claim that these regulations

subsidy
A grant of money from a government to a producer to achieve some desired outcome, such as the installation of pollution-control equipment.

Pigouvian tax
A tax levied on the production and/or sale of any good or service that causes a negative externality such as pollution; named after economist Arthur Pigou.

DID YOU KNOW?

- Canada's CO_2 equivalent emissions (a measure used to convert the emissions of different GHGs into a common unit) in 2016 were 704 Mt, down from a peak of 745 Mt in 2007.

- CO_2 emissions per capita in Canada peaked in 2000 at 23.8 tonnes. In 2016, they had fallen to 19.4 tonnes.

- In Canada, heating an average home for four months creates 1 tonne of CO_2 emissions. Commuting 10 km (each way) to work in a Honda Civic creates 1 tonne of CO_2 emissions in one year.

United Nations Framework Convention on Climate Change (UNFCCC)

An international agreement negotiated in 1992 that establishes how future treaties called "protocols" or "agreements" are to be negotiated to address the issue of climate change.

Kyoto Protocol

An international agreement arrived at in 1997 that set international targets and standards to generate mandatory greenhouse gas emission reductions in 41 industrialized countries and the European Union.

Paris Agreement

An international agreement signed in 2015 to replace the Kyoto Protocol. It focuses on consensus building and co-operation, allowing countries to set their own greenhouse gas emission targets with mandatory reporting of progress every five years.

carbon pricing

Requires firms to pay for costs of production associated with releasing greenhouse gas emissions in an attempt to control global warming and climate change. Sometimes referred to as a *carbon tax*.

DID YOU KNOW?

The Latin American country of Costa Rica has one of the lowest ratios of GHG emissions to electricity consumption in the world. In 2017, Costa Rica generated its electricity needs using 100 percent renewable energy sources for 300 days in a row. Over 99 percent of Costa Rica's electricity needs are served by renewable resources such as water (78.26 percent), wind (10.29 percent), geothermal (10.23 percent), and solar and biomass (0.84 percent).

are often treated as taxes, in the sense that those who break the law are fined; if offenders feel that paying the fine is cheaper than taking the action necessary to prevent the external cost, they may just pay the fine. Another problem is that such regulations can be costly and difficult to administer. In times of budget cuts, the policing of regulations may be cut back. This complaint was levied against the Ontario government during the Walkerton water inquiry in 2001, convened after the deaths of people who drank municipal water that was contaminated with E. coli bacteria. It has been suggested that economic tools, such as taxes and subsidies, tend to be more efficient than regulation because compliance is built in through market pricing mechanisms.

CLIMATE CHANGE AND THE KYOTO PROTOCOL

Addressing the issue of climate change requires governments around the world to co-operate using the economic tools at their disposal. The first international agreement was the **United Nations Framework Convention on Climate Change (UNFCCC)**, negotiated in 1992. This framework continues to exist and establishes how treaties, called "protocols" or "agreements," are to be negotiated to address the issue of climate change. In all, 192 parties (that is, countries or economic organizations) signed the agreement.

The parties convene annually in a meeting called the Conference of the Parties (COP) to evaluate and discuss their progress in dealing with climate change. In 1997, at COP3 in Kyoto, Japan, members agreed to the **Kyoto Protocol**. This agreement set international targets and standards that were supposed to have legal force, creating mandatory GHG emission-reduction targets in 41 industrialized countries plus the European Union. The collective reduction targets were set at GHG emission levels 5.2 percent below 1990 levels by 2012.

The protocol laid out three main strategies for countries to achieve their targets. First, countries could receive emission-reduction credits for natural processes (called "carbon sinks") that remove GHGs from the atmosphere. Carbon sinks include forest and agricultural land (natural environments that absorb and store CO_2). The maintenance of carbon sinks would count as credits to meet "reduction goals." Second, under the clean development mechanism (CDM), countries could receive emission-reduction credits for investing in technology and infrastructure that reduced emissions in less developed countries. For example, if Canada replaced a coal-fired powerplant with a solar power farm in a less-developed country, Canada would receive emission-reduction credits. Third, countries could receive emission-reduction credits through emissions trading, which allows for the buying and selling of emission credits. Those who were ahead of their goals could sell their extra emission-reduction credits to those who were unable to meet their goals.

The Kyoto Protocol has had a limited effect on GHG emissions for a number of reasons. China and India were not included in the agreement, as more than 100 developing countries were exempt. Moreover, the United States ultimately refused to participate because developing countries were not required to meet emission targets. Canada withdrew from the agreement in 2012, claiming that it would not be successful without the participation of China and the United States, but also facing $14 billion in penalties for failure to meet its mandatory target. Few countries reached their target, and many of those that did managed to do so using credits from other countries as opposed to actually reducing their own emissions.

Some say that the real success of the Kyoto Protocol lies in the fact that it started the international community on a path toward GHG emission reductions. As the world's first emission-reduction treaty, it has raised awareness about greenhouse gases, established ways to measure emissions, and spurred technological innovations to reduce emissions. It has also demonstrated just how difficult it is to reduce GHG emissions.

Solar power farms like the one pictured here reduce GHG emissions. The Sarnia Photovoltaic Power Plant in Ontario, for example, covers 450 hectares of land and produces 120,000 MWh of energy, which, if produced in a coal-fired plant, would generate 39,000 tonnes of CO_2 emissions.

CLIMATE CHANGE AND THE PARIS AGREEMENT

In 2015, at COP21 in Paris, members of the UNFCC created an agreement to replace the Kyoto Protocol. Called the **Paris Agreement**, it has some important differences when compared with the Kyoto Protocol. Many countries most affected by climate change argued that a weakness of the Kyoto Protocol was the fact that it ignored dealing with adaptation to climate change, which is just as important as reducing GHG emissions. Others argued that the existence of legally binding requirements, difficult to enforce internationally, took the focus off international co-operation. In addition, being able to claim credits to achieve goals meant that actual reductions were largely ignored.

The Paris Agreement focuses on consensus building, allowing countries to set their own goals and targets, achieving a climate of co-operation as opposed to a requirement of fulfilling legal obligations. With an aim to take effect in 2020, the agreement has an overall goal of limiting average global temperature increases to less than 2°C above pre-industrial levels. Parties are to report their progress every five years, and goals should demonstrate a progression, with each new pledge tougher than the previous one. Initial efforts should be focused on stopping increases in GHG emissions, followed by efforts to reduce the level of emissions, and then dealing with the removal of existing carbon from the atmosphere. As of June 2018, 178 countries had committed to participating in the agreement.

In 2017, the federal government of Canada announced the Pan-Canadian Framework on Clean Growth and Climate Change as part of its commitment to the Paris Agreement. This framework established four pillars: setting prices on carbon pollution, pursuing complementary measures to further reduce carbon emissions, establishing measures to adapt to climate change, and taking actions to accelerate innovation and technology. Canada's first pledge under the Paris Agreement is a target of GHG emission levels 30 percent below 2005 levels by 2030.

There is hope. Previous environmental crises such as acid rain and depletion of the ozone layer have largely been mitigated through international co-operation.

Self-Reflect

1 Why do you think the Coase theorem has limited influence in controlling major pollution problems such as the greenhouse effect or toxic-waste dumps?

2 What is tort law, and how does it address the issue of externalities?

3 Create a table that compares the advantages and disadvantages of subsidies, taxes, and regulations as means of controlling pollution.

4 Compare the Kyoto Protocol and the Paris Agreement, identifying key similarities and differences.

5 What are the four pillars of Canada's Pan-Canadian Framework on Clean Growth and Climate Change?

Thinking like an Economist

Carbon Emission Regulations versus Carbon Pricing: Which Is More Effective in Reducing Emissions?

Let's assume that electricity production in the economy is made up of two coal-burning producers. Government planners want to reduce CO_2 emissions from these two power plants by a total of 20 megatonnes (Mt) (1 megatonne = 1 million tonnes). Which strategy would be more effective in reducing CO_2 emissions: carbon emission regulations or carbon pricing?

CARBON EMISSION REGULATIONS

This reduction could be achieved by regulating both firms to reduce their CO_2 emissions in proportion to the amount they create. Power Plant A (PPA) is responsible for 75 percent of CO_2 emissions, and Power Plant B (PPB) is responsible for 25 percent. Because of the age of PPA's equipment, the technology required to meet the goal will cost PPA $20 per tonne of CO_2. Its total pollution abatement costs as a proportion of the industry total (that is, the two power plants together) would be $300 million ($0.75 \times 20$ Mt $\times$ $20).

Suppose, on the other hand, that through its more efficient CO_2 abatement technology, PPB faces a CO_2-reduction cost of $10 per tonne of CO_2. Its total cost would be $50 million ($0.25 \times 20$ Mt $\times$ $10). Thus, the total cost of 20 Mt of CO_2 abatement in the industry would be $350 million ($300 million + $50 million).

CARBON PRICING

Carbon pricing forces firms to consider the cost of CO_2 emissions in their production processes. Let's assume that the government could achieve a 20 Mt reduction in CO_2 emissions by placing a $14-per-tonne price on any CO_2 emissions above a 20 Mt reduction of each producer's current level. For example, if a firm's current level is 130 Mt of CO_2 emissions, it would face a $14-per-tonne price on any CO_2 emissions above 110 Mt (the 20 Mt reduction). Firms could choose to reduce their CO_2 emissions by 20 Mt through abatement technology and avoid the carbon pricing. Alternatively, they could choose to continue to release the same level of CO_2 emissions and pay the cost for the 20 Mt of CO_2 emissions they did not reduce.

In our scenario, PPA would have such high CO_2-reduction costs that it would probably choose to continue to pollute and pay to release the current level of CO_2 emissions. Under the government's carbon pricing policy, PPA would pay $280 million (20 Mt $\times$ $14) if it continued to release the same level of CO_2 emissions. However, if it used abatement technology to reduce CO_2 emissions by 20 Mt, PPA would pay $400 million (20 Mt $\times$ $20). Since it costs much more to clean up the CO_2 than to keep releasing CO_2, PPA would likely continue to pollute.

However, PPB would use abatement technology to clean up all 20 Mt of CO_2 emissions because the cost of carbon pricing is much higher than abatement. Under the government's carbon pricing policy, PPB would pay $280 million, the same as PPA. Yet, if it used abatement technology to reduce CO_2 emissions by 20 Mt, PPB would pay only $200 million (20 Mt $\times$ $10).

The carbon pricing policy may seem unfair to PPB, in that it bears the brunt of the CO_2 abatement costs. Keep in mind that the goal is to achieve a total benefit for society, not individual firms. From the point of view of society, the desired reduction in CO_2 has taken place. In addition, both PPA and PPB were given a choice—reducing their emissions or paying to emit CO_2.

COMPARING BOTH APPROACHES

In our scenario, the total cost of reducing CO_2 emissions by 20 Mt through carbon emission regulations was $350 million (without factoring in the cost of legal enforcement). Under the carbon pricing policy, the same net reduction would be achieved at a cost of $200 million and an increase in government revenue of $280 million.

With the carbon pricing policy, the government would receive $280 million in revenues from PPA, which could be used to pay expenses related to climate change. Those expenses could include paying a subsidy to farmers who lose crops to drought or supporting homeowners who lose property due to flooding. At the same time, the government would achieve its targeted CO_2 emission reduction because of the abatement actions of PPB.

The financial impact of carbon pricing gets even more interesting. Carbon pricing would cost PPA $280 million as an income transfer from the firm to the government. The government could use this revenue to address external costs, or it could return the revenue to the provinces or consumers it came from (as per Canada's Greenhouse Gas Pollution Pricing Act [2018]). Thus, the cost to society for the cleanup of 20 Mt of CO_2 emissions would be the $200 million abatement cost for PPB. Because the industry costs of reducing CO_2 emissions are cheaper in the carbon pricing approach, consumers would likely find that price increases for goods and services that involve the emission of carbon are minimized.

As long as the carbon price set by government is higher than the cleanup costs of most firms in an industry, a carbon pricing policy will be more effective than carbon emission regulations in reducing CO_2 emissions.

APPLYING ECONOMIC THINKING

1   Make a T-chart listing the pros and cons of implementing a policy requiring carbon pricing.

2   In the scenario presented in this feature, what would be the consequences of setting a carbon price of $8 per tonne on CO_2 emissions? What about a carbon price of $22 per tonne on CO_2 emissions?

DID YOU KNOW?

- Many Canadian economists prefer to use *carbon pricing* instead of *carbon tax* because *carbon pricing* implies the intent of payment for resource use, while *carbon tax* implies the intent of revenue generation by government.

- To reduce emissions by 80 percent, some estimates suggest that the carbon price would need to exceed $100 per tonne.

- Canada's Greenhouse Gas Pollution Pricing Act set a carbon price of $20 per tonne starting in 2019, which will rise by $10 per tonne each year until 2022, when it reaches $50 per tonne. A $20-per-tonne carbon price would increase gas prices by about 4.5 cents per litre.

How can government policy reduce GHG emissions by polluters such as this coal-fired power plant in Trenton, Nova Scotia?

Chapter 19
Consolidation Activities

KNOWLEDGE

1 How does David Suzuki argue that economics and ecology should be "companion disciplines"?

2 The United Nations report *Our Common Future* introduced the concept of sustainable development with an environmental focus. In economics the idea of sustainable development has grown to include what three pillars? Explain using an example for each pillar.

3 Why are externalities called "neighbourhood effects"?

4 Why should discharge of effluent into a river or emission of GHGs into the air count as inputs in the production process?

THINKING & INQUIRY

5 Some say that sustainable development is impossible, given advances in technology and the demand that these advances place on the use of more and more resources. Others see technology as the key to finally achieving sustainable development, as it allows us to be more efficient and creative in the use of resources such that we do not exhaust them. Identify an example of technology used in each of these roles. To which of these two views do you subscribe? Prepare a list of arguments that you could use to support your point of view.

6 Research the rules in your municipality for the disposal of household wastes. (Most municipalities send a brochure to households once a year or post this information on a municipal website.) How does your municipality attempt to limit the impact of waste disposal on the environment? Is there any attempt to make households accountable for the external costs associated with waste disposal? Explain.

7 Research the debate surrounding an oil or gas pipeline proposal. Examples include the Mackenzie Valley Pipeline, Trans Mountain Pipeline, and Keystone Pipeline. Create a table that lists the pros and cons claimed by both proponents and opponents of the project.

8 Each of the following quotations can be linked to concepts explored in this chapter. Explain each quotation, referring to at least one key term from the chapter.

a) "We do not inherit the earth from our ancestors; we borrow it from our children." (Indigenous proverb)

b) "We're finally going to get the bill for the Industrial Age. If the projections are right, it's going to be a big one: the ecological collapse of the planet." (Jeremy Rifkin, *World Press Review*, December 30, 1989)

c) "In an underdeveloped country, don't drink the water; in a developed country, don't breathe the air." (Jonathan Raban, 1976)

d) "I am one of the patients of air pollution. When the Japanese economy grew very rapidly, my asthma deteriorated. . . . For the last ten years I can hardly work. And when the law was enacted, the law concerning the abatement of pollution, it has given me compensation. That is my only income, from the compensation that this law provides." (Yoshi Suzuki, World Commission on Environment and Development hearing, February 1987)

COMMUNICATION

9 Investigate an environmental agreement or program that attempts to address an externality. Create a one-page summary that briefly outlines the problem, how it attempts to solve the problem, and, if possible, how effective it has been. Some suggestions include:

   a) Canada–United States Air Quality Agreement, 1991

   b) Canadian Environmental Protection Act, 1999

   c) Great Lakes Water Quality Agreement, 2012

   d) Pan-Canadian Framework on Clean Growth and Climate Change, 2016

10 Write a brief report about a class-action lawsuit related to environmental or economic concerns. Address the following questions:

   a) What was the cause of the problem?

   b) Who was claimed to be responsible?

   c) Who was affected?

   d) What was the outcome?

   e) Are there any laws or programs in effect today to prevent a similar occurrence?

11 Create a poster that displays the externalities related to a particular economic transaction. At the centre of the poster, create an image that conveys an economic transaction such as someone buying fish at a market or using electricity generated by a coal-fired power plant. Radiating out around the central image, present images representing external costs borne by third parties as a result of the transaction.

12 Prepare a brochure that promotes an environmental organization or movement. Possible organizations include Greenpeace, Rainforest Alliance, Earth Rangers, Ecojustice, World Wide Fund for Nature (WWF), Sierra Club, and Ducks Unlimited.

   a) When and where was it formed?

   b) How was it formed?

   c) In which country(ies) does it operate?

   d) What issue is its focus?

   e) What kind of externalities is it trying to address?

   f) What methods does it use to try and affect change?

APPLICATION

13 Using supply and demand analysis, explain the process by which a subsidy for electric cars would reduce GHG emissions.

14 Think about the route that you take when travelling from your home to your school. Identify five negative externalities that you have experienced that were likely not factored into the cost of production.

15 Examine your neighbourhood, comparing the appearance of litter in a local ravine or an empty lot with that of private homes. Take photos with a smartphone to document your observations. Explain your observations using the concept of "tragedy of the commons."

16 Use the Internet or a newspaper database to research one of the environmental disasters listed below. Explain what happened during the event and the impact of its aftermath. Utilize at least three key terms or concepts learned in this chapter as part of your explanation.

   a) Tokaimura, Japan (1999)

   b) Deep Water Horizon, Gulf of Mexico (2010)

   c) Exxon Valdez, Alaska (1989)

   d) Love Canal, New York (1978)

   e) Bhopal, India (1984)

   f) Three Mile Island, Pennsylvania (1979)

   g) Chernobyl, Ukraine (Soviet Union) (1986)

   h) Seveso, Italy (1976)

Unit 5 Performance Task

Advocating for the Most Appropriate Role of Government

In this unit, we have investigated economic decision making from the perspective of government involvement in the economy, full employment, income distribution, and sustainable growth and development. The following authentic challenge requires you to put your learning to effective use.

YOUR TASK

As a promising economic thinker, you are asked to assume the role of social advocate by your employer, a foundation that promotes public policy alternatives. You are required to produce a seven- to ten-minute informative video or podcast that advocates for the most appropriate role of government in the Canadian economy. The video or podcast must be designed as an "Economics in the News" segment for local news broadcasts, dealing with issues arising from each of these five topics:

- **Government spending and taxation** (for example, Should deficit financing be promoted, discouraged, or made illegal? Should penalties be increased for participating in the underground economy to avoid taxes?)
- **Regulating competition** (for example, Should mergers, alliances, and business practices be regulated?)
- **Recession, recovery, and full employment** (for example, How much responsibility should government assume for job creation?)
- **Income distribution** (for example, Should an inheritance tax be introduced to redistribute income?)
- **Sustainable development** (for example, Does the pollution credit program require government support or supervision?)

As the producer of the video or podcast, you are required to advocate for the most appropriate role for government, providing your assessment to an audience with a limited background in economics. Your video or podcast must be informative and persuasive; be interesting enough to be broadcast by several news outlets; and be persuasive enough to influence thinking about public policy alternatives. To confirm success, your boss expects to see a 10 percent increase in the number of YouTube views, podcast downloads, and/or news outlets picking up the segment, as well as the volume of audience responses.

STEPS AND RECOMMENDATIONS

1   Use economic publications, news reports, expert opinion, and the Internet to research the topic you choose to present. Reflect on the issues to identify policy goals, implications, and required economic trade-offs.

2   Conduct a cost-benefit analysis to determine the most appropriate role of government. When addressing a critical question like this, remember to make a reasoned judgement. That will require appropriate criteria to base your decision and solid evidence to support it.

3   Take a definite position, advocating a specific course of action (or public policy) to address social services, employment levels, citizens with low incomes, and the environment, while promoting such goals as growth and stability, economic freedom, productivity, sustainability, competitiveness, and equity. Keep the language appropriate for an audience with a limited background in economics.

4   Design your presentation to achieve maximum persuasive impact from the chosen medium. Your teacher may provide additional layout and content instructions, and models of high-quality work for your reference.

5   Prepare a convincing presentation to gain support for the position being advocated.

ADAPTING THE TASK

To capitalize on your personal skills, consider creating a web page that a related foundation can add to its website to inform public policy and invite feedback from citizens. Alternatively, you might produce a position paper or public information pamphlet to be presented at the foundation's next policy conference. Search websites of organizations that influence policy-making to find examples of the direction (medium and strategy) that your work might take. Share drafts with your teacher, classmates, and parents or guardians for useful feedback.

ASSESSMENT CRITERIA

The following criteria will be used to assess your work:

- **Knowledge:** accurately using appropriate economic terms, concepts, principles, and supporting data
- **Thinking and Inquiry:** locating and assessing information from a variety of reliable sources; using sound economic reasoning and thorough analysis to explain the impact of policy on economic goals
- **Communication:** properly using language and style conventions to support the chosen medium and presentation format and strategy; presenting economic information and analysis clearly
- **Application:** effectively applying cost-benefit analysis to support the position taken; building and presenting a persuasive and economically sound argument

Use the rubric provided by your teacher as a coaching tool to help complete this task successfully.

Unit 6
The Global Economy

Canadians sell a large amount of goods and services to buyers around the world and are dependent on goods and services bought from other countries. International trade (also known as *global trade*) is the exchange of goods and services between countries. These transactions are conducted between individuals, companies, government organizations, or even non-profits located in different countries. As a result of international trade, Canadians can choose from a wider variety of products, and Canadian businesses can access new markets and expand, have greater opportunities to attract capital investment, and share in the discoveries made by other countries.

Since the Second World War, countries addressed the movement of goods and services by pursuing open, freer trade. Many worldwide trade agreements exist and focus on reducing or eliminating trade barriers, establishing more open terms of trade, and encouraging foreign investment. Although international trade has many positive effects, nationalist movements across Europe, the United States, and other countries argue that globalization is failing and attempt to reverse this trend by renegotiating trade agreements and reducing or restricting free trade. In this unit, you will learn about Canada's role in the global economy, look at the role of currency exchange rates in trade, and consider the issues surrounding international trade and the global economy.

How are people's lives affected by international trade?

As you read this chapter, consider the following questions:

- What evidence of international trade can you find in your home? In your school? In your community? How has technology connected people globally?

- How important are imports to your lifestyle? How would your shopping habits change if you were to buy only Canadian-made products?

- What do you think would happen if everyone in the world only purchased domestic products?

- How does international trade impact your leisure and entertainment choices (travel, music, movies, and sports)?

- What current issues have you read or heard about in the media that relate to international trade?

LOOKING AHEAD ⟶

The performance task at the end of this unit will require you to investigate the inquiry question above. It provides an opportunity for you to:

- Assume the role of an adviser to Canada's minister of international trade

- Apply economic knowledge and skills to provide an analysis and recommendation on a new free trade agreement

- Conduct online research on country-specific data, trade profiles, and tariffs

- Use a performance task rubric and feedback to prepare a high-quality case study

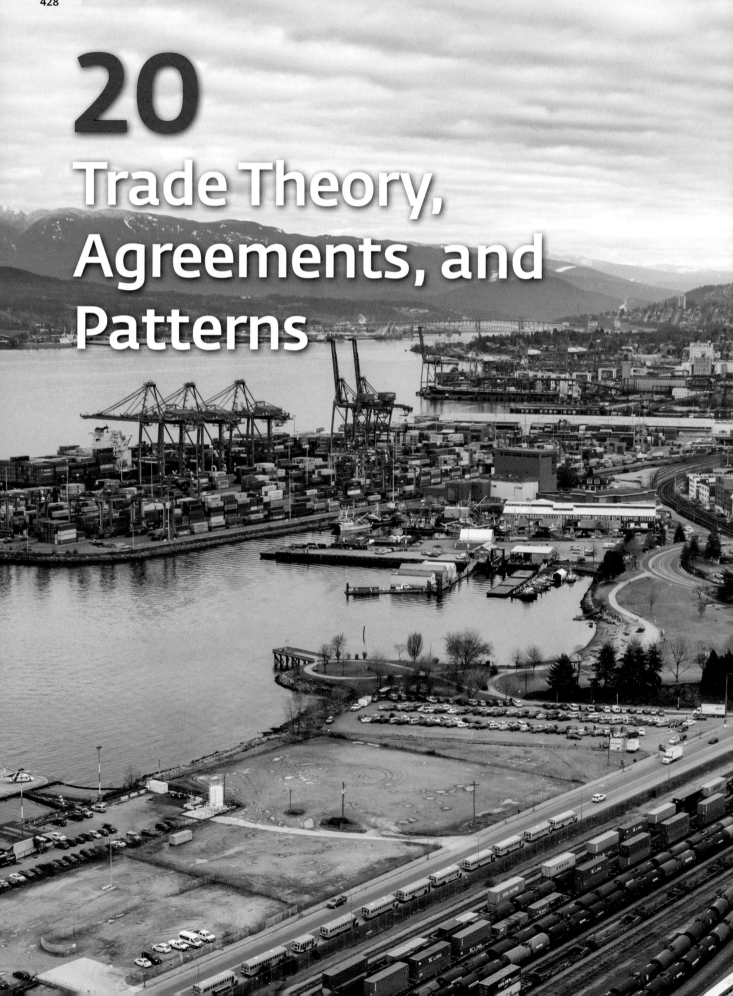

20
Trade Theory, Agreements, and Patterns

INTRODUCTION

Signs of international trade are everywhere. Just look around and you will see how this is true. What did you to wear today? There is a good chance your clothing was made in India, China, or Bangladesh. The new smartphone you just bought? Probably made somewhere in Asia. What about the plastic and metal in a computer? It's likely that the copper was mined in South America and the oil used for making the plastic came from the Middle East. What was the last meal you ate? If you had coffee this morning, the beans probably came from a country in South America (perhaps Colombia or Brazil). The oranges and orange juice you enjoyed? Likely from the United States, either Florida or California. Throughout history, individuals, groups, and countries have traded. Why do people trade? They trade to get the goods they do not have in exchange for the goods they have. Buying, selling, or exchanging goods and services is known as *trade*.

KEY TERMS

international trade

globalization

absolute advantage

comparative advantage

protectionism

dumping

terms of trade

tariff

subsidy

sanctions

embargo

quota

General Agreement on Tariffs and Trade (GATT)

World Trade Organization (WTO)

multilateral

WTO Dispute Settlement Body

trading bloc

North American Free Trade Agreement (NAFTA)

free trade area

United States-Mexico-Canada Agreement (USMCA)

customs union

common market

Canada-US Automotive Products Trade Agreement (or Auto Pact)

Free Trade Agreement (FTA)

intellectual property rights

Asia-Pacific Economic Cooperation (APEC)

Comprehensive and Progressive Agreement for Trans-Pacific Partnership (CPTPP)

Reciprocity Treaty

National Policy

merchandise trade (or visible trade)

non-merchandise trade (or invisible trade)

balance of merchandise trade

trade surplus

trade deficit

LEARNING GOALS

Once you have completed this chapter, you should be able to:

- Explain the benefits of specialization and international trade, using the concepts of absolute and comparative advantage

- Analyze the costs and benefits to Canadian stakeholders and to the Canadian economy of the global trend toward freer international trade

- Describe the nature and role of the World Trade Organization as an international institution

- Explain the nature of the North American Free Trade Agreement and assess its impact on Canadian stakeholders and the Canadian economy

- Apply economic inquiry to an analysis of public policy issues arising from Canadian trade policy

international trade
The exchange of goods or services across international borders.

DID YOU KNOW?

Freer trade can promote peace between countries. Many economists believe that freer trade can help nations foster peace and avoiding conflict. Why? Trade is a mutually beneficial relationship that is a human activity; businesses from both countries have an incentive to maintain goodwill with one another. Conversely, protectionism (such as tariffs and quotas) can increase hostility between countries. An increase in tariffs by one country is usually met with retaliation of tariffs in return; increasing tensions as seen in 2018 with a "trade war" between the U.S. and China.

Trade Theory

Throughout history, countries have traded with one another, selling some of their surplus products and buying other products that they needed. Today, **international trade** is more important than ever and continues to grow rapidly. International trade is absolutely essential in Canada's economy to maintain the lifestyles enjoyed by Canadians. The value (and volume) of international trade continues to grow each year, as Figure 20.1 shows.

Why do countries prefer to trade instead of attempting to become more self-sufficient? Why do they prefer to rely on other countries for certain goods and services instead of developing domestic industries to provide those same goods and services?

Countries buy goods from other countries for the same reasons that individuals buy from other individuals. No single person can afford to be totally self-sufficient. The economic costs would be too great. A person cannot independently produce all the food, clothing, construction materials, machines, medicines, entertainment, and information systems that are needed. Your productivity—and, therefore, your standard of living—is much higher if you can specialize in what you do best and buy the rest of what you need from others who are specialists at what they do. Everyone's needs are more efficiently met through this specialized environment.

In this way, trade allows industries (and countries) to specialize, thus achieving greater economic efficiency. This improved productivity, along with the benefits of operating at a larger scale, usually improves market prices and living

FIGURE 20.1
The value of Canada's trade in goods, from November 2013 to November 2018

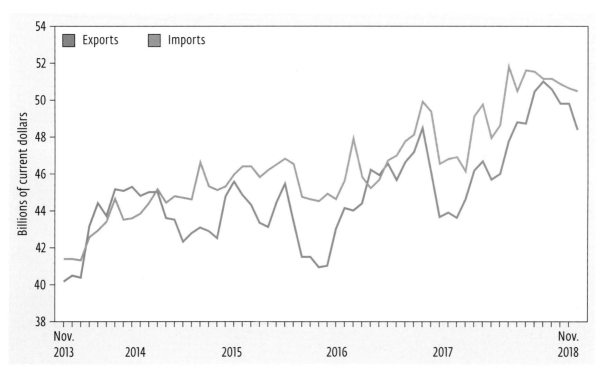

standards for people in both the importing and the exporting countries. The trend toward increased international trade and investment flows are all part of an economic trend known as globalization. **Globalization** is a process whereby national or regional economies become integrated through new global communication technologies, foreign direct investment, international trade, immigration, and the flow of money. One reason globalization has occurred is that trade barriers across national borders have been reduced or removed. In recent times, globalization is seen as freer trade across borders. The pace of globalization has increased dramatically because of several changes that have taken place within the past few decades.

TRADE BENEFITS ALL PARTIES

One of the important economic principles of international trade is that both buyer and seller benefit from the transaction. Specialization is often identified as the most important mutual benefit from international trade. There are clear economic advantages in allowing countries to concentrate their industrial activity on the mass production of goods for which they have the necessary resources and the ability to use them most efficiently. However, to understand the economic benefits of international trade, we need to examine absolute and comparative advantage, concepts that were introduced in Chapter 5.

Absolute Advantage

One country has an **absolute advantage** if it makes a product or service more productively than other countries. The country manufactures more products with the same amount of resources. The country with an absolute advantage has better technology or labour, or higher-quality resources. For example, it can be said that Zambia has an absolute advantage in producing copper, and that Canada has an absolute advantage in producing forest products. Countries export products or services in which they have an absolute advantage, and they import products or services in which other countries have an absolute advantage.

The concept of absolute advantage can easily be presented through the following hypothetical situation. Assume that there are only two countries in the world: Canada and the United States. They can each produce apples and peaches, but if each country uses half of its resources to produce each product, they produce different amounts. This scenario is illustrated in Figure 20.2.

Generally, it makes more sense for each country to specialize in products in which they have an absolute advantage. In this example, each country would make twice as much of the product in which it has an absolute advantage and none of the other product. This scenario can be seen in Figure 20.3.

Notice the difference in totals? Overall, more apples and peaches are produced in the second scenario. Canada has an absolute advantage in apples,; the United States has an absolute advantage in peaches.

globalization
A process whereby national or regional economies become integrated through communication technologies, foreign direct investment, international trade, immigration, and the flow of money.

absolute advantage
The capacity of one economy to produce a good or service with fewer resources than another.

FIGURE 20.2
Each country uses its resources to produce two products

Country	Apples	Peaches
Canada	1 000	600
United States	800	1 400
Total	1 800	2 000

FIGURE 20.3
Each country specializes in one product

Country	Apples	Peaches
Canada	2 000	0
United States	0	2 800
Total	2 000	2 800

comparative advantage
The capacity of one economy to produce a good or service with comparatively fewer resources than another (for example, having a lower opportunity cost).

Comparative Advantage

Let's now complicate our model to see if specialization and trade continue to provide similar economic benefits when one country has an absolute advantage in the production of both goods being traded. Surprisingly, the answer is still yes. To understand why, we must explore the concept of **comparative advantage**, first outlined by David Ricardo (see Chapter 5) almost 200 years ago. To put it succinctly, even if one country has an absolute advantage in every field of production, it will likely hold a greater advantage in some fields than in others. These differences in relative efficiencies, or comparative advantage, are all that is required to make specialization and trade economically beneficial for individuals, regions, and countries.

In Figure 20.4, the United States is shown to have an absolute advantage in producing both apples and peaches. To understand whether Canada and the United States should trade in this example, we need to revisit the concept of opportunity cost (see Chapter 2), and then apply it to the production of apples and peaches. Remember that opportunity cost is the cost of giving something up to get something else. For example, if you put all your money, energy, and resources into producing one product, you must give up producing its alternative. The same goes for consumption.

FIGURE 20.4
Absolute advantage of the United States in producing both apples and peaches

Country	Apples	Peaches
Canada	1 000	500
United States	1 200	800
Total	2 200	1 300

Applying the concept of opportunity cost to trade, let's look at how efficient each country is at producing each fruit, based on the scenario in Figure 20.4, beginning with peaches:

- In Canada, 1 peach costs 1 000 ÷ 500 = 2 apples
- In the United States, 1 peach costs 1 200 ÷ 800 = 1.5 apples

As you can see, the opportunity cost of peaches—giving up the alternative of producing apples—is lowest in the United States; therefore, the United States should produce peaches.

Now let's look at apples:

- In Canada, 1 apple costs 500 ÷ 1 000 = 0.5 peaches
- In the United States, 1 apple costs 800 ÷ 1 200 = 0.667 peaches

As you can see, the opportunity cost of apples—giving up the alternative of producing peaches—is lowest in Canada; therefore, Canada should produce apples.

In this example, Canada has a comparative advantage in apples, and the United States has a comparative advantage in peaches. A country can be said to have a comparative advantage over another when it can produce a good or service at a lower opportunity cost.

Continuing with our hypothetical situation, Figure 20.5 shows what would happen if Canada and the United States each specialized in the fruit for which they have a comparative advantage. From this, you can see that trade is advantageous. Why? Because the total number of apples and peaches has increased (3 600 total fruit by specializing, compared with the 3 500 in Figure 20.4). Canada and the United States together have given up 200 apples to gain 300 peaches.

Production in both countries can also be adjusted so that no apples are lost (see Figure 20.6). If the countries traded after specializing, the same number of apples would be produced as before (Figure 20.4), and 167 peaches would still be gained.

Comparative advantage is the foundation for specialization and trade. If countries produce items in which they have a comparative advantage and import from other countries the products in which those other countries have a comparative advantage, both countries benefit. The lessons from absolute and comparative advantage are general and simplistic; however, they can be applied to the real world. Although international trade involves millions of products and many countries, the study of absolute and comparative advantage demonstrates that trade is beneficial to all countries.

Clearly, the productive efficiency of both countries has been improved by specialization and trade. As a result, more apples and more peaches are available each month to consumers in both trading countries. Over time, it is likely that the quality and price of both products will also improve as a result of specialization and trade.

FIGURE 20.5
Canada and the United States specialize and trade

Country	Apples	Peaches
Canada	2 000	0
United States	0	1 600
Total	**2 000**	**1 600**

FIGURE 20.6
Adjustments

Country	Apples	Peaches
Canada	2 000	0
United States	200	1 467*
Total	**2 200**	**1 467**

*The opportunity cost for the United States to produce 200 apples is 133 peaches (recall: 1 apple costs 0.667 peaches), which are then subtracted from 1 600 for an adjusted total of 1 467.

Canada often finds its comparative advantage in industries that extract and process natural resources, like this potash mine in Belle Plaine, Saskatchewan.

protectionism
An economic policy that aims to restrict imports through tariffs, quotas, and regulations in an effort to boost domestic industry.

dumping
The deliberate practice of selling a product internationally at a price lower than its domestic price.

Protectionism and Trade Barriers

Even though the gains from trade normally benefit both trading partners, historically, arguments have been made for the restriction of trade. **Protectionism** is an economic policy that aims to restrict imports through tariffs, quotas, and regulations in an effort to boost domestic industry. Protectionist arguments usually focus on the protection of domestic industries from foreign competition and on the protection of the domestic economy from foreign influence and control.

ECONOMIC ARGUMENTS

The following economic arguments are sometimes used to support a country's policies restricting international trade.

- *Protection of domestic employment*. When a country imports goods and services, it is simultaneously providing employment opportunities for foreign industry. Importing goods, without increasing exports, results in the exporting of jobs.

   As imports flow into a country, money must flow out to pay for them. The demand for domestic products is diminished, and production levels are reduced. Lower demand and production can slow down economic growth and create unemployment. Conversely, a reduction in the level of imports can stimulate economic activity in a country and provide more jobs for domestic workers, at the expense of foreign workers.

- *Retaliation.* When a trading partner adopts a strategy of import reduction to combat domestic unemployment, it is effectively exporting some of its unemployment to the other country's economy. This other country may try to recapture some of the lost jobs by imposing new import restrictions of its own. This retaliation generally leaves both partners worse off by reducing the benefits of specialization and trade. However, each country tries to punish the other more than it will suffer itself. Domestic producers often argue that we should not let foreign goods into our country if our goods are excluded from their markets. This, too, is a retaliatory argument.

- *Protection against dumping.* Sometimes foreign competitors attempt to dump production surpluses abroad to protect domestic prices. **Dumping** refers to the deliberate practice of selling a product abroad at a price lower than the domestic price. For example, a shirt that sells for the equivalent of $100 in the country in which it was made might be sold to foreign buyers for $50 to unload large quantities of stock without affecting the $100 selling price at home. Dumping makes it very difficult for shirt producers in the second country to compete. They may not be able to sell their shirts for $50 without incurring heavy losses. Trade restrictions can help reduce the frequency and limit the impact of dumping.

- *Diversification.* Trade restrictions can help to diversify an economy whose prosperity is closely tied to the export of a few products or to trade with a single country. Relying on a few export products or on a single trading partner can leave an economy vulnerable to market fluctuations abroad. Trade restrictions allow for the development of new domestic industries and export markets. The more a national economy is diversified, the more self-sufficient it will be in times of conflict or crisis.

- *Protection of "vital" industries.* Trade restrictions can also be used to protect national security and public health. For example, the uncontrolled export of military equipment, biotechnology, and nuclear technology can compromise national and global security if these resources fall into the wrong hands.

- *Protection of developing industries.* Trade restrictions can be used to protect developing, or "infant," industries from foreign competition. Because of their recent origin and small size, newer domestic industries may lack the efficiency and economies of scale needed to compete head to head with established foreign producers.

- *Improvement of terms of trade.* When a country's volume of trade is large enough to affect global markets, it can use trade restrictions to improve its terms of trade. For example, by restricting its exports of petroleum, the world's largest oil-exporting country could affect the global market price for crude oil by producing a supply shortage. By imposing restrictions on its imports, the world's largest importer of newsprint could decrease the global demand for that product enough to lower the market price. On a smaller scale, trading partners can impose temporary trade restrictions to help negotiate more favourable terms of trade.

- *Protection of environmental and safety standards.* To protect workers and the natural environment, many governments impose industrial standards. However, these standards vary greatly. When a country imposes high standards, the result is increased production costs for domestic industries. These increased costs are generally passed on to consumers in the form of higher prices. Countries with lower environmental and safety standards effectively reduce the operating expenses and product prices of domestic industries. In a global economy, firms may choose to relocate to countries with lower environmental and safety standards to gain a competitive advantage and to improve profits.

- *Protection from foreign influence and control.* Trade restrictions can be used to protect key domestic industries from foreign control. Various Canadian laws restrict or limit foreign ownership in different industries in Canada. The federal Broadcasting Act restricts broadcasting licences to non-Canadians or to companies that are owned or controlled by non-Canadians. Other industries where foreign investment is regulated or restricted by the Canadian government include telecommunications, banking, oil and gas, farming, and book publishing.

DID YOU KNOW?

In 2018, the United States imposed tariffs on billions of dollars of imports from many of its trading partners, including Canada, Mexico, the European Union (EU), and China. The United States claimed that these tariffs were in defence of national security, though many critics pointed out that it was an effort to reduce the supply of steel on the world market.

In response, countries including Canada retaliated by imposing tariffs of their own on a proportional (equal dollar) value of US exports. The EU retaliated with tariffs on US products such as motorcycles, denim, cigarettes, and orange juice. Some of the countries filed legal challenges with the World Trade Organization (WTO). The result was the largest trade war in history.

Thinking like an Economist

Working with Absolute and Comparative Advantage

Economists use the concept of comparative advantage to determine the benefits of specialization and trade among countries. Calculations involving opportunity costs to determine the most appropriate specializations and the **terms of trade** can help quantify these mutual benefits.

Figure 20.7 indicates the amounts of steel and copper that can be produced in the countries of Arcticona and Tropicona, using 1 000 hours of labour. Refer to the data in this table to answer the questions that follow.

FIGURE 20.7
Production opportunities with 1 000 hours of labour

Country	Steel Production (tonnes)	Copper Production (tonnes)
Arcticona	4	10
Tropicona	3	2

terms of trade
The rate at which a country's exports are exchanged for its imports.

APPLYING ECONOMIC THINKING

1   Which country has an absolute advantage in steel production and which in copper production?

2   Calculate the opportunity cost of each product in each country. Explain your calculations.

3   Which country has a comparative advantage in the production of steel? Explain.

4   Which country has a comparative advantage in the production of copper? Explain.

5   Assume that each country has 4 000 labour hours to use each month and, without trade, each country would use half of its labour in the production of each good. Produce a set of tables similar to Figures 20.2 and 20.3 to prove that the two countries would benefit from specialization and trade. Support your conclusions by explaining your calculations.

6   Explain how the two countries can co-operate to correct a simultaneous shortage of steel and a surplus of copper. Produce a revised total production table to show this correction, similar to Figure 20.6.

7   Arcticona and Tropicona have an economic incentive to maintain peaceful relations. Explain why.

BARRIERS TO TRADE

There are many arguments in favour of restricting trade, but, generally speaking, at the heart of most arguments is the trade-off between global economic efficiency and the political and economic pursuits of a country. International trade is restricted by various barriers outlined in Figure 20.8.

FIGURE 20.8
Barriers to trade

Barrier	Description
Tariffs, or import duties	**Tariffs** are special taxes imposed on certain imported goods. They act to control import levels by making imported goods more expensive to consumers. Generally, as tariffs are increased, the quantity of imports decreases. Tariffs are also used by governments to generate revenue.
Subsidies	**Subsidies** are government payments made to producers to stimulate economic activity and to protect jobs. In subsidized markets, the price that producers receive is more than the price that consumers actually pay for the product. Subsidies for agricultural commodities, softwood lumber, and aircraft construction have been challenged on the grounds of fairness and efficiency.
Transportation costs	Increases in **transportation costs** tend to make imports more expensive. Generally, as these costs increase, the quantity of imports decreases.
Export taxes	Governments can levy a tax on exports to control the goods leaving the country. **Export taxes** generally make exports more expensive and, therefore, less desirable.
Voluntary export restraints	A country's government may negotiate to persuade an exporter to limit voluntarily the amount of a product being sold in the country. Administrative delays, health and safety standards, and licence requirements can be used to pressure exporters into accepting voluntary export restraints. In 1986, the Canadian government used administrative delays to tie up Japanese cars in the Port of Vancouver to help "persuade" Japanese manufacturers to accept export restraints and to produce more cars in Canada to protect Canadian jobs.
Trade sanctions and embargoes	Governments may impose trade **sanctions** on a country whose political practices are unacceptable. Sanctions effectively stop or severely curtail trade with the offending country. For example, Canada and many other countries imposed trade sanctions on South Africa until the government renounced its policy of apartheid. (This policy favoured a select cultural group and oppressed the majority of its citizens.) Trade sanctions are intended to apply economic pressure to bring about political change. In 1973, many Arab oil-exporting countries decided to impose a trade **embargo** on their oil. This decision meant that the oil was not allowed to leave the home port, thus creating a global shortage. The intent was to secure better prices for exports and to demonstrate the advantages of maintaining good relations with the Arab world.
Quotas	Governments can establish **quotas**, or limits, on the total quantity of imports allowed to enter the country. Quotas control the flow of imports and actually reduce the volume of international trade.

tariff
The transfer of part of a firm's production costs (such as cleaning up pollution caused by the release of wastes into the air, soil, or water supply) to the public (the third party).

subsidy
A grant of money from a government to a producer to achieve some desired outcome, such as the installation of pollution-control equipment.

sanctions
Restrictions on trade with one country levied by another for some political purpose.

embargo
An action taken by one country against another for some political purpose to prevent import or export of goods or services.

quota
A restriction placed on the amount of product that domestic producers are allowed to produce; also, a limit on the total quantity of goods imported into a country.

Self-Reflect

1 Why do countries trade?

2 Define *globalization*.

3 Define *protectionism*. Summarize three arguments for restricting international trade.

4 What are some key industries protected by the Canadian government from foreign control?

General Agreement on Tariffs and Trade (GATT)

An international trade agreement signed by 23 countries, including Canada, in 1947. It was designed to reduce trade barriers among member countries.

World Trade Organization (WTO)

The successor (in 1995) to the General Agreement on Tariffs and Trade (GATT); the WTO has expanded and strengthened the procedures for reducing trade barriers.

multilateral

Pertaining to many countries, as an agreement reached among many countries.

WTO Dispute Settlement Body

A mechanism for settling a trade dispute between two or more countries; it involves setting up expert panels to arrive at a decision.

The WTO headquarters are located in Geneva, Switzerland.

Major International Trade Agreements

GENERAL AGREEMENT ON TARIFFS AND TRADE

Since the global failure of protectionist trade policies during the 1930s, the prevailing trend has been to liberalize trade through a general reduction in tariffs. In 1947, as the international community attempted to build a lasting peace in the aftermath of a destructive war, Canada, the United States, and 21 other countries (representing well over 90 percent of the world's trade) signed the **General Agreement on Tariffs and Trade (GATT)**. This international agreement was designed to reduce trade barriers among member countries. Tariffs in member countries fell from an average of 40 percent in 1947 to an average of 5 percent in 1988, while the volume of international merchandise trade multiplied 20-fold. The **World Trade Organization (WTO)** institutionalized, strengthened, expanded, and ultimately replaced the GATT in 1995.

World Trade Organization

The most inclusive, sustained, and successful **multilateral** negotiations to promote global trade were the eight rounds of GATT meetings that eventually culminated with the establishment of the international institution known as the World Trade Organization (WTO) on January 1, 1995.

The WTO promotes trade liberalization (easing trade restrictions) throughout the world. Economic prosperity and social development are at the heart of the WTO. It has 164 member countries, and its decisions are made by consensus. The WTO is involved in the following five activities:

- **Trade negotiations.** The WTO is a place where countries can discuss their trade disparities and come to mutually agreeable solutions.

- **Implementation and monitoring.** The WTO regularly monitors whether WTO agreements have been adopted and properly implemented.

- **Dispute settlement.** The **WTO Dispute Settlement Body** is a forum for countries to consult, mediate, and arbitrate discrepancies in how countries have interpreted their trade agreements.

- **Building trade capacity.** The WTO supports developing countries with trade through skills development, training, and aid for the infrastructure needed for trade.

- **Outreach.** The WTO engages with various international organizations, the general public, and the media to build awareness about WTO activities.

REGIONAL TRADE AGREEMENTS

A *trade agreement* is an enforceable treaty between two or more countries that addresses the movement of goods and services, eliminates trade barriers, establishes terms of trade, and encourages foreign investment.

Given the increased number of countries participating in recent WTO talks, the negotiation process has become far more complex. Some observers believe that the new trend may be toward more specialized regional trade agreements, such as the Free Trade Agreement between Canada, Mexico, and the United States. These regional agreements, negotiated outside of the WTO, are known as **trading blocs**. The WTO recognizes these regional initiatives as complements (rather than alternatives) in the pursuit of more open trade. There are presently three types of trading blocs: free trade areas, customs unions, and common markets.

The **North American Free Trade Agreement (NAFTA)**, which came into effect in 1994, established a **free trade area** that includes the countries of Canada, Mexico, and the United States. Over the 25 years of its existence, NAFTA more than doubled Canada's total merchandise trade with the United States. In 2018, NAFTA was renegotiated and updated for the modern economy and became known as the **United States-Mexico-Canada Agreement (USMCA)**.

A **customs union** represents a stronger degree of regional integration. This type of regional trade agreement includes not only free trade among its members but also a common set of trade restrictions imposed on the rest of the world. However, restrictions on the movement of capital and workers among member countries remain in force. The 12-member Caribbean Community and Common Market (CARICOM) is an example of a customs union.

A **common market** is the strongest form of regional integration. Common market agreements include the free trade of goods and services within the bloc, the free movement of capital and labour within the bloc, and the imposition of a common set of trade restrictions on non-members. The 28-member European Union (EU) is the largest common market. Since the agreement was signed, trade across European borders has dramatically increased, and the EU has become a trading superpower. In 2016, its gross domestic product (GDP) was the second largest in the world at US$16.4 trillion, according to the World Bank.

EU members are party to a trade agreement encompassing 28 countries in Europe (as of 2018) and a population of almost half a billion people. The EU has its own flag, anthem, and currency. It also has common financial, security, and foreign policies. The purposes of the EU are to promote peace, economic growth, government co-operation, strong bonds between people, political integration, and to ensure that the population can prosper in a safe society. This single market allows labour, goods, services, and investments to flow freely across borders. The agreement eliminates protectionism and allows all governments to purchase goods from each of the EU countries.

trading bloc
Regional trade agreements, such as NAFTA and those of the European Union, negotiated outside the World Trade Organization.

North American Free Trade Agreement (NAFTA)
The 1994 free trade agreement among Canada, the United States, and Mexico.

free trade area
The region encompassing a trade bloc whose member countries have signed a free trade agreement.

United States-Mexico-Canada Agreement (USMCA)
The 2018 free trade agreement between the United States, Mexico, and Canada that was designed to replace NAFTA; it is often referred to as "NAFTA 2.0."

customs union
Extension of a free trade agreement among members to include a common policy on trade restrictions on non-members.

common market
The strongest form of free trade agreement, which includes free movement of labour and capital among members, tariff-free movement of goods, and a common policy on trade restrictions against non-members.

Canada-US Automotive Products Trade Agreement (or Auto Pact)

A 1965 trade agreement between Canada and the US to eliminate tariffs on auto parts and automobiles.

Free Trade Agreement (FTA)

An agreement between two or more countries to eliminate tariffs between them while retaining the right to impose tariffs upon non-members. In 1989, the FTA between Canada and the United States was meant to phase out trade restrictions. It was superseded by NAFTA, which came into force in 1994.

intellectual property rights

Patents for technology, recorded music, and pharmaceutical drugs.

THE ROAD TO THE UNITED STATES-MEXICO-CANADA AGREEMENT

- *Auto Pact, 1965.* Before 1965, a 15 percent tariff was imposed on American automobiles imported into Canada. To avoid the tariff, US automakers opened branch plants in Canada. Given the relatively small size of the domestic market, Canadian plants were unable to benefit from economies of scale. As a result, production was less efficient, car prices were significantly higher, and Canadian auto workers earned less than their American counterparts. The **Canada-US Automotive Products Trade Agreement (or Auto Pact)** was signed in 1965 to establish free trade in automotive vehicles and parts between the two countries. This integration and rationalization of the auto industry increased auto production efficiency in both countries, protected auto industry jobs, increased the wages of Canadian auto workers, and reduced the relative price of automobiles.

- *Free Trade Agreement, 1989.* After the recession of 1982, the rising tide of protectionism in the United States threatened to restrict Canadian exports from its major markets. To improve its access to US markets, the Canadian government negotiated a free trade agreement with its biggest trading partner. The **Free Trade Agreement (FTA)** came into effect on January 1, 1989. As a benefit of this agreement, trade between the partners has increased significantly, but there have also been costs. Workers in some formerly protected industries lost their jobs. Trade theory suggests that, in the long term, jobs lost in declining industries should be replaced by expanded employment opportunities in competitive export industries. Critics argue that an important second cost of free trade is Canada's increased dependence on the US economy and increased US ownership and control of Canadian industries.

- *North American Free Trade Agreement, 1994.* In January 1994, Canada, the United States, and Mexico launched what was at the time the world's largest free trade zone. The North American Free Trade Agreement (NAFTA) set rules surrounding the movement of goods and services, labour, and investments across North America. It eliminated tariffs and other trade barriers, and promoted fair competition among the three countries. **Intellectual property rights**, including patents, copyrights, trademarks, and technical designs, were also protected across the continent. Under NAFTA, goods traded between Canada and the United States became tariff-free on January 1, 1989, while tariffs between Canada and Mexico were eliminated in 2008. NAFTA set an example of mutually beneficial free trade to the rest of the world by being the first comprehensive trade agreement of its type.

- *United States-Mexico-Canada Agreement, 2018.* NAFTA created the world's largest free trade area more than two decades ago. With member economies generating $20.8 trillion, the agreement was hailed by free trade supporters as highly successful. However, opponents claim that globalization does not benefit everyone. The fears of globalization have caused a protectionist movement around the world, as demonstrated by the United States in its notice to Mexico and Canada that it wanted to renegotiate NAFTA.

That notice fulfilled a key election promise from President Donald Trump to renegotiate or tear up the agreement. After more than a year of negotiations between its member countries, an updated NAFTA—called the United States-Mexico-Canada Agreement (USMCA)—was announced, and the agreement was modernized after more than 25 years in existence.

CANADA'S KEY TRADE AGREEMENTS WITH THE ASIA-PACIFIC REGION

- *Asia-Pacific Economic Cooperation, 1989.* **Asia-Pacific Economic Cooperation (APEC)**, created in 1989, is a trade organization that unites many of the countries surrounding the Pacific Ocean. Its mission is to support economic growth and prosperity in the Asia–Pacific region. APEC's 21 member countries (including Canada) comprised about 2.8 billion people and represented approximately 59 percent of world GDP and 49 percent of global trade in 2015. APEC is not established by treaties, but is based on consensus, and commitments are voluntary.

  APEC's goals are to foster open and free trade among its members, increase prosperity and economic growth, and develop the Asia–Pacific community. APEC's work focuses on its three pillars: trade and investment liberalization, business facilitation, and economic and technical co-operation. Beyond trade, APEC also discusses climate change, security and terrorism, global economic success and integration, and emergency preparedness. The organization has decreased tariffs and trade barriers among its members, which has caused a dramatic increase in exports. Since APEC was created, trade among participating members has increased significantly.

  As a result of APEC's work, growth has soared in the region, with real GDP increasing from US$16 trillion in 1989 to US$20 trillion in 2015. As a result, residents of the Asia–Pacific area experienced a per capita income increase of 74 percent, bringing millions out of poverty and creating a growing middle class in just over two decades.

- *Comprehensive and Progressive Agreement for Trans-Pacific Partnership, 2018.* Canada was involved in the Trans-Pacific Partnership (TPP) trade deal, a free trade agreement among 12 countries over four continents with a market of 800 million people. The combined GDP of these countries accounted for 40 percent of the world's economy at the time of its first signing in 2016. The TPP was a key issue in the US presidential election of 2016, and in January 2017 the United States withdrew from the TPP. Since that time, the remaining 11 countries moved ahead without the United States, and the deal has been renamed the **Comprehensive and Progressive Agreement for Trans-Pacific Partnership (CPTPP)**. On December 30, 2018, the CPTPP entered into force among the six countries (including Canada) that have ratified it so far.

Asia-Pacific Economic Cooperation (APEC)

A regional forum established in 1989, mainly of Pacific rim countries, that promotes free trade among its members.

Comprehensive and Progressive Agreement for Trans-Pacific Partnership (CPTPP)

A new free trade agreement including Canada and 10 other countries. The CPTPP will be one of the largest free trade agreements in the world once it is ratified by all member countries.

Self-Reflect

1 What is a trade agreement?

2 What are the five main activities of the WTO?

3 How did NAFTA impact trade between Canada, the United States, and Mexico?

4 What effect has APEC's work had on its member countries?

Reciprocity Treaty
A free trade agreement between British North America and the United States, lasting from 1854 to 1866.

National Policy
A policy of tariff protection for Canadian industry, linked to railroad building and western settlement, that was launched by the Conservative government of Sir John A. Macdonald in 1879.

Canadian Trade Policies and Patterns

DEVELOPMENT OF CANADIAN TRADE POLICY

During the past 150 years, trade restrictions (most often occurring in the form of protective tariffs) have generally decreased globally, with a few notable exceptions. The United States has greatly influenced the evolution of Canada's national trade policy—not surprising given its historic role as our country's major trading partner.

- *Reciprocity Treaty.* In 1854, the British and US governments signed the **Reciprocity Treaty**. This established a qualified free trade relationship between what was then called British North America and the United States. By 1866, this reciprocal trade agreement had fallen victim to political and economic pressures. As a result, it was cancelled, and trade tariffs rose sharply prior to and immediately after Confederation in 1867.

- *National Policy.* In 1879, Canada's first prime minister, Sir John A. Macdonald, succeeded in passing the **National Policy** into law. Creating a "tariff wall," the National Policy persuaded many US manufacturers to open branch plants on the Canadian side of the border so that they could continue selling in Canadian markets without facing tariffs. Tariff rates peaked around 1890, after which the prevailing trend was to slowly reduce trade tariffs. This liberalizing trend was primarily driven by the general economic prosperity of the times and lasted into the 1930s.

- *The Great Depression and Second World War.* During the Great Depression of the 1930s, Canada attempted to combat rising domestic unemployment by raising protective tariffs. Governments in most industrialized countries increased tariffs, partially to stimulate domestic employment and partially to retaliate against restrictions imposed on their products in foreign markets. In the end, this general decline in international trade hurt the economies of all industrialized countries.

By 1939, the economic crisis of the Great Depression had been effectively addressed. In most industrialized countries, Canada included, tariff rates had been once again reduced to promote higher levels of international trade. With the outbreak of the Second World War in 1939, international trade was once again adversely affected. Canadian tariff rates were quickly increased during the early 1940s.

The idea of globalization began to gain prominence when representatives from many countries met at the Bretton Woods Conference in July 1944. The conference established stable currency exchange systems and free trade. It laid the foundations for the International Monetary Fund (IMF) and the International Bank for Reconstruction and Development (now called the World Bank). In subsequent years, a variety of other trade organizations were formed. These trade organizations led to a series of trade agreements throughout the world.

TRADE PATTERNS

To understand the magnitude and scope of international transactions, we need to clarify further the terminology of trade. Goods that are grown, extracted, or manufactured in one country and sold to another form part of the global **merchandise trade**. Merchandise trade is also referred to as **visible trade** because of the tangible nature of the goods being transacted. The exchange of services, tourism, investment incomes, and other transfers of funds is known as **non-merchandise trade** (also referred to as **invisible trade**). Invisible trade consists of money flows often without tangible products flowing in return. Given its intangible nature, this type of service-based trade is more difficult to document and measure statistically. For example, merchandise imports arriving in Canada from Germany can be easily tracked by government officials. Imports (in the form of both goods and services) bought by Canadian tourists travelling abroad are far more difficult to track.

On a global scale, the volume and value of imports must always equal the volume and value of exports because one country's imports are, automatically, another country's exports. However, for individual countries, the **balance of merchandise trade**—the difference between the value of merchandise exports and merchandise imports—will not necessarily be at equilibrium at any given time. A country is said to have a favourable balance when the value of exports is greater than the value of imports—referred to as a **trade surplus**. A country is said to have an unfavourable balance when imports exceed exports—referred to as a trade **deficit**. Canada's balance of trade from 2008 to 2018 is shown in Figure 20.9.

merchandise trade (or visible trade)
Tangible goods that are grown, extracted, or manufactured.

non-merchandise trade (or invisible trade)
Services, tourism, investment income, and other transfers.

balance of merchandise trade
The difference between a country's merchandise exports and imports.

trade surplus
The amount by which a country's exports exceed its imports.

trade deficit
The amount by which a country's imports exceed its exports.

FIGURE 20.9

Canada's balance of trade, 2008–2018

Canada has run a trade deficit (that is, it imports more than it exports) for most years since 2012. From 2008 to 2009, Canada had a large trade surplus, with exports exceeding imports.

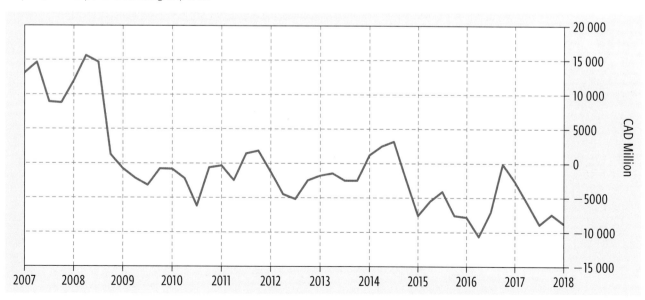

The United States continues to be Canada's largest trading partner, and lumber remains one of Canada's most significant exports.

FIGURE 20.10

Canada's top six merchandise exports and imports, Q3 2018 (in CAD millions)*

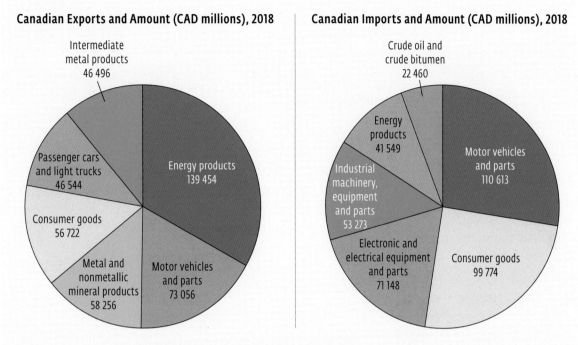

Canadian Exports and Amount (CAD millions), 2018

- Intermediate metal products 46 496
- Passenger cars and light trucks 46 544
- Consumer goods 56 722
- Metal and nonmetallic mineral products 58 256
- Energy products 139 454
- Motor vehicles and parts 73 056

Canadian Imports and Amount (CAD millions), 2018

- Crude oil and crude bitumen 22 460
- Energy products 41 549
- Industrial machinery, equipment and parts 53 273
- Electronic and electrical equipment and parts 71 148
- Motor vehicles and parts 110 613
- Consumer goods 99 774

* Data is accurate as of publication and subject to updating by Statistics Canada.

Figure 20.10 shows Canada's top six merchandise exports and imports for the third quarter of 2018. At the time, Canada's top three merchandise exports were energy products, motor vehicles and parts, and metal and non-metallic mineral products. The top three merchandise imports were motor vehicles and parts, consumer goods, and electronic and electrical equipment and parts.

The United States, with a population of over 320 million, continues to be Canada's largest trading partner. The United States also has the largest consumer market in the world, with consumer spending three times larger than that of China, Canada's second-largest trading partner. The United States still relies on Canada's raw materials, notably oil, lumber, and water. Canada's exports to the United States in 2016 amounted to $392 billion, and our imports from the United States were over $359 billion. Manufacturing jobs have decreased in both Canada and the United States as cheaper labour and improved technology make it more economical to send these manufacturing jobs to Asia and Mexico.

Self-Reflect

1 What is meant by visible and invisible trade?

2 What is a country's balance of merchandise trade?

3 Define *trade surplus* and *trade deficit*.

4 What are Canada's main merchandise exports and imports?

Chapter 20
Consolidation Activities

KNOWLEDGE

1 Define *international trade*.

2 Why is trade important to Canadian businesses?

3 What is a trading bloc? Identify the following as free trade areas, customs unions, or common markets.
   a) European Union (EU)
   b) North American Free Trade Agreement (NAFTA)
   c) Caribbean Community and Common Market (CARICOM)

4 What is the Comprehensive and Progressive Agreement for Trans-Pacific Partnership (CPTPP)? Which country withdrew from membership?

5 What was the Bretton Woods Conference? How did it impact international trade?

6 Which country is Canada's top trading partner? In 2016, did Canada have a trade surplus or a trade deficit with this country?

THINKING & INQUIRY

7 What is a bilateral trade agreement? Using the Internet, search Global Affairs Canada and provide examples of Canada's bilateral trade agreements.

8 Explain the difference between a quota and a tariff. Which do you think would be preferred by governments?

9 Explain dumping as it relates to international trade. How does it impact a domestic business?

10 Consider Canada's trade with the world. What are the main products that are exported? What are the main products that are imported?

11 What is the purpose of the European Union?

COMMUNICATION

12 Explain the following phrase: "Free trade needs to be fair trade."

13 A number of controversial issues surrounded the renegotiation of NAFTA and the creation of the new agreement between its partners Canada, Mexico, and the United States: the USMCA. Research current issues surrounding the USMCA agreement and provide an update on its status. Write a news report to present your findings.

APPLICATION

14 Use Figure 20.11 to answer the following questions:
   a) Which country has the absolute advantage in producing each product?
   b) Which country has a comparative advantage in producing each product? Prove it!
   c) Prove that both countries can benefit from specialization and trade.

FIGURE 20.11
Production opportunities: possible output of snowshoes and running shoes per worker per day

Country	Steel Production (tonnes)	Copper Production (tonnes)
Myopia	8 pairs	5 pairs
Utopia	10 pairs	25 pairs

21

Financing International Trade

INTRODUCTION

The economic systems of the world have become increasingly connected through globalization. For example, Canadians can purchase goods from other countries, spend their income on tourism and services on other countries, and invest in businesses in other countries through foreign direct investment. Likewise, foreigners can enter Canada, enjoy Canadian tourist attractions, and invest in Canadian businesses.

Imagine that you decide to take a trip to an international destination. You purchase an airline ticket, book a hotel room, travel to your destination, eat your meals at a local café, visit nearby attractions, and buy a ticket to a concert. As a Canadian, you have Canadian dollars, yet all of these purchases in the foreign country require a different currency. What makes these transactions possible? Exchange rates play a crucial role in allowing international trade to occur; companies, governments, and consumers purchase goods and services from foreign markets.

This chapter will examine how massive amounts of goods and services flowing in and out of Canada are financed. You will learn the importance of exchange rates, why different currencies complicate trade, how currencies are converted, and how countries track their transactions with other countries.

LEARNING GOALS

Once you have completed this chapter, you should be able to:

- Describe how different currencies complicate trade among countries
- Explain how currencies are converted
- Understand why exchange rates fluctuate
- Compare fixed and flexible exchange rates
- Demonstrate an understanding of Canada's balance of payments

KEY TERMS

export (or receipt)

import (or payment)

exchange rate

appreciation

depreciation

flexible (or floating) exchange rate

fixed exchange rate

devaluation

managed float

balance of payments account

current account

capital and financial account

capital account

inflow

outflow

financial account

direct investment

Canadian direct investment (CDI)

foreign direct investment (FDI)

portfolio investment

official international reserves

statistical discrepancy

export (or receipt)
A good or service that is produced in one country, but sold to consumers, businesses, or governments in another country.

Buying and Selling Internationally

We learned in Chapter 20 how important international trade is to the Canadian economy. Canadian exports account for over one-third of our gross domestic product (GDP), or the total wealth our economy produces in a given year (see Figure 21.1). These exports provide income for Canadians, produce tax revenues for our federal and provincial governments, and pay for our imports.

The major difference between buying and selling internationally and buying and selling domestically, is the need to use different currencies. Exporters demand payment for the goods they sell in their own country's currency. Suppose that a Canadian manufacturer is selling $10 million worth of industrial machinery to an American company. The American importer would have to exchange US dollars for Canadian dollars to complete the sale. If the exchange rate is US$1.00 = CDN$1.30, the importer would pay US$7 692 307 ($10 000 000 ÷ $1.30) to obtain the $10 000 000 necessary to pay the Canadian exporter.

But where would the American bank obtain Canadian funds? Let's suppose that Canadian importers want to buy $10 million worth of fruit from the United States. They would have to exchange CDN$10 000 000 for US$7 692 307 at a Canadian bank to pay the American fruit exporters. The American bank has US dollars and needs Canadian dollars; the Canadian bank has Canadian dollars and needs US dollars. Both banks can meet their customers' needs by getting together and completing a transaction.

In the past, currency exchanges were carried out on a bank-to-bank basis. Today, the bank can obtain foreign currency from the foreign exchange market, which is a computerized global network of banks, investment dealers, and financiers. The conversion of currencies is a service provided for a fee, or *commission*. Note an important point from the example above: when the United States and Canada buy products from one another, each country supplies the currency—its own—that the other country needs.

FIGURE 21.1
Canada's exports as a percentage of GDP, 1960–2017
Why is trade growing in importance to Canada? What has happened to the percentage of Canada's GDP attributed to exports over the past 20 years?

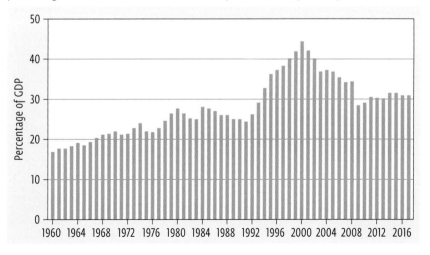

In Chapter 20, we learned that a number of intangible transactions are also defined as either exports or imports. Known as invisible, or non-merchandise, trade, these transactions include exchange of services, tourism, and interest and profits earned abroad—all the payments and receipts made between two countries and that require a conversion of one currency into another. A Canadian **export** (or **receipt**) is defined as an international transaction in which a foreign currency must be converted into Canadian dollars.

A Canadian **import** (or **payment**) is an international transaction in which Canadian dollars must be converted into a foreign currency.

A Canadian tourist visiting Japan is actually considered a Canadian import. The Canadian tourist must convert Canadian dollars into Japanese Yen to pay for hotels, meals, and so on, all of which constitute a Canadian import, or payment. Alternatively, Canadians who earn interest from deposits in foreign banks and convert the interest earned into Canadian dollars are creating Canadian exports, or receipts.

EXCHANGE RATES

An **exchange rate** is defined as the price at which one currency can be purchased for another. The exchange rate of the Canadian dollar is usually expressed in terms of US dollars. For example, the statement "the Canadian dollar is worth 0.75 US dollars" means that CDN$1.00 will obtain US$0.75 in the exchange market.

Another way of looking at the exchange rate of our dollar is to price other currencies in terms of Canadian dollars. For example, the statement "the US dollar is worth 1.30 Canadian dollars" means that US$1.00 will obtain CDN$1.30 in the exchange market.

How Exchange Rates Are Determined

The value of a currency is measured by its price in terms of other currencies. If that price increases, the currency is said to have appreciated in value. For example, if the Canadian dollar rises from US$0.75 to US$0.77, an **appreciation** of the Canadian dollar, in terms of the US dollar, has occurred. A currency depreciates when its price falls in terms of other currencies. In Figure 21.2, we can see that, in terms of the US dollar, the Canadian dollar depreciated from 2011 to late 2015. A dollar **depreciation** occurs when the value of a foreign currency rises in terms of the Canadian dollar.

To understand how these rates are determined, we apply a familiar economic tool—demand and supply analysis—to Canadian exchange rates, assuming that the exchange rates are **flexible**, or **floating** (meaning that they are determined entirely in the market by the forces of demand and supply, with no government intervention).

import (or payment)
A good or service that is purchased by consumers, businesses, or governments that was produced in another country.

exchange rate
The price at which one currency can be purchased with another.

appreciation
An increase in a domestic currency's value in terms of another currency.

depreciation
A decrease in a domestic currency's value in terms of a foreign currency.

flexible (or floating) exchange rate
An exchange rate determined entirely in the market by the forces of demand and supply, with no government intervention.

FIGURE 21.2
The value of the Canadian dollar in relation to the US dollar, 2009–2018
How did the Canadian–US dollar exchange rate change from 2009 to 2018? How do you think this change affected international trade during that time?

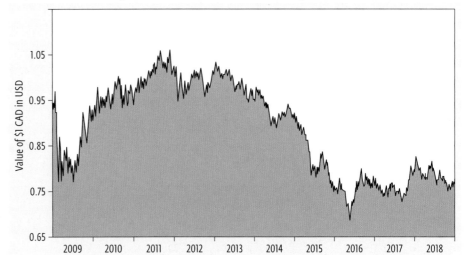

CURRENCY MARKETS

The Demand for Canadian Dollars

Remember that when Canadians export goods or services, we want to receive payment in Canadian dollars. A demand for Canadian dollars is thus created in the foreign exchange market by the foreign importers of our goods or services. Figure 21.3(a) shows the demand for Canadian dollars by US importers.

The vertical axis represents the exchange rate between the US dollar and the Canadian dollar. Note that the dollar appreciates in value as the numbers rise along the vertical axis. The horizontal axis represents the quantity of Canadian dollars demanded by US importers. When the exchange rate falls, or depreciates, US importers demand more dollars because our exports become less expensive to them; in other words, the US dollar "buys" more Canadian dollars.

Dollar depreciation (which, as we have learned, causes the US dollar to appreciate) increases the demand for our exports; thus, the quantity of Canadian dollars demanded will rise as well. If the Canadian dollar appreciates, our exports become more expensive to US importers, so they demand fewer Canadian dollars. Therefore, the demand curve has the familiar inverse, or negative, relationship between the vertical axis (representing the exchange rate) and the horizontal axis (representing the number of dollars demanded). As the Canadian dollar appreciates, fewer Canadian dollars are demanded; as it depreciates, more Canadian dollars are demanded.

FIGURE 21.3

Demand and supply of Canadian dollars

Canadian exports create a demand for Canadian dollars by foreign importers. Foreign imports purchased by Canadians create a supply of Canadian dollars.

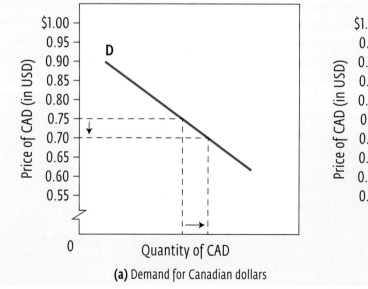

(a) Demand for Canadian dollars

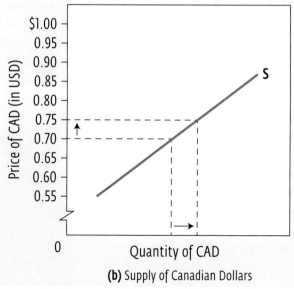

(b) Supply of Canadian Dollars

The Supply of Canadian Dollars

When Canadians import goods and services, we must pay foreign exporters in their own currency. We supply Canadian dollars in the exchange market and demand foreign currency in exchange. The supply curve in Figure 21.3(b) illustrates that when the Canadian dollar appreciates in terms of the US dollar (one Canadian dollar now buys more US dollars), Canadians find that US goods and services are less expensive. By demanding more US dollars to buy these goods and services, Canadians supply more Canadian dollars.

Alternatively, dollar depreciation makes foreign imports more expensive for Canadians; thus, fewer US dollars are demanded and fewer Canadian dollars are supplied. Therefore, the supply curve has the familiar direct, or positive, relationship between the vertical and horizontal axes. As the Canadian dollar appreciates, more Canadian dollars are supplied; as it depreciates, fewer Canadian dollars are supplied.

The Exchange Rate at Equilibrium

The actual exchange rate will be set at the point where the quantity of US dollars demanded equals the quantity of Canadian dollars supplied—that is, where demand and supply are at equilibrium. As shown in Figure 21.4, demand and supply intersect when the value of the Canadian dollar is US$0.75. This graph illustrates that if the exchange rate were set at CDN$1.00 = US$0.80, the supply of Canadian dollars would exceed the demand for them, causing the rate to fall to CDN$1.00 = US$0.75. If the exchange rate were set too low, at CDN$1.00 = US$0.65, the demand for Canadian dollars would exceed the supply of them, causing the exchange rate to rise to CDN$1.00 = US$0.75. Assuming no other forces are operating in this market, the exchange rate moves toward equilibrium at CDN$l.00 = US$0.75. However, other forces are always present, and the exchange rate does change.

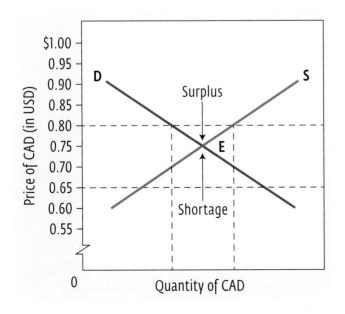

FIGURE 21.4
The exchange rate market equilibrium

If the exchange rate is set too high (for example, CDN$1.00 = US$0.80), the surplus created will cause the exchange rate to fall (depreciate) and return to equilibrium. If the exchange rate is set too low (for example, CDN$1.00 = US$0.65), the shortage created will cause the exchange rate to rise (appreciate) to correct the shortage created.

Thinking like an Economist

A Closer Look at Exchange Rates

CONVERTING CURRENCIES WITH EXCHANGE RATES

Canadians are very conscious of exchange rates, particularly between our country and the United States, because we trade with and travel to the United States extensively. To understand how the prices of goods and services in the United States compare with those in Canada, we need to know how to calculate the value of our dollar in terms of the US dollar.

The exchange rate can be quoted in two ways: the value of one Canadian dollar to the US dollar or the value of one US dollar to the Canadian dollar. Currency can be converted using either exchange rate.

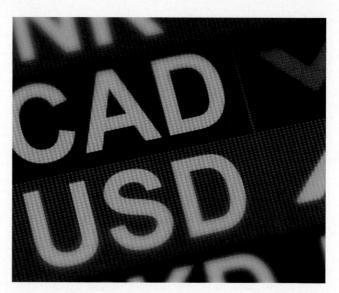

1 Converting currency with an exchange rate quoted in terms of the Canadian dollar—for example, US$1.00 = CDN$1.33:

   a) To convert US dollars into Canadian dollars, multiply the original amount by the exchange rate.

Example: You received a gift of US$150 from an American relative and want to convert it to Canadian dollars. How much Canadian money does this equal?

$$\$150 \times \$1.33 = CDN\$199.50$$

   b) To convert Canadian dollars into US dollars, divide the original amount by the exchange rate.

Example: Your cousin is visiting from Boston and has CDN$100 left over at the end of the visit. How much American money does this equal?

$$\$100 \div \$1.33 = US\$75.18$$

2 Converting currency with an exchange rate quoted in terms of the US dollar—for example, CDN$1.00 = US$0.75:

   a) To convert Canadian dollars into US dollars, multiply the original amount by the exchange rate.

Example: You are planning a short vacation to New York City. You have budgeted CDN$1 000 for your expenses. How much American money does this equal?

$$\$1\,000 \times \$0.75 = US\$750$$

   b) To convert US dollars into Canadian dollars, divide the original amount by the exchange rate.

Example: You have US$150 left over from your US vacation. How much will you receive in Canadian dollars when you exchange this money?

$$\$150 \div \$0.75 = CDN\$200$$

WINNERS AND LOSERS OF A LOW CANADIAN DOLLAR

Exchange rates are important to trade and can affect international businesses in a variety of ways. Canadian trade favours a low dollar because exports leaving Canada are less expensive and, therefore, foreign countries purchase more Canadian goods. There are many winners and losers of a low Canadian dollar.

Winners of a Low Canadian Dollar	Losers of a Low Canadian Dollar
Canadian exporters. It is easier for Canadian exporters to compete when the Canadian dollar is low. Canadian companies selling goods and services to countries with higher currency rates can sell more because of the relative decrease in price.	**Canadian importers.** As consumers, we like a high dollar because it allows us to cross-border shop for good deals. Companies also gain when they purchase US-made equipment, raw materials, and software.
Canadian tourism. Many Americans choose to visit Canada as tourists because a lower Canadian dollar decreases the price of their trip.	**Canadian travellers.** A low Canadian dollar makes it more expensive for Canadians to travel to the United States.
Canadian retailers. Retailers benefit when the Canadian dollar is low because many consumers will decrease their number of cross-border shopping to the United States or reduce online shopping for products from other countries.	**Canadian major league sports teams.** Professional sports teams operating in Canada pay their players in US dollars to entice them to play here. When the Canadian dollar is low, it is more expensive to pay players.

APPLYING ECONOMIC THINKING

1 You have CDN$800 to spend during a beach vacation in Florida. How much in US dollars will you have to spend if the exchange rate is US$1.00 = CDN$1.30?

2 a) A British company wants to invest £5 million in Canadian government bonds. The exchange rate is £1.00 = CDN$1.70. How many dollars' worth of Canadian bonds can the company buy?

   b) The bonds pay the company CDN$200 000 in interest. How much will that convert to in pounds?

3 A tourist travelling in Italy converts CDN$2 000 into euros. How many euros will this tourist be able to spend if the exchange rate is CDN$1.00 = €0.66?

4 How would an appreciation of the Canadian dollar against the US dollar impact the following?

   a) Canadian exporters

   b) Canadian importers

   c) US tourists visiting Canada

CAUSES OF FLUCTUATIONS IN THE EXCHANGE RATE

Up to this point, we have learned how changes in the exchange rate of the Canadian dollar affect our exports and imports. Yet, what causes the exchange rate itself to change? Although economists do not agree on the exact causes of a decline in the exchange rate, let's consider some of the reasons that *usually* explain fluctuations in the exchange rate.

A Change in Demand for Canadian Goods

Figure 21.5 illustrates a rise in Canadian exports as the demand curve moves to the right from D_1 to D_2. Such an increase creates an increased demand for Canadian dollars because Canadian exporters want to be paid in their own currency. The exchange rate rises, or appreciates, from $0.75 to $0.80, where the demand for dollars equals the supply of them. Conversely, a decrease in exports would move the demand curve to the left, causing the exchange rate to fall, or depreciate, as a result of the new equilibrium point. To understand what causes these changes in demand, let's explore two factors:

- ***Canadian exports tend to increase when the economies of our trading partners, particularly the United States, are growing.*** Ultimately, the demand for exports depends, to a large extent, on the economic health of our trading partners. As Canada's trading partners demand more Canadian products, they increase the demand for Canadian dollars in the foreign exchange market. Thus, when the Canadian dollar appreciates, a shift in demand from D_1 to D_2 takes place, as illustrated in Figure 21.5.

- ***Canadian interest rates affect the demand for Canadian dollars.*** If interest rates in Canada rise, Canadian bonds and bank deposits become more attractive to foreign financiers and traders, increasing the demand for Canadian dollars. If Canadian rates fall, the inflow of foreign capital seeking interest rate profits declines, and the demand for the dollar falls.

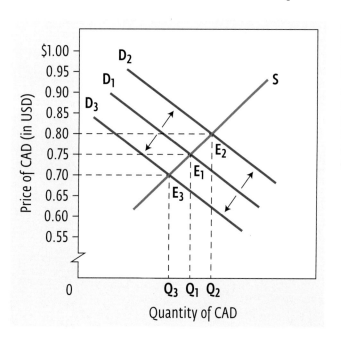

FIGURE 21.5

Exchange rate changes: changes in demand for the Canadian dollar

An increase in demand, from D_1 to D_2, will cause the Canadian dollar to appreciate; a decrease in demand, from D_1 to D_3, will cause the Canadian dollar to depreciate.

A Change in the Supply of Canadian Dollars

Figure 21.6 illustrates a rise in Canada's imports as the supply curve moves to the right from S_1 to S_2. Such an increase creates an increased supply of Canadian dollars and causes the equilibrium point to shift to E_2, where the supply of Canadian dollars equals the demand for them. The value of the dollar has depreciated from $0.75 to $0.70. A decrease in imports would move the supply curve to the left, causing the equilibrium rate (E_3) to rise to $0.80, or to appreciate to the point where supply equals demand. These different equilibrium rates also cause changes in the quantity of Canadian dollars (Q_1, Q_2, Q_3) actually transacted. Imports tend to increase when the Canadian economy is growing and to decrease when it is in recession, similar to the demand for domestic goods.

FIGURE 21.6
Exchange rate changes: changes in supply of the Canadian dollar
An increase in supply, from S_1 to S_2, will cause the Canadian dollar to depreciate; a decrease in supply, from S_1 to S_3, will cause the Canadian dollar to appreciate.

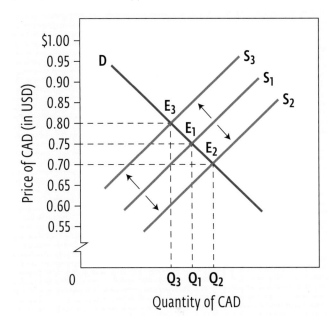

What effect would an economic downturn in the United States have on Canadian exports and the demand for Canadian dollars in the foreign exchange market?

fixed exchange rate

An exchange rate for a currency that is fixed in relation to another currency, such as the US dollar.

devaluation

A depreciation or fall in the exchange value of a currency resulting from intervention on the part of a government or its central bank.

managed float

A policy of allowing a currency's exchange value to be set by the international market, with intervention by the country's central bank from time to time to smooth out fluctuations.

EXCHANGE RATE SYSTEMS

Fixed Exchange Rates

Until the 1970s, most countries had **fixed exchange rates**, meaning that they fixed, or pegged, their exchange rate to the US dollar. To maintain the pegged rate, governments bought or sold their own currencies in the foreign exchange market and kept foreign currencies in special reserve funds.

Suppose that the Canadian dollar were pegged at US$0.75, and, because of a fast-growing US economy, demand for Canadian exports increased. The demand for Canadian dollars would move upward, pressuring the Canadian dollar upward. To prevent the dollar from appreciating beyond its pegged rate of US$0.75, the Bank of Canada would intervene in the exchange market by purchasing US dollars and supplying Canadian dollars. Figure 21.7 illustrates the result, showing the supply curve moving to the right, which causes the exchange rate to move down to its pegged rate.

Conversely, the Canadian dollar could be pressured downward by a fall in exports or by a rise in Canadian imports. Suppose that Canadian imports were rising from S_1 to S_2, as shown in Figure 21.8. To prevent the Canadian dollar from depreciating, the Bank of Canada would have to use the US dollars in its reserve fund to buy Canadian dollars on the foreign exchange market. This purchase would increase the demand for Canadian dollars from D_1 to D_2, restoring the exchange rate to its pegged value of US$0.75. However, if increases in the market demand for dollars were met with equal increases in market supply, the government would not have to intervene to support the pegged value.

Although central banks tried to prevent the **devaluation** or depreciation of their country's currency by using foreign reserves to purchase it, the actions of corporations and individual speculators often nullified the central banks' efforts. For example, if these groups believed that the Canadian dollar was pegged too high, they would cash in their Canadian investments and invest the money in other countries. They were counting on the fact that the amount of money they were moving out would be so large that the Bank of Canada could not possibly buy back Canadian dollars with the limited foreign exchange reserves on hand. If they were proved correct, and the dollar could not be defended at the official rate, the Bank of Canada would be forced to devalue the dollar—in other words, reduce its value in relation to other currencies. The businesses and speculators would then reconvert their investments into Canadian funds at a profit. For this and other reasons, fixed exchange rates were abandoned in 1973.

At this point, it is important to clarify terminology. If a currency loses value in money markets as a result of some government or central bank intervention, this is described as *currency devaluation*. If a currency loses value as a result of the transactions of businesses and speculators, this is described as *currency depreciation*. *Revaluation* and *appreciation* both refer to currency value gains, but they result from different actions.

DID YOU KNOW?

In 2018, Venezuela's economy faced hyperinflation that, according to the International Monetary Fund (IMF), could hit 1 million percent. In response, Venezuela introduced a new currency with five fewer zeroes to replace the country's previous currency, the bolivar. The new currency was pegged or fixed to the country's cryptocurrency, called the *petro*.

FIGURE 21.7
To prevent the Canadian dollar from appreciating beyond a fixed rate of US$0.75, prior to 1973, the Bank of Canada would buy US dollars

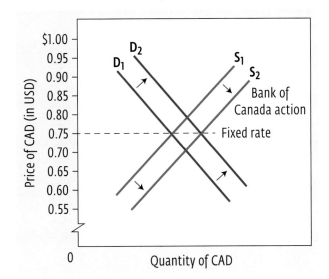

FIGURE 21.8
To prevent the Canadian dollar from depreciating beyond a fixed rate of US$0.75, prior to 1973, the Bank of Canada would buy Canadian dollars

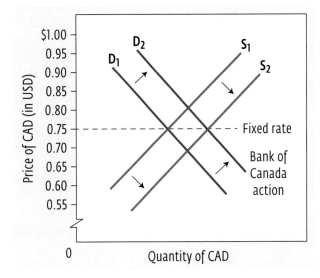

Flexible Exchange Rates

A flexible, or floating, exchange rate is set solely by market forces (demand and supply), without government intervention. Few countries are willing to allow their exchange rate to float without some intervention from time to time. Some countries use a system called a **managed float**, a compromise between flexible and fixed rates.

Under this system, the government allows the international market to set the exchange rate in the long run, as it would under a flexible exchange rate system, but intervenes from time to time to smooth out short-term fluctuations. Under a managed float exchange rate system, the government and/or central bank of a country may decide to intervene in the currency market to adjust the exchange rate in a certain direction.

In Canada, the Bank of Canada allows market forces (supply and demand) to determine the exchange rate for the Canadian dollar (a flexible or floating rate). It uses interest rates to control short-term fluctuations in the exchange rate. If the dollar depreciates, the Bank of Canada can raise interest rates to increase the demand for the dollar; if the dollar appreciates, it can lower interest rates.

Self-Reflect

1 Explain whether each of the following is a Canadian export (receipt) or Canadian import (payment):

a) Canadians increase their travel to Cuba.

b) A Canadian auto parts supplier sells automotive safety equipment to a US auto company.

c) A Canadian investor receives a dividend payment from a South Korean tech company.

2 Indicate whether each of the following would increase the demand for (or the supply of) the Canadian dollar:

a) The US economy experiences record levels of economic growth, with GDP increasing by 4 percent.

b) A protectionist government is elected in the United States, Canada's largest trading partner. As a result, the United States places tariffs on many Canadian industries.

c) The Bank of Canada raises its interest rate as a result of strength in the Canadian economy.

balance of payments account

National account of international payments and receipts, divided into the current account and the capital and financial account.

current account

A bank account for a business that operates like a chequing account, paying little or no interest and serving as a medium of exchange; also, part of a balance of payments account that records totals for three components: goods, services, and investment income.

The Balance of Payments

Countries keep track of their transactions with other countries in their **balance of payments account**. This account is divided into two main parts: the current account, and the capital and financial account.

THE CURRENT ACCOUNT

The **current account** includes three components: goods (or visible trade), services (or invisible trade), and investment income. Goods include raw materials and processed or manufactured goods. Services include tourism; transportation charges for shipping goods by rail, sea, and air; commercial services such as management and consulting; and government assistance to other countries, the United Nations, and other international organizations. Investment income is composed of dividends and interest earned from investments in Canada and abroad.

Figure 21.9 shows the structure of Canada's current account from 2013 to 2018. It indicates whether Canada has a surplus or deficit. In relation to goods, from 2013 to 2018, Canada imported more goods than it exported (except during the first three-quarters of 2014). A deficit balance was recorded for services for all years, which is in line with Canada's international trade record of running a current account deficit for each year since 2009.

Investment income also shows a deficit balance in Figure 21.9. This means that from 2013 to 2018, foreign investors collected more interest and dividends from their investments in Canada than Canadian investors collected from their investments abroad. This investment income deficit is large enough that, when combined with the other two balances on goods and services, Canada usually records a current account deficit. How can a country pay out more than it receives? The answer is found in the capital and financial account, which must record a surplus. Alternatively, if the current account records a surplus, then the capital and financial account must record a deficit.

FIGURE 21.9

The structure of Canada's current account, 2013–2018

Why do you think Canada has a current account deficit?

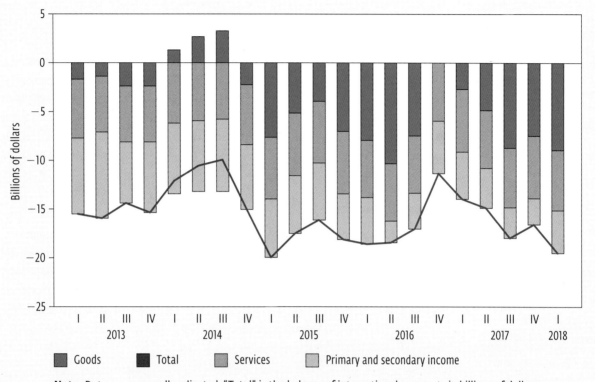

Note: Data are seasonally adjusted. "Total" is the balance of international payments in billions of dollars.

DID YOU KNOW?

For many years, China's currency, the renminbi (referred to often as the yuan) was fixed (pegged) to the US dollar. Officially "unpegged" in 2005, it is now fixed to a basket of currencies, including the US dollar. Many critics point to China's intervention in devaluing its currency (to keep its exports cheap) as a cause of the United States' trade war with China under President Donald Trump, who placed over $50 billion in tariffs on Chinese imports to the United States, as a result of the United States' trade deficit with China.

capital and financial account

Part of an economy's balance of payments account that measures flows of capital and investment.

capital account

Part of a balance of payments account that records totals for migrants' funds, inheritances, and government pension payments.

inflow

A receipt that flows into Canada and is recorded on the capital account, such as an inheritance received by a Canadian from another country.

outflow

A payment that flows out of Canada, recorded on the capital account, such as a pension paid to a Canadian living outside of the country.

financial account

The part of the balance of payments that records totals for direct investment and portfolio investment.

direct investment

Investment in the form of building a new plant, establishing a new business, or taking over an existing one, carried out by Canadians abroad or by foreigners here.

Canadian direct investment (CDI)

Canadian direct investment abroad, in the form of building a new plant, establishing a new business, or taking over an existing one.

foreign direct investment (FDI)

Foreign direct investment in Canada in the form of building a new plant, establishing a new business, or taking over an existing one.

THE CAPITAL AND FINANCIAL ACCOUNT

The **capital and financial account** is made up of two components: the capital account and the financial account.

Capital Account

The **capital account** includes migrants' funds, inheritances, and government pension payments to Canadians living abroad. These items are further divided into **inflows** and **outflows**. For example, when Canadians receive an inheritance from a relative in another country, it is considered an inflow. When immigrants to Canada want to send money to their home country, the money sent is considered an outflow. A pension paid to a "snowbird" (retiree) living in Florida is also considered an outflow.

Financial Account

The **financial account** includes two types of investment. The first type is **direct investment**, either by Canadians abroad (**Canadian direct investment, or CDI**) or by foreigners in Canada (**foreign direct investment, or FDI**). Direct investment involves investors who either establish a new plant or business or take over an existing one by purchasing controlling shares. When foreigners invest in our country, it is an inflow, or receipt, for Canada; when Canadians invest abroad, it is an outflow, or payment. CDI abroad exceeded FDI in Canada from 2002 to 2016, as Figure 21.10 shows.

FIGURE 21.10

Canada's direct investment position, 2002–2016

This graph shows foreign direct investment in Canada and Canadian direct investment abroad. How does foreign direct investment benefit Canadians?

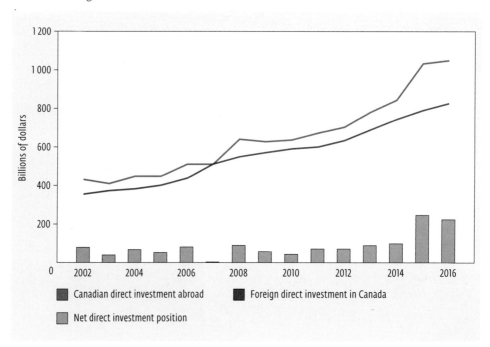

The second type is **portfolio investment**. This type of investment involves investors who receive dividends or interest on stocks or bonds, but who do not control a company, as is the case with direct investment. Purchases of Canadian stocks or bonds by foreigners represent an inflow, or receipt, for Canada, while similar purchases of foreign stocks or bonds by Canadians represent an outflow, or payment.

Official International Reserves

The **official international reserves** are another important component of the financial account. Managed by the Bank of Canada, the official reserves totalled $81 billion in 2018. Composed of mostly US dollars (CDN$48 billion), other foreign currencies (CDN$22 billion), and $11 billion in other reserves and drawing rights, the reserves are similar to a bank account held by an individual. When income exceeds expenditures for a period of time, the individual's bank account increases. However, when expenditures exceed income, the individual must use the savings in the account to make up the difference. The official reserves can be used by the Bank of Canada in the same way. If Canada's current account and capital account are in surplus, then the Bank of Canada increases the official reserves. If Canada's current account and the capital account are in deficit, then the Bank of Canada draws down on the official reserves to pay for the shortfall.

Balancing the Account

When the accounts are totalled, the current account and capital and financial account should balance, as indicated in Figure 21.11. Why? Foreign buyers need Canadian dollars to buy Canadian exports. Canada supplies these dollars by importing foreign goods—that is, when Canadians import goods and services, they convert Canadian dollars into foreign currency. If Canada is exporting more goods and services than it is importing, the supply of Canadian dollars will be insufficient for foreigners to buy our exports. This is where the capital and financial account comes into play. It must finance foreign demand for our dollars by recording more outflows of Canadian money than inflows of foreign money. It runs a deficit to pay for the surplus on Canada's current account.

Conversely, if Canadians import more than they export, they are demanding more foreign money than foreign buyers are supplying, and Canada's capital and financial account records more inflows of foreign money than outflows. In this case, the capital and financial account runs a surplus to pay for the deficit on the current account.

It is impossible to track all transactions, and thus the current account does not balance exactly with the capital and financial account. A required adjustment called the **statistical discrepancy** is calculated to bring the balance of payments account (current and capital/financial accounts) into balance.

portfolio investment
Investment in the form of purchases of stocks or bonds.

official international reserves
The foreign currencies and gold held by the Bank of Canada.

statistical discrepancy
An adjustment made to bring the current account into balance with the capital and financial account on a country's international balance of payments.

FIGURE 21.11
Canada's balance of international payments (in CAD millions), 2017
The minus signs indicate an outflow of Canadian money.

Current account balance	-63 268
Capital account balance	-76
Financial account balance	+51 962
Capital and financial account balance	51 887
Current account balance minus capital/financial account balance	-11 381
Statistical discrepancy	+11 381
Balance of payments	0

Self-Reflect

1 Determine whether each of the following represents a payment or a receipt and whether it is part of the current or capital and financial account.

a) A company in British Columbia sells lumber to the United States.

b) A business in Ontario buys industrial machinery from Germany.

c) A Canadian consulting firm wins a contract to advise a Chilean firm.

d) A Japanese bank purchases an issue of Canadian government bonds.

2 Explain how the official international reserves play an important part in the balance of payments account.

Chapter 21
Consolidation Activities

KNOWLEDGE

1   How do flexible exchange rates differ from fixed exchange rates?

2   Explain the difference between a depreciation and devaluation in a country's currency.

3   What two parts make up the balance of payments account?

4   What three components are included in the current account?

THINKING & INQUIRY

5   What would each of the following likely prefer—a higher or a lower exchange rate for the Canadian dollar?

   a) A Canadian sports team owner with American players who want to be paid in US dollars.

   b) A Canadian forestry company selling on world markets.

   c) A Canadian company that must import equipment from abroad.

   d) A Canadian retiree who spends the winter in Florida.

   e) Canadian hotels, resorts, and restaurants catering to foreign tourists

6   Calculate the following:

   a) If €1.00 = CDN$1.70, how many Canadian dollars would be equal to €300?

   b) How many euros would be exchanged for $100 Canadian dollars?

   c) If the exchange rate for CDN$1 = Mex$14 (Mexican pesos), how much would Mex$1 be worth in Canadian dollars?

7   Suppose that the exchange rate of the euro in terms of our dollar changes from €1.00 = CDN$1.50 to €1.00 = CDN$1.60. Would Canadian exporters to Europe gain or lose by this fluctuation? How would Canadian imports of European goods be affected?

8   What would be the effect of the change in the exchange rate described in the preceding question for European travellers visiting Canada and Canadian travellers vacationing in Europe?

9   a) Suppose that the inflation rate is rising in Canada. Would a lower or higher exchange rate for our dollar be more beneficial in addressing this problem? Explain.

   b) What action could the Bank of Canada take to achieve the solution you chose in (a)?

10 a) Suppose that the unemployment rate is rising in Canada. Would a lower or a higher exchange rate for our dollar be more beneficial in addressing this problem? Explain.

   b) What action could the Bank of Canada take to achieve the solution you chose in (a)?

COMMUNICATION

11 Using online research, write a short news report on the current situation of one of the following topics:

   • Canada's balance of trade

   • Foreign portfolio investment in Canada and Canadian portfolio investment abroad

   • The Chinese yuan

   • The currency crisis in Venezuela and/or Argentina

   • The trade war between the United States and China

Video-record or audio-record your report and present it to the class.

APPLICATION

12 For the following examples, indicate whether the Canadian dollar would appreciate or depreciate:

a) Bombardier of Montreal lands a big contract to build aircraft to be sold in the United States.

b) A Canadian mining company invests in developing a new mine and smelter in Indonesia.

c) A Hollywood movie company decides to make its next two movies in St. John's and Toronto.

d) A Canadian auto manufacturer buys parts from a manufacturer in Mexico.

e) A provincial government borrows money from financial institutions in the United States.

13 The following table shows a hypothetical demand and supply schedule for the Canadian dollar (in US dollars).

Price of Canadian Dollar (in USD)	Quantity of Canadian Dollars Demanded (in CAD billions)	Quantity of Canadian Dollars Supplied (in CAD billions)
$0.85	60	140
$0.80	80	120
$0.75	100	100
$0.70	120	80
$0.65	149	60

a) What will be the value of the Canadian dollar at the exchange rate market equilibrium (see Figure 21.4, on page 453)?

b) Explain what would happen to the Canadian exchange rate at CDN$1.00 = US$0.80.

c) Explain what would happen to the Canadian exchange rate at CDN$1.00 = US$0.70.

14 a) Determine the balance on the current account below. Explain whether the account has a deficit or surplus.

Investment income payments	$100
Merchandise exports	$300
Non-merchandise payments	$100
Investment income receipts	$40
Merchandise imports	$300
Non-merchandise receipts	$150

b) Determine the balance on the capital and financial account below. Explain whether it has a deficit or surplus.

Direct investment abroad	$200
Foreign direct investment in Canada	$275
Portfolio investment abroad	$250
Portfolio investment in Canada	$200
Capital account balance	-$15

Explain whether this account balances with the current account.

15 What is the purpose of a statistical discrepancy when calculating the balance of payments for a country?

22

International Economic Issues

INTRODUCTION

In this unit, you have learned about international trade and how international trade agreements focus on reducing or eliminating trade barriers, establish more open terms of trade, and encourage foreign investment. The integration of markets and the reduction of barriers to the flow of products, goods, and investment among countries have led to *globalization*. Although globalization provides benefits to economies around the world, many people from different countries feel that the costs associated with globalization have negatively affected their quality of life. Some people believe that globalization promotes the exploitation of the poor by the rich through the spread of capitalism and results in job losses in developed economies. In this chapter, we will investigate key issues arising from globalization and examine how governments and organizations respond to various international economic issues.

LEARNING GOALS

Once you have completed this chapter, you should be able to:

- Understand globalization and related issues
- Assess global economic disparities and explain the main causes and effects of economic marginalization
- Identify barriers to economic development
- Describe development strategies to reduce poverty
- Assess responses to economic disparity by intergovernmental organizations
- Conduct research to locate information from a variety of reliable sources to assess countries for a new free trade agreement and communicate recommendations clearly, effectively, and accurately

KEY TERMS

globalization

multinational corporation (MNC)

outsourcing

subsidiary

protectionism

gross national income (GNI) per capita

high-income economy (or industrially advanced country)

upper middle-income economy

low-income economy (or less-developed country)

economic development

Global Affairs Canada

fair trade

xenophobia

non-governmental organization (NGO)

Fairtrade

United Nations

United Nations Declaration on the Rights of Indigenous Peoples (UNDRIP)

United Nations Development Programme (UNDP)

United Nations Educational, Scientific and Cultural Organization (UNESCO)

World Health Organization (WHO)

UN Women

International Monetary Fund (IMF)

World Bank

globalization

A process whereby national or regional economies become integrated through communication technologies, foreign direct investment, international trade, immigration, and the flow of money.

multinational corporation (MNC)

A firm that operates in more than one country; a corporation with a global production and selling strategy, having headquarters in one country and branch plants in several other countries.

outsourcing

The practice of moving some internal business operations to third-party firms to save on costs.

Globalization

Globalization is the process whereby national or regional economies become integrated through communication technologies, foreign direct investment, international trade, and the flow of money and people. When industrially advanced countries open their markets to goods (especially labour-intensive manufactured goods) produced by low-income economies, in the long run and in a fair trade arrangement, both parties share the benefits of the law of comparative advantage (see Chapter 20). Many countries have removed barriers to crossborder trade, resulting in a huge increase in the volume of international trade. Figure 22.1 shows the top 10 exporters and importers of goods in world merchandise trade in 2017.

Globalization has provided benefits to many economies around the world. However, globalization is also considered to be the main culprit behind the global financial crisis of 2008–2009. The global financial crisis resulted in a Great Recession that has led to a rise in protectionism in a number of countries. The global financial crisis has also led to slower economic growth in Canada and other countries.

THE MULTINATIONAL CORPORATION

The **multinational corporation (MNC)**—any company registered in one country that conducts business in two or more countries—is fundamental to globalization. MNCs are large firms that produce goods and services on a global basis and market them around the world.

The business arrangement of hiring outside contractors to produce either parts or finished products is called **outsourcing**. Using an outsourcing strategy, multinationals can "shop around" in many countries for the subcontractor

FIGURE 22.1

Top 10 exporters and importers in world merchandise trade, 2017

Rank	Exporter	Value (USD billions)	Share (%)	Rank	Importer	Value (USD billions)	Share (%)
1	China	2 263	12.8	1	United States	2 410	13.4
2	United States	1 547	8.7	2	China	1 842	10.2
3	Germany	1 448	8.2	3	Germany	1 167	6.5
4	Japan	698	3.9	4	Japan	672	3.7
5	Netherlands	652	3.7	5	United Kingdom	644	3.6
6	Republic of Korea	574	3.2	6	France	625	3.5
7	Hong Kong, China	550	3.1	7	Hong Kong, China	590	3.3
8	France	535	3.0	8	Netherlands	574	3.2
9	Italy	506	2.9	9	Republic of Korea	478	2.7
10	United Kingdom	445	2.5	10	Italy	453	2.5

that will produce their goods for the least amount of money. The business arrangement of setting up a **subsidiary**, or branch plant, in another country is another way of conducting an international operation.

Today, the debate over foreign multinationals has shifted from concern over their presence in a country to concern over whether they will move their operations—and jobs—to other countries. Many foreign multinationals have moved their operations into and out of Canada. Over the past 30 years, a considerable number of manufacturing jobs have shifted from industrialized countries (including Canada) to China and less-developed countries. At the same time, many Canadian firms have expanded their operations to sell their products and services to markets in other countries. For example, Canadian clothing manufacturer Canada Goose has expanded rapidly into international markets. It now has stores in the United States, England, Japan, and China.

In the past 40 years, China has emerged as a major global economic power. Free-market policies have been promoted in many Chinese districts, transitioning the country from a centrally planned economy to a social market economy. Many subsidiaries of foreign multinationals are located in China. However, as wages in China have begun to rise, some multinationals have relocated operations to other countries in the South Asia region, such as India and Bangladesh.

subsidiary
A branch plant of a multinational corporation.

RECOVERING FROM THE GLOBAL FINANCIAL CRISIS

In 2008, the subprime mortgage crisis in the United States triggered a global financial crisis that caused economic turmoil around the world. The subprime mortgage crisis occurred after financial institutions in the United States approved numerous mortgages to buyers who did not meet the standard requirements for buying a home. The original intent of subprime loans had been to allow more lower-income Americans to own a home. However, over time, financial institutions approved loans they knew would go into default, since they could remove these loans from their balance sheets before their impact was registered on the bottom line. However, this system was not sustainable and eventually failed; the crisis sent the world economy into a global recession to a level not seen since the Great Depression of 1929. Note the drastic dip in total world merchandise trade in 2009 shown in Figure 22.2, which was mainly the result of the global recession. At the time, domestic and global economies shed many jobs, putting many out of work. This outcome sparked a protectionist movement that has become a very real danger to the global economy.

FIGURE 22.2
Total world merchandise trade (imports and exports), 2008–2017
What caused world exports and imports to decline in 2009? Describe merchandise trade from 2010 to 2014 and trade levels after that period. What caused the change from 2015 onward?

Year	Exports (US$ millions)	Imports (US$ millions)
2008	16 165 329	16 572 352
2009	12 560 643	12 782 052
2010	15 311 089	15 505 508
2011	18 337 997	18 503 649
2012	18 495 998	18 711 911
2013	18 956 495	19 021 197
2014	18 970 332	19 136 180
2015	16 524 682	16 794 444
2016	16 032 338	16 298 574
2017	17 706 706	18 065 141

protectionism
An economic policy that aims to restrict imports through tariffs, quotas, and regulations in an effort to boost domestic industry.

RESHAPING GLOBALIZATION: THE RISE OF PROTECTIONISM

Over the past 30 years, the removal of numerous barriers to international trade has been a major driving force for globalization. Most of these 30 years witnessed an increase in the volume of international trade resulting directly from the theories of trade you learned about in Chapter 20: absolute and comparative advantages. Those theories promised great gains from trade if it is open and free from trade barriers such as tariffs. Industrialized countries made a determined effort among themselves to lower trade barriers that prevented the gains that freer trade would provide. However, a decade after the global financial crisis sparked the Great Recession, many countries are struggling with modest economic growth, and their workers face a changing job market due in part to disruptive technological change. As a result, a rise in **protectionism** and a movement away from global co-operation among countries is sweeping the world.

An example of this trend occurred when citizens of the United Kingdom voted in a referendum in 2016 to leave the European Union, a move referred to as *Brexit*. In the year following the Brexit vote, Britain went from being one of the fastest-growing economies of the G7 (Group of Seven richest countries in the world) to one of the slowest, according to the International Monetary Fund (IMF).

Protectionism fuelled the renegotiation of the North American Free Trade Agreement (NAFTA), which the United States threatened to terminate, and Canada, the United States, and Mexico attempted to protect their own business interests. Ultimately, NAFTA was preserved, albeit in a new agreement titled the United States-Mexico-Canada Agreement, or USMCA. In 2018, the United States placed tariffs on over $200 billion of Chinese goods, triggering a trade war between the world's two largest economies. In response, China imposed retaliatory tariffs on US imports, halting US imports of oil and soybeans. The United States–China dispute continued to hover over international trade agreements and global economic growth in 2019.

The 2016 referendum in the United Kingdom resulted in a vote for Brexit, but it was not a landslide: 48.11% voted to remain in the European Union. Pictured here is a pro-remain rally in London.

THE CANADIAN ECONOMY IN THE AFTERMATH OF THE GLOBAL FINANCIAL CRISIS

Globalization leads to the interdependence of economies as well as possible economic instability and fluctuations. Since the global financial crisis, the Canadian economy has grown slowly. The Bank of Canada predicted gross domestic product (GDP) growth of 2.8 percent in 2017, 2.0 percent in 2018, and a decline to 1.6 percent in 2019. Like many governments around the world, Canada's federal and provincial governments have been running budget deficits to grow the Canadian economy. Some view globalization as a threat to a country's sovereignty that could lead to a rise in protectionism.

In 2017, the Organisation for Economic Co-operation and Development (OECD) reported that Canadian households were global leaders in debt. The Bank of Canada and the IMF have been raising the alarm over the state of Canada's economy, particularly over the enormous increase in personal debt that Canadian consumers have accumulated. Many middle-class Canadians are alarmed by the growing cost of living in Canada's cities, especially since wages have not kept pace with the price of housing or the price of consumer goods. In the United States, the Federal Reserve began tightening monetary policy with a series of interest rate increases, as did the Bank of Canada after a decade of unusually low interest rates. In 2018, the Bank of Canada increased the interest rate to 1.5 percent, the highest since 2008. Interest rates are increasing and are expected to climb over the next decade. Higher interest rates will put pressure on consumers, posing increased risk for the Canadian economy.

Self-Reflect

1 Explain the difference between outsourcing and creating a subsidiary.

2 According to the IMF, what happened to Britain's economy the year following the Brexit vote?

3 Describe how protectionism created a trade war between the United States and China in 2018.

4 What are some of the concerns facing the Canadian economy since the global financial crisis?

gross national income (GNI) per capita

A measurement of a country's income divided by its population. It includes all the income earned by a country's residents and businesses, including any income earned abroad. It was formerly called *GNP per capita*.

high-income economy (or industrially advanced country)

A country with high enough GNI per capita (set at US$12 056 in 2019) to provide the majority of its citizens with prosperity.

upper middle-income economy

A country in which a minority of the population lives in poverty, with incomes at GNI per capita from $3 896 to $12 055 (in 2019).

low-income economy (or less-developed country)

A country in which a majority of citizens live in poverty, with incomes at or below about GNI per capita of US$995 (in 2019).

Underdevelopment: The Status Quo?

Although the proportion of poor Canadians continues to increase statistically, most Canadians live a relatively comfortable lifestyle in contrast to the majority of people in the world. To help recognize the disparities that exist between rich and poor countries, the World Bank classifies economies into four income groups based on annual **gross national income (GNI) per capita** data: high-income, upper middle-income, lower middle-income, and low-income economies.

High-income economies (also known as **industrially advanced countries, or IACs**) are those with a GNI per capita that is high enough to provide a substantial majority of citizens with prosperity. In 2019, the World Bank set US$12 056 (about CDN$16 100) as the minimum GNI per capita for this group. In all, 81 countries were classified as high-income economies. This category includes Canada, the United States, most European countries, Israel, and Japan.

Upper middle-income economies are those in which a minority of the population lives in poverty. In 2019, the World Bank set US$3 896 to $12 055 (about CDN$5 200 to $16 100) as the range of GNI per capita for this group. In all, 56 countries were classified as upper middle-income economies. This category includes Brazil, China, Colombia, Cuba, and Mexico.

Lower middle-income economies are those with a GNI per capita in the range of US$996 to $3 895 (about CDN$1 300 to $5 200). In all, 47 countries were classified as lower middle-income economies. This category includes El Salvador, Honduras, Cameroon, Egypt, India, and Vietnam.

Low-income economies (also known as **less-developed countries, or LDCs**) include the poorest countries in the world. They are countries with a GNI per capita of US$995 (about CDN$1 300) or less. In all, 34 countries were classified as low-income economies. This category includes Afghanistan, Haiti, Syria, Somalia, and Zimbabwe.

Many contemporary economists have concluded that the gap between high- and low-income countries continues to widen. It has been stated by various economists, relief workers, and religious leaders that in order for the world to experience lasting peace, it must first do away with existing injustices that serve to keep low-income countries from achieving sustained economic progress.

BARRIERS TO ECONOMIC DEVELOPMENT

Economists judge the economic success of a country by whether its standard of living is rising. An economy shows **economic development** when a country's standard of living has improved, something we can easily see when there is a measurable increase in per capita GDP that is shared by the bulk of its population. To achieve economic development, a country requires both economic growth and a widespread distribution of the benefits of this economic growth. In attempting to facilitate economic growth, low-income countries generally face a series of obstacles.

Lack of Economic Freedom and Stability

Many low-income countries have politicoeconomic systems in place that limit economic freedom and the individual pursuit of self-interest. In some low-income countries, military and other forms of dictatorship control the government. The stability present in a strong dictatorship comes at the price of lost personal and economic freedom. In these "controlled" economies, national wealth rarely manages to trickle down to the majority of citizens.

Malnutrition

Countries with a low GNI per capita usually have insufficient food supplies to distribute, resulting in a malnourished population. Other goods and services that contribute to improved health standards are also in short supply. To complicate matters, available food and productive resources may be controlled by a small minority of the population and used only for their benefit. For example, many low-income countries grow cash crops intended for export. These cash crops are usually grown on huge plantations owned by a small minority. The majority may be powerless to do anything about this imbalance.

Low Capital Investment

Because individuals, households, and firms must use most of their income to purchase essential goods and services, only a minor portion of income can be saved. Without substantial savings in banks, the financing of investment projects and the development of a capital-goods infrastructure are very difficult to achieve. Further, when foreign interests supply money or real capital, their interests (profit maximization) may not always be in the best interests of the host country, so they may be unwelcome. Finally, traditions that discourage self-interest, competition, and profit may inhibit local entrepreneurship.

Political Instability

Political and economic stability is a prerequisite for lasting development and discourages the flight of investment funds and profits out of a less-developed economy to safer markets. Political stability permits long-term planning and promotes capital investment by multinational companies. If foreign investors are confident that their investments will not be seized by government, they are more likely to invest. Political stability is usually not assured until a country experiences a substantial period of rule by a democratically elected government.

economic development
A rise in a country's standard of living as measured by a rise in per capita GDP.

DID YOU KNOW?

Many Canadian and American multinationals have ceased operations in Venezuela. In 2017, Air Canada suspended flights to Venezuela over safety concerns and civil unrest. In 2017, US car company General Motors had its factories and plants taken over by Venezuela's government. In 2018, cereal maker Kellogg's decided that it would leave Venezuela due to the country's economic crisis.

Natural Resource–Intensive Production

For many of the world's less-developed countries, economic enterprise is limited largely to primary industrial activity. Their economic revenue is based on the exportation of limited natural resources, such as bauxite, latex rubber, coffee, bananas, cocoa, and sugar cane. A country that exports relatively inexpensive natural resources and imports expensive manufactured goods usually experiences a steady drain of money out of its economy. This imbalance serves to limit the economy's ability to grow. If less-developed countries receive discounted prices (whether as a result of market forces or exploitation) for their resources, then their economic growth potential can be even more adversely affected. This situation is made worse if foreign interests control the natural resources, taking potential profits out of the country.

Consider the real cost of a chocolate bar. A large majority of cocoa production occurs on small farms in African countries such as Ghana and the Ivory Coast. The farmers that grow cocoa (the main resource in chocolate) receive the least (3 percent) of the price of an average chocolate bar. The largest portion of the average price of a chocolate bar (43 percent) goes to the sellers, such as supermarkets and variety stores. Most cocoa farmers remain in poverty, with many farming families struggling on an income of less than $1 per day. As Figure 22.3 shows, cocoa growers receive very little for their crops.

FIGURE 22.3

Breaking down the real cost of a chocolate bar for consumption in North America

What percentage of the sales price do cocoa farmers receive? Who has the most power to set prices?

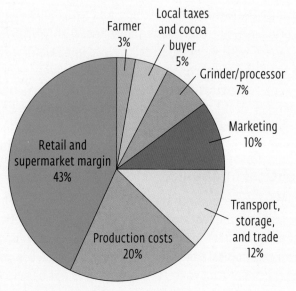

Debt Burden

Many less-developed countries have borrowed money from foreign banks, governments, and international institutions, such as the World Bank and the IMF. Money was borrowed to finance infrastructure projects (to build roads, schools, and water works), to feed hungry citizens, to prevent the collapse of the domestic currency and banking system, and to pay for imports. Debt repayment can happen only when the country that owes the debt has a surplus of exports over imports, resulting in a positive flow of money into the country and, ultimately, in economic growth. To achieve this surplus, industrialized countries must open their markets to exports from less-developed countries. Few low-income economies have ever managed to achieve a surplus of exports over imports, particularly because many more-developed countries maintain trade barriers to protect their own industries. As a result, many less-developed countries fall deeper and deeper into debt, and the interest payments on their debt get larger. Having to pay the interest on the incurred debt becomes a further burden for debtor economies and limits their ability to invest and grow.

Population Growth and Child Labour

Population growth in most low-income economies tends to be too high to be sustained by the existing levels of production growth. Consequently, the standard of living declines steadily over time. Rapid population growth and low incomes are linked. Large families are seen as an economic necessity in low-income countries. In many low-income countries, children are required to work in factories or in dangerous conditions, such as mining for precious metals used in smartphones. One of the most dangerous activities involves scavenging through refuse dumps to find materials that can be sold. As a direct result of child labour, millions of children miss the chance to go to school, and most never learn to read or write. High levels of illiteracy are always associated with high levels of poverty.

June 12 is the World Day Against Child Labour. Many intergovernmental and non-governmental organizations have inititives to curb the practice of child labour, but it is still prevalent, affecting more than 200 million children worldwide.

Global Affairs Canada
The Government of Canada department that manages Canada's diplomatic relations, provides consular services to Canadians, promotes the country's international trade, and leads Canada's international development and humanitarian assistance.

Development Strategies: Breaking the Vicious Cycles of Poverty

Although a difficult task, it is not impossible to break the vicious cycles of poverty shown in Figure 22.4. Breaking these cycles involves the efforts of many individuals and organizations, working on many different fronts. Direct aid from developed countries is needed to help break the vicious cycle of poverty that is at work in less-developed countries. Relief programs are needed to deal immediately with crises resulting from drought, famine, civil war, earthquakes, and other natural disasters. Structural programs are necessary to help build the infrastructure, education systems, and capital resources necessary to provide a foundation for lasting economic development. In Canada, international assistance is administered by **Global Affairs Canada**.

Significant progress has been made in reducing poverty in the world over the past few decades. According to the most recent estimates by the World Bank, 10 percent of the world's population lived on less than US$1.90 per day in 2015. This figure was 11 percent in 2013 and 35 percent in 1990.

INVESTING IN PRODUCTIVE RESOURCES

For many low-income economies, natural resources are limited. In economies with few natural resources, government programs can work toward developing human resources by investing in their citizens' education, health care, and nutrition. Education and training increase the supply of skilled labour, which in turn increases productivity and the standard of living. Government programs can also work toward developing capital resources by encouraging savings. Financial institutions that have capital can use those funds to lend to entrepreneurs. Developing and implementing "intermediate technology" (simple and practical tools, and basic machines such as a hand-operated pump) that makes good use of plentiful, low-cost labour is an effective strategy for less-developed countries.

FIGURE 22.4

The vicious cycles of poverty

At what point in each cycle could a change be made that might help people trapped in poverty break out of the cycle? Who would be capable of making this change?

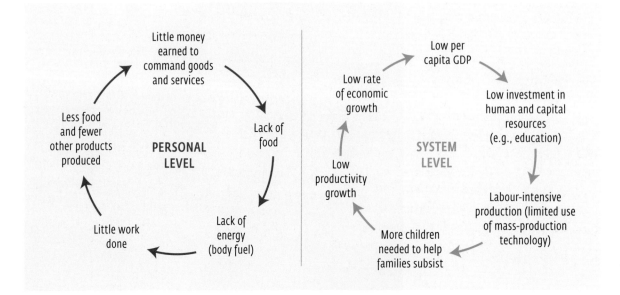

PROMOTING SUSTAINABLE GROWTH

Less developed countries sometimes need international cooperation to achieve sustainable growth. When an oppressive dictatorship limits a country's economic growth and shared prosperity, strong international sanctions can help force a correction. When the population is growing faster than the economy, birth control can be promoted to help improve living standards. For many poor countries now crippled by massive debt, debt reduction or forgiveness can free up more funds for sustaining economic growth. Given that sustainability ultimately requires economic, ecological, and social justice, development can be fostered by a concerted global effort to promote fair trade over free trade. The principal elements of fair trade are:

- Fair prices
- Empowerment of disadvantaged workers and producers
- No child or forced labour
- Safe and clean working conditions
- Respectful treatment of the environment
- Commitment to non-discrimination and gender equity

Globalization and Immigration

Globalization connects economies through trade and investment and the flow of goods and services across borders. It has also resulted in greater migration of people from one country to another, many in search of a better future and quality of life.

Many foreigners continue to seek a permanent home in Canada, as it continues to be recognized as one of the best countries in the world in which to live. In 2017, the Economist Intelligence Unit ranked Canada as home to three of the top five most liveable cities: Toronto, Calgary, and Vancouver. As the Canadian population ages, new immigration is easing labour shortages in the country and adding to the country's human capital.

In 2015 and 2016, an unprecedented number of refugees and migrants—more than 1 million people—arrived in the European Union. Many came from underdeveloped countries where they faced civil war, oppression, and poverty, and wanted to call Europe home.

On this continent, the impoverished countries of Honduras, Guatemala, and El Salvador have seen thousands of migrants flee to the United States in recent years in an attempt to escape violence and poverty. In South America, thousands of migrants from Venezuela have left the country in recent years due to its struggling and collapsed economy. In 2017, Canada witnessed a rise in the number of illegal migrants crossing into the country from the United States, mainly due to a crackdown on undocumented immigrants in the United States. The rise of populism, partially fuelled by political parties and politicians, has spurred a rise in **xenophobia**, an intense dislike or fear of people from other countries. Massive migrations are most effectively addressed at the problem's source.

fair trade
Trade deals where the most vulnerable trading partners are treated with dignity and respect rather than being exploited by wealthy traders or large multinational corporations.

xenophobia
The fear and intense dislike of strangers or foreigners or of anything that is considered strange or foreign.

CHECK IT OUT!

Zambian-born economist Danbisa Moyo (see page 99), a specialist in international development, argues that government-to-government foreign aid has actually hurt economic development in Africa because it has encouraged dependency and corruption. Aid is often provided with conditions that favour the developed nation. She recommends market-driven, private sector investments over government handouts.

Self-Reflect

1 List and describe the four income categories used by the World Bank to classify economies. Provide an example of a country for each category.

2 What are the causes of low levels of economic development? Create a rank order of the causes, giving justification for your choices.

3 What is xenophobia? Why is it increasing?

Thinking like an Economist

Beyond GDP per Capita: Measuring Happiness and Well-Being

GDP per capita (the total value of a country's annual production of goods and services divided by its population) is a useful statistic used by economists to measure a country's output, income, and standard of living. While GDP per capita is an important indicator of economic performance, it is a statistic that is limited because it is not able to measure the overall well-being of citizens in an economy. When comparing countries on the basis of their overall well-being, it is important to look beyond the traditional economic indicators, such as GDP per capita, inflation, and employment rates.

By considering other indicators, a better assessment of a country's overall well-being can be made. That is the goal of the World Happiness Index, an annual publication by the United Nations that measures "the overall happiness" of 156 countries. In 2011, the UN General Assembly recognized happiness as a "fundamental human goal," and the following year the first ever UN Conference on Happiness was held. The World Happiness Index has been published every year since 2012. Figure 22.5 shows the six variables that the World Happiness Index considers in its annual assessment.

FIGURE 22.5
The six variables of the World Happiness Index

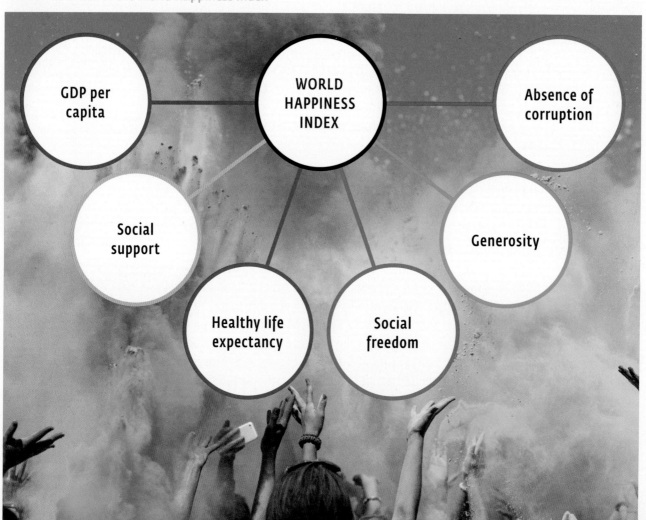

In 2018, Canada ranked seventh in the World Happiness Index. The top 10 happiest countries for that year were as follows:

1. Finland
2. Norway
3. Denmark
4. Iceland
5. Switzerland
6. Netherlands
7. Canada
8. New Zealand
9. Sweden
10. Australia

While the United States ranked 14th from 2014–2016, it dropped four places to the 18th spot in 2017, despite having a higher GDP per capita than most countries in the top 10. In 2018, it remained 18th. Since 2008–2010, the five countries that experienced the largest drop in ranking were Ukraine, Yemen, Syria, Malawi, and Venezuela, all of which are countries facing violence, war, and human rights issues. Measuring happiness is not an exact science, as factors other than GDP per capita are considered. Additional factors that could be considered when assessing a country's overall well-being are the distribution of income in society, the health of citizens, life expectancy, the quality of education, housing and homelessness, pollution, and corruption and violence.

Is there a connection between happiness and economics? Perhaps, since many of the top 10 countries on the World Happiness Index also rank the highest for labour productivity, according to the OECD. So, the next time you encounter GDP per capita in a comparison of countries, remember to think like an economist and consider the limitations of this statistic and consider extra factors that can better measure happiness and well-being.

APPLYING ECONOMIC THINKING

1. Why is GDP per capita a limited statistic when measuring quality of life?

2. Use the Internet to access the latest World Happiness Report. Which countries experienced the greatest increase/decrease on the most recent happiness report? Why? What happened to Canada's rank?

3. With reference to the World Happiness Index, create a collection of photos on what defines happiness using technology. What photos would you choose to represent what happiness means? Why did you select these images? Write a one-paragraph reflection justifying your photo selections and how they represent well-being. Be sure to properly source all images.

NGOs and Intergovernmental Organizations

Non-governmental organizations (NGOs) are usually non-profit, international organizations that are independent of government and focused on improving humanitarian issues, such as poverty, health care, disease, or the environment. As one example, **Fairtrade** is an NGO that works to improve trade conditions for producers in developing countries. Fairtrade works to secure improved trading relationships for producers, many of them low income, from around the world. It guarantees that the prices paid for products are adequate to cover the costs of sustainable production. Under this system, workers are treated fairly, and they are ensured safe working conditions, adequate housing, and decent wages.

UNITED NATIONS

One of the largest and likely most influential organizations in addressing global poverty and injustices is the **United Nations**. The United Nations is an international organization that strives for world peace and social advancement. It was established by world leaders in 1945 at the end of the Second World War as a mechanism to create peace and eliminate war. It has grown to include 193 countries. Its representatives discuss and collaborate on issues that affect the entire world. Today, the United Nations works on a number of global issues, such as alleviating poverty, improving food production, advancing human rights, advocating for democracy, organizing disaster relief, and promoting social justice.

United Nations Declaration on the Rights of Indigenous Peoples

According to the United Nations, there are an estimated 370 million Indigenous people worldwide living in 70 different countries. Indigenous people throughout the world have faced discrimination, oppression, and exploitation, and are arguably among the most disadvantaged and vulnerable populations in the world. Indigenous people have had their rights violated as they sought recognition of their identities, their way of life, and their right to traditional lands and natural resources.

In an attempt to have the international community recognize the need to protect Indigenous rights, culture, and way of life, the **United Nations Declaration on the Rights of Indigenous Peoples (UNDRIP)** was adopted in 2007 by a majority of 144 states. UNDRIP established a universal framework of minimum standards for the survival, dignity, and well-being of all Indigenous people. Originally voting against this framework, Australia, Canada, New Zealand, and the United States have since reversed their positions and adopted the declaration.

UNITED NATIONS DEVELOPMENT PROGRAMME

United Nations Development Programme (UNDP) works in 170 countries and territories to help eradicate poverty and reduce inequality and exclusion. It is the lead developer of climate action programs within the United Nations.

In 2015, UNDP and 150 world leaders adopted the 2030 Agenda for Sustainable Development and its Sustainable Development Goals, or SDGs (the 17 SDGs appear in Figure 22.6). Setting priorities for global development, the 2030 Agenda for Sustainable Development aims to protect the planet, end poverty, and ensure peace for everyone on the planet.

The United Nations Framework Convention on Climate Change (UNFCCC) was adopted in 1992, with the objective to combat climate change. Within the UN system, UNDP works with countries to turn their climate goals into action in conjunction with the UNFCCC. Over 20 years later, parties to the UNFCCC signed a new agreement to combat climate—the Paris Agreement—which is the largest international climate agreement to date. For the first time, both developed and developing countries agreed to fast-track and increase the investment required to battle climate change and take the necessary steps to ensure a low-carbon future for all countries. The Paris Agreement entered into force on November 2016. As of April 2018, 194 states and the European Union, representing more than 88 percent of global greenhouse gas emissions, have signed the agreement. In 2017, US President Donald Trump announced his intention to withdraw from the Paris Agreement. Despite this setback, all other signatories, including Canada, have reaffirmed their commitment to the agreement. The United Nations Intergovernmental Panel on Climate Change continues to stress that the world, including Canada, remains far from its goals on cutting greenhouse gas emissions, furthering concerns of irreversible changes, damage, and loss of some ecosystems.

UNITED NATIONS EDUCATIONAL, SCIENTIFIC AND CULTURAL ORGANIZATION

Based in Paris, the **United Nations Educational, Scientific and Cultural Organization (UNESCO)** is a specialized agency of the United Nations. The purpose of UNESCO is to help build peace and security by promoting collaboration among countries in the areas of education, science, and culture. The agency helps people live as global citizens free of hate and intolerance, works to increase access to quality education, and promotes cultural heritage and the dignity of all cultures. It also stands up for freedom of expression, which is fundamental to democracy and development. UNESCO was an active participant in the development of the SDGs and is contributing to their implementation through its activities in education, natural sciences, social and human sciences, culture, communication and information, and sustainable development for oceans.

United Nations Development Programme (UNDP)

Part of the United Nations system, UNDP works to achieve the eradication of poverty and the reduction of inequality and exclusion. UNDP focuses on helping countries build and share solutions in three main areas: sustainable development, democratic governance and peacebuilding, and climate and disaster resilience.

United Nations Educational, Scientific and Cultural Organization (UNESCO)

The United Nations Educational, Scientific and Cultural Organization. It seeks to help build peace and security by promoting collaboration among countries in the areas of education, science, and culture.

FIGURE 22.6

UNDP's Sustainable Development Goals

The Paris Agreement seeks to address one of the 17 sustainable development goals of the 2030 agenda: climate action. In 2015, Canada and 192 other UN members adopted this 15-year global framework for addressing these 17 social, economic, and environmental goals.

1   No poverty
2   Zero hunger
3   Good health and well-being for people
4   Quality education
5   Gender equality
6   Clean water and sanitation
7   Affordable and clean energy
8   Decent work and economic growth
9   Industry, innovation, and infrastructure
10 Reduced inequalities
11 Sustainable cities and communities
12 Responsible consumption and production
13 Climate action
14 Life below water
15 Life on land
16 Peace, justice, and strong institutions
17 Partnerships for the goals

World Health Organization (WHO)
Established in 1948, WHO is a specialized agency of the United Nations whose role is to be the direct authority on international health within the United Nations system and to provide leadership in global health responses.

UN Women
An entity of the United Nations that is dedicated to gender equality and the empowerment of women. It supports member states in setting global standards for achieving gender equality.

WORLD HEALTH ORGANIZATION

Globalization has brought people together across the world so that they can share each other's products, services, and cultures. Increased global travel has brought something else as well: global pandemics, or outbreaks of disease that can spread around the world. Greater awareness of the possibility of pandemics by national health organizations and co-ordination with the **World Health Organization (WHO)** have prevented the spread of some diseases. WHO, a specialized agency of the United Nations, directs international health within the United Nations system and provides leadership in global health responses.

UN WOMEN

Gender equality is a basic human right, and yet inequalities between men and women remain in society and result in social, political, and economic consequences. **UN Women** focuses on areas of gender equality and the empowerment of women. In a number of developing and underdeveloped economies, women face many barriers to economic participation, such as a lack of education, reduced access to employment, violence, discrimination, and pay inequity.

Investing in women's economic empowerment is one of UN Women's initiatives, and "sets a direct path towards gender equality, poverty eradication, and inclusive economic growth." Their programs promote women's ability to secure decent jobs, accumulate assets, and influence institutions and public policies for positive change.

DID YOU KNOW?

Providing women with the same opportunities as men can improve a country's economy. According to the World Bank report *Doing Business 2017*, eliminating discrimination against women could raise per capita productivity by 40 percent around the globe. This increase in competitiveness can increase economic growth and reduce poverty. What policies could governments implement that would reduce gender discrimination?

INTERNATIONAL MONETARY FUND

The **International Monetary Fund (IMF)**, an organization that is part of the United Nations system, tracks economic trends, analyzes countries' financial performance, warns governments of potential financial problems, provides expertise to governments, and provides a forum for discussion. The IMF represents 186 member countries, including Canada. The people who work at the IMF are principally economists with expertise in macroeconomic issues. The purpose of the IMF is to promote financial stability, prevent and solve economic crises, encourage growth, and prevent and relieve poverty.

The IMF also provides loans to governments with specific economic conditions, such as cutting government spending to prioritize short-term economic goals. In 2017, the IMF stepped in to help Greece with its crushing debt problems, providing a loan of almost $2 billion. In 2018, Pakistan applied for its 13th loan since the 1980s in an attempt to stop a cycle of economic crashes. Not all IMF policies have positive effects, and the IMF is often accused of increasing poverty. The strict conditions that are part of loans to countries often emphasize a limit on government spending that result in cutbacks to social programs in areas such as health care and education.

WORLD BANK

The **World Bank** is not a bank in the traditional sense. Established in 1944, it is an organization of 189 member countries, including Canada, that provides monetary and technical support for developing countries. It too is an organization within the United Nations system. Its mission is to end extreme poverty and to promote shared prosperity.

It has set the following two goals for the world to achieve by 2030:

- End extreme poverty by decreasing the percentage of people living on less than $1.90 a day to no more than 3 percent
- Promote shared prosperity by fostering the income growth of the bottom 40 percent for every country

The World Bank provides loans and grants to poor countries to assist with education, health, infrastructure, farming, environmental issues, resource management, and other economic concerns. It provides funds to support HIV/AIDS assistance, biodiversity projects, clean water, electricity, and transportation. It also seeks to help poor countries move toward self-sufficiency.

Many criticisms have been directed at the World Bank. Critics say that the World Bank has caused many countries to suffer because of the conditions it imposes on a country to obtain a loan. In addition, many of the projects that are funded by the World Bank have been criticized by human rights groups for environmental damage, displacing poor communities, forced labour, and child labour.

International Monetary Fund (IMF)

An organization of 186 member countries that lends money to help members facing balance of payments and exchange rate problems.

World Bank

An international agency financed by the richer countries that attempts to help less-developed countries by providing direct grants and programs.

Self-Reflect

1 What are NGOs? Describe their purpose.

2 What is the purpose of the United Nations? What are some social justice issues that the United Nations works to address?

3 What is the Paris Agreement? Why is it important?

4 What does "WHO" stand for? What is its role?

Chapter 22
Consolidation Activities

KNOWLEDGE

1 Define *globalization*.

2 Why did the global financial crisis of 2008–2009 occur?

3 What is Brexit?

4 What is the purpose of the 2030 Agenda for Sustainable Development?

THINKING & INQUIRY

5 Create a list and investigate where common products you use on a daily basis are made. Consider your food, electronics, clothing, music, entertainment, and sports equipment. Share your results with your class or a classmate.

6 How has the world economy changed since the global financial crisis of 2008–2009?

7 Describe Canada's economic recovery since the global financial crisis. What are some concerns?

8 Using the Internet, conduct research on current United States–China trade relations.

9 A multinational corporation decides to move a plant from Canada to another country. What responsibility do you think each of the following have to the employees who will lose their jobs?

a) the government

b) the multinational

c) the employees themselves

10 Using the Internet, find the most recent census data from Statistics Canada on "immigration and ethnocultural diversity." Provide an overview of how immigration and culture are shaping Canada's economy, workforce, and communities. Which countries do most of Canada's recent immigrants come from today? How about over the past few decades? Which Canadian cities do most new immigrants move to today?

11 Are developed countries doing enough to address climate change? Research and report on the Paris Climate Agreement and compare the commitment of Canada, the United States, and Mexico to the agreement.

COMMUNICATION

12 In small groups, discuss the following quotations. Choose one quotation and create a graphic to depict its meaning and the current issues that it represents.

- *"I'm not opposed to free trade if it's fair trade. But I am opposed to bad trade deals."*
  —Martin O'Malley, former US governor of Maryland

- *"Free trade is not based on utility but on justice."*
  —Edmund Burke, Irish statesman and philosopher (1729–1797)

- *"We have to remember we're in a global economy. The purpose of fiscal stimulus is not simply to sustain activity in our national economies but to help the global economy as well, and that's why it's so critical that measures in those packages avoid anything that smacks of protectionism."*
  —Stephen Harper, former prime minister of Canada

13 Visit the Division for Sustainable Development Goals website and select one of the 17 SDGs. Conduct research and write a news report informing your readers about the world's progress in meeting the target for your selected goal.

14 Does freer trade bring people closer together, or do trade disputes and import competition force them apart? Write a letter to the editor of your local newspaper, presenting your viewpoint. Provide economic evidence to support your opinion.

APPLICATION

15 Draw a supply and demand graph to help explain why the price of labour in less-developed countries tends to be low. What other factors contribute to low wages?

16 Explain the reasoning behind the argument that foreign aid does little good. What is your position on this issue?

Unit 6 Performance Task

Evaluating Trade Partners for a Free Trade Agreement with Canada

International trade is a major contributor to the Canadian economy, and its importance has increased since the Second World War as countries have become increasingly interconnected through globalization. Economists believe that free trade is beneficial because specialization, comparative advantage, and gains from trade improve the overall well-being of people in countries with free trade agreements. However, as we have seen in this unit, international trade has its downsides and can also negatively affect people's lives.

The following task asks you to analyze the economies of two countries and propose which country would be the best candidate for a new free trade agreement with Canada.

YOUR TASK

You are an adviser to Canada's minister of international trade. The minister has asked you to review two countries with which Canada is exploring a new free trade agreement. Using research from trade organizations, your challenge is to produce a case study that analyzes the two countries and recommends with which country Canada should pursue a new free trade agreement.

STEPS AND RECOMMENDATIONS

1 Review the work you have done in this unit to refresh your understanding of related economic concepts and skills.

2 Visit the Global Affairs Canada website and navigate to the "Trade and investment agreements" web page to find free trade agreements that are currently in "exploratory discussions" (instead of agreements that are in force). Select two free trade agreements currently in "exploratory discussions." You will conduct research on the foreign country named in each agreement.

3 Conduct online research on the two countries in the free trade agreements you chose in step 2. For country information, search the International Monetary Fund (IMF) website and the Organisation for Economic Co-operation and Development (OECD) website; and for trade profiles and tariff profiles, search the World Trade Organization (WTO) website. Find the following information on each country:

- GDP per capita, inflation rate, employment rates, health and education expenditure, mortality and life expectancy rates, balance of payments, balance of trade, and currency and exchange rates

- Issue(s) that exist in each country (political, labour, environmental, and human rights)

- Trade barriers (such as tariffs or quotas) that currently exist in each country

4 Write a case study on each country, using the data collected in step 3. In the case study, consider the alternative choices that you have identified, evaluating them and selecting the most appropriate recommendation on the country with which Canada should pursue a future free trade agreement. Justify and defend your decision: Why did you choose one country over the other?

Use the following structure for your case study:

- Executive summary
- Introduction
- Alternatives
- Analysis
- Recommendation
- Appendix

ADAPTING THE TASK

Discuss with your teacher the option of collaboratively working on this case study in small groups and presenting your case study to the class using presentation software. Research what makes an effective presentation, and practise your communications skills prior to the presentation date. Consider adapting this task to advise a less developed country in proposing a new trade deal with Canada.

ASSESSMENT CRITERIA

The following criteria will be used to assess your work:

- **Knowledge:** accurately using economic concepts, principles, and theories
- **Thinking and Inquiry:** using sound economic thinking to focus analysis and make appropriate connections
- **Communication:** clearly presenting and communicating your recommendation to the intended audience in an appropriate format and style
- **Application:** presenting an interesting and persuasive argument in response to the question being investigated

Use the rubric provided by your teacher as a coaching tool to help complete this task successfully.

Take a seat at the table: the WTO's meeting room in Geneva, Switzerland.

Epilogue
Looking Ahead to a Better Tomorrow

With its many variables, looking ahead in the economic world is always a challenge. However, without being able to project forward, economic thinking becomes less helpful. Human behaviour creates social, economic, technological, and political change. In the collective sense, for the most part, we create our own future. Managing change will be a big part of this future. Tying together the concepts and issues addressed in the previous chapters, the following ideas are offered as standards for progressive and sustainable growth for the Canadian economy.

SUSTAINABLE GROWTH

Economic, ecological, and social justice (see page 366) are required to achieve sustainability. Economic sustainability must be based on the wise use of productive resources. In recent years, the vision of limitless growth under free enterprise has come under closer scrutiny. Such growth is seldom sustainable. Consumer confidence is an essential ingredient in sustainable growth. If investors forecast consumer demand to be healthy, they will be more confident about securing a comfortable return on their investments. This investor confidence can stimulate innovation and increases in productivity. Consumer confidence requires optimism about income prospects, economic security, and the ability to achieve greater prosperity.

Ecological sustainability can only be achieved through responsible stewardship of natural resources and protection of our fragile environment. We owe it to future generations to minimize the waste of resources and the contamination of air, land, and water. Sustainability is also rooted in the fair treatment of all stakeholders to minimize exploitation by the rich and powerful. As larger numbers of a population become disadvantaged or marginalized, they become more vulnerable to exploitation. Social injustice is not sustainable. In the long term, only shared prosperity can prevent violent confrontation.

DEMOGRAPHIC TRENDS AND CHANGING JOB MARKETS

Thanks to medical advances and healthier lifestyles, Canadians are living longer. As baby boomers (those born between 1946 and 1966) continue to age, the average age of Canadians continues to increase. In an aging society, the demand for healthcare services will grow substantially and become a higher priority. Furthermore, a labour shortage may arise if large numbers of young immigrants do not continue to join the Canadian workforce each year.

As artificial intelligence (AI) and robotics continue to change production methods, more jobs once done by humans will be assumed by computerized machines. The implementation of AI must be carefully monitored to maximize its promise while minimizing the hazards.

Sometimes, workers do not have the exact skills that employers need. To remain employable, the labour force will require ongoing education and training. In addition, contract work and part-time employment are increasing at a faster rate than full-time and permanent jobs. Rather than expecting one job for life, your generation must be open to changing careers and employers, and becoming self-employed. As the workplace continues to evolve, people will focus their energies on tasks that machines cannot complete effectively, including services and the advancement of digital technology.

Some experts claim that technology can create as many jobs as it replaces. From an economic perspective, high-skill jobs are usually created, while low-skill jobs are replaced. With this redefinition of work and the workplace, some economists believe that the concept of income will also need revision. They suggest that guaranteed income policies will be required to support service-based productivity and keep consumer demand at healthy levels.

As more Canadians retire relative to the active workforce, there will be increased pressure on government pension and healthcare plans. Critics have suggested that these plans will not be able to meet future obligations without substantial infusions of cash. In response, many Canadians have started registered retirement savings plans and tax-free savings accounts to provide for their own needs. Unfortunately, a large number of Canadians have not planned well for retirement, expecting to receive sufficient government benefits. In addition, the escalating costs associated with socialized health care (medicare) will be a source of public debate for years to come.

SHARED PROSPERITY, EQUITY, AND SOCIAL JUSTICE

Aside from temporary and cyclical setbacks, business profits continue to grow, and stock market indicators continue to inch upward. From 2014 to 2015, the earnings of the top 1 percent of the population rose from 10.3 to 11.2 percent of the country's total income. Most of these increased incomes were in the provinces of Ontario, Alberta, and British Columbia, and most increases were from corporate dividends rather than pay increases. In addition, average earnings data for the 2016 census reveal a persistent gender bias. In most fields, men continue to earn more than their female counterparts.

Canada's focus on the common good requires reflection, not only on the achievement of prosperity but also on the equitable distribution of wealth. As governments cut spending to reduce taxes and fiscal debt, an increasingly larger portion of the Canadian population ends up living in poverty and with food insecurity. As a result, an increasing number of households and individuals are vulnerable in the event of an economic or a personal crisis.

The number of homeless people in Canada and the number of Canadians forced to use food banks continue to increase. At the same time, corporate profit levels continue to grow and provide additional income for investors. At what point do profit levels become excessive? At what point do they suggest that resources, workers, or consumers may have been exploited? Many Canadians still believe that one important role of government is to ensure a more equitable distribution of income by providing direct assistance to those most in need. Others maintain that dependence on government assistance discourages self-reliance. Whatever the case, Canadians will most probably need to continue the fight against poverty and to rebuild the self-esteem of those pushed to the margins of society. Education and employment training are essential in reversing the vicious cycle of poverty.

THE ROLE OF GOVERNMENT

What do Canadians expect from our government? How much are we willing to pay in taxes to receive the social programs that we expect? How can we ensure that government dollars are spent efficiently? Ultimately, how much of our economic freedom are we prepared to trade for increased government involvement and regulation in the economy? At present, Canadian public opinion is divided. Some people favour the continued downsizing of government to reduce debt. Others want public health care and other social benefits protected.

Most Canadians expect government to remain closely involved in protecting competition and ensuring fair business practices, especially as businesses continue to grow and become more powerful. Some business leaders advocate the adoption of more "American-like" practices

that will allow Canadian firms to compete on a level playing field. The US model calls for less government involvement in the economy and emphasizes individual freedom and self-reliance. The traditional Canadian model reflects a more collectivist, or common good approach, similar to the economies of Sweden and France. Public debate on the most appropriate role of government will likely continue. The principal tasks of this course have been to help you recognize opinion for what it is; decide whether an assertion is based on fact, logic, and acceptable assumptions; and, ultimately, evaluate the impact that suggested changes will have on economic conditions.

PRODUCTIVITY AND INNOVATION

Many factors influence productivity growth, including the amount and quality of technology available per worker, the quality of the workforce, and the pace of innovation and investment in new technology. To sustain and improve living standards, Canadians must work hard to create efficiencies or productivity gains in every field of economic endeavour. Unemployment rates in Canada are expected to remain slightly higher than those in the United States. If the productivity of Canadian labour increases through training and technological advances, then wage rates and working conditions could improve without adversely affecting business profits. If worker productivity does not increase, then wage rates and working conditions might have to be adjusted downward to keep Canadian labour globally competitive. If Canadian workers are paid more without proportionate gains in productivity, then price inflation could increase and employment levels could fall as employers shed surplus workers. Ultimately, the international value of the Canadian dollar might also decline.

Some firms have improved worker productivity by instituting profit-sharing programs and allowing workers to become shareholders. These strategies give workers an added interest in the firm's success and an additional income stream. Many economists argue that Canadian industries face a formidable challenge in narrowing the productivity gap with their American counterparts. The quality of the workforces in Canada and the United States is comparable in terms of education and skill. US businesses, however, tend to invest in more technology per worker and adopt the latest technologies faster than their Canadian counterparts. In recent years, a significant boost to productivity in Canada has come from advances in the information and communications technology industry. For example, Canadians are world leaders in fibre optic technology.

To continue to improve productivity, Canadian businesses must increase their investment in innovation. The Canadian government can support innovation by providing investment incentives (such as tax breaks) to Canadian businesses and promoting increased research and development (R&D) in Canada rather than importing this expertise from abroad. As long as interest rates remain low, businesses will be more likely to invest in innovation and improve productivity.

Several public and private challenges remain if productivity and innovation are to keep Canadian industry competitive. What specific measures and funding (both private and public) will be required to achieve this goal? Will Canadian entrepreneurs be able to turn new ideas into job-creating, profitable businesses? Will Canadian universities be able to train a large number of high-calibre scientists, researchers, and engineers without substantial financial assistance from government? Will quality researchers opt to stay in Canada or accept lucrative offers abroad? Will talent and expertise be drained out of Canada, or will the Canadian economy attract knowledge and expertise from abroad? Will the private sector generate sufficient investment funds for the large-scale innovation ventures and infrastructure improvements required, or will the government have to participate? The answers to these questions will help to determine how successful Canadians will be in increasing productivity.

CORPORATE POWER AND THE MARKETPLACE

Canadians are living in a "golden age" for corporations and big business, both in Canada and globally. In a free-enterprise market, successful businesses will continue to expand their capital assets, their scale of operations, and their ability to acquire smaller rivals. As a result, the concentration of corporate power in Canada is expected to continue to grow. In addition, successful businesses will continue to enter into more alliances with other large enterprises to share technology, reduce operating expenses, and gain additional market share. As long as healthy levels of competition are maintained in the marketplace and unfair business practices are regulated and held accountable, the benefits of this corporate concentration can include efficiencies from large-scale operations, increased ability to compete in larger global markets, competitive prices for Canadian consumers, and substantial returns on investment for Canadian firms.

At the same time, it cannot be assumed that all big businesses will automatically be good for Canada and Canadians. Many do not behave as good corporate citizens by displaying a clear social conscience in their decision making. They prefer "profit maximization" strategizing (often including pollution, outsourcing, and laying off domestic workers), leaving it to governments to deal with the harmful consequences. The 2018 decision by General Motors to shut down its assembly plant in Oshawa, Ontario, and move its vehicle production to Mexico (where employment costs are a fraction of Canadian costs) is a classic example of profit-driven decision making. Yet when General Motors was on the brink of bankruptcy, during the financial crisis of 2008, the Canadian and Ontario governments were asked to provide billions of dollars in job-protecting bailout money.

CLIMATE CHANGE, CLEAN ENERGY, AND ENVIRONMENTAL PROTECTION

Climate change resulting from global warming is a confirmed scientific fact. Given our country's cold climate, great distances between communities, and highly industrialized economy, Canadians will most likely continue to be high per capita consumers of energy reserves. The search for alternative forms of energy, if successful, will reduce both our reliance on imported fossil fuels and the emission of greenhouse gases. As these carbon-based gases continue to warm up our atmosphere, urgent action is needed in all industrialized countries. The damage caused by more frequent episodes of extreme weather will cost more money to address each year. To tackle climate change, Canada and 194 other countries signed the Paris Agreement (2015) to limit carbon emissions. Others will have to be forced to cut harmful emissions significantly through international pressure. China, the United States, and the European Union (EU) account for half of all carbon emissions.

Canadians have been interested in the development of solar energy since the global fuel crisis of the mid-1970s. From an economic perspective, capital investment in solar energy technology and wind power technology should increase proportionately as more ventures demonstrate the profitability of these clean energy investments. Advances in turbine technology have led the governments of Ontario, Alberta, Quebec, New Brunswick, and Newfoundland and Labrador to include wind power in their energy mix.

The challenge of meeting Canada's energy needs while reducing harmful carbon emissions will continue to require sizable capital investment. With the potential for great profits, renewable energy initiatives should continue to attract investor interest and create employment opportunities. For example, Ballard Power Systems of

Vancouver, British Columbia, is recognized as a world leader in developing, manufacturing, and marketing zero-emission, proton-exchange membrane (PEM) fuel cells to power buses, trains, cars, drones, and electrical equipment. PEM fuel cells produce electric power through the reaction of hydrogen and oxygen. Since water is the only by-product, these fuel cells are a clean power solution.

In spite of this progress, important economic questions remain. Can the impacts of climate change be dealt with effectively within the present economic system through carbon taxes, pollution credits, subsidies, grants, and regulations? Or is an existential emergency required to force the drastic actions necessary to avoid disaster? How can the largest countries (China, the United States, the EU, and India) be pressured into more responsible stewardship of our ailing planet? How far can we get with consumer-based programs that rely on lifestyle changes (reduce, reuse, and recycle) without a parallel initiative to affect more socially responsible corporate citizenship? How can emission reductions and pollution controls be effectively monitored to confirm actual achievement?

Ultimately, if all other strategies fall short, the present economic system may have to shift toward a "no growth" economy where consumerism is sharply reduced and stability becomes the focus. Strict legislation (including fines) and consumer action (protests, boycotts, and targeted stock acquisition) may be required to force co-operation, regardless of the impact on corporate profits.

GLOBALISM, NATIONALISM AND LOCALISM

As we continue down the path of globalization, no country can isolate itself from economic events abroad. Today, each national economy is a "province" of the global economy. Canadian workers are now part of the global labour pool, and jobs will be created where market forces dictate.

Present levels of globalization demonstrate both good and bad effects. It is hoped that Canadian business and government leaders will have a positive impact on the future direction of globalization. For globalization to succeed, it must be seen to work for people and not just for profits. If we are able to achieve this goal, the biggest dividends will be sustainable development and peace. If we are unable to achieve this goal, political unrest may escalate. The flood of desperate refugees migrating away from oppressive and exploitative conditions in some developing countries will continue to grow exponentially, unless the international community is able to address the root causes of this desperation in their original homelands.

The recent wave of refugees attempting to cross national borders has been one catalyst in the rise of populist movements toward renewed nationalism and local control. These ultra-conservative sentiments are often fuelled by xenophobia and the fear that migrants will take jobs and social benefits away from citizens. Britain's emotional Brexit strategy to leave the EU was greatly influenced by the desire to regain control over national borders.

Some critics suggest that a return to a renewed form of communism or socialism is one likely political reaction to capitalist exploitation in some less developed countries. However, the economic collapse in 2018 of oil-rich Venezuela, under a socialist dictator backed by military leaders, is confirmation that economic correction is not a simple matter of ideology, because corruption, exploitation, and mismanagement can exist under any system.

To date, globalization has promoted free trade, but the full potential of free trade has not been achieved. Wage stagnation and the loss of manufacturing jobs in developed countries can be linked directly to globalization. These outcomes have fuelled anti-globalization sentiments in many developed economies. What is now needed is a united movement toward fair trade. It is not enough for trade to be free of barriers to maximize profits. To serve humanity best, trade must also be free of exploitation and environmental contamination. Companies doing business with oppressive governments help to perpetuate injustice. Until fair trade and democratic government prevail, developed countries can expect desperate refugees in unprecedented numbers.

As manufacturing continues to be outsourced to less developed economies, Canada's economic future does not rest in the manufacturing sector, but rather in the natural resources sector and the post-industrial services and technology sectors. According to World Bank data, high- and medium-technology goods are the fastest-growing components of international trade, while resources and other primary products are in decline. This pattern is expected to continue, further highlighting the importance of the services and technology sectors in Canada's future.

AND SO IT COMES DOWN TO THIS . . .

The economic challenges awaiting you are both problems and opportunities. Use the knowledge and skills acquired through this course to think both critically and economically when analyzing important issues. To make sound decisions, be sure to recognize and weigh the costs and benefits of each available alternative. Welcome to the complex adventure that being Canadian entails. Now, roll up your sleeves and help build a better tomorrow.

Congratulations! You have steadily progressed through this course, and now is the time for you to demonstrate the full extent of your learning by applying your acquired knowledge and skills to a final, culminating task.

YOUR TASK

As a recent graduate of economics, you are searching for work in your field. The following prospective employers have indicated an interest in hiring a new economics consultant/adviser:

- Canadian Broadcasting Corporation (CBC)
- Royal Bank of Canada (RBC)
- Toronto Stock Exchange (TSX)
- Magna International
- PCL Construction
- The largest municipality in your province

Along with your job application, you will submit a short report outlining the following:

- Your assessment of the current state of the Canadian economy
- A forecast of future trends
- Recommendations (identifying and advocating the wisest course of action) to help grow the economy

Your report should also identify current economic patterns and issues to prioritize economic goals and recommend strategies to effectively achieve them. Review Canada's 10 principal economic goals discussed in Chapter 4 (pages 52–55) and prioritize the goals you think are most relevant to your report.

PERFORMANCE TARGET

You need to impress your preferred employer, so demonstrate that you can use economic information, data, and graphs to effectively interpret and communicate useful information for personal, corporate, or political (collective) decision-making. Your challenge is to analyze economic ideas and activity patterns thoroughly, while clearly communicating important observations and forecasts. Even those with a limited background in economics should be able to recognize the significance of what you present. The CBC job is for an on-air analyst/adviser who would need to explain important economic ideas in news reports. The other employers are looking for in-house expertise to inform decision making.

STEPS AND RECOMMENDATIONS

1 Determine which employer and sector of the economy would represent the best fit for your interests and abilities.

2 Review the critical-thinking questions that follow, and keep them in mind as you prepare the report showcasing your knowledge and skills.

3 Conduct research to summarize current economic conditions and to identify and prioritize issues and available options.

4 Perform a cost-benefit analysis to identify the wisest strategies to address issues and promote Prepare a persuasive argument to confirm the soundness of the strategies being advocated.

5 Create a concise, informative, and persuasive report to present and support your ideas. Remember that many people do not have a background in economics, so you will need to be informative, concise, and persuasive.

CRITICAL-THINKING QUESTIONS

1 Presently, what are the most important events, activities, or patterns in the Canadian economy that your prospective employer would be most interested to hear about in your report?

2 Which reliable sources of information would be most helpful to project and support your predictions of future trends?

3 What criteria can be used to determine the most appropriate course of action to recommend, and what evidence can be used to confirm the soundness of this recommendation?

4 What is the most effective way to communicate your knowledge and skills to the members of the hiring committee?

ADAPTING THE TASK

Discuss with your teacher alternative employers and industries for which you are most interested in adapting this task. Format options for your report can also be discussed with your teacher so that you select the most appropriate vehicle to demonstrate your knowledge and skills, along with your ability to use them effectively.

You may choose to organize your presentation into a written, video, PowerPoint, or online report. Diagrams, graphs, and tables are essential for communicating your ideas most effectively, regardless of the format you choose. Share drafts with your teacher, classmates, parents, or guardians to obtain useful feedback about improving your presentation.

ASSESSMENT CRITERIA

The following criteria will be used to assess your work:

- **Knowledge:** accurately using economic terms, concepts, principles, and theories
- **Thinking and Inquiry:** using sound economic thinking to focus analysis and make appropriate forecasts and connections
- **Communication:** presenting economic information clearly and accurately, and in an appropriate format and style
- **Application:** presenting a relevant account of economic patterns and a persuasive argument for the course of action being advocated

Use the rubric provided by your teacher as a coaching tool to help complete this task successfully.

Glossary

Absolute advantage: The capacity of one economy to produce a good or service with fewer resources than another.

Absolute poverty: Poverty defined as lacking the basic essentials for survival such as food, shelter, or clothing.

Accounting profit: The excess of a firm's revenues over its costs.

Acquisition: The purchase of controlling interests in one company by another.

Actual output: The GDP that the economy actually produces, which may be lower than its potential GDP.

After-tax income: Total annual income after federal and provincial taxes are deducted.

Aggregate demand: The total demand for all goods and services produced in an economy.

Aggregate supply: The total supply of all goods and services produced in an economy.

American antitrust law: Federal laws to protect competition and to prevent a company or enterprise from becoming too powerful or dominant in the marketplace.

Analytical economics: The branch of economics that deals with facts and direct observation of the world; also called *positive economics*.

Appreciation: An increase in a domestic currency's value in terms of another currency.

Aquaculture: The breeding and raising of marine life in tanks, ponds, and reservoirs; also known as fish farming.

Arithmetical progression: A number sequence (such as 1, 3, 5, 7, 9, 11, 13...) that has the same difference (in this case, by 2) between each number in the sequence; it is associated with food production in the pessimistic theories of Thomas Malthus.

Articles of incorporation: A legal document, filed with the government, that incorporates a business.

Asia-Pacific Economic Cooperation (APEC): A regional forum established in 1989, mainly of Pacific rim countries, that promotes free trade among its members.

Asset: Anything that is owned by a business, company, or government.

Asset income: Income received by an individual in the form of interest, dividends, or rent.

Asset value: A corporate share's portion of the corporation's net worth, represented by its assets minus its liabilities.

Automatic stabilizers: Mechanisms built into the economy that help to stabilize it by automatically increasing or decreasing aggregate demand, such as Employment Insurance, welfare programs, and progressive taxes; often contrasted with discretionary fiscal policy.

Balance of merchandise trade: The difference between a country's merchandise exports and imports.

Balance of payments account: National account of international payments and receipts, divided into the current account and the capital and financial account.

Balance sheet: A snapshot of the financial health of a business such as a bank, recording its assets and liabilities.

Balanced budget: The situation that occurs when a government spends an equal amount to what it has collected in tax revenue.

Bank deposit money: Money composed of people's deposits and loans granted by the banks, exchangeable by cheque or electronic transfer.

Bank note: Paper currency issued by a country's central bank.

Bank rate: The rate of interest charged by the Bank of Canada to the chartered banks, which serves as a benchmark for the interest rates charged by financial institutions to their customers.

Barter: The trading of goods and services without the use of a monetary system; such transactions are common in traditional economies.

Bear market: A stock market under the influence of traders expecting prices to fall, an expectation that is usually self-fulfilling.

Before-tax income: Total annual income before federal and provincial taxes are deducted.

Black market: The illegal exchange of goods in short supply, as when some people buy up as much of a good as possible, stockpile it, and sell it at a higher price.

Blue-chip stock: Shares of large corporations that are commonly regarded as safe and stable investments.

Bond: A financial asset that represents a debt owed by a corporation to the holder, on which interest is paid by the corporation to the holder.

Book value: The value of a share when it was first issued; also known as face value.

Bourgeoisie: The term used by Karl Marx for industrial capitalists who, he theorized, would be overthrown by the working class.

Boycott: A union tactic of bringing pressure upon an employer by encouraging the public not to purchase the employer's product.

Brain drain: Emigration of highly skilled Canadian workers to the United States and other countries.

Branch banking system: A banking system, such as Canada's, that restricts the number of banks that can operate, but allows them to have as many branches as they want.

Branch plant: A firm or factory owned by a multinational corporation that operates in another country.

Bull market: A market influenced by investors expecting prices to rise, an expectation that is usually self-fulfilling.

Bureaucracy: The administrative structure of government responsible for delivering programs such as Employment Insurance and medicare.

Business cycle: A rise and fall in national economic performance characterized by four phases: peak, contraction, trough, and expansion.

Canada Assistance Plan (CAP): A federal transfer of money to the provinces to help fund welfare programs for Canadians.

Canada Pension Plan (CPP): A pension paid to all retired workers who have made compulsory payments to the plan during their working years.

Canada-US Automotive Products Trade Agreement (Auto Pact): A 1965 trade agreement between Canada and the US to eliminate tariffs on auto parts and automobiles.

Canadian direct investment (CDI): Canadian direct investment abroad, in the form of building a new plant, establishing a new business, or taking over an existing one.

Canadian Labour Congress: A federation of Canadian unions, which lobbies the federal government on labour legislation and other social and economic policies affecting workers.

Capital: A factor of production that refers to the machinery, factories, warehouses, and equipment used to produce goods and services.

Capital account: Part of a balance of payments account that records totals for migrants' funds, inheritances, and government pension payments.

Capital and financial account: Part of an economy's balance of payments account that measures flows of capital and investment.

Capital goods: Goods, such as tools or machinery, used to produce consumer goods.

Capital-intensive production: Production in which machinery rather than labour dominates the process, characteristic of the factory system.

Capitalism: An economy characterized by private ownership of business and industry, the profit motive, and free markets.

Carbon pricing: Requires firms to pay for costs of production associated with releasing greenhouse gas emissions in an attempt to control global warming and climate change. Sometimes referred to as a carbon tax.

Carrying capacity: Environmental term referring to the number of people that the earth's resources can support indefinitely if those resources are managed effectively.

Cartel: A group of competitors collaborating together to limit competition or to increase profits.

Cash drain: The proportion of a bank deposit that a person chooses to hold in cash outside the bank, reducing the bank's excess reserves and, thus, its ability to lend.

Cause-and-effect fallacy: See *Post hoc fallacy*.

Ceiling price: A restriction imposed by a government to prevent the price of a product from rising above a certain level.

Ceteris paribus: Latin for "other things being equal" or "as long as other things do not change"; an assumption made when economists want to understand the cause-and-effect relationship between any two factors and want other factors affecting that relationship to be held constant.

Chartered bank: A bank established by a charter passed by the Canadian federal government.

Chequing account: An account that serves primarily as a medium of exchange, paying little or no interest.

Child Tax Credit: A federal payment to low-income households with children under 18 years; replaced the Family Allowance in 1978.

Circular flow of income: A model of the economy that sees GDP as a total of all the money payments made to businesses and individuals.

Class-action lawsuit: A lawsuit brought by one or more persons who file a complaint on behalf of themselves and others affected by a problem, such as pollution caused by a firm's activities.

Climate change: The varied consequences of global warming, including excessive rainfall and drought, and other extreme weather events, linked to the release of greenhouse gases.

Closed shop: A clause in the collective agreement between a union and an employer that stipulates that the employer may hire only union members.

Coase theorem: Theory of economist Robert Coase, which states that in some circumstances private negotiations are more efficient than government intervention in dealing with negative externalities such as pollution.

Cohort: A group with similar statistical characteristics, such as all Canadians between 18 and 25 years of age.

Collective agreement: A contract lasting a specific period of time, negotiated by a union with the employer through the process of collective bargaining.

Collective bargaining: A process whereby a union negotiates wages and working conditions with the employer on behalf of all members of the union.

Collusion: An illegal agreement among competing firms to set prices, limit output, divide the market, or exclude other competitors.

Combines Investigation Act (1889): Canada's first act to prevent firms from fixing prices or lessening competition to the detriment of consumers; replaced in 1986 by the Competition Act.

Command economy: An economic system in which production decisions are made by government-appointed central planners.

Commodity: A raw or semi-processed good (such as minerals, lumber, or grain) that is often sold in bulk.

Commodity money: Money that has value in itself; for example, cattle, wheat, or salt.

Common good: The well-being of society at large, sometimes referred to as the most good for the greatest number.

Common market: The strongest form of free trade agreement, which includes free movement of labour and capital among members, tariff-free movement of goods, and a common policy on trade restrictions against non-members.

Common resources: Productive resources (such as forests, pasture lands, and fishing waters) that are owned by no one but are available for use by different people.

Communism: A political system on the extreme left, founded on the theory of Karl Marx, that calls for government or community ownership of the means of production.

Comparative advantage: The capacity of one economy to produce a good or service with comparatively fewer resources than another (for example, having a lower opportunity cost).

Competition Act (1986): The act that replaced the old Combines Investigation Act to address problems caused by business mergers, acquisitions, and price fixing.

Competition Bureau Canada: Government agency that administers the Competition Act.

Competition Tribunal: The board empowered to make decisions on disputes between corporations and Competition Bureau Canada that cannot be decided through negotiation.

Complementary goods: Goods that are interrelated and used together (for example, gasoline and automobiles).

Comprehensive and Progressive Agreement for Trans-Pacific Partnership (CPTPP): A new free trade agreement including Canada and 10 other countries. The CPTPP will be one of the largest free trade agreements in the world once it is ratified by all member countries.

Compulsory arbitration: A process in which a government forces both sides in a labour dispute to accept the decision of a third party.

Conciliation: A process in which a third party helps a union and an employer reach an agreement; also called *mediation*.

Conglomerate: A group of companies involved in different industries, but controlled by a central management group.

Conjecture: An opinion or guess based on inference or assumption.

Consequence: The result, effect, or outcome of an action taken or the refusal to take an action.

Consumer equilibrium: The state of satisfaction a consumer reaches when the marginal utility divided by price is equal for two or more products bought by that consumer.

Consumer goods: Those goods or services that an economy produces to satisfy human needs.

Consumer price index (CPI): A price index that measures changes in the level of prices of consumer goods and services.

Consumer sovereignty: A principle of market economies that the production choices of the economy are ultimately made by the buying decisions of consumers.

Consumer surplus: The difference between what consumers are willing to pay for an item and what they actually pay.

Consumption: Household spending on goods and services.

Contractionary fiscal policy: Government policies to decrease aggregate demand through tax increases and/or decreased spending.

Co-operative: A business owned equally by its members who have a common relationship, goal, or economic purpose.

Copyright law: A law that protects the intellectual property rights of writers and the creative works of artists.

Corn Laws: Early nineteenth-century taxes on grains imported into Britain that drove up the market price of domestic grain to benefit aristocratic landlords. These taxes became a focus of opposition for David Ricardo's wage and free trade theories.

Corporate alliance: A group of companies that agree to operate as a single company while retaining separate ownership.

Corporate income tax: A tax paid to the federal and provincial governments by corporations as a percentage of their profits.

Corporation: A business firm recognized legally as a separate entity in its own right.

Cost per unit: A measure of a firm's efficiency, obtained by dividing total costs by the number of units produced.

Cost-push inflation: Inflation caused by the passing down of increased production costs to consumer goods and services.

Craft unions: See *Trade unions*.

Crowding out: The theory that government borrowing drives up interest rates and reduces the amount of loanable funds, thereby making it more difficult for businesses to borrow.

Crown corporation: A business owned by the federal government.

Crown land: A Canadian term for government-owned land.

Currency: Coins and notes that compose the money supply of an economy.

Current account: A bank account for a business that operates like a chequing account, paying little or no interest and serving as a medium of exchange; also, part of a balance of payments account that records totals for three components: goods, services, and investment income.

Custom duty: A tax charged on foreign goods entering the country; also called *tariff*.

Customs union: Extension of a free trade agreement among members to include a common policy on trade restrictions on non-members.

Cyclical deficit: The part of a deficit that is incurred when the government is trying to pull an economy out of a recession.

Cyclical unemployment: Unemployment caused by a downturn in the business cycle.

Debt: The total amount that a government owes on money it has borrowed to fund deficit budgets in the past.

Decision lag: The time required for a government to decide on an appropriate fiscal policy after recognizing that an economic problem exists.

Deferred savings: A policy of bringing foreign peoples under the control of one country for its economic benefit; pursued in the nineteenth and twentieth centuries by European countries over sizable areas of Asia, Africa, and South America.

Deficit budget: The situation that occurs when the government spends more than it collects in taxes, causing a shortfall (or deficit), which it must cover through borrowing.

Deflation: A general fall in the price levels of an economy.

Demand: The quantity of a good or service that buyers will purchase at various prices during a given period of time.

Demand curve: A straight line or curve on a graph illustrating the demand schedule for a product.

Demand deposit: A bank deposit (such as a chequing account) that can be used to make immediate payment.

Demand-pull inflation: Inflation caused by excessive increases in consumer demand relative to available production.

Democracy: A political system characterized by a freely elected government that represents the majority of its citizens.

Deposit (or money) multiplier: The amount by which a change in the monetary base is multiplied to determine the resulting change in the money supply.

Depreciation: A decrease in a domestic currency's value in terms of a foreign currency.

Depression: A prolonged recession characterized by falling GDP, very high unemployment, and price deflation.

Deprivation: A term associated with the idea of absolute poverty; that is, income so low that an individual cannot afford the basic necessities of life.

Deregulation: The opening of a market to more competition by eliminating government regulations originally put in place to limit competition.

Derived demand: Demand for resources (such as labour) that is dependent on, or derived from, the direct demand of consumers for the goods and services being produced.

Devaluation: A depreciation or fall in the exchange value of a currency resulting from intervention on the part of a government or its central bank.

Developmentalist: A school of economic thinkers who believe that economic development makes social and political progress possible.

Dictatorship: A political system in which a single person exercises absolute authority over an entire country.

Direct demand: Consumer demand for goods and services that directly determines the kind and quantity produced; see also *Derived demand*.

Direct investment: Investment in the form of building a new plant, establishing a new business, or taking over an existing one, carried out by Canadians abroad or by foreigners here.

Direct relationship: A positive association between two variables where when one variable is increased the other variable also increases, and when one variable is decreased the other also decreases.

Direct tax: A tax (such as income tax) whose burden cannot be passed on to others by the taxpayer.

Discouraged workers: Those who would like to work but have stopped looking because they believe nothing is available for them.

Discretionary fiscal policy: Deliberate government action taken to stabilize the economy in the form of taxation or spending policies; often contrasted with automatic stabilizers.

Dividend: Corporation profits distributed to shareholders on a per-share basis.

Division of labour: The specialization of workers in a complex production process, leading to greater efficiency.

Double coincidence of wants: The problem of barter: for a trade to occur, both parties must want what the other is willing to trade.

Dow Jones Industrial Average: The most widely known indicator of stock market activity based upon the daily closing prices of 30 blue-chip US corporations.

Downsize: Reduce the number of employees in a company to lower production costs.

Drawing down: An environmental term referring to the process of using up resources (such as minerals or forests) or abusing ones (such as fresh water or air) in the present that should be available for future generations.

Dumping: The deliberate practice of selling a product internationally at a price lower than its domestic price.

Dynamic pricing: The practice of changing price as demand increases or decreases within a short time frame.

Easy money policy: A monetary policy of low interest rates, easy availability of credit, and growth of the money supply.

Economic development: A rise in a country's standard of living as measured by a rise in per capita GDP.

Economic growth: An increase in an economy's total production of goods and services.

Economic profit: The excess of a business's revenue over its economic costs (implicit and explicit costs).

Economic system: The laws, institutions, and common practices that help a country determine how to use its resources to satisfy as many of its people's needs and wants as possible.

Economics: The study of the way society makes decisions about the use of scarce resources.

Economies of scale: The greater efficiency a firm can achieve when it produces very large amounts of output.

Economize: To use limited resources efficiently in production.

Economy: A self-sustaining system in which many independent transactions in a society create distinct flows of money and products or services.

Effective (use of resources): A particular use of resources that achieves a desired end, such as consumption.

Efficiency: A firm's ability to produce at the lowest possible cost, measured by either its cost per unit or its unit labour cost.

Efficient (use of resources): The use of a bare minimum of resources to achieve a desired end, such as consumption.

Elastic coefficient: A coefficient for a product of more than one, indicating that a given percentage change in price causes a greater percentage change in quantity demanded.

Elasticity of supply: The responsiveness of the quantity supplied by a seller to a rise or fall in its price.

Embargo: An action taken by one country against another for some political purpose to prevent import or export of goods or services.

Employment Insurance (EI): A federal program to assist those temporarily out of work due to job loss, illness, or birth or adoption of a child; called *Unemployment Insurance (UI)* until 1996.

Employment rate: The total number of employed divided by the total labour force.

Entrepreneurship: The contribution made by an owner, manager, or innovator who organizes land, labour, and capital to produce goods and services.

Environment for enterprise: A society's social values and institutions, such as stable government, that are favourable to businesses attempting to produce and sell goods and services.

Equilibrium price: A price set by the interaction of demand and supply in which the absence of surpluses or shortages in the market means there is no tendency for the price to change.

Equity: Fair and just distribution of income within an economy.

Essential Skills: Skills defined by Employment and Social Development Canada that people require if they are to learn, work, and live.

Excess reserves: The amount of cash over and above what is needed to meet demand from depositors and so can be lent.

Exchange rate: The price at which one currency can be purchased with another.

Excise tax: A tax paid to the federal and provincial governments, as a set dollar amount per unit, on items such as liquor, gasoline, and tobacco.

Exclusion: A term associated with the idea of relative poverty; that is, income so low that an individual cannot enjoy the standard of living of the majority of society.

Expansionary fiscal policy: A government policy to increase aggregate demand through tax cuts, increased spending, or both.

Expenditure approach: A calculation of GDP that totals all that the economy spends on final goods and services in one year.

Explicit costs: Costs that appear on a business's accounting statements, such as payment for material, machines, rent, utilities, and taxes.

Export: A good or service that is produced in one country, but sold to consumers, businesses, or governments in another country.

Externality: A side effect of production, either positive or negative, experienced by a third party who is neither a producer nor a consumer of the product.

Factors of production: Resources (such as land, labour, and capital) that are used to produce goods and services. Also called *productive resources*.

Fair trade: Trade deals where the most vulnerable trading partners are treated with dignity and respect rather than being exploited by wealthy traders or large multinational corporations.

Fairtrade: A non-government organization that works to empower disadvantaged producers in developing countries by tackling conventional trade, in particular by promoting and licensing the Fairtrade label.

Fallacy: A hypothesis that has been proven false but is still accepted by many people because it appears to be true.

Fallacy of composition: A mistaken belief that what is good for an individual is automatically good for everyone, or what is good for everyone is good for the individual.

Fallacy of single causation: A mistaken belief, based on oversimplification, that a particular event has one cause rather than several causes.

Family Allowance: A program of monetary support, started in 1942, for all Canadian households with children under 18; replaced by Child Tax Credit in 1978.

Fascism: A political system on the extreme right, combining a free-market economy with a non-democratic form of government.

Fiat money: Money that represents value because governments have declared it to be legal tender, not because it is valuable in itself or exchangeable for gold.

Financial account: The part of the balance of payments that records totals for direct investment and portfolio investment.

Firm: A privately owned organization engaged in business activities.

Fiscal policy: Government taxation, spending, and borrowing policies used to try to stabilize the economy.

Fixed costs: Costs (such as rent and property taxes) that remain the same at all levels of output and must be paid whether the firm produces or not.

Fixed exchange rate: An exchange rate for a currency that is fixed in relation to another currency, such as the US dollar.

Flexible exchange rate: An exchange rate determined entirely in the market by the forces of demand and supply, with no government intervention.

Floating exchange rate: See *Flexible exchange rate*.

Floor price: A restriction that prevents a price from falling below a certain level.

Foreign aid: Assistance and economic support given from one national government to another to combat poverty and to facilitate economic growth.

Foreign direct investment (FDI): Foreign direct investment in Canada in the form of building a new plant, establishing a new business, or taking over an existing one.

Foreign exchange reserve: The store of foreign currencies and gold held by the central bank, used at times to intervene in the foreign exchange market.

Fractional reserve banking: The discovery made by goldsmiths that they could lend much of the gold deposited with them for safe keeping because only a fraction of it was usually withdrawn by the depositors.

Free Trade Agreement (FTA): An agreement between two or more countries to eliminate tariffs between them while retaining the right to impose tariffs upon non-members.

In 1989, the FTA between Canada and the United States was meant to phase out trade restrictions. It was superseded by NAFTA, which came into force in 1994.

Free trade area: The region encompassing a trade bloc whose member countries have signed a free trade agreement.

Frictional unemployment: Unemployment caused by workers who are between jobs or who are entering or re-entering the labour force.

Frontier: The curve on a production possibilities graph representing the maximum numbers of two items that can be produced with a given amount of resources.

Full employment: The lowest possible rate of unemployment, seasonally adjusted, after allowing for frictional and structural unemployment.

Full-employment equilibrium: The intersection of aggregate demand and supply, at which full employment is reached and prices have just started to rise.

Futures market: A market for commodities that are bought and sold for future delivery.

GDP gap: The cost of unemployment to the economy, measured by the difference between the actual GDP produced and the potential GDP that could be produced if the unemployment rate equalled the natural rate of unemployment.

GDP per capita: The total value of a country's annual production of goods and services divided by its population; also called *per capita GDP*.

General Agreement on Tariffs and Trade (GATT): An international trade agreement signed by 23 countries, including Canada, in 1947. It was designed to reduce trade barriers among member countries.

Geographical unemployment: Unemployment created in specific parts or geographical regions of a country due to a weak economy in the area that is overly reliant on one or two struggling industries. Ultimately, this unemployment is caused when the skills and location of available workers do not match or support the limited economic opportunities that exist in the region. It is also known as regional unemployment.

Geometrical progression: A number sequence (such as 2, 4, 8, 16, 32, 64...) that has the same ratio (in this case, × 2) between each number in the sequence; it is associated with population growth in the pessimistic theories of Thomas Malthus.

Gig economy: A shift in the labour market that sees firms using more freelance workers and independent contractors instead of full-time employees.

Global Affairs Canada: The Government of Canada department that manages Canada's diplomatic relations, provides consular services to Canadians, promotes the country's international trade, and leads Canada's international development and humanitarian assistance.

Globalization: A process whereby national or regional economies become integrated through communication technologies, foreign direct investment, international trade, immigration, and the flow of money.

Gold standard: A promise by a government that it will exchange gold for the national currency on demand.

Goods and Services Tax (GST): A Canadian federal government sales tax levied on a range of goods and services.

Government enterprise: A business that provides services owned by the federal, provincial, or municipal government.

Greenhouse gases (GHGs): Gases such as carbon dioxide, methane, and nitrous oxide released by the burning of fossil fuels that are contributing to global warming and climate change.

Gross domestic product (GDP): The total market value of all final goods and services produced by an economy in a given year.

Gross national income (GNI) per capita: A measurement of a country's income divided by its population. It includes all the income earned by a country's residents and businesses, including any income earned abroad. It was formerly called *GNP per capita*.

Guaranteed Income Supplement (GIS): A program of extra support for older Canadians whose primary income source is Old Age Security (OAS).

Harmonized Sales Tax (HST): A single tax that blends together the federal goods and services tax with the provincial sales tax.

Hidden unemployed: The total of all underemployed workers plus all discouraged workers, a number not included in calculating the official unemployment rate.

High-income economy: A country with high enough GNI per capita (set at US$12 056 in 2019) to provide the majority of its citizens with prosperity; also called *industrially advanced country*.

High-tech industries: Industries that develop, provide, or use highly complex technology.

Holding company: An enterprise that holds shares in other producing companies.

Horizontal integration: The joining together of two firms that produce the same product or service to operate as one firm.

Horizontal merger: A consolidation of two firms producing the same product or service.

Human capital: The knowledge, skills, and talents possessed by workers.

Human Development Index (HDI): Established by the United Nations, a measurement of a country's achievements in three aspects of human development: life expectancy, literacy and education levels, and GDP per capita. In 2018, Canada ranked 12th among the 189 countries included in the HDI.

Humanitarian aid: Life-saving assistance from one country to another in times of emergencies such as famine, drought, earthquakes, tsunamis, and destructive weather storms.

Hyperinflation: A particularly serious period of price inflation when the inflation rate exceeds 50 percent per month.

Hypothesis: A speculative theory requiring proof or verification.

Impact lag: The time required for a fiscal policy to bring about a change in the economy.

Imperfect competition: A common market situation where competition is less than perfect (where many buyers interact with many sellers) but still competitive (unlike monopoly).

Samples include monopolistic competition and oligopoly.

Implementation lag: The time required to implement an appropriate fiscal policy after making the decision to carry it out.

Implicit costs: Costs not included among expenses on the income statement of a business, such as the amount of owner's time spent devoted to his or her business and the money invested in the business that could have earned interest if invested somewhere else.

Import: A good or service that is purchased by consumers, businesses, or governments that was produced in another country.

Inadequate demand unemployment: Unemployment caused by declining aggregate demand; another term for cyclical unemployment.

Income approach: A calculation of GDP that totals all the incomes earned by the different factors of production in producing all final goods and services in one year.

Indexing: An adjustment made to some wages and pension payments to offset year-to-year price increases, using the CPI as a guide.

Indirect tax: A tax (such as sales taxes) whose burden is passed on by the seller to the buyer of the good.

Industrial Revolution: The period of technological innovation and factory production, beginning in Britain in the late eighteenth century, that eventually changed an economy from one largely agricultural and rural to one that was industrial and urban.

Industrial unions: Unions that represent all workers in a given industry, regardless of the type of job they do.

Industrially advanced country (IAC): See High-income economy; also referred to as developed country.

Inelastic coefficient: A coefficient for a product of less than one, indicating that a given percentage change in price causes a smaller percentage change in quantity demanded.

Inequity: A condition or privilege that benefits some to the detriment of others because fairness and distributive justice have been overlooked.

Inflation: A general rise in the price levels of an economy.

Inflation premium: An allowance for inflation that is built into all interest rates.

Inflation rate: The annual percentage by which the CPI has risen.

Inflationary gap: The gap between aggregate demand and full employment equilibrium; characterized by high inflation, low unemployment, and high GDP growth.

Inflow: A receipt that flows into Canada and is recorded on the capital account, such as an inheritance received by a Canadian from another country.

Infrastructure: The foundation of goods and services (such as roads, power grids, transit systems, communications systems, schools, and hospitals) that allows an economy to operate efficiently.

Injection: Any expenditure (such as investment, government spending, and exports) that causes money to be put into the income–expenditure stream of the economy.

Input: A productive resource (such as land, labour, or capital) used to produce an output.

Intangible resources: Resources that are necessary for production, such as entrepreneurship, knowledge, and an environment for enterprise. Intangibles are not as visible as tangible resources, but they are no less important.

Intellectual property rights: Patents for technology, recorded music, and pharmaceutical drugs.

Interest rate: The price charged for borrowing money.

International Monetary Fund (IMF): An organization of 186 member countries that lends money to help members facing balance of payments and exchange rate problems.

International trade: The exchange of goods or services across international borders.

Inverse relationship: A negative association between two variables where when one variable is increased the other decreases, and when one variable is decreased the other increase.

Investment: A business's purchase of capital goods, construction of new buildings, or changes to inventories, with a view to increasing production and profit.

Invisible hand: Adam Smith's notion that the unintended result of individual producers' desire for profit is to supply society with the goods and services it needs, at prices consumers are willing to pay, as a result of competition.

Invisible trade: See *Non-merchandise trade*.

"Jobless" recovery: A phenomenon, not fully understood, of a rise in GDP unaccompanied by a fall in unemployment.

Kyoto Protocol: An international agreement arrived at in 1997 that set international targets and standards to generate mandatory greenhouse gas emission reductions in 41 industrialized countries and the European Union.

Labour: A factor of production comprising the physical and mental effort contributed by people to producing goods and services.

Labour demand curve: A graphical representation of the relationship between the quantity of labour demanded and the wage rate.

Labour force: The total of all Canadians holding jobs plus all of those actively seeking work.

Labour-intensive production: Industry in which labour, rather than machinery, dominates the production process.

Labour supply curve: A graphical representation of the relationship between the number of people willing to offer their services in the form of labour and the wage rate.

Labour union: A workers' organization that negotiates with employers and promotes the interests of its members.

Labour value: Karl Marx's notion that the value of any item is equal to the value of the labour used to produce it.

Laissez-faire: A French term meaning "leave to do" or "let alone," which became associated with the idea that an economy operates best if individuals are allowed to pursue their own self-interest without government interference.

Land: A factor of production that includes all natural resources used to produce goods.

Law of accumulation: Adam Smith's theory that business people who invest a percentage of their profits in new capital equipment increase the economy's stock of capital goods, thus ensuring economic growth and future prosperity.

Law of demand: A law stating that the quantity demanded of a good or service varies inversely with its price, as long as other things do not change.

Law of diminishing returns: The eventual decline in the rate of extra outputs produced that occurs when one input used in production of the output is held constant and the others are increased.

Law of increasing relative cost: The increase in the relative cost of producing more of item A, measured by the numbers of another item, B, that could be produced with the same resources.

Law of increasing returns to scale: The increase in the rate of extra outputs produced when all inputs used in production are increased and no inputs are held constant.

Law of population: Adam Smith's theory that the accumulation of capital by business people requires more workers to operate the equipment, leading to higher wages, which in turn lead to better living conditions, lower mortality rates, and an increase in population.

Law of supply: A law stating that the quantity supplied of a good or service will increase if the price increases and fall if the price falls, as long as other things do not change.

Leakage: Any use of income (such as saving, paying taxes, and spending on imports) that causes money to be taken out of the income–expenditure stream of the economy.

Legal tender: Money that a government has declared must be accepted within the national economy as payment for goods and services.

Less-developed country (LDC): See *Low-income economy*; also referred to as *developing country*.

Liability: Anything owed by an individual, a business, or a government.

Liquidity: The relative ease with which an asset can be used to make a payment. Money is the most liquid asset.

Lockout: The shutting down of the workplace by an employer to force the union to accept the employer's contract offer.

Long run: A time period in which the firm can adjust both its fixed and variable costs to increase its maximum capacity.

Lorenz curve: A graph used to show the degree of inequality that exists among groups of income receivers of the same size.

Low-income cut-off (LICO): A Statistics Canada measurement of low income, defined as any household spending more than 55 percent of its before-tax income on food, shelter, and clothing.

Low-income economy: A country in which a majority of citizens live in poverty, with incomes at or below about GNI per capita of US$995 (in 2019); also called *less-developed country*.

M1: The narrowest measurement of the money supply, comprising cash in circulation along with chequing and current accounts.

M2: A larger measurement of the money supply than M1, comprising M1 plus all types of personal savings accounts, term deposits, and non-personal notice deposits.

M2++: A larger measurement of the money supply than M2, comprising M2 plus deposits at non-bank deposit-taking institutions, money market mutual funds, and annuities.

M3: A larger measurement of the money supply than M2++, comprising M2++ plus foreign currencies held by Canadians and large term deposits held by businesses.

Macroeconomics: The study of the economy as a whole in contrast to microeconomics, which studies its individual parts.

Managed float: A policy of allowing a currency's exchange value to be set by the international market, with intervention by the country's central bank from time to time to smooth out fluctuations.

Marginal benefit (MB): The additional revenue generated by a firm as additional units are produced, thereby increasing the use of an externality, such as a lake for dumping waste.

Marginal cost: The additional cost for a firm of producing one more unit of its product.

Marginal private cost (MPC): Part of a process to assess the impact of production decisions, marginal private cost is the additional production cost incurred privately by a firm as it increases units of output. It does not take into account the cost of negative externalities.

Marginal product: The change in output that occurs from adding an additional unit of input.

Marginal propensity to consume (MPC): A measurement of the tendency to spend a change in income on consumption, calculated by dividing the change in consumption by the change in income.

Marginal propensity to withdraw (MPW): A measurement of the change in withdrawals from national income due to savings, taxes, and buying of imports divided by a change in income.

Marginal revenue: The additional revenue gained by a firm from producing one more unit of its product.

Marginal revenue product of labour (MRPL): The amount of additional, or marginal, revenue that is generated for a firm as a result of adding one more worker to the production process.

Marginal social cost (MSC): Part of a process to assess the impact of production decisions, marginal social cost is the additional cost to society in terms of an increase in externalities caused by an increase in production.

Marginal tax rate: The tax rate paid on an increase in an individual's income.

Marginal utility: A measure of the extra satisfaction that a consumer achieves from consuming one more unit of a product.

Marginal utility theory of consumer choice: A theory stating that the extra satisfaction that a consumer achieves from consuming successive units of a good diminishes. With two or more items, consumers maximize their satisfaction when they receive the same amount of satisfaction per dollar for each item, a condition called *consumer equilibrium*; also called *utility theory*.

Market demand schedule: The sum total of all the consumer demand for a good or service.

Market economy: An economic system in which production decisions are made by the actions of buyers and sellers in the marketplace.

Market value: The actual price at which a share will sell on the stock market.

Marketing board: An agricultural organization established to administer quotas and market the products of its producers.

Mean average income: An average income figure that is calculated by dividing the total income by the total population.

Means testing: An income test applied to an individual as a prerequisite to receiving social welfare programs such as the Child Tax Credit or Guaranteed Income Supplement.

Measure of value (or standard unit of account): A function of money that allows comparisons of the value of various goods and services.

Median income: An average income figure that represents the middle income, dividing an economy's range of incomes into two equal parts.

Medicare: Canada's national health care program, which is administered by the provinces and territories. It covers all Canadians and is funded by taxation.

Medium of exchange: The main function of money, allowing the exchange of goods and services.

Mercantilism: An economic system that emphasized state control of trade, with the goal of exporting as many goods as possible and importing as few foreign goods as possible.

Merchandise trade: Tangible goods that are grown, extracted, or manufactured; also called *visible trade*.

Merger: The joining together of two firms or companies to operate more effectively as one.

Microeconomics: The branch of economics that studies the behaviour of individuals and firms in the economy in contrast to macroeconomics, which studies the economy as a whole.

Mill rate: The property tax rate; a percentage of the value of a property as assessed by the local tax authorities.

Minimum wage: A government-established wage, higher than one set by the demand for, and supply of, workers.

Mixed economy: An economic system, such as Canada's, that contains elements of market, command, and traditional systems.

Mixed market economy: An economic system predominantly featuring characteristics of a free market system but also incorporating some qualities of command economies, such as government-owned enterprise.

Monetarist: A school of economic thought based on the belief that the most effective way for government to affect the economy is by regulating the money supply.

Monetary policy: A process by which the government affects the economy by influencing the expansion of money and credit.

Money: Anything generally acceptable in an economy to purchase goods and services.

Money capital: The funds used to acquire real capital.

Money market mutual fund: Mutual funds specializing in short-term governmental and corporate securities.

Money multiplier: See *Deposit multiplier*.

Money supply: The total amount of cash in circulation plus bank deposits.

Monopolistic competition: A market structure in which many small to medium-sized firms sell a differentiated product, each having some control over price.

Monopoly: A market structure in which one firm has complete control over supply, allowing it to set a profit maximizing price.

Monopoly bank: A hypothetical example of a single bank with no competitors.

Monopsony: The reverse of a monopoly market, where there are many sellers (usually workers) but only one buyer (usually an employer).

Multilateral: Pertaining to many countries, as an agreement reached among many countries.

Multinational corporation (MNC): A firm that operates in more than one country; a corporation with a global production and selling strategy, having headquarters in one country and branch plants in several other countries.

Multiplier effect: The multiplied effect upon GDP that results from a change in people's income.

Mutual fund: A fund comprising the investments of many clients; it is invested in the shares of other companies and managed by professional managers.

Nasdaq: Commonly used acronym for the National Association of Securities Dealers Automated Quotation, one of the largest stock markets in the world. It is an electronic network that functions as a stock market for over 4 100 companies, including many technology companies.

Nasdaq Composite Index: The indicator used by Nasdaq to monitor and summarize its daily trading activities and to report general or overall changes in the market value of the many stocks listed on this exchange.

National Policy: A policy of tariff protection for Canadian industry, linked to railroad building and western settlement, that was launched by the Conservative government of Sir John A. Macdonald in 1879.

Nationalization: Another term for state ownership of business enterprise.

Natural monopoly: A field with high fixed costs (such as public utilities) in which greater efficiencies result when one firm supplies the product or provides the service.

Near bank: Financial institutions (such as credit unions, caisse populaires, trust, and mortgage companies) that perform several functions similar to those of chartered banks, but do not have the power to expand or contract the money supply as the chartered banks are able to do.

Near money: Deposits or assets that can act as a store of value and can be converted into a medium of exchange but are not themselves a medium of exchange.

Negative externality: A cost suffered by a third party as the result of production or consumption.

Neighbourhood effects: See *Spillover costs*.

Nominal GDP: The total value of GDP before it is adjusted for price increases; also called *current dollar GDP* or *money GDP*.

Nominal interest rate: An interest rate that includes an inflation premium, an allowance for risk, and credit worthiness.

Non-governmental organization (NGO): A non-profit group that functions independently of government. NGOs can be organized on a local, national, or international level to serve specific social or political purposes.

Non-merchandise trade: Services, tourism, investment income, and other transfers; also called *invisible trade*.

Non-price competition: Competition among firms in areas other than price (for example, quality of product).

Non-price factor: A factor held constant in the relationship between price and quantity demanded and supplied. Non-price factors include, on the demand side, income, population, tastes and preferences, expectations, and prices of substitute and complementary goods; and on the supply side, costs, number of sellers, technology, nature and the environment, and prices of related goods.

Non-profit/charitable organization: A government-registered form of business created not for profit but to provide a service or to organize and perform works of charity.

Normative economics: The branch of economics that deals with value judgements about economic subjects rather than facts and observations; also called *policy economics*.

North American Free Trade Agreement (NAFTA): The 1994 free trade agreement among Canada, the United States, and Mexico.

Notice account: A deposit that requires the depositor to give some notice to the bank before withdrawal of funds.

Official international reserves: The foreign currencies and gold held by the Bank of Canada.

Offshoring: A geographical business activity that takes advantage of lower costs of production in other countries by outsourcing parts of the production process.

Okun's law: A formula that states that for every percentage point that the actual unemployment rate exceeds the natural employment rate, a GDP gap of 2 percent occurs.

Oikos: A Greek word meaning "household" or "estate," which historically was the first subject of economics analysis.

Old Age Security (OAS): A program whereby all Canadians are paid a monthly benefit after the age of 65.

Oligopoly: A market structure characterized by a few large firms, selling an identical or differentiated product, each with some to substantial control over price.

Open shop: A clause in the collective agreement between a union and an employer that allows union membership to be voluntary.

Operating band: The range of 0.5 percent between the bank rate charged by the Bank of Canada and the interest it pays on deposits; the overnight rate target is set at its midpoint.

Opportunity cost: The value or benefit that must be given up to achieve something else. For example, by choosing to produce item A, a business gives up the benefit that it could have gained from producing item B using the same resources.

Origin: As used in graphs, the point at which the vertical and horizontal axes meet.

Outflow: A payment that flows out of Canada, recorded on the capital account, such as a pension paid to a Canadian living outside of the country.

Output: The products produced by using resources or inputs such as land, labour, or capital.

Outsourcing: The practice of moving some internal business operations to third-party firms to save on costs.

Overnight rate: The rate of interest, controlled by the Bank of Canada, that is charged by financial institutions on short-term loans made between them; it is set within the operating band.

Overnight rate target: A monetary tool used by the Bank of Canada to control the overnight rate; it is set by the Bank of Canada at the midpoint of the operating band.

Paradox of value: A seeming contradiction in the economy in which the demand for necessities needed for survival is not high enough to ensure that their prices at least match the prices of luxury items, which are unnecessary for survival.

Paris Agreement: An international agreement signed in 2015 to replace the Kyoto Protocol. It focuses on consensus building and co-operation, allowing countries to set their own greenhouse gas emission targets with mandatory reporting of progress every five years.

Participation rate: The labour force expressed as a percentage of the total employable population.

Partnership (general and limited): A business or firm owned by two or more people that is bound by the terms of a signed agreement.

Partnership agreement: The legal agreement between individuals in a partnership.

Patent law: Laws that protect the rights of product inventors and developers by giving them the sole right to benefit from product sales for a set period of time.

Patronage: Profits made by a co-operative enterprise that are paid out to co-operative members based on the individual member's activity as a customer.

Payment: See *Import*.

Perfect competition: A rare market structure characterized by many sellers (selling exactly the same product) and many buyers, no barriers to entry into the market for new firms, and perfect knowledge of prices (so there are no price differences and no individual can influence them); also called *pure competition*.

Personal income tax: A tax paid to the federal and provincial governments by individuals on their income.

Phillips curve: A diagram demonstrating an inverse relationship between inflation and unemployment rates.

Physiocrat: A believer in the eighteenth-century philosophy that argued that laws created by humans are artificial and unnecessary because they interfere with natural laws (such as an individual's pursuit of self-interest), which would ultimately benefit all of society.

Pigouvian tax: A tax levied on the production and/or sale of any good or service that causes a negative externality such as pollution; named after economist Arthur Pigou.

Policy economics: See *Normative economics*.

Political orientation: The placement of specific ideas within a spectrum of political views ranging from extreme far-right thinking (fascism) to moderate views (capitalism and socialism) before extending to far-left thinking (communism).

Portfolio investment: Investment in the form of purchases of stocks or bonds.

Positive check: Thomas Malthus's theory that war, famine, and disease would check population increases to some extent, but not enough to prevent the geometrical progression of the world's population to unsustainable levels.

Positive economics: See *Analytical economics*.

Positive externality: A benefit to a third party as the result of an economic transaction; for example, an increase in the property values of homes near the construction of a new subway.

Post hoc fallacy: A mistaken belief that what occurs before some event is logically the cause of it; also called *cause-and-effect fallacy*.

Potential GDP: The output that the economy can produce if the unemployment rate is equal to the natural unemployment rate.

Potential output: The GDP that the economy could produce with full employment.

Poverty line: The unofficial term used for the Statistics Canada low-income cut-off.

Preventive check: Thomas Malthus's theory that restraints such as late marriage and sexual abstinence would help reduce the birth rate to some extent, but not enough to prevent the geometrical progression of the world's population to unsustainable levels.

Price elastic: If the quantity of a good or service bought changes a lot when price rises or falls, it is said to be price elastic.

Price elasticity of demand (PED): An expression of how much more or less consumers will buy of a product if its price changes.

Price elasticity of supply (PES): An expression of how responsive the quantity supplied by a seller is to a rise or fall in the price of a product.

Price inelastic: If the quantity of a good or service bought does not change much when price rises or falls, it is said to be price inelastic.

Primary market: The first time a ticket is sold for an event by an event organizer such as Ticketmaster.

Primary, secondary, tertiary, and quaternary industrial activity: Primary industries are those enterprises concerned with the harvesting or extraction of natural resources. Secondary industries are concerned with the manufacturing of marketable products. Tertiary industries are concerned with providing a marketable service. Quaternary industries are enterprises concerned with providing extremely specialized and high-tech services.

Prime rate: The lowest rate of interest a financial institution offers to its best customers, such as large corporations.

Principal: The original amount a corporation borrows with a bond, repayable to the bondholder, and on which interest is paid.

Priority: The favouring of one available option over another in making a decision or choice.

Private corporation: A company that privately controls all sales of its ownership shares, instead of publicly trading in a stock market.

Private enterprise: A term applied to the private ownership of productive resources, a characteristic of market economies.

Privatization: The sale of public assets in a government enterprise to private firms.

Privatize: To turn over the ownership and operation of a government enterprise to the private sector.

Product differentiation: The attempt by competing firms to distinguish their product in some desirable way from that of their competitors to gain greater control over price.

Production possibilities curve: A graphical representation of the production choices facing an economy.

Productive resources: Anything that can be used to manufacture goods or services. Also called *factors of production*.

Productivity: A firm's ability to maximize output from the resources available, usually measured as the firm's output per worker.

Progressive tax: A tax (such as income tax) in which the tax rate increases as an individual's income increases.

Progressive tax system: A taxation system that taxes higher incomes at a higher percentage rate than lower incomes; it is designed to reduce income inequalities and finance social spending.

Proletariat: The term used by Karl Marx to describe the working class who, he theorized, would rise up and overthrow the bourgeoisie, or industrial capitalists.

Propaganda: Concerted messaging efforts used to influence thoughts and opinions by repeated emphasis, distortion, deception and misinformation.

Property tax: A tax paid to local governments (such as cities and towns) by holders of houses and commercial properties.

Proportional tax: A tax that takes a constant percentage for all income earners.

Prosperity cycle: An increase in aggregate demand leading to a cycle of higher production, more jobs, increased income, and greater consumption, resulting in even higher aggregate demand.

Protectionism: An economic policy that aims to restrict imports through tariffs, quotas, and regulations in an effort to boost domestic industry.

Protectionist: This is a term used to characterize an economic policy that restricts imports through tariffs, quotas, and regulations in an effort to boost domestic industry.

Provincial Sales Tax (PST): A Canadian provincial government sales tax levied on a range of goods and services.

Proxy: A document signed by a shareholder appointing another person to vote on behalf of that shareholder.

Public corporation: A firm or company that freely trades its ownership shares in a stock market, subject to government supervision.

Public debt: The total debt held by federal and provincial governments accumulated from their past borrowings, on which interest must be paid.

Public goods: Goods produced to serve the greater good, such as schools, highways, hospitals, and parklands.

Public policy issue: A matter that impacts members of a society that a government oversees through its positions, actions, and laws.

Public sector unions: Unions representing workers employed by governments.

Pure competition: See *Perfect competition*.

Quebec Pension Plan (QPP): The pension plan similar to the Canada Pension Plan (CPP), but administered by the Quebec government.

Quintile: One-fifth (or 20 percent) of the total number of income earners in an economy; it is used to examine income distribution.

Quota: A restriction placed on the amount of product that domestic producers are allowed to produce; also, a limit on the total quantity of goods imported into a country.

Rand Formula: A 1945 ruling stating that all workers in a workplace in which a union exists and bargains for all workers must pay union dues, even if they are not union members.

Rate of return: The amount of extra revenue an investment by a business in new machinery, new technology, or a new plant will bring in.

Raw materials: All natural resources used in production.

Real capital: A more precise term than capital for the machinery, factories, warehouses, and equipment used to produce goods and services. It is distinct from money capital.

Real GDP: The total value of all goods and services produced in Canada in a given year, adjusted for price changes; also called *constant dollar GDP*.

Real rate of interest: The nominal rate of interest minus the expected rate of inflation.

Receipt: See *Export*.

Recession: A contraction of the economy in which real GDP declines for a minimum of two consecutive business quarters (six months).

Recessionary gap: The gap between aggregate demand and full-employment equilibrium, characterized by high unemployment, low inflation, and low GDP growth.

Reciprocity Treaty: A free trade agreement between British North America and the United States, lasting from 1854 to 1866.

Recognition lag: The time it takes a government to recognize a problem in the economy that requires an appropriate fiscal policy to correct.

Recovery: The first part of an expansionary period following a downturn in the economy.

Regressive tax: A tax rate that takes a proportionally lower percentage from higher-income earners.

Regulation: Government rules that oversee, standardize, and control markets, industries, and business practices.

Relative cost: The cost of producing one item, A, expressed in terms of the numbers of another item, B, which must be given up to produce A (that is, A's opportunity cost).

Relative poverty: Poverty defined as lacking the conditions of life enjoyed by most people in the same economy.

Relief strategy: An anti-poverty program that provides immediate relief for poor Canadians, such as government transfer payments and community food banks.

Rent: The price people pay for accommodation, determined by demand and supply for rental accommodation.

Rent-control program: A government program that limits the amount landlords can increase rents.

Replacement unemployment: Unemployment caused by the movement of firms with labour-intensive production to foreign countries in which labour rates are lower.

Reserve ratio: The ratio between the reserves a bank keeps on hand and the amount it has on deposit.

Residential school: A government-sponsored system that was established to assimilate Indigenous children into the dominant "white" Canadian culture. The residential school system ran from 1849 to 1996.

Rightsize: Review the size of a company's workforce to correct the previous overuse of labour.

Risk premium: An additional bonus or compensation paid to individuals for the risks voluntarily assumed and handled responsibly as part of their work. For example, fire fighters and other first responders are paid a premium for having to risk their lives to save others. High-rise construction workers and oil riggers are also paid a bonus for the dangerous work they do.

Rotating strike: A union strategy, used when an employer has several workplaces, of withdrawing services for a short time from each workplace on a rotating basis.

S&P/TSX Composite Index: The indicator of stock market activity used in Canada.

Sales revenue: A practice of adjusting price according to changing demand in a very short time frame.

Sales tax: A tax (such as the Goods and Services Tax or the Provincial Sales Tax) paid to the federal and provincial governments on the purchase and consumption of goods and services by the end user.

Sanctions: Restrictions on trade with one country levied by another for some political purpose.

Savings account: A bank account that allows holders to earn interest on saved money.

School of economic thought: A group of economists who share and promote common ideas on how economies function.

Scientific method: A method of study used to make discoveries in natural science and social sciences (such as economics) that has four steps: observation, data collection, explanation, and verification.

Seasonal unemployment: Unemployment caused by recurring climatic factors, such as the impact of winter on construction, tourism, farming, and so on.

Seasonally adjusted unemployment rate: An unemployment rate adjusted to eliminate recurring and unavoidable unemployment due to seasonal factors.

Secondary market: The reselling of tickets bought from buyers in the primary market at a higher price than the stated ticket price.

Self-interest: An idea, central to the philosophy of Adam Smith, that each individual's strongest drive is to better his or her own condition.

Shareholders: The owners of the shares of a corporation; they are entitled to voting rights and a share of the corporation's profits.

Shares: Corporate assets divided into equal parts that are sold to buyers, giving them ownership and a share of the corporation's profits.

Short run: A time period in which the firm's maximum capacity is fixed by the shortage of at least one resource.

Social costs: Production costs that are not paid by either the product's producer or consumer but passed on to others; for example, environmental pollution, garbage disposal, and resource depletion; also called *third-party costs*.

Social science: Sciences, such as economics, history, and sociology, that study some aspect of human behaviour.

Social welfare safety net: Government programs, such as Employment Insurance and the Child Tax Credit, established to help vulnerable members of the population.

Socialism: A political system of the moderate left that calls for public ownership of the principal means of production, to be achieved in a democratic and peaceful manner.

Sole proprietorship: A business owned and operated by one person.

Spillover costs: Costs (such as those associated with cleaning up pollution) that are borne by a third party instead of the producers and consumers of the product; also called *neighbourhood effects*.

Spot market: A market (such as the Ontario Food Terminal) for commodities that are bought and sold for immediate delivery.

Stabilization policies: Government intervention in the economy to try to stabilize it, using fiscal and monetary policies.

Stagflation: A period of slow growth when both unemployment and inflation increase, as seen from 1973 to 1982 in Canada.

Stakeholder: A person with a vested or personal interest (or stake) in an economic decision.

Standard of living: The quantity and quality of goods and services that people are able to obtain to accommodate their needs and wants.

Standard unit of account: See *Measure of value*.

Staple: Products requiring little processing; fish, fur, and lumber were Canada's main exports from the sixteenth to the eighteenth centuries.

Statistical discrepancy: An adjustment made to bring the current account into balance with the capital and financial account on a country's international balance of payments.

Stock exchange: The actual building in which shares are traded.

Stock market: Either a physical place or an electronic network through which shares can be bought or sold.

Stockbroker: An agent who buys and sells shares on the stock market for individuals and companies.

Store of value: A function of money that allows value to be stored for the future, allowing it to be used in the purchase of goods and services.

Strike: A temporary work stoppage by employees to force their employer to accept the union's contract demands.

Structural deficit: The deficit that would exist even if the economy were at full employment due to the structure of government spending and taxation policies and not current economic conditions.

Structural strategy: A long-term program to reduce poverty, such as retraining and relocating workers.

Structural unemployment: Unemployment caused by long-term changes in the economy, such as shifts from goods production to services, or the introduction of technology that replaces labour.

Subsidiary: A branch plant of a multinational corporation.

Subsidy: A grant of money from a government to a producer to achieve some desired outcome, such as the installation of pollution-control equipment.

Substitute goods: Goods that are similar to other goods and that serve as an alternative if the price of a particular good rises.

Supply: The quantities that sellers will offer for sale at various prices during a given period of time.

Supply schedule: A table showing the quantities of a product supplied at particular prices.

Surplus budget: The situation that occurs when a government spends less than it collects in taxes, causing it to have money left over (a surplus).

Surplus value: The difference between the value of a good measured in terms of the labour used to produce it, and its higher selling price, a surplus that Karl Marx believed was stolen from labour by capitalists.

Sustainability: Practices and conditions that can be expected to continue safely for the long term because they minimize waste and inefficiency of resources, environmental damage, and the unfair treatment of vulnerable stakeholders.

Sustainable development: Economic development that considers how current production and consumption patterns affect the ability of future generations to meet their needs with respect to economic prosperity, social justice, and environmental sustainability.

Swedish Competition Authority (Konkurrensverket): An agency of the Swedish government assigned the responsibility to regulate competition and to ensure fair business practices, especially by companies holding a dominant position (40 percent or more of a market share) in the marketplace.

Tangible resources: Physical resources (such as land and labour) that are necessary for production and are visible.

Tariff: The transfer of part of a firm's production costs (such as cleaning up pollution caused by the release of wastes into the air, soil, or water supply) to the public (the third party).

Technological unemployment: Unemployment caused by replacement of workers with more capital-intensive production methods; a type of structural unemployment.

Technology-intensive production: Manufacturing goods or providing services that involve the extensive use of highly specialized technology, such as medical research laboratories and computer software design and engineering facilities.

Term deposit: Bank accounts in which the holder agrees to deposit a fixed amount of money for a fixed period of time for a fixed interest rate.

Terms of trade: The rate at which a country's exports are exchanged for its imports.

The Atlantic Groundfish Strategy, The (TAGS): A $1.9 billion federal aid program from 1994 to 1998 for the 31 000 people who lost their livelihood with the collapse of the North Atlantic cod fisheries.

Theory of the firm: The relationships that exist between a firm's revenues, costs, and profits.

Third-party costs: See *Social costs.*

Tight money policy: A monetary policy of high interest rates, more difficult availability of credit, and a decrease in the money supply.

Tort law: The body of law that allows a person injured by another to seek compensation by suing; it is used as a basis for class-action lawsuits against companies causing environmental externalities.

Total cost: The total of a firm's fixed and variable costs, which includes all the purchases made by a firm for productive resources to produce a good or service.

Total revenue: The price of a product multiplied by the quantity demanded of the product.

Trade deficit: The amount by which a country's imports exceed its exports.

Trade surplus: The amount by which a country's exports exceed its imports.

Trade unions: Unions that represent workers in a single occupation; also called *craft unions.*

Trade-off: The sacrifice of one resource or production choice for another.

Trading bloc: Regional trade agreements, such as NAFTA and those of the European Union, negotiated outside the World Trade Organization.

Traditional economy: An economic system in which production decisions are determined by the practices of the past.

Tragedy of the commons: When a shared resource is depleted or destroyed by individual self-interest acting contrary to what is good for society as a whole.

Transfer payments: Direct payments from governments to other governments or to individuals; a mechanism for providing social security, income support, and alleviation of regional disparities.

UN Women: An entity of the United Nations that is dedicated to gender equality and the empowerment of women. It supports member states in setting global standards for achieving gender equality.

Underground economy: Economic activity for which no paper trail exists because it is illegal or conducted "under the table" to avoid following regulations or paying taxes on the transaction.

Underemployment: A situation in which workers hold jobs that do not fully utilize their skills or that employ them only part time when they wish to work full time.

Unemployment Insurance (UI): A federal program started in 1942 to assist those temporarily out of work due to job loss, illness, or birth or adoption of a child; it was renamed Employment Insurance (EI) in 1996.

Unemployment rate: The percentage of the labour force that is not working at any given time; the total number of Canadians unemployed divided by the total labour force.

Union dues: The amount of money that each member of a union pays to support its activities.

Union shop: A workplace where all employees, upon being hired, must become members of the union.

Unit labour cost: A measure of a firm's efficiency, obtained by dividing its total labour costs by the number of units it produces.

Unitary coefficient: A coefficient for a product equal to one, indicating that a given change in price causes an equal percentage change in quantity demanded.

United Nations: Founded in 1945, it is an international organization with 193 state members. It works to address global issues such as peace and security, climate change, sustainable development, human rights, disarmament, terrorism, humanitarian and health emergencies, gender equality, governance, food production, and more.

United Nations Declaration on the Rights of Indigenous Peoples (UNDRIP): A declaration adopted by the United Nations in 2007 that established a universal framework of minimum standards for the survival, dignity, and well-being of all Indigenous people.

United Nations Development Programme (UNDP): Part of the United Nations system, UNDP works to achieve the eradication of poverty and the reduction of inequality and exclusion. UNDP focuses on helping countries build and share solutions in three main areas: sustainable development, democratic governance and peacebuilding, and climate and disaster resilience.

United Nations Educational, Scientific and Cultural Organization (UNESCO): The United Nations Educational, Scientific and Cultural Organization. It seeks to help build peace and security by promoting collaboration among countries in the areas of education, science, and culture.

United Nations Framework Convention on Climate Change (UNFCCC): An international agreement negotiated in 1992 that establishes how future treaties called *protocols* or *agreements* are to be negotiated to address the issue of climate change.

United States-Mexico-Canada-Agreement (USMCA): The 2018 free trade agreement between the United States, Mexico, and Canada that was designed to replace NAFTA; it is often referred to as "NAFTA 2.0."

Universality: A principle of the Canadian welfare state specifying that some benefits, such as health care, should be available to all citizens, regardless of income.

Unlimited personal liability: When the owner or owners of a business are personally responsible for all debts incurred by the business.

Upper middle-income economy: A country in which a minority of the population lives in poverty, with incomes at GNI per capita from $3 896 to $12 055 (in 2019).

Util: A theoretical unit of satisfaction that a person gains from consuming an item.

Utility: The usefulness, satisfaction, or benefit derived from each available option to help make a rational choice among them.

Utility theory: See *Marginal utility theory of consumer choice*.

Value added: The increase in market value of a product resulting from additional processing or refinement of that product.

Variable costs: Costs that change or vary with the level of output, such as labour and raw materials.

Vertical integration: The merging of two firms involved in different stages of the production process of a good or service.

Visible trade: See *Merchandise trade*.

Voluntary arbitration: A process during a labour dispute in which the parties agree to submit proposals to a third party who is given the power to decide which proposal, the union's or the employer's, is fairer.

Wage: The price a worker receives for supplying labour to a business with a demand for it.

Wage differentials: Differences in wage rates among different labour markets.

Wealth: Accumulated assets of individuals and families less their total debts.

Welfare poor: Non-working people who are poor because they are ill, disabled, elderly, or single parents, or for other reasons.

Welfare state: A philosophy that government should intervene to help people who are poor, sick, or unemployed as well as provide equal access to education, health care, and social services.

Work-to-rule: A union tactic of performing only the duties required in the contract, and not extra work carried out voluntarily or after hours.

Working poor: People who work for low wages and are defined as poor.

World Bank: An international agency financed by the richer countries that attempts to help less-developed countries by providing direct grants and programs.

World Health Organization (WHO): Established in 1948, WHO is a specialized agency of the United Nations whose role is to be the direct authority on international health within the United Nations system and to provide leadership in global health responses.

World Trade Organization (WTO): The successor (in 1995) to the General Agreement on Tariffs and Trade (GATT); the WTO has expanded and strengthened the procedures for reducing trade barriers.

WTO Dispute Settlement Body: A mechanism for settling a trade dispute between two or more countries; it involves setting up expert panels to arrive at a decision.

Xenophobia: The fear and intense dislike of strangers or foreigners or of anything that is considered strange or foreign.

Index

Credits